A History of Women's Writing in Russia

A History of Women's Writing in Russia offers a comprehensive account of the lives and works of Russia's women writers from the Middle Ages to the present. Based on original and archival research, much of it never published before, this volume forces a re-examination of many of the traditionally held assumptions about Russian literature and women's role in the tradition. In setting about the process of reintegrating women writers into the history of Russian literature, contributors have addressed the often surprising contexts within which women's writing has been produced. Chapters reveal a flourishing literary tradition where none was thought to exist, they redraw the map defining Russia's literary periods, they look at how Russia's women writers articulated their own experience, and they reassess their relationship to the dominant male tradition. The volume is supported by extensive reference features including a bibliography and guide to writers and their works.

ADELE MARIE BARKER is Professor of Russian and Slavic Languages and Comparative Cultural and Literary Studies at the University of Arizona. She is the author of *The Mother Syndrome in the Russian Folk Imagination* (1986) and co-author of *Dialogues/Dialogi: Literary and Cultural Exchanges between (ex-) Soviet and American Women* (1994). She is the editor of *Consuming Russia: Popular Culture, Sex, and Society since Gorbachev* (1999).

JEHANNE M GHEITH is Associate Professor of Slavic and Women's Studies at Duke University. She is the editor, with Barbara Norton, of *An Improper Profession: Women, Gender, and Journalism in Late Imperial Russia* (2001).

A History of
Women's Writing in
Russia

Edited by
ADELE MARIE BARKER

and

JEHANNE M GHEITH

CAMBRIDGE
UNIVERSITY PRESS

PUBLISHED BY THE PRESS SYNDICATE OF THE UNIVERSITY OF CAMBRIDGE
The Pitt Building, Trumpington Street, Cambridge, United Kingdom

CAMBRIDGE UNIVERSITY PRESS
The Edinburgh Building, Cambridge CB2 2RU, UK
40 West 20th Street, New York, NY 10011–4211, USA
477 Williamstown Road, Port Melbourne, VIC 3207, Australia
Ruiz de Alarcón 13, 28014 Madrid, Spain
Dock House, The Waterfront, Cape Town 8001, South Africa

http://www.cambridge.org

First published 2002

Printed in the United Kingdom at the University Press, Cambridge

Typeface LexiconNo2 RomanA-Txt 9/13 pt.   *System* QuarkXpress 4.1   [TB]

A catalogue record for this book is available from the British Library

ISBN 0 521 57280 0 hardback

For Lena Koshkareva:

For luminous scholarship and friendship,

for the light in her kitchen,

for nuances, travels, poets

JG

For Noah

with love

AB

Contents

Notes on contributors

OLGA BAKICH is Senior Tutor in the Department of Slavic Languages and Literatures at the University of Toronto. She is the editor of the Russian language literary and historical journal *Rossiiane v Azii*. She has written several articles on the history of the Russian community in Harbin and is compiling a forthcoming bibliography *Harbin Russian Imprints: Bibliography as History, 1898–1963*.

ADELE MARIE BARKER is Professor of Russian and Comparative Cultural and Literary Studies at the University of Arizona. She is the author of *The Mother Syndrome in the Russian Folk Imagination* (1986), co-author with Susan Hardy Aiken, Maya Koreneva, and Ekaterina Stetsenko of *Dialogues/Dialogi: Literary and Cultural Exchanges between (ex-) Soviet and American Women* (1994), and editor of *Consuming Russia: Popular Culture, Sex, and Society Since Gorbachev* (1999).

CATHERINE CIEPIELA is Associate Professor of Russian at Amherst College. She has published on Tsvetaeva, Bakhtin, Zhukovsky, and Pasternak, and is the author of a forthcoming book entitled *The Same Solitude: Boris Pasternak and Marina Tsvetaeva*.

JEHANNE M GHEITH is Associate Professor of Russian Literature and Women's Studies at Duke University. She is the author of *Finding the Middle Ground: Krestovskii, Tur and the Power of Ambivalence in Nineteenth-Century Women's Prose* (forthcoming), and co-editor with Barbara Norton of *An Improper Profession: Women, Gender, and Journalism in Late Imperial Russia* (2001) and with Robin Bisha, Christine Holden, and William Wagner of *Russian Women 1698-1917: Experience and Expression. An Anthology of Sources* (forthcoming). She has also written the introductions to *The Memoirs of Princess Dashkova* (1995) and Evgeniia Tur's *Antonina* (1996). She is currently working on a book entitled *Out of the Whirlwind: Interviews with Survivors of the GULag.*

HELENA GOSCILO is Professor of Slavic at the University of Pittsburgh and Professor at the University Center of International Studies. She specializes in gender and contemporary culture, and her most recent publications include *Dehexing Sex: Russian Womanhood During and After Glasnost* (1996), *The Explosive World of Tatyana N. Tolstaya's Fiction* (1996; Russian version 1999), and *Russia. Women. Culture* with Beth Holmgren (1996). She has also translated Anastasia Verbitskaia's *Keys to Happiness* with Beth Holmgren (1999), and Svetlana Vasilenko's *Shamara and Other Writings* (1999). She is editor of *Russian Culture of the 1990s* (forthcoming). Currently she is co-writing two books: a cultural study of the New Russians, with Nadezhda Azhgikhina and a volume on Russian illustrators of children's books with Beth Holmgren.

KATHARINE HODGSON is Head of the Department and Lecturer in Russian at the University of Exeter. She is the author of *Written on the Bayonet: Soviet Russian Poetry of World War Two* (1996) and of articles on twentieth-century Russian poetry and women's writing. She is currently preparing a monograph on the Leningrad poet Olga Berggol'ts.

BETH HOLMGREN is Professor and Chair of the Department of Slavic Languages and Literatures at the University of North Carolina–Chapel Hill. Her publications include *Women's Works in Stalin's Time: On Lidiia Chukovskaia and Nadezhda Mandelstam* (1993), *Russia. Women. Culture,* edited with Helena Goscilo (1996), and *Rewriting Capitalism: Literature and the Market in Late Tsarist Russia and the Kingdom of Poland* (1998). She is also the editor and translator along with Helena Goscilo of Anastasia Verbitskaia's *Keys to Happiness* (1999).

CATRIONA KELLY is Reader in Russian at Oxford University. Her publications include *A History of Russian Women's Writing 1820–1992* and *An Anthology of Russian Women's Writing 1777–1992.* She is co-editor of *Constructing Russian Culture in the Age of Revolution* and of *An Introduction to Russian Cultural Studies.* She is currently finishing work on *Refining Russia: Gender and the Regulation of Behavior from Catherine to Yeltsin.*

ANNA KRYLOVA is an Assistant Professor of Modern Russia and the Soviet Union at the University of South Carolina. Her book manuscript is entitled "Emplotting the New Soviet Person: Social Change and Representation in Stalin's Russia." Her publications have focused on Soviet and Russian identity and its generational and gender aspects during the Soviet and post-Soviet periods.

ROSALIND MARSH is Professor of Russian Studies at the University of Bath. She is the author of *Soviet Fiction Since Stalin: Science, Politics and Literature* (1986), *Images of Dictatorship: Stalin in Literature* (1989), and *History and Literature in Contemporary Russia* (1996). She is the editor of *Women in Russia and Ukraine* (1996), *Gender and Russian Literature: New Perspectives* (1996), and *Women and Russian Culture* (1998). She is currently President of the British Association of Slavonic and East European Studies.

ROSALIND MCKENZIE received her doctorate from the School of Slavonic and East European Studies at the University of London where she worked on secularizing tendencies in medieval hagiographic literature. She is currently working in the field of humanitarian aid and development in the former Soviet republic of Georgia.

JENIFER PRESTO is Assistant Professor of Slavic and Comparative Literature at the University of Southern California. She is currently at work on a comparative study of Zinaida Gippius and Aleksandr Blok and has published articles on both Gippius and Gogol.

STEPHANIE SANDLER is Professor of Slavic Languages and Literatures at Harvard University. She is the author of *Distant Pleasures: Alexander Pushkin and the Writing of Exile* (1989), co-editor of *Sexuality and the Body in Russian Culture* (1993), and editor of *Rereading Russian Poetry* (1999). She is the author of numerous essays on contemporary Russian women poets, poetry in the Pushkin period, and myths of Pushkin in Russian culture.

CAROL UELAND is Associate Professor of Russian, Chair of the German and Russian Department, and Director of Russian Studies at Drew University in Madison, New Jersey. She is the author of *The Symbolists' Pushkin* (forthcoming Harriman Institute Series) and co-translator with poet Paul Graves of *Apollo in the Snow: Selected Poems of Alexander Kushner* (1991). She has published several articles on Russian women writers, including Yunna Moritz, Anna Barkova, Olesia Nikolaeva and others, as well as translating Russian women's poetry.

JUDITH VOWLES is an independent scholar and translator. She is co-editor of *Sexuality and the Body in Russian Culture* (1993) and *Russia Through Women's Eyes: Autobiographies from Tsarist Russia* (1996). She is also a contributor to *Women Writers in Russian Literature* (1994) and *Russian Subjects: Empire, Nation, and the Culture of the Golden Age* (1998). She is currently working on Batiushkov and Bunina.

MARY ZIRIN is an independent researcher-translator specializing in prerevolutionary women writers. With Marina Ledkovsky and Charlotte Rosenthal she edited *Dictionary of Russian Women Writers* (1994). She is also the translator of Nadezhda Durova's *The Cavalry Maiden* (1988).

Acknowledgments

The editors wish to thank the Duke University Arts and Sciences Council, Duke Women's Studies, and at the University of Arizona, the Dean's Office of the College of Humanities, and the Department of Women's Studies for the support and time we needed in order to work on this volume. Our thanks also to Robin Bisha and to Peter Maggs for invaluable technical assistance above and beyond the call of duty. Our friends Julia Clancy-Smith and Carl Smith ran interference for us from a continent and an ocean away. And our contributors to this volume showed uncommonly good cheer and patience in putting up with seemingly endless delays, editing, cutting, and last minute queries. They were models for collaboration. And to our friends and family – Susan Aiken, Barbara Andrade, Al Babbitt, Noah Barker, Chris Carroll, Richard Eaton, Dorothy Gheith, Mohamed and Aida Gheith, Georgia and Katherine Maas, Ron, Barbara and Megan MacLean, Eileen Meehan, David Need, Barbara Norton, and Del and Lafon Phillips – we can finally say "we are finished!"

In closing, we would like to thank two unlikely contributors to this volume: Coach K. of the Duke Blue Devils and Coach Olsen of the Arizona Wildcats. To both of you, "You may never have expected to be the motivating force behind *A History of Women's Writing in Russia.*" Over the years the two editors of this volume have shared an intense love of basketball, rooting for two teams that became national rivals for the NCAA Men's Championship as we were putting the finishing touches on this book in March, 2001. We celebrated the first submission of this manuscript by standing under the basket at Cameron. And we have cheered and mourned for these two teams, clutching at the buzzer, arguing with the officiating, and wondering what we would do when basketball season was over. This rivalry nurtured our friendship as it nurtured this book.

Note on transliteration

In general, we have adhered to a modified Library of Congress system of transliteration. However, in the representation of the names of authors who are familiar to the English-speaking reader, we have eliminated the *ii* and *yi* endings, replacing them with the more familiar *y* as in the case of Dostoevsky, Tolstoy, Brodsky, etc. Soft and hard signs have been retained in the endnotes and bibliographical material but in some cases have not been denoted in the text proper to facilitate reading for the non-specialist.

Abbreviations

Editions of works by Russian authors

Izb	*Izbrannoe* (Selections)
IzbPr	*Izbrannye proizvedeniia* (Selected works)
IzbS	*Izbrannye sochineniia* (Selected compositions)
PSS	*Polnoe sobranie sochinenii* (Complete collected works)
Soch	*Sochineniia* (Works)
SS	*Sobranie sochinenii* (Collected works)

Abbreviations used in archive entries

ATKP	Arkhiv tvorcheskikh kadrov Soiuza Pisatelei
RGALI	Rossiiskii gosudarstvennyi arkhiv literatury i iskusstva (Russian State Archive of Literature and Art)
RTsKhIDNI	Rossiiskii tsentr khraneniia i izucheniia dokumentov noveishei istorii (Russian Center for Preservation and Study of Records of Modern History)

English-language periodicals

CSS	*Canadian Slavonic Studies*
RL	*Russian Literature* (includes some articles in Russian)
RLJ	*Russian Language Journal* (includes some articles in Russian)
RLT	*Russian Literature Triquarterly*
RR	*Russian Review*
ScotSR	*Scottish Slavonic Review*
SEEJ	*Slavic and East European Journal*
SEER	*Slavonic and East European Review*
SovLit	*Soviet Literature* (Moscow)
SR	*Slavic Review*

Russian periodicals

BdCh	*Biblioteka dlia chteniia* (Library for Reading)
DN	*Druzhba narodov* (Peoples' Friendship)
LitGaz	*Literaturnaia gazeta* (Literary Gazette)
LitOb	*Literaturnoe obozrenie* (Literary Review)
LitZ	*Literaturnye zapiski* (Literary Notes)
MGv	*Molodaia gvardiia* (The Young Guard)
NlitOb	*Novoe literaturnoe obozrenie* (New Literary Review)
NM	*Novyi mir* (New World)
NSovr	*Nash sovremennik* (Our Contemporary)
NZh	*Novyi zhurnal* (New Review)
OZ	*Otechestvennye zapiski* (Notes of the Fatherland)
RBog	*Russkoe bogatstvo* (Russian Wealth)
RLit	*Russkaia literatura* (Russian Literature)
RMysl'	*Russkaia mysl'* (Russian Thought)
ROb	*Russkoe obozrenie* (Russian Review)
RRech'	*Russkaia rech'* (Russian Speech)
RSlovo	*Russkoe slovo* (Russian Word)
RV	*Russkii vestnik* (Russian Herald)
SevV	*Severnyi vestnik* (Northern Herald)
SPVed	*Sanktpeterburgskie vedomosti* (St. Petersburg News)
VE	*Vestnik Evropy* (Herald of Europe)
VopLit	*Voprosy literatury* (Questions of Literature)
ZR	*Zolotoe runo* (Golden Fleece)

Abbreviations of frequently cited works

Andrew	Andrew, Joe (ed. and tr.), *Russian Women's Shorter Fiction: An Anthology, 1835–60*. Oxford, 1996.
Balancing Acts	Goscilo, Helena (ed.), *Balancing Acts*. Bloomington, IN, 1989.
Bannikov	Bannikov, N. V. (ed.), *Russkie poetessy XIX veka*. Moscow, 1979.
Bisha *et al*	Bisha, Robin, Jehanne Gheith, Christine Holden, William Wagner (eds.), *Russian Women, 1698–1917: Experience and Expression: An Anthology of Sources*. Bloomington, IN, 2002.
Chester and Forrester	Chester, Pamela and Sibelan Forrester (eds.), *Engendering Slavic Literatures*. Bloomington, IN, 1996.

Clyman and Greene	Clyman, Toby W. and Diana Greene (eds.), *Women Writers in Russian Literature*. Westport, CT, 1994.
Clyman and Vowles	Clyman, Toby W. and Judith Vowles (eds.), *Russia through Women's Eyes: Autobiographies from Tsarist Russia*. New Haven, CT and London, 1996.
Contemporary Russian Poetry	Smith, Gerald S. (ed.), *Contemporary Russian Poetry*. Bloomington, IN, 1993.
Costlow, Sandler and Vowles	Costlow, Jane T., Stephanie Sandler and Judith Vowles (eds.), *Sexuality and the Body in Russian Culture*. Stanford, 1993.
Dacha	Uchenova, V. (ed.), *Dacha na Petergofskoi doroge*. Moscow, 1986.
Dialogues	Aiken, Susan, Adele Barker, Maya Koreneva, and Ekaterina Stetsenko (eds.), *Dialogues/Dialogi: Literary and Cultural Exchanges Between (ex-) Soviet and American Women*. Durham, NC, 1994.
DRWW	Ledkovsky, Marina, Charlotte Rosenthal, and Mary Zirin (eds.), *Dictionary of Russian Women Writers*. Westport, CT, 1994.
Gender Restructuring	Liljeström, Marianne, Eila Mäntysaari, and Arja Rosenholm (eds.), *Gender Restructuring in Russian Studies*. Slavic Tamperensia, 2. Tampere, 1993.
Goscilo and Holmgren	Goscilo, Helena and Beth Holmgren (eds.), *Russia. Women. Culture*. Bloomington, IN, 1996.
Heldt	Heldt, Barbara, *Terrible Perfection*. Bloomington, IN, 1987.
Hoisington, *Out Visiting*	Hoisington, Thomas H. (ed. and tr.), *Out Visiting and Back Home*. Evanston, IL, 1998.
Kelly *History*	Kelly, Catriona, *A History of Russian Women's Writing 1820–1992*. Oxford, 1994.
Kelly *Anthology*	Kelly, Catriona (ed.), *An Anthology of Russian Women's Writing*. Oxford, 1994.
Kelly *Utopias*	Kelly, Catriona (ed. and tr.), *Utopias: Russian Modernist Texts, 1905–1940*. London, 1999.
Lives in Transit	Goscilo, Helena (ed.), *Lives in Transit*. Ann Arbor, MI, 1995.
Markov and Sparks	Markov, Vladimir and Merrill Sparks (eds.), *Modern Russian Poetry: An Anthology with Verse Translations*. Indianapolis, IN, 1967.

Marsh *Gender*	Marsh, Rosalind (ed.), *Gender and Russian Literature. New Perspectives*. Cambridge, 1996.
Marsh *Women*	Marsh, Rosalind (ed.), *Women in Russian Culture: Projections and Self-Perceptions*. New York, 1998. (Studies in Slavic Literature, Culture and Society, 2).
Novye amazonki	Vasilenko, Svetlana (comp.), *Novye amazonki*. Moscow, 1991.
Pachmuss *Modernism*	Pachmuss, Temira (ed. and tr.), *Women Writers in Russian Modernism*. Urbana, IL, 1978.
Perkins and Cook	Perkins, Pamela and Albert Cook (eds.), *The Burden of Suffering: Women Poets of Russia*. New York, 1993.
Present Imperfect	Kagal, Ayesha and Natasha Perova (eds.), *Present Imperfect*. Boulder, CO, 1996.
Serdtsa	Iakushin, N. I. (ed.), *"Serdtsa chutkogo prozren'em"… Povesti i rasskazy russkikh pisatel'nits XIXV*. Moscow 1991.
Soviet Women Writing	Decter, Jacqueline (ed.), *Soviet Women Writing*. New York, 1990.
Svidanie	Uchenova, V. (ed.), *Svidanie*. Moscow, 1987.
Third Wave	Johnson, Kent and Stephen M. Ashby (eds.), *Third Wave: The New Russian Poetry*. Ann Arbor, MI, 1992.
Todd and Hayward	Todd, Albert C. and Max Hayward (eds.) *An Anthology of Twentieth Century Russian Poetry*, selected by Evgenii Evtushenko. New York, 1993.
Tol'ko chas	Uchenova, V. (ed.), *Tol'ko chas*. Moscow, 1988.
Tomei	Tomei, Christine D. (ed.), *Russian Women Writers*, 2 vols. New York and London, 1999.
Tsaritsy muz	Uchenova, V. (ed.), *Tsaritsy muz: russkie poetessy XIX-nachala XXvv*. Moscow, 1989.

Introduction

> What we know does not satisfy us. What we know constantly reveals itself as partial. What we know, generation by generation, is discarded into new knowings which in their turn slowly cease to interest us . . . The facts cut me off. The clean boxes of history, geography, science, art. What is the separateness of things when the current that flows each to each is live? It is the livingness I want.
>
> JEANETTE WINTERSON, Gut Symmetries (82–3)

In presenting the history of women's writing in Russia from its beginnings to the present day, we have been guided by the desire to incorporate the "livingness" of which Jeanette Winterson speaks. To capture that essential living quality of the women writers presented in this volume, the eras in which they lived, the literary lives they led, and the places they occupied within a tradition long dominated by men is the task we have set before ourselves in this volume. Women's literary endeavors have, with few exceptions, occupied obscure, indeed often unseen places in the history of Russian literature. As we set about the process of reintegrating women writers into the history of Russian literature, we wanted to recover lost literary lives, address factual gaps in our knowledge, and rethink the contexts within which women's writing has been produced. Our journey has led us to examine questions of gender and genre, to reconsider traditional periodization and classifications of literary versus non literary, high versus low, public versus private, and to query the relationship between women's literary productivity and mainstream Russian literature.

The essays that follow are in an important sense the product of many hands over many years. Our approaches and insights have benefited immeasurably from the pioneering work of Slavic feminist scholars such as Barbara Heldt, Catriona Kelly, and Mary Zirin, and from feminist scholarship in the field of European and American women's writing.[1] Much of our initial research was prompted by the same questions feminist scholars had asked about European and American women's writing. Were Russia's women writers, under the influence of the liberal social and political movements of the middle of the nineteenth century, writing what could be termed feminist fiction, and, if so, how does the understanding of what it means to write feminist fiction differ between cultures? Several of the essays (see Catriona Kelly's and Rosalind Marsh's in particular) struggle with these different cultural definitions of feminism in moving towards an understanding of how women's political and social views translated themselves into fiction.

Like much feminist scholarship, ours was often guided by the question of whether women's writing comprises a separate tradition or not. The chapters in this volume suggest that while there was not a separate tradition of women's writing in Russia, neither was that writing a part of what has come to be known as the mainstream. From the second third of the nineteenth century and perhaps even earlier, women writers were influential and widely read. Their writings interacted with those penned by men at every level; men and women read each other's drafts, their published works, reviewed each other's works in the literary journals of the day, and were influenced by each other's literary productions. In the twentieth century Russia's women writers have likewise been powerfully engaged with the male tradition. Stephanie Sandler notes in her chapter on "Women's Poetry Since the Sixties" that women poets' primary allegiance in Russia has not been to other women poets and that their works do not make genuine and complete sense outside the context of their male contemporaries and precursors. By the same token, however, the pervasive presence of the male tradition within their works has in no way prevented women writers in both the nineteenth and twentieth centuries from seeking out "models of an authoritative female voice" (Hodgson, 208). Thus, the twin strands of Russian literary tradition have been inseparable while simultaneously drawing upon their own distinctive role models.

Despite the inseparability of the two traditions, women's writings have been largely lost, and, when recovered, have rarely been studied in relation to writings by men. It is precisely because Russia's women writers were as much a part of mainstream literary life as they were that the act of omitting them from a history of Russian literature leaves one with a radically incomplete picture of Russia's literary life during the formative years of its development.

If some of our questions replicate those asked by our colleagues study-ing women's literature in other countries, some are also specific to the Russian historical and cultural experience, notably how certain long-held cultural stereotypes played themselves out in the lives and works of the women writers represented in this volume. How, for example, did the semi-sanctified role of the mother, so deeply embedded in Russian thought as to border on national obsession, both enable and impede women who took up the pen? Likewise, how did certain Orthodox concepts such as that of humility or *smirenie*, deeply ingrained in the Russian religious imagination, become, as Judith Vowles points out in "The Inexperienced Muse," a source of both pride and ambivalence for the women poets she discusses?

As we set out to compile this history, we wanted to avoid replicating the paradigms of literary histories we were trying to rethink. Any history, after all, is by definition arbitrary, providing closure and periodization, defining schools and movements in ways that, while often useful, also seem artificial. How, we wondered, could we at once construct a history and yet remain true to what Jeanette Winterson calls its "livingness"? Thus, we have tried to discuss these writers in ways that do not com-partmentalize them and that question standard periodizations and con-textualizations. Further, we have deliberately avoided trying to reconcile contradictions between contributors, preferring instead to assemble a history that is open ended, allowing the contributors to engage in dia-logue with each other. Marsh and Kelly, for example, disagree over the degree to which women's involvement in major public campaigns affected the development of women's writing. Marsh also challenges the argument that Russia lacked an earlier tradition of women's prose writ-ing, arguing that by the turn of the century Russian women writers had a number of literary precursors on whom to draw, both Russian and foreign.[2] In her view, the tradition of poetry has deeper roots than that of prose in Russian women's writing, partly because poetry is a more intimate, confessional genre particularly well suited to women's talents, and partly because women's prose has frequently been denigrated as a genre devoted exclusively to love and trivial themes (180). Further, she argues, Russian women were heirs to a problematic prose tradition in which women were expected to conform to images of what Heldt has termed "terrible perfection."[3] Jehanne Gheith, in "Women of the Thir-ties and Fifties" takes issue with Marsh, avoiding what she sees as essen-tializing women's talents. We regard these different approaches as productive to our critical thinking and as opening dialogue regarding the primacy of and preference for certain genres at particular moments in literary history.

The essays in this volume also open up a variety of methodological approaches. Several of the chapters (Zirin's, Vowles's, and Gheith's) reconstruct the contexts within which women's writing was produced and acquired meaning. Women writers in the eighteenth century, as Vowles points out, were largely "left out of the familiar circles, formal associations, salons, and 'society' where so much of literary life then took place" (63). Thus women rewrote and invented myths, according to Vowles, "as a way of establishing female legitimacy and authority" (70). In her essay on the Silver Age, Jenifer Presto similarly shows how the Symbolist perception of the world and women's place in it blinded an entire generation of poets to facets of women's lives and works that lay outside their mystical constructs of the Beautiful Lady or *Prekrasnaia Dama*. It was left to Symbolist poets such as Mirra Lokhvitskaia, Poliksena Solov'eva, and Zinaida Gippius to create an image of woman as agent rather than muse or ideal, whose unique function was to inspire male poets to take up their lyres.

The context within which women's writing was produced is also discussed in the chapters on Soviet women's writing by Anna Krylova and Adele Barker. Krylova argues that the categories many Russians and western Slavists have used in analyzing the Soviet period have tended to valorize dissident voices at the expense of those who occupied central places in official Soviet literary life. She calls for different ways to understand the narratives of those who were "official" and to develop new categories of analysis from within their works. Looking at literary life not from the margins but from the center out, forces us to reorganize the ways in which we have traditionally viewed both moral and aesthetic categories within the Soviet context. Likewise, Barker finds the problem of identities a much more telling prism through which to view women writers from the late 1950s on than the positioning of these writers within the binary hierarchy of official versus non-official. Barker argues that irrespective of where they stood vis-à-vis the center, since the end of the Stalin period women writers have been engaged in negotiating a complex system of identities articulated for them during the Soviet period. Beth Holmgren similarly contends that we need to re-evaluate some of the common assumptions upon which our approaches to Soviet literature have been based. Taking issue with the long-standing notion that *embourgeoisement* is necessarily equated with bad literature, Holmgren posits that positioning a text somewhere between "authentic" folk art and the highbrow does not mean that it is "therefore aesthetically inferior and morally suspect" (Holmgren, 232). Traditionally, for example, western Slavists' use of the term Socialist Realism or even "official literature" to describe a work of literature was tantamount to a critical kiss of death. In her essay on perestroika and post-perestroika literature, Helena Goscilo takes the need to recontextualize Russian women's writing a step further by celebrating the ways in which women's writing simultaneously participates in both high and low culture and in the breakdown of these categories.

The two chapters that discuss women's literary productions outside of Russia also implicitly question some of the traditional frameworks within which Russian women's writing has been studied. In her discussion of the Paris emigration, Catherine Ciepiela demonstrates that Marina Tsvetaeva's influence was much larger within the Paris circle than had previously been thought. Olga Bakich and Carol Ueland, in their chapter on Russian women writers in Harbin, open up new perspectives about the relationship of Russia to the East and to the Far Eastern emigration, a topic which until now has been treated from an almost entirely ungendered perspective.

Juxtaposing the essays with one another in order to create new ways of seeing is an important part of the process of recontextualization. Moving between Ciepiela's essay on the Paris emigration, for example, and Bakich and Ueland's article on the Far Eastern emigration creates a sense of the importance of locale and culture for art in exile: in both emigrations maintaining that link to Russian culture was vital, but the means by which that link was secured were often different.[4] While Gippius, Tsvetaeva, and others defined themselves within and against Parisian norms, the Harbin writers such as Marianna Kolosova or Natal'ia Il'ina were working in a country where they lived a completely segregated life from Chinese culture and were, in fact, viewed as lower class citizens by the local Chinese community. Other juxtapositions emerge as well. To read Zirin's discussion of Verbitskaia's autobiography alongside Marsh's discussion of Verbitskaia's fiction gives us a richer sense of the interrelationship between fictional and autobiographical selves at the turn of the century. Similarly, if we look at Zirin alongside Krylova, we are able to see not only the shift in autobiographical discourse in the Bolshevik period but the similarities in political and social pressures at very different times in history that occasioned the production of less than completely truthful autobiographies.

The reader will also note that several authors appear in more than one chapter. For example, Nadezhda Khvoshchinskaia is discussed by both Vowles and Gheith; Zinaida Gippius is dealt with by both Presto and Ciepiela; Tsvetaeva appears in chapters authored by Presto, Ciepiela, and Hodgson; I. Grekova is taken up by Holmgren and Barker, and Liudmila Petrushevskaia by Barker and Goscilo. We have purposely overlapped these discussions in order to present Russian literature through a different prism, one that does not allow for a neat movement from Sentimentalism to Romanticism to Realism, slowly merging into the Silver Age and then Socialist Realism and beyond. We also wanted to allow multiple facets of these authors to emerge.

Another way in which this volume re-envisions the history of Russian writing is through reperiodization (e.g. Kelly's, Gheith's and Zirin's essays). Unlike traditional histories of Russian literature of the eighteenth and nineteenth centuries, Kelly's neither starts with the reign of Catherine II nor ends with the death of Pushkin; rather her essay covers the years 1760 to the early years of Pushkin's literary development in the 1820s. Although in general she subscribes to Pushkin's centrality, by redrawing the map of the eighteenth and early nineteenth centuries, Kelly allows other developments in literary life at the time, such as the importance of conversations between sisters in literary works, to emerge from Pushkin's shadow. Gheith's essay also forces a re-examination of common assumptions about period as she focuses on the 1830s and 1850s within the context of women's writing rather than the more commonly held divisions of the 1840s and 1860s. Zirin's chapter presents an unlikely periodization, one that begins with 1783 and ends in 1971, tracing moments in between that look like no traditional division used to characterize these periods. She discusses the rhythms of women's self-writing, which moved from memoirs or autobiography based on western European models in the early nineteenth century, then departed from this model in the middle of the century, and finally returned to an autobiographical voice with the rise of Modernism in the late nineteenth century. By discussing women's writing within a different kind of time frame, Zirin suggests an alternative way to place women's autobiographical writings, one that reveals the historical and social developments that make certain kinds of life writing possible. Through this kind of realignment, we hope to challenge some of the traditional categories and judgments usually made about a work of art based on the period to which it has traditionally been assigned. Although most critics will agree that such categories are useful classifying devices rather than representations of literary and social realities, these periodizations are so common that it is often difficult to see beyond them, thus limiting our ability to account for developments that do not fit within traditional parameters. To call received historical periodizations into question is to understand Russian literary history as messier, more complex, less predictable, and hence more vital than it has heretofore been understood.

Traditionally, little attention has been given to how women articulated their own experience. Tracing the evolution of women's writing through their autobiographical statements reveals much about the articulation and the aesthetics of female self-representation; it also shows how those representations interacted with the public and political world. When asked, for example, how women are portrayed in Russian literature, most readers will refer to *Anna Karenina*, which is, of course, a brilliant representation of a woman – but through a man's eyes. Further, most readers will not be aware that there are also female-authored texts that powerfully inscribe female experience. The appearance of autobiography at once marks the entry of genres once thought to be non-literary into the literary canon and at the same time enables us to talk about the ways women inscribed their own experiences. In her chapter on prerevolutionary autobiography, Mary Zirin discusses the growth of autobiography in mid-nineteenth-century Russia, a phenomenon she connects to the rise of journals devoted to history and a concomitant increase of autobiographical accounts in socio-literary journals. Zirin sees an inherent contradiction in women's autobiographies of this period: torn between the "impulse to disclose the 'truth' of their lives and social imperatives that discouraged disclosure" (102) nineteenth-century Russian women's autobiography interrogates the notion of autobiography as "truthful disclosure" when composed under certain kinds of political and social pressures. Zirin's essay thus suggests how autobiographical statements could also be reflective of women's participation in both the social and literary realms. Similarly, Anna Krylova's "In Their Own Words? Soviet Women Writers and the Search for Self" takes up this relationship between political pressure and personal statement as she discusses how women's official autobiographies were constructed during the Stalinist era. Krylova argues that biography was something one was not necessarily born with but had to acquire as a way of legitimizing oneself in Soviet society, an argument that encourages us to rethink the traditional divide between the personal and the political as the two became conflated within the Soviet era. Looking at these two essays together suggests among other things that the imperative to write politically correct autobiographies was not limited to the Stalin period alone.

The essays on autobiography in this volume thus question our traditional assumptions of what it means to write autobiography and the longstanding insistence that autobiography be truthful. Given the social dictates of several of the eras we discuss, where full disclosure was discouraged, the way in which autobiography came to be composed adds a different perspective to how political and personal identities become conflated at certain moments in history. Finally, Holmgren in "Writing the Female Body Politic (1945–1985)" adds yet another dimension to the argument as she discusses how the image of the whole woman threatened to displace the Socialist Realist hagiography with normal biography, as High Stalinism gave way to the more domestic fictions of the forties.

The theme of autobiography also raises the question of the way in which these writers fashioned their authorial personae. As Kelly notes in her chapter, when women began to set pen to paper in the eighteenth century, they were "trapped in a net of *topoi* that precluded original expression" (48). From the images of the Amazonki, to Sappho, Corinna, and Niobe, Russia's women writers were the recipients of models of self-presentation that did not necessarily speak to their experience. One recalls Tatiana in Pushkin's *Eugene Onegin* sitting down and attempting to write her famous love letter to Onegin but having no words or images on which to draw in her own language. With whom then were these women to identify? Although many of the images they inherited were outworn, Vowles makes the point that women reached for them anyway, transforming them in the process, as did the poet Anna Bunina with Sappho, as a way of "resisting the formation of boundaries between men's and women's writing and language" (68). Part of the impetus to revise these images and make them useful to women's experience in the eighteenth and nineteenth centuries was the women writers' fear of being overly identified with the male tradition, particularly with the male-dominated tradition of poetry in Russia. Even into the twentieth century, the paucity of past models continued to be a problem for women writers. Although the hallowed images of woman as the incarnation of suffering Mother Russia resurfaced powerfully during the Stalin era, the tendency towards self-mythologization Hodgson notes in poets such as Akhmatova (216) suggests that the images and *topoi* that were part of women's received poetic inheritance were not always sufficient to their poetic imaginations.

The question of *topoi* raises the larger question of the tradition, a question which underlies most of the essays in this volume. The problem of literary tradition is a particularly charged one in Russia because of the panoply of male stars produced in the nineteenth century. Many of the women writers discussed in this volume were not simply responding to a male literary tradition into which they had wandered – one comprising Pushkin, Dostoevsky, Tolstoy, and Chekhov – but were active creators of that same tradition, working alongside and often independent of their male colleagues. In the eighteenth and nineteenth centuries, Russia's women writers experienced a complex relationship to the tradition, positioned as they were simultaneously within and outside it. The situation for Soviet women writers has been no less complex. Throughout most of the twentieth century, Soviet writers received different and often conflicting signals as to how to respond to and integrate the literary and historical past into their works. In the early days of the Bolshevik state, Lenin and others sought to find a way to incorporate the elitist literature of the past into the education of the worker. Later, after the death of Stalin, the historical and literary past would provide the values necessary for the re-evaluation of Soviet society. Both Holmgren and Barker look at how Soviet women writers responded to the call either to distance themselves from the past or to embrace it when it was expedient to do so. Both, for example, discuss how it was in the best interests of women writers during the Stalin era to dissociate themselves from the past and from women writers both past and present who were perceived to be "scribblers."

One of the most persistent *topoi* that Russian women writers have struggled with has been that of the body – a set of constructs and paradigms so deeply embedded in Russian national and cultural consciousness that even now they are still powerfully deployed as metaphors within contemporary Russian women's fictions. In western feminist theory the relationship between women's writing and the body has been informed by the age-old binary division between mind and body – spirit and matter. From the time of the early Christian fathers, women's bodies have been consigned to the dual domains of the maternal or the sexual, venerated on the one hand, damned on the other. This cultural bifurcation of the female body has created a social scenario in which to dwell too much within the body is to be sexually provocative, risking being branded promiscuous; yet, to be too little of the body is to be barren. Finding the middle ground between these two becomes nearly impossible.[5] Thus women appear to lose on all counts. And as writers they find themselves even more conflicted, for the very act they are engaged in – the articulation of self and body – is antithetical to woman's socially constructed identity which renders her, whether whore or madonna, outside verbal discourse. Yet, as Terry Eagleton has recently noted, such dichotomies are invalid, as aesthetics and intellect cannot be separated from the body. Ultimately, maintains Eagleton, to the degree that aesthetics has its origins as a discourse of the body, the creative act thus becomes as much a function of physical selves as of the intellect.[6]

These same tensions which are present in western thinking about women's bodies are pervasive as well throughout Russian literary and cultural history, with the added difference that a powerful folk tradition linking the image of the mother with the "damp mother earth" (mat' syra zemlia) placed the image of the Russian mother not only in close proximity to the Mother of God "Bogoroditsa" but to the land itself in all its various incarnations – as fertile, as suffering, as depleted, garnering ever more loyalty and love the more she suffered.[7] The ensuing social and cultural tensions caused by these complex images of the feminine engage many of the writers represented in this volume. In "The Inexperienced Muse" Vowles notes that anxiety about the body is often manifest as a fear of appearing immodest (68). Thus the image of the constrained body, created by women writers themselves in the nineteenth century, suggests that while women writers manifested a certain transgressiveness in taking up the pen, in all other matters of gender stereotypes, they conformed to cultural norms of femininity. Ciepiela discusses the appearance of the deformed or mutilated self (128) as an important category for women, one to which they increasingly retreat as their poems are branded ugly. Presto notes in her essay that the Silver Age poet Mirra Lokhvitskaia, unlike other women poets of her generation, focuses on the corporeal in her lyrics, enacting a metonymic relationship to the body. Lokhvitskaia fantasizes about transforming her heart into an unmediated organ of song, thereby creating an identity between poetic voice and female body – an identity that would later become central in French feminist theory of writing the female body.[8] The image of the female body acquired a particular configuration during the Stalin era in which, in Holmgren's words, "the good body was the hard body," (225) and in which woman's body, paired with the male worker in the visual propaganda of the day, "accented both her likeness and subservience to a stereotypically masculine model." And yet, while exhorted to hone their bodies to help build the socialist workers' paradise, Soviet women were also called upon to make the maternal body available to the state by producing more workers. It is the response to these tensions and contradictions, both from Soviet ideology and from Russia's past, that underlie and explain the often grotesque, free-spirited depictions of the body that Goscilo describes in what she terms the "unheavenly bodies" of late Soviet and post-Soviet women's prose.

Much of the anxiety about the body in Russian women's writing has been linked to anxiety specifically about the maternal body and how that body has been made to conform to the semi-sanctified mother figure in Russian cultural and religious history. Not surprisingly, then, many have been engaged in rewriting the traditional narratives of motherhood that have informed both Russian religious and secular thought since the Kievan period. Presto notes that most women and men associated with Symbolism were anti-procreative. Ciepiela, in "The Women of Russian Montparnasse," notes the complications of this movement away from motherhood in the poetry of Gippius, Tsvetaeva, and in the emigration in general. During the Stalin years the image of the mother figure came to be used as a way of unifying the nation during difficult times. Thus Stalin drew on nationalist symbols of Mother Earth and Mother Russia to evoke nationalist sentiment, a theme taken up by both Hodgson and Holmgren, who argue that the images of the bereft mother and the female mourner were compelling for women writers during the Soviet era. Ironically, as Hodgson suggests, one of the ways to show strong allegiance to the Stalinist state was by appropriating and reinforcing images from the Russian past.

While one of our goals in this volume has been to show the ways in which women writers have dealt with many of the subjects traditionally taken up by male writers, we have also sought to highlight those areas more specific to the female experience. Hodgson argues in "Women and Gender in Post-Symbolist Poetry and the Stalin Era" that women's poetry was particularly well received in the middle of the twentieth century because "it met a real need for confessional poetry which recognized specifically female experience" (209). Further, the relationship between mothers and daughters, an area remarkable for its absence in most male-authored fictions, becomes central to many of the authors represented here. Several essays also address what women's lives were like, how women were educated, and how they earned their living. Issues of women's social mobility are also addressed differently and more sympathetically by women writers than by their male contemporaries.

Literary relationships among women receive the attention here that they fail to receive in more traditional histories. It is in looking at these relationships that we are able to understand more fully the complexities of women's relationship to male traditions and how women's literary endeavors took place simultaneously within and outside that tradition. Vowles, Marsh, Ciepiela, and Hodgson all look at how women engaged with other women of their generation and formed close female friendships. Marsh discusses how both Verbitskaia and Dmitrieva were encouraged in their writings by Khvoshchinskaia and Nazar'eva. Ciepiela talks about how Tsvetaeva's power set the example for younger women poets, such as Anna Prismanova and Alla Golovina, living in the Paris emigration. Presto cites Lokhvitskaia's passionate, exotic poetic persona (138) as the prototype for the early poetic personae of Nadezhda Teffi (Lokhvitskaia's sister), the Soviet prose writer Marietta Shaginian, and Anna Akhmatova. But it is also important to note that the influence of these women writers on each other was a function not only of their perceived similarities but of differences as well. Ciepiela, for example, discusses how Marina Tsvetaeva, writing in the Paris emigration, influenced poets such as Irina Knorring, whose sensibility was entirely different from Tsvetaeva's.

In addition to themes more common to the female experience, the essays in this volume revisit aspects of women's experience that have previously been defined for them by male writers. Such, for example, is the theme of love. Counter to the received wisdom – mostly male in origin – about the primacy of love in a woman's life, many of the women writers represented here explicitly wrote against the theme of love as the highest pinnacle of a woman's existence. Instead, writers such as Kheraskova (see Kelly's essay) view love as damaging to a reasonable, autonomous existence in a way that prefigures the work of Mary Wollstonecraft on women's rights in England. Holmgren, Barker, and Goscilo discuss the fate of love within the context of the great Soviet romance of boy meets girl meets tractor. Holmgren finds permutations of that paradigmatic romance even under Stalinism, while Barker sees romance in the post-Stalin era as the arena within which larger issues of self and state are worked through. Finally Goscilo explores the tendency among post-Soviet writers such as Marina Palei and Liudmila Ulitskaia to reinvigorate romance with a heavy dose of female sexuality, strikingly absent, and consciously so, in most Soviet literature.

Many of the chapters in this volume take up the relationship between women's writing and the volatile social and political issues of the day.

Since the eighteenth century, writing has served as the chief vehicle through which Russian women have negotiated their way through the complex maze of social and political issues. Since the 1830s and the advent of the Natural School, social commitment has always been a central category in Russian literary criticism. But with few exceptions women have scored badly here, often being accused of paying insufficient attention to social developments, or of writing about them clumsily, or inartistically. Many of the essays in this volume show that women did, in fact, participate in the social realm and did so in ways that are complex and often breathtaking. Gheith, for example, argues that the ways in which women took part in the discourse on women's emancipation in Russia were very different from those subscribed to by Chernyshevsky and the other social critics of the middle of the nineteenth century and that this knowledge changes the parameters of the woman question and necessitates a re-evaluation of what constitutes the social. Marsh, in discussing twentieth-century prose authors, addresses how women writers participated in the representation of the social and in the movement of literature as social and moral action. Some writers raised social issues through their writing (Gurevich, Dmitrieva, Runova) as they took up issues from women's emancipation to the evils of child labor, while still others took on social questions through the venue of political activism (Krestovskaia, Verbitskaia, etc.).

The essays in this volume suggest that women's relationship to the social was multi-faceted. Not all women writers made social themes primary; some, in fact, deliberately eschewed them. In her essay on late twentieth-century women poets, Stephanie Sandler argues that "Russia's notorious habit of politicizing culture has virtually ensured an apolitical stance in many poets" (266). And yet, at the same time, Sandler notes the ways in which women incorporate the details of *byt* (the details of everyday life) in their poetry. In our schema, this act of claiming *byt* as the material of poetry becomes a social act, one that expands traditional notions of what constitutes social engagement in literature and leads to a re-evaluation of Russian women writers as being socially and politically unengaged.

Although this volume provides extensive coverage of the history of women's writing in Russia, we recognize that much still remains to be done. Much of the research reflected on these pages is still in its incipient stages. Often the work of recovery has been complicated by the difficulty of establishing such basic facts as bibliography, for such information is not always readily available for women writers. There were also questions we could not answer, topics that, in the interest of space, we could not treat. Drama, for example, is still an area where, as Kelly notes, women's literary endeavors were rendered problematic because of the existence of non-publishing dilettantes in the late eighteenth and early nineteenth centuries. The relationship between the oral and the written tradition in women's writing in the Soviet period is an area that still needs much study. Thus far the study of orality has largely been confined to folklore. During the Soviet period, however, workers and peasants dictated their biographies and memoirs for local Party organizations. Their oral biographies provide fertile fields for examining how women fashioned their own life stories against the larger historical narratives of their times.

Finally, because of the unusual time lag between the writing of these essays and their appearance in print, we were unable to include in this volume many new writers and much new literary production, a good deal of which is available on the Internet. Indeed, the very means by which we access literary production these days has changed both the way new writers reach their audience and the dynamics of literary response on the part of readers. While we have tried to be as inclusive as possible in the Guide to Women Writers and Their Works, in a volume such as this, those chapters dealing with contemporary culture are the hardest hit by the inevitable delays in the production process. For example, even as this volume was entering production Tat'iana Tolstaia's first novel *Kys'* was published, reminding us once again that a volume such as this always lags just behind what is being written by those whom we study.

The essays assembled in this volume invite us to rethink and re-measure Russia's literary tradition, allowing us to see it with different eyes. Much of what the writers represented in this volume have to say enables us to look beyond their literary texts to re-envision social and familial relations, aesthetics, and gender and genre norms during the eras they were writing in. As we embarked on the process of recovering their works and their voices, moving between well-known and little-known writings and writers, we refound a tradition that was not always shaped *for* these writers, but one that was often shaped *by* them. Their lives and their literary texts all suggest the livingness – the constantly changing interaction between writer and reader and between writer and the tradition itself – that constitutes the heart of a vital and volatile literary history.

NOTES

1. See, for example, Nina Auerbach, *Woman and the Demon: The Life of a Victorian Myth* (Cambridge, MA, 1982); Judith Butler, *Gender Trouble: Feminism and the Subversion of Identity* (New York, 1990); Hélène Cixous, *Readings: The Poetics of Blanchot, Joyce, Kafka, Kleist, Lispector, and Tsvetaeva*, ed., tr., and intro. by Verena Andermatt Conley (Minneapolis, MN, 1991); Marilyn Frye, *The Politics of Reality: Essays in Feminist Theory* (Freedom, CA, 1983); Diana Fuss, *Essentially Speaking* (New York, 1989); Gayle Greene and Coppelia Kahn (eds.), *The Making of Feminist Literary Criticism* (New York, 1993); Marianne Hirsch, *The Mother/Daughter Plot: Narrative, Psychoanalysis, Feminism* (Bloomington, IN, 1989); bell hooks, *Feminist Theory: From Margin to Center* (Boston, MA, 1984); Audre Lorde, *Sister Outsider* (Freedom, CA, 1984); Toril Moi, *Sexual/Textual Politics: Feminist Literary Theory* (New York, 1985); Mary Poovey, *Uneven Developments: The Ideological Work of Gender in Mid-Victorian England* (Chicago, 1988); Adrienne Rich, *On Lies, Secrets and Silence: Selected Prose 1966–1978* (New York, 1979); Naomi Schor, *Breaking the Chain: Women, Theory, and French Realist Fiction* (New York, 1985); Elaine Showalter, *A Literature of Their Own: British Women Novelists from Bronte to Lessing* (Princeton, NJ, 1977); Gayatri Chakravorty Spivak, *In Other Worlds: Essays in Cultural Politics* (New York, 1988).
2. For an opposing view to Marsh's see Charlotte Rosenthal, "Achievement and Obscurity: Women's Prose in the Silver Age," in Clyman and Greene, 164–5.
3. In her groundbreaking book *Terrible Perfection: Women and Russian Literature*, Barbara Heldt argues that while women were valorized and often venerated in nineteenth-century Russian male-authored fictions, those same women were also condemned to silence by their authors.
4. For a comparable set of analyses of Anglo-European women authors, see Mary Lynn Broe and Angela Ingram (eds.), *Women's Writing in Exile* (Chapel Hill, NC, 1989).
5. Among the many excellent studies on women's bodies, see Susan Bordo, *Unbearable Weight: Feminism, Western Culture, and the Body* (Berkeley, CA, 1993); Wendy Chapkis, *Beauty Secrets: Women and the Politics of Appearance* (Boston, MA, 1986); Costlow, Sandler and Vowles; Susan Suleiman, *The Female Body in Western Culture: Contemporary Perspectives* (Cambridge, MA, 1986); and Marina Warner, *Alone of All Her Sex: the Myth and the Cult of the Virgin Mary* (New York, 1983).
6. Terry Eagleton, *The Ideology of the Aesthetic* (Oxford, 1990), 13.
7. See in particular, Joanna Hubbs, *Mother Russia: The Feminine Myth in Russian Culture* (Bloomington, IN, 1988).
8. See Hélène Cixous and Catherine Clement, *The Newly Born Woman* (Minneapolis, MN, 1986) and Luce Irigaray, *This Sex Which is Not One* (Ithaca, NY, 1985) and *Speculum of the Other Woman* (Ithaca, NY, 1985).

1
_____

Women's image in Russian medieval literature

Until comparatively recently, both literary and historical criticism of the female image in medieval Russia has too often drawn a gloomy picture of inequality, repression, and suffering. With very limited exception, prerevolutionary analysis of the female image was occupied with women's legal, sociopolitical, and family status. Even the stalwarts of twentieth-century criticism, such as D. S. Likhachev and I. P. Eremin, produced no specific examination of the evolution of female characters, concentrating rather on questions of form and generic classification.[1] Furthermore, the absence of women writers in the medieval period and a preponderance of ecclesiastical female stereotypes have encouraged primarily historically based analysis, to the detriment of the literary portrait.

No work of literature written by a woman has come down to us; indeed, it was very rare for women to be literate as access to education was denied to them. In the cases where aristocratic ladies were taught to read, this was solely for devotional purposes such as reading of the Holy Scriptures and life-stories of the Orthodox saints. Until the seventeenth century, there was little alternative reading material – only a few travel accounts and historical works. Writing (and reading) was quite simply considered neither a profession, nor a general instructive or pleasurable activity; rather, it was a sacred task undertaken by the male clergy for the teaching and dissemination of Orthodox Christianity. The seventeenth century, the beginning of the modern period, saw the gradual appearance of creative secular writing as literacy became more widespread and foreign cultural influences gained more attention; yet only in the eighteenth century did women start producing creative literature, doubtless spurred on by the determination of Catherine II finally to establish a formal system of education for women.

Thus, throughout the medieval era, the portrayal of the female literary image and identity was dependent upon men working in a strictly patriarchal and ecclesiastical environment which did little to promote the less stereotypical image of women. Pre-seventeenth-century literary characters tended to be based (albeit at times very loosely) on historical figures whose sociopolitical status was reflected in the portrayals in the literary text. In the case of women, these spheres were restricted and controlled, resulting in likewise limited literary depictions.

How is it, then, that such inauspicious beginnings spawned so many original, admirable and enduring female literary prototypes, recognizable in both men and women's writing throughout the nineteenth and twentieth centuries? Whether as a reflection of prevailing social conditions or a study in psychological analysis, there are countless examples of modern heroines who have inherited characteristics from their medieval counterparts. The treatment of early prototypes has varied depending on the sociopolitical situation, whether the author is male or female, and whether the response to earlier models is positive or negative. With the advent of Socialist Realism, many of the traditional female role models were no longer appropriate, and modern prototypes were created, more suitable for the political and cultural ethos of Communism. Having evolved in diverse ways over nine centuries, the original prototypes were not easily usurped, and they surface in literature throughout the Soviet period, re-emerging once again with Russia herself in the 1990s.

This chapter will discuss in detail the most important female literary prototypes of the medieval period and point to some of the later works in Russian literature which draw inspiration from them. The main sociopolitical influences that affected women and their literary portrayal will also be mentioned, for their significance cannot be ignored in the construction of any medieval literary characters.

The creation of female prototypes was, of course, never a conscious exercise, but rather a response and/or reaction to the contemporary needs and desires of the author. Neither did the evolution of the female image run a smooth course; the earliest female literary characters were subjected to constant and most often unjustified misogyny for centuries. This did not lead to unchallenged submission on the part of women, however, even if a written response was not an option available to them. "Love your wives, but give them no power over you": these words, attributed to Vladimir Monomakh and found *sub anno* 1096 in the *Povest' vremennykh let* (Primary Chronicle), strongly indicate that the wise and respected

Monomakh had come to the conclusion even at this early date that women were not so powerless and held considerably more influence over their menfolk than many contemporary historians would care to admit.

Reinforcing this distrust of women, the first seven centuries of medieval Russian literature saw the rapid development of an ever-present tradition of the denigration of women, in comparison to which Monomakh's words are in fact comparatively meek. Far less ambiguous, for example, was the anonymous author of the twelfth-century *Molenie Daniila Zatochnika* (Supplication of Daniil the Exile), who seldom hesitated to employ imaginative descriptions in his tirades against the fairer sex. The *Slovo o zhenakh o dobrykh i o zlykh* (Discourse on Women, both Good and Evil) continued the misogynistic tradition, claiming that a virtuous wife is more valuable than precious gems, while an evil wife is like an aggravating itch. The fourteenth-century *Izmaragd* (Emerald), a miscellany of devotional readings, warned unsuspecting husbands to beware of the perfidious intentions of malicious-tongued women; and the sixteenth-century *Domostroi* (Household Management) offered advice to husbands on how they might best whip their erring wives to keep them under control and left no doubt as to who remained master of the household. Variations on this theme continued well into the seventeenth century when works such as the *Beseda ottsa s synom o zhenskoi zlobe* (A Father's Conversation with his Son about Woman's Evil) merely presented a more sophisticated and narratively detailed version of the *Slovo o zhenakh*.

Such a sustained level of misogyny was not, however, a feature inherited from Slavonic antiquity. When Vladimir I, Grand Prince of Kiev, instituted Orthodoxy as the official Russian religion in 988, he also opened the door to Byzantine cultural influence which entered the earliest Russian state of Kievan Rus' alongside the wider transplantation of necessary ecclesiastical texts.[2] As the eastern territory of the Holy Roman Empire, Byzantium was subject to canon law, and Orthodox Christianity proved to be no less misogynistic than its predecessor in Rome. Byzantine thought, for example, subscribed to a Neoplatonic asceticism regarding sexuality, which claimed that "women's reproductive function tied them more intimately to the physical world and made them even less capable [than men] of spiritual growth,"[3] rendering women more vulnerable to satanic forces and impurity. Many translations of misogynistic Byzantine sermons found in tenth-century Kievan collections stress the weakness of woman and her propensity to sin. The clergy actively disseminated this notion in Rus'—with evident success if judged by the mere handful of female native Russian saints compared with the array of male saints, several hundred strong.[4] The process of selective translation of only the most necessary texts for the teaching of Christianity further re-inforced this prototype: deprived of the wider Byzantine literary heritage (the vast collections of philosophy, historical works or classical literature which were not translated), Rus' was provided only with a very specific ecclesiastical model for female characters.

The Byzantine model conflicted strongly with the traditions of Slavonic antiquity where it appears that women enjoyed respect and sta-tus in society. This was not merely connected with the importance of their role as mothers and home-keepers, but was rather deeply embedded in the complex hierarchy of ancient pagan gods and goddesses. Various sources have unearthed pagan goddesses worshiped in Rus', including the popular and important Mokosh', goddess of fertility, women, childbirth, and woman's work such as spinning. The worship of Mokosh' possibly grew out of the ancient Slavonic cult of Damp Mother Earth (*Mat' syra zemlia*), all-powerful and creative embodiment of fertility and spring. These female pagan images commanded great reverence, their powers being regularly invoked to help, heal, and comfort. With the arrival in Rus' of the Christian Church, however, such powers were decried as witchcraft, the devil's work, and every aspect of pagan worship was denounced by the Orthodox authorities. Vladimir I, perhaps sensing an opportunity to weaken matriarchal domestic-based power and shift control to a more state-governed basis, supported this concept.

This transition was not without problems. Confusion arose between traditional pagan practices and nascent Russian Christianity, leading to a phenomenon known as *dvoeverie* (double faith) in which pagan ritual was carried over and mingled with Christian practices. Disparities in the teaching and acceptance of the new faith became an issue between rural and urban societies, upper and lower social classes, and it was not until the fifteenth century that the state and Church began in earnest to work together – ultimately in vain – to eradicate *dvoeverie*.[5] One of the best-known female Orthodox images strongly influenced by *dvoeverie* is Saint Paraskeva Piatnitsa: identified with many of the powers attributed to Mokosh', Paraskeva protected those who obeyed her rules of work, but most horribly punished those who broke them (a good example of pagan-style retribution in a supposedly Christian saint).

This change of attitude to women was reinforced by the exclusively male clergy responsible for copying manuscripts and ecclesiastical texts, and for disseminating the teachings of the Orthodox Church. Early Christian literature is hardly famed for impartial generosity towards the female image: stark black and white contrasts in many early Russian literary works tended to associate women either with Mary Mother of God (although no earthly woman could ever hope to approach her degree of perfection), or with the fallen figure of Eve, the temptress and destructor of good men. This duality may have felt more like a vicious circle for medieval Russian women who could never hope to attain the respected position of mother without participating in the sins of Eve. This idealization–reality conflict is frequently found in later female characters as well. Many of Fedor Dostoevsky's heroines, for example, both reflect and further complicate this dilemma as can be seen in the case of the prostitute Sonia in *Prestuplenie i nakazanie* (Crime and Punishment, 1866); for all her saintly goodness and compassion, which play a critical role in the redemption of Raskolnikov, Dostoevsky also marks her as the fallen woman, the prostitute.

Mention should briefly be made here, however, of the twelfth-century apocryphal tale *Khozhdenie bogoroditsy po mukam* (Travels of the Virgin Around Hell) found in early translated collections. In the tale, Mary attempts to intercede on behalf of those suffering in hell after she witnesses their torments. Although finally successful, alone she is unable to persuade God and Christ to take heed of her pleas – only when the angels and male saints join in does Christ relent and grant an annual period of leniency. Thus, we see even Mary portrayed as a weaker and less effectual character in the divine hierarchy – although far greater in compassion. The importance of compassion and intercession provided by female characters held great attraction for later writers: Dostoevsky's Ivan in *Brat'ia Karamazovy* (The Brothers Karamazov, 1881), for example, cites the unwillingness of God and Christ to release man from suffering (as opposed to Mary's determination to provide relief) in this apocryphal tale as one justification for rejecting the teachings of Christ.

With the gradual spread and entrenchment of ecclesiastical misogyny, the spheres of influence women had enjoyed in pagan Rus' were drastically curtailed, and women were forced to adapt to a system in which their role was always secondary. One of the most potent factors which contributed to the downward spiral of pre-Christian female authority and which nurtured the rise of misogynistic literature was the practice of selective literacy. The zeal with which manuscripts were composed and copied in the monasteries of Rus' was not to be found in the convents, as women were excluded from all such literary activity. While convents were often known to have libraries, thus indicating the possibility of at least some nuns being literate, there is no evidence to suggest that they also engaged in composition or copying of any type. A statement in the twelfth-century saint's life *Zhitie Evfrosinii Polotskoi* (Life of Evfrosiniia of Polotsk) that Evfrosiniia "wrote books in her own hand" is intriguing, but sadly cannot be substantiated. The *beresty* (birchbark documents, dating from the eleventh to the fifteenth centuries) discovered in the old city of Novgorod, on the other hand, do provide conclusive evidence that some women were actively literate. Messages, written and received by both men and women, were almost always for purposes of commerce, jurisdiction, and household management, rather than recreation or even devotional pursuit, although there are a small number of intimate letters such as one recently discovered in Novgorod. It is written by a woman who gently but insistently asks a gentleman friend why he has not come to see her – she has already written three times. Emotive yet frank, she appears anxious that she has offended him in some way and cannot understand his silence. Such fragmentary relics penned by women are not overly unusual in Novgorod, although even here no substantial evidence has come to light to suggest an active participation in the far more extensive official ecclesiastical literature.

It thus appears that women's contribution to early written culture was of a limited and practical nature. This understandably led to an imbalance of authorial perspective: the literary image of woman was seen almost exclusively through the prism of the Orthodox Church. The final and inevitably distorted impression cannot be considered an accurate reflection of reality, but rather the product of imagination, fear, fantasy, discrimination, and desire on the part of the male clergy. This distortion was possibly further promoted by some secular social structures such as the *terem*, loosely defined as the part of elite households where female members of the family lived and entertained their lady friends. Commonly blamed for the introduction of the *terem* tradition into medieval Russia are either Byzantine cultural influences or else the invading Tatar Hordes; and it is often assumed that the *terem* simply dealt women yet another misogynistic blow in the form of enforced control, "banishment" from the public arena, thus effectively depriving them of opportunity to become actively involved within a wider social context. These are, however, dangerously simplistic explanations which mask a far more complex issue: did the *terem* function purely as a repressive tool against women, or was it also designed and employed to protect female members of a patriarchal society where the importance of pure bloodline and arranged marriage was still paramount to ensure vital political allegiance among the various branches of the aristocracy? Furthermore, how did women react to the limited freedom of movement imposed upon them? Nancy Shields Kollmann convincingly suggests that the *terem* tradition may have grown up in Russia as "a native response to the development of elite society," citing, for example, "its utility in the political context and its compatibility with Russian Orthodox values about women."[6] As for women's reaction, it is very possible that within their physically restricted lives, they did enjoy power and sway in several important matters: they were largely responsible for selecting future spouses for their children and arranging the marriages; and they could ingratiate themselves with other families whenever need arose. Whatever the possible advantages of the *terem*, however, physical isolation still meant that there was little opportunity to record the positive aspects of woman's life, or to influence literary activity in the outside world where woman's image remained distinctly disadvantaged: increasingly absent in real life from the social arena, female literary characters through many centuries of Christianized Rus' continued to be depicted for the greater part as pious – and silent – wives of the heroic male protagonist. This was only to change when Peter the Great denounced the *terem* tradition and brought the elite women out into society at the end of the seventeenth century.

The restricted medieval perspective, however, did not mean that the literary image of women was purely negative. An exploration of female characters throughout the medieval period uncovers many exceptions to the black and white Christian stereotyping of women and presents enlightening and positive portraits. The oldest documented record of an influential woman, for instance, is the richly detailed legend surrounding Princess Ol'ga of Kiev, wife of Prince Igor. The colorful entry *sub anno* 945 in the *Primary Chronicle* (*Povest' vremennykh let*), has more than a hint of folkloric motif, attributing many of the traditional *mudraia devitsa* (Wise Maiden)[7] characteristics to Ol'ga, including an element of cunning which neatly complements her natural intelligence. She is respected for her gracious nature, yet remembered more for her resourceful and imaginative acts of revenge against the Derevlians who had slain Igor in battle. By dint of superior wit and tactical maneuvering, Ol'ga is ultimately far more effective than all her husband's warriors: according to the chronicle, she prevents the lands of Rus' from falling into enemy hands and upholds the honor of her dead husband. For this, she is compared favorably to any man, yet still retains all the traditionally attractive qualities of a woman.

Although hers is far from the perfect image of women advocated by the Church, the chronicler clearly relishes Ol'ga's feats of vengeance and recounts the tale with great enthusiasm. It must be emphasized, however, that Ol'ga undoubtedly received preferential treatment (not to mention leniency in the face of her un-Christian actions) from the ecclesiastical scribes, as she was the first member of the Rus' nobility to convert to Christianity. It was certainly politically astute for the relatively young Orthodox Church to make the most of such a popular and strong figure as Ol'ga, protector of the Kievan lands, who chose conversion: her example, correctly used, could well have helped to shore up the Church's efforts to instill Orthodoxy in Rus'.

One of Ol'ga's most popular traits is her similarity to figures from Russian folklore: as mentioned above, she possesses the wit and ingenuity of the Wise Maiden; her unconquerable warlike spirit casts her in the role of a *polenitsa* (legendary female warrior); and her leadership and annihilation of the enemy men recall the exploits of the legendary Amazons.[8] A similar early exception to the silently pious female character, and one who shares Ol'ga's dichotomous roots in ecclesiastical literature and folkloric tradition, is the mother of Feodosii of the Kievan Caves. In Nestor's revered twelfth-century saint's life *Zhitie Feodosiia Pecherskogo* (Life of Feodosii of the [Kievan] Caves), she is portrayed as an overpoweringly strong character of the negative type: determined to prevent her son from entering a monastery, she beats and abuses him mercilessly, attempting to break his religious resolve. A masculine, monster-like harridan, she must surely embody many of the clergy's worst apprehensions about women, and only when she takes the veil is she finally brought under control. To find such vivid violent descriptions in the hagiography of such an important ecclesiastical figure as Feodosii is unprecedented: hagiographical canons dictated that all individual characteristics be erased in favor of a common stereotypical embodiment of Christian values. Nestor, however, did not hesitate to contrast a bold catalogue of this mother's Herculean strength and attempts at selfish emotional blackmail to prevent her child leaving her for the Church, with the meekness and genuine humility of her son's temperament along with his determination to devote his life to God. The final effect is, of course, that Feodosii triumphs over his mother's iron rule (in a stark gender reversal of Ol'ga's triumph over the Derevlian Prince Mal), and the terrible excesses of his mother's character serve simply to emphasize the goodness of his own.[9] The Church is also left with an unforgettable portrait of a woman who acts directly against the Christian forces of Good, until repentance (or enlightenment) forces her to take the veil.

Ol'ga and Feodosii's mother are two of a kind; they bridge the chasm created deliberately by the clergy's efforts to eliminate all traces of pagan culture from ecclesiastical texts. As the Church expanded and grew more powerful, however, the female role in literature was increasingly consigned to black and white background stereotypes, and the more vivid female characters were to be found predominantly in folklore, even though the colorful wealth of oral tradition is populated for the most part by men. The Russian *skazki* (fairy tales), for example, generally depict women as a trophy to be won. Fairy tales fall into three main groups: animal tales; *volshebnye skazki* (magical tales), originating in pre-Christian times; and the later *bytovye skazki* (everyday tales), which incorporate a moral aspect – albeit of often dubious quality – and may also be satirical. The everyday and magical tales are the most pertinent to this study with the former tending to produce stereotypical female character casts, whilst the latter portray some positive heroines, such as in "Mar'ia Morevna." Mar'ia is a beautiful princess and champion warrior who so impresses Ivan-Tsarevich that he marries her. The stereotype of woman as the weaker sex is frequently reversed in this tale: disobeying Mar'ia's instructions when she goes off to war, Ivan-Tsarevich unleashes a terrible ogre kept prisoner by Mar'ia, who is consequently carried off by the ogre. Ivan-Tsarevich, continually breaking down in tears when presented with yet another seemingly impossible task to perform, must spend many years being "tested" to win her back.

Females are also often cast in the "helper" role in fairy tales, where only they are able to save the hero. This is certainly the case in the tale "Mudraia zhena" (The Wise Wife), where the traditional *durak* (fool) marries a wise maiden capable of magical acts and who always saves him by offering precious advice or completing the necessary tasks herself. Mention should also briefly be made of Baba-Iaga, the evil witch who also, however, has her more generous moments.

Rather more fertile ground for a stronger depiction of women are the *byliny* (epic folk songs). The principal characters of these were the fearless *bogatyri* (warrior heroes) who reveled in traditional manly exploits and shows of unimaginable strength to overcome all the odds and win a woman and land for their king. Reminiscent once again of the legendary

Amazons, there is a sizable collection of *polenitsy* (warrior maidens), women who challenge the epic heroes and prove their physical superiority over them. Predictably, the warrior maidens are normally then "tamed" by the men who woo and win them. One famous Kievan *bogatyr'*, for example, Dobrynia Nikitich, is challenged by a mysterious *bogatyr'*, who is identified as the warrior maiden Nastas'ia just before they engage in battle. Dobrynia and Nastas'ia are eventually married, after which Nastas'ia hangs up her sword and rapidly settles into domesticity with her husband. In the *bylina* "Dunai," however, the *bogatyr'* weds his longtime love Nastas'ia, only to kill her later when she proves more skillful than her husband in archery. Dunai is seemingly unable to cope with the humiliation of his wife outdoing him, although when he realizes that Nastas'ia was carrying his child, he takes his own life in despair and grief. The image of the warrior maiden captured the imagination of many later writers, both men and women, and was used to great effect in, for example, Nadezhda Durova's early nineteenth-century *Kavalerist-devitsa: Proisshestvie v Rossii* (The Cavalry Maiden).

Another important female figure in *byliny* is the hero/heroine's mother. Invariably old and wise and often widowed, she is able to foresee calamities which will befall her child and offer advice. Examples of this are the widowed mothers of Dobrynia in "Dobrynia i zmei" (Dobrynia and the Dragon), and in "Vasilii Buslaev": they warn their sons against certain actions and even take preventive measures to save them. These wise mother figures differ strongly from the weak-willed wives of countless *byliny*, who are lured into unfaithfulness either by evil spirits or more simply temptations of the flesh.

Occasionally elements of oral tradition did find their way into official Church literature, and among these fragments it is not unusual to discover laments (*prichitaniia* or *plachi*) sung by women. Included in the fourteenth-century hagiographical *Slovo o zhitii velikogo kniazia Dmitriia Ivanovicha* (Discourse on the Life of Grand Prince Dmitrii Ivanovich), for example, is the lament of his widow, Ovdotiia. Replete with themes and motifs from oral tradition, it also incorporates eloquent and sincere exhortations to Mary Mother of God not to forget Ovdotiia in her hour of need and miserable loneliness. Another widow, Iaroslavna, is found in the twelfth-century epic *Slovo o polku Igoreve* (Tale of Igor's Campaign) lamenting her husband Igor, believed to have been slain in battle against the Polovtsians. Her lyrical lament abounds with folklore imagery; amidst comparisons to the strength and beauty of nature, she likens herself to a seagull (the bird of mourning) flying to tend her fallen husband and cleanse his wounds. These are among the earliest examples of recorded Russian oral traditions, and one may only speculate in what way the image of women in medieval Russian literature may have been improved had such poetic sentiment been more regularly recorded in written form.

Another case of documented folklore on a far more extensive level is found in one extraordinary work which stands out for its unique composite structure of fairy tales and hagiographical *topoi*. The mid-sixteenth-century *Povest' o Petre i Fevronii muromskikh* (Tale of Petr and Fevroniia of Murom) was composed by the cleric-publicist Ermolai-Erazm, ostensibly for the canonization of the thirteenth-century historical figures of the same name and about whom very little is known. It is clearly modeled, however, upon much older fairy tales and is of the same genus as Gottfried von Strassburg's tale of Tristan and Isolde, thus illustrating the widespread influence of migratory folklore motifs. Petr is a prince who is mortally wounded by a dragon while defending the honor of his sister-in-law and can be cured only by Fevroniia, a peasant girl who speaks in riddles and mixes magical potions for Petr, eventually making him – not too unwillingly – marry her. After a few troublesome social problems, in which Fevroniia's wit, cunning, and magical powers inevitably save the day, they live happily ever after. The tale was christianized in order to emphasize the supposed saintliness of the couple: the dragon is the devil, the magical curative potion a divine miracle, and the conclusion reads more like a moralistic religious parable than a fairy tale. The fusion of folklore and hagiography is not without its problems; the work is memorable principally for its rich and colorful folk motifs, with the hagiographical elements tending to be relegated to the background. This was clearly a highly successful formula, however; the number of extant manuscript copies, even allowing for natural loss over time, attests to great popular demand for the tale in the medieval era.[10]

Fevroniia is a complex character who contravenes most of the submissive female stereotypes of religious hagiographical literature, but does not fully conform to the usual mold of folkloric Wise Maiden. She comprises a synthesis of both sets of characteristics: intelligent yet cunning, proud yet humble, and always the stronger of the partnership. Indeed, after slaying the dragon, Petr is passive, almost a secondary character, all further action being initiated by the dominant figure of Fevroniia. Despite their harmonious and loving mutual relations, this appears to be exactly what Monomakh warned against, and, true enough, it turns out to be the cause of great political problems. Petr's *boiars* (noblemen) claim that their wives do not approve of Fevroniia (coming from a peasant family, she is deemed too lowly to be queen), and they do not cease to harass their husbands until the latter persuade Petr to get rid of Fevroniia. The situation is turned on its head, however, when Fevroniia states that the one item she is permitted to take with her will be Petr. The ensuing inter-factional squabbling that breaks out between the *boiars* is sufficient to bring them to their senses and plead with Petr and Fevroniia to return and rule jointly over them. This appears to be authorial advocation of the political concept of a centralized state, ruled over by an autocratic leader sufficiently strong and respected to put an end to interference and problems arising from the *boiar* ranks – suitable (not to mention sensible) approbation for the reign and policies of Ivan the Terrible. With the positive conclusion of the tale, Monomakh's notion is both confirmed – had the *boiars* not listened to their wives, they would not temporarily have lost Petr as their prince – and debunked, as Fevroniia remains the dominant half of a successful ruling partnership.

Only the tale of Ol'ga's revenge against the Derevlians can begin to rival the obvious hybrid of ecclesiastical and fairy-tale elements found in the *Povest' o Petre i Fevronii muromskikh*; no other extant work from the medieval period incorporates folkloric tradition to such a great degree. It must be remembered that local tales connected to the Church were easily confused with folklore in a society where the transmission of information, both fact and fiction, was predominantly oral. Thus, the possibility of ecclesiastical tales being filtered through and corrupted by popular myth was very likely, and complicated further by the subtleties and unconscious practice of two-fold belief.

The seventeenth century in Russia is marked as a time of definitive political, social, and ecclesiastical transition which brought the medieval era to an end and heralded the dawning of the modern period with the accession to the throne of Peter the Great in 1682. The Time of Troubles (1605–13) between the death of Boris Godunov and the accession of Mikhail Romanov to the throne dominated the beginning of the century with the terrors of invasion, civil war, and uncertainty. As a consequence, many Russians were left questioning long-held precepts concerning the political and moral state of Russian affairs. The religious revivals, and later the Schism[11] of the Orthodox Church simply compounded the confusion felt by a people who may have been justified in believing Russia, the Third Rome, was now floundering hopelessly.[12] Invasion from the West resulted in renewed contact with the Catholic lands of Europe, and the accompanying influences of culture and education. A growing awareness of the secular world outside Russia slowly gave birth to dissatisfaction with the moralistic didacticism of previous centuries, and answers to the malaise of Russia and her people began to be sought beyond the confines of a purely ecclesiastical world view.

The radical sociopolitical changes of this time were equally reflected in literary developments; ecclesiastical dominance over literary activity began to wane and the rise of literacy in secular society introduced exciting new influences. In this respect, two works in particular mark an important milestone in the evolution of medieval literature: composed as hagiographies, both the *Povest' ob Ul'ianii Osor'inoi* (Tale of Ul'ianiia Osor'ina) and the *Povest' o boiaryne Morozovoi* (Tale of the Boiaryna Morozova) present detailed portraits of strong and determined women as their protagonists. Both works testify to the birth of a new attitude towards literary heroines.

The *Tale of Ul'ianiia Osor'ina* tells how Ul'ianiia followed the expected course of marriage to a virtuous man, Georgii, and the raising of his children, while managing the household and estate with common sense and success during the frequent and prolonged absences of her husband. Following the death of two of their sons, Georgii refused Ul'ianiia's request to retire to a convent, explaining to her that she still had a husband and family who needed her care. She accepted his decision and concentrated solely on her charitable deeds in the secular world. One extraordinary feature of this work, which purports to be a hagiography, is that neither protagonist nor author (Ul'ianiia's son Kallistrat) ever took monastic vows, thus making it the first Russian hagiography both to be devoted to a layperson and composed by one. Unlike the majority of previous hagiographers, Kallistrat was thus able to present an unusually rich account of Ul'ianiia's lifestyle, with far greater accuracy and fewer of the hagiographical clichés of embellishment used in cases where insufficient original material was available to the hagiographer. He builds up Ul'ianiia's character in a way previously unseen in Russian literature: he describes how she relates to others, her family and servants; he is defensive of her goodness and saintly qualities as well as her practical nature; we hear how her actions stem from reasoned motive instead of divine preordination; and we feel her despair as well as her happiness. Together, these factors present a very intimate picture of Ul'ianiia, one sufficiently realistic for many women to be able to identify with.[13]

Ul'ianiia is the first genuinely good Russian heroine, cast in realistic terms of human value rather than simply in the ecclesiastical mold of sinful woman who must redeem herself. Practical common sense mixed with her irreproachable *smirenie* (humility; considered one of the most important virtues in Orthodox Christianity) is starkly at odds with the centuries-long formulaic patterns of inherent female wickedness and clearly marks a turning point in attitudes towards women. The emphasis placed upon her great feats of charity in the real world can further be seen as recognition that women, as well as men, could contribute positively, in a material and spiritual sense, to society.

Ul'ianiia provides the prototype for later literary characters such as Matrena in Aleksandr Solzhenitsyn's "Matrenin dvor" (Matryona's House, 1963). Matryona's life and total selflessness, mirroring those of Ul'ianiia, act as authorial expressions of morality and spiritual belief. Both Kallistrat and Solzhenitsyn, furthermore, choose to voice their dissatisfaction with elements of the Orthodox Church by creating female characters who have no strong links with the established Church, yet whose faith is undiminished and productive.

Far less subtle an attack than Kallistrat's against the Church was made by the author of the *Povest' o boiaryne Morozovoi*, which tells of the campaign waged against the ecclesiastical hierarchy by Feodosiia Morozova, seventeenth-century aristocratic courtier and most famous female Old Believer, in the aftermath of the Nikonian ecclesiastical reforms. As in the case of Ul'ianiia, the author of Feodosiia's hagiography was well-acquainted with her daily life and routine and thus able to furnish his tale with convincingly realistic detail. He describes how Feodosiia is moved from nunnery to nunnery in Moscow, before finally being exiled to the far northern territories. Further, he records many of the conversations Feodosiia has with her adversaries on this voyage of imprisonment. Slowly, a portrait emerges of a devoted mother, a loyal sister and friend, but also a supremely intelligent woman extremely well-versed in theology as well as the Holy Books, and a favorite debating partner of learned men. A rational thinker, she cannot accept the Nikonian reforms as they contravene traditional Orthodox rituals and would lead to blasphemy. Through an emotive and penetrating analysis of her thoughts and motives, the reader is encouraged to form a favorable and admiring impression of Feodosiia.

For all the emphasis laid upon the emotional and intellectual sides of her nature, however, Feodosiia is undoubtedly made of stern material; she stands her ground in the face of terrible persecution, eventually starving to death in a desolate northern fortress dungeon. She is not the type of character to cede to another merely because she is a woman, never hesitating to contradict – albeit in a civil tone – the senior clergy and statesmen who attempt to dissuade her from her chosen path. Feodosiia is not, however, cast in the mold of earlier religious super-ascetics: the author creates a measured balance of tender "womanly" characteristics together with elements of great strength and fighting spirit, resulting in a genuinely multi-dimensional character. The author, himself an Old Believer, naturally wished to hold Feodosiia aloft as an example of forti-tude and resolution, and by emphasizing her womanly qualities and virtues, he increases the impact and sympathy of the reader. This, in turn, imparts to the work a sense of realism; no longer are we dealing with literary ideals of womanly virtue but with virtue tested against the back-drop of real life. The first truly revolutionary female prototype in Russian literature, Feodosiia's example may well have inspired later voices of protest against the seemingly invincible forces of state and Church.

It is worth noting that up to this point the greater majority of strong female literary characters are widows (Ol'ga from the *Povest' vremennykh let*, Feodosii's mother, Ovdotiia and Iaroslavna, Ul'ianiia and Feodosiia). This is a repeated pattern originating in the traditional respect afforded to eld-erly women – the usual time of widowhood. Widows were deemed to have fulfilled their duty to society, cared for husbands and raised families, and, more importantly, they were no longer considered a threat, either in terms of sexual temptation (leading potentially to family dishonor) or possible contamination of the bloodline, as their child-bearing years were consid-ered to be past. Moreover, after the death of a husband, his widow would commonly shoulder the responsibilities and duties of managing the fam-ily estate and affairs if her sons were still minors. As a result, widows became more active members of the commercial and social spheres and even held higher positions at the royal courts than married women. The Church likewise decreed that the only women permitted to bake the com-munion host were widows aged fifty and over. The inherent implication in this attitude towards widows is that "desexualization" brings more privilege, influence, and freedom, in line with Neoplatonic ascetics regarding sexually active woman as a spiritual inferior. Monomakh would perhaps have been wiser to beware the widow rather than the wife.

One endearing seventeenth-century portrait of womanly tenderness and strength, however, is not that of a widow. The dynamic, belligerent, and fanatical Old Believer Archpriest Avvakum found his most patient and devoted supporter in his wife Anastasiia Markovna. In his lengthy autobiographical *zhitie* (life), detailing his staunch and often violent protest against the Nikonian reforms, subsequent persecution, and exile in Siberia, Avvakum describes how Anastasiia faithfully followed him, sharing his privation with no complaint. Despite all of Avvakum's outward shows of strength and domination in the narrative, he hides from his wife neither his own insecurities nor the brutal truth that their hardships will end only when they die – he knows her to be sufficiently strong in mind and in faith to accept their fate – and his descriptions of Anastasiia are tender and admiring, recognizing both her patience and feats of endurance. She never offers unsolicited advice, yet always inspires him to continue teaching the true faith when he becomes discouraged; and Avvakum always complies with her advice.

Anastasiia can furthermore be seen as the earliest in a long tradition of compassionate female characters and writers who support their menfolk when all others have turned against them. Princess Natal'ia Dolgorukaia, for example, later recorded in her *Zapiski* (Notes) the hardships of exile in Siberia with her husband in the eighteenth century, and the wives of the Decembrists likewise stoically followed their husbands into exile.[14] Slightly over one century later, Nadezhda Mandel'stam recounted the last four years of her husband Osip's life in exile in *Vospominaniia* (Hope Against Hope: a Memoir), at the same time as Evgeniia Ginzburg recorded her own experiences of life in the camps in the 1930–40s in *Krutoi marshrut* (Within the Whirlwind).

The later decades of the seventeenth century witnessed a dramatic acceleration of secular influences in Russia, prompted by the reforms of Peter the Great. Increased literacy outside the ranks of the clergy led to several compositions of a more secular nature; suddenly the characters, their motivation and the ability to entertain an audience with a compelling plot became important factors. This was the nascent form of a semi-secular genre, the *povesti* (tales), which no longer strove to nourish merely the spiritual requirements of the reader, but also the creative. One especially welcome development was in character portrayal; having already witnessed an apparent authorial desire to reflect a more realistic literary protagonist in the tales of Ul'ianiia Osor'ina and Boiaryna Morozova, the later seventeenth-century *povesti* began to sweep aside many more of the medieval stereotypes of character depiction. A curiosity arose about the psychological motivation and rationale of the protagonist, as well as the psychology of human relations. Slowly, medieval stereotypes became less viable which, in turn, meant that the image of woman as an evil inferior to man began to recede. It should be noted, though, that there were still no women writers and so even this new progressive female literary identity was still constructed from a male viewpoint.

The move towards secular writing was gradual, however, and many *povesti* continued to rely upon traditional moralistic instruction for their denouement. The *Povest' o Savve Grudtsyne* (Tale of Savva Grudtsyn), for example, while presenting a detailed picaresque-style storyline, still cast the main female character in the mold of devil's advocate, and the didactic import was clearly that monastic retreat remained the only way to ensure salvation. The *Povest' o Karpe Sutulove* (Tale of Karp Sutulov), on the other hand,[15] does illustrate the trend towards a more advanced type of secular composition, and at the same time it demonstrates that familiar international themes and plots had indeed penetrated Russian literary culture. In a satirical commentary upon corruption and dissolute behavior in both the merchant and clerical milieux, Tat'iana, loyal and loving wife of the wealthy merchant Karp, succeeds in reducing three lustful would-be seducers (a merchant, a priest, and an archbishop) to unwilling actors in an improvised pantomime. Taking advantage of her husband's absence and her need to take up a pre-arranged financial loan, all three of these traditionally respected characters demand to spend one night with her. She neatly and amusingly sidesteps their advances (even persuading the archbishop to dress up in her own clothes), takes their money and exposes their shameful intentions to the local *voevoda* (provincial governor), who recognizes not only Tat'iana's wit and intelligence, but also the humor of the situation. Karp likewise fully appreciates the talents of his extraordinary wife, applauding the fact that she acted independently of him and profited so handsomely – like Avvakum and Anastasiia, Karp and Tat'iana present another example of a positive and rewarding partnership.

What is most interesting about Tat'iana is that she is not the most obvious choice for a literary heroine. A perfectly ordinary woman – a merchant's wife who enjoys entertaining her well-to-do female friends while awaiting the return of her husband – she is described as increasingly perplexed at almost every turn, and she pursues the unadventurous path of seeking advice from her priest and then the archbishop. Only when these options simply further confuse the issue does she combine a daring mixture of impulse and improvisation. This works firmly in her favor as the reader does not necessarily expect Tat'iana to show such panache, yet at the same time remain in control of the situation. The entire tale, in fact, illustrates just how far the female image had progressed from the medieval prototype, and how successful a woman could be in both business and self-defense: Tatiana secures the money she needs without compromising her honor, and even lectures the failed suitors on their moral conduct – in stark contrast to their vacuous honeyed words to her – before mischievously delivering them up to the *voevoda*.

At times reminiscent of Princess Ol'ga, Tat'iana's "revenge" is far more humorous and also free to address a serious contemporary issue in its outspoken condemnation of corruption in the Church. Seldom before had such senior ecclesiastical figures found themselves the butt of such humiliating escapades – and never before at the hands of a woman! No longer was the restrictive Byzantine female literary prototype fully enforceable: the ecclesiastical monopoly on literacy had been broken and lay writers were not subject to the strict censure of the Church. Female sexuality was recognized as more than simply an instrument of the devil, it became a part of real life and could be incorporated in more progressive literary works to great humorous effect. The author of this tale created a very suitable protagonist to expose corruption in the Church; so many centuries of repression by the Church of every type of female depiction would surely have made Tat'iana's revenge all the sweeter. On a wider scale, later in the eighteenth century female writers themselves took up the challenge and directed many satirical and witty epigrams against those male authors who still scorned the position and abilities of the fairer sex.

Annushka is the unusually strong female protagonist of another tale from the end of the seventeenth century, *Povest' o Frole Skobeeve* (Tale of Frol Skobeev), which presents a broader and colorful portrait of contemporary Muscovite society. Frol, infamous and incorrigible scoundrel, makes no attempt to disguise his scurrilous desire to obtain position and wealth by any available means. He cheats and bribes his way into marriage with Annushka, daughter of a Muscovite aristocrat, by dressing up in his sister's clothes and attending Annushka's name-day party which culminates in Frol's forcible – albeit hesitant – seduction of his innocent hostess. Cross-dressing per se is a daring and highly uncommon concept in medieval Russian literature: in the *Povest' o Karpe Sutulove*, it is used as a momentary stalling tactic (designed to buy time for Tat'iana until the next suitor arrives) just as much as an appropriately comic/moralistic device (making the archbishop exchange his long ecclesiastical robes for one of Tatiana's long dresses). For Frol, on the other hand, it is an important and calculated part of his seduction plan, which imbues it with a far more risqué element. It is furthermore unusual to find cross-dressing of men as women, as opposed to women as men: in this case, however, it anticipates the future dominant/submissive roles of Annushka and Frol.

What Frol clearly does not count upon is the speed with which his new wife acquires from him the art of dissemblance and deception. She rapidly develops a talent for turning every situation to her advantage, exploiting every possibility. In fact, Annushka consistently appears to be the dominant character in their partnership both in terms of intelligence and emotional sensibility. On more than one occasion in the text, Annushka is described as feeling pity for Frol, which suggests at least some degree of emotional or rational superiority. In contrast to the other female characters of the tale, including her complicit nurse, Annushka is ready and determined to stand up for herself, risking parental rage and abandonment, in order to decide her own actions and fate.

Intrigue and plot are essential in this tale: a complex storyline with several detailed digressions provides not only variety and humor, but also an opportunity for diverse interaction between different characters. This in turn gradually reveals more about the psychology of the central characters, how they reason and react in different situations. The anonymous author offers neither commentary nor moral judgment on the behavior of his two wayward protagonists; instead he describes the thoughts and desires of the main characters as well as some secondary figures, allowing readers to come to their own conclusions – a freedom not found previously in Russian literature. He does, however, appear at times inclined to favor Annushka over Frol: while much of the humor of the latter's character rides on his reputation as the stereotypical rogue, Annushka is developed in a more distinctive manner. She is a more realistic figure, having to cope with pertinent female problems of the time ranging from undesirable amorous advances to arranged marriages. Neither Frol nor Annushka, however, show much respect for the traditions of honor and obedience, even though they succeed in establishing very comfortable lives at the expense of Annushka's family. While this may have been the expected behavior of a rogue such as Frol, to disobey one's parents is not appropriate for a lady of breeding such as Annushka, who can be seen as breaking completely with all medieval prototypes and clearing the path for more independent heroines in the future. The fact that the tale was immensely popular, and is known in many versions and copies, suggests that this theme was appreciated by a wide audience. Undoubtedly, the comic aspects of Muscovite high society would have been appealing, but

Annushka is such an attractive, daring, and novel type of heroine, it is very likely that her character also played an important role in its success.

In conclusion, it is clear that the literary image of medieval Russian women suffered mixed fortunes. What can be gleaned and interpreted from the earliest chronicles and folklore sources concerning women's status in pre-Christian times lends support to the notion that women enjoyed considerable sway in many spheres of life, but that the arrival of the Orthodox Church in Rus' began a long process of erosion of women's image and powers. Ecclesiastical propaganda nourished misogynistic attitudes and complex dilemmas of idealization *versus* condemnation, commonly reflected in both medieval and modern literary works. Despite much vilification, however, women slowly learned to function within the new parameters of Christianity and build upon their remaining areas of influence. Male writers, in turn, created several strong female literary prototypes, choosing to emphasize traditional folkloric elements alongside the ecclesiastical image of women.

In the seventeenth century the old-fashioned Christian stereotype of women finally gave way to a new and radically different literary heroine. Catering to a more sophisticated and increasingly secular audience, greater interest in psychological motivation and analysis of the individual characters became a focal point in literary endeavor. Throughout the seventeenth century, several important female literary protagonists mark a more modern and realistic form of expression and genre. By the time of Peter the Great, the female prototype had finally begun to "answer back," and to challenge the accepted Orthodox stereotype; Monomakh's words of warning had at last been rendered anachronistic and redundant.

NOTES

The author would like to thank the editors, referees and Faith Wigzell for their help and suggestions in the writing of this chapter.

1. For an overview of critical attitude, see N. L. Pushkareva, *Zhenshchiny drevnei Rusi* (Moscow, 1989), 177–209.

2. See D. S. Likhachev, "The Type and Character of the Byzantine Influence on Old Russian Literature," *Oxford Slavonic Papers* 12–13 (1965–7), 14–32.

3. See Eve Levin, *Sex and Society in the World of the Orthodox Slavs, 900–1700* (Ithaca, NY, 1989), 36; and Joanna Hubbs, *Mother Russia: The Feminine Myth in Russian Culture* (Bloomington, IN, 1988), 92.

4. This contrasts also with the Byzantine Orthodox calendar which dedicated many festivals to female saints.

5. See T. A. Bernshtam, "Russian Folk Culture and Folk Religion" in Marjorie Mandelshtam Balzer (ed.), *Russian Traditional Culture: Religion, Gender, and Customary Law*

(Armonk, NY, 1992), 34–47; and Francis Conte, "Paganism and Christianity in Russia: 'Double' or 'Triple' Faith?" in *The Christianization of Ancient Russia. A Millennium: 988–1988* (Paris, 1992), 207–15.

6. For a history of the *terem* in Russia, see Nancy Shields Kollmann, "The Seclusion of Elite Muscovite Women," *Russian History* 10: 2 (1983), 170–87.

7. The Wise Maiden is a positive character found in Russian folktales; commonly of peasant origin, she speaks in riddles, possesses supernatural talents and offers precious advice to the hero (without which he would be lost), and often marries him.

8. The Amazons were a nomadic tribe of female warriors who, according to Herodotus, operated a matriarchal society and roved the southern steppe of ancient Rus' in the fifth century BC; see Herodotus, *The Persian Wars*, Book IV, chapters 110–17.

9. Twelfth-century scribes in Rus' would have applied the canons of Byzantine rhetoric to their composition, one common feature of which was to provide exempla through contrast, an easily comprehensible and very effective means of differentiating good from bad for the reader.

10. Manuscripts were expensive and time-consuming to produce, with very few literate scribes able to reproduce them. Thus, a manuscript which has survived extant in many copies indicates a popular demand for that particular work.

11. The Schism in the Russian Orthodox Church came about in the mid-seventeenth century as a result of the reforms introduced by the Patriarch Nikon in an effort to bring the Russian Orthodox Church in line with other Orthodox communities. Nikon's reforms brought about strong opposition from the more conservative elements in the church who, under the leadership of the Archpriest Avvakum, formed a group of schismatics known as the Old Believers.

12. Moscow as The Third Rome was a doctrine developed in the sixteenth century which supplied the Muscovite autocracy and the church with both historical and genealogical justification. According to this doctrine the first Rome had fallen because it had betrayed true Christianity; Constantinople had fallen for similar reasons which left Moscow the only true remaining Christian capital, one that would rule forever.

13. Kallistrat did not compose this masterpiece without a second agenda, however: it is likely that he supported the trans-Volga hermit movement, which repudiated the highly ritualistic form of worship commonly practiced in the established Orthodox Church during the sixteenth and seventeenth centuries, and instead encouraged an individual striving towards salvation without need of holy vows. Thus, Kallistrat possibly chose Ul'ianiia as his subject not simply from filial admiration and love, but also precisely because he could offer a more realistic portrait of someone worthy of sainthood, yet who had lived and worked only in the secular world.

14. The Decembrists were a group of army officers who, under the reign of Nicholas I, organized an uprising on December 14, 1825 in an effort to bring about a more liberal, constitutional Russia. Badly organized, the officers were arrested and subsequently were either hanged or exiled to Siberia.

15. The subtitle of this *Povest'* is particularly interesting: "Povest' o nekotorom goste bogatom i slavnom o Karpe Sutulove i o premudroi zhene ego, kako ne oskverni lozha muzha svoego" (The Tale of a Certain Rich and Famous Merchant Karp Sutulov and of his Extremely Wise Wife, Who Did Not Defile her Husband's Bed). This is one of the very rare occasions in medieval Russian literature where a female character is mentioned in the title of a work.

2

Sappho, Corinna, and Niobe: genres and personae in Russian women's writing, 1760–1820

Introduction: the cultural background

The westernization of Russian culture that began in earnest during the reign of Aleksei Mikhailovich (1645–1676) affected women's writing slowly. Up to the middle of the eighteenth century, the only genre of writing to which women made any significant contributions was the private letter (as had been the case in pre-Petrine times too). Most letters, as in previous generations, remained routine and ungrammatical communications of mundane content. Only in the late eighteenth century did the letter turn into something resembling an art form. The letters of Catherine II, or of Masha Protasova, niece and protégée of the poet Vasilii Zhukovskii, are just as "literary", if not – in the second case, at least – as playful, as the more famous missives of the "Pushkin pleiad" two decades later.[1]

But private correspondence, if still the main genre to which women contributed (in terms of numbers involved), was, from the 1750s, no longer the only, or indeed the most important, vehicle for their work. It was at this date that women began, at first hesitantly, to become involved in the creation of *literatura*, the new tradition of imaginative writing that had been implanted in Russia about a century earlier. One important factor that prompted their participation was the increased social and political prominence of women in the post-Petrine period. Introduced to a greater public role by Aleksei Mikhailovich, emancipated by proxy during the regency of Sophia, his successor, then forced by her brother Peter the Great to take their place alongside men in public assemblies, women had, after Peter's death, been thrust by the quirks of succession to the ultimate heights of autocratic power. Women in Russia, therefore, went in three generations from near-invisibility (though with the possibility of manipulation behind the scenes) to the greatest degree of political and public prominence their society could offer.

What was more, the most successful and longest-lived Russian woman ruler, Catherine II, was (unlike, for instance, Elizabeth I of England) genuinely interested in bettering the lot of her female subjects, a task to which she devoted a great deal of time and energy. Though Catherine herself took pride in her "masculine" intellect, her insistence on the need to combat the triviality of women's lives, and inculcate in them a love of intellectual pursuits, including writing, had far-reaching effects on the aristocratic circles of her day. It is clear that her efforts were greeted with approbation verging on adulation by many aristocratic women, and that Catherine inspired in them aspirations to self-betterment. In the "Invocation" to her *Heroides: Dedicated to the Muses* (1777), Ekaterina Urusova encapsulated literary history in heroic couplets:

> Soon all the Russian land burst into bloom,
> Racines and Pindars issued from her womb,
> Singing in praise of CATARINA's day . . .
> Now, clustering about the sacred Muses' throne
> The female sex begins to lift its song . . .
> Russia has Sapphos now, and de la Suzes . . .[2]

In "Stanzas on the Founding of the Russian Academy of Sciences," Mar'ia Sushkova paid tribute not only to Catherine, but also to her cultural lieutenant Ekaterina Dashkova, President of the Academy, as a pioneer of intellectual liberty for women:

> And You, the co-worker of respected writers,
> The honour of Your sex, complete Your glorious path,
> O Favourite of the Muses given unto Your Care,
> Be one of their number, and be an ornament to them;
> A wonderful phenomenon of this century, and a new one,
> In you, O Dashkova, the scholar sees the light;
> The Minerva of our days, driving away prejudice,
> Herself pays tribute to your qualities.[3]

The importance of Catherine and Dashkova's prominence as an aid to women's intellectual self-confidence should not be underestimated, given that this was a culture where the lives of famous men and women of the past and present were used to inspire young pupils in the schoolroom. On the other hand, one should perhaps not overemphasize the direct influence of Catherine and Dashkova as literary models. Neither contributed to the genres of lyric verse and fiction, the two main areas of other women's literary activities, while both participated significantly in spheres normally outside the span of "feminine" ambition (journalism, satirical comedy, and, in the case of Catherine II, narrative history and historical plays).

There were factors other than distinguished example, too, which facilitated women's growing participation in literature, as in other domains of public life. One was the huge disruption of native traditions witnessed by aristocratic Russia during the eighteenth century. Political and social reform, the development of industry, commerce, and education, changes in custom, dress, and manners were so manifold that conventional notions of appropriate behavior were suspended, if not reversed. *Commedia dell'arte* and the Baroque court masquerade, in which women disguised themselves as men and men as women, enjoyed great popularity in Russia throughout the eighteenth century.[4] In a society where power presented itself as theater, the conventions of spectacle inevitably spilled over into life. Catherine II and Dashkova adopted masculine dress in order to lead the coup deposing Peter III in 1762; the young male courtiers of the later part of Catherine's reign were to become at least as dandified as their female counterparts, who themselves exercised considerable authority over their own lives and incomes. If the ridiculously Francophile *zhemanikha* (affected society lady) was a favorite satirical object of male authors, such as Iakov Kniazhnin, women writers were equally ready to poke fun at the folly of men. Here, for example, is an extract from a poem by the Moskvina sisters, "To a Looking-Glass," published in their collection *Aoniia* of 1802, but still in the late eighteenth-century manner:

> And when a young beau has a meeting
> With his sweetheart, he too comes
> To find how he'd be best completing
> His dress, to please his lady love.
> How he smirks and twirls and giggles,
> How he stamps his pretty feet,
> And spends quite half an hour rehearsing
> His complimentary, flattering speech.[5]

The new social prominence of women, and concomitant superfluity of men, might be the subject of bilateral mockery, but it also had significant effects on the composition of serious literature. Women could now perfectly well act as literary patrons; like men in the same position, female patrons could be the recipients of works of routine flattery, but they could also be the inspirations of works of genuine merit. As early as 1734, for example, the cleric Fedor Buslaev published a syllabic-verse eulogy to his late patron Baroness Mariia Iakovlevna Stroganova, a woman whose virtue and philanthropy were generally admired. The poem, "Umozritel'stvo dushevnoe" ("Spiritual Contemplation"), a vision of the dead woman first lying on her deathbed, and then being greeted by personifications of her various virtues in Heaven, is a work of deep religious feeling and true eloquence. The virtues of prominent women were also celebrated in funeral eulogies and name-day sermons by numerous other eighteenth-century clerics, some of them holding the highest ranks in the Orthodox Church. Such works reflected a profound change in attitude by the Orthodox Church, which in the sixteenth and seventeenth centuries had emphasized the inherent sinfulness of all but the Mother of God and a few women of extraordinary virtue (for example, virgin saints). It is scarcely surprising that the new secular literature proved at least as ready to celebrate the achievements of women in its turn. In 1783, for example, Kniazhnin addressed a humorously self-deprecating poetic epistle to Dashkova, celebrating her erudition and acknowledging her patronage of the arts.

Besides such broad social tendencies, certain more immediate factors also encouraged women's literary activities. Though all the evidence suggests that women from the elite of Russian society (in particular, from the royal household) had always been taught their letters, their education (like that of most Russian men) had been intended in the first place to equip them for the reading of sacred texts. Peter the Great's emphasis on education as a channel for vocational training was obviously more relevant to boys than girls; the Petrine conduct manual *Iunosti chestnoe zertsalo* (The Honest Looking-Glass of Youth, 1717) suggests that the primary purpose of women's education should be to inculcate morality, and especially filial piety, philanthropy, and modesty (both in a sexual and in a social sense). However, even in the first half of the eighteenth century some enlightened upper-class parents had their daughters educated privately to a higher intellectual standard than *The Honest Looking-Glass* anticipated. The norm, especially in the provinces, was still represented by Anna Labzina, who remembered teaching herself to read and write from the Gospels, or by Derzhavin's first wife, of whom Ivan Dmitriev recalls in his *Vzgliad na moiu zhizn'* (Glimpse of My Life, 1823, 40–1), "she had had the most run-of-the-mill upbringing, of the kind then offered in private schools, but after her marriage acquired a passionate interest in the best works of French literature." But some aristocratic households spared no expense in engaging tutors for their daughters; and even more negligent parents or guardians sometimes gave girls free range of the books in the library, or at any rate those that they did not consider immoral (as happened with Princess Dashkova in her youth). The educational theories propagandized by behavior books of the late eighteenth century, most of them translations from the French of such authors as François Fénelon and Anne-Thérèse de Lambert, emphasized the benefits to girls' morals of reading worthy books. The need for aristocratic girls to have a good grammatical grasp of their own language, and also of foreign languages, in particular French, was something else stressed in educational treatises; it was given an equal prominence in the curriculum of Catherine II's showpiece "Institutes for Daughters of the Nobility," where education to the highest international levels was offered to a select few.[6]

Aristocratic women's command of foreign languages naturally gave them access to literary texts from abroad, particularly from France. Translation into Russian was, therefore, one way in which a well-educated young woman could make a contribution to the literary world, and, in the 1790s, women such as Mar'ia Sushkova and Ekaterina and Anastas'ia Svin'ina did indeed translate various works from the French, German and even English. However, the importance of women's contribution to translation should not be overstated: the majority of translations carried out during the late eighteenth century were the work of men, many of them impecunious university students, and some acting under the aegis of the Society Concerned with the Study of Foreign Literature, founded by Catherine herself, which operated between 1768 and 1783. It was not until at least the 1820s that translation began to become a female-dominated profession in Russia (a development that, predictably enough, coincided with a decline in its profitability, and perhaps also prestige). And while translation definitely dominated work produced by women, there were still at least a dozen writers active before 1800 with original texts to their credit.

Before 1800, the overwhelming majority of women (and for that matter men) were dilettantes: that is, they wrote for pleasure rather than to earn money. The upper-class women who alone had the education and leisure to attempt writing were not usually in need of remuneration. Also, while writing was generally accepted as an attractive accomplishment for young unmarried women, this did not make it a respectable long-term profession, comparable with, say, a position at court; only women who remained unmarried, such as Urusova, Mar'ia Pospelova, Anna Volkova or Anna Bunina, or widows, such as Dashkova, could expect to have an extended career. A considerable number, therefore, produced original work before disappearing from the scene when their careers were interrupted by marriage (as with Mar'ia Izvekova), or by some other event (biographical materials are so scanty that it is impossible to say why Aleksandra Murzina, Aleksandra Magnitskaia, or Elisaveta and Mariia Moskvina, for instance, ceased writing after having published work of some distinction).

Women poets

Two significant problems beset any attempt to recover the history of Russia's pioneering women poets. The first is the fact that much material never appeared in published form: it was read aloud, or circulated in letters or manuscript copies, or was noted in albums of the kind kept by most upper-class ladies in the late eighteenth and early nineteenth centuries. Verse of this kind usually comes to light only when its composer already has a publication history (as in the case of Anna Bunina's *Khot' bednost' ne porokh* [Though Poverty's No Stain, 1813], which circulated in manuscript, but was not published until 1971), or when she has distinguished male connections (as in the case of Elizaveta Lanskaia-Villamova, whose album tribute to Derzhavin was published in the latter's *Collected Works*). The second, and related, problem is that the undoubted existence of a "buried tradition" has sometimes prompted commentators to exaggerate the importance of women poets, crediting anonymous works to specific women on very slender evidence.[7] Therefore, the account given here errs towards conservatism, including only women who published work in journals or collections.

Not surprisingly, the earliest women writers came from exceptional families, not only in terms of rank, but in terms of intellect and education as well. Both Ekaterina Kniazhnina-Sumarokova and Elisaveta Kheraskova were married to writers, and the former was the daughter of the poet Sumarokov; Ekaterina Urusova at one stage nearly became engaged to the most talented poet of the late eighteenth century, Gavrila Derzhavin, who described her in his memoirs as "a famous poet of the day" (*Zapiski*, 124). For her part, Kheraskova was portrayed by the journalist Nikolai Novikov (in his *Slovar' russkikh pisatelei*) as "the Russian de la Suze," and she, Urusova, and Sumarokova were indeed the equivalents of de la Suze and her contemporaries, the French *précieuses* of the seventeenth century. All of them were not only well-educated, but even, in the first two cases at least, erudite; all had connections with salon culture, and adopted a literary language that was based on the lexis and syntax of polite conversation.[8]

Of the three, the least interesting in terms of achievement is Kniazhnina-Sumarokova. She can with certainty be credited with only one elegy, published under the initials "E. S." in her father's magazine *The Industrious Bee*; the poem is more or less indistinguishable from his work, right down to the use of a masculine speaker. The fact that Kniazhnina-Sumarokova continued writing after her marriage is clear from Ivan Krylov's scurrilous portrayal of her in *Prokazniki* (The Mischief-Makers, 1793), as "Mrs Chatterbox" (Taratora), who scribbles occasional verses as she has her hair done (consulting her hairdresser for help with rhymes the while). However, this later work has been lost.

Both Kheraskova and Urusova were women of more diverse talents. Kheraskova was the author of hymnic verses, all moral or religious in orientation and intensely introspective. Some of these are conventional enough in subject matter, diction, and intonation, but in others she did manage to shape her own characteristic voice. In "Molitva" ("Prayer," 1760), for example, she asks God's help in an affliction that results not from unhappy love, but from the disdain of "former friends," by whom her "services are not recalled." In "Stans" ("Stanza," 1760), she sees love not as the pinnacle of female existence (as it was for the Sentimentalists), but as something damaging to a reasonable and autonomous existence:

> The fearsome bitterness of love
> Makes no stirring in my veins.
> My heart is happy, being free;
> I neither sigh, nor shed salt tears;
> Soul within me, be detached,
> Obedient to my intellect.[9]

Kheraskova's declaration of independence, while influenced by the Masonic ideas of her husband, is also consonant with enlightened eighteenth-century feminism, forerunning, in some senses, Mary Wollstonecraft's strictures against the cult of love by women in *A Vindication of the Rights of Women*, written nearly thirty years later (though it should be noted that eighteenth-century Russia did not develop a discourse on women's rights, as opposed to their duties, the more radical part of Wollstonecraft's treatise). Urusova's writings elaborate similar themes. In the charming "Ruchei" ("Brook," 1796), the speaker sees the foaming waters of a stream as exemplifying her own rebellious passions, which she resolves to control. And in "Chasy uedineniia" ("Hours of Solitude," 1796), she offsets melancholy contemplation by showing how the company of the Muses saves her from loneliness:

> O hours of solitude!
> Do not hasten to flow away:
> Your forceful current
> Brings me a taste of sweetness.
> I have fled from vanity,
> And walled myself in peace:
> In my heart I feel serenity.
> The Muses, seeing me at liberty,
> Command me to drink the Castalian waters
> And begin conversing with me.[10]

Urusova's representation of herself as a friend of the Muses is not unlike Pushkin's, in his early work, though she employs neo-classical *topoi* ("Castalian waters") rather than the witty references to the everyday found in Pushkin's most original pieces (for example, "To my Inkwell" of 1821).

Philosophical verse was by no means the only genre espoused by the *précieuses*. Urusova, the most ambitious of them, was the author of a mock-epic, *Polion* (1774), describing a hero rather like Euripides' Hippolytus, whose learning has led him to spurn women. Unlike Hippolytus, however, Polion escapes a tragic fate: feeling the onset of "pleasant love," he cheerfully abandons his Seneca in the woods, visits the Temple of Sound Sense, and joins Pomona, Ceres, and his friends for a celebration. Four decades later, Anna Bunina, another equally ambitious poet, and self-created *précieuse* (as an orphan from a well-off, but provincial, family, she lacked Urusova's educational advantages) also wrote a mock-epic, likewise with a male protagonist, choosing the hubristic Phaeton, who disastrously borrowed Apollo's chariot, as her eponymous hero.

But the major genre of neo-classical poetry that attracted most female practitioners, especially from the 1790s, was the solemn ode. Mar'ia Sushkova, Aleksandra and Natal'ia Magnitskaia, Aleksandra Murzina, Anna Bunina, and especially Mar'ia Pospelova all essayed their hands at this, producing competent and literate pieces of work. A stanza from Sushkova's ode on the founding of the Russian Academy has already been quoted; here is a comparable stanza from Pospelova's "Oda na vsera-dostnyi den' vosshestviia na Vserossiiskii Prestol EGO IMPERATORSKOGO

VELICHESTVA ALEKSANDRA PERVOGO "(Coronation Ode, 1801) for Aleksandr I, which contains a ringing address to his wife, Elisaveta:

> And Your Most Delightful Spouse,
> Who causes the Graces' beauty to be dimmed,
> May She be the glory of the world,
> Protection to the unhappy, a shield for the weak,
> And may ELISAVETA be for me
> A token of the Highest bounties,
> The Joy of half the world,
> The enormity of my delight
> Is increased by her many perfections.[11]

Interesting as texts produced within a specifically feminine patronage culture, women poets' odes had, however, only limited aesthetic importance. They remained conventional in themes and handling, without the forceful originality to be found in the best work by men writing at the same period, particularly Derzhavin. The crucial factor here was surely the emphasis, in women's education, on foreign languages; though many aristocratic women were at least as well-educated and well-read, in some respects, as their male contemporaries, few (if any) had an adequate grasp of the Church Slavonicisms and archaisms demanded by the Lomonosovian "high style" that was considered proper to the ode.

At any rate, women poets' ventures into minor genres of neo-classical verse, such as the fable or the epigram, were considerably more successful. A gifted practitioner here was Natal'ia Sumarokova (first cousin once removed of Ekaterina, and the sister of a minor Siberian writer, the editor of *Irtysh'*, in which all her work was published). Sumarokova's work included witty epigrams, such as the following on a workaholic judge (her strictures are still applicable to over-active professionals of all kinds, such as academics!):

> Here lies a judge, Damon by name,
> Who fretted over papers morn to night
> So that he never slept. Alas, he was not right
> To work himself so hard; he could instead
> More usefully have spent his time in bed.[12]

Wit was equally evident in women's attempts at the satire, a genre in which Aleksandra Murzina particularly distinguished herself. Like the Moskvina sisters, she aimed shrewd sallies at preening male peacocks, while "Prevrashchenie, ili Nebylitsa" ("Metamorphosis, or a Fable," 1799) was a delightful tale of an exceptionally silly (even by pastoral standards) shepherd and shepherdess. Best of all, though, is "K chitateliam" ("To My Readers," 1799), a poem defending women writers, and women generally, against slurs on their intellect. Having denied that she is personally offended by criticism ("authors every one / Must groan beneath that fate") she launches into a sparkling comparison of men and women:

> One other thing, you know
> Makes me surprised and vexed
> Far more: that satire's blows
> Are aimed against my sex;
> As though we ladies all
> Existed without light,
> Whilst men, fearing no fall,
> Soared in the starry heights.
>
> As though our Father God
> Had given us no brains,
> But only tender hearts
> That guide with iron reins;
> They say vanity impure
> Doth hold us in its sway,
> Since beauty's the only lure
> We have, to catch our prey.
>
> Yes, so they, puffed with pride
> In their talents, like to think:
> As they scornfully deny
> Our place in reason's ranks.
> But if they were more bright,
> They'd use their brains to delve:
> The weaknesses they slight
> In us, they have themselves.[13]

Most neo-classical poems by women, whatever genre they belonged to, took an ironic view of love, and indeed of emotional outbursts generally. However, from the 1790s such lightly mocking work was increasingly challenged by poetry belonging to the Sentimentalist tradition, which moved in precisely the opposite direction, making romantic sighings and tearful eloquence ubiquitous. The verbosely entitled *Priiatnoe i poleznoe preprovozhdenie vremeni* (A Pleasant and Instructive Manner of Passing the Time, which I shall abbreviate *PPPV*, for obvious reasons), as well as *The Hippocrene* (Ippokrena), *Irtysh' prevrashchaiushchiisia v Ipokrenu, ezhemesiachnoe sochinenie, izdavaemoe ot Tobol'skogo glavnogo narodnogo uchilishcha* (here abbreviated to *Irtysh'*), and Karamzin's journals *Aonidy*, and later *Vestnik Evropy* (The European Herald), all aimed much of their material at women readers. Karamzin's "Poslanie k zhenshchinam" (Epistle to Women), a classic of Russian Sentimentalism, appeared in the first volume of *Aonidy* (1796). After describing women's power to inspire, nurture and delight men, Karamzin imagines the epitaph that will be engraved on his tomb: "He loved . . . / He was the tenderest bard of tender women!". Not all contributors to Sentimentalist journals were so fawning: Ippolit Bogdanovich's "Pis'mo gospozhe F — o russkom stikhoslozhenii" ("Letter to Miss F — on Russian Verse Composition"), published in *PPPV* volume 1 (1794) is an eminently practical guide to the norms of late eighteenth-century Russian verse. Assuming his pupil's knowledge of "the essence of poetry, that sweetener of our woes, that favourite daughter of Mother Nature," and also of what is meant by the terms idyll, ode, tragedy and *poema* (epic), Bogdanovich dispensed detailed advice on the crafting of different measures.

Bogdanovich's words seem to have been heeded: much of the verse published over the next decade by women was technically competent and pleasing to the ear. But women's attraction to writing was, perhaps, due rather to factors other than such practical advice, or even the gallant idealization of their qualities. The journals' willingness to publish work by women writers was one. Another was the link of Sentimentalism and enthusiastic religiosity: the practices of Protestant sects, such as the Pietists, had encouraged women to express their spirituality in a way that the Orthodox Church in Russia historically had not. Certainly, between 1790 and 1820, a number of important spiritual works by women were published: these included Aleksandra Khvostova's essay "Sovety dushi moei, tvorenie khristiianki, toskuiushchei po gornem svoem otechestve" ("Advice of my Soul, the Work of a Christian Longing for her Heavenly Fatherland," 1816), and Anna Volkova's long poem "Gimn sovesti" ("Hymn to Conscience," 1816), which advises a withdrawal from the world so that the spiritual self may be cultivated:

> Why, alas! why should I possess treasures?
> Dearer to me is poverty with a feeling soul,
> Dearer to me than fame is my soul's tranquility.[14]

But it was above all Sentimentalism's fascination with unhappy love that drew Russian women, no doubt because themes of parting, betrayal, and parental coercion had a very real resonance in a society where women were legal minors, subject to the whims first of their fathers, and later of their husbands, or other male relatives, and where forced marriages were common. At the same time, Sentimentalism could provide models of ideal relationships in which men were more sensitive (*chuvstvitel'nye*) than was likely in reality, as well as providing denunciations of behavior types to be avoided (the plausible rake). That women readers also responded to such themes is indicated by the subscription lists of books published during the period, some of which list significant numbers of female names alongside those of male subscribers.[15]

The massive shift in poetic tastes since the late eighteenth century, brought about most particularly by the Romantic movement's emphasis on "inspiration" and "originality," has made it difficult for modern readers to see late eighteenth-century women's poetry with an unjaundiced eye. Often well-turned and harmoniously phrased, in the conversational "Karamzinian" manner, it is also often remarkably trite in its themes, genteel in its emotions, and formulaic in its imagery. Like their male counterparts, such as Ivan Dmitriev, or Karamzin himself, and in stark contrast to some of the British women poets collected by Roger Lonsdale in his anthology *Eighteenth-Century Women Poets*, Sentimentalist women poets seemed trapped in a net of *topoi* that precluded original expression. Apart from unhappy love, evoked, say, in Anna Svin'ina's "Pesnia" (*Zhurnal dlia milykh 7* [1804], 9), or Anastas'ia Svin'ina's "Milonova pechal'" (Milon's Sadness, *Aonidy* 1 [1796], 84), the favorite subject was sentimental friendship. The anonymous "Bratu moei vospitatel'nitsy" ("To the Brother of my Governess"), published in *The Hippocrene*, vol. 3, 366–8, selects a male addressee: commoner still are evocations of friendship between women, of which a late example is Mar'ia Lisitsyna's "K nezabvennoi" ("To One Unforgotten," *Stikhi i proza*, Moscow, 1829, 13–14). As this last example suggests, the death of a friend or relation was considered an especially appropriate occasion for outpourings. Elisaveta Mikhailovna Dolgorukova's "Elegy on the Death of my Beloved Sister Countess A. M. Ermakova, October 29, 1798," is exemplary in its smoothness of phrasing and banality of expression: "Friendship, the precious gift of heavenly spheres, / Can be for us the cause of bitter tears . . ."[16] Nature poetry was just as routine, with a range of predictable references used emblematically to point some standard theme. Roses suggest transience (Natalia Magnitskaia, "K roze", *PPPV* 12 [1796], 237), the return of spring, the fading of the poet's own beauty (Urusova, "Vesna",

Aonidy 1, 67–9). There is a superabundance of gurgling brooks, greening groves, songbirds in descant, and other such props of pastoral or "anacreontic" poetry. Uniformity of landscape is matched by uniformity of emotion – gentle melancholy predominates. Many poems read like prize pieces from a school magazine (which, given the age of the contributors, and the importance of literary writing as a school exercise of the time, is approximately what they were).

Among so much blandness, it is almost a relief to come across work by a poet such as Liubov' Krichevskaia, a young provincial girl, whose "On the Death of the Most Delightful N.N. Ia-voi," published in her first collection *Moi svobodnye minuty, ili sobranie sochinenii v stikhakh i proze, Khar'kov* (My Hours of Leisure, 1817), offsets conventional grief with touching references to the realia of provincial Russian life. Her work, like the Moskvina sisters' verses, is often clumsy in phrasing and stumbling in metre, but like their nature poetry (where snow-covered trees are compared to "bunches of grapes"), has a spontaneity missing from the more polished efforts published in *Aonidy*, *PPPV*, or later *Damskii zhurnal* and *The European Herald*. But occasionally the poets working for these journals also produced more heartfelt pieces.[17] And the Sentimentalist tradition also offered some women poets, particularly those from outside the aristocracy, the chance to voice real pain. It is doubtful whether Anna Bunina's superb poem "The Sick Woman's Maytime Stroll" written when the author was dying from cancer, would have been possible without the new tradition of introspection brought to Russia by the cult of sensibility.[18]

A word now about the masks that Russian women used in order to write their poetry, since there were interesting differences between genres of poetry, as between poetry and prose traditions. The characteristic feminine persona of neoclassical tradition (in Russia as elsewhere) was the Greek poet Corinna, who, as biographical legend had it, had been both modest (rebuking her female contemporary Myrtis for daring to rival Pindar) yet ambitious (she had herself, tradition stated, beaten Pindar in competition no less than five times). The characteristic persona of Sentimentalist verse, on the other hand, was Sappho, who was viewed in the eighteenth century not as a lesbian pioneer, but as the unhappy spurned lover of the shepherd Phaon, and the sentimental friend and mentor of younger women. Another female role that began to be increasingly important from the late 1790s was that of Niobe. The accession of Paul I to the throne, ending decades of female rule in Russia, was followed by an assiduous propagation of the ideology of "separate spheres," with

Paul's consort Maria Fedorovna presented as the archetype of female virtue: the devoted wife and mother, whose philanthropic and educational activities made her the "mother" of Russia in a symbolic sense.[19] As the anonymous "N S---a" put it in her "Pol'skoi, sochinennyi dlia vseradostnogo Vysochaishego pribytiia IKH IMPERATORSKIKH VELICHESTV ... v Blagorodnoe Moskovskoe Sobranie, Aprelia 29 dnia" (Polonaise on the Most Joyful Occasion of a Visit by THEIR IMPERIAL MAJESTIES ... to the Moscow Assembly of the Nobility, 1797):

> And Maria with her gentle gaze,
> Enlivens our soul,
> Lights us like the sun.
> Glory to thee, PAUL the incomparable,
> Glory, Greatest Tsar in the world.[20]

But, as the refrain of S---a's lyric indicates, it is Paul, rather than Maria, who was its true subject. Few women poets were to endorse the "royal mother" cult quite so wholeheartedly as Vasilii Zhukovskii, whose "Poslanie Velikoi Kniazhne Aleksandre Fedorovne" ("Epistle to Grand Duchess Aleksandra Fedorovna," 1818) saw the birth of the heir to the throne, Prince Aleksandr Nikolaevich (later Aleksandr II), as the apotheosis of imperial maternity. When royal maternity is invoked, it is maternal education, rather than fertility, that is the issue: women poets seeking patronage for themselves refer to themselves as daughters of the Tsaritsa. In her "Ode on the Marriage of Grand Prince Konstantin Pavlovich and Grand Princess Anna Pavlovna," Aleksandra Murzina abandoned her usual tone of light irony in order to place herself under the protection of Maria Fedorovna:

> The Universe is warmed by enthusiasm
> For You — and I too am warmed:
> O Mother of an entire hemisphere!
> Deign to gaze on me — be my mother too![21]

However, it was above all in prose where idealization of motherhood was evident, and where Sapphos and Niobes, more or less unchallenged by any ironical Corinnas, were free to express their enthusiasms.

Prose writers

So far, there have been few discoveries of major poetic works written by women for a private audience in the decades before and after 1800. But posthumous publications have made clear the existence of a vigorous tradition of prose-writing for private consumption, including not only letters, but also diaries and especially memoirs. The memoir tradition may not have thrown up any works of great introspection, in the manner of Rousseau's *Confessions*, but then (as feminist critics, such as Shari Benstock, have pointed out), women's memoirs in the West have also found the confessional memoir a problematic genre. In any case, a number of animated and poignant autobiographies survive, which, besides their literary worth, also offer invaluable evidence about the lives of women around 1800. From determinedly independent figures such as Catherine II (whose numerous memoirs include a short, but powerful, account of her childhood, and an extended chronicle of her marriage to Peter III), and Ekaterina Dashkova, to those who more willingly subordinated themselves to family duties, such as Natal'ia Dolgorukaia (whose account of following her husband to Siberia later became an inspiration for the wives of the Decembrist rebels), or Anna Labzina, who was able only gradually to escape from the tyranny of the predatory husband she had married as a vulnerable teenager, pre-1820 memoir literature offers an extraordinary range of female experience, and makes fascinating reading.

It is a good deal more accessible, for a modern reader, than the "public" prose tradition of the day, which was totally dominated by the Sentimentalist adventure tale. The plot based on lovers' vicissitudes was standard from the moment the earliest fiction by Russian women appeared in the late 1770s. The short tales of Natal'ia Neelova and the anonymous woman writing as "A Certain Russian Lady," unravelled such plots within the small compass of the *povest'*, (novella, *conte*). Some of their successors, however, such as Mar'ia Izvekova, writing in the first years of the nineteenth century, or Mariia Lisitsyna, who came into literature in the 1820s, spun the material out to far greater length (two- or three-volume novels). Whatever their length, though, such tales shared various common features. Whether they are supposed to be set in Russia or abroad, their setting is mythically abstract: town names are not mentioned, and landscapes are never described. Characters are equally archetypal: either models of virtue or monsters of vice. There is an abundance of preposterous plot retardation devices – kidnappings, fires, mistaken identities, resurrections of dead bodies. Exemplary in all these ways is Izvekova's *Milena, ili redkii primer velikodushiia* (Milena, or a Rare Example of Magnanimity, 1809). The admirable Milena, who is brought up in an unnamed and uncharacterized "provincial town", falls in love with

Viktor, but after he is reported drowned at sea, she marries the wicked Erast (a name whose villainous connotations had been established by Karamzin's *Poor Liza*, 1792). She bears Erast a son, Milovzor (Sweet Gaze). Then, however, Viktor reappears, having escaped drowning after all; his reappearance leads to accusations by Erast that Milena is an "undeserving mother." During the next hundred pages she sets out to prove the opposite, even refusing to renounce Erast when the latter turns out to be a bigamist and murderer. His heart softened by Milena's staunchness, Erast finally commits suicide (in an interesting reversal of *Poor Liza*!), leaving Milena and Viktor to enjoy a "quiet wedding" and a blissfully happy marriage. (The above outline considerably simplifies the plot, which also includes the supposed death of Milovzor, who is rescued living from his grave, a fire, a tense encounter between Milena and Erast's other wife, and a large number of fainting fits.) The style of *Milena* is as preposterous as its plot: characters do not marry, but "lay on themselves the eternal fetters" (though perhaps one should allow for unconscious irony here), babies are invariably "innocent," and joys "inexpressible."

Some life was injected into the hackneyed plot of amorous misadventure by Liubov' Krichevskaia, whose "Korinna" (published in *Dve povesti*, Moscow, 1827), is the tale of a girl whose ideal upbringing, organized by an enlightened mother, has given her an appreciation of beauty and virtue, but not the ability to control her passions. In representing an intensity so great that it makes Korinna waste away, Krichevskaia displays a certain psychological insight, and her work looks forward to that of Nadezhda Durova in the 1830s. But the prose of Krichevskaia's contemporary Mariia Lisitsyna was in no sense innovative, reverting once more to the traditions of Izvekova. Though her two-volume novel *Emilii Likhtenberg* (Moscow, 1826), unusually, is a first-person narrative, and one written in quite a lively manner (the hero describes himself in the opening pages as heir to a million "clanking thalers"), the novel has as few pretensions to psychological verisimilitude as to narrative inventiveness.

Another genre occasionally espoused by women writers was the prose fable, or didactic *conte*: a narrative expounding through exemplary instances the benefits of philanthropy, the perils of vanity and pride. At their worst, as in the case of Ekaterina Svin'ina's "Suguboe blagodeianie" (An Outstandingly Good Deed, *PPPV* 8 [1795], 386), or the same author's "Ballada" (*PPPV* 2 [1794], 406–11), these works make still more forbidding reading than the novels of Izvekova or Lisitsyna. The moral insights offered are leaden, and the zestful absurdity of the adventure novels absent. However, there are also wittier examples to be found. Svin'ina herself was also the author of a prose fable slyly showing the dangers to artists of working for patrons. When the Monkey depicts other animals as they really are, this inspires fury; however, when the Vixen flatters them (giving the Lion a "pleasing charm" [liubeznaia priiatnost'] of mien as well as a hairy mane), she is rewarded with a patent and a pension. And Catherine II's own "allegorical tales" combine transparent propaganda of enlightenment values with endearing citations of genuine folk-tale formulae. In "Skazka o tsareviche Khlore," for example, the hero is brought up by "seven nannies, all rational women and skilled in the upbringing of children." ("The Tale of Prince Chloros," *Sochineniia Imperatritsy Ekateriny II*, ed. A. I. Vvedenskii [St. Petersburg, 1893], 367–73.)

A very different kind of imaginative prose (if the term "prose" is appropriate for what are really prose poems) was represented by Aleksandra Khvostova's "fragments," "Kamin" ("The Fireplace") and "Rucheek" ("The Brook"), meditative outpourings in the Ossianic manner, with rhythmic cadences that render more effective the gloomy *topoi* to which the speaker resorts. Here she is, for example, contemplating the fireplace and drawing moral reflections from it, and viewing the grave of her father:

> O joys! where are they? They are the stuff of fancy, vanishing like thin smoke, and only occasionally rising before us like visions! . . .
> But my groans could not disturb his sound sleep, his deep sleep, the wind carried off afar my fading voice, and the name of my Friend resounded in vain on the thin air![22]

Such intense Gothic fancies made Khvostova's *Fragments* immensely popular: in an era where print-runs of two or three hundred copies were more than respectable, the prose-poem had a first edition of 2,400; it went on being reprinted regularly until 1833, and was translated into several other European languages. In a similar vein of melancholic nature-worship (though never achieving Khvostova's astonishing popularity) was Pospelova's collection of poems and prose texts, *Nekotorye cherty prirody i istinny [sic.], ili ottenki myslei i chuvstv moikh* (Some Traits of Nature and Truth, or Reflections of my Thoughts and Feelings [Moscow, 1801]).

At the other end of the spectrum from vaporous perorations of this kind was prose journalism, one interesting branch of which, an offshoot of Sentimentalist regard for the woman reader, was literary criticism, sometimes but not always offered in the form of the "reader's letter." The short-lived *Zhurnal dlia milykh* (Sweethearts' Journal) published material by a "Pr. El. Tr-ia" (perhaps Princess Elizaveta Trubetskaia), who offered her opinions on recent publications, mostly of poetry. She wrote with wit and sarcasm, commenting on male poets in ways that echoed the patronizing views of gentleman critics on "ladies' verse," and so rendered these ridiculous. On a poem published in *The European Herald*, for example, she comments: "For me, these verses are incomprehensible, but that is perhaps because I am a woman." In similar vein, her "Otryvok" (Fragment), published in part 6, showed two sisters discussing recent literature while sitting in a garden pavilion (*besedka*): one says to the other: "Look, here is a fable by Count Khvostov! [a verbose author of occasional verse – CK] See, ma soeure [sic], what simplicity, what innocence!"[23]

An essayist of more substantial achievements was Katerina Puchkova, a friend of Anna Bunina's, whose *Pervye opyty v proze Ekateriny Puchkovoi* (First Attempts in Prose, 1812), offered not only incentive models for emulation ("On the Successes of Russian Women," 118–22), but also a defense of women's intellectual capacities voiced by the spirited *Vsemila* (Allsweet: "On Women," 82–93), and a discussion of literature, including literature written by women ("Letter to a Woman Friend on Russian Literature," 127–39). Not until the late 1850s were women again to offer their views on literature so directly to the public.

Nor was literary criticism the only branch of journalism in which Russian women were engaged. The work of Trubetskaia and even Puchkova is dwarfed, in quantitative terms, by the huge contributions made by Catherine II and Dashkova, who were among the most important editors and periodical authors of the late eighteenth century, irrespective of gender. Catherine II's journal *Vsiakaia vsiachina* (Allsorts), in which the Empress disguised herself as the bossy but sensible "Madame Allsorts," while goodnaturedly plagiarizing much material from Addison's *Spectator*, laid the foundations of satirical journalism in Russia. In "Byli i nebylitsy" ("Truths and Fables"), her column in Dashkova's *Sobesednik liubitelei rossiiskogo slova* (Interlocutor of Lovers of the Russian Word), Catherine adopted a masculine mask: a fussy squire prosily prating of his grandfather, while also recording the doings of his indolent, fashion-obsessed, empty-headed and snobbish younger relations. Dashkova's activities included, besides involvement with the journal just mentioned, her editorship of the scholarly *Novye ezhemesiachnye sochineniia* (New Monthly Essays), for which she herself occasionally wrote articles.

Finally, this nutshell-sized account of Russian women's prose writing before 1820 would not be complete without mentioning the works written by aristocratic women in court circles whose first language was French. These included not only the memoirs of Dashkova and Catherine II already mentioned, but also fiction, most notably the novels of Julie (or Juliane) Krüdener, Baltic German wife of a Russian diplomat, and author of the massively popular *Valérie*, an elegant reworking of Goethe's *Werther* that conveys the heroine's feelings a good deal more intensely than its model.

Dramatists

Drama, like poetry, is an area where composing an overview of women's activities is made problematic by the existence of non-publishing dilettantes. Many sources, such as Ivan Dolgorukov's 1820s memoir dictionary *Kapishche moego serdtsa* (Temple of My Heart), record that aristocratic women were keen amateur actresses; some certainly wrote dramatic pieces for home performance, but scarcely any have survived (an exception being the salon hostess Zinaida Volkonskaia's Italian opera libretto *Giovanna d'Arco: dramma per musica ridotto da Schiller*, published in Rome in 1821). Therefore, I have been forced to concentrate here on the few and unrepresentative writers whose work did reach print and the professional theater.

Outstanding among these, both in terms of opportunity and of ability, was Catherine II, whose lively comedies of the 1770s, such as *O vremia!* (O tempora! O mores!), spicing didacticism with humor, are among the better eighteenth-century excursions in the vernacular style; Catherine's Shakespearian histories were interesting attempts to break the neo-classical mold, if scarcely classics of the stage.

Two other women who attempted drama espoused the tradition of "lachrymose comedy" (comédie larmoyante), transferring the plots and characters of didactic sentimental fiction to the stage. In Elisaveta Titova's *Gustav Vaza, ili torzhestvuiushchaia nevinnost'. Dramma v piati deistviiakh* (Gustav Vasa, or the Triumph of Innocence [St. Petersburg, 1810]; the title page adds "performed at the Court Theatre on 27 June, 1809"), the eponymous hero, a virtuous (for which read "well-meaning and dim") Swedish ruler, is the victim of a court intrigue, as an ambitious older courtier tries to sideline a younger one, exploiting the fact that the latter's beloved has taken the fancy of the king. The dramatic "conflict," if such it can be called, is set out with many lamentations on the conflicts of virtue ("O cruel Virtue! But I shall do as you command . . . so used am

I to hearing your voice, that I dare resist no longer ... Let me see Matilda once more, and then die in peace," [15]), and leaden sententiae ("O what an ornament of humanity is the memory of a noble ruler!" [7]).[24] Moments of unintentional humor spice what is by any standards a very bad play indeed. And Mar'ia Izvekova's *Al'fons i Florestina, ili schastlivyi oborot, dramma v 4 deistviiakh* (Alphonse and Florestina, or a Turn for the Better, Moscow, 1807) contains still more unlikely reversals than Izvekova's novels. The virtuous Albertina is discovered lost in a wood, with her son Isidor; after many vicissitudes, she (now revealed as "Florestina"), is united with the father of her child, Alphonse, despite the machinations of his wicked father Count Dunkelwald, who has contrived a false marriage between the two, then spirited Alphonse away, and who is now trying to marry him off to Eliza. Perhaps, though, rather than poking fun at the literary infelicities of these texts, one should see them primarily as pieces of theater, part of a melodramatic tradition that continues in the soap operas of today, ephemeral creations meant to satisfy the hunger for intense emotion and spectacular event felt by an immediate audience, rather than the numinous cravings of an unpredictable posterity. That Titova and Izvekova successfully attained the former goal, if not the latter, is suggested by the fact that their plays not only reached print, but also the professional stage, a significant achievement given both the underdeveloped character of the Russian theater, and the domination of dramatic tradition by male writers.

Conclusion

It would be foolish to overstate the achievements of Russian women writers of the earliest generations. Known to the tiny fraction of Russian society that purchased books and literary journals, they depended on the goodwill of the male writers who edited journals, if they did not have the resources to publish themselves. Almost every book published by a woman writer opened with an apology for the writer's modest talents. Even Ekaterina Urusova, whose social standing might have been assumed to put her beyond assault, craved the indulgence of Polion's first readers:

> I flatter myself with the hope that my readers, out of respect for my sex, and for my first attempts in this kind of verse composition, might forgive the faults to be found here: in this manner they will encourage my timid Muse to further efforts.[25]

Alternatively, a male (or much less frequently, female) acquaintance might contribute a preface praising the talents of the debutante writer: in this manner the "publisher" (interestingly and rarely, a feminine one, izdatel'nitsa) introduces Khvostova's *Fragments* by saying:

> Wishing to perform a service to sensitive Readers [the masculine/neutral form chuvstvitel'nye chitateli is used], I am publishing the works of a certain Russian Lady Writer, who conforming to the modesty that is proper to our sex, long resisted my desires, and wanted to hide her talents from the Public.[26]

The sense that writing (or at least publishing) was an immodest activity, fostered not only by famous men of the day, but (more than a mite hypocritically!) by such women writers as Madame Genlis (see, for example, her "La Femme auteur," published in Russia by *The European Herald* during 1804), was to have long-lasting inhibitory effects on Russian women. It can be felt still in the laments on the general view of women writers as "freaks" to be found in the works of such 1830s writers as Elena Gan.

As Madame de Staël warned in her "Women who Practise the Art of Letters" (1800), those who wrote risked seeming not only immodest, but ridiculous. Sappho might be a convenient mask for women love poets, but her eventual suicide allowed male epigrammatists to poke fun at women poets, who, it was suggested, would have been better to fling themselves into the sea quite a lot earlier (along the lines of Charles Lamb's rhyme: "Swans sing before they die / 'Twere no bad thing / Should certain persons die before they sing"). (Or as Batiushkov put it, perhaps to Anna Bunina: "You're Sappho, I'm Phaon, I do admit / But must regret / You haven't jumped off Levkas yet.")[27] Prose writers did not escape either: the unfortunate Mar'ia Izvekova was the subject of a rude anonymous epigram comparing her own bulk with that of her novel:

> This novel and its authoress
> Are quite alike: their portliness
> Unites them, and their uselessness.[28]

But one should also not overstate the disadvantages under which women labored before Romanticism. Epigrams aimed at men abounded, many of a scatological offensiveness beside which the jejune humor of jibes at women poets seems harmless. Nor was "modesty" an exclusively female attribute, given authors' uncertain status in a society still dominated by the tastes of the court. Numerous male writers of the day, especially those of aristocratic birth, published under initials, rather than using their full names; male writers were also capable of breaking into protestations of modesty for their "feeble efforts," in dedications aimed to please powerful patrons.[29] It was only when Romanticism had made such strategies seem craven and unmanly that modesty was reinforced as a trait not only proper to women writers, but exclusive to them. Besides, in the late eighteenth and early nineteenth centuries, there was no sense that women were necessarily made unfit by physiology and intellect for composition. One cannot imagine any important writer between 1820 and 1835 (at the earliest) giving women such sympathetic and uncondescending support as Sumarokov had rendered Kheraskova in his 1761 fable addressed to her, "The Vixen and the Statue":

> You breathe, I know, the air of high Parnassus,
>   For you write verses.
> Well, no-one can chain up a woman's reason:
> Who says a lady writing verse is treason?
> The Muses are women all, and so's Minerva,
>   And not one man inhabits Helikon,
>   So pray write on:
> A fair mind makes the fairest more deserving.[30]

As we have seen, several women did indeed write in the manner referred to by Sumarokov, producing light verse of intelligence and wit. And some serious work by women, notably the writings of Anna Bunina and Ekaterina Urusova, is as competent, intellectual, and interesting as much work by their male contemporaries; no special pleading is required in order to argue for its merits. So far as prose and drama were concerned, there is perhaps less of lasting interest, though prose fiction in French sometimes reached a higher standard (particularly in the case of Krüdener's work), and "private" prose – letters and memoirs – was often remarkably spirited and absorbing. Finally, as Russian scholars such as Boris Uspenskii have pointed out, some women's texts, exemplary excursions in Lomonosov's "middle style," a literary idiom based on the language of polite conversation, made a vital contribution to the development of the Russian literary language. And even the least polished writers, such as Izvekova and Lisitsyna, can be granted a small place in literary history, as women who spurred both other women (for example, Mariia Zhukova), and men (for example, Pushkin in his *Tales of Belkin*) to imitate or to parody their efforts in sensational writing.

NOTES

The author would like to express her gratitude to the British Academy for its generosity in financing a research visit to Russia under its Small Personal Research Grants scheme, and to Melanie Anstey and David Chater, who acted as her hosts during the visit. She also acknowledges useful comments on earlier versions of this article from Judith Vowles, Barbara Heldt, Gerry Smith, Jehanne Gheith, and Adele Barker.

1. On pre-Petrine letters see, e.g., A. A. Zalizniak, "Uchastie zhenshchin v drevnerusskoi perepiske na bereste," in Luigi Magarotto and Daniela Rizzi (eds.), *La cultura spirituale russa* (Trento, 1992), 127–46; A. A. Medyntseva, "Gramotnost' zhenshchin na Rusi XI–XIII, po dannym epigrafiki," in *Slovo o polku Igoreve i ego vremia* (Moscow, 1985), 218–40. For an example of eighteenth-century workaday correspondence, see the letter by A. I. Kurakina (1711–1786) in *Arkhiv dekabrista S. G. Volkonskogo*, ed. S.M. Volkonskii and B.L. Modzalevskii, vol. I (Petrograd, 1918), 1. M. Protasova-Moier's letters are available in *Utkinskii sbornik: Pis'ma V. A. Zhukovskogo, M. A. Moier i E. A. Protasovoi*, ed. A.E. Gruzinskii (Moscow, 1904), 135–286.

2. Kelly *Anthology*, 1–2, 397–8. В кратчайши времена Россия процвела, / Расинов, Пиндаров, она произвела, / ЕКАТЕРИНИН век те ныне воспевают . . . / И чтобы окружать священных Муз престол, / То начал воспевать у нас и женский пол; . . . / В России видимы Сапфоны, де ла Сюзы.

3. И Ты, сотрудница писателей почтенных, / Честь пола Твоего, свершай толь славный путь; / Любительница Муз, Тебе препорученных, / Участвуй в лике их, и им красою будь; / Чудесное в сей век и новое явленье, / В Тебе, о Дашкова, ученый видит свет, / Минерва наших дней, гоня предрассужденье, / Достоинствам твоим награду подает. *Sobesednik liubitelei russkogo slova* 9 (1783), 18–22.

4. On masquerades, see, e.g., Catherine II, *Zapiski* (London, 1859), 107, 112.

5. К милой подойти захочет / Коль красавец молодой: / То с тобою похолочет, / В милость чтоб прийти у той. / Повертится, посмеется / И пошаркает ногой, / Будто к милой обернется — / В речь взойдет тотчас с тобой. *Aoniia, ili sobranie stikhotvorenii: sochinenie Gzh. ***[Moskvinykh]*, Book 1 (all published, Moscow, 1802), 156.

6. On eighteenth-century education, including Catherine's flagship Smol'nyi Institute, the best source is still E. Likhacheva, *Materialy dlia istorii zhenskogo obrazovaniia v Rossii, 1086–1796* (St. Petersburg, 1890). A good English-language study is J. Black, "Educating Women," in his *Citizens for the Fatherland: Education, Educators and Pedagogical Ideals in Eighteenth-Century Russia* (New York, 1979), 152–72. On advice books, see Catriona Kelly, "Educating Tatiana: Manners, Motherhood and Moral Education (Vospitanie), 1760–1840," in Linda Edmondson (ed.), *Gender in Russian History and Culture, 1800–1990* (Basingstoke, 2001).

7. See, for example, S. Vengerov's *Russkaia poeziia: sobranie proizvedenii russkikh poetov* (Russian Poetry: A Collection of the Works of Russian Poets [St. Petersburg, 1897–1903]).

8. On salon culture and the *précieuses* in France, see Joan DeJean, *Tender Geographies: Women and the Origins of the Novel in France* (Columbia, 1991). The part of salons in Russian literary history awaits detailed study: M. Aronson and S. Reiser, *Literaturnye kruzhki i salony* (Leningrad, 1929), is valuable as a selection of primary materials, but

the commentaries are badly outdated. See also Laura Schlosberg, "Converging Realms: The Literary and Palace Salons of the Russian Nobility, 1820–1870," (Ph. D. dissertation, Duke University, 2000).

9. Огорчение любовно / Не тревожит кровь мою; / Сердце я имею вольно; / Не вздыхаю, слез не лью. / Ты душа во мне бесстрасна, / Будь уму всегда подвластна. *Poleznoe uveselenie* 2: 20 (1760), 189–90.

10. О часы уединенья! / Не спешите протекать: / Сила вашего теченья / Сладость мне дает вкушать. / От сует я удалилась, / Тишиною оградилась, В сердце чувствую покой. / Музы, зря мою свободу, / Пить велят Кастальску воду, / И беседуют со мной. *Aonidy* 1 (1776), 135–6.

11. Любезная Твоя Супруга, / Что Грациев красу затмит, / Да будет честь земного круга, / Покров нещастных, слабых щит; / Да будет мне ЕЛИСАВЕТА / Залогом Вышнего щедрот, / Отрадой половины света, / Участница Твоих доброт, / Великость моего блаженста / Ее возвысят совершенства. M. Pospelova, "Nekotorye cherty prirody i istinny [sic], ili ottenki myslei i chuvstv moikh," *Soch* (Moscow, 1801), 208.

12. Лежащий здесь судья, по имени Дамон, / Спал мало и почти всегда в бумагах рылся. / Но больше б прибыли гораздо сделал он, / Когда бы время то, в которое трудился, / Употреблял на сон. *Irtysh'* 6 (1791), 22–3.

13. Но более тому / Я слушая дивилась; / Что к полу моему / Сатира вся клонилась, / Как будто женский пол / Жизнь в мраке провождает; / Мущина ж, презря дол, / Умом в звездах летает; // Что будто б нас Творец / Не наградил умами, / А нежности сердец / Дал вдаствовать над нами; / Что нами суета / Едина обладает, / И только красота / К нам прочих привлекает. // Се! — как они любя / Свои таланты, мыслят, / Призревши нас, себя / В разумных только числят. / Но есть ли в их умы, / В их нравы вникнут строже; / То, в чем коль слабы мы, / И в них во всем бы тоже. A. Murzina, *Raspuskaiushchaiasia roza, ili raznye sochineniia v proze i stikhakh* (Moscow, 1799), 46–7.

14. Почто! Увы! почто сокровищем владею? / Милее бедность мне с чувствительной душой, / Милее знатности души моей покой; *Syn otechestva* 30 (1816), 229.

15. On subscription lists in poetry books, see Wendy Rosslyn, "Anna Bunina's 'Unchaste Relationship with the Muses': Patronage, the Market and the Woman Writer in Early Nineteenth-Century Russia," *SEER* 74: 2 (April, 1996), 223–42. Prose texts sometimes also contained such lists: Mar'ia Lisitsyna's *Emilii Likhtenberg*, for example, credits 112 subscribers (including merchants and actors), of whom 8 are women.

16. И дружество само, безценный дар Небес! / Причиною для нас бывает горьких слез. *Ippokrena* 4 (1799), 231–9.

17. See, for example, Aleksandra Magnitskaia's "Na smert' zhavoronka, Avgusta 15" (On the Death of My Sky-Lark upon August 15 Last, 1798).

18. For an excellent account of Sentimentalist poetry, much fuller than that attempted here, see Vowles, "The 'Feminization' of Russian Literature," in Clyman and Greene.

19. On empresses, see Richard Wortman, *Scenarios of Power: Myth and Ceremony in Russian Monarchy*, vol. I (Princeton, NJ, 1995), 250–1, 260–5. Empress Maria Feodorovna's monument to her husband Tsar Paul is particularly relevant to my discussion here, given that it represented the Empress as inconsolable widow weeping over her husband's urn. The Lazar'evskoe Cemetery at the Aleksandr Nevsky Monastery, St.

Petersburg, has other fine examples of "weeper" monuments, many with accompanying epitaphs.

20. И МАРИЯ кротким взором, / Тихих прелестей собором / Наши души оживит, / Будто солнцем озарит. / — Славься, ПАВЕЛ несравненный, / Славься, Первый в мире царь. *Aonidy* 2 (1797), 291–4.

21. Вселенная — и с нею я — / О Матерь целого подсвета! Воззри — будь Матерь и моя! Murzina, *Raspuskaiushchaiasia roza* 72.

22. Радости! Где оне? — В одном воображении, исчезли как тонкий дым, и только иногда как легкие привидения мечтаются. / Стон мой не мог нарушить крепкого его сна глубокого, ветер уносил далеко умирающий голос мой, и имя Друга моего напрасно в тонком воздухе рассталося! A. Khvostova, *Otryvki* (St. Petersburg, 1796), 10, 35.

23. *Zhurnal dlia milykh* 5 (1840), 245, 360. Male editors (e.g. Novikov) were known to compose letters from fictional "ladies" in order to express points they themselves wanted to make, but these were not usually signed, so it seems likely that "El. Tr-ia" was a real figure. The 1820s memoir dictionary of I. M. Dolgorukov (1764–1823), *Kapishche moego serdtsa*, recalls a poetry-writing Varvara Trubetskaia of Kostroma, perhaps the mother of Elizaveta and her sister Ek[aterin]a.

24. "О жестокая добродетель! Но ты повелеваешь . . . привыкши внимать гласу твоему, не смею даже оному противиться . . . Увижу еще раз Матильду и спокойно умру." "Память доброго Государя есть украшение человечеству!"

25. Я ласкаю себя надеждою, что мои читатели, уважая пол мой, и первые мои опыты в роде сего исполнения, могут извинить находящиеся здесь погрешности; чем ободрят робкую Музу мою, к дальним упражнениям.

26. Желая сделать услугу и удовольствие чувствительным Читателям, издаю я сочинение одной Российской писательницы, которая держась скромности, нашему полу свойственной, долго противилась моему жеданию и хотела скрыть от Публики свои дарования.

27. Мадригал новой Сафе: Ты — Сафо, я — Фаон, об этом я не спорю, / Но, к моему ты горю, / Пути не знаешь к морю. *Russkaia epigramma*, ed. M. I. Gippel'son and K. A. Kumpan (Leningrad, 1988), no. 641.

28. Извековой роман с Извековой и сходен: / Он так же, как она, дороден / И так же ни к чему не годен! *Ibid.*, No. 1180.

29. See, e.g., the preface by Ivan Novitskii to one of the first Russian cookbooks (in fact an embellished translation from the German), which consists of a deeply respectful dedication to Natal'ia Andreevna Strekalova, with apologies for the translator's "humble efforts": Anon., *Novaia polnaia povarennaia kniga* (St. Petersburg, 1780).

30. "Лисица и статуя": Я ведаю что ты Парнасским духом дышешь; / Стихи ты пишешь. / Не возложил ни кто на женский разум уз: / утоб дамам не писать, в котором то законе? / Минерва женщина, и вся беседа Муз, / Не пола мужеска на Геликоне; / Пиши! не будешь тем ты менше хороша; / В прекрасной быть должна прекрасна и ыа. *Poleznoe uveselenie* 3:19 (1761), 161.

3

The inexperienced muse: Russian women and poetry in the first half of the nineteenth century

When Anna Bunina (1774–1829), the first major Russian woman poet of the nineteenth century and one of the first Russian women to sustain a literary career, entitled her first collection of poetry *Neopytnaia muza* (The Inexperienced Muse, 1809–1812), she marked not only her own inexperience as a poet but the broader absence of women from the ranks of Russian poets. Only a generation later the situation had changed dramatically. By 1845 the young religious poet Elisaveta Shakhova (1822–1899) could style herself the "youngest sister of sisters who have gone before" ("K zhenshchinam-poetam" ["To Women-Poets"]), and could have named a score of women writing poetry. Had she attempted a female genealogy she might have named among her older "sisters" not only Bunina, but Bunina's peers, the Sentimentalist writers Mar'ia Pospelova (1780–1805), Anna Volkova (1781–1834), and Liubov' Krichevskaia (d. after 1841), or the scholarly poet and classicist Ekaterina Kul'man (1808–1825).[1] Although the names of many women who inspired poets in the 1820s are remembered, only a few women are known to have written poetry themselves, among them Princess Zinaida Volkonskaia (1789–1862), Anna Gotovtseva (1799–1871), Elizaveta Timasheva (1798–1881), and Mariia Lisitsyna (d. 1842?). From the 1830s onward, however, women published poetry in sufficient numbers to attract critical attention. Shakhova's genealogy would have continued with the leading women poets of her time, Evdokiia Rostopchina (1811–1858) and Karolina Pavlova (1807–1893), less well-known poets like Aleksandra Fuks (1805–1853), Ol'ga Kriukova (1815/17–1885), Avdot'ia Glinka (1795–1863), and Varvara Annenkova (1795–1866), as well as a few women of non-gentry birth, including Nadezhda Teplova (1814–1848) of the Moscow merchant class, and Domna Anisimova (1812–after 1868), the daughter of a village sexton. Even as Shakhova wrote, other women were making their poetic debuts, most notably Iuliia Zhadovskaia (1824–1883) and Nadezhda Khvoshchinskaia (1820?–1889).

There is still much that we do not know about the lives and circumstances of these and other women who aspired to become poets in the Romantic period. Unlike educated men for whom literary activities were an accepted, even expected part of their lives, and who were often sustained by close friendships and professional ties forged as they passed through schools, government, and military service, women of comparable classes were educated to take their place in society and become wives and mothers. They were not expected to become poets, although a little versifying was acceptable, even desirable, as a social grace. In an age when poets demanded a high degree of skill and a rigorous command of the Russian language from one another, women's education often neglected Russian language and literature in favor of French, which remained the dominant language of educated Russian society, among women even more than men. This circumstance earned many women a reputation for wide knowledge of Western European literatures, and enabled some women to write in languages other than Russian; conversely, however, in a time of rising literary nationalism these same women were regularly faulted for their ignorance of Russian and their preference for foreign literatures and languages.[2] Bunina was sensible of this difficulty when, in her translation and adaptation of a manual of versification, *Pravila poezii* (The Rules of Poetry, 1808), she urged her fellow countrywomen to learn their native language and master the craft of poetry. Although by the 1840s Rostopchina could assume a large female readership for her Russian verse, her grammatical errors and faulty use of rhyme and meter could still jar on even her admirers.

Women's difficulties with the Russian language were compounded by their position in the familiar circles, formal associations, salons, and "society" where so much of literary life then took place.[3] A number of women poets expressed a sense of isolation, as did Bunina in "Otrechenie" ("Renunciation," 1809) and Teplova in "Uedinenie" ("Solitude," 1845); isolation and the absence of response became one of Pavlova's central themes. Although some women formed significant ties with individual literary men, propriety and the fear of scandal evidently constrained friendships with men other than husbands and family members.[4] A few were invited to become honorary members of literary societies, as Bunina, Volkova and the elderly poet Ekaterina

Urusova (1747–after 1817) were of Aleksandr Shishkov's "Beseda liubitelei russkago slova" ("Colloquium of the Lovers of the Russian Word," 1811–1817).[5] However, most groups like the "Arzamas" circle, and the looser gathering of poets around Pushkin (the "Pushkin pleiad") which acted as "laboratories" for the Russian literary language, and often combined literary activities with the pleasures of wine, women, and song, did not readily include ladies.[6]

In these circumstances "society" ("svet") and the "mixed" or "feminine" salons evidently played an important role for aspiring women poets. The character of such assemblies varied, and, according to memoirists, French rather than Russian was more often the language of conversation. Others, however, offered places where men and women could converse in Russian, read their work and listen to the readings of others, and engage in intellectual discussion and games. The young Pavlova regularly attended the brilliant Moscow salons of Princess Volkonskaia in the 1820s, and the gatherings of Avdot'ia Elagina (1789–1877) from the 1820s to the late 1840s. Rostopchina, fond of society and a salon *habituée*, was a frequent visitor in the St. Petersburg drawing rooms of Aleksandra Smirnova (1809–1882), Sof'ia Karamzina (1802–1856) and her step-mother Ekaterina Karamzina (1780–1851), and Prince Vladimir Odoevskii (1803–1869) among others. She dedicated many of her poems to this world and its members. Avdot'ia Glinka (1795–1863) and her husband Fedor Glinka (1786–1880) welcomed several generations of young women to their Moscow home from the late 1820s onward, including Nadezhda Teplova, her sister Serafima, and their friend Lisitsyna. Later, Shakhova and Zhadovskaia both appreciated the religious and philanthropic atmosphere of the Glinkas' household. A similar tone distinguished the less aristocratic home of Evgeniia Maikova (1803–1880), who was at the heart of a literary circle in St. Petersburg from 1834 onward. Shakhova and her friend and mentor, the poet Vladimir Benediktov (1807–1873), visited her gatherings, as well as those of Elizaveta Karlgof (1816/17–1884) who held literary evenings in St. Petersburg in the late 1830s and in Moscow from the middle of the 1840s to the late 1850s.[7] Many of these hospitable women also wrote prose and poetry themselves, including Avdot'ia Glinka, whose translations of German poetry as well as her own religious verse circulated in the 1830s and 1840s, and Maikova, who contributed much verse to the domestic journals and magazines produced by her circle. Aleksandra Fuks, who opened one of the few provincial salons, in Kazan, also published poetry and prose. Both Rostopchina and Pavlova organized salons after their marriages gave them the means and the independence to do so, and both used these gatherings to read their own work. Rostopchina opened her St. Petersburg home in 1836 to writers and art and music lovers. Pavlova and her husband organized their more political and literary salon in Moscow in the 1840s. Important as these salons were to literary women, they had to endure repeated assertions that the presence of ladies at such gatherings produced a coldness and frivolity that were hostile to serious literary and intellectual endeavors. Indeed, Pavlova herself gave a devastating portrayal of one such literary salon in her novel *Dvoinaia zhizn'* (A Double Life, 1848). By the late 1840s and 1850s the tone of such gatherings was changing as a new generation of young men, many of the "raznochintsy" class, scorned "aristocratic" salon society and echoed the old complaints about "feminine" company.[8]

Both men and women circulated their writings in manuscript or gave readings at such gatherings. Literary correspondence, albums, handmade books, and domestic journals and magazines were all common. In general it is difficult to gauge the extent and workings of that manuscript tradition; moreover, women's manuscript writings were less commonly published subsequently. Sometimes only a few poems of a larger body of work are all that found their way into print.[9] When women began to publish work, they did so more slowly than men. The gentlemen's disdain for commercial publishing was felt even more keenly by ladies as a violation of propriety. A white hand stained with ink and a frowsy woman who neglected her dress were common images for a woman who published. Even more forbidding was criticism likening a woman writer to an adventuress, an immoral creature. Almanacs, elegant literary collections modeled on Karamzin's *Aonidy*, offered a middle ground between private circulation and commercial publication; they were a favored place to make a debut.[10]

From the late 1820s on, most literary journals regularly published women's poetry. Of these, *Sovremennik* (The Contemporary) was particularly important. Under Petr Pletnev's editorship, work by Avdot'ia Glinka, Rostopchina, Pavlova, and Shakhova regularly appeared in the same issues. When the civic critic Nikolai Chernyshevsky (1828–1889) became editor, this practice ceased, and Rostopchina and Pavlova, as well as Zhadovskaia, moved to *Moskvitianin* (The Muscovite), edited by Mikhail Pogodin (1800–1875). Individual volumes of verse also appeared more frequently. In 1833 volumes by Kul'man, Teplova, and Kriukova were published. Fuks's poems appeared in 1834, and Shakhova published the first of several collections in 1837. Rostopchina's first collection of verse appeared in 1841. Volumes of verse by Annenkova and Zhadovskaia were published in 1844. Critics regularly reviewed these and other volumes as well as individual poems in almanacs and journals.[11] Yet even as more women poets appeared in print, poetry was in decline and the novel was fast becoming the dominant genre. Pavlova's first and only collection of Russian poetry was largely ignored when it appeared in 1863. Not until the Silver Age did women again publish poetry in such numbers.[12]

A number of influential and persistent assumptions about the woman poet and woman's poetry first took hold in the late eighteenth and early nineteenth centuries, emerging with the "feminization" of Russian culture associated with the Sentimentalist and westernizing orientation of Nikolai Karamzin (1766–1826) and his followers.[13] Almost from the moment that women writers emerged in significant numbers, critics and scholars attributed their appearance to the literary and linguistic program of the Karamzinists. In this view, the Karamzinists turned to the French salon tradition as a model for Russian literary life, and sought to establish as the Russian literary language a single "middle" style based on the spoken language of polite society and on ladies' refined taste, thus granting the "tender sex" an authority and prestige hitherto unknown. They were opposed by the politically conservative Aleksandr Shishkov (1754–1841) and his supporters who remained committed to neoclassicist ideals. Although they differed in their literary and linguistic views, the Shishkovites and Karamzinists shared the assumption that physiological differences, exemplified by women's perceived physical weakness and softness, and greater sensibility, was the basis for determining social roles, moral codes, as well as the literary possibilities open to women. Both groups assumed that "woman's poetry" was characterized by "tenderness" ("nezhnost'") of language and subject, and that it was a poetry of the heart and sensibility, concerned primarily with love and the emotions.

Of the women writing verse in the early nineteenth century when such attitudes had yet to take firm hold, Anna Bunina was quickly singled out by her contemporaries as the leading Russian woman poet. A familiar figure in St. Petersburg literary circles from 1802 onward, she contributed prose and poetry to a variety of journals and almanacs, much of it collected in *Neopytnaia muza* and the three-volume *Sobranie stikhotvorenii* (Collected Poetry, 1819–1821) published by the Russian Academy. Born into a gentry family that placed little value on education for girls, but encouraged by Enlightenment ideals that credited women with rational minds and the capacity for learning, Bunina spent her inheritance on a broad, rigorous, classical education. Although the labels "learned woman" and "bluestocking" became increasingly pejorative in her lifetime, Bunina remained committed to Enlightenment ideals and opposed to the "feminization" of Russian culture that led to separate literary spheres for men and women. Certainly physiological differences might impose some limitations on women's sphere of action, for example on a military career, as she acknowledges in "Na vystuplenie rossiisko-imperatorskikh voisk" ("On the Campaign of the Russian Imperial Troops," 1809); and certainly love was a necessary and indeed civilizing condition of relations between the weaker and the stronger sex, although she carefully distinguished between love as respect and erotic love in her essay "Liubov'" ("Love," 1799). She did not concede, however, that these assumptions entailed a separate sphere of literary activity. If a woman's tender sensibilities and physical weakness prevented her from fighting on the battlefield, they did not prevent her from writing of warfare in bloody detail (e.g. "Na istreblenie frantsuzov, naglo v serdtse Rossii vtorgnuvshikhsia" ["On the Destruction of the French upon Their Impudent Incursion into the Heart of Russia"]). Bunina claimed for herself as a poet the language, subjects, and genres she could master through her own intellect and competence. Denying that love and the nuances of feeling were her only true subjects, and that a delicate, "feminine" language and style suited to polite society and ladies' sensibility her appropriate register, she mocks such attitudes and the ladies who encouraged them in her witty "Razgovor mezhdu mnoiu i zhenshchinami" ("A Conversation Between Me and Women," 1812).

Often named the "Russian Sappho," Bunina symbolized her attitude towards Sappho in the frontispiece to the first volume of *Neopytnaia muza* and *Sobranie stikhotvorenii*.[14] She depicts Sappho triumphant rather than silenced by the loss of her lover. Bunina represents her not as she was conventionally represented, flinging herself from the White Rock in despair, but borne safely on the back of a dolphin. Beneath the engraving are the words "The lyre saved me from drowning." She sought to revise the Sapphic model by her poetic practice and set an example to other women through her wide range of subjects, language, metrical skill and innovations, and emotional tone. The genres and the subjects she attempted (odes and fables, patriotic verse and political allegory, idylls and elegies, epigrams and large-scale compositions, didactic verse and Greek translations) and her use of her native language with all the elements that a refined "feminine" sensibility would purge as "vulgar" and "harsh," including Church Slavonicisms, colloquialisms, and proverbs, were a way of resisting the formation of boundaries between men's and women's writing and language.

If much of Bunina's original poetry, as well as her translations of Batteux and Boileau, demonstrated her adherence to eighteenth-century neoclassicist ideals and situated her on the side of the Shishkovites, she was drawn towards a more romanticist emphasis on the poet when she reflected on her own experience as a woman poet. Bunina was increasingly subject to the fear that she erred, even sinned, in her poetic ambitions. She valued qualities of restraint and order, calm and stability ("prochnost'" and "prochnyi mir" are favorite words), and wrote numerous poems celebrating a life of quiet moderation (e.g. "Na schastii" ["On Happiness," 1811], "Shchastlivyi Menalk. Idillia" ["Happy Menalchus. An Idyll," pub. 1819], "Poslanie k Leonu" ["Epistle to Leon," 1812]). Her concern with legitimacy, authority, and social order is evident in *Padenie Faetona* (The Fall of Phaeton, 1811). The poem relates the disastrous consequences to himself and the world of Phaeton's hubristic desire to drive the chariot of his father, the sun-god; and it figures Bunina's own position as a woman poet aspiring to realms she feared she had no right to.[15] While she praised the qualities of meekness and humility as virtues in the abstract, she could write angrily of them when they were required of her and other women ("Ei zhe" ["To Her," 1812]). Nor did she feel that she possessed them ("Pokhvala liubvi" ["In Praise of Love," publ. 1819]). Many of her most personal and powerful poems are bleakly inspired by depression, slander and betrayal by friends, ridicule as a woman poet, as well as by worsening health and a painful and ultimately fatal breast cancer which took her to England in an unsuccessful search for a cure in 1815 ("Pri vstreche vesny" ["Meeting the Spring," 1809], "Uprek drugu" ["Reproach to a Friend," publ. 1819], "Pesn' smerti" ["Song of Death," 1812], "Maiskaia progulka boliashchei" ["The Sick Woman's Maytime Stroll," 1812]). The dark and often angry mood of such poems contrasts sharply with the gentler and more accepting tones of such poets as Pospelova, Volkova, Krichevskaia, and Kul'man.

An anxiety about writing and the body, often manifested in women's work as a fear of appearing immodest, emerges in Bunina's poetry as a fear that her disease is a punishment. In "Maiskaia progulka boliashchei" she drew together themes and images scattered throughout her poetry to suggest that the poet's ambition and painful illness are inextricably, even causally, linked. The external destructive forces of enemies, poverty, and isolation that beset her, now attack her from within. Her fear that women's involvement in poetry is destructive had already appeared in the early poem "S primorskogo berega" ("From the Seashore," 1806), in which a girl's song shatters a calm domestic scene. In "Maiskaia progulka boliashchei" the images of the burning flame and poison coursing through the veins in the earlier poem reappear, intensified as hell fire, a volcano in her breast, and a viper poisoning her blood and devouring her from within. The exhilarating strength, power, speed, and physical control over nature the poet possesses in such poems as "Sumerki" ("Twilight," 1808) and "Razgovor mezhdu mnoiu i zhenshchinami" become in "Maiskaia progulka boliashchei" symptoms of disease as the woman poet is driven, racked and restless with pain, through an orderly, pastoral landscape in which she, accursed, can find no place and in which she seeks in vain for respite and relief from man or God.

Similar to Bunina in her poetic ambitions, although milder and more optimistic in tone, was Bunina's younger contemporary, the prodigy Elisaveta Kul'man. Kul'man shared Bunina's love of learning and aspired to membership in the Russian Academy. Unlike Bunina, however, Kul'man found her gifts encouraged early on, and mastered eleven languages (Russian and Church Slavonic, French, German, Italian, English, classical and modern Greek, Latin, Spanish, and Portuguese). Her death at age seventeen ended a promising literary career. Her work was largely unknown until 1833 when her former tutor Karl Grossgeinrikh succeeded in bringing a selection of her translations and original poetry from her voluminous manuscripts into print with Shishkov's assistance at the Russian Academy.[16]

Kul'man's inventive and scholarly reworking of classical mythology in *Piiticheskie opyty* and her poems of a richly imagined land and time of Ancient Greece reflect the revival of interest in Greek and Roman culture among early nineteenth-century scholars and poets looking for models and ideals for their own time. Contemporary scholars were impressed by the erudition evident in her translations of Anacreon and in *Pamiatnik Berenike* (Memorial to Berenice), a recreation of the lost work of classical poets (including Bion, Moschus, Callimachus, Apollonius of Rhodes, and Homer the Younger) presented as a tribute to the Empress Berenice, mother of Ptolemy and patron of education and the arts circa 200 BC. *Pamiatnik Berenike* opens with an invocation to the "all-embracing goddess" (Isis) and reflects Kul'man's sustained effort to place women and the woman poet at the origins of culture and literature. In the two original poetic cycles *Venok* (Wreath) and *Stikhotvoreniia Korinny ili Pamiatnik Elise* (The Poems of Corinna or Memorial to Elis), Kul'man composed a series of myths that formed a coherent and intricate whole, and even charted names, events, and places on a map of Greece to give them geographical and historical substance. Her poetry thus belongs to a tradition of women's revisionary writing that rewrites and invents myths as a way of establishing female legitimacy and authority.[17] *Pamiatnik Elise*, for example, offers an account of a kingdom founded by the mythical queengoddess Elis, presided over by female deities, and rich in stories of women. The nine myths of metamorphosis retold in *Venok* share the same focus. "Mak" ("Poppy") relates the story of Demeter's search for her daughter Persephone, a favorite subject of women revisionary poets. In "Nartsiss" ("Narcissus"), Kul'man transforms Narcissus into a girl. Nartsissa, daughter of Diana and Endymion, is a young huntress, who becomes enamored of her own reflection in a pool, and drowns trying to embrace the "young man." Emphasizing the maternal element in the virgin goddess, Kul'man relates how Diana mourns her daughter, and wears the narcissus she has become on her breast as a remembrance. Aphrodite figures prominently in a number of poems: "Fialka" ("Violet"), "Roza" ("Rose"), and "Anemona" ("Anemone"). Like Bunina, Kul'man made a firm, moral distinction between erotic, frivolous love, and love as respect and devotion. She represented the goddess of love as a benign, gentle figure, a beneficial and civilizing influence, typically emphasizing Aphrodite's modesty, rather than using her as an occasion for erotic description. In "Gvozdika" ("Carnation") Kul'man performed a similar transformation in her variation on the ever popular myth of Acteon surprising Diana bathing that usually served as the occasion for erotic description.[18] Kul'man reworked the encounter as one between the goddess and a young girl. The girl performs an act of kindness for Diana and is rewarded with the goddess's protection for herself and her family. Kul'man's retelling of the myth "domesticates" the virgin huntress goddess, just as she stresses the goddess's maternal feelings in "Nartsiss."

Stories of female creative and poetic power have a special place in Kul'man's mythology as a source of authority and inspiration for herself. A central poem in *Stikhotvoreniia Korinny* relates the story of Corinna's first competition, and how Pindar crowns her with laurels for her song telling how the laurel originated when the nymph Daphne is transformed into a laurel tree to escape Apollo's pursuit. A sequel to the tale in "Lavr" tells how the laurel tree withers despite all Apollo's care, until Daphne herself speaks of her sorrow at being shut out of the temple of Apollo–poetry. The tree thrives once more when granted the right to crown the heads of Apollo and all poets. Kul'man, like Bunina, did not take Sappho as her model. Although she offered as a female precursor, Myrtis, the mature woman poet and teacher of Corinna and Pindar, to whom she pays tribute in "K Mirto" ("To Myrtis"), she preferred the youthful figures of Corinna and Evdora. In "Nezabudka" ("Forget-Me-Not"), she describes how Evdora's poetic gifts briefly blossom only to fade in death. Unwittingly Kul'man created a figure that became a poignant reminder of her own early death.

When Kul'man's work appeared in print in the heart of the Romantic period, approximately fifteen years after its composition, it joined that of a number of other women just venturing to publish poetry. Aleksandr Nikitenko's introduction to *Piiticheskie opyty* praises Kul'man as a poet, but minimizes both her learning and her insistence on the poet's public role. He emphasizes her modesty and extreme timidity, and declares that she would have rather died than be seen as a learned woman, and that she concealed her gifts from all but her tutor: "No one would have realized she was a woman writer," he observes approvingly. "She guarded under a cloak of secrecy the fruits of her poetic passions."[19] His assertions reflect the difficulties facing women poets then coming into print: the constraints of modesty had become increasingly narrow at the same time as the figure of the poet had become central. Even Ivan Kireevskii, who wrote one of the first, gallantly admiring essays about the rise of women poets, was reluctant to name them, even when they themselves put their signatures to their work. His reluctance originates in the belief that women *were* their poetry, and that their poems were "mirror verse" and "confessions."[20] Thus the romantic identification of art and life, poet and man, was peculiarly charged for women poets for whom the demands of being a woman and being a poet were potentially both a source of poetic power and authority and also a source of division and conflict. In these circumstances, certain incarnations of the Romantic poet were particularly appealing to women. Such poems as Teplova's "Sovet" ("Advice," 1837), Rostopchina's "Kak dolzhny pisat' zhenshchiny" ("How Women Should Write," 1840), and Pavlova's "Est' liubimtsy vdokhnovenii" ("There are favorites of inspiration," 1839) and "Net, ne im tvoi dar sviashchennyi!" ("No, your sacred gift is not for them!" 1840), draw more or less subtle parallels between the woman who silently and shyly escapes notice and whose heart is full of poetry, and the solitary, melancholy, and reflective poet dreamer who emerged in the poetry of pre-Romantic writers like Vasilii Zhukovskii (1783–1852) and who appears again in such poems as Dmitrii Venevitinov's "Poet" (1826). The poet's sacred, quiet dreams, his secret, silent inner life, his artless, instinctive utterances, even his sudden shame, are profoundly feminine, and represent the way many women poets imagined their work when the demands of propriety and romantic imagery coincided. The isolated poet, alone in a crowd, would become a useful persona for the woman poet, and the Russian poet with his useless gift ("naprasnyi dar") was a figure in whom women poets could recognize themselves.[21]

The feminine aspects of the poet were the more striking given the reaction against "feminine" influence, as many writers and critics scorned the direction in which Russian poetry had developed and railed against the "feminization" of Russian language and literature.[22] Anxious to free themselves of this feminine influence and to redefine the poet's place in Russian society and create a "poetry of thought," an antidote to the frivolous, light poetry suited to drawing rooms and ladies' taste, they declared with renewed insistence that woman's poetry was a special category and the woman poet a different creature.

One of the first women poets to publish in the 1830s and whose work reveals some of these tensions was Nadezhda Teplova. The small body of lyric poetry she wrote between the late 1820s and her death in 1848 treats many of the themes explored by such poets as Venevitinov (1805–1827), Fedor Tiutchev (1803–1873), and the Decembrist Andrei Odoevskii (1802–1839), as well as thinkers like Nikolai Stankevich (1813–1840) and his circle, who brought the philosophy of Schelling and German idealism to their attempts to forge a "poetry of thought." There are many parallels between the work of these "poets of thought" and Teplova's poetry, as in "Iazyk ochei" ("The Language of Eyes," 1831) where she writes of the poet's inexpressible world beyond speech or song; "Vesna" ("Spring," 1841) which tells of the poet's penetration of the veil of nature and the soundless, wordless world open to her senses and heart; and "Soznanie" ("Consciousness," 1831) where she writes of her yearning for a realm of art and beauty she cannot attain. In contrast to her male peers, whose idealism has been explained as an attempt to escape the restrictive atmosphere of Nikolai I's repressive rule and to transcend the barriers to political action and change erected after the failure of the Decembrist revolt in 1825, Teplova's idealism, her abandonment of the material world and her longing to escape the body, flow rather from her desire to free herself from the dreariness of her life ("Tsel'" ["Purpose," 1835] and "Zhizn'" ["Life," 1842]), as well as the restrictions imposed on a woman poet, and the demands of modesty that forced her into concealment and made poetry a "dangerous gift."

The reception of Teplova's work justified her fears. Readers like Stankevich who should have most appreciated her "poetry of thought" praised it as "charming," a product of woman's true and natural sphere, "the sphere of love and feeling."[23] He faulted her, moreover, for the "indefiniteness" of her verse which kept the poet herself out of her poetry. However, if Teplova kept herself and her body out of her poetry, she made the body itself, its boundaries and limits, its senses and sensibility a central theme. Many of her poems explore the workings of sensibility, the ways in which the subject and the object are connected, how feeling and its expression shape and are shaped by the world, and how the workings of love and sympathy make the world knowable. Her concern is with the very nature of knowledge and how the moment of apprehension is related to the poetic imagination. Love, a favorite word, is the prelude to and basis for understanding and knowledge, in the sense that Kireevskii, reflecting on Venevitinov's philosophical ideas, suggests that "to love is to comprehend."

Teplova explores the ways in which the body and its senses operate in several poems about poetry, the poet, and poetic receptivity of the world. Apprehension of the world becomes identical with the dissolution of boundaries, and the tension or differentiation between body, world, and the mediating senses/feelings is dissolved in ways that may be seen as akin to the death of the body as in "Fleita" ("Flute," 1835), or as an expansion of the body beyond all boundaries as in "K charodeiu" ("To the Enchanter," 1831) and "Pererozhdenie" ("Regeneration/Degeneration," 1835).

Teplova's response to the conflict between art and life, poetry and love facing a woman poet was to expunge the body and the poet herself from her poems. Her fate as a poet, little reviewed and despite her sister's efforts to reprint her work, little read, was very different from that of Evdokiia Rostopchina, the "Russian Corinna" (an allusion to Germaine de Staël's eponymous heroine) and the "Russian George Sand" as she was styled, the most celebrated Russian woman poet of the 1830s and 1840s, who, far from obscuring herself, placed herself and her life at the very heart of her poetry. Wealthy and socially prominent by marriage, a well-known figure in literary circles, with a reputation for enjoying society's pleasures, she was, after Lermontov's death in 1841, considered by some not only the leading woman poet, but the leading poet of her generation. For the women poets of her time, Rostopchina was a formidable figure because in such poems as "Sovet zhenshchinam" ("Advice to Women," 1838), "Kak dolzhny pisat' zhenshchiny," and "Iskushen'e" ("Temptation," 1839, published 1841), she sought to speak for all women, and thus define "woman's poetry" and the "woman poet" for her contemporaries.

Rostopchina grounded her work firmly in the Russian tradition, specifically the "feminization" of culture associated with Karamzin. Written in a style that follows the cadences and speech patterns of the gentry and educated society, her tender "woman's poetry" was perceived by admiring readers as the fulfillment of the Karamzinists' vision. Her verse is rich in echoes of the poetry of the Golden Age. As her eclectic and prolific use of epigraphs shows, she was equally well-read in Western European literature of the Romantic period. In particular, she was unique in her recognition and promotion of contemporary women poets and novelists in France, Germany and Britain. The names she cites most often include the British novelist Sidney Owenson (married name Lady Morgan), the French poetesses Mélanie Waldor (1796–1871), Anaïs Ségalas (1814–1895), and Amable Tastu (1798–1885), the German writer Countess Ida von Hahn-Hahn (1805–1880), the British writer Laetitia Landon (1802–1838) and the French poet Marceline Desbordes-Valmore (1786–1859).[24]

Rostopchina embraced an ideal of womanhood as a separate sphere, physically, emotionally, and poetically. Whether she is comparing the dashing, active life of a soldier in the Caucasus to her own more retiring, passive, and silent life in her quiet country "cell," as she does in "Serezhe" ("To Serezha," 1839), the preface to her first collection of verse in 1841, or whether she is contrasting the rough masculine living quarters on a man o' war to the delicate arrangements made to accommodate ladies in "Bal na fregate" ("Ball on the Frigate," 1842), she readily accepts that men and women inhabit different worlds. Unlike Bunina, however, Rostopchina does not find her literary sphere limiting. Thus in "Chernovaia kniga Pushkina" ("Pushkin's Notebook," 1838) Rostopchina gently declares that she is only a weak woman in whom thought and inspiration must be fettered by meek modesty, but nonetheless manages to give the impression that she is Pushkin's rightful heir. In "Oda Poezii. Anakhronizm" ("An Ode to Poetry. An Anachronism," 1852) she takes the whole realm of poetry to be feminine as she celebrates the Golden Age of Russian poetry as a Golden Age for women when Art and Beauty reigned supreme, and swears her devotion to the presiding goddess of Poetry and refuses to bow to the apostates who would desecrate Her temple.

Her poems about poetry and the woman poet repeat familiar claims: that woman's poetry comes from the heart, as in " 'Ona vse dumaet!'," (" 'She is always thinking!'," 1842), with its epigraph "'Plus rêver que penser!' Devise de femme"; that the woman poet is artless, her poetry a spontaneous overflowing of the self and the emotions; that improvisation is appropriate in women poets for whom body, self, and poetry are inextricably intertwined; that love is woman's essential subject ("Sovet zhenshchinam" and "Kak dolzhny pisat' zhenshchiny"). Her verses are presented as confession, a mirror of her soul, and she spoke of her work as a diary of her heart, identifying each poem by date (the year, month, and usually day) and place. At the same time she carefully concealed anything in her life that did not fit the poetic persona she created for herself in her poetry and life.[25]

She describes the life of a society lady in many poems set in St. Petersburg, Moscow, the family estate of Selo Anna, fashionable spas, and the cities of Germany, Italy, and France. She takes her scenes from a life of ease and leisure in gentry circles and polite society, and she was a knowledgeable, shrewd, and often witty observer of that world. Behind the poise of the society lady, however, she also hints at hidden depths and tragedy in her life. Many poems echo the Sapphic story of love and loss (e.g. "Moim dvum priiatel'nitsam" ["To My Two Friends," 1848]). That story was the basis for her poetic cycle *Neizvestnyi roman* (An Unknown Romance, 1847), as well as the novel *Schastlivaia zhenshchina* (A Fortunate Woman, 1851–1852), and she skillfully let her readers believe that these narratives of other women's lives were based on her own sorrows. As she writes in "Kak dolzhny pisat' zhenshchiny," women's writings are necessarily half-hidden and elusive. Hints, unanswered questions, and vague allusions are the poetic equivalent of woman's downcast eyes and retiring life and characterize much of Rostopchina's poetry. Thus she prefaced one group of poems ("Zelenaia kniga" ["Green Book," 1834–1838]) with a dedication "Posviashchenie" ("Dedication," 1855) in which she talks of a secret unnamed figure, both lover and reader, who has inspired the poems but whose name she will never divulge.[26] Lies, secrets, dissemblance, and the masks and costumes that women must assume in life become subjects in themselves, as they do in "Nadevaia albanskii kostium" ("Putting on an Albanian Costume," 1835) and "Pochemu ia liubliu maskarada?" ("Why Do I Love A Masquerade?" 1850).

Rostopchina found critics early on who faulted this "poet of the ball," as she was dubbed, and who criticized her frivolity and saw in her only a society lady, whose encounter even with the great Russian poet Pushkin takes place at a ball ("Dve vstrechi" ["Two Meetings," 1839]). Critics like Vissarion Belinsky (1811–1848), and Chernyshevsky castigated her as the incarnation of a cold-hearted society woman symbolizing the irresponsible "aristocratism" and moral failure of Russian literature.[27] Rostopchina attempted to adapt to the changing times and in "Tsirk deviatnadtsatogo veka" ("The Circus of the Nineteenth Century," 1850), she emulated the critical social realism of Nekrasov's poetry with a fresh interpretation of her old subjects, the ball and the mask, in a series of vignettes depicting the lives of misery and want that men and women dancing at a ball conceal behind elegant manners and fashionable clothes. More typical, however, were her attempts to revive and reaffirm the past and to restore the society and the tradition in which she had flourished, as she does in such works as her verse drama *Vozvrat Chatskogo v Moskve* (Chatskii's Return to Moscow, 1856), her sequel to Aleksandr Griboedov's *Gore ot uma* (Woe from Wit, 1822–3), and "Dom sumasshedshikh v Moskve v 1858" ("The Madhouse in Moscow in 1858"), her continuation of Aleksandr Voeikov's verse satire of the same name. By her death in 1858, she had ceased to be the central figure she once was, and her reputation never recovered from the criticisms leveled at her in her lifetime.

Rostopchina's confident declarations defining woman's character and woman's poetry, however powerful, did not go undisputed among women. Among those who disagreed was the girl poet Elisaveta Shakhova who first appeared in print just as Rostopchina was making her reputation. Between the publication of her *Opyty v stikhakh piatinadtsatiletnei devitsy* (Experiments in Verse of a Fifteen-Year-Old Girl) in 1837 and 1845, when she entered the newly founded Spaso-Borodinskii Monastery, one of the first and most famous of the nineteenth-century women's religious communities, Shakhova's prose and poetry regularly appeared in the leading journals, and she published two more collections of verse (1839 and 1840), as well as a volume of narrative poems (1842).

Deeply devout, Shakhova became one in a line of women religious poets that can be traced back through Elizaveta Kheraskova (d. 1809) and Aleksandra Murzina (active in the 1790s) in the eighteenth century, and that included several of Shakhova's contemporaries, Avdot'ia Glinka prominent among them, as well as twentieth-century poets like Mariia Shkapskaia (1891–1952) and Elizaveta Kuz'mina-Karavaeva (Mother Mariia, 1891–1945).

Shakhova's reflections on being a woman poet became intertwined with working out her religious vocation. Her piety and the atmosphere of the literary circles she frequented, contrasted sharply with Rostopchina's world. There were several antagonistic exchanges between the two women. Most of these propound different versions of womanhood. Rostopchina's poem "Ravnodushnoi" ("To the Indifferent Girl") dated 1830, but published in 1838 and evidently directed at Shakhova, declares that giving up love and romance as the stern, cold, and moralistic girl with a religious vocation does in the poem is unnatural and unwomanly. Shakhova's condemnation of the "poet of the ball" was no less sharp in her poem "Zhenshchina i bal" ("Woman and the Ball," 1840), in which she rebuts "Iskushen'e," one of Rostopchina's most famous poems, in which the poet, a young mother, reproaches those who chastise women for their innocent pleasures, and declares that as a woman she is subject to all feminine inclinations and longs for balls. Sundering the two female images that Rostopchina brings together, Shakhova moralizes in conventional terms against the meaningless display of fashion, dancing, empty words, and glances. She reprovingly declares that a woman pure in heart and mind finds balls and society's pleasures dull. She extols instead a domestic scene of calm simplicity, genuine friendship, and rational virtue presided over by an "angel in the house," an image drawn partly from her circle's interest in British domestic life and Victorian ideals of womanhood, and exalted in Benediktov's poem to their mutual friend and patron Evgeniia Maikova, "K zhenshchine" ("To a Woman," 1839). In poems like "Galopad" ("Gallop," 1841), a poem of a demonic dance and a tribute to his famous "Val's" ("Waltz," 1840), Shakhova adopted Benediktov's convoluted syntax, mixture of styles, and striking and extravagant use of metaphor and hyperbole as a way of distinguishing herself stylistically from Rostopchina's smooth style. In "Mechtatel'" ("Dreamer," 1840), Shakhova excoriates the dreamer, one of Rostopchina's favorite self-images and a central aspect of her poetic persona. Shakhova scorns this romantic figure as one who hates life and lives only in the past and the future, never the present, eaten up with hatred and resentment. In "Reshimost'" ("Resolution," 1840), Shakhova makes a declaration that is both a step toward religious renunciation, and an aesthetic statement that she is not a confessional poet like Rostopchina. Rejecting all hope and dreams of love, she resolves that her maidenly, private thoughts as she lies in bed will remain unknown to the world. She takes a vow of silence, swearing that her murmurs, tears, and whisperings will go unheard. Paradoxically, despite her assertions to the contrary,

Shakhova wrote for publication, although as her later poetry shows, she remained torn.

In "K zhenshchinam-poetam," written in 1845 on the eve of entering a convent, Shakhova tried to sum up her conclusions about women and poetry, and in lines set off at the end of the poem, she proposes reconciling the claims of poetry and the claims of life on a woman poet by writing for oneself and for God as a "bird free on the wing." She continued writing secular verse, but the religious note already apparent in her work was becoming predominant; the divide between secular and religious life formed the basis for her 1849 collection *Mirianka i otshel'nitsa* (The Secular Woman and the Nun). In 1863 Shakhova finally took the veil, adopting the name Mother Mariia. As she wrote in her poem "Avtobiograficheskii otzyv iz glushi" ("Autobiographical Response from a Backwater," c. 1865), this sharpened the conflict she faced as a poet poised between the religious life and worldly concerns.

Shakhova's religious beliefs found little favor with the civic critics. More popular as a contrast to Rostopchina was the young provincial poet Iuliia Zhadovskaia. Zhadovskaia has gone down in literary history primarily as the woman writer critics contrasted to Rostopchina.[28] Her prominence in critical essays of the period had as much to do with what she symbolized as with the quality of her verse. Zhadovskaia's plight as a young woman mired in provincial life was contrasted favorably to Rostopchina's aristocratic world of luxury and frivolity. While Nikolai Dobroliubov (1836–1861) criticized the harsh, prosaic qualities of Zhadovskaia's poetry as incompetent, he simultaneously valued these "failings" as a sign that her poems were truly written from her heart, unlike Rostopchina's insincere, polished lyrical outpourings.[29] Nevertheless, if they differed stylistically, critics agreed that both were characteristically feminine poets in their preoccupation with love. Indeed, if Zhadovskaia's settings are more provincial, taking place in woods, steppe land, and gardens, in thunderstorms and under night skies, rather than at balls and in drawing rooms and salons, she shares the more worldly poet's intimate tone. The first-person voice predominates and tells similar stories of a young woman's disappointment in love in poems that are often addressed to her lover. Stylistically, however, Zhadovskaia more closely resembles Shakhova in her attempts to break free of a poetic language associated with Rostopchina and her tradition. In "Monolog," for example, Zhadovskaia writes of the difficulty in finding a language in which to describe her sensations as she gazes at the stars. She imagines a (male) reader sneering and calling her a dreamer ("mechtatel'nitsa"). In several poems Zhadovskaia suggests that there is a natural language of trees, stars, flowers, and elemental powers that she strives to understand and emulate by paring away clichés, abandoning smooth diction and ready rhymes, and experimenting with meter and prosaic elements.[30] Critics in Zhadovskaia's day, however, had little interest in this aspect of her work, and, furthermore, faulted her for a lack of interest in social problems.

More successful in this respect, although better known as a novelist than a poet, was Nadezhda Khvoshchinskaia (1820?–1889). She began her literary career with poetry in the Nekrasovian manner in the 1840s, and published a considerable number of poems before abandoning poetry altogether in the 1860s.[31] In a version of the ball theme, "Detskii bal" ("Children's Ball," 1848), the writer assumes a quasi-maternal persona who is horrified at the sight of children being corrupted, and determines to reform society and preserve their innocence. In "Slovo" ("Word," 1856) she characteristically argues that literature should be placed in the service of social reform rather than Beauty and Art. Realism rather than romantic idealism, moral indignation and love of the people, work, and action ("delo") rather than melancholy dreaming and love and passion absorb her energies. Instead of the first person singular, the "I" dominant in Rostopchina's poems, Khvoshchinskaia uses the first person plural, "we," and imagines herself speaking for a generation of like-minded men and women urging social reform. There are poems that sound a wistful note, longing for love and dreams, as in "Ne mogu ia priniat'sia za delo" ("I cannot settle down to my work," 1851), but the poet more often rejects such idle daydreaming, resolutely determined to work and be useful to society. The realism and psychological subtlety that came to characterize her fiction are already evident in her poetry, and indeed in this she bears comparison with Pavlova.

Although Karolina Pavlova had been active in literary life from the 1820s onward, and had earned a reputation as a precise and talented translator with two volumes of poetry, Das Nordlicht (1833) and Les préludes (1839), she turned to writing her own Russian poetry relatively late, at the end of the 1830s.[32] Pavlova's dedication to her "sacred craft," her technical virtuosity and her complex exploration of meter and rhyme, which later gave her a reputation as "a poet's poet" and made her much admired in the Silver Age, came from her early "apprenticeship" as a translator. Her insistence on the craft of poetry sharply distinguished her from Rostopchina with her "poetry of the heart" and improvisational manner.

Pavlova was alert to the ways in which the different positions men and women occupied in social and literary life had affected the development of poetry and the poet's understanding of his or her calling. In a number of poems, she explores the ways in which some genres were more or less accessible to men and women.[33] In "Da, mnogo bylo nas, mladencheskikh podrug" ("Yes, we were many, young girls and friends," 1839), for example, she employs the conventions of the friendly epistle, in which poets addressed one another, affirming their fellowship and their identity as poets, to suggest the absence of such a community for women poets. In "A. D. B[aratynsk]oi" ("To A. D. B[aratynsk]aia," 1858), she plays with the conventions of the flirtatious album verse that assume a male poet and a female addressee. She adopts a "masculine" stance and addresses a beautiful woman to whom she is dictating her verses, thus creating a tension that leads the reader to consider the underlying assumptions about such poems.

The isolated woman was a recurrent figure in Pavlova's poetry and prose–as she was in the work of other women poets (e.g. Bunina's "Pesn' svobody" ["Song of Freedom," 1812], Teplova's "Uedinenie" ["Solitude"])– and closely linked in her poetry also to the image of the solitary Romantic poet (e.g. "Est' liubimtsy vdokhnovenii," and "Net, ne im tvoi dar sviashchennyi!"). In Pavlova's poetry that isolation was intensified by her sense that the age of poetry was passing, not only because realism and the novel were supplanting poetry, but because so many of the poets she had known as a young woman had died ("Zovet nas zhizn'" ["Life calls us," 1846] and "Dumy" ["Meditations," 1847]). She explored these themes in a group of self-reflective poems written between 1840 and 1844, each entitled "Duma" ("Meditation"), that had particular significance in her development as a poet. In these poems she reflects on the nature of thought itself, the workings of memory and emotion – an inquiry that places her alongside those poets who attempted to forge a "poetry of thought." She links the isolation and alienation of the Romantic poet to her own sense of isolation as a woman poet outside the larger community of (male) poets and to the alienation from herself that her rigorous analysis of her own emotions, thoughts, and memories brings.[34] The critical, analytical voice she defined in the "Duma" poems became characteristic of her work as a whole. Thus in "Laterna Magica" (1850), the introduction to an unfinished poem about women, the poet expresses her fear of writing in a literary climate that despises poetry as frivolous and of interest only to children and foolish women; she relates how suddenly she is inspired to write by a vision of herself at work, outside looking in through a window at a young woman sitting sadly in a darkened room, who asks the poet to tell her story and understand her. In her narrative poem *Kadril'* (Quadrille, 1843–1857) Pavlova brought her talent for psychological analysis and realism to representing women's lives in the sad, tragic, and comical stories four women tell as they sit together before a ball. It is that clarity of vision that Pavlova's heroine Cécile acquires in her innovative novel in prose and poetry *Dvoinaia zhizn'*. Realism by no means destroys poetry for Pavlova (as it does for Rostopchina in her story of the girl poet, *Dnevnik devushki. Poeziia i proza zhizni* (Diary of a Girl. The Poetry and Prose of Life, 1842–1850); rather it makes poetry all the more necessary. In *Dvoinaia zhizn'*, the young girl's poetic gifts seem to emerge as she becomes more thoroughly entangled in the snare of a bad marriage. The critical vision the young heroine attains by the end of Pavlova's novel and the alienation and otherness Cécile experiences were central to Pavlova's own conception of poetry.

By the 1850s, Pavlova, beset by marital troubles and increasingly beleaguered in a hostile political and literary climate, found herself isolated, for a time falling almost silent as a poet. A renewal of her creative energies came after 1853, associated with a brief affair with the young Russian lawyer Boris Utin. From this period came not only the cycle of poems to Utin, memorializing their friendship, in which she returns to her themes of isolation, conversation, and friendship, but many of her historical and philosophical poems, among them "Razgovor v Kremle" ("Conversation in the Kremlin," 1854), "Prazdnik Rima" ("Rome Holiday," 1856), and "Uzhin Polliona" ("Pollion's Supper," 1857). She brings to these subjects the same concern with memory, emotion, and thought. In 1858 she moved permanently abroad, settling finally in Dresden. During these years, she traveled extensively for the first time in her life, visiting the cities of Italy and going as far as Constantinople, journeys that inspired the beautiful poetic cycle *Fantasmagorii* (Phantasmagorias, 1856–1861). She arranged for the publication of her first collection of poetry in 1863; it met with little attention and less praise.[35] In this she shared the common fate of poets in Russia at that time as the novel became the dominant genre. She was one of the last women poets of the Golden Age of Russian poetry; Rostopchina had died in 1858, Zhadovskaia and Khvoshchinskaia had both turned to prose; Shakhova had retired to a convent and was writing very little. Nevertheless, some of their work survived. When women poets again emerged at the end of the nineteenth century, if they found that attitudes towards women's poetry and the woman poet were unchanged, unlike Bunina at the beginning of the century, they found a more experienced muse and turned back to these earlier women poets for instruction and inspiration.

NOTES

I would like to thank Adele Barker, Jehanne Gheith, Louis Goldring, and Catriona Kelly for their helpful readings at different stages in writing this essay.

1. On Volkova, Pospelova, and Krichevskaia, see Catriona Kelly's essay in this collection.

2. On Franco-Russian ties see: G. Ghennady, *Les écrivains franco-russes* (Dresden, 1874); *Russkaia kul'tura i Frantsiia, Literaturnoe nasledstvo*, nos. 29–30, 31–2, 33–4 (Moscow, 1939); Kelly *History*, 53–6; Frank Göpfert, "Das Schicksal Sarra Tolstajas und die Frage nach einer Geschichtsschreibung russischer Frauenliteratur," in his *Russland aus der Feder seiner Frauen zum Femininen Diskurs in der Russischen Literatur* (Munich, 1992), 51–68. Women who wrote original poetry in languages other than Russian include Kul'man, Pavlova, Elizaveta Ulybysheva, and Volkonskaia. Many women were also active as translators.

3. On literary life, see William Mills Todd III, *Fiction and Society in the Age of Pushkin. Ideology, Institutions and Narrative* (Cambridge, MA, 1986); Wendy Rosslyn, "Anna Bunina's 'Unchaste Relationship with the Muses': Patronage, the Market and the Woman Writer in Early Nineteenth-Century Russia," *SEER*, 74:2 (1996), 223–42; Wendy Rosslyn, *Anna Bunina (1774–1829) and the Origins of Women's Poetry in Russia* (Lewiston, 1997).

4. See, among other friendships between men and women, those of Bunina and Aleksandr Shishkov, Kul'man and her tutor Karl Grossgeinrikh, Teplova and Mikhail Maksimovich, Pavlova and Evgenii Baratynskii, Shakhova and Vladimir Benediktov, Rostopchina and Vladimir Odoevskii and Mikhail Lermontov.

5. S. I. Ponomarev, *Nashi pisatel'nitsy, Sbornik otdeleniia russkogo iazyka i slovesnosti imperatorskoi akademii nauk*, 52 (1891), 16.

6. I. M. Semenko, *Poety pushkinskoi pory* (Moscow, 1970); Lydiia Ginzburg, *O lirike* (2nd edn, Leningrad, 1974); M. I. Gillel'son, *Ot arzamasskogo bratstva k pushkinskomu krugu pisatelei* (Leningrad, 1977); William Mills Todd III, *The Familiar Letter as a Literary Genre in the Age of Pushkin* (Princeton, 1976); *"Arzamas,"* ed. V. E. Vatsuro and A. L. Ospovat (2 vols., Moscow, 1994). As far as we know, women did not organize their own societies.

7. Karlgof (b. Oshanina; Drashusova by her second marriage) also had salons in Kiev (1839) and Odessa (1840–1).

8. See, for example, the account of Rostopchina's Moscow salon in the late 1840s and early 1850s, E. P. Rostopchina, *Schastlivaia zhenshchina* (Moscow, 1991), 391–411; Lina Bernstein, "Women on the Verge of a New Language: Russian Salon Hostesses in the First Half of the Nineteenth Century," in Goscilo and Holmgren, 209–24.

9. This is the case with Gotovtseva (m. Kornilova), Ekaterina Timasheva (b. Zakriazhskaia), Praskov'ia Bakunina (1810–80?), Varvara Maksheeva (m. Bistrom, 1822–after 1867), and Evgeniia Maikova. On these writers see *DRWW* and *Russkie pisateli 1800–1917. Biograficheskii slovar'*, ed. P. A. Nikolaev (4 vols. of projected 5, Moscow, 1989–1999); on Bakunina see also Diana Greene, "Praskov'ia Bakunina and the

Poetess's Dilemma," in F. Göpfert, *Russland aus der Feder seiner Frauen*, 43–57. A handful of poems by Timasheva and Gotovtseva appear in Bannikov and *Tsaritsy muz*.

10. N. P. Smirnov-Sokol'skii, *Russkie literaturnye al'manakhi i sborniki XVIII–XIX vekov* (Moscow, 1965).

11. See, for example, Ivan Kireevskii, "O russkikh pisatel'nitsakh" [1834], *PSS*, vol. I (Moscow, 1861; repr. Ann Arbor, 1983), 114–25; Vissarion Belinsky, "Sochineniia Zeneidy R- Voi," [1843], in Belinsky, *PSS* (13 vols., Moscow, 1953–9), vol. VII, 648–78; Mikhail Katkov, "Sochineniia v stikhakh i proze grafini S. F. Tolstoi," in *Syn otechestva* 12:2 (1840), 19–50.

12. Jane A. Taubman, "Women Poets of the Silver Age," in Clyman and Greene, 171–88; Charlotte Rosenthal, "Achievement and Obscurity: Women's Prose in the Silver Age," *ibid.*, 149–70; Rosenthal, "The Silver Age: A High Point For Women?" in Linda Edmondson (ed.), *Women and Society in Russia* (Cambridge, 1992), 32–47; Svetlana Boym, *Death in Quotation Marks. Cultural Myths of the Modern Poet* (Cambridge, MA and London, 1991), 191–240.

13. On "feminization" and the "feminine pen" see: Gitta Hammarberg, "The Feminine Chronotope and Sentimentalist Canon Formation," in G. S. Smith (ed.), *Literature, Lives, and Legality in Catherine's Russia* (Nottingham, 1994), 103–20; Judith Vowles, "The 'Feminization' of Russian Literature: Women, Language, and Literature in Eighteenth-Century Russia," in Clyman and Greene, 35–60; Wendy Rosslyn, "Conflicts over Gender and Status in Early Nineteenth-Century Russian Literature: The Case of Anna Bunina and Her Poem *Padenie Faetona*," in Marsh *Gender*, 55–74; Kelly *History*. See also Kelly's essay in this collection.

14. On Sappho (and Corinna) as models, see Kelly's essay in this collection and Diana Lewis Burgin, "The Deconstruction of Sappho Stolz. Some Russian uses of the 'Tenth Muse'" in Chester and Forrester, 13–33. On Bunina as Sappho see, for example, K. N. Batiushkov's mocking "Madrigal novoi Safe" (c. 1809), in *Soch* (2 vols., Moscow, 1989), vol. I, 240.

15. See Rosslyn's excellent reading of this poem in Rosslyn, "Conflicts over Gender and Status."

16. *Piiticheskie opyty* appeared in two parts in 1833. They contained only the Russian texts, although Kul'man typically wrote each piece in Russian, German and Italian. It was reprinted as the first of three volumes in 1839, together with the German and Italian versions. Volumes two and three contained Kul'man's Russian fairy tales and tales from the *Arabian Nights*. On the publication history, see G. I. Ganzburg, "K istorii izdaniia i vospriiatiia sochinenii Elizavety Kul'man," *RLit* 1 (1990), 148–55; Grigorii Izrailevich Ganzburg (ed.), *Stat' i o poetesse Elisaveta Kul'man* (Kharkov, 1998).

17. See Alice Ostriker, "The Thieves of Language. Women Poets and Revisionist Mythmaking," [1981] in Elaine Showalter (ed.), *The New Feminist Criticism. Essays on Women, Literature and Theory* (New York, 1985), 314–38.

18. See, for example, Nikolai Karamzin's "Rytsar' nashego vremeni" ("A Knight of Our Time," 1802) or Anton Del'vig's "Kupal'nitsy" ("The Women Bathers," 1824).

19. A. Nikitenko, "Zhizneopisanie devitsy Elisavety Kul'man" [1833], *Polnoe sobranie russkikh, nemetskikh i italiianskikh stikhotvorenii. Piiticheskie opyty Elisavety Kul'man* (St. Petersburg, 1839), i–xxv, quoted p. xxi.

20. Kireevskii, "O russkikh pisatel'nitsakh," 117.

21. See Elena Gan's portrayal of the effects of class and gender on the formation of a girl poet in her unfinished "Naprasnyi dar" ("A Futile Gift," 1842).

22. On women's effeminizing influence see, for example, Nikolai Nadezhdin, "Evropeizm i narodnost'" (1836), quoted in V. V. Vinogradov, *Ocherki po istorii russkogo literaturnogo iazyka XVII–XIX vekov* (1934) (3rd edn, Moscow, 1982), 335; A. S. Pushkin, "O predislovii g-na Lemonte k perevodu basen I. A. Krylova" (1825), in Pushkin, *PSS* (10 vols., Leningrad, 1977–9), vol. 7, 19–24. For further examples see Vinogradov, *Ocherki*, 329–77, and Vinogradov, "Russko-frantsuzskii iazyk dvorianskogo salona i bor'ba Pushkina s literaturnymi normami 'iazyka svetskoi damy'," in V. V. Vinogradov, *Iazyk Pushkina* (Moscow and Leningrad, 1932), 195–236.

23. V. E. Vatsuro, "Zhizn' i poeziia Nadezhdy Teplovoi," *Pamiatniki kul'tury. Novye otkrytiia. Ezhegodnik 1989* (Moscow, 1990), 29.

24. See *An Encyclopedia of Continental Women Writers*, ed. Katharine M. Wilson (2 vols., New York and London, 1991). On prose writers in Russia, see Olga Demidova, "Russian Women Writers of the Nineteenth Century," in Marsh *Gender*, 98–102, and 105–10. Rostopchina focuses on Desbordes-Valmore's early collections *Poésies* (1830) and *Les Pleurs* (1833) in which the French poet writes of love and loss. On Desbordes-Valmore, see Michael Danahy, "Marceline Desbordes-Valmore (1786–1859)," in Eva Martin Sartori and Dorothy Wynne Zimmerman (eds.), *French Women Writers: A Bio-Bibliographical Source Book* (Westport, CT and London, 1991), 121–33. On Landon see Angela Leighton, *Victorian Women Poets. Writing Against the Heart* (New York, 1992), 45–77; Susan Brown, "The Victorian Poetess" in *The Cambridge Companion to Victorian Poetry*, ed. Joseph Bristow (Cambridge, 2000), 180–202. De Staël's *Corinne* is a powerful presence in the work of both poets, as it was in Rostopchina's. See also Angela Leighton (ed.), *Victorian Women Poets: A Critical Reader* (Oxford, 1996).

25. She is almost silent on her experience of motherhood, strikingly so given Desbordes-Valmore's emphasis on this subject.

26. Vladimir Kiselev-Sergenin, "Russkaia muza: Zagadki i tainy. Taina grafini E. P. Rostopchinoi," *Neva* 9 (1994), 267–84.

27. V. Belinsky, "Stikhotvoreniia grafini E. Rostopchinoi" (1841), in Belinsky, *PSS*, vol. v, 456–60. N. G. Chernyshevsky, "Stikhotvoreniia grafini Rostopchinoi" (1856), in Chernyshevsky, *PSS* (15 vols., Moscow, 1939–53), vol. iii, 453–68.

28. See Diana Greene, "Nineteenth-Century Women Poets: Critical Reception vs. Self-Definition," in Clyman and Greene, 108. Many of these earlier views were repeated by A. Skabichevskii in his essay "Pesni o zhenskoi nevole" (1886), in Skabichevskii, *Soch*, 2 vols. (2nd edn, St. Petersburg, 1895), vol. ii, 545–59.

29. N. A. Dobroliubov, "Stikhotvoreniia Iulii Zhadovskoi" (1858), in Dobroliubov, *SS* (9 vols., Moscow, 1961–4), vol. iii, 133–47.

30. M. L. Gasparov places Zhadovskaia's innovations in context in Gasparov, *Ocherki istorii russkogo stikha* (Moscow, 1984), 161–205.

31. A bibliography of Khvoshchinskaia's poems and prose can be found in Ponomarev, *Nashi pisatel'nitsy*, 60–70.

32. With the exception of "Sfinks" ("Sphinx," 1831).

33. Stephanie Sandler and Judith Vowles, "Beginning to Be a Poet: Baratynskii and Pavlova," in Monika Greenleaf and Stephen Moeller-Sally (eds.), *Russian Subjects: Empire, Nation, and the Culture of the Golden Age* (Evanston, IL, 1998) 151–72.

34. Kelly examines Pavlova's "otherness" in Kelly *History*, 94–107.

35. See, for example, Mikhail Saltykov-Shchedrin's review, "Stikhotvoreniia K. Pavlovoi" (1863), in Saltykov-Shchedrin, *PSS* (20 vols., Moscow, 1966), vol. v, 362–7.

4

Women of the 1830s and 1850s: alternative periodizations

In Russia, female authors came to the fore in the 1830s and 1850s, a fact which raises questions about one of the central ways that discussions of Russian literature are usually organized: the periodization of the forties and sixties. The men of the forties and those of the sixties are well-known figures in the world of nineteenth-century Russian politics and prose. This division signals a movement from diagnosis to action, from the superfluous man to the New Man, from apathy to activity.[1]

In the nineteenth century, women's writings were an essential part of the development of Russian realism; including discussion of these writings in our analyses of realism today would reshape the century in terms of theme, periodization, and style as this essay seeks to show. In addition, the writings I will discuss propose a different model of literary evolution from Harold Bloom's theory of literary paternity as a battle between fathers and sons. While there are certain differences among the writings of the women of the thirties and fifties, there are also many, many points of connection. I contend that, unlike the men of the sixties, the "sons" who came into being in conscious opposition to the "fathers" of the 1840s, the women of the fifties continue many of the themes of their predecessors without taking on an oppositional stance and that Russian women's writings of the middle of the nineteenth century follow a model of connection and development rather than the Bloomian paradigm of struggle that has become canonical for their male counterparts.

The second third of the nineteenth century was crucial in the development of Russian women's writing. In the 1830s, as Russian letters shifted from poetry to prose and from a salon culture to a print culture, women, like men, began publishing prose in (relatively) large numbers; in the 1850s, women's fiction attained new prominence.[2] In this period,

[85]

social responsibility was one of the major evaluative categories for literature, and it was widely thought that women's writings did not contribute to the work of social progress. But, I will argue, female authors (of
both the thirties and fifties) address social issues in a variety of ways:
through an insistence on communication, through giving major narrative roles to characters of lower estates, and by protesting the position of
women in Russian society, often through a critique of arranged marriage.[3] Though many of these works do not directly advocate reform, they
diagnose problems so clearly as to constitute a call for change.[4]

Elena Gan and Mar'ia Zhukóva were two of the most prominent
authors of the late 1830s and early 1840s. They, like many other writers of
the day (e.g. Pavlova, Sollogub, Rostopchina), often wrote some version
of the society tale (*svetskaia povest'*),[5] a genre popular in the 1830s and one
that is considered to have gained women entry to the field of Russian
letters as both authors and characters.[6]

Gan frequently portrays the fate of the unusual woman, one who goes
beyond *prilichie* (propriety), and, in doing so, moves beyond the bounds
of society's norms. In *Sud sveta* (Society's Judgment, 1839) and *Naprasnyi
dar* (A Futile Gift), Gan concentrates specifically on female authors. In
Society's Judgment, when a woman writer, the wife of a military man, comes
to town, she is described as a "pedant," an "oddity," and "a dancing monkey";[7] she cannot be part of high society nor can she be a member of the
confraternity of men of letters. Rather, she is located in a liminal social
space of present loneliness but great intellectual and moral power and
potential (this is analogous to the Romantic hero's alienation).[8] *Society's
Judgment* gains much of its poignancy from the play between fiction and
autobiography as Gan herself was both military wife and writer. *A Futile
Gift,* unfinished because of Gan's death in 1842, describes Aniuta, another
author-heroine: she is a poor, talented woman who wastes away in a
netherworld of insanity caused by the dissonance between her great
talent and the lack of a societally sanctioned outlet for it (the dilemma of
the superfluous man in a different key). Here, the gift is futile because it
has been bestowed on a poor, rural woman, and so, cannot be appreciated
in Russian society, given that society's make-up and prejudices.

Gan's works, like those of many Russian writers, often turn on
(mis)communication (*Ideal, Futile Gift, Society's Judgment*). And, while most
(all?) narrative engages communication in some way, the fictions of
Russian women, in both the thirties and the fifties, are often metanarra-
tives on the topic.[9] Communication has multiple valences in the works of

these authors: it functions as plot motivator, metaphor, thematics, social commentary, form, as index of morality, and as (potential) social critique.

Many female writers focus on orality as morality and make a distinction between society "talk" and honest conversation. Society talk is poisonous: aristocratic women, in works like Gan's *Ideal*, Rostopchina's *Chiny i den'gi* (Rank and Money), and later Tur's *A Mistake* and Nadezhda Khvoshchinskaia's *Anna Mikhailovna* destroy others by means of gossip as effectively as men kill one another in duels or on the field of battle. Honest conversation, however, can heal both individual and collective ills. These fictions frequently depict the damage that society talk can do; most also indicate the importance of a different kind of communication (one with Romantic resonances), often wordless, emotional, and deep – and usually between two women.[10] It is the capacity (or lack thereof) for certain kinds of talk that defines female morality in many works by women: female character is thus, on one level at least, defined in terms of communication.

Regarding the larger social dimension, private communication poses a threat to an autocratic state (hence censorship of letters), so this emphasis on honest conversation may also be seen as subtly subversive of larger structures – certainly in effect and perhaps in intent. If the open communication that many women authors advocate were to be achieved, it would change both high society and social structures: when communication is direct, the results are potentially explosive in a state that explicitly relies on controlling information.

Zhukova's *Vechera na Karpovke* (Evenings by the Karpovka, 1837–8) is a complicated experiment in narration that explores the transition from oral to written storytelling, and the effects of the telling on both audience and narrator. The six stories plus frame tale deploy different narrators (male and female), different styles, and different genres ranging from society tale to historical tale.[11]

In *Evenings*, at least once a week, one of the regular guests at the summer dacha of Natal'ia Dmitrievna Shemilova tells a story based in Russia and "on his or her own memories" (10); this emphasis on "true Russian tale" establishes a framework for a critique of Russian mores. *Evenings* models a kind of communication in which stories have concrete effects on protagonists' lives. Most notably, two of the characters (Liubin'ka and Vel'skii) become engaged partly as a result of the information that has been communicated and the barriers that have been broken down in the various narrations. Such an approach privileges narrative and suggests that one goal of storytelling is to change lives, which is, of course, an important element of social reform.

One of these stories, *Medal'on* (The Locket), details the life of an unattractive orphan, Mar'ia,[12] who is brought up in the home of Prince Z, together with his beautiful and pampered daughter, Sof'ia. Mar'ia falls in love with the doctor Vel'skii[13] who initially seems to be attracted to her as well; Sof'ia, not to be outdone, competes for Vel'skii's attentions. Having won his love, Sof'ia abruptly rejects him and agrees to an arranged and advantageous marriage to a count. Mar'ia, having watched all this, dies at an early age. On one level this story points to the problems of arranged marriage, and on another it points to larger social problems. The moral lesson of *The Locket* is repeated in many works by women:[14] Mar'ia, loyal, learned, and pure, with a deep inner world, dies, a victim of society; Sof'ia, shallow and calculating, "wins out" in society's terms. This comparison serves as a diagnosis of an ailment in Russian life: there is a serious problem in a society in which the Sof'ias succeed and the Mar'ias die.

Like *The Locket* and *Evenings* in general, many works by women (Gan, Tur, Panaeva, Nadezhda Khvoshchinskaia) are what I will call "diagnostic" texts. That is, stories like *The Locket* and Gan's *Society's Judgment* present problems in Russia – here, specifically the difficult position of Russian women – as a way of bringing them to the attention of the reading public. "Diagnosis" was a fairly common strategy at the time (Gogol's texts were considered diagnostic by Belinsky and other prominent critics; see also the satiric version of the diagnostic text in Lermontov's *Hero of Our Time*), yet works by women have not been considered part of this tradition.[15]

Concurrently with diagnostic texts, society tales, and works focusing on the problems of women (sometimes these three overlap in a single text), women were engaging in other kinds of writing as well. Nadezhda Durova, most famous for her account of her years in the army during the Napoleonic wars, published prose fiction roughly contemporaneously with Gan and Zhukova – and Durova's works do not fit into these three categories. Even when she focuses on themes similar to those of Gan and Zhukova (such as the problems of arranged marriage), her approach differs radically. *Igra sud'by ili protivozakonnaia liubov'* (Play of Fate or Transgressive Love, 1839), for example, begins with a theme common to many society tales, a mother who wants to see her daughter "settled" (the number of times the verb *pristroilas'* is repeated is distinctly unsettling). But the tale quickly swerves from the usual drawing room decorum of the society tale and becomes the story of the downward spiral into syphilis of the heroine, the formerly beautiful Elena. Married off at an early age to an officer who introduces Elena to alcohol, she soon progresses to taking lovers and to disease. (This is the earliest tale I am aware of in which a female protagonist is profoundly affected by alcohol.)

Most of Durova's works evidence a marked Gothic influence and indicate a fascination with the non-Russian. This includes the sympathetic focus on the Tatars in the historical and gender-bending tale *Nurmeka* (1839), the Lithuanian myths in *Gudishki* (1839), the Polish Gothic in *Pavil'on* (1839), and the Jewish-Moslem parents and brothers in *Klad* (Treasure Trove, 1840). Even more than national origin, gender is a remarkably fluid category in many of Durova's works, especially in *Nurmeka* and *Treasure Trove* (and in her formally autobiographical writings). Durova's fictions are not simply anomalous, though; rather, they provide early examples of later developments like the complex engendering of Nadezhda Khvoshchinskaia's works or the exotics of Lydiia Charskaia.[16]

The next major period in women's writing is that much-maligned decade, the 1850s, a period of tight censorship during which authors like the Khvoshchinskaia sisters, Panaeva, Pavlova, Sokhanskaia, and Vovchok published some of their finest prose. The works of the fifties expand many of the themes and styles of the thirties; they also develop new ones.

Many of these writings are elaborated society tales, such as Sof'ia Engel'gardt's *Skol'zkii put'* (A Slippery Slope, 1861), Karolina Pavlova's *Dvoinaia zhizn'* (A Double Life, 1848) and *Za chainym stolom* (At the Tea Table, 1859), and several of Evgeniia Tur's works. Women's fiction in this period, too, often critiques society by showing the negative effects of familial and other social structures on their female characters' lives, and encourages a strong identification of the reader with the heroine (Panaeva's *Semeistvo Tal'nikovykh* [The Tal'nikov Family, 1848], Nadezhda Khvoshchinskaia's *Anna Mikhailovna*, 1850, Marko Vovchok's *Sasha*, 1858).

But there are also some differences between the two periods: even more than in the thirties, writers of the fifties describe the inner lives of their female protagonists in absorbing detail; there is a move to a greater focus on psyche. And more fiction by women in the later period features male protagonists and/or acknowledged social issues (Nadezhda Khvoshchinskaia, *Pervaia bor'ba* [First Struggle, 1869]; Sof'ia Khvoshchinskaia, *Mudrennyi chelovek* [An Enigmatic Man, 1861]; Vovchok's peasant tales). Also, an open-ended style which poses questions and leaves them unresolved, becomes more common (e.g. Pavlova, *At the Tea Table*, Sokhanskaia's *Posle obeda v gostiakh* [A Conversation after Dinner, 1858], Tur's *Oshibka* [A Mistake, 1849], and many works by Nadezhda Khvoshchinskaia including *Kto zhe ostalsia dovolen?* [Who Ended Up Satisfied?, 1853], *Schastlivye liudi* [Lucky People, 1876],[17] and *First Struggle*.

Tur's debut novella, *A Mistake*, is a good example of the elaborated society tale. The plot is simple: Slavin, an aristocrat par excellence and Ol'ga, who is of the lower aristocracy, love one another, but Slavin is wooed away by the Princess Gorskina. Ol'ga rarely ventures into society, but she makes the mistake (?) of attending a ball at which the Princess Gorskina, by cleverly juxtaposing Ol'ga to herself, shows Slavin that Ol'ga will never belong to high society. From that point on, Slavin slowly moves away from Ol'ga, and, at the end of the novella, Slavin and Gorskina have just married while Ol'ga is alone. In an extension of the ways that Gan and Zhukova position talented women in their fictions, Ol'ga is morally superior to the other characters in *A Mistake*: like many of the heroines of the two earlier authors, the sign of Ol'ga's superiority is the fact that she cannot fit into high society.

A Mistake extends the work of earlier women writers in other ways as well, as it questions both the institution of marriage, and the norms of evaluation in high society. Because Slavin loves another, Ol'ga rejects marriage to a man she loves, and in which she would be financially secure. But Ol'ga does not go mad or die, as was common in the earlier works; rather, she chooses a life of integrity outside of marriage. This choice and the ways it is validated in the novella again suggest that women may be better off alone or in their families of origin rather than in a loveless union.[18] In addition, *A Mistake* emphasizes the importance of relationships between women, for Ol'ga is able to choose independence partly because of the support of her sister Sof'ia and (eventually) her mother.

Nadezhda Sokhanskaia, in *A Conversation after Dinner*, also focuses on female friendship; the tale depicts the instant sympathy that can spring up between women even in a chance encounter. In *A Conversation*, Sokhanskaia's first major work, an irresolvable question is being discussed at the local Marshal's house: who is to blame if a married couple separates, the wife or the husband? A private conversation based on this theme arises between the female narrator and Liubov' Arkhipovna, a woman of the lower gentry. Liubov' (Love) maintains that it is always the wife's fault if there is discord in a marriage. To support her position she tells how she learned to appreciate the man she had been forced to

marry despite the fact that she loved another, Sasha Cherny. Liubov'
claims that arranged marriage is necessary and women's submission to it
vital, but Sokhanskaia raises questions about these claims as Liubov' describes her own early misery in the marriage, and even more dramatically,
Cherny's fate: he died shortly after Liubov''s marriage.

A *Conversation*, then, returns to the theme of arranged marriage, and
presents arguments both for and against it.[19] But the interpretation is
left ambiguous: should one applaud Liubov' Arkhipovna's reconciliation
to her marriage, as, through it, she has managed to eke out a measure of
happiness, or does this resignation merely perpetuate the system of
arranged marriage? Portraying a problem and leaving the conclusion to
the reader, as noted above, is fairly common in women's writings of the
period. This device emphasizes communication between (implied) author
and reader; it also encourages readers to tangle with a moral/social problem even after they have finished the work.

A *Conversation* also models another way in which women's writings
commonly represent the social world, as issues of class are addressed
throughout the novella. Sokhanskaia's central narrator is an outsider to
high society, a woman of the impoverished gentry. The fact that the narrator ranks lower in the social scale is not incidental; many works of the
fifties (and some earlier writings) focus on women of lower estates, giving crucial narrative authority to these characters. Sof'ia Engel'gardt
(Olga N) in *Semeistvo Tureninykh* (The Turenin Family, 1863), places a
female servant in the key narrative role; Tur in *Antonina* and *Zakoldovannyi
krug* (A Vicious Circle, 1854) gives the central narration not to servants or
peasants but to that ambiguously classed creature, the governess; in several of Marko Vovchok's peasant stories (published before the emancipation of the serfs in 1861), the primary narrator is a peasant woman who
describes both her own life and that of the gentry in harrowing terms
(*Sasha*, 1858; *The Plaything*, 1859; *The Schoolgirl*, 1860). The difference in
social estate is sometimes handled in other ways: in Panaeva's *Women's
Lot*, women are joined by a common unhappiness that transcends (some)
class differences.

This focus on interaction between women of different estates is
another variation on the theme of communication as social commentary,
as it emphasizes the central importance of non-nobles in social discourse.
It is also a subversion of literary convention, for female authors often
depict friendship between women as a strong and powerful bond in a way
that is rare in male-authored works. While women's texts do often depict

rivalries between female characters (e.g. Zhukova's *The Locket*, Pavlova's *A Double Life*), many also present a different kind of relationship – often between sisters: a friendship based on shared integrity, mutual understanding, honesty, and intelligence. Female authors frequently present both kinds of relationships in a single text.[20] This depiction of female friendship differs from better-known portrayals of relationships between female protagonists (cf. Ol'ga and Tat'iana in Pushkin's *Evgenii Onegin* or Zinaida and Vladimir's mother in Turgenev's *First Love*).

Many of the themes and styles discussed above are repeated, refined, or overturned in Panaeva's *Women's Lot*, a tripartite work that was published in 1862 in the foremost radical journal of the day *Sovremennik* (The Contemporary). *Women's Lot* fulfills many of the worst prophecies and prejudices about women's writing; it is the kind of text people have in mind when they dismiss women's writing as "wordy" or "maudlin." It is precisely for that reason that I discuss it here: both because Panaeva's novel represents one common strain of Russian women's writing, and because, while this has usually been labeled "bad" writing, it is also, as I argue later, an important work both historically and aesthetically. Further, my reading of *Women's Lot* hints at the ways that "good" and "bad" writing are historicized categories, categories that were being created and reiterated at the time the novel was written.

Women's Lot is a didactic text whose aim is to re-form society: "I am writing this for youths [young men] to teach them what to do," notes Panaeva's narrator (52). The work is at once a call for improvement in women's lives and a challenge to the terms in which the "woman question" had been posed in public discussion. Male radicals like Mikhailov and Pisarev focused mainly on educational, economic, and familial reform as ways to improve women's lives.[21] *Women's Lot* advocates change in all these areas, but argues that legislated familial reform will be dangerous for women unless there is a concomitant change in male morality.

In an address to "honorable" (*chestnye*) women, the (male) narrator states: "And don't expect anything *for now* from the emancipation of women" (50, my emphasis). The reasons given for this are that the emancipation of women will lead only to men advocating free love and thus loving and leaving women freely; the burden of the children will then fall on women, and society will be merciless in its judgment of them (50–2). Thus, unless men's morals change, legislation can bring no advantage to women, for: "Living with an honorable man, a woman needs no legal rights; she is under his protection; but if she is in the hands of an egotist, she is his victim" (52). The rest of the novel bears this out, by showing the fates of women who are dependent on dishonorable men, men who use women as they choose, yet hold in contempt those women who have no societally sanctioned claim (marriage) on them.[22]

Although Panaeva unquestioningly assumes women's dependence on men, she also suggests an aspect of the woman question that has usually been ignored both by her contemporaries and later scholars: what are the practical consequences of legal emancipation for women in a country not known for its adherence to the rule of law, and what would happen to women if men turned out to be less honorable than the radical critics assumed? Further, Panaeva's emphasis on the importance of moral rather than legislative reform is a common theme in Russian women's writing and in Russian varieties of feminism.

Women's Lot traces the story of Sof'ia, who enters the novel reading, an occupation that in many works by women signals moral superiority and an inability to negotiate high society.[23] Sof'ia is caught between the worlds of her mother and father. She spent her childhood in the idyllic setting of the country estate and almost exclusively in the pure, moral world of her mother, Anna Antonovna while her father, Grigorii Andreevich, lives mainly in Petersburg with a woman of ill repute (*loretka*). When Sof'ia comes of age, at her father's instigation (but with her own eager acceptance), she marries a wastrel, Petr Vasil'evich. Although it is clear from the outset that this will be a disastrous relationship, the legal and customary power of the father in Russia means that the mother is powerless to stop the marriage; and, in fact, she dies soon after the wedding.

Sof'ia moves to the estate of Petr Vasil'evich's selfish, depraved grandfather, where she discovers life in all its un-idealized ugliness. In a scene set up by the grandfather, Sof'ia meets Lizaveta, a former mistress of Petr Vasil'evich who has had a child by him. The same day, Sof'ia discovers that Olimpiada Fedorovna (the grandfather's daughter) has also been seduced by Petr and that Petr is off with a third mistress, Katia (who soon moves in). The grandfather, expecting a fight, then orchestrates a meeting of the four women (Sof'ia, Olimpiada Fedorovna, Lizaveta and Mar'ia Vasil'evna, one of the women living in the grandfather's household). But instead, through conversation ("true talk"), they are united by a common unhappiness created by the betrayal of men. In this scene, Panaeva counters patriarchal expectations by presenting a community based on the ability to communicate, and on a conscious sense of oppression.

The final two sections of the novel are much shorter than the first, and they serve to reinforce the importance of friendship among women. In addition, one positive relationship between a man (Snegov) and a woman (Anna Vasil'evna) is introduced.

Women's Lot provides a social critique on many levels. Panaeva's work calls for the "woman question" to be articulated in new terms, terms that will take into account morality, emotions, and the inner worlds of both men and women. And, like the texts discussed above, it is diagnostic, showing the evils of Russian society – specifically, the difficulties of women's position – without suggesting a realizable resolution of them. The novel posits a solution: that men become more moral – but given the depiction of men in the novel, this cannot be considered likely to happen any time in the next millennium or so. *Women's Lot* also suggests the need for another kind of change: propriety (*prilichie*) is a large part of what keeps women in a downtrodden position, and this set of rules also must be changed in order to improve women's position.

Panaeva's novel is an example of the kind of didactic work that many women (Elena Gan) and men (Nikolai Chernyshevsky) produced in Russia in the second third of the nineteenth century. *Women's Lot* raises and reworks issues and motifs seen in other women's writings, namely, the difficulty of women's lives in Russian society; the poisonous nature of society talk; the importance of education for women; the problem of attaining the right balance between books and real life; the importance of communication among women; self-sacrifice as a proof of femininity; the central position of the daughter; the orphan; the contrast between two women; and a focus on the interior life of the female characters. In concentrating on women's personal worlds, Panaeva implicitly proposes changes for all of society – a diagnostic text par excellence. And, in terms of aesthetics, Panaeva's exaggerated pathetics have become the definition of bad writing; her novel is, therefore, an important indicator of how the categories of "good" and "bad" writing have been constructed in Russia. Critics have defined the novel as quintessentially "bad": this judgment misses both Panaeva's radical critique of the terms in which the "woman question" had been posed, and her refinement of the motifs of earlier women's fiction such as the centrality of communication and the various levels of "talk" that Panaeva proposes in *Women's Lot*.

Panaeva clearly hit a nerve with her critique of current articulations of the woman question: *Women's Lot* called forth some strong reactions in the Russian press. The radical critic Dmitrii Pisarev, for example, argued that the work was retrograde and that, in *Women's Lot*, Panaeva was working against the emancipation of women.[24] Although this debate is too complicated to engage here in any detail, I do want to note that many liberals and radicals critiqued women's writing in similar terms. This phenomenon reflects a contradictory ethos: on the one hand, liberals and radicals argued for women's rights and on the other, resisted, ignored, or did not see women's opinions on the matter. As in the case of Panaeva and Pisarev, at the middle of the century, women and men often had different ideas about what it meant to liberate women: women's perspectives are only now beginning to be recovered.

Khvoshchinskaia's *First Struggle* represents a very different kind of writing from Panaeva's work. *First Struggle* is told in the first-person, by a male narrator, and it directly addresses the issue of generational change – a topic that is often considered central in the political, literary, and social life of Russia. *First Struggle* reverses the relationships between the generations depicted in Turgenev's novel, *Fathers and Children*, a work that became the locus of a major debate about Russian society.[25] In *Fathers and Children*, Bazarov, a member of the younger generation, embodies radicalism, and so (despite the ambiguity of the ending) one could, and many did, posit a schema of political progression. In Khvoshchinskaia's novella, it is the son who wants to retain the aristocratic values of a former time, while the father emblematizes a deeper, more generous world view. Khvoshchinskaia, then, presents the political dynamics depicted in *Fathers and Children* as cyclical or regressive rather than progressive.

In Khvoshchinskaia's novella, the narrator, by telling his own story, condemns himself in the eyes of the reader. "Serge," as he calls himself, whose mother died when he was five, has been brought up by an aunt in Moscow, from whom he has learned urban high society aristocratism. After eight years, his father (provincial gentry) takes Serge back to the provincial town of N (where many of Khvoshchinskaia's tales are set), and the rest of the story details Serge's attempts to negotiate his father's ideals and provincial life.

Serge opens his account by explaining that he, unlike most people, has not compromised his values: "I have not become petty," he says (*Ia ne izmel'chal*). It soon becomes clear that what he has resisted are the ideals of the sixties (values with which most of his readers would sympathize), instead retaining what he understands as aristocratic values.

The power of the narrative comes from the discrepancy between Serge's self-depiction and the reader's evolving perception of him. In

Serge's terms, this is the story of his "struggle" to survive in a world where very few people are equipped to understand and appreciate him. Yet Serge is totally focused on himself and as long as his actions serve the goal of his aristocratism, any means are justified. He treats the other characters in a utilitarian and often cruel way, including those who are most generous to him, his father and Mar'ia Vasil'evna, a quasi-romantic interest. Because Serge is unconscious of his own egotism and arrogance, there is no possibility of moral redemption: he thinks he is in the right. This bland unconsciousness of his own morally repugnant self creates a horrifying and fascinating character.

First Struggle is a study in competing frameworks and a complicated collusion not only between the characters of father and son, but also between the implied author and reader. Serge's framework is narrow, and the text turns on the assumption that the reader will react against Serge's cold treatment of his father and the son's inability to understand his father's values.

But this story can also have the effect of undercutting these values, for the power of the narrative relies on the fact that Serge is so utterly wrong about morality while so completely believing that he is right. By extrapolation, Serge's position can lead the reader to question his or her own perspective, for it demonstrates that a strong belief in one's own goodness – and even having others who share that view – is no proof against behavior/essence that most readers would regard as morally reprehensible. Khvoshchinskaia's novella thus removes the comfort of the possibility of an absolute moral ground. It, like many of her works, leaves the reader with more questions than answers.

Critics largely ignored *First Struggle* when it was first published in 1869. There were a few notable exceptions, including a review entitled "Women's Soullessness" by the prominent radical Nikolai Shelgunov, who argued that the Russian reading public was not yet sophisticated enough for this novella. Therefore, he claimed, *First Struggle* was a socially retrograde and immoral work. (Shelgunov later apologized to Khvoshchinskaia for this review.)[26] After *First Struggle* was issued as a separate edition in 1879 and 1880, noted critics like Nikolai Mikhailovskii described Khvoshchinskaia's novella as being both socially progressive and artistically sophisticated.[27] This reversal of the earlier judgment indicates the dawn of a new era in the understanding of Russian women's writing, one in which fiction by women could be seen as part of the work of social progress.

Panaeva's and Khvoshchinskaia's works describe two different strains of women's writing in Russia. Some may question my choice of *Women's Lot* as a representative text: it is not as incisively ironic as the works of the Khvoshchinskaia sisters, nor as tightly plotted as Panaeva's own *The Tal'nikov Family*. As stated above, I have, perhaps perversely, chosen it precisely because it exhibits the qualities that many consider typical of women's writing: it is didactic, overwritten, and appeals to the emotional; it focuses on female character, and it plays on the sympathy of the reader for the heroine; it tries to create an identification of reader and heroine. But *Women's Lot* had the power to move audiences of its own time and has the potential to do so today; the novel also raises new questions and illuminates old debates – like those around the woman question – from new angles. *First Struggle* works very differently. Rather than insisting on an identification of reader and character, it demands the reader's distance from the main protagonist (who is male); it is narrated in an ironic, less emotional style; it is open-ended, rather than overtly didactic, and it engages many of the moral and social questions common in discussions of nineteenth-century Russian literature. These works suggest the range of styles and themes in women's writing of the middle of the nineteenth century. When compared with the writings of the 1830s, these writings also demonstrate a number of continuities, such as a focus on class difference, and, particularly in *A Conversation*, *A Mistake*, and *Women's Lot*, a concentration on women's interior worlds, and on diagnosis of the difficulties of women's position in Russian society. Such continuities suggest that the later authors built on the themes of their predecessors.

The ethos of the 1830s and 1850s cannot be as neatly divided as the 1840s and 1860s have traditionally been (though the latter, too, are less distinct than is usually thought). Literature forms in a continuum, and examining the works of women writers indicates the artificiality – and the uses – of periodization: dividing the century up into the forties and sixties allows for certain facts to emerge and specific narratives to be told. Alternative periodizations highlight a different set of narratives, such as the ones described in this essay, and in this volume in general. This more fluid imagining allows for greater possibilities and a different kind of accuracy of historical understanding than does either a narrative of progress or insistence on sharp distinctions between periods. And, as these writings by women are (re?)integrated into the Russian literary tradition, a new and more dynamic picture of what constitutes Russian writing will emerge.

NOTES

I am grateful to several people who gave superb readings of a draft of this essay: Adele Barker, Catriona Kelly, Laura Schlosberg, and Mary Zirin.

1. The "superfluous man" is a character common in Russia throughout the first two thirds of the nineteenth century (and arguably beyond). Superfluous men are figures whose great potential is wasted because they cannot find outlets for their talents. These characters were interpreted as commentary against the autocratic government and the mores of high society. The New Man is the man of the sixties, capable of revolutionary action.

2. The thirties and fifties (like the forties and sixties) do not necessarily represent the decades in which works were published, but rather the ethos that shaped these writers and their fictions. So, although Panaeva's *Zhenskaia dolia* (Women's Lot, 1862) and Khvoshchinskaia's *Pervaia bor'ba* (First Struggle, 1869) were published in the 1860s, I consider them here under the rubric of the 1850s.

3. The relationship between literature and social reality is mediated in complex ways; my aim here is to show how women's works may be recuperated even into traditional understandings of Russian literature, which assume a very close connection between literature and the work of social progress.

4. See Gan, *Ideal, Sud sveta* (Society's Judgment); Zhukova, *Vechera na Karpovke* (Evenings by the Karpovka); Rostopchina, *Chiny i den'gi* (Rank and Money); Pavlova, *Dvoinaia zhizn'* (A Double Life), *Za chainym stolom* (At the Tea Table); Tur, *Oshibka* (A Mistake), *Plemiannitsa* (The Niece); Sokhanskaia, *Posle obeda v gostiakh* (A Conversation after Dinner); Nadezhda Khvoshchinskaia, *Anna Mikhailovna*, and Sof'ia Khvoshchinskaia, *Mudrennyi chelovek* (An Enigmatic Man).

5. Society tales are tales of manners and thwarted love, usually between people of (slightly) different social origin. These stories often represent the heroine's interior world in greater detail than was common previously, and juxtapose this honorable inner life to the falseness of relations in the "beau monde."

6. V. G. Belinsky, "O kritike i literaturnykh mneniiakh 'Moskovskogo nabliudatelia,' " *SS* (Moscow, 1976), 267, 302; Elizabeth Shepard, "The Society Tale and the Innovative Argument in Russian Prose Fiction of the 1830s," *RL* 10 (1981), 112.

7. Gan, *Sud sveta* in V. Uchenova (ed.), *Dacha na Petergofskoi doroge* (Moscow, 1986), 150–3.

8. Catriona Kelly makes a similar point: Kelly *History*, 112.

9. See Tur, *Antonina* and *Zakoldovannyi krug* (A Vicious Circle); N. D. Khvoshchinskaia, *Vera*; Sokhanskaia, *A Conversation after Dinner*.

10. See, for example, Gan, *Ideal*, Durova, *Ugol* (The Nook), Zhukova, *Baron Reikhman*, Rostopchina, *Schastlivaia zhenshchina* (A Fortunate Woman), and Tur, *A Mistake*.

11. All references are to Zhukova, *Vechera na Karpovke* (Moscow, 1986).

12. Many heroines in Russian fiction of this period are orphans (having lost one or both parents). In women's works, the orphan plot is often used to set up a contrastive pair of female heroines of about the same age (the orphaned and the familied) as in Gan's *Ideal*, Tur's *The Niece*, or Zhadovskaia's *V storone ot bol'shogo sveta* (Apart from the Great World, 1857).

13. This is a different Vel'skii from the character in the frame tale, a play on names that again serves to blur the boundaries between various kinds of narration and between "story" and "life."

14. See Tur, *Oshibka* (A Mistake), *Plemiannitsa* (The Niece), *Dve sestry* (Two Sisters); Panaeva, *Women's Lot*; Vovchok, *Institutka* (The Schoolgirl), *Sasha*.

15. Nikolai Gogol (1809–1852) was known for his serio-comic tales, and in particular for "humanizing" the petty clerk; Mikhail Lermontov (1814–1841), a poet and prose writer whose *Hero* sets out (ironically) to diagnose, but not to cure, Russia's ills.

16. On these aspects of Khvoshchinskaia's and Charskaia's work, see (on Khvoshchinskaia) my "Do Pseudonyms 'Have' Biographies?: The Case of V. Krestovskii," paper presented at *Double Lives*, Berkeley, CA, February 1996; on Charskaia, Susan Larsen, "Girl Talk: Lidiia Charskaia and Her Readers," in Laura Engelstein and Stephanie Sandler (eds.), *Self and Story in Russian History* (Ithaca, 2000), 141–67.

17. These dates are from the Kaspari edition and refer to the date of composition.

18. Many works by women advance this position: see S. D. Khvoshchinskaia, *Gorodskie i derevenskie* (City Folks and Country Folks, 1863), Marko Vovchok, *Tri doli* (Three Fates, 1861).

19. For a counterview, see Joe Andrew's reading of *A Conversation*, in which he argues that the arranged marriage is not the narrative center of the story. Andrew, "The Matriarchal World in Nadezhda Sokhanskaia's *A Conversation After Dinner*," in Jan Ivar Bjørnflaten, Geir Kjetsaa and Terje Mathiassen (eds.), *A Centenary of Slavic Studies in Norway. The Olaf Broch Symposium* (Oslo, 1998), 3–22.

20. For texts that depict primarily positive relationships between female characters, see Gan, *Ideal*; N. D. Khvoshchinskaia, *Bratets* (Brother Dearest), *Pansionerka* (The Schoolgirl); Tur, *Two Sisters*. Works that depict both supportive and competitive relationships between female characters include Panaeva, *Women's Lot*; Tur, *A Mistake*; Vovchok, *Sasha*. Quotes here are taken from *Zhenskaia dolia* (Women's Lot) (*Sovremennik*, March–May, 1862).

21. M. L. Mikhailov (1829–1865) was a poet, prose writer, and radical, who was instrumental in public formulations of "the woman question" in Russia; D. I. Pisarev (1840–1868) was a leading nihilist, journalist, and critic. See Costlow, "Love, Work and the Woman Question in Mid Nineteenth-Century Women's Writing," in Clyman and Greene, 61–75; and Rosenholm, *Gender Awakening: Femininity and The Russian Woman Question of the 1860s* (Helsinki, 1999); and "The 'Woman Question' of the 1860s and the Ambiguity of the 'Learned Woman'," in Marsh *Gender*, 112–28 for cogent discussions of women's public explorations of the woman question.

22. This emphasis may be partly based on Panaeva's biography: she was unhappily married to the author Ivan Panaev and in a long-term liaison with the poet Nekrasov; both relationships were differently torturous. See Marina Ledkovsky, "Avdot' ya Panaeva: Her Salon and Her Life," *RLT* 9 (1975), 423–32.

23. See, for example, Gan, *Ideal*, Tur, *A Mistake*, Zhadovskaia, Zhukova. Joe Andrew makes a similar point regarding Gan's *Ideal* in *Narrative and Desire in Russian Literature 1822–49: The Feminine and the Masculine* (New York, 1993), 87–8.

24. D. I. Pisarev, "Kukol'naia tragediia s buketom grazhdanskoi skorbi," *RSlovo* (1864); repr. *Sochineniia v shesti tomakh*, vol. IV (St. Petersburg, 1901), 147–96. Nadezhda Khvoshchinskaia also reviewed *Zhenskaia dolia*; she agrees with Panaeva's interpretation of women's emancipation. See V. Porechnikov, "Provintsial'nye pis'ma o nashei literature," *OZ* (May 1862), 39.

25. M. S. Goriachkina also notes the relationship of *First Struggle* to Turgenev's *Fathers and Children* in her afterword to N. D. Khvoshchinskaia, *Povesti i rasskazy* (Moscow, 1984), 374, 375. Khvoshchinskaia's title is, perhaps, a reference to Turgenev's well-known tale *Pervaia liubov'* (First Love).

26. See Shelgunov, "Zhenskoe bezdushie," *Delo* (September 1870), 1–34. His 1874 apology was published in *RMysl'* (February 1892).

27. *Sochineniia N. K. Mikhailovskogo*, vol. VI (St. Petersburg, 1897), 653–5.

5

"A particle of our soul": prerevolutionary autobiography by Russian women writers

"... the great truth [is] that we love our past no matter what it gave us; ... that the places where we left a particle of our soul, a fragment of our life, are sacred."

—ANASTASIIA VERBITSKAIA

Autobiography plays a pivotal role in the dialog between past and present that we call history: our foremothers' first-person accounts are often the only records we have of past women's lives.[1] Autobiographies and memoirs by Russian women developed in rhythmic interconnection with fiction.[2] Women began publishing imaginative narrative prose in the first decade of the nineteenth century, and fiction has remained an important genre for them since the 1830s. The first recorded autobiographies by Russian women date from the last third of the eighteenth century, but early works even by public figures (those of Catherine II and Ekaterina Dashkova) circulated in manuscript and were published only decades after their authors' death.[3]

Quantity is as remarkable as quality in the autobiographical legacy left us by prerevolutionary Russian women: at least 200 substantive works of retrospective life-writing, including memoirs of "great men," "family chronicles," and travel accounts, have appeared in print to the present day.[4] In the literary-historical context, two points in time are important: when the work was written, and when it was published. The former tells us something about the contemporary culture, the models of writing about the self the author was subscribing to or contesting, and the audience she saw herself as addressing. At the latter point the work was dropped into the cultural stream, to sink into obscurity or to float as a text that could influence the development of the genre.

As to date of publication, fewer than twenty retrospective autobiographical works by Russian women were published before 1860, and some twenty more came out in the 1860s. From the 1870s there was a steady accretion in the appearance of autobiographies and memoirs, a phenomenon connected with the rise of journals devoted to history and a corresponding increase in autobiographical accounts in socio-literary journals.[5] Throughout most of the Soviet period, autobiography, like all other writing, was repressed or exploited in accordance with the prevailing sociopolitical environment. The rich legacy of prerevolutionary female self-expression was mostly ignored except for memoirs describing the lives of prominent men. Among the autobiographies that did appear in censored print, those by women from radical movements were given preeminence. In emigration, Russian women from a wide spectrum of political and social thought wrote accounts of the lost Eden of their prerevolutionary youth. It is impossible to estimate the number of unpublished autobiographies/memoirs from all periods that still languish in state and private archives in Russia and abroad.

When we consider the period in which they were written, Russian women's prerevolutionary life-writings fall roughly into three periods. During the first, through the early nineteenth century, the few women who wrote retrospectively about their lives drew on Western European models. In these works the narrator was usually the chief actor (i.e., these were autobiographies proper). By the middle of the century, women seem to have reconfigured the genre along lines influenced by Russo-Victorian norms of feminine modesty, writing self-censored works in which the narrator tends to be an observer or chronicler of others' lives (memoirs).[6] Only gradually, with the rise of modernist movements that emphasized individual psychology, did women reacquire the impetus to center themselves within their autobiographical narratives.

From the legacy of Russian women's prerevolutionary autobiography in print, I have chosen eight that represent a variety of styles and approaches: idiosyncratic personal accounts by Nadezhda Durova and Nadezhda Sokhanskaia written in the first half of the nineteenth century; works by Avdot'ia Panaeva, Mariia Kamenskaia, and Ekaterina Iunge, dating from the latter decades of the nineteenth century and published at the turn of the twentieth; and autobiographies by Anastasiia Verbitskaia, Valentina Dmitrieva and Anastasiia Tsvetaeva written and published in the twentieth century. All but Iunge wrote fiction as well as autobiography and were skillful in structuring narrative. All their texts represent individual resolutions to the conflict between the impulse to disclose the "truth" of their lives and social imperatives that discouraged such disclosure; as we study them today, it seems clear that, in Leigh Gilmore's terms, "Whether and when . . . any particular text appears to tell the truth, ha[s] less to do with that text's presumed accuracy . . . than with its apprehended fit into culturally prevalent discourses of truth and identity."[7]

From 1836 to 1841, Nadezhda Durova published a corpus of interlinked autobiographical and fictional works that reflect the life she led within a doubly fabricated persona.[8] The upheavals of the Napoleonic wars gave Durova unprecedented opportunity to fulfill her quixotic drive for masculine freedoms when, disguised as a man, she served as an officer in the Russian light cavalry from 1807 to 1816. In her remarkable *Kavalerist-devitsa* (The Cavalry Maiden, 1836), and the fragmentary autobiographical works that followed it, Durova is most creative in writing about her life, playing fast and loose with aspects she chooses to omit or distort, either for fear of alienating a potential audience or through self-censorship. She frames her self-portrait in the mythic tradition of virgin warrior, but both "virgin" and "warrior" are artificial constructs: Durova was a capable soldier, but her motivation for running away to the army was more a need to escape from intolerable domestic constraints than a burning desire to fight for her country. She was no virgin: she left behind a broken marriage and a son whom she never mentioned.

Durova was as unique in the Russian autobiographical tradition as in her military career. At the time she published *Cavalry Maiden* one autobiography by a Russian woman, Natal'ia Dolgorukaia, had appeared in print (in 1810) and that, as indicated by the title of S. N. Glinka's laudatory article, "A Model of Love and Conjugal Fidelity" (Obrazets liubvi i supruzheskoi vernosti), was greeted as an exemplary portrait of self-sacrificing Russian womanhood rather than as an account of the trials of a very human girl thrust into demanding circumstances. The depiction of childhood as a formative period did not become a commonplace of Russian autobiography until after Tolstoy's *Detstvo. Otrochestvo. Iunost'* (Childhood. Boyhood. Youth) and S. T. Aksakov's *Detskie gody Bagrova vnuka* (The Childhood Years of Bagrov's Grandson) appeared in the 1850s.[9] Durova was their unacknowledged precursor, prefacing *Cavalry Maiden* with an account of her upbringing and the conflicts in childhood that led to her adult decision to flee the fate of her sex.

While the clash of female voice and male plot made *Cavalry Maiden* a unique document, Durova also drew on an established tradition of travel literature and its offshoot, the military memoir. The work was assembled from (or framed as) journals Durova kept at sporadic intervals during her cavalry years. It is the selection she made from raw notes, tracing intended and unintentional ironies of her complex personality, that gives it auto-biographical depth: she moves from hotheaded recruit to an officer blasé in battle but always eager for "adventures" prohibited her female con-temporaries, wandering alone at night and interacting with a wide vari-ety of people met by chance; and from proud officer riding a beloved warhorse to bereft woman bewailing the death of a pet dog.

Cavalry Maiden has had a checkered history in Russian literature and history. In the 160 years since its publication, Durova's story has been treated as something between curiosity and legend, and she as an Amazon only slightly less mythic than the female steppe warriors of prehistory. In times of crisis, however, when heroism was demanded of all Russia's citizens, her story has been resurrected and used as a model for heroism by Russian women, with appropriate embroidery – usually involving a lover. The fresh audience the work has recently found in Russia and abroad indicates that, within the double deception, Durova conveyed some basic "truth" of her restless, sexually ambiguous character.

By 1847 Nadezhda Sokhanskaia, living on her mother's small, struggling farm on the Ukrainian steppes, had begun sending stories by mail to journals in the capitals, but she received little encouragement from their editors. Among the problems she faced in establishing herself as a writer was lack of access to current publications: the letter and manuscript she sent to Petr Pletnev in St. Petersburg reached him only after he had relinquished the editorship of *Sovremennik* (The Contemporary). Pletnev saw flashes of talent in Sokhanskaia's descriptions of Ukraine, but overall her tales were mannered imitations of Sandian romanticism. As a writing exercise, Pletnev asked her to describe her own life – and she took up the challenge, at first timidly and then with increasing verve.[10] While Durova led a wandering life divorced from the feminine sphere, Sokhanskaia's adventures were internal, a cruel process of psychological adaptation to a circumscribed milieu. Durova published *Cavalry Maiden* in 1836, indicating to her editor, Aleksandr Pushkin, that she had women in mind as the audience that could best understand her; Sokhanskaia's "Autobiography" appeared posthumously only in 1896 and was patterned for a single male reader. Durova blurred the boundaries between fiction and fact to protect personal secrets, to give her female audience an image they could accept, and to create a more gripping story. Sokhanskaia seems determined to tell Pletnev the "truth," but she glides over aspects of her emotional development to stress intellectual struggles she hopes he will sympathize with. The text, produced when she was still in her mid-twenties, has a rare immediacy that matches Durova's "journals." No account of the development of Russian autobiography can afford to omit either.[11]

There is a duality in Sokhanskaia's attitude to Pletnev. In the flowery style of the times, she expresses gratitude to the great man who has deigned to correspond with her, but there is an underlying note of defiance throughout: how could Pletnev, rector of St. Petersburg University, tutor to the royal family, and professor at the Patriotic Institute for Girls, imagine all the petty insults and major deprivations she had suffered as a poor girl studying on government stipend in a sequestered boarding school (an "institute") in Khar'kov?[12] The shock of coming home not to her beloved childhood manor surrounded by trees and flowers but to a dirt-floored cottage in the Ukraine? What it was like to live in a society that expected her to marry, but in surroundings that saw eligible men only occasionally – and a man willing to marry a dowryless girl almost never? To be unable to find a suitable post as governess, the only work for which she was in principle trained? To lead an existence where journals and books were rare, and paper and ink a luxury?[13]

From her scattered readings in Russian journals, Sokhanskaia assumes that the conservative Petersburg society which Pletnev represents does not approve of women writers. She writes her life story as one of a vocation that develops virtually against her will: she invents tales for a rapt audience of girls over a clandestine candle in the institute dormitory; her despair at her arid surroundings is cured by slow awakening to the beauties of the steppe and the richness of its lore; and she experiences a religious epiphany that frees her to follow her need to write – even if she will end up "sit[ting] on the doorstep of the poorhouse and . . . tell[ing] tales of wonders to passersby . . ." Eight years later Sokhanskaia began publishing mature works of fiction to the greatest acclaim that any Russian woman writer had yet been accorded.

From the 1870s, autobiographical works by women began appearing in substantial numbers, most of them accounts focused outside the self, on their genealogical line ("family chronicle") or on people of note they had known. As the title under which Avdot'ia Panaeva's reminiscences appeared as a book, *Russkie pisateli i artisty, 1824–1870* (Russian Writers and Actors, 1824–1870) indicates, she saw her readers primarily as those interested in the history of St. Petersburg Imperial Theaters in which she grew up and the intellectual circles around *The Contemporary* in which she moved from the late 1840s.[14] In her memoir Panaeva adopts the curious stance of observer rather than participant. She says almost nothing about the multifarious roles she played in the journal: under the signatures "N. Stanitskii" or "N.S." she wrote two long novels with Nekrasov and published at least twenty shorter works of fiction, read manuscripts and proofs, and for some years ran a fashion column with Panaev. She depicts herself mainly as a housekeeper, passing through *The Contemporary* editorial offices on her rounds of domestic duties and serving endless meals to famished contributors.

Her ambiguous status might have inhibited self-disclosure: married to Ivan Panaev from 1837, she became the lover of Nikolai Nekrasov in 1847 or 1848, just as the three of them took over *The Contemporary*. In the memoir, however, she neither hides the fact that they all lived together until Panaev's death in 1862 nor exploits it, but simply treats her daily interactions with both men as a fact of life. Even by the late 1880s, earlier autobiography offered Panaeva no prototype for a narrative that would have recorded Panaev's frivolous abandonment of her and her often ugly affair with Nekrasov, although irresponsible men's abusive relationships with women did become a basic theme of her fiction.[15] *The Contemporary* was revered as a beacon of liberalism, and a frank presentation of its owners' private lives would undoubtedly have shocked many of her readers. Instead, she devoted her pages to fond observations of contributors like the radical critics Vissarion Belinsky, Nikolai Dobroliubov, and Nikolai Chernyshevsky. These men played a major role in shaping the ideals of the 1860s, when all the sacred verities of society came under question and young women found themselves at a crossroad between the life their mothers had known and the need (financially and spiritually) for independence, between self-fulfillment and service to the community. Iunge, Verbitskaia, Dmitrieva, and Anastasiia Tsvetaeva all mention the impact Nekrasov's poems had on them in their youth.

Panaeva's impersonal approach suggests that the ideals the circle espoused were more important than their failure to live up to them. Growing up in the theater, a *déclassé* milieu, Panaeva was profoundly democratic in spirit. Her marriage to a man who was noble by birth if not

by conviction brought her into her first contact with the cruelties of serf-
dom, and one boast she does make is that she encouraged Panaev to use
his share of an inherited estate to buy the journal. Her reminiscences
abound in pithy observations and brisk asides, but her convictions and
character are expressed more directly in her fiction, with its portraits of
women used cruelly by their society.

Among the hybrid works – a blend of family chronicle, memoir, and
account of their own lives – that appeared at the turn of the century are
those by the half-sisters Mariia Kamenskaia and Ekaterina Iunge. Durova
and Sokhanskaia describe lives led on the geographical and social
peripheries of Russia; like Panaeva, Kamenskaia and Iunge lived in
Petersburg, but their privileged circumstances were far removed from her
bohemian milieu. Like Panaeva also, they recreated a distant past in old
age. Kamenskaia's "Vospominaniia" ("Reminiscences") were begun when
she was in her seventies and published in monthly installments in
Istoricheskii vestnik. Her spirited voice, digressive narrative, and lack of
retrospective angst or apology bear out the reader's impression that she
was the rare Russian woman to have had a genuinely happy childhood.

Kamenskaia's work intertwines a family chronicle centered around the
history of the Tolstoy clan from Catherine the Great's reign to the late
1830s and her own anomalous life as a "daughter of the regiment of
artists." "Our Tolstoi elders used to say, 'In our clan nobody's rich; the only
rich men are those who married rich wives'" (1: 35), and the life Kamenskaia describes is that of a largely landless nobility dependent on military
or civil appointments for their livelihood. Kamenskaia's father, Count
Fedor Petrovich Tolstoy, was one of the first nobles to desert traditional
paths of advancement and take up the unheard-of career of artist, serving as vice-president of the Academy of Arts from 1838 to 1860. Tolstoy
married young, for love, and both parents surrounded their daughters,
frail Liza and sturdy Mariia, with a devotion seconded by unmarried
female relatives who shared the household. Kamenskaia does not dwell
on the grief caused by the deaths of her mother and older sister within a
year of one another in 1838, but passes gallantly on to the life of young
womanhood she entered upon after the period of mourning. Her narrative ends abruptly with her marriage to a young writer, Pavel Kamenskii.
She planned to continue her life story further, but "my hope for health
deceived me . . . and I no longer have the strength to write" (12: 637).
Kamenskaia's failure to complete her enchanting memoir is a loss to
letters and history.

Sheltered in an outgoing and charitable family, Kamenskaia recounts what she felt to be an ideal childhood. Her intention is "in my old age, to relive my fine past at least on paper," using the words of "my father, mother, uncles, aunts, and my father's nanny" (1: 34). Lovingly, she reconstructs the layout of the modest "pink house" in which they lived before they moved into grander apartments on the Academy grounds. She furnishes affectionate portraits of her father's colleagues in all their eccentric quiddities. She remembers events that have historical resonance: encounters with the imperial family; the great flood of 1824; Pushkin's funeral. Her many tales of relatives' foibles and pranks are presented in a way that informs readers that she is aware of the occasional barbarity of their behavior. As close as she comes to overt political commentary is to remark, "My dear father and mother, for as far back as I remember them, seemed a bit compulsive in their desire to free all their serfs as rapidly as possible" (6: 625–6). For reasons that will become clear below, the only note of bitter reproach in Kamenskaia's "Vospominaniia" is directed at her father's second wife, Ekaterina Iunge's mother.

While Kamenskaia's memoirs are marked by what the Russians still define as a central "feminine" characteristic, integration of character (*tsel'nost'*, literally "wholeness"), those of her half-sister, Ekaterina Iunge, lack singularity of voice and reveal a concomitant structural confusion. Some of this discord might be due to the fact that, unlike the other autobiographers treated here, Iunge never wrote artistic prose; what we sense, however, is that she never reached psychological equilibrium. Although she was approaching old age when she wrote her "Vospominaniia," there is no feeling of closure in her mixed autobiography/ memoir. Although she promises to keep her account affirmative ("After all, positive aspects rather than negative are precious to mankind" [7]), her mother's image hovers over the book like a storm cloud. Iunge seems to have few pleasant memories of the second Countess Tolstaia to share, and there was clearly no later period of reconciliation between the two like that which softens Verbitskaia's later reminiscences of her own difficult mother.

Iunge was born when Kamenskaia was twenty-six. The setting of Kamenskaia's youth and Iunge's life from birth is the same: the official apartments of the Academy of Arts. Iunge, however, knows her father only as an eternally occupied, kind, but remote icon. She devotes a major section of the book to an adulatory biography of him (referring readers to Kamenskaia's earlier memoir for the period of his first marriage – the half-sisters are careful to defer to one another). Iunge's only overt criticism of Tolstoy is that he was too soft in domestic matters, an oblique reference to her mother's domination. While Kamenskaia and her sister Liza had been raised by their parents and had the run of the Academy, Iunge and her younger sister Ol'ga were relegated to the care of a spinster aunt.

Kamenskaia's memoir ends with her return to her father's apartments after her marriage: Count Tolstoy has asked the young couple to live with him, and for Mariia this conjunction of childhood and marital life is a perfect resolution. By Iunge's account, Kamenskaia's stepmother has driven the young woman from her father's house. The little girl sees her half-sister only as a fleeting presence, visiting her aunt clandestinely or weeping in Tolstoy's study. At fourteen Iunge developed a romantic friendship with a man she designates as "K.," who later turned cold toward her, mocking the ideas and ideals they had shared. Only later does Iunge learn that her mother had demanded that K. deliberately destroy her daughter's attachment to him. Iunge's mother also attempted to control her husband's posthumous image: her daughter relates a horrifying anecdote in which the countess burns a portion of Tolstoy's memoirs before her eyes.

Both girls were educated at home, Kamenskaia by her parents and Iunge by a succession of governesses; both memoirs offer valuable information on the haphazard domestic education of girls in early and mid-nineteenth-century Russia. The Academy of Arts was off limits to Iunge, but in adolescence she shared the rich intellectual milieu that her mother cultivated, and her life was enriched by an interchange of ideas and even polemics with a variety of prominent men who paid her the compliment of taking her seriously, including the historian Nikolai Kostomarov, the Ukrainian poet and artist Taras Shevchenko, and the American-born black actor Ira Aldridge. When women were first permitted to sit in on lectures at St. Petersburg University in 1859, the countess attended the first before deciding that they were suitable for her daughters as well.

Iunge's account is most integrated when she depicts her early childhood and her friendships with men. Her suitor K. persuaded her to keep a diary, and the memoir displays affecting flashes of unmediated emotion when Iunge inserts excerpts from it devoted to that affair. Later, however, passages from the diary turn the memoir into an uninspired travelogue. The Tolstoys took Ekaterina and Ol'ga on a two-year "Grand Tour" of Europe from 1860–1862. Ekaterina had decided to follow her father's example and become an artist, and at each extended stay in France, Italy, and Germany, diary excerpts dutifully record her (admittedly) juvenile impressions of great works of art. Mariia Kamenskaia was forced by ill health to cut short her delightful reminiscences; Ekaterina Iunge chose to end her unstructured book abruptly at the same point, the traditional "happy ending" of her marriage to a prominent doctor.

The prose and poetry of the late nineteenth-century Silver Age were marked by renewed emphasis on individual psychology; the period inspired women's autobiographies similar in unmediated self-disclosure to Durova's and Sokhanskaia's idiosyncratic early works. Anastasiia Verbitskaia, born in 1861 on the cusp of Aleksandr II's great reforms, was the wildly prolific writer of self-published popular novels that depicted the "new woman" of the turn of the century. Her autobiography of childhood and youth echoes the impassioned rhetoric of her fiction and records the beginnings of her evolution into an ardent individualist at odds with the self-sacrificing spirit of the revolutionaries. She entitled the work, *Moemu chitateliu* (To My Reader), and in a brief foreword she defined that (grammatically masculine) reader as: "a distant kindred soul sounding in unison with my own," a person who considered "art" [*tvorchestvo*] the "highest value in life."

The autobiography begins as a family chronicle, as Verbitskaia recounts her grandmother's and mother's lives, often in their own words. They were the most important presences in her early life and that of her elder sister, Aleksandra (married name Sorneva, died 1891), who also became a writer. Her grandmother, Anastasiia Mochalova (c. 1816–1879), was a respected provincial actress. Depiction of her failing health and approaching death becomes a counterpoint to her granddaughters' coming of age. Verbitskaia's mother, Mariia Ivanovna Ziablova (c. 1836–1906), a restless and dissatisfied woman, was no more suited for the maternal role than Iunge's mother: mercurial and nervous, always seeking escape from boredom and unfulfilled ambitions, she often left her daughters and young son for months at a time to the mercies of a rigid housekeeper, and created emotional turmoil at home when she was tempted to leave her tolerant elderly husband for another man. The difference between Iunge's portrait and Verbitskaia's, however, is that mother and daughter, in the latter's adulthood, had a period of reconciliation that enabled Verbitskaia to portray her mother's struggles sympathetically.[16]

Verbitskaia depicts early childhood in Iaroslavl, where her father commanded a military regiment, as stubborn resistance to her mother's capricious despotism. Like Sokhanskaia, Verbitskaia and her sister were educated in a boarding school under royal patronage, but where Sokhanskaia focuses on her struggle to get an education in her Khar'kov institute, Verbitskaia depicts all the broad mood swings of girlhood. Her splendid singing voice, cherubic looks, and reputation as a rich heiress make her an instant favorite with the headmistress and students at the Elizavetinskii Institute in Moscow, but she falls abruptly from her pedestal when the fact that her grandmother was an *actress* is bruited throughout the school. Verbitskaia portrays herself as ugly when she falls from favor and regains her sense of being attractive only as she forms loving friendships and becomes the favorite student of her geography and history professors. Even though institute girls were no longer completely sequestered after 1864 – the girls were permitted to leave for weekends, holidays, and vacations – by Verbitskaia's account, the intensity of the girls' claustrophobic preoccupations had not changed. The climate of hothouse sexuality fostered passionate crushes (*obozhanie*) on any likely objects – male professors, matrons, older students, and contemporaries. Some of the girls were strongly attracted to the *narodnik* (populist) movement of the 1870s, but revolutionary fervor weakens and adulatory monarchism sweeps over the students when Tsar Aleksandr II visits the school.

The second volume covers the first year of Verbitskaia's life after graduation. Her father died while she was in the institute, and home becomes the small estate he had bought a few years earlier. The rhythms of the narrative slow from the frenetic activity of school days to the lyrical pace of country life. Her mother is working intensively to turn the property into a model of modern agriculture, and Verbitskaia and her sister, who in school days went their separate ways, are drawn together for companionship. Aleksandra is the first to discover a vocation for writing fiction and drama; several times in her autobiography Verbitskaia refers to her sister's suicide in 1891, which she blames on her difficulties in establishing herself as a writer.[17] Another sudden shift in their lives occurs the following winter when their mother, famous as a dilettante actress in Iaroslavl days, is invited to take part in a season of amateur theater in Moscow. The girls enter a heady world of rehearsals, performances, social visits, and parties, and their emotional life is complicated by attentions from worldly men. Finally, their mother realizes that this enchanting circle smacks more of the *demi-monde* than the respectable society she sought for her daughters. She is reluctant to spare capital from the estate for a marriage settlement and, in ironic counterpoint to their earlier expectations, her two daughters become dowryless girls like those they had pitied in the institute. At the end of the second volume, Verbitskaia, determined to earn her living, persuades her mother to let her take a post as governess, even in the late 1870s one of the few respectable jobs open to a gentry girl of reduced means. Up to this point Verbitskaia has portrayed herself as the typical naive "institute girl"; she planned, but apparently never produced, further volumes which would have addressed her transformation into a "new woman."

Valentina Dmitrieva led the life of dedication to the cause of revolution that her close contemporary Anastasiia Verbitskaia rejected. Durova, Sokhanskaia, and Verbitskaia all had roots in the provincial gentry; Kamenskaia and Iunge came from aristocratic stock; Panaeva's parents were among the *déclassé* caste of actors; Dmitrieva was one of the rare peasants to become a professional – both writer and doctor – by dint of both luck and hard work. She wrote her autobiography, *Tak bylo* (The Way it Was), in the 1920s, and, unlike Kamenskaia's, its even, generally cheerful tone was probably at least to some degree generated by Soviet norms of semi-hagiographic depiction of revolutionaries' fates. There is a troubling suggestion of self-censorship in her account, which, like Panaeva's, merges her life with that of her immediate community.

Autobiographers traditionally define the onset of conscious existence from their first memory: Dmitrieva's is the poignant one of her father tossing his daughter, nearly two years old, into the air and telling her, "Now we are free [as] Cossacks." Her parents were literate serfs, educated by their former owner to occupy responsible posts on his estates, and the 1861 emancipation brought them periods of relative prosperity when the family had work and desperate poverty when it did not. They had little time and energy to worry about Dmitrieva's upbringing. Her childhood came to a *de facto* end at age nine when she became nanny to younger siblings. The family's fortunes were repaired three years later, at cost to her father's pride, when they went to live with Dmitrieva's maternal grandfather.

Dmitrieva learned to read and write and took advantage of the libraries on the estates where her parents worked. She was jealous when her favorite brother was sent to school in Tambov, but he managed to interest the town's intelligentsia in the gifted fourteen-year-old's plight and they arranged for her to attend the local *gimnaziia* for girls. Before long Dmitrieva was involved in *narodnik* (populist) circles, and her experience mirrors in miniature the tragic cycle of repression and resistance that scars Russian history of the late imperial period: subjected to repeated searches and interrogations from the tsarist police, she describes herself as steadily more radicalized and more implacably determined to keep to her course as propagandist and teacher of revolutionary ideals. After secondary school, the Tambov *zemstvo* (local government) sent Dmitrieva to medical courses in St. Petersburg, where she became involved in public protests. Her subvention was cut off, and from 1880 she earned a meager living as a writer. Dmitrieva's extensive fiction refracts the settings and ideals of her life in the same seemingly objective way that she portrays them in *The Way it Was*. She completed her medical education and used those skills mainly to serve isolated peasant communities during epidemics. When she was finally offered a post as a rural doctor, she rejected it: "A quiet haven, a well-fed life, quiet work . . . No, I couldn't do it. The narcotic atmosphere of cards, vodka, rude backwoods flirtation, and vulgar gossip suffocated me . . ." (246).

Dmitrieva's life before the Revolution was spent, first in exile and later by choice, in Tver' and Voronezh. She describes the polemic engagement and clash of opinions of the fragmented provincial revolutionary movements of the 1880s and 1890s as stimulating rather than threatening. There is no trace of feminist thought in *The Way it Was*. Like Panaeva, her account appropriates male discourse. Unlike Panaeva, however, who did not grant most other women even the dignity of names, but referred to them as, for instance, "Belinskii's wife," Dmitrieva gives no hint of preference for male over female company: activists of both sexes are portrayed as her associates. Except for one early infatuation, Dmitrieva downplays intimate emotions; the husband she acquires along the way is depicted as just another comrade.

All in all, Dmitrieva's work, like Iunge's, is an unsettling mixture of memoir and autobiography: there is too much left unsaid in her account, too much focus outward on the social component of her life, and too little on personal priorities. She ends her account with the 1905 revolution, which brought Russia limited parliamentary government, and we might take this as an oblique hint that for Dmitrieva this was the country's flashpoint of the change she had long worked to bring about.

Of all these attempts to recover the past, Anastasiia Tsvetaeva's *Vospominaniia* (Reminiscences) is the most Proustian: she reconstructs in painstaking detail the settings, mores, and psychological shifts she went through in her first twenty years. Like Kamenskaia, she examines her young life from the stance of tolerant old age. The work is clearly a labor of love, an attempt to share with readers a past from which, although she remained in the Soviet Union, she was abruptly cut off by war and revolution. It is also an intimate portrait of her elder sister, Marina Tsvetaeva. Although Anastasiia depicts herself as less obsessed by books than Marina, she shares the poet's love for and skill with language. The texture of her work is rich in flights of alliteration and imagery and lyrical passages that stand alone as prose poems. What might have become an overpowering recitation of details is redeemed by precise observation and keen insight – ironically, perhaps the more closely focused because she and Marina, like Verbitskaia, were nearsighted and viewed the world clearly only by squinting or wearing glasses. Defective vision might partially explain Tsvetaeva's sensitivity to olfactory stimuli: the characteristic odors of new and familiar localities are a motif throughout her account of childhood.

Tsvetaeva's autobiography marches steadily forward through the years and, within each year, through the seasons. Occasional lapses of memory – for instance, details of her mother's funeral, lost in the haze of grief – only serve to highlight the remarkable range of what may well be called re-creation rather than simple recall. In a litany, she marks off Marina's and her birthdays in September, exactly two years apart: for instance, "That was in autumn 1906. We turned fourteen and twelve years old" (223 [all quotes taken from 3rd expanded edition]). She defines the stages of life they pass through as well, framing the tale in the quadripartite structure that Tolstoy planned for his trilogy: in addition to his published account of childhood, adolescence (often translated into English as boyhood/girlhood), and youth, Tsvetaeva heads the last section of her memoir, well over 600 pages long, with the fourth part Tolstoy never completed: young wo/manhood (*molodost'*). Anastasiia's childhood ends with her mother's death in 1906; adolescence and youth for both sisters are closely linked and extend through their early marriages; their father's death, the loss of the Moscow house in which they grew up, and the outbreak of the First World War in 1914 mark the beginning of young womanhood.

"My first memory of Marina. It doesn't exist. It is preceded by a feeling of her presence around me that originated in that mist where memories are born" (4). Tsvetaeva's *Reminiscences* are a remarkable psychological study of the individuation of a second child, as she wavers between the "we" of a cozy unity with Marina and the development of her independent "I." Tsvetaeva depicts the girls in early years as moving through the rhythm of winters in Moscow and summers in Tarusa with a healthy dose of sibling rivalry. "Musia took 'Undina,' and – in exchange – I got 'Rustem i Zorab.'

That's how we divided – everything. Not in a niggardly way, no – from passion" (24). Unity becomes more important as, "like tumbleweed," they accompany their tubercular mother from Italy to Switzerland to Germany to the Crimea (1902–1906). (Travel abroad also separates them from their father and elder half-siblings, to whom they were also close.) The girls rapidly take on the coloration of their surroundings. In Nervi, they become friendly with a colony of Russian revolutionaries in exile and are transformed into radicalized atheists; at a convent-like school in Lausanne they are equally rapidly converted into devout Christians. After their mother's death, the two girls return to the family home in Moscow and education at separate *gimnazii* and soon revert to a secular bohemianism. Their intimacy continues, but it is shared now both with girlfriends and, increasingly, with older male intellectuals. Marina brings her sister into the literary and artistic circles the precocious poet frequents, and the two develop a sister act of chanting Marina's poems together in perfect unison.

Anastasiia portrays their youth by contrast as well as by solidarity. Marina is miserable in girlhood and even attempts suicide. Her early marriage to a boy a year younger than she, Sergei Efron, and the birth of her daughter, Ariadne, lend Marina a bloom of happiness that Anastasiia denotes by commenting repeatedly on the radiant beauty she will never have again. In contrast, Anastasiia depicts her own happy-go-lucky adolescence and unhappy premature young womanhood in sober and matter-of-fact fashion: she falls in love – symbolically depicted during her first meeting with the moody man as a mad endurance contest on racing iceskates – and, pregnant at sixteen, marries him. They soon separate, leaving her with a son to raise. Her happiest days are during her brief second marriage, but, soon after the war breaks out, her husband dies of a ruptured appendix and within weeks her second son succumbs to diphtheria. The narrative loses its shape and control at that point: Anastasiia treats the terrible events of the sisters' separation between late 1917 and 1921 – all the horrors of civil war, famine, and universal destruction – in retrospect in a chapter as the two spend their first night of reunion in Marina's Moscow apartment bringing each other up to date. Anastasiia's jumbled depiction of the last year before Marina's emigration is of a fight for survival in which the two sisters in desperation go their separate ways.

These autobiographical works cover a broad reach of Russian history from the moment in 1783 when Nadezhda Durova's mother refused to nurse her newborn daughter to 1922 when Marina Tsvetaeva chose to follow her husband abroad; Durova published *Cavalry Maiden* in 1836, and Anastasiia Tsvetaeva's *Reminiscences* first appeared in print in 1971. As we read these autobiographies/memoirs by Russian women, the extreme variations in their social and economic status seem less central to their depictions than the overall prescriptions for the female sex in patriarchal Russia that underlie their accounts, whether they accept, defy, or are denied the common expectation of marriage and child-bearing. Childhood and girlhood are the epochs they describe most uninhibitedly. Even the few who extend their accounts into womanhood treat sexual maturation and married life with a discretion mandated by the norms of contemporary Russian discourse. Old age is not an epoch they describe directly, but it is present in the voice of an elderly narrator remembering her youth or expressed in portraits of older women in the family. Relationships with mothers are complex and significant, varying from outright neglect and abuse to warm, unstinting support. Other female relatives, aunts, and sisters in particular, are important in some lives, but Kamenskaia's father is the only man depicted as playing a substantive role in his daughters' upbringing. The extent to which the masculine and feminine spheres are separate is striking, although it diminishes late in the nineteenth century with the expansion of women's opportunities to enter a variety of vocations. How typical these works are of Russian women's autobiographical literature overall will only become apparent after a thorough analysis of the corpus as a whole. This truncated survey is necessarily only a bare indication of the rich panorama of prerevolutionary Russian life to be found in its women's life-writings.

NOTES

1. In *Terrible Perfection* 64–102, Barbara Heldt examined autobiography as a congenial genre for Russian women. Nine years later Judith Vowles and Toby Clyman expanded on her insight in their authoritative introduction to *Russia Through Women's Eyes*, an anthology of translated selections from nineteenth-century Russian women's autobiographical works. The anthology includes an extensive bibliography.

2. Postmodern theory tends to view autobiographical writings and fiction as related, equally unreliable forms of narrative, but my nineteenth-century authors saw them as separate genres and distinguished accounts of their own lives ("truth") from first-person fiction closely based on events they had lived through by giving the narrator and other characters invented names. For a cogent reformulation of the interaction among gender, class, and nationality and the relation between "truth" and "falsity" in women's autobiography, see Leigh Gilmore, *Autobiographics: A Feminist Theory of Women's Self-Representation* (Ithaca, NY and London, 1994), especially chapter 1.

3. For autobiographies dating from the late eighteenth and early nineteenth centuries (Catherine II, Dolgorukaia, Dashkova, and Labzina), see Catriona Kelly's article in this volume; Clyman and Vowles, 14–19; and articles in *DRWW*. Kelly Herold's "Russian Autobiographical Literature in French: Recovering a Memoiristic Tradition" (Ph.D. dissertation, UCLA, 1998) analyzes autobiographical works written between the early

1750s and 1825, half of them by women, and casts light on the European roots of the genre in Russia.

4. By "substantive," I mean works over roughly fifty pages in length, some of which may have been printed as a series of shorter pieces.

5. See Clyman and Vowles, 26–7. The three most prominent historical journals were *Istoricheskii vestnik, Russkaia starina* and *Russkii arkhiv*. I know of no phenomenon in other western societies like the proliferation of historical journals in Russia in the last third of the nineteenth century.

6. The distinction I make for the purposes of this article between *autobiography* (as works focused on the self) and *memoir* (as those centered on the ambient milieu) is based on criteria outlined by Zoya Vatnikova-Prizel in *O russkoi memuarnoi literature. Kriticheskie analizy i bibliografiia* (East Lansing, MI, 1978), 17–39. In critical works and reviews of Anglophone literature, the terms are often used interchangeably. The most common term for life-writing in prerevolutionary Russia was *vospominaniia* (reminiscences) with *zapiski* (notes) often used as well. *Avtobiografiia* tends still to be reserved for short, factual statements.

7. Gilmore, *Autobiographics*, ix.

8. This section condenses themes from my "Introduction" to the English translation of *The Cavalry Maiden; Journals of a Russian Officer in the Napoleonic Wars* (Bloomington, IN, 1988), ix–xxxiii, and my later article, "A Woman in the 'Man's World': The Journals of Nadezhda Durova," in Marilyn Yalom and Susan Groag Bell (eds.), *Revealing Lives: Gender in Autobiography and Biography* (Albany, NY, 1990), 43–51. On Durova, see also Heldt, 80–6; and Clyman and Vowles, 20–1.

9. For the development of "childhood" as a genre in Russia, see A. Wachtel, *The Battle for Childhood: Creation of a Russian Myth* (Stanford, CA, 1990).

10. An unpublished paper by Hilde Hoogenboom, "From Sandian Idealist to Russian Realist: The Transformation of Nadezhda Sokhanskaia," explores the exchange between Pletnev and Sokhanskaia from both archival and published sources.

11. On Sokhanskaia, see Heldt, 87–93; Clyman and Vowles, 22–5; and Paul Debreczeny, *Social Functions of Literature: Alexander Pushkin and Russian Culture* (Stanford, CA, 1997), 49–53.

12. For a detailed portrait of life in a contemporary institute, see "N." [Sof'ia Khvoshchinskaia, 1828–1865], "Vospominaniia institutskoi zhizni," *Russkie vedomosti* 9–10 (1861). The first half appears as "Reminiscences of Institute Life" in Clyman and Vowles, 76–108, translation by Valentina Baslyk.

13. This crisis in her life is featured in the excerpt from Sokhanskaia's "Autobiography" in Clyman and Vowles, 48–59, also translated by Valentina Baslyk.

14. For a summary of Durova's, Sokhanskaia's, and Panaeva's pre-Tolstoian depictions of Russian girlhood, see Zirin, "Butterflies with Broken Wings? Early Autobiographical Depictions of Girlhood in Russia," in *Gender Restructuring*, 255–66.

15. For Panaeva's life with Nekrasov, see Richard Gregg, "A Brackish Hippocrene: Nekrasov, Panaeva, and the 'Prose of Love,'" *SR* 34: 4 (December, 1975) 731–51.

16. The excerpts from Verbitskaia's *Moemu chitateliu* that appear in Clyman and Vowles (335–80, translated by Judith Vowles) are those devoted to her grandmother's and mother's lives. Verbitskaia also published a two-volume novel *Igo liubvi* (Yoke of Love), based on their story.

17. Her sister's sad example may have been one factor impelling Verbitskaia to establish her own publishing house.

6

The women of Russian Montparnasse
(Paris, 1920–1940)

The Russians who left their homeland during the years just after the Bolshevik Revolution remained a "society abroad," to use Marc Raeff's phrase.[1] Deprived of their citizenship by Soviet decree in 1921, many of those who emigrated to Europe did not receive foreign passports until after World War II, when others, inspired by war-era patriotism, finally applied for Soviet citizenship. (A small number repatriated earlier.) This generation of post-revolutionary émigrés, known as the First Wave, made little effort at assimilation within their host countries, choosing instead to recreate Russia in microcosm. They established their own cultural institutions – newspapers, theaters, publishing houses – and sustained a vital intellectual scene. In Berlin and Prague, the early centers of the emigration, this process was linked to cultural developments in the "metropolis," as Soviet Moscow was called. It was only in Paris, which became the acknowledged capital of émigré Russia in the mid-1920s and remained so until the war, that a distinct émigré culture evolved.

The situation of Russian émigré writers in Paris is thrown into relief by their literal proximity to a second foreign literary community, that of expatriate American writers. Both the Russians and the Americans wrote primarily in their native tongue, though they had personal and creative ties with the French intelligentsia. The expatriate conclave featured a number of women, such as Natalie Barney, Gertrude Stein, H. D. (Hilda Doolittle), Kay Boyle, and Djuna Barnes. These "women of the left bank," as Shari Benstock has called them in her book of that title, published in prestigious venues, set up their own bookshops and presses, and presided over literary gatherings.[2] Natalie Barney, who ran the most famous Paris salon, was the type of the expatriate female Modernist, an intellectually and sexually independent woman whose autonomy was secured by family prestige and income. Not all of these women were, like Barney, openly lesbian, but most were declared feminists who freely chose to live and work outside what they regarded as a hidebound native culture.

Russian women writers abroad, by contrast, were living in exile, with no opportunity to be published and read back home. (The single exception was the Communist Elsa Triolet, whose three Russian novels were published in Soviet Russia during the 1920s.) Certainly they were both popular and influential within the émigré literary world. Nadezhda Teffi was among the best loved authors of the Russian emigration, Zinaida Gippius hosted its most prestigious salons, and Marina Tsvetaeva was perhaps its greatest poet. However, few émigré writers could hope to support themselves on earnings from publications in such a restricted literary market, and even those who held jobs often lived in poverty. (French law barred Russians from high-paying jobs in the professions.) The fortunate ones had family money, such as Irina Odoevtseva and Sofia Pregel, who was supported by a physicist brother living in America. One had fabulous luck: Anna Prismanova's husband, the poet Aleksandr Ginger, won a large sum in damages from a French bus company after injuring his shin in an accident. But most writers relied on the generosity of Russian and French patrons (*metsenaty*), mainly through the auspices of the Union of Russian Writers and Journalists. Their yearly fundraising ball at the Hotel Lutèce was attended by all the major writers and editors, who put on entertainments for the donors; Nina Berberova, for example, recalled pulling a wealthy lawyer around the ballroom in a carriage.[3]

An episode from 1930 brings home the contrasting material circumstances of Russian and American women writers in Paris. Marina Tsvetaeva was among the poorest of the émigré writers: the main breadwinner in her family of four for most of her years in emigration, she nevertheless insisted on earning solely as a literary professional. She more frequently wrote prose (more saleable than poetry), relentlessly pursued her editors for payment, and took every opportunity to meet wealthy patrons. She also sought to broaden her readership by rewriting in French her narrative poem "The Swain" ("Molodets," 1922) for an edition illustrated by the émigrée artist Natalia Goncharova. As part of a campaign to place the book with a French press, Tsvetaeva read the poem at one of Barney's "Fridays." Nothing came of the encounter, but several years later Tsvetaeva responded to Barney's *Pensées d'une Amazone* (1918, 1920) with another French composition, her "Lettre à l'Amazone," a controversial reflection on lesbianism. (Tsvetaeva had at least one homosexual affair, to which she devoted a poetic cycle.)[4] In her "Lettre," she argues that lesbian love is doomed by one partner's desire to bear children, which leads her to marry "the enemy," as men are called throughout the essay. She thus simultaneously affirms and renounces lesbianism as woman's most profound sexual experience. Tsvetaeva's logic may be puzzling to today's reader, as it must have been to Barney, but few other émigrées addressed matters of sexuality and gender as boldly as Tsvetaeva, with the exception of Zinaida Gippius.

Tsvetaeva and Gippius belonged to the so-called "older generation" of literary émigrés, meaning that they arrived in the West as mature writers. It also meant that they came of age during the flourishing of prerevolutionary Russian Modernism: Gippius, whose work is discussed in chapter 7, was a founder of Russian Symbolism, while Tsvetaeva belonged to the star-studded generation of poets that followed (Mandel'stam, Akhmatova, Pasternak, Mayakovsky). Both women made outstanding contributions to the reinvention of Russian verse form. They also challenged traditional notions of gender and sexuality in their writing and sexual choices, in ways both like and unlike the American women Modernists in Paris. If Tsvetaeva was engaged by Barney's example, Gippius could be compared to Stein. Gippius was bisexual in her erotic attachments but, like Stein, claimed a masculine creative identity and had competitive relationships with male colleagues. (Berberova compared Gippius's disregard for Vladimir Nabokov to Stein's dislike of James Joyce.)[5] As Jenifer Presto has recently emphasized, however, Gippius also cultivated an extravagant femininity that parodied stereotypes of the female poet.[6]

After leaving Russia in 1919, Gippius devoted her energies to the political cause of defeating Bolshevism and rescuing the cultural tradition that, in her view, was being destroyed in Soviet Russia. She hosted meetings of "Zelenaia lampa" ("The Green Lamp"), modeled upon the Pushkin-era salon, and helped establish several journals designed to foster a new generation of Russian writers. As a writer, she turned to non-fiction – diaries of her years in revolutionary Petersburg, memoirs of Symbolist contemporaries, and essays on literary and political topics. However, Gippius also published a series of new stories in émigré periodicals and a new book of verse, *Sianiia* (Radiances), thus continuing to exemplify the Silver Age writer who works in all genres but is above all a lyric poet. Even Nadezhda Teffi, an older generation writer who was famous in prerevolutionary and émigré Russia for her humorous sketches of everyday life, published several volumes of poetry. The model remained deeply influential in émigré culture. Nina Berberova and Irina Odoevtseva, who are perhaps properly called "middle generation" writers since they began their careers as poets in prerevolutionary Petersburg under the tutelage of Nikolai Gumilev, both focused on short fiction and novels after emigrating but returned to poetry during their lengthy careers. (Both also lived to see the end of the Soviet era and in the late 1980s visited Russia, where Odoevtseva spent her final years.) Poetry, that is, had the greatest prestige in émigré culture, such that among younger émigrée writers, only Elena Deisha (pseud. Georgii Peskov) published no verse.

In this cultural context, Marina Tsvetaeva was an inescapable presence. In contrast to Gippius, Tsvetaeva reached her creative peak after leaving Russia, and she became the premier émigré poet of the 1920s. (Some contemporaries actually regarded her as the premier Russian poet, a defensible claim, given the diminished lyric output of Akhmatova, Mandel'stam, Pasternak, and her fellow émigré Khodasevich during this period.) At the start of the decade, Tsvetaeva had not published a collection of verse since her debut in her early teens. However, she had since accumulated a large body of poetry that encompassed several stages in her development, involving sophisticated use of linguistic masks, greater rhythmic variety, and a punning, "etymological" semantics. Between 1921 and 1923, around the time she emigrated to Berlin, Tsvetaeva flooded the literary market with eight new books of poetry. Most of this work was enthusiastically received by émigré critics, but Tsvetaeva did not rest on her laurels. In Berlin (1922), and later in Prague (1923 to 1925), she wrote her last and greatest collection of lyrics, *Posle Rossii* (After Russia, 1928). At the same time, she was channeling more lyric energy into longer verse genres, writing two verse tragedies based on Greek mythology and a dozen or more narrative poems. In these works, which may be considered her masterpieces, the concentrated, elliptical line of her lyric poetry is worked into elaborate rhythmical compositions akin to those of the Russian Modernist composers.

Soon after Tsvetaeva moved to Paris in late 1925, she gave a public reading that took the émigré capital by storm. At the same time, however, the high Modernist aesthetic of her latest work was drawing criticism from Parisian reviewers, notably Georgii Adamovich. Tsvetaeva's acid response in her 1926 essay "Poet o kritike" ("The Poet on the Critic"), with a selection of Adamovich's worst critical gaffes, alienated much of the literary community. Nor did her admiration of the "Soviet" poets Pasternak and

Mayakovsky play well in the politicized environment of Russian Paris. Later that year, when the first number of the literary almanac *Versty* (Milestones, 1926) appeared, featuring Tsvetaeva's "Poema gory" ("Poem of the Hill,"1923) alongside works by Sergei Esenin and Isaac Babel, Gippius led the attack, criticizing the journal's "pro-Soviet mood."[7] In fact, Tsvetaeva's husband, Sergei Efron, was to become increasingly involved in the returnee movement; he ended by taking part in an NKVD assassination attempt and was repatriated to Soviet Russia in 1937. Two years later Tsvetaeva followed the rest of her family there and, after Efron and her daughter were arrested, committed suicide in 1941.

According to the reigning narrative of Tsvetaeva's years in emigration, the émigré literary world spurned its greatest poet, finally driving her back to Soviet Russia and to her death. It is a narrative of neglect and remorse that does not address the full reality of Tsvetaeva's situation. Though her "lyrical flood," as she put it, had ceased by the mid-1920s, she continued to write and publish prolifically. The lyrical prose style of her portraits of contemporaries, reflections on literature, autobiographical essays, and a few short stories, were praised by contemporaries, including women writers.[8] Tsvetaeva also continued to participate in public literary life, giving regular readings, appearing at major events, and patronizing the literary circle "Kochev'e" ("The Ark," 1928–39).[9] Far from being invisible to her fellow émigrés, Tsvetaeva seems to have embodied the alienation and isolation experienced by all Russians abroad. As one contemporary observed, Tsvetaeva influenced the émigré literary community less through her poetic practice than "the whole atmosphere of tragic genius associated with her."[10] The power of Tsvetaeva's example for younger women poets is attested by recently published materials belonging to Kristina Krotkova, a minor émigrée poet, and by dedicatory poems by Irina Knorring, Alla Golovina, and Anna Prismanova.

Tsvetaeva's own work provided a script for the role she played in émigré culture. In her manifesto poem "Na krasnom kone" ("On a Red Steed," 1921), the poet pursues her calling at the price of childhood innocence, romantic fulfillment, and motherhood. This theme of the poet's withdrawal from the world sounded ever more strongly in her poetry of the 1920s. Concomitantly, Tsvetaeva devoted more of her creative powers to representing "the other world" ("tot svet") as a place of ecstatic experience. In several of her later long poems – "Popytka komnaty" ("Attempt at a Room," 1926), "Poema lestnitsy" ("Poem of the Staircase," 1926), and "Poema vozdukha" ("Poem of the Air," 1927) – the poet creates dream-spaces she may temporarily inhabit. Often they have the shape of familiar urban interiors (staircases, corridors), which are transformed and expanded in what might be called a domestic sublime, taking a cue from her phrase "domesticity of distance" ("domashnest' dali").

For such a poet, the alienated condition of exile is a natural one, as Tsvetaeva proclaims in a poem that appeared in a Prague journal under the title "Emigrant-Poet" ("Émigré-Poet," 1923) in 1925. She is "Vega's émigré" on earth, a visitor from the constellation formed from Orpheus's lyre:

> Here among you: your mansions, money, smogs,
> Matrons, ministries.
> Neither beating you nor joining you,
> Like some—
> Schumann, whirling spring beneath his hem:
> Higher! Out of view!
> Suspended like a nightingale's tremolo—
> Like some–chosen one.
>
> Wary, since you lick his feet
> When he crests high!
> Lost among aches and obstacles,
> A god in a den of sin.
>
> Extra! Exceptional! Émigré! Accustomed
> To upward... not accepting the gallows . . .
> In tattered suit of visas and valiuta—[11]
> Vega's émigré.[12]

Tsvetaeva's conviction that the poet "rises above" her circumstances shaped her views about the future of émigré literature. She took exception to the idea, expressed by others of her generation, that young émigré writers would be crippled by *bespochvennost'*, by their lack of "grounding" in their native culture. As she stated in an admiring review of the young poet Nikolai Gronskii, "everything here is 'ground'" ("Vse zdes' — pochva") for the true poet, whose deepest roots are in poetry itself.[13]

Gronskii was one of the few young émigré poets who worked in Tsvetaeva's beloved genre of the long poem (*poema*). There is, however, one notable instance of a younger woman poet writing in this genre. Nina Berberova's "Liricheskaia poema" ("Lyric Long Poem," 1924–6), which appeared in the prestigious journal *Sovremennye zapiski* (Contemporary Notes) in 1927, addresses her "double life" ("*dvoinaia zhizn'*") as a Russian living in the indifferent bourgeois environment of Paris. As in Karolina Pavlova's novel of that title, and in Tsvetaeva's poetry, the female protagonist has her richest experience in dreams. "Lyric Long Poem" opens with the speaker's claim that she has forgotten Russia, supplanted in her psyche by a recent dream. This dream is cast as a personal memory of the first day of creation: she becomes Adam before our very eyes, when she switches to grammatically masculine forms ("I ia vosstal na lone raia"). Berberova plays up this gender transformation by describing the physical sensation of God removing his/her rib to create Eve. The point of her striking identification is to claim a kind of "original innocence":

> And if I'm among strangers here—
> I've not been exiled, I've been sent forth,
> And there was never any exile,
> No sins were ever mine![14]

The phrase "ia v poslan'e", borrowed from Gippius, has evangelical overtones, but the poem seems less a testament of faith than an extraordinary assertion of the will to survive unburdened by her past. Berberova speaks here and in her other writings as an "iron woman," as she later titled her biography of Gorky's companion, Moura Budberg. Even the émigré theme of solitude is treated in this register: "Solitude, your step is regal,/ Defiance, your pitiless voice is lofty."[15]

Berberova's tone presents a sharp contrast to the "Paris Note" of jaded despair that dominated the writings of the younger generation. The phrase has been attributed to the poet Boris Poplavskii, who died an exemplary "Paris Note" death by overdosing on heroin. However, it was the poet and critic Georgii Adamovich (mentioned earlier for his conflict with Tsvetaeva) who cultivated the idea that a distinctive tonality was emerging among Parisian émigrés. The young émigré poets, he argued, were finding legitimate outlet in "psychologism," turning inward in reaction to their blighted situation (and to a perceived decline of European culture generally).[16] In championing the value of poetry as human document, he downplayed issues of composition, sparking a lengthy polemic with Vladislav Khodasevich. Khodasevich, who viewed himself as working to sustain the Pushkinian tradition, urged young poets to achieve formal mastery by studying the verse canon. In this debate between Adamovich and Khodasevich over the importance of craft, which took place in the early 1930s, women's poetry became an important exhibit. In a 1931 review essay on "Women's Poetry" ("Zhenskie stikhi"),

Khodasevich states that a poem's confessional power does not guarantee its literary quality and that "poetesses," due to "certain features of the female character," rely overmuch on the unmediated expression of feeling.[17] Akhmatova is put forward as both the model and the exception: her feminine self-preoccupation is redeemed by her poetic skill. Khodasevich finds that most women poets fail to pull this off, making recent volumes by Ekaterina Bakunina and Irina Knorring cases in point.

Bakunina, at least, turned Khodasevich's argument to her advantage in the pages of *Chisla* (Numbers, 1932–4), which showcased the work of young Parisian writers and for which Bakunina served as secretarial editor. In her response to a regularly featured questionnaire, "For Whom and Why to Write," Bakunina characterizes herself as a "writing nonwriter" – in no sense an apology, since she takes Adamovich's view that, in this historical situation, with a declining readership and unstable literary culture, there simply is no such thing as a "writer." She goes on to assert that women are naturals for the role: "There is one inspiration – the intolerability of silence. It is particularly difficult for women, placed under pressure by their nature. And every woman – potentially – is an hysteric."[18] Women's need to speak, that is, will ensure that culture, albeit of a different sort, will be sustained. Bakunina's own poetic persona is markedly feminine, and she devotes separate sections of her *Stikhi* (Poems, 1931) to "Motherhood" and "Womanliness." Her literary specialty, however, was the graphic depiction of woman's sexual experience, which she achieved more fully in two novels that were enough of a *succès de scandale* to be translated into several European languages.

Lydiia Chervinskaia, who was known as the Greta Garbo of Russian Montparnasse, was the model Paris Note poet. In line with Adamovich's pronouncements, her poems express profound skepticism about the possibility of communication, often rendering moments of silence. These typically occur during scenes of lovers parting at dawn, occasions for the lyric subject to reflect on essential human solitude. (She dedicated one such poem to her husband, the poet Lazar Kel'berin.) Chervinskaia's concern with female emotional experience, in particular the experience of the failed affair, places her in the Akhmatovan tradition. Her tendency to chart the movements of her heart with analytical distance ("consciousness and feeling are divided" ["soznanie i chuvstvo razdvoilas'"]), also recalls the work of the Symbolist poet Aleksandr Blok, exemplar of cynical despondence. As she states in her poem "Khochetsia Blokovskoi shchedroi napevnosti..." ("I'd like the generous singsong of Blok . . ."),[19] she also strives for his musicality by mixing meters, lines, and stanzaic forms in a one-off, improvisational spirit.

Another woman poet closely associated with the Paris Note is Irina Knorring. In the above-mentioned review essay, Khodasevich identified her as a self-obsessed "Akhmatovan" while praising her mastery of Akhmatova's spare poetic idiom. However, Knorring's lyric persona has a very different profile than Akhmatova's. The opening poem of her first collection *Stikhi o sebe* (Poems About Myself, 1931) announces the defining condition of the feminine self she shapes throughout her *oeuvre*: "I will be long and horribly sick" ("Budu dolgo i strashno bol'na"). In actuality, Knorring struggled with diabetes for fifteen years, to die of it at age thirty-seven. Her poems are less concerned with physical illness, however, than with the speaker's spiritual state. To be precise, they register the symptoms of clinical depression: she is dull, forgetful, and deprived of will ("Mysli tonut v matovom tumane" ["Thoughts drown in a matte fog"]). The volume's concluding five-poem cycle *Ballada o dvadtsatom gode* (Ballad of 1920, 1924), depicting her family's flight from revolutionary Russia, suggests that her malaise stems from the loss of her homeland. Knorring thus follows the script Akhmatova wrote for the Russian émigré: "But I forever pity the exile, / A prisoner, an invalid" ("No vechno zhalok mne izgnannik, / Kak zakliuchennoi, kak bol'noi"). By historical chance, Akhmatova herself became acquainted with Knorring's verse in the sixties and endorsed her enactment of the role, praising her work as a sincere document of émigré misery.[20]

Knorring's second collection, *Okna na sever* (Windows to the North, 1937), focuses on the prospect of death, and without consolation (cf. "It will be painful. Not frightening, but strange . . ." ["Budet bol'no. Ne strashno, a stranno . . ."]). In the final poem, the speaker instructs the reader how to memorialize her:

> Wind my cross about with green ivy,
> Mark the outline of my grave.
> That's all. No pity, not a moan.
> Don't have the church bells rung,
> And never come again.
>
> Let my grave be overgrown
> With prickly weeds.
> – After all, you won't find me
> In this somber churchyard.

> Only, at the dining-room window,
> In the night's oppressive silence,
> Let a meager memory of me
> Be quiet and severe. (1939)[21]

By dismissing the mourner from her gravesite, Knorring appears to negate the poet's aspiration to be memorialized, most famously expressed in the Russian tradition by Aleksandr Pushkin's lines "I have raised to myself a wondrous monument, / The people's path to it will never be overgrown" ("Ia pamiatnik sebe vozdvig nerukotvornyi, / K nemu ne zarastet narodnaia tropa, . . ." 1836). But she actually represents a change of venue, from the cemetery to her dining-room: she will be remembered in the home, representing the inescapably private fate of the émigré poet. Knorring also departs from tradition by omitting any mention of poetry as vehicle of the poet's immortality. In fact, throughout her poetry, she represents her poems as no more vital than herself ("my unanimated verse" ["moi nezhivye stikhi"]). But the final stanza of "Wind my cross, . . ." acknowledges that she has created a space for remembrance through writing: memory's place at the dining-room window is the very spot from which her lyric persona speaks in poem after poem. What seems like a modest request ("a meager memory") is a demand that we "put ourselves in her place" when we read her poetry.

Knorring so effectively personified the "helplessly sick" that interesting moments of anger and defiance in her poetry are obscured. In her love poetry, for example, the speaker often appears far from long-suffering, and she wrote some forceful poems on the arrogance of male poets in her circle, including her husband Iurii Bek-Sofiev. Vera Bulich was another poet whose embrace of a conventional female persona was "troubled rather than quiescent," as Catriona Kelly has phrased it in her analysis of Bulich's poetry.[22] Bulich spent all her émigré years in Helsinki, but her view of poetry as a sincere document of personal experience unites her with the Paris Note poets, and, like Knorring, she speaks from a consciously marginal position. Raisa Blokh, who spent most of her writing career in Berlin, was yet another poet of female suffering. Her modest persona speaks of self-erasure in language that has both Christian and pantheistic overtones: "And I have lived on this earth only / To be nothing and to merge with everything" ("I ved'tol'ko zatem na zemle zhila ia, / Chtob nichem ne byt' i vo vsem proiti"). (Blokh was a medieval scholar and a translator of Christian mystical poetry.)

This attitude of humility is occasionally complicated by a note of childlike impatience ("Send me a very simple golden earthly happiness / Or let me fall back asleep" ["Ty poshli mne sovsem prostoe / Zolotoe schast'e zemnoe, / Ili dai mne usnut' opiat'"]), and by veiled references to her Jewish background, which Blokh was forced to confront by the rise of Nazism.[23] A poet whose persona explicitly conforms to a Christian ideal of self-sacrifice, and whose poetry was associated with the Paris Note, was Elizaveta Skobtsova (Kuz'mina-Karavaeva), who published as Mat' Mariia after taking her monastic vows in 1932.[24]

A different strain in émigrée poetry is represented by the work of Sofia Pregel, Galina Kuznetsova, and Ekaterina Tauber, who belonged to the Parisian literary establishment: Pregel was a leader in publishing and writers' organizations; Kuznetsova was the protégée of Nobel Prize-winner Ivan Bunin and lived at his homes in Paris and Grasse; Tauber, who lived first in Belgrade and then in the South of France, was a member of Khodasevich's literary circle "Perekrestok" ("Crossroad"). Although their thematics and poetic style are Akhmatovan, their poetry is less confessional than that of the Paris Note poets and more given to description. At least at the beginning of their careers, the poetic impulse arises from the desire to capture images from the Ukrainian childhood they happened to share, images that are vivid and pleasing. The different tonality of their verse is conveyed in part by frequent reference, literal and metaphoric, to sunlight. Of the three poets, Pregel focuses most on social *byt* (daily life), rendering scenes from southern urban life; some of her most evocative poems concern her Jewish family milieu, to which she devoted a separate section of her first book, *Razgovor s pamiat'iu* (A Conversation with Memory, 1935). The pleasure with which she describes Ukrainian shops and meals led several reviewers to compare her to the Flemish painters. Pregel also displays appealing self-irony, as when she imagines that, absorbed in her remembrances, she must seem mad to passers-by. Kuznetsova's *Olivkovyi sad* (Olive Garden, 1937), her only book of poetry, opens with recollections of the Ukrainian landscape, which glimmers through her current surroundings in the South of France. Her sensual renderings of these two southern climes are interwoven with a metaphysical argument that develops around the biblical image of the garden.[25] Tauber also employs southern European landscapes as palimpsests of her native Ukraine, landscapes that are suffused with Christian spirituality: "The evangelical and Provençal / Landscape was all around . . ." ("Evangel'skii i provansal'skii / Povsiudu peizazh obstupal . . .")

The only émigrée poet who departed entirely from Akhmatova's example was Anna Prismanova. Prismanova was a "Parisian" poet only in the sense that she was, along with her husband the poet Aleksandr Ginger, an enduring presence on the capital's literary scene from its inception in the mid-1920s. She belonged to a minority of writers in Paris, Tsvetaeva among them, who admired the work of the Russian and Soviet avant-garde and adopted elements of their style. Though Prismanova's prosody is extremely conventional, other aspects of her poetics bespeak the influence of Pasternak and Mayakovsky. Her playful sound orchestration, for example, is reminiscent of early Pasternak: "Sweetie, my soul, you're / not coddled by cotillions" ("Dushen'ka, moia dusha, ty / ne balovana balami"). She also shared the Futurists' penchant for peculiar and highly elaborated visual imagery: "Eggs are two-faced, in their brittle swaddling / nursing the origin of sun and moon" ("Dvuliki iaitsa, v khrupkoi pelene / leleia solntsa i luny nachalo"). Prismanova was no less daring in representing her own lyric persona, who is variously compared to a fish, a snail, and a scuba-diver. Like Mayakovsky, she often describes a deformed lyric self in raw anatomical detail ("bone and blood"; "windpipe and esophagus"). Prismanova's distorted self-representation has an analogue in her practice of cutting up or defacing photographs of herself and could be viewed as an assertion of authorial control over the shaping of her own image (a right one reviewer challenged by lamenting the absence of a portrait in her collected works).[26]

Prismanova, however, had no illusions about autonomous selfhood; her poetry is an ongoing, ambivalent reflection on legacies, on family legacies, in particular. As she suggests in a famous poem about the Brontë sisters ("Sestry Brontë")[27], her "deformities" are inherited: "The sins of the past generation live on: / The children's flaws go back to their fathers" ("Zhivut grekhi bylogo pokoleniia: / porok detei voskhodit k ikh ottsam"). The poem openly refers to her father's medical vocation, juxtaposing him with the Brontës' father, a pastor. In fact, there are striking parallels between the two families, each of which had three (surviving) daughters, one named Anna, who lost their mother to cancer at a very young age. Prismanova's work includes several graphic descriptions of her mother's throat cancer, in particular, her poem "Gorlo" ("The Throat"), which features a metal feeding tube. Her damaged mother is more subtly evoked in poems like "Kameia" ("Cameo"), in which the speaker's soul is as "one-sided" ("odnobokaia") as the image on her mother's cameo – an image which is also cut off at the throat, as it were. The poem speaks of permanent confinement within the cameo frame, suggesting a paralyzing identification with the mother, one that dictates "muteness" ("nemota"). In other poems, Prismanova's lyric speaker similarly identifies with a second female forebear, a grandmother who went mad ("Babushka," ["Grandmother"]). She often speaks of losing her mind, and an excellent longer poem, "Zheltyi dom" ("The Loony Bin," 1947), renders childhood impressions of the local insane asylum. Interestingly, the child acquires a female identity in the course of the poem, appearing first as a neuter "rebenok" and "ditia," to finally become a feminine "devochka." Like Tsvetaeva, then, who also lost her mother at an early age, Prismanova explores her own psychological formation with sensitivity to gender, particularly as it bears upon her poetic vocation.

Some of Prismanova's best poetry also concerns Russian cultural legacies. Catriona Kelly has discussed how in her cycle *Pesok* (Sand), which describes her childhood town of Libau, Latvia, Prismanova depicts a site that was virtually unrepresented in Russian culture.[28] Yet Prismanova also freely appealed to Russian Christian mythology, despite her Jewish origins. (She altered her family name "Prisman" to the Slavic "Prismanova.") Christian imagery often appears in her representations of the poet, as when she speaks of poets as "zealots of the writing trade" ("podvizhniki slovesnogo truda"). The poet-martyr is the subject of her final book of verse, a lengthy "lyrical story" ("liricheskaia povest'") entitled "Vera" ("Faith," 1960). The book concerns the sufferings and attainment (*podvig*) of Vera Figner, the nineteenth-century Russian radical who was imprisoned for twenty years in the Schlusselburg fortress. The introductory poem clarifies Prismanova's purpose in choosing what was, for an émigré writer, an unusual subject: "Will I succeed in confessing / my primary sin to the pen? ("V svoem osnovnom pregreshenii / uspeiu l' priznat'sia k peru?"). The sin she hopes to expiate is the sin of the émigré, the "rat" who has deserted the "sinking ship" that is Russia. (Prismanova and Ginger applied for and received their Soviet citizenship in 1946, but decided against returning.) As she tells Figner's story, the speaker compares herself to her hero, to find that she crucially lacks Figner's willpower ("sila voli"). However, she is able to reconceive her sin as the discovery of a new kind of wisdom gained in emigration:

> I have lived a quarter century abroad
> and learned in these foreign lands
> to seek the simply human in a hero,
> Leaving the heroic to one side.[29]

Prismanova thus brings herself to relinquish a Russian cultural model she deeply honors – a striking gesture in the context of an émigré culture that generally sought to preserve rather than question the prerevolutionary heritage.

Another distinctive voice in the Parisian context was that of Alla Golovina, a graduate of the so-called Prague School headed by the literary scholar Alfred Bem. Bem, like Khodasevich, viewed poetry as artifact rather than document, but was more oriented toward avant-garde poetics. (Tsvetaeva was an important presence in this circle during her years in Prague.) The work of the young Prague poets – whose female representatives, along with Golovina, were Emiliia Chegrintseva and Tat'iana Klimenko-Ratgauz – featured greater formal variety and freedom of invention than the poetry of their Parisian colleagues. The fanciful element is especially pronounced in Golovina's work, as the title of her *Lebedinaia karusel'* (Swan's Carousel, 1935) suggests. In a characteristic poem, "V gorodskie sady vosvrashchaiutsia ptitsy" ("Birds are returning to the city gardens," 1930), the lyric persona undergoes a springtime, night-time transformation that is rendered with charming actuality:

> Tonight I feel no weakness behind my shoulders:
> People and angels stroll along the same bridge, –
> I clumsily tangle wings with oncomers,
> Like a girl in a crowd with her first umbrella.[30]

Elsewhere in the poem, Golovina displays a Pasternakian liking for foreign terms ("kaktus," "makintosh," "parashut," "linolium") and uses them to the same whimsical effect. In general, her voice has a quality of wonderment that is rare among the émigrée poets.

Golovina is representative, however, in having written short stories as well as lyrics. Kuznetsova started her publishing career with a collection of stories, while Tauber, Bulich, and Chervinskaia published a number of uncollected stories in émigré periodicals. In general, the genre of the short story was well represented among émigrée writers, perhaps influenced by the older generation writer Nadezhda Teffi. Teffi's humorous satires of social *byt* had been hugely popular in prerevolutionary Russia, and her depictions of hapless émigrés were equally so in Russian Paris: the title of her story "Ke fer?" ("Que faire?"), which appeared in the first issue of the main Russian newspaper, *Poslednie novosti* (The Latest News), became the catchword of the Russian emigration. Berberova published her first stories, about the milieu of Russian workers at the Renault factory, as a reporter for *The Latest News*; her literary reputation rests on her work in the genre.[31] Avgusta Damanskaia published a well-received collection of stories, *Zheny* (Wives, 1929), depicting the experience of émigrée women. Most interesting is the work of Elena Deisha, who focused exclusively on the genre. Like the writers previously mentioned, her stories are largely based on the realia of émigré life, which she casts, however, in a fantastic-realist mode in the tradition of Gogol and Dostoevsky.

Emigrée writers also produced a number of novels, again usually drawing upon émigré *byt*: Berberova, Odoevtseva, Kuznetsova, Gorodetskaia, Teffi, and even Mat' Mariia all tried their hands at the genre. Irina Saburova wrote novels in a variety of modes (historical, anti-utopian), in addition to the fairy-tale novellas that were her trademark. Generally speaking, novels by women were not as well received as their short fiction and poetry. However, Shakhovskaia and Elsa Triolet wrote novels in French that were highly regarded in their host country: Shakhovskaia received the Prix de Paris for *Europe et Valèrius* (1949), while Triolet won the Prix Goncourt in 1945 for *Le premier accroc coute deux cents francs* (c. 1945). (Triolet published seventeen French novels.) They were the only younger generation émigrée writers to achieve reputations outside the émigré community, belatedly joined by Berberova when her stories began to appear in French and English translation during the 1980s.

The younger generation émigrées did not match the creative achievements of their elders, Tsvetaeva and Gippius. However, they made essential contributions to émigré culture between the wars, participating in literary life on a scale and to a degree perhaps unprecedented in Russian history. Pregel, Berberova, and Shakhovskaia all served as editors of important émigré journals. Bulich, Chervinskaia, Tauber, Odoevtseva, Shakhovskaia, and Berberova wrote reviews for major periodicals. Shakhovskaia and Berberova also published book-length critical studies and biographies. (Berberova wrote a popular biography of Tchaikovsky that was the first to mention his homosexuality.) In the area of scholarship, Blokh made contributions to medieval studies, and Shakhovskaia won the Prix Therouanne de l'Academie Française for her books on "daily life" in historical Moscow and Petersburg. Most of the writers mentioned above translated prose and poetry, mainly between French and Russian; Avgusta Damanskaia deserves special recognition as the author of some fifty-four volumes of translations. Finally, women authored some of the most important émigré memoirs: Kuznetsova's *Grasskii dnevnik* (Grasse Diary, 1967), Pregel's *Moe detstvo* (My Childhood, 1973–4), Odoevtseva's

Na beregakh Nevy (On the Banks of the Neva, 1967) and *Na beregakh Seny* (On the Banks of the Seine, 1978–81), and Berberova's controversial *The Italics are Mine* (1967). One may expect that, as twentieth-century Russian literature is remapped after the end of Soviet rule, these writers' contributions will become more visible.

NOTES

1. Marc Raeff, *Russia Abroad: A Cultural History of the Russian Emigration, 1919–1939* (Oxford, 1990).

2. Shari Benstock, *Women of the Left Bank. Paris, 1900–1940* (Austin, TX, 1986).

3. Nina Berberova, *Kursiv moi*, vol. 2 (2nd edn, New York, 1983), 469–70.

4. "Podruga" ("The Girlfriend," 1914–15).

5. Berberova, *Kursiv moi*, vol. I, 282.

6. Jenifer Presto, "The Fashioning of Zinaida Gippius," *SEEJ* 1 (Spring, 1998), 58–75.

7. Anton Krainii (Zinaida Gippius), "O 'Verstakh' i o prochem," *Poslednie novosti*, no. 1970 (August 14, 1926), 2–3.

8. Alla Golovina's admiration for Tsvetaeva's prose, as well as her poetry, has been attested by Irina Sokolova in Alla Golovina, *Villa "Nadezhda"* (Moscow, 1992), 357.

9. Mark Slonim, "O Marine Tsvetaevoi" in L. A. Mnukhin and L. M. Turchinskii (eds.), *Vospominaniia o Marine Tsvetaevoi* (Moscow, 1992), 337.

10. Iurii Terapiano, *Literaturnaia zhizn' russkogo Parizha za polveka* (Paris and New York, 1987), 170.

11. "Valiuta" is the Russian term for foreign currency.

12. This and all subsequent translations are the author's. Здесь, меж вами: домами, деньгами, дымами, / Дамами, Думами, / Не слюбившиь с вами, не сбившись с вами, / Неким —/ Шуманом пронося под полой весну: / Выше! из виду! / Соловьиным тремоло на весу — / Некий — избранный. // Боязливейший, ибо взяв на дыб —/ Ноги лижете! / Заблудившийся между грыж и глыб / Бог в блудилище. //Лишний! Вышний! Выходец! Вызов! Ввысь / Не отвыкший . . . Виселиц / Не принявший . . . В рвани валют и виз / Веги — выходец.

13. Marina Tsvetaeva, "O knige N. P. Gronskogo 'Stikhi i poemy'," *SS*, vol. v (Moscow, 1994), 461.

14. И если здесь я средь других — / Я не в изгнанье, я в посланье, / И вовсе не было изгнанья, / Падений не было моих!

15. Одиночество, царственна поступь твоя, / Непокорность, высок твой безжалостный голос!

16. Gleb Struve, *Russkaia literatura v izgnanii* (New York, 1956; repr. Moscow, 1996), 142.

17. Vladislav Khodasevich, *Koleblemyi trenozhnik. Izbrannoe* (Moscow, 1991), 578.

18. Ekaterina Bakunina, "Dlia kogo i dlia chego pisat'," *Chisla* 6 (1932), 255.

19. Undated.

20. Anna Akhmatova, *SS*, vol. II (Moscow, 1986), 217.

21. Обвей мой крест плющем зеленым, / Чертой могилу обведи. / И — все. Ни жалости, ни стона. / Не поминай церковным звоном, / И никогда не приходи.// Пусть зарастет моя могила / Колючей сорною травой. / — Ведь ты на кладбище унылом / Уже не встретишься со мной. // И только у окна в столовой, / В ночной, томящей тишине, / Пусть будет тихой и суровой / Скупая память обо мне.

22. Kelly *History*, 321.

23. See her letters in T. P. Voronova, "Raisa Blokh — russkaia poetessa i istorik zapadnogo srednevekov'ia (iz perepiski s O. A. Dobiash-Rozhdestvenskoi)," *Problemy istochnikovedcheskogo izucheniia istorii russkoi i sovetskoi literatury* (Leningrad, 1989), 54–85.

24. See Catriona Kelly, "Writing an Orthodox Text: Religious Poetry by Russian Women, 1917–1940," in Joe Andrew (ed.), *Poetics of the Text* (Amsterdam, 1992), 153–70; and her *History*, 280–1.

25. See Marina Ledkovsky, "Paradise Lost to Paradise Regained: Galina Kuznetsova's 'Olive Orchard'," *Canadian-American Slavic Studies* 1–4 (1993), 148–56.

26. Vadim Kreid, "O sobranii sochinenii Anny Prismanovoi," *NZh* 182 (1992), 392.

27. Many of Prismanova's poems are undated.

28. Catriona Kelly, "Finding a Home: the Poetry of Anna Prismanova," manuscript. See also Kelly, "Painting and Autobiography: Anna Prismanova's *Pesok* and Anna Akhmatova's *Epicheskie motivy*," in C.K. Kelly and S. Lovell (eds.), *Russian Literature. Modernism and the Visual Arts* (Cambridge, 2000), 58–87.

29. Живу я на чужбине четверть века / и научилось в этой стороне / искать в герое просто человека, /геройское оставив в стороне.

30. В эту ночь за плечами не чую бессилья: / Ходят люди и ангелы общим мостом,—/ С непривычки сцепляю со встречными крылья, / Как на улице девочка первым зонтом.

31. "Billancourt Holidays" (Biiankurskie prazdniki) appeared serially from 1928 to 1940 in *The Latest News*. The stories were reprinted as a group in *Oktiabr'* 11 (1989) and *IzbS*, 2 vols. (Moscow, 1997).

7

Women in Russian Symbolism: beyond the algebra of love

Introduction: on signs, functions, and celebrated equations

"The wife of [Aleksandr Aleksandrovich Blok] and suddenly . . . !" they knew what I should be like, because they knew what "function" I was equal to in the equation of the poet and his wife. But I was not a "function." I was a human being, and I myself often didn't know what I was equal to, let alone what was equal to the "wife of a poet" in the celebrated equation. It was often the case that I was equal to nothing; and thus I stopped existing as a function and went off into my own "human" existence.

LIUBOV' MENDELEEVA-BLOK, *I byl', i nebylitsy o Bloke i o sebe*
(Facts and Myths About Blok and Myself)

Many of the women who occupy a place in western histories of Russian Symbolism[1] do so not because they distinguished themselves as poets or writers in their own right, but rather because they fulfilled important "functions" in the "celebrated equations" of male poets.[2] To be sure, most students of Russian literature can without much difficulty elaborate on the ways in which Liubov' Mendeleeva-Blok and Lydiia Zinov'eva-Annibal fulfilled the "wife-function" and "muse-function" for Aleksandr Blok and Viacheslav Ivanov respectively or even how Nina Petrovskaia fulfilled the "muse-function" for Valerii Briusov and Andrei Belyi, but they are much less likely to be familiar with the memoirs, plays, poetry, and short stories of these women. The notable exception to this rule is the poet Zinaida Gippius, whose literary accomplishments have not been overshadowed by her marriage to the Symbolist poet and theoretician Dmitrii Merezhkovskii. I would suggest that the tendency for the "wife-" and "muse-function" of the vast majority of women in Symbolism to supersede what Michel Foucault would refer to as the "author-function"[3] was, to a great extent, conditioned by the philosophical underpinnings and aesthetic practices of Russian Symbolism itself. And before I turn to a discussion of Symbolist women writers, I will examine the ways in which some of the major practitioners of Russian Symbolism fostered mythologies of women which de-emphasized their role as artists and creators.

The Russian Symbolist movement, which began around the turn of the century and lasted until approximately 1910, was influenced not only by French Symbolist poetry and continental philosophy, but also by the writings of the nineteenth-century Russian religious philosopher and poet, Vladimir Solov'ev. It was, in part, due to Solov'ev's writings on the Divine Sophia that women in Symbolist circles were frequently positioned as muse, rather than as writing subject. Solov'ev envisioned the divine feminine principle of Sophia as a necessary catalyst in the movement of human history and as a mediatrix between the cosmic and earthly realms. In his lyrics, Solov'ev typically positions his poetic persona as a passive figure who is visited by the figure of Sophia. Though the figure of Sophia is presented as all-powerful and is often conflated with the Woman Clothed in the Sun from the Apocalypse, it is ultimately the role of the male lyrical persona to make sense of her appearance and to interpret the meaning of the signs she reveals to him.

Under the influence of Solov'ev's sophiology, many Russian Symbolist poets were inclined toward envisioning their amorous interests as intimations of the Divine Sophia caught in the liminal zone between the earthly and the divine. Perhaps the most notable example of this phenomenon involved the poet Aleksandr Blok and his wife, Liubov' Mendeleeva-Blok, daughter of Dmitrii Mendeleev, founder of the periodic table of elements. Blok not only conflated his wife Liubov', whose first name means "love" in Russian, with the figure of the Beautiful Lady (*Prekrasnaia Dama*) of his early poetry, but Blok's contemporaries, Belyi and Sergei Solov'ev, viewed Liubov' as the earthly embodiment of the Beautiful Lady of Blok's poetry and made her the subject of cult adoration. The manner in which Belyi and Solov'ev responded to Blok's wife owed much to the way in which Blok's own poetic persona positioned himself vis-à-vis his all-powerful muse in his early lyrics. Similar to the way in which Blok's poetic persona in his *Stikhi o Prekrasnoi Dame* (Verses about the Beautiful Lady, 1901–2) attempts to interpret the signs of the arrival of the androgynous figure of the Eternal Feminine, Blok's contemporaries attempted to interpret the signs and gestures of Liubov' Dmitrievna in her daily life. As Blok's aunt and first biographer, Mariia Beketova, indicates:

> They gave Lyubov' Dmitrievna positively no peace, drawing mystic
> conclusions and generalizations from her every gesture, movement,
> the way she happened to have done her hair. It was enough for her to
> have put on a bright ribbon, sometimes even to gesticulate with her
> hand, and the "Blokites" would exchange significant glances and
> pronounce portentous conclusions.[4]

This obsession with reading the signs of the woman-muse and
attempting to reconstruct them into a comprehensive narrative was not
limited to Aleksandr Blok and his circle but was endemic to the Symbolist movement as a whole. Though Vladimir Solov'ev has generally been
considered to have had a greater influence on second generation Symbolists, including Blok, Belyi and Ivanov, his legacy can be seen in the
writings of the Decadent or first-generation Symbolist, Valerii Briusov as
well. For example, in his occult novel, *Ognennyi angel* (The Fiery Angel,
1907–8), which was based on his tumultuous triangular relationship with
the writers Nina Petrovskaia and Andrei Belyi, Briusov implicitly adheres
to a mode of reading the feminine that is vaguely similar to that of Blok
and Solov'ev. The novel, set in Germany against the background of the
Reformation, is narrated by a soldier of fortune named Ruprecht, who
upon returning to Germany from the New World meets a hysterical witch
by the name of Renata, whom he attempts to save from her visitations by
a fiery angel. By depicting the feminine as a hysterical figure whose bodily signs are open to interpretation and speculation by the first-person
male narrator, Briusov implicitly imagines the feminine as a "dark continent," whose geography must be mapped by the male narrator and
thereby espouses a type of reading of woman not unlike that of Blok and
his contemporaries. Though Blok and company may have interpreted the
gestures and signs of Liubov' Dmitrievna as a symbol of the arrival of the
Eternal Feminine (or the Woman Clothed in the Sun from the Apocalypse), rather than the demonic fiery angel as in the case of Briusov, they
all viewed women as a series of signs or signifiers that await interpretation by the male writer.

This tendency to envision women as a sign of an impending historical narrative or as a "function" in a mystical equation need not continue
to guide the way in which we read women in Russian Symbolism. By
allowing ourselves to adhere too closely to the philosophical tenets of
Russian Symbolism, we are likely not only to overlook women such as
Poliksena Solov'eva (Allegro) who did not serve as wife or muse for one of
the male Symbolists, but also to overgeneralize their role as sign, rather

than as purveyor of signs. The latter tendency is particularly true in the case of the prose writer Nina Petrovskaia, whose literary reputation has been confined largely to that of muse or plot-function in Briusov's novel, thanks in part to Vladislav Khodasevich's essay on the Symbolist method, "Konets Renaty" ("The End of Renata," 1928).[5] While Khodasevich makes a convincing case for the fact that Petrovskaia identified too closely with the figure of Renata and allowed her life to become emplotted within Briusov's novel in the final years of her life, Joan Delaney Grossman has recently argued that Petrovskaia's relationship to Briusov and his literary creation may not have been as slavish as Khodasevich implies.[6] Drawing on Petrovskaia's own writings, Grossman demonstrates that Petrovskaia was engaged in a complicated battle of philosophical principles with Briusov that fails to make its way into Briusov's text and that she was a creative personality in her own right.

In the brief discussion of Russian Symbolism that follows, I hope to move beyond this practice of reading women Symbolists as simply a series of signs or "functions" in the "celebrated equations" of male poets, that is to say, beyond an interpretive strategy that amounts to viewing women poets within what I would term the algebra of love. To be sure, the metaphysics of love or the "arithmetic of love" (*arifmetika liubvi*), as Zinaida Gippius referred to it in her lecture of the same title,[7] was an underlying principle in the way in which the Russian Symbolists organized their lives.[8] Nevertheless, I will focus on the role that women played as poets and writers in their own right, rather than on the role they played in the Symbolist family romances of the period. It is my contention that many of the women associated with Symbolist circles were acutely aware of this tendency to assign them the role of muse and implicitly or explicitly challenged this fact through their own self-fashioning as poets and writers. In order to demonstrate this, I will concentrate on five key figures, Mirra Lokhvitskaia, Poliksena Solov'eva (Allegro), Zinaida Gippius, Lydiia Zinov'eva-Annibal, and Elizaveta Dmitrieva (Cherubina de Gabriak), who employed different strategies to negotiate a space for themselves as writing subjects.

From sign to purveyor of signs: muse into poet

A transitional figure, Mirra (Mariia) Lokhvitskaia was probably the most popular female poet in her day as well as one of the most interesting in terms of how she forged her poetic identity. Hailed by critics as "the

Russian Sappho" for her status as prominent female poet, rather than her sexual orientation, she was awarded the prestigious Pushkin prize twice, including once posthumously. While Lokhvitskaia was not officially a member of any Symbolist circles, she was involved with the Symbolist poet Konstantin Bal'mont, with whom she shared a Decadent interest in exoticism and ecstatic "moments" or *migi*. Lokhvitskaia wrote lyrics on highly religious and meditative themes, as well as on the distinctly un-Symbolist theme of the experience of motherhood (most of the women in Symbolist circles, like their male counterparts, were virulently anti-procreative). Lokhvitskaia, though, is probably best known for her love lyrics which were unabashedly passionate, sensuous, and feminine and were often tinged with biblical and eastern symbolism. In her self-presentation, Lokhvitskaia called attention to her exotic and passionate nature, opting to employ the name "Mirra," which is a homograph for the Russian word "myrrh" (*mirra*).[9] In poems such as "Poludennye chary" ("Southern Charms," 1896), Lokhvitskaia describes an exotic setting filled with myrrh, thereby inscribing herself within the poem as a scent and calling attention to the eastern and sensual nature of her poetry.

Lokhvitskaia's decision to present herself within her poetry in an ultra-feminine manner distinguishes her from many of the other prominent female poets of the time. Whereas female Symbolist poets such as Poliksena Solov'eva (Allegro) and Zinaida Gippius often employed a masculine poetic persona in their lyrics, Lokhvitskaia employed a feminine persona in her poems and called attention to the femininity of her poetic persona through direct references to her persona's feminine appearance and even her body. For instance, in her early poem, "Pesn' liubvi," ("The Song of Love," 1889), Lokhvitskaia effaces the boundaries between the female poet and her song, expressing the desire in the poem's central stanza to contain a lyre within her chest so as to transform her feelings directly into song:

> I would like to have a lyre
> In my chest, so that the tender, young feelings
> Would begin to sound like songs,
> But . . . my heart strings would burst.[10]

Lokhvitskaia fantasizes here not just about assuming, but about subsuming the lyre and transforming her heart into an unmediated organ of her song. In expressing the desire to metamorphose the self literally into an instrument of song, she expresses the dream to enact an identity between poetic voice and female body that would later become central to French feminist theories of *écriture féminine* or writing the female body.

The corporeal, passionate and seemingly unlimited economy of desire of Lokhvitskaia's love lyrics differs sharply from the otherworldly, restrained, and sublimated love lyrics of later Symbolist poets such as Gippius and perhaps can only be matched in tone by the "boundless" (*bezbrezhnye*) lyrics of the young Konstantin Bal'mont, who frequently envisioned himself as conqueror of the sunny realm of the New World. There is an almost hedonistic quality to some of Lokhvitskaia's love lyrics, which puts her closer to the camp of the Decadents than of the Symbolists. Sensory and tactile images of flowers, sparkling stones, diaphanous fabrics, and perfumes typically occupy a central place in her love poetry as do sultry, exotic settings; and in this Lokhvitskaia's verse reflects a pre-occupation with *orientalia* that can be found among many Russian artists and writers of the *fin de siècle*, including such figures as Leon Bakst and Valerii Briusov.

Orientalism and exoticism, in fact, do not simply provide the setting of some of Lokhvitskaia's lyrics, but become a crucial facet of her self-fashioning as a female poet. In her programmatic poem, "Ia ne znaiu, zachem uprekaiut menia" ("I don't know why they reproach me"), which appeared in her second volume of verse (1898) and was ostensibly addressed to her critics and detractors, Lokhvitskaia self-consciously positions herself as a queen (*tsaritsa*), whose fieriness incites the ire of her staid contemporaries:

> I don't know why they reproach me,
> Because there is too much fire in my creations,
> Because I move right toward a living light
> And I do not want to heed the slander of languor.
>
> Because I sparkle like a princess in elegant verses,
> With a diadem in my luxurious tresses,
> Because I weave myself a necklace of rhymes,
> Because I sing of love and of beauty.
>
> But I will not buy my immortality with my death,
> And for songs I love sonorous songs.
> And my burning, feminine verse will not betray
> The madness of my worthless reveries.[11]

Here through the defiant act of attacking her detractors, Lokhvitskaia's poetic persona is dressed in the garments of poetry and transformed simultaneously into both the muse and the maker of her own poem. By calling attention to her poetic persona's diadem, necklaces, and luxurious tresses, Lokhvitskaia would appear to evoke the biblical figure of Salomé, who is depicted as bejeweled and veiled in the paintings of the French Symbolist painter Gustave Moreau as well as in the poem "Hérodiade" by the French Symbolist poet Stéphane Mallarmé. However, unlike the icy, virginal figure of Salomé that appears in Mallarmé's poem and serves as a figure for Mallarmé's poetics of restraint and even impotence, Lokhvitskaia's poetic persona "sparkles," embodying the very sensuous nature of her "burning, feminine verse." While imagining her poetic persona as a *femme fatale*, Lokhvitskaia manages to eschew the tragic script that is traditionally associated with such a figure, particularly in the Russian Romantic tradition, where the transgressive female is often punished. Lokhvitskaia refuses to be disciplined by her readers or to succumb to a tragic romantic ending to ensure their undying affection ("But I will not buy my immortality with my death").

Lokhvitskaia's interest in oriental themes may have had an influence on the early poetry of her sister Nadezhda Teffi (Nadezhda Lokhvitskaia) and the Soviet prose writer Marietta Shaginian, as well as on Anna Akhmatova. As is well known, Akhmatova relied heavily on eastern stereotypes in her own self-presentation, assuming the surname of her Tatar great-grandmother for her poetic signature and imagining her poetic double as elemental and pagan in her narrative poem, *U samogo moria* (By the Very Sea, 1914), and elsewhere. But perhaps even more importantly, Lokhvitskaia's tendency to envision herself both as the maker and muse of her own poem anticipates Akhmatova's lyrics, where she presents the self both as speaking subject and objectified female figure by calling attention to her attire and appearance.[12]

While Mirra Lokhvitskaia created an exotic poetic persona that might be seen as the feminine counterpart to Konstantin Bal'mont's orientalist figure of the poet-conquistador, Poliksena Solov'eva constructed a markedly different poetic self that was no less a reaction to the poetic circles with which she was associated. Sister of the poet and religious philosopher Vladimir Solov'ev, whose poetry sang the praises of the Divine Sophia, Solov'eva distinguished herself as an artist, author of children's tales, and a poet. In her poetry, she clearly resisted identification with the figure of the muse or with the Solov'evian concept of the Eternal Feminine. Solov'eva adopted the genderless poetic signature "Allegro," which bore no trace either of femininity or of a connection to the Solov'ev family, and she regularly appeared in the salon and in official portraits in menswear. In her poetry, which often takes nature for its theme, Solov'eva identified with the masculine gender (or refrained from marking the gender of her lyrical "I" altogether through the use of present tense verbal forms which are unmarked in Russian).

In addition to concealing her gender in her poetry, Poliksena Solov'eva avoided the exoticism typical of Lokhvitskaia and the so-called Bal'mont school. Whereas sultry landscapes or fanciful moonlit gardens of roses typically provided the backdrop for Lokhvitskaia's poetry, wistful fall and winter settings of the Russian North were typical subject matter for Solov'eva, who often accompanied her nature poems with her own black-and-white vignettes of pastoral scenes, reflecting the tone of her poetry in their subtlety and grace. Moreover, whereas Lokhvitskaia addressed her love poems to a real or imagined male addressee, the addressee in Solov'eva's poetry is almost always feminine, either an actual woman or a feminine embodiment of nature.

In terms of the male-female dynamic of her lyrics, Solov'eva seems to operate within the tradition of the love lyric, practiced by her brother Vladimir, where the speaking subject is posited as masculine and the addressee appears as a powerful feminine figure, be it the Divine Sophia or the feminine World Soul as expressed through nature.[13] But, if in Vladimir Solov'ev's poems this dynamic is clearly heterosexual (this in spite of the androgynous attributes of the all-powerful figure of the Eternal Feminine), in Poliksena Solov'eva's poems, as Burgin and Forrester have noted, the heterosexual nature of this same male-female dynamic is called into question, particularly when we consider that the sex of the author does not correspond with the gender of her lyrical "I."[14] Through the use of an unmarked masculine lyrical "I," she expresses desire for a feminine other, thereby transposing the traditional (male) love lyric into a masked lesbian love lyric.

Solov'eva's subtle subversion of the tradition of the love lyric is something that could be overlooked in many of her verses, where her lyrical "I" appears only as a trace (with no specified gender). Solov'eva typically makes nature scenes, rather than the lyrical "I," the focal point of her poems. In this sense, she enacts a relationship to her subject much like that of the landscape painter, who typically does not depict herself within the diegetic continuum of the nature scene, though her thoughts may influence the depiction of the events. Such a tendency toward authorial effacement can be seen in her four-line poem, "V osennem sadu" ("In the

Autumnal Garden," 1908), which ostensibly deals with the sounds of an autumn day:

> Silence reigns golden-like in the autumnal garden,
> All that's audible is linen being hammered in the pond.
> And how somewhere an apple falls with a heavy sound,
> And how someone's heart whispers quietly with my heart.[15]

Reminiscent of a *haiku* in terms of its brevity and compression, this lyric treats one discrete moment in time, where the silence of an autumnal garden is broken by three different sounds: the sound of linen being slapped against a rock, the fall of an apple, and finally the whispering of two hearts. It is only in the fourth and final line of the poem that Solov'eva interrupts this description of the sounds of nature – sounds which simultaneously evoke a quotidian country setting (with the washing of laundry) and the Garden of Eden (the garden, the falling apple) – with a description of the sounds of two lovers whispering. Significantly, these sounds are only indirectly associated with the poetic speaker at the very end of the poem, where we learn that one of the hearts in communion is that of the poetic speaker referred to only through the adjective "my" (*moi*).

What Solov'eva does in encapsulated form in her poem, "In the Autumnal Garden," can be seen in greater detail in her frequently anthologized poem, "Den' dogorel, v iznemozhen'e" ("The day burned itself out in exhaustion"). As in her shorter lyric, Solov'eva refrains from employing the first-person pronoun and disperses the thoughts and emotions of her lyric speaker throughout the nature description. The first two of the poem's three stanzas are devoted entirely to a highly eroticized description of the changes in nature as the day draws to a close:

> The day burned itself out in exhaustion,
> Panting, the wind ran through,
> Babbled away still for a moment –
> And dozed off and became numb.
>
> The misty dusk of the night embraced everything,
> And still glittering from the darkness
> The silvery apparition of the birch
> And the pale flowers of the lime.[16]

Here Solov'eva relies heavily on personification to cast nature in a highly erotic light. Exploiting the gender inherent in Russian nouns, she configures the day (*den'*) as a masculine entity, ostensibly exhausted after love-making, and the night (*noch'*) as a feminine entity, embracing everything and glittering with the silvery apparition of the birches (*berezy*) and the pale flowers of the lime (*lipa*). Though we might infer that she projects the feelings and characteristics of lovers onto these grammatically masculine and feminine natural entities, Solov'eva refrains from making this explicit in the first two stanzas.

Only in the very last stanza of the poem does Solov'eva hint at a connection between this erotic landscape and the relationship of two lovers, when she reveals the presence of the lovers' table:

> To our brightly illuminated table
> Winged throngs fly
> And a semi-burned moth
> Is enveloped in death throes.[17]

The manner in which Solov'eva constructs her poetic persona is, in some ways, similar to that of her friend and contemporary, Zinaida Gippius, a highly influential figure who distinguished herself as a poet, dramatist, novelist, short story writer, critic, and *salonière* in Petersburg and later in emigration in Paris. Gippius, whose poetry often takes religious and philosophical themes for its subject matter, strove in her own words to write "like a human being, and not just like a woman" (*kak chelovek, a ne tol'ko kak zhenshchina*).[18] Accordingly, she frequently used the unmarked masculine voice in her poetry, rather than the feminine voice typical for a female poet, and she signed her poetic works as Z. Gippius, rather than as Zinaida Gippius or Zinaida Gippius-Merezhkovskaia, which would emphasize her status as wife of the famous Symbolist poet and theoretician. In addition, she employed the male pseudonyms, Anton Krainii (Anton "The Extreme") and Tovarishch German (Comrade Herman), among others for her literary criticism. Yet while Gippius shared Solov'eva's predilection for the masculine voice in her poetry, she relished in flaunting her femininity in the salon. If at the turn of the century she sometimes appeared in the salon in menswear (as was the style not only in Russia but elsewhere in Europe and America), in later years, particularly while in emigration in Paris, she exhibited a penchant for exaggerated feminine costumes and hairstyles that, according to her contemporaries, overstepped the boundaries of good taste.

And, in creating a public persona that was distinctly at odds with her poetic persona, Gippius deviated from the typical Symbolist practice of blurring the boundaries between life and art known as *zhiznetvorchestvo* or life-creation. Unlike, for example, a poet such as Aleksandr Blok who created a seemingly seamless identity between his poetic and public personae and transformed his life into a "book" that could be read and interpreted like a literary text, she created a series of contradictory images of the self in her life and art that ultimately served to make her a virtually unreadable text. For instance, Gippius posed for a famous turn-of-the-century photograph dressed in a long flowing white gown, evoking the image of the Eternal Feminine. Yet, she also appeared at a meeting with members of the Holy Synod of the Russian Orthodox church in a seemingly modest black dress, whose pleats opened upon the slightest movement revealing light-pink fabric that created the illusion that she was nude underneath. Though after ten years of marriage she wore a single braid, which signified virginity among the peasantry, she was also known to sport a necklace that supposedly contained the wedding bands of her numerous married suitors. In all of these instances, Gippius put herself and her body on display, simultaneously inviting and defying her audience to read and understand her. In such a fashion, she may be seen as playing with and against the general tendency within Russian Symbolism to construct the feminine as a subject that must be read and interpreted by the (male) viewer.

The play with expectations that we see in her salon performances carried over into much of her poetry as well. For instance, in her second volume of poetry, published in 1909, Gippius included two poems back-to-back entitled "Ona" ("She"), both of which are dated 1905 and therefore could not be differentiated by title and date. In the first of these two poems, Gippius's masculine poetic speaker would appear to describe a female being in highly negative and corporealized terms that correspond to negative stereotypes of femininity, and it is only in the very last line of the poem that the speaker reveals that the feminine entity being described is not a woman of flesh-and-blood, but his soul (*dusha*), a feminine noun in Russian:

> In her dishonest and pathetic lowliness,
> She is, like dust, grey, like the dust of the earth.
> And I am dying from her proximity,
> From her indivisibility with me.
>
> She is scaly, she is prickly,
> She is cold, she is a snake.
> She has wounded me with her abhorrent, burning
> Elbow-shaped scales
>
> Oh, if I had felt the sharp stinger!

She is sluggish, dumb, quiet.
She is so heavy, so listless.
And there is no getting to her, she is deaf.

With her rings she, impudent,
Snuggles up to me, suffocating me
And that dead, and that black
And that awful one – my soul.[19]

Were we to limit ourselves to reading all but the last line of the poem, we might accuse Gippius of evoking all of the characteristics of the castrating woman, who is suffocating, fleshy, snake-like, and phallic. However, when we read the last line of the poem, we have to question whether Gippius is merely appropriating misogynistic male discourse or, indeed, subverting it by applying this language not to a female being, but the soul – a concept which in western metaphysics is generally configured in completely opposite terms. This subversion is further complicated, though, by the fact that Gippius evokes an implicit identification between self and soul in the poem's final stanza.

To be sure, Gippius held many views about women and femininity that could hardly be termed feminist in the modern, socially-committed sense of the word. She reportedly refused to participate in women's poetry readings or to contribute to collections of women's poetry, claiming in a personal exchange with the émigrée writer Irina Odoevtseva: "Once in Petersburg they approached me for poems for a women's salon album, and I told them: I do not form affiliations on the basis of sex!"[20] And in an essay entitled "O zhenskom pole" ("On the Female Sex"), which appeared in *Zveno* on May 7, 1923, Gippius, writing under the male pseudonym of Lev Pushchin, refuted the very categories of "women's poetry" and "women's art." Nonetheless, in the idiosyncratic way in which she appropriated feminine stereotypes in her poetry and in her life, she may be seen as operating against images of femininity fostered by many of the Russian Symbolists.

Another figure whose relationship to reigning male mythologies of women was extremely complicated was Lydiia Zinov'eva-Annibal. According to the reports of her contemporaries, she adeptly played the role of wife of the poet, serving as the "soul and psyche" of Viacheslav Ivanov's Wednesday meetings at the Tower, their Petersburg apartment.[21] Clad in garlands and Greek chlamyses, she would often lead their guests in ring dances and bacchanalian songs, indulging Ivanov's fascination with Dionysian ritual. Though best known for her salon theatrics,

Zinov'eva-Annibal distinguished herself as a writer of considerable note, composing poetry, several plays, short stories, a draft of a novel, and the fictionalized childhood memoirs, *Tragicheskii zverinets* (The Tragic Menagerie), which received rave reviews from her contemporaries upon their publication in 1907 and have since attracted considerable critical attention in the West.[22] Until only very recently, though, her literary reputation in the West has rested almost entirely on her novella, *Tridtsad'-tri uroda*, (Thirty-Three Abominations, 1907), which in its day enjoyed something of a *succès de scandale* with its sensationalized depiction of lesbian love and its cult of the female body. Though this work has been critiqued for the stereotypical ways in which it represents female same-sex love,[23] the novella does more than offer a titillating representation of female sexuality that appeals to male voyeuristic pleasure: it also addresses the problem of female subjectivity in very compelling ways.

Framed as a diary, *Thirty-Three Abominations* focuses on the highly eroticized relationship between the unnamed female narrator, an aspiring actress, and her older lover, a famous actress named Vera. The relationship between these two women is by no means idyllic and is, from the very onset, fraught with the specter of infidelity and romantic rivalry. In fact, as the narrator recalls, her love affair with Vera began on the eve of her wedding, when Vera burst into the loge where she and her betrothed, who happened to be Vera's former lover, were sitting and whisked her off behind the scenes of the theater. Although the narrator's fiancé commits suicide, effectively dissolving the love triangle, the women's relationship is not fated to remain free of the intrusion of men. Eventually Vera disturbs the course of their love affair, which is repeatedly described as an essentially narcissistic relationship where the narrator is reflected in the eyes of her beloved, when she encourages the narrator to pose nude for a society of thirty-three male artists. It is at this point that the narrator's vision of the self as a specular opposite of her female lover is disrupted, precipitating a sense of loss of identity. As the narrator gazes on the thirty-three portraits of herself composed by the thirty-three artists, referred to ironically as her "lovers," she wonders:

> Me? Is this me? Is it really me whom both Vera and I loved?
> This one and this one and this one? . . .
> I ran from one canvas to another, through the entire studio.
> In all directions as they sat around me, painting, I saw myself.
> Or did I not recognize myself from the back? From the side?
> In a three-quarter view, or a quarter.

And directly in front . . . did I not recognize myself?
These are of someone else. They are not ours.
Someone else's, someone else's. Simply someone else's.
This was not our beauty, not that which Vera owned.
Thirty-three abominations. Thirty-three abominations.
And they were all me. And not all me.[24]

By presenting the renderings of the male artists as unfaithful repro-
ductions of female beauty, Zinov'eva-Annibal turns to an issue that preoccupied many of the Symbolists, namely whether the feminine can ever
be incarnated in its pure and unadulterated form in this world. For instance, in his early poem, "Predchuvstvuiu Tebia. Goda prokhodiat
mimo" ("I have a foreboding of You. The years go by," 1901), Aleksandr
Blok expresses the fear that the Beautiful Lady will betray his image of
her when she finally appears to him; his poetic speaker in the poem
repeatedly laments: "But it is terrible to me: You will alter Your appearance" (*No strashno mne: izmenish' oblik Ty*).[25] But if Blok is concerned with
the way in which the Eternal Feminine might manifest herself in a manner that is unfaithful to the *poet's* image of her (something that would be
borne out in his later poem "Neznakomka" ["The Stranger," 1906], where
she makes her appearance in the guise of a prostitute), Zinov'eva-Annibal
is concerned with the ways in which the *woman's* image of herself may be
betrayed by the male artist. (It bears noting, though, that Zinov'eva-
Annibal acknowledges that women may be complicit in this process: she
clearly implicates Vera, whose name ironically means "faith" in Russian,
in being untrue to the nameless female narrator by encouraging her to
give herself over to the male artists.)

Indeed, many of the women writers in Symbolist circles felt compelled
to respond to the reigning cult of female beauty either directly in their
works or indirectly through their self-presentation. This was particularly
the case for the writer Elizaveta Dmitrieva, who was immortalized on the
pages of *Apollon* as "Cherubina de Gabriak" in 1909 and 1910, the same
years that Anna Akhmatova began making her literary debut in Petersburg. Though a highly talented poet, Dmitrieva, a schoolteacher with a
slight limp, did not outwardly embody the ideal of feminine beauty
expected of female poets of the day and was unable to garnish the support of the editors of *Apollon*, where she regularly read her poems. However, this all changed when, under the guidance of the Symbolist poet
Maksimilian Voloshin, she fabricated the literary persona of Cherubina
de Gabriak. Under the name of Cherubina, Dmitrieva sent her poems to

Apollon via post along with tamarisk and olive leaves, initiating a highly seductive epistolary relationship that piqued the interest of the editorial board and enabled her to get her poems published.

For her poetic alter ego Dmitrieva constructed a literary biography that differed considerably from the curriculum vitae of her own life. Whereas Dmitrieva led the ordinary existence of a schoolteacher – an existence which, it should be noted, did not deter Mallarmé from being esteemed as one of the foremost French Symbolist poets, Cherubina, with her exotic-sounding Franco-Spanish surname and her Catholic inclinations, lived the kind of romantic life one reads about in novels. In a poem which appeared in *Apollon* in 1909, Dmitrieva portrays her poetic double as a medieval nun, who is consigned to live her life in isolation under the shadow of a dark force:

> They have locked the door to my abode
> With a key that is forever lost;
> And a Black Angel, my protector,
> Stands with a burning sword.
>
> But the brilliance of the crown and the purple of the throne
> Are not to be seen by my anguish,
> And on my virginal hand
> Is the unnecessary ring of Solomon.
>
> My dark gloom will not be illuminated
> By the rubies of great pride ...
> I have accepted our ancient sign –
> The sacred name of Cherubina.[26]

This poem, which bears all of the earmarks of the Gothic tale (the nun, the cell, and the Dark Angel),[27] may be read as a metaliterary commentary on the production of "Cherubina de Gabriak" with the nun guarded by the Dark Angel referring to the heavily guarded literary mask of Dmitrieva. Certainly, when the poetic speaker states in the final stanza that she will not allow her "dark gloom" to be illuminated by "great pride," we can assume that Dmitrieva refers to her decision to forego publicity to preserve the sanctity of her literary creation.

To be sure, for the members of the editorial board of *Apollon* it was the elusiveness of the poet's identity, rather than her virtuoso versification techniques (Dmitrieva imported unusual poetic forms such as the rondeau, villanelle, and rondel into her verse), that was most attractive. In his reminiscences, *Portrety sovremennikov* (Portraits of Contemporaries, 1955), Sergei Makovskii, the editor of *Apollon*, maintains:

All of the "apollonians" fell in love with her. No one doubted that she was indescribably beautiful, and positively required of me, those that were younger, that I immediately "explain" [*raz" iasnit'*] the brazen "stranger" [*neznakomka*]. It is necessary to remember that all of three or four years separated Cherubina from the heartfelt poems of Blok addressed to the "Beautiful Lady" [*Prekrasnaia Dama*]; the time was filled with romanticism.[28]

Gradually, however, the veil of Cherubina began to unravel. Suspecting that Dmitrieva and Cherubina were one and the same, Nikolai Gumilev confronted Voloshin with this idea. Voloshin responded by challenging Gumilev to a duel to preserve the "honor" of Cherubina. The true identity of Cherubina was finally revealed by Sergei Makovskii, who simply paid a visit to the woman who had been reading poetic parodies of Cherubina, Dmitrieva herself. Once unmasked, Dmitrieva vowed to stop publishing her poems under the pseudonym of Cherubina, with the exception of those that had already been accepted by the journal, signaling an end to Cherubina de Gabriak. The death of Cherubina did not, however, mark the death of the poet. Elizaveta Dmitrieva continued to write poetry and to publish children's literature until her death in 1928; however, she never attained the notoriety of her poetic alter ego.

In many ways, Cherubina de Gabriak represents an extreme example of the way in which the "muse-function" could take precedence over the "author-function" for the woman poet in Symbolism. But in spite of the overriding tendency in this period to identify the woman with the muse, this did not deter women from writing or from actively engaging in salon life. Besides the writers discussed above, there were numerous other women who made their mark in Symbolist circles, including such figures as Anastasiia Chebotarevskaia, Adelaida Gertsyk, Liubov' Stolitsa, and Liudmila Vil'kina to name just a few.[29] Some of these women openly embraced feminine images in their verses, much as Lokhvitskaia had earlier. Gertsyk, for example, envisioned her poetic self as "sister of all living things,"[30] while Stolitsa sang the praises of the maidenly world soul. Others, however, adopted the masculine voice in their poetry and polemicized with the tendency to conflate the female author with the Eternal Feminine. For many of the women Symbolists, becoming a writer was intimately connected with reconfiguring the amorous scripts of the period and resisting identification with, though not the power of, the muse. And in doing so, they paved the way for the important creative experiments of later women writers in Russian Modernism.

NOTES

1. Partly a reaction to Russian Realism, Symbolism was a complex and evolving artistic movement, taking place in Russia in the late nineteenth and early twentieth centuries. In Symbolism, writers attempted to access the world beyond through language and the reconfiguration of traditional signs.

2. This holds true for Avril Pyman's *History of Russian Symbolism* (New York, 1994) as well as Ronald E. Peterson's *History of Russian Symbolism* (Philadelphia, 1993). Paradoxically, the criticism of Inokentii Annenskii and Valerii Briusov on Russian poetry offers a much more balanced discussion of the contribution of women poets to Russian Modernism. See I. Annenskii, "O sovremennom lirizme. One," *Apollon* 3 (December 1909), 5–29 and V. Briusov, "Zhenshchiny poety," *SS*, vol. VI (Moscow, 1975), 318–23.

3. See Michel Foucault, "What Is an Author?" in David Lodge (ed.), *Modern Criticism and Theory: A Reader*, (New York, 1988), 197–210.

4. Quoted in Avril Pyman, *The Life of Aleksandr Blok*, vol. I: *The Distant Thunder 1880–1908* (New York, 1979), 170.

5. Khodasevich's focus in this essay is on the Symbolist method of blurring the boundaries between life and art known as *zhiznetvorchestvo* or "life-creation," not on the role of women within Symbolist circles. Nonetheless, I find it highly significant that he upholds the woman writer Nina Petrovskaia as the consummate example of this fatal tendency to confuse life and art, proclaiming that "more artfully and decisively than others she created 'a narrative poem out of her very life'" (*Nekropol'*. *Vospominaniia*, Paris, 1976, 9).

6. See Joan Delaney Grossman, "Valery Briusov and Nina Petrovskaia: Clashing Models of Life in Art" in Irina Paperno and Joan Delaney Grossman (eds.), *Creating Life: The Aesthetic Utopia of Russian Modernism* (Stanford, 1994), 122–50.

7. This lecture has been reprinted in *Russkii eros ili filosofiia liubvi v Rossii* (Moscow, 1991), 208–14.

8. Olga Matich has treated this phenomenon extensively in her essay, "The Symbolist Meaning of Love: Theory and Practice" in Paperno and Grossman, *Creating Life*, 24–50.

9. As N. A. Petrovskii points out in *Slovar' russkikh lichnykh imen* (Moscow, 1966), 159, the Russian name Mirra is actually derived from the Greek word *myrrine* meaning 'myrtle' (or *mirt* in Russian).

10. Хотела б лиру я иметъ / В груди, чтоб чувства — робкие, / Как песни начали звенеть, / Но . . . порвались бы сердца струны. Mirra Lokhvitskaia, *Tainykh strun sverkaiushchee pen'e: Izbrannye stikhotvoreniia* (Moscow, 1994), 30.

11. Я не знаю, зачем упрекают меня, / Что в созданьях моих слишком много огня, / что стремлюсь я навстречу живому лучу / И наветам унынья внимать не хочу. // Что блещу я царицей в нарядных стихах, / С диадемой на пышных моих волосах, / Что из рифм я себе ожерелье плету, / Что пою я любовь, что пою красоту. // Но бессмертья я смертью своей не куплю, / И для песен я звонкие песни люблю. / И безумью ничтожных мечтаний моих / Не изменит мой жгучий, мой женственный стих. *Tsaritsy muz*; 227.

12. For a discussion of the connections between the poetry of Lokhvitskaia and Akhmatova, see Christine D. Tomei's essay "Mirra Loxvickaja and Anna Axmatova: Influence in the Evolution of the Modern Female Lyric Voice" in Nina Efimov, Christine D. Tomei, and Richard Chapple (eds.), *Critical Essays on the Prose and Poetry of Modern Slavic Women* (Lewiston, NY, 1998), 135–60.

13. For an excellent discussion of the ways in which Solov'eva subverts the poetic and philosophical conventions of her brother Vladimir Solov'ev, see Nancy L. Cooper, "Secret Truths and Unheard-of Women: Poliksena Solov'eva's Fiction as Commentary on Vladimir Solov'ev's Theory of Love," *RR* 56:2 (April 1997), 178–91.

14. See Diana Lewis Burgin in her essay, "Laid Out in Lavender: Perceptions of Lesbian Love in Russian Literature and Criticism of the Silver Age, 1893–1917" in Costlow, Sandler, and Vowles, 177–203 and Sibelan Forrester in her essay, "Wooing the Other Woman: Gender in Women's Love Poetry in the Silver Age" in Chester and Forrester, 107–34.

15. Тишина золотовейна в осеннем саду, / Только слышно, как колотят белье на пруду, / Да как падает где-то яблоко звуком тугим, / Да как шепчется чье-то сердце тихо с сердцем моим. Bannikov, 212.

16. День догорел, в изнеможенье / Вздыхая, ветер пролетел, / Пролептал еще мгновенье — / И задремал и онемел. // Все обнял ночи сумрак мглистый, / И лишь блестят из темноты / Березы призрак серебристый / И липы бледные цветы. *Ibid.*, 203–4.

17. На стол наш ярко освещаный, / Толпы крылатые летят. / И мотылек полусожженный / Предсмертным трепетом объят. *Ibid.*, 204.

18. Quoted in Temira Pachmuss, *Zinaida Hippius: An Intellectual Profile* (Carbondale, IL, 1971), 17. It bears noting that this quotation would seem to imply that writing "like a woman" was incompatible with writing "like a human being." In stressing the importance of writing as a human being or *chelovek*, which is a masculine noun in Russian, Gippius would appear to identify with a universal masculine subject in her poetry.

19. В своей бессовестной и жалкой низости, / Она, как пыль, сера, как прах земной. / И умираю я от этой близости, / От неразрывности ее со мной. / Она шершавая, она колючая, / Она холодная, она змея / Меня изранила противна-жгучая / Ее коленчатая чешуя. // О, если б острое почуял жало я! / Неповоротлива, тупа, тиха. / Такая тяжкая, такая вялая, / И нет к ней доступа — она глуха. // Своими кольцами она, упорная. // Ко мне ласкается, меня душа. / И это мертвая, и эта черная, / И эта страшная — моя душа! Z. N. Gippius, *Sochineniia. Stikhotvoreniia. Proza*, ed. K. M. Azadovskii and A. V. Lavrov, (Leningrad, 1991), 140.

20. Quoted in Irina Odoevtseva, *Na beregakh Seny* (Paris, 1983), 414.

21. Quoted in Beth Holmgren, "Stepping Out/Going Under: Women in Russia's Twentieth-Century Salons" in Goscilo and Holmgren, 232.

22. See Jane Costlow's discussion in "The Gallop, the Wolf, the Caress: Eros and Nature in *The Tragic Menagerie*" in *RR*, 56:2 (April 1997), 192–208.

23. See, for example, Burgin's discussion of Zinov'eva-Annibal's novella in "Laid Out in Lavender" (182–4).

24. *Thirty-Three Abominations*, tr. Sam Cioran, in Carl Proffer and Ellendea Proffer (eds.), *The Silver Age of Russian Culture* (Ann Arbor, MI, 1975), 112.

25. Aleksandr Blok, *SS*, vol. I (Moscow, 1960), 94.

26. Замкнули дверь в мою обитель / Навек утерянным ключом: / И черный Ангел, мой хранитель, / Стоит с пылающим мечом. // Но блеск венца и пурпур трона / Не увидать моей тоске, / И на девическом руке — / Ненужный перстень Соломона. // Не осветят мой темный мрак / Великой гордости рубины . . . / Я приняла наш древный

знак— / Святое имя Черубины. Cherubina de Gabriak, *Avtobiografiia. Izbrannye stikhotvoreniia*, ed. E. Ia. Arkhipov (Moscow, 1989), 35.

27. Many of these Gothic motifs, for instance, occur in Charlotte Brontë's novel, *Villette* (1853), which is narrated by an English schoolteacher named Lucy Snowe who finds herself in the exotic surroundings of Villette. Marina Tsvetaeva briefly compares Cherubina de Gabriak with Brontë, albeit not directly with her schoolteacher heroine, in *Zhivoe o Zhivom* (A Living Word about a Living Man, 1933).

28. Sergei Makovskii, "Cherubina de Gabriak," in *Portrety sovremennikov* (New York, 1955), 339–40.

29. Due to space constraints, I am unable to go into greater detail about the accomplishments of these writers.

30. Quoted in *DRWW*, 201.

8

The eastern path of exile:
Russian women's writing in China

No one will hear your voice
in the depth of the night
Whether you cry out or not . . .[1]

MARIIA VIZI, *Noktiurn* 2
(Nocturne 2, 1970s)

Histories of Russian literature have all too often ignored the Far Eastern emigration. Part of the reason for this neglect lies in the very nature of the emigration itself. Unlike the émigré communities in Paris, Berlin, and New York where in time the Russian community gradually became integrated with the native population, the Russian émigrés in China never assimilated. Essentially they remained outsiders to the country and culture which they inhabited, living an entirely Russian life with rare instances of understanding or assimilating Chinese culture. Apart from specialists and interpreters, ordinary Russians did not learn Chinese the way émigrés learned French, Czech, or Serbo-Croatian or the other languages of Europe. Estranged from Chinese life, the émigré population was similarly cut off from émigré life in Europe. Distance and political upheavals prevented many of their literary journals and newspapers from finding their way to the West. Thus it was that the Russians living in China from 1917 through the post World War II years found themselves torn not only from the country they had left but from the European émigré communities as well, a fact which may account for why so little critical attention has until recently been paid to this chapter in Russian literary history.

Historical background

Since the Far Eastern emigration produced fewer names of note than did the Paris emigration, some historical background is in order as a way of providing the context within which several generations of Russian women were writing in China. Ironically, the first wave of émigrés who fled eastward after the Revolution, via Siberia and the Russian Far East, encountered a land which had, in part, already been settled by Russians. Since the end of the nineteenth century, the Chinese Eastern Railway (hereafter CER) built and operated by Russia in the Chinese North-East (known as Manchuria by foreigners at the time), had given rise to Russian communities of railway employees and settlers. The largest such settlement, with some 40,000 Russian subjects of varying nationalities, developed at the central railway junction of Harbin. The Russian Imperial Diplomatic Corps and the Russian Ecclesiastical Mission established themselves in Beijing, while consular officials, businessmen and some settlers lived in other cities such as Tianjin, Hankou, Qindao, and Shanghai. By the 1920s the émigrés of the first wave swelled the number of former Russian subjects in China to somewhere between 250,000 and 400,000.

Harbin, with its distinctly Russian character and way of life, was, not surprisingly, the major, and for many, a lengthy stop in the diaspora. The city welcomed all those who were deemed unsuitable in the new Soviet state and came to reflect the social, political and cultural make-up of prerevolutionary Russian society.[2] Gradually some émigrés found work on the CER or in private businesses, others set up small enterprises. Life was hard, and the Harbin press often published appeals from charities and reports of suicides. By the mid-1920s, the century's turbulent political events caught up with the Russian émigrés in their Chinese refuge. In 1924 China and the USSR signed an agreement on the joint operation of the CER. The Soviet side insisted on employees being exclusively Soviet or Chinese citizens: no émigrés. Many Harbin Russians took Soviet citizenship driven either by patriotic feelings or the need to keep their jobs. The latter became known as "kharbinskie rediski" ("Harbin radishes") – red on the outside, white inside. Some émigrés took Chinese citizenship. Over the years, Sino-Soviet relations deteriorated and led to the brief armed conflict of 1929, from which the USSR emerged victorious, only to face another enemy.

In 1931–2, Japan occupied the Chinese North-East and established its puppet state of Manchukuo. By 1935 aggressive Japanese policies forced the USSR to sell its share of the CER and pull out. The railway's Soviet employees and many former émigrés with Soviet passports went to the USSR. Others, faced with the growing Japanese domination of all spheres of life, left the disintegrating Russian cocoon of Harbin for Shanghai, Beijing, Tianjin, Qindao, Hankou, and Hong Kong.

Not all Russians could or would leave Harbin in the 1930s. Some 40–60,000 stayed in China only to endure Japanese rule, the closure of Russian institutions, strict censorship, gradual Japanization, and the harsh years of the War for Great East Asia, as Japan called its participation in World War II. By the end of the 1930s, the Japanese rulers of Manchukuo forced émigrés into one central organization, the Bureau for the Affairs of Russian Emigrés in the Manchurian Empire (Biuro po delam rossiiskikh emigrantov v Man'chzhurskoi imperii), which had been established to regulate every aspect of émigré life.

With the defeat of Japan and the victorious entry of the Red Army into North-East China in August 1945, many émigrés were arrested for true or perceived collaboration with the Japanese and for anti-Soviet activities. Prominent figures were executed, while many others received harsh sentences to labor camps. In the early 1950s, survivors either accepted a Soviet offer to be resettled on the virgin lands of the USSR or succeeded in emigrating to countries which were willing to accept them, particularly Australia, Belgium, Brazil, Chile, Paraguay, South Africa, Venezuela, and much later the USA and Canada. By the mid-1960s, the Russian émigré community in China had disappeared.

Memoirs of the emigration

Some of the most valuable testaments as to what life was like for Russians living in the Far Eastern emigration are contained within the memoirs and autobiographical novels of Russian women, many of whom had not necessarily been writers, after they left China for other countries or for the USSR.[3] The earliest recollections of life in China were presented in the novels of Nina Fedorova who settled in the US before World War II and whose semi-autobiographical novels were published first in English and much later in Russian. The first account of Russian émigré life in China to appear in the USSR was a two-volume semi-autobiographical novel, *Vozvrashchenie* (The Return), by the journalist Natal' ia Il'ina, which described the life of a patriotic émigré girl and her eventual decision to leave China for her homeland. Her viewpoint is best explained by the circumstances of the immediate postwar period. After the Soviet Union's sufferings and losses of World War II, patriotic feelings, coupled with the influence of Soviet propaganda, led a number of Russian émigrés in China to return to the Soviet Union in hope of participating in the postwar reconstruction of their homeland. Il'ina chose this path, and having returned to Stalin's Russia, it is not surprising that her portrait of most émigrés and life in emigration is extremely negative. But it became one of the few glimpses of émigré life available to Russians in the Soviet Union. Many émigrés abroad were appalled and angered by the novel. Anti-Soviet feelings were particularly strong among Russians in China, especially in Harbin where over 15,000 Russians were arrested and taken to Soviet camps. In the 1980s, in the changing climate of the late Soviet period and under the influence of liberal friends and colleagues, Il'ina published a book of memoirs, *Dorogi i sud'by* (Roads and Fates), which takes a more balanced and objective view.

A number of memoirs of Russian émigré life in China were published abroad in the 1980s, after their authors had resettled and adjusted to yet another emigration. The memoirs of Elizaveta Rachinskaia and Zinaida Zhemchuzhnaia and a fictionalized account by Ol'ga Sofonova portray Russian life in China nostalgically and poetically, yet without concealing their hardships and suffering. Rachinskaia called her impressionistic recollections a "kaleidoscope"; her detailed pictures of the Harbin epoch serve as a memorial to both her lost Russia and the Russian émigré families of Harbin. The unfinished recollections of Iustina Kruzenshtern-Peterets vividly describe her happy childhood in prerevolutionary Harbin, then her later difficulties in émigré Harbin and Shanghai, when she had to support her widowed mother and younger brother on a journalist's salary. Her recollections bring to life many significant figures of the emigration to China and portray a resilient and independent young woman with passionate convictions and a wonderful sense of humor. Nina Mokrinskaia, with endearing honesty, recollects her poverty-stricken childhood and youth in Harbin. Helen Yakobson's memoirs, unlike those mentioned above, were published in English, thus making them accessible to a broader audience. They include observations on life as a Russian émigré in the US and on her earlier life in China. The Yakobson and Mokrinskaia memoirs provide a fascinating comparison of two very different mother-daughter relationships under the strains of émigré life.

The Russian literary community in China

In the 1920s and the first half of the 1930s, Harbin was the major Russian cultural center in East Asia. Interest in literature was strong. Bookstores and libraries stocked books by prerevolutionary, émigré, and some Soviet writers, and subscribed to many Russian-language periodicals. Local newspapers and journals not only reprinted excerpts from works published in Paris, Berlin, Prague, and Belgrade and occasionally from Soviet works, but also became the forum for debates between the various intellectual factions – monarchist, anti-Soviet and even pro-Soviet – residing in Harbin at the time. Some fifty poets and prose writers published their own works both in these journals and newspapers and as separate editions.

The Russian literary community in Harbin was dominated by male writers (Aleksei Achair, Arsenii Nesmelov and Valerii Pereleshin) most of whom wrote poetry. Among them, however, were two gifted women poets – Marianna Kolosova and Mariia Vizi – whose works will be discussed later in this chapter. While poetry remained the dominant genre within the Harbin literary community, some women, along with their male colleagues N. A. Baikov, Vsevolod Ivanov, and Ia. Lovich, worked within the genre of prose fiction. Penned in the 1920s and 1930s, the novels of Rozaliia Donbrovskaia, Sofiia Zaitseva, and Elena Shchirovskaia described life in old Russia.[4] In Ol'ga Morozova's novel *Nevozvratnoe* (Unreturnable, 1932) and its lengthy sequel *Sud'ba* (Fate, 1934), the life of its Russian heroines and heroes unfolded before and during the Revolution and in Polish emigration. Several works dealt with the life of Russian émigrée women in China. Galina Morozova's *Lana* (1939) was a love story of a young Harbin girl who patriotically worked in White Russian organizations. Some of K. V. Shendrikova's works also dealt with the émigré experience. Her novel *V pautine Shankhaia* (In the Web of Shanghai, 1937) described the fates of girls, drawn by poverty into working in night clubs in Harbin and Shanghai, becoming kept women or prostitutes.

Women's literary output increased in the second half of the 1920s and 1930s as new names from the growing second generation brought to Harbin as young children started to appear on the pages of Harbin periodicals. Many of them participated in the activities of the literary circle "Molodaia Churaevka" (Young Churaevka), founded by the Harbin poet Aleksei Achair under the auspices of the Harbin branch of the YMCA. The circle provided support and encouragement to aspiring writers and became a major event on the Harbin literary scene. At its regular meet-ings, works of both émigré and Soviet writers were discussed; literary styles and techniques, particularly those of the Symbolists and Acmeists, were studied. Writers read their works and had them critiqued. While most of the gifted young poets in "Churaevka" were male – among them Valerii Pereleshin, Georgii Granin, Sergei Sergin, Nikolai Svetlov, Nikolai Shchegolev, Vladimir Slobodchikov, Petr Lapiken, and Nikolai Peterets – there were also several important women's voices among them, notably Larissa Andersen's, Lydiia Khaindrova's, and Nataliia Reznikova's.

Despite the level of talent in the "Churaevka" group, their voices, as mentioned earlier, remained muted outside their immediate literary community. While some of the writers succeeded in publishing books, funding, as in Europe, was a constant problem and print runs were small. Moreover, as Elizaveta Rachinskaia pointed out later, they were all "too young and unsure of their strength to send their work to Paris journals."[5] Their poetry was confined to various Harbin and Shanghai periodicals, as well as anthologies such as *Lestnitsa v oblaka* (Staircase to the Clouds, 1929), *Semero* (Seven, 1930), *Izluchiny* (Curves, 1935), and *Gumilevskii sbornik* (Gumilev Collection, 1937). The last volume of Russian poetry in Harbin, *Lira* (The Lyre), a joint effort of nine poets, came out in April 1945. Three months later, the Red Army invaded Manchuria and brought an end to émigré Harbin.

As more and more Russians left Harbin for other Chinese cities in the second half of the 1930s, Shanghai became the next important center of Russian cultural activity. Newly arrived writers founded literary circles such as "Shanghai Churaevka" and "Khlam," – an acronym of "Painters, Writers, Artists, Musicians" – which, with deliberately playful irony, also formed the word "rubbish" in Russian. Shanghai writers and poets pub-lished their works in a number of short-lived journals of the 1930s, such as *Parus* (The Sail), *Ponedel'nik* (Monday), *Prozhektor* (Searchlight), *Vrata* (Gates), *Segodnia* (Today), and *Feniks* (Phoenix).

Shanghai did not remain a safe refuge for very long. By 1943, many former Harbin poets, as well as Mariia Korostovets from Beijing, found themselves caught in war-time Shanghai. They formed a literary circle, "Piatnitsa" ("Friday") which, as one participant recalled, became a way of coping with the Japanese occupation, war, and the threat of death. For the next two years, they met on Fridays to read and discuss their poetry and practice their art in a poetic "exercise," modeled on a typical Chinese custom. A scrap of paper with a topic written on it would be pulled from a bowl, and at the next meeting everyone brought a poem devoted to the topic. In 1946 the results were published in a collection, *Ostrov* (The Island, 1946), a title which reflects their sense of isolation in the midst of war. It was the last collection of Russian poetry to be published in China.

Russian women writers in China

While Russian émigré writers in Europe included such well-known names as Zinaida Gippius, Nadezhda Teffi, Marina Tsvetaeva, and others, the names of their counterparts in the Far East – Aleksandra Parkau, Marianna Kolosova or Mariia Vizi – remained virtually unknown outside their own literary community. Moreover, their literary fortunes within their own community were often fraught with difficulties. On the one hand, women writers were extolled. A women writers' section appeared occasionally in the Harbin journal *Rubezh* (Border). Similarly, women writers were acknowledged in an article in that same journal as occupying "a prominent place among the prose and poetry writers of our Far East emigration."[6] Despite the lip-service paid to women's literary endeavors, the fact remained that in terms of productivity they were vastly outnumbered by the male writers who dominated the émigré literary scene in the Far East.

Given the constraints under which these women were writing, their choice of poetry as the primary genre within which they worked becomes especially significant in assessing how they negotiated the multiple displacements in their lives. The fact that women writers wrote poetry reflects, on the one hand, the current trend in Harbin in the 1920s. But their choice of genre also suggests how they perceived their role vis-à-vis the Russian cultural tradition which they had left behind. Because Harbin was in many ways a continuum of prerevolutionary Russia on the political, social, and cultural fronts, women had a much greater role to play as preservers and perpetuators of Russian (non-Soviet) culture. As our subsequent analysis of the poetry of several of these women will show, the commitment to preserving Russia's rich cultural heritage provided a strong motivating force for their work. They drew inspiration from the poetic schools (Symbolism and Acmeism primarily) that had dominated the Russian literary landscape at the time these writers had been forced to leave their homeland. Poetry would transpose memory into verse and simultaneously keep those tremendously valued cultural traditions alive.

One other compelling reason why poetry became the preferred genre of the time for both male and female writers was the very nature of the displacement they experienced. Prose requires extended periods of time, peaceful existence, continuity, and reams of paper, most of which were lacking in the Harbin emigration. Moreover, the traumatic events of the Russian Revolution and Civil War were still too incomprehensible in their proximity and horror; distance was needed to reflect upon them in a large creative form. Poetry, both lyrical and political, offered the solution that the larger form of the novel could not, at least not yet. Poems could be composed orally, written down on scraps of paper, passed from person to person, memorized, and recited at social gatherings. Poetry expressed feelings and experiences in brief, quotable lines, and therefore was easier to publish in newspapers, journals, and small collections, especially for women just beginning their literary careers.

Women poets

The history of Russian women poets writing in China has just begun to be studied and many figures merit individual critical analysis. As a beginning step, we will present an overview of this material by drawing on the lives and works of eight poets: Aleksandra Parkau, Marianna Kolosova, Mariia Vizi, Elizaveta Rachinskaia, Ol'ga Skopichenko, Lydiia Khaindrova, Nataliia Reznikova, and Viktoriia Iankovskaia. After briefly surveying their biographies, we will place their lives and their poetry within a broader context, examining first their common experiences as émigrée women and how these experiences found thematic expression in their verse. The study of these women living in this kind of confined cultural tradition – cut off from China, their homeland, and to some extent the other émigré communities abroad – raises interesting questions regarding literary influence. Although these women were working within a relatively small community, it is unclear to what degree they were aware of and used one another's works as models given the pull of the literary tradition they had left behind.

Aleksandra Parkau, the first of these poets to settle in Harbin, arrived there during World War I. Like many other early settlers, she and her husband became émigrés by virtue of their decision not to return to Russia after the Revolution. The leading poet of the first generation of Russian women in China, Parkau was often published in Harbin periodicals and held a literary salon in Harbin. In 1933 she moved to Shanghai where she continued to write poetry and participate in literary circles. In the late 1940s, she followed her son and his family to the USSR; nothing is known of her subsequent life.

Unlike Parkau with her prerevolutionary ties to Harbin, Marianna Kolosova fled to China in her teens after her father, a priest, was shot in the Civil War. She married A. N. Pokrovskii, co-founder of the Russian Fascist Party in Harbin and began writing in 1925 under the pseudonym of Marianna (instead of her given name Rimma) Kolosova or Elena Insarova. The latter name was taken from that of the heroine in Ivan Turgenev's novel *Nakanune* (On the Eve), who marries, against her family's wishes, an exiled fighter for the liberation of his native Bulgaria and continues working for the cause after his death. Marianna Kolosova became known as "the bard of the White Army" for her patriotic poetry filled with an uncompromising spirit of struggle against the Bolsheviks and calls for revenge. In contrast, her poems as Elena Insarova spoke of love, jealousy, sorrow, and loneliness. (Some readers, who preferred these themes, actually suggested to the amused Kolosova that she emulate Insarova.) When Pokrovskii left the Fascist Party in protest over the pro-Japanese collaborationist stand of its leader K. V. Rodzaevskii and formed his own faction, he and other opponents were arrested by the Japanese. His patriotism and refusal to work with the Japanese, fully shared by Kolosova, made it dangerous for them to remain in Manchukuo, and they departed for Shanghai. After World War II, in the spirit of patriotism which seized many émigrés, Kolosova took Soviet citizenship, but publicly rejected it after the Soviet denunciation of the writers Anna Akhmatova and Mikhail Zoshchenko in 1946. In the early 1950s, she and her husband emigrated to Chile.

Mariia Vizi (the Russian rendering of her name, Mary Vezey) had a Russian mother and an American father, Custis H. Vezey, the publisher of an English-language newspaper in St. Petersburg. During the Civil War, he moved his family to Harbin where he published an English-Russian newspaper *The Harbin Daily News*. Vizi grew up bilingual, and her first collection included poems in Russian and in English, as well as translations of Sara Teasdale, Edna St. Vincent Millay, and George Santayana into Russian and of Aleksandr Blok and Nikolai Gumilev into English. She also left Harbin for Shanghai and later for the US, where she continued to write and publish.

Elizaveta Rachinskaia emigrated to Harbin in 1918. Although she did not publish a collection, her poems and short stories, as well as a translation of Arthur Rimbaud's "Drunken Ship," ("Le Bateau ivre") appeared in Harbin journals. Her husband, the lawyer I. A. Gusel'nikov, was arrested in 1945 and disappeared in Soviet camps. Rachinskaia left China for Australia and then Great Britain where she worked for the BBC and wrote memoirs.

Ol'ga Skopichenko also contributed to Harbin periodicals and produced one book of poetry in Harbin and another in Shanghai. Many of her poems were devoted to love, but she also wrote patriotic verses inspired by the White resistance, though softer in register than those of her friend, Marianna Kolosova. In the late 1940s, like many Russians in Shanghai, she and her husband were moved to a temporary émigré camp in Tubabao, Philippines, where they waited for two years for permission to emigrate to North or South America. In Tubabao, she produced hectographed books, a play, and children's stories and later continued to write in San Francisco.

Lydiia Khaindrova, brought to Harbin at the age of six during the Civil War, belonged to a family of Russified Georgians who had settled in Harbin well before the Revolution. She published several collections of poetry in Harbin, then, in the wave of exodus, moved to Qindao, Tianjin, and then Shanghai. In 1947 she went to the USSR, where her collection of poetry *Daty, daty . . .* (Dates, dates . . ., 1976) included a few Harbin and Shanghai poems. She died in 1986.

Nataliia Reznikova grew up in Harbin, leaving the city in the late 1930s for Shanghai and then the US. Quite prolific, she published two collections of poetry as well as the novels *Izmena* (Betrayal), *Raba Afrodity* (The Slave of Aphrodite), and *Pobezhdennaia* (The Defeated), and a semi-historical novel *Pushkin i Soban'skaia* (Pushkin and Sobanska).

A poet from outside China, Viktoriia Iankovskaia, a granddaughter of the Far East hunter and naturalist M. I. Iankovskii, was brought to Korea in 1922. Her father set up an estate and a hunting lodge in an isolated place where she wandered in the taiga, hunted, and imagined herself to be a "female Tarzan." On visits to Harbin, Iankovskaia appeared at meetings of the "Churaevka" circle and contributed to Harbin and Shanghai periodicals. In 1945 most of the family was arrested and deported to Soviet camps. In 1951 she left for Chile and in 1961 moved to the US.

As is clear from these brief sketches, all of these women experienced enormous displacement and rupture in their lives, yet found the time and strength to express themselves in verse. Most continued to write after they left China. While in their temporary eastern refuge, they managed to leave a record of themselves as both women and artists. Their poetry spoke of the experiences that all Russian women faced in China. Given the hardships dealt women in emigration, their courage, quest for self-determination, and devotion to their art are truly impressive.

Identity themes in poetry

The major theme of Russian émigré literature of the first wave was, as Marina Tsvetaeva, an émigré poet in Europe, put it in one of her poems, "toska po rodine," which may be translated as "nostalgia" or "an anguished longing for home."[7] It found expression in such related themes as memories of home and homeland, an intense concentration on Russian images, dreams of returning home, mourning Russia's tragic fate, a refusal to forgive or forget losses, a call for resistance to and a struggle against Soviet power, ruminations over the life and destiny of émigrés, often coupled with despondency and resignation. The role of the poet in the preservation of cultural heritage, and, indeed, the purpose of poetry itself become themes as well. In this poetry, the persona frequently assumes the stance of an exile, someone "who inhabits one place and remembers or projects the reality of another."[8]

Nostalgia was so powerful that, like a wall, it often blocked any perception or understanding of the country in which these poets found themselves. China had a very limited impact on the thematic content of their works, which, as a result, contained very little, if anything, to indicate that they were written in China and not, say, in France or Czechoslovakia. Life in China was perceived as temporary, and most Russians in China did not bother to learn the Chinese language because knowledge of it was not imperative for survival in the Russian enclaves. In most cases, Chinese culture and literature were ignored except for a superficial acquaintance with some images and symbols.[9] On the few occasions when Chinese themes and images made their appearance, they were intended to simply add local color. Parkau portrayed the burning of incense, dragon processions, firecrackers, and enjoying Chinese dumplings during the celebration of Chinese New Year.[10] Khaindrova presented a peaceful and melancholy picture of ploughed Chinese fields and ancestral graves.[11] Some poems described the beauty of nature and the feelings it arouses, but nothing in them, except the title, indicated that the landscape is Chinese and not Siberian or Far Eastern. Thus, Rachinskaia's poems are entitled "Osen' na Sungari" ("Autumn on the

Sungari"), referring to the Sungari River on the shores of which Harbin was built, or "Barim" ("Barim") and "Iz Barimskoi tetradi" ("From the Barim Notebook"), Barim being a picturesque railway station at the Xing'anling Mountain Range. In Parkau's "Vesna v Kharbine" ("Spring in Harbin") again only the title places the poem in China. In her poem "Po kitaiskomu kalendariu" ("According to the Chinese calendar . . ."), the description of autumn in all its glory of color and its stormy destruction of summer ends with a remark by "a loud and unbearable" Chinese servant, that according to the Chinese calendar, autumn has arrived.

Iankovskaia was perhaps unique in drawing on the Asian part of her Russian identity. The sight of the former Chinese graves on the French concession in Shanghai brings to mind her father's estate in Russia.[12] On leaving Korea, the first country of her emigration, she says:

> I will part with this country as well,
> Because all life is parting.
> But with you, as with the last spring,
> The parting is harder, more painful.[13]

The parting is particularly painful due to the fact that Iankovskaia spent her youth in Korea and learned there how to mourn her homeland, her mother, and other losses. Iankovskaia, who was said to have Buriats among her ancestors, creates a romantic image of herself as "a descendant of Genghis-khan," with "wide cheekbones" and "zigzags of black eyebrows." In one poem she lights a bonfire on the starry night in the Mongolian steppes, and a passing Mongol, "her brother, separated by centuries," joins her:

> Casting seven centuries off twenty,
> I see myself walking along the steppes:
> Years cannot sprinkle with darkness
> Indelible pictures in the heart . . .
> Years cannot ladle away from the blood
> A stream poured into the body by Asia,
> And eyebrows above the slanting eyes,
> Often grow dark in a Slavic land.[14]

Others draw on more traditional images of Russian culture. Vizi, the most skilled poet of the group in terms of her mastery of poetic form, conveys her nostalgia in a chant imitating Russian peasant speech:

> There is God. The heart knows this and prays:
> "God grant me a small peasant hut by the village fence.

Grant me a spring well by the hut's earthen mound.
Grant me bast shoes and felt boots.
Grant me a small pail for gathering mushrooms.
And wouldn't it be nice to get at least a small pot instead of a pipe.
Grant me also a red cow,
And a small plot to plant my carrots.
And also, please don't forget, lend me
at least a little rye.
And the main thing – a birch tree by the threshold.
How could You not grant it? Is it too much?"[15]

Despite her own citified and multicultural background, Vizi's longings for her homeland lead her to associate with archetypal images of rural Russia.

Nostalgia, in its many variations, finds powerful expression in Marianna Kolosova's poetry:

And here, in an alien, cold world,
Suddenly I will lose my restraint and shout:
"Hey, how far is it to Siberia?
Hurry up the horses, coachman! I want to go home!"[16]

Visions of her beloved Russia haunt her:

Tormented by thoughts, I can't sleep all night . . .
My doleful one, how can I help You?
How long will you suffer?
How shall I help you?
What can I give you?[17]

Kolosova's first collection was entitled *Armiia pesen* (An Army of Songs): although she did not know how to use a rifle or operate a machine-gun, she would "send forth her army of thundering songs!" (Dvinu armiiu pesen gremiashchikh! [Epigraph to *Armiia pesen*]. In her "Dinamitnaia lirika,"[18] ("Dynamite-Laden Lyrics,") she declares that while she did not invent gunpowder, her persona has been its by-product.[19] Her "army of songs" praises "the knights of the White idea" who heroically fought against the Reds in the Civil War and continued their struggle in emigration. Her poems mourn victims of the struggle, including the murdered Tsar Nicholas II and the Tsarevich Aleksei, pray for God's punishment upon those who caused the suffering, and passionately, insistently, issue a battle call to fight for the salvation of Russia, and seek vengeance.[20]

Nostalgia for Russia was often accompanied by political coloration. Skopichenko's patriotic poems turn to Russia's past: the Holy Princess Ol'ga, whose conversion to Christianity in the middle of the tenth century was instrumental in bringing Christianity to Kievan Russia; the assassination of Aleksandr II in 1881, the Russian Navy, the murder of Nicholas II and his family, and other tragic events. She writes that her love and pride in her homeland stems not from the beauty of its nature and the glory of its history but from its mortal wounds, suffering, anguish, and refusal to submit: "With this thought, exile is more comforting, / With this thought I too will not bow down!"[21] It is better, she says in another poem, to be shot than to forget one's homeland.[22] One poem compares her love for Russia to a samurai's love for Japan, and she vows to commit spiritual *harikari* if she accepts the impossibility of returning to the Volga and Siberia.[23]

Voices of other poets are gentler in their expressions of love and deep longing for their homeland and ground their poems in everyday experience. In Parkau's poem "Rodnoe" ("Home," 1930), after a hard day's work an émigré audience in China is watching a newsreel. Images of different countries flash by, when, suddenly, the viewers sigh as if one person. What has affected them so deeply?

> It is nothing really . . . A trifle . . . A broken fence,
> A rye field, a forest, – a squalid landscape . . .
> Two peasant women with pails, huts of villages,
> And peasants in a cart on the road.
> By the field, at its border, birch trees,
> Transparent and thin, bow down in the wind,
> And native cornflowers, crushed by the heavy wheel, slowly
> straighten up . . .[24]

In "Gadan'e" ("Fortune Telling," 1933), the cards predict imminent news from afar and "distant roads" for two grim old émigrés. Both vainly hope that the news would be from Russia and the roads would lead them to see, at least once more, their beloved homeland.[25]

Khaindrova's lyrical heroine, unlike other young girls in spring, dreams only about Russia and about a new moon which looks daily with the heroine's eyes over her native fields and lakes.[26] In another poem, she writes with resignation of the ultimate impossibility of holding onto a sense of the place of her origin:

> We rush swiftly, not knowing where,
> We laugh, cry, hide our sorrows,

And soon our exile will become our homeland,
And our homeland become like drifting smoke.[27]

Despondency and resignation to fate dominate her poetry.[28] Reznikova dreams of her troubled snowbound homeland[29] and of a home in Russia with the ever-present white birches:

But Russia is like a dream – it is inaccessible,
We can't build our little white house.
And I quietly cry at night, alone,
About you and the house . . . and about everything.[30]

For both poets memory may be ephemeral but emotional pain persists.

If Kolosova urges women to an active role in the anti-communist struggle, poems in Khaindrova's first collection bear such titles as "Submission," "What Sorrow . . .," "Loneliness," "Acceptance," and speak of calm sadness, resignation, despair, loss of hopes, empty days, and beauty and youthful dreams destroyed by mind-numbing work in an office. In one poem she bitterly blesses misfortune for taking away her homeland:

Submission to everything that will happen,
Submission to a new anguish as well, –
This a stop not on the first road taken
and sorrow not in the last line written.
. . . Submission, indifference to everything,
A chill in the soul amidst the warmth.
Propriety causes a smile,
And pain ends in a volume of poetry on the table.[31]

Traditional Russian Orthodox virtues such as humility and meekness and the need to find consolation in religion are manifested in many poems of Khaindrova, Rachinskaia, and others.

The image and fate of women in general, and émigrée women in particular, are another major theme employed by these poets. In one of Kolosova's poems, a man ponders the fate of a woman he used to know: is she now toiling in the potato fields of Canada, or sitting behind a cash register in a butcher's shop? Is she married to a busy, arrogant foreigner in New York? Is she dancing in a ballet in Paris, or has she become a prostitute in Berlin?[32] Many of Kolosova's poems describe émigrée women as experiencing a modern Golgotha and offer prayers for lost fathers, brothers, husbands, fiancés, and other loved ones. One section of her *Armiia pesen* is entitled "How Could She Help the Homeland?" in which, among poems depicting women's suffering and exhaustion, is also one deriding well-off émigrée women who forget the horrors of the Revolution and enjoy dances, champagne, and diamonds.[33] Other poets, like Vizi and Khaindrova, write tender and affectionate poems dedicated to or about their female friends who have helped sustain them in emigration.

Like women poets of other times, those in the emigration in China often look to historical and mythic precursors as role models to help them surmount their sense of displacement. Not surprisingly, one of Kolosova's heroines is Joan of Arc, who with "a girl's unswerving hand" ("Nedrognuvshaia devich'ia ruka") held on to the flag and led an army.[34] In contrast, Parkau sings the praises of Napoleon's beloved Josephine, whose name also deserves to remain in history because she was a tender wife who stood by him in defeat as well as victory.[35] Others look to Russian history and culture for their role models. Rachinskaia, in a poem from an unfinished cycle entitled *Russian Women*, paints an idealized portrait of a Russian noblewoman. A mythic figure whose lifetime spans over a century, she is a graduate of the prestigious Smolnyi Institute for Girls in St. Petersburg. Her fragile beauty is such that at a ball old men forget their cards, an old senator whispers compliments to her, and the Emperor honors her with his attention at the Jubilee Ball. During the Revolution, however, she fights like a fearless eagle for her children, her beloved, and for the dignity of Russian women. In emigration, she bears with dignity her change in situation:

> Now these poor hands grew rough,
> But work and poverty bring no fear, – never mind!
> No, different, truly cross-bearing torments
> Became the cruel lot of a Russian mother.[36]

Given how often ruptured relationships occurred in their lives, it is not surprising that love lyrics make up a large part of these women's poems, in which they relive the suffering of separations in the past or fear for those to come in the ongoing Asian diaspora. Often political issues fuel such ruptures. In several poems Kolosova addresses the question of loving someone from the enemy camp. These poems were rooted in personal experience: back in Russia, she and the much older V. V. Kuibyshev, the well-known Red Army commander, fell in love, but political differences drove them apart. She writes in a poem addressed to him:

> We are forever strangers.
> I am not yours and you are not mine.

> Don't call me back to Soviet Russia
> Don't call me home to you.[37]

In another poem addressed to him, she melodramatically warns:

> But I will lie in wait for your step,
> And I promise you, as my enemy,
> That in my black Browning
> I will save a bullet for you.
> For the many whom you spitefully torment,
> For the many whom you have killed, –
> You will receive a fatal bullet
> From the one whom you loved![38]

For other poets, love is inseparable from nostalgia. Skopichenko's love poems are filled with images of peasant Russia: laughter and stolen kisses in the snow as a sled with a happy couple overturns; a young village wife exchanging glances and kisses with a young neighbor when her husband is away; or wanderings and courtship in a forest on the pagan night of Ivan Kupala.[39]

Nostalgia often takes a different turn and merges with issues of patriotism in the verse of these women as they fear for the future of émigré children. In a poem by Parkau, a postcard from Paris, another center of Russian emigration, occasions gloomy reflections on young émigré men who became cab-drivers, chauffeurs, vagrants or beggars, and young women who slave, with a needle in hand, over sewing to feed their families.[40] In another, people walk past two young boys, lying dead drunk on a Harbin street, and only a pathetic little girl desperately tries to revive them.[41] Another poem bemoans the large number of suicides among émigré youth. As a few friends place a wreath on the snow-swept grave of a young girl who took her life, her boyfriend stands nearby:

> Perhaps this homeless boy,
> Who knows no God, no home, no fatherland,
> On an impulse of momentary sorrow,
> Like you, like you, will depart from life! . .
> Our young, faced with a pauper's lot
> And losing strength early in the journey,
> Are departing for the quiet gloom of the cemetery,
> Under the vault of untimely graves.[42]

One of their worst fears expressed in verse is that their children will grow up not knowing about or caring for Russia. In a poem of Khaindrova's, an

émigré is married to a foreign woman, and their son cannot understand his
father's nostalgia. Like an angry wolf cub, he hates his father's country and
the city called Moscow.[43] Skopichenko feels bitter despair when a little
Russian girl, born in emigration, listening to a Russian folktale, asks,
"Russia – what is it? / A city like ours, or simply a village?" The poet
continues,

> The storm of the revolution, our narrow daily life . . .
> Much is lost . . . much is gone . . .
> They will grow up in exile, grow up not as Russians,
> Thinking that the Homeland is a city or a village.[44]

Since the preservation of their Russian cultural heritage, as mentioned
earlier, was such an important motivation for their work, these poets turned
to precursors and contemporaries for inspiration, drawing mainly on the
Symbolists and Acmeists. For many poets, Nikolai Gumilev and Aleksandr
Blok, both of whom met tragic deaths in 1921, were guiding lights. Gumilev
was particularly revered and studied. Mariia Vizi translated some of their
poems into English, and has the honor of being Gumilev's first translator.
One of his poems, in her translation, begins with prophetic words:

> You will remember me forevermore
> and all my world of magic and light,
> a flaming world, with music held in store,
> amid the rest – the only that is right.[45]

In one of her own poems, she mourns the victims of the Civil War, among
them Gumilev:

> When the snow falls, flickering,
> the memory will pain me,
> that death, so unnecessary, covered him in snow,
> That he suffered, and that even
> the frozen sound of the word
> that he wished to say
> did not reach the empty shore.[46]

Khaindrova also fondly recollects the image of the "slim officer
Gumilev."[47] Her poem was reprinted in *Gumilevskii sbornik* (The Gumilev
Collection) published in Harbin in 1936, on the twenty-fifth anniversary
of his death. Blok, "God's ray," "a miracle," as Mariia Vizi describes him
in one of her poems, is another source of inspiration for her:

> He died, and I know
> neither the words nor incantations

to return at least a part of his spell to the world.
The disaster was not his death,
but the fact that it was not in my power to find
and sprinkle magic water
over his distant grave.
I would give half of my life
just to know truly
that my song is at least a weak echo
of his broken reed-pipe.[48]

What is reflected in the selections above is a wide range of views on the purpose of poetry and the role of the poet. Kolosova passionately argues that art for art's sake is unacceptable, and art inseparable from ideas. In her own words she ironically becomes a mirror image of her politically engaged contemporaries in the Soviet Union: "a singer of the coming dawn," "a drummer," and "a propagandist."[49] Her "doomed Muse," born in the fire which engulfed Russia, appears in the smoke of battle and orders the poet to rise and protect her.[50] In contrast, Khaindrova entitles her first collection *Stupeni* (Steps), referring to the steps trodden on the difficult path of an émigré poet, while the second bears the title *Kryl'ia* (Wings), creating an image of poetry as wings capable of raising the poet above her sad existence. Others delight in the power of art to transcend prosaic reality. Vizi boldly declares: "I am a sorceress. I have power over everyone / who crosses my path!"[51] The epigraph to her first collection of poetry is taken from a poem by Anna Akhmatova: "It is impossible / for a body to live without sun and for the soul without songs."[52]

By the time that World War II was sweeping across Europe and Japan was launching its war for Great Eastern Asia, several young women poets of the third generation of Harbin Russians had launched their poetic careers under even more difficult circumstances. Japanese-occupied China was as severe in its censorship as was Stalinist Russia, thus making it impossible to publish anything political or critical of local conditions. Most of the third generation poets were born in emigration and had no memories of Russia but, as one of them, Alla Kondratovich, writes:

I am young. I did not know Russia
and grew up far from the homeland.
Nevertheless, I have longed for Great Russia,
and wonderful feelings have grown in my heart.[53]

The poem is entitled "Over a book of verse of M. Kolosova" ("Nad knizhkoi stikhov M. Kolosovoi"), proving that, at least in one instance, the bequeathal of cultural heritage between generations of Russian women poets in China was fully achieved.

In conclusion, the emigration of Russian women writers to China and beyond was fraught with danger, emotional pain, and enormous loss. Lyrical poetry – whether intended for publication or as private consolation – became the primary outlet for these experiences. As in other diasporas, the writing of these women was informed by a vision of exile on multiple levels. Yet, despite the constant sense of the fragility of their existence, and the pain of their own displacement, their desire to preserve their common cultural heritage became a task of paramount importance, which they continued to fulfill as writers, translators, and teachers.

NOTES

1. И никто не услышит твой голос в ночи, / кричи, не кричи. . . (*Голубая трава*, 30).

2. Helen Yakobson, *Crossing Borders. From Revolutionary Russia to China to America* (Tenafly, NJ, 1994), 45.

3. The titles and other information on these memoirs are provided in the "Bibliographical guide to writers and their works" following the last chapter of this book.

4. The names given are those under which these poets published; for full information see the "Bibliographical guide to writers and their works".

5. E. Rachinskaia "Perechityvaia knigu *Azef*" *Novoe russkoe slovo*, 21782 (February 1, 1970), 5.

6. "Smotr zhenskikh literaturnykh sil emigratsii Dal'nego Vostoka," *Rubezh* 47 (November 17, 1934), 24–5. *Rubezh* (1927–45), published by E. S. Kaufman, was a light entertainment weekly of some thirty pages, and succeeded in lasting longer than other journals by capturing a wide audience with brief accounts of international and local news, fiction, and poetry, interspersed with photographs, advice on fashion, cartoons, etc. Its literary merit lies in having published many short stories and poems of Harbin writers.

7. Marina Tsvetaeva, "Toska po rodine! Davno. . ." *IzbPr* (Moscow, 1965), 304–5.

8. Paul Tabori, *The Anatomy of Exile: A Semantic and Historical Study* (London, 1972), 27.

9. See Catherine Ciepiela's chapter for the contrasting experience among Russian women writers in Paris.

10. "Lunnyi Novyi God," private collection.

11. "Kitaiskaia pashnia," *Kryl'ia*, 47.

12. "Shankhaiskoe," in *Po stranam rasseianiia* (San Francisco), 30.

13. Я расстанусь и с этой страной, / потому что вся жизнь — расставанье. / Но с тобой, как с последней весной, / Тяжелее, больнее прощанье. "Proshchanie s Koreei" ("Parting with Korea"), *ibid.*, 14.

14. Из двадцати столетий — семь столетий откинув, / Вижу идущей себя по степи: / Неизгладимые сердцу картины —/ Годы не могут их тьмой окропить. . . / Годы не могут отчерпать из крови / Влитую Азией в тело

струю, / И над глазами раскосыми — брови / Часто чернеют в славянском краю. "Ot odnogo kostra" ("From the Same Fire"), *ibid.*, 16.

15. Есть Господь. Сердце ведает, молится — «Боже, дай избушку мне — у околицы. / Дай колодец ключевой у заваленки. / Дай лапти и валенки. / Дай ведрышко, ходить по грибы, / Хорошо бы еще хоть горшочек, вместо трубы. / Дай еще — красную корову, / И землицы — посадить свою морковку. / И еще, не забудь, одолжи / Хоть полдесятинки ржи. / А главное — березку у порога. / Неужели не дашь? Разве много?» "Molitva," *Stikhotvoreniia* (Poems), 65.

16. И здесь, в чужом холодном мире, / Вдруг, не сдержавшись, закричу: / «Эй, далеко ли до Сибири? / Гони, ямщик! Домой хочу!» "Na postoialom dvore," *Rubezh* 9 (February 24, 1934).

17. Думами томясь, я не сплю всю ночь . . . / Скорбная моя, как Тебе помочь? / Долго ли еще будешь Ты страдать? / Как тебе помочь / Что тебе отдать? "Chto tebe otdat'?," *Armiia pesen*, 18.

18. *Gospodi, spasi Rossiiu! Kniga vtoraia*, 31.

19. "Sklad porokhovoi," *ibid.*, 77.

20. "Po patronchiku — za krovinochku!" *ibid.*, 25–6.

21. С этой мыслью отрадней изгнание, / С этой мыслью и я не согнусь! "Rodine," *Put' izgnannika*, 6.

22. "Veruiu," *ibid.*, 6.

23. "Gordost' samuraia," *ibid.*, 14.

24. Да ничего . . . Пустяк . . . Поломанный плетень, / Ржаное поле, лес, — пейзаж убогий . . . / Две бабы с ведрами, избушки деревень / Да мужики в телеге на дороге. / У поля, на меже, прозрачны и тонки, / Березки клонятся от ветра долу, / И медленно встают родные васильки / примятые под колесом тяжелым . . . *Rubezh* 28 (July 5, 1930).

25. *Rubezh* 13 (March 25, 1933).

26. "Sny o Rossii," *Stupeni*, 15.

27. Стремительно бежим — куда, не зная, / Смеемся, плачем, горести таим, / И скоро станет родиной изгнанье, / А родина — как стелющийся дым. "Stremitel'no bezhim," *Stupeni*, 54.

28. "Ne zakrichu i ne zaplachu," *Rubezh* 7 (February 12, 1938), 14.

29. For example, "Zanesennaia meteliami . . ." *Rubezh* 5 (January 29, 1938), 1.

30. Но Россия, как сон, — недоступна она, / Не построить нам беленький дом. / И я плачу тихонько ночами одна / О тебе и о нем…обо всем. "Ia skuchaiu v schastlivye tikhie dni . . .," *Pesni zemli*, 23.

31. Покорность всему, что случится, / Покорность и новой тоске — / Не в первой дороге станица, / Печаль не в последней строке. / . . ./ Покорность, во всем безразличье, / Душевная стужа в тепле, / Рождает улыбку приличье, / А боль — том стихов на столе. "Pokornost'," *Stupeni*, 5.

32. "No vstretit'sia boius' . . ." *Armiia pesen*, 64–6.

33. "Poklonnikam fokstrota," *ibid.*, 62–4.

34. "Zhanna d'Ark," private collection.

35. "Zhozefina," *Rubezh* 42, (October 14, 1933), 4.

36. Загрубели теперь эти бедные руки, / Но работа, нужда не страшны, — что за дело! / Нет, иные, поистине крестные муки / Стали матери русской жестоким уделом. "Smolianka," *Rubezh* 39 (September 24, 1938), 1.

37. С тобой мы навеки чужие. / Я не твоя и ты не мой. / К себе в советскую Россию / Ты не зови меня домой. "Pis'mo narkomu," *Na zvon mechei*, 34.

38. Но я твой след подкараулю / И обещаю, как врагу, / Что в черном браунинге пулю / Я для тебя приберегу. / За то, что многих злобно мучишь, / За то, что многих ты убил, — / Ты пулю смертную получишь / От той, которую любил! "V ogromnykh zalakh Sovnarkoma," *ibid.*, 35.

39. *Put' izgnannika*.

40. "Pod siren'iu," private collection.

41. "Na paneli," *Rubezh* 40 (September 26, 1931), 1.

42. А может, мальчик бесприютный, / Без Бога, дома и отчизны, / В порыве горести минутной, / Как ты, как ты, уйдет из жизни! . . . / Наш молодняк от доли нищей, / В пути теряя рано силы, / Уходит в тихий мрак кладбища, / Под свод безвременной могилы. "Gor'kie puti," private collection.

43. "Pod chuzhim nebom," *Stupeni*, 20.

44. Это что — Россия? / Город вроде нашего, или так — село? . . . Буря революции, наши будни узкие… / Многое потеряно . . .многое ушло . . . / Вырастут в изгнании, вырастут не русскими, / Думая, что Родина — город иль село. "Dni moi v izgnanii," *Put' izgnannika*, 20.

45. "Eshche ni raz vy vspomnite menia . . .," *Stikhotvoreniia*, 46.

46. Когда посыплет снег, мелькая, / мне будет память тяжела, / что смерть — ненужная такая — его ведь снегом занесла. / Что он страдал, и даже слово, / которое сказать хотел, / до края берега пустого / замерзший звук не долетел. "Kogda posyplet sneg, mel'kaia . . .," *Stikhotvoreniia*, 45.

47. "V sumerkakh," *Stupeni*, 6.

48. Он умер, — и ведь я не знаю / ни слов таких, ни заклинаний / чтоб возвратить земному краю / хоть часть его очарований. / Не смерть его была бедою, / а то, что я найти не в силах и / окропить живой водою / его далекую могилу. / И я пол-жизни отдала бы, / чтоб только знать на самом деле, / что песнь моя — хоть отзвук слабый / его разбившейся свирели. "Bloku," *Stikhotvoreniia*, 137.

49. "Kruzhku literatorov," *Armiia pesen*, 111–13.

50. "Obrechennaia muza," *Na zvon mechei*, 93.

51. Я колдунья. Я властна над всеми, / кто мою дорогу пересек! "Ot luny do solntsa," *Stikhotvoreniia*, 41.

52. . . . . Невозможно жить / без солнца телу и душе без песни. (Epigraph to *Stikhotvoreniia*).

53. Я молода. России я не знала, — / От родины я выросла вдали, / За Русь великую, однако, я страдала, / И чувства чудные в груди росли. *Rubezh* 39 (September 24, 1938).

9

Realist prose writers, 1881–1929

By the end of the nineteenth century, the number of women prose writers in Russia had increased to an unprecedented level. The critic V. Chuiko stated in 1889, "There have never been so many women in Russian literature as now. A woman writer with a reputation, a woman who translates or writes for a newspaper is far from being a rare phenomenon in Russian society."[1] By 1899 the critic A. Skabichevskii further emphasized the significant increase in the number of women writing prose, claiming that Russia was being "inundated" by women's prose fiction, and that almost as many female prose writers as male were being published in the "thick journals."[2]

This chapter can deal with only a small number of the numerous texts by women realist prose writers who rose to prominence during the period 1889–1929. Although some reference will be made to writers' differing stylistic techniques, the main focus will be on the themes of women's prose that (with the possible exception of works by accomplished stylists such as Ol'nem and Teffi) constitute its main interest and originality. "Realist" and "feminist" writing will be treated separately, although it is difficult to draw any clear distinction between them, since women realists, while providing general insights into contemporary society, are often particularly successful at depicting female characters and raising issues of interest to women. For the purposes of this essay, "feminist" texts will be defined as writings by women writers which "show, in content or form or both, a critical awareness of women's role and status in society,"[3] and sometimes demonstrate women attaining a measure of success in achieving their goals.

The political and intellectual background

One important reason why the number of female prose writers was grow-ing by the late nineteenth century was women's enhanced ability and ambition to participate in the Russian literary process. This was largely a result of the extension of women's rights: in particular, the greater edu-cational and social opportunities open to women. By the end of the century it became possible for a larger number of women to obtain a secondary and higher education (although the percentage of the female population which benefited from education was still very small, and it was not until the revolutionary years 1905–7 that significant progress was made in women's higher education).[4] Nevertheless, many of the women writers who emerged in the late 1880s had attended the Higher Women's Courses, first established in Russia in the 1860s, or the Bestuzhev Courses for women in St. Petersburg.

The social status of many women was changing, as Russia was being transformed by the forces of industrialization and urbanization. In other countries, such as Britain, Germany, and America, similar social changes had, somewhat earlier, led to an increase in the number of working women, and the development of the women's movement.[5] In Russia, after the emancipation of the serfs in 1861, the gentry class fell into gradual decline, and could no longer provide for many of its unmarried young women, who had to search for employment. It became necessary for a growing number of Russian women to work, and to attain economic independence through work. It has been estimated that by 1897 there were already six million women in Russia living on their own salaries.[6]

Since many other professions, such as the law, the universities, the local *zemstvo* assemblies, and the government bureaucracy, remained largely closed to women until 1905, literature and journalism became some of the most accessible and popular professions for educated Russian women. Many women writers, such as Anastasiia Verbitskaia, Varvara Tsekhovskaia ("Ol'nem"), and Nadezhda Lokhvitskaia ("Teffi"), began their careers as journalists. The most prominent woman journalist was Liubov' Gurevich, who from 1891 until its closure by the censorship in 1898 became the publisher and co-editor of the journal *Severnyi vestnik* (Northern Herald, 1885–98), which played a significant role in publishing women writers. In the early twentieth century a number of new journals aimed specifically at women were established, such as *Zhenskoe delo* (Women's Cause, 1899–1900), *Zhenskii vestnik* (Women's Herald, 1904–16), and *Zhurnal dlia zhenshchin* (Journal for Women, 1914–26); and in 1899, Verbitskaia set up her own publishing house from the proceeds of her best-selling novels. As women became more influential in the literary world, the Russian literary establishment in turn became more tolerant of women's writing.

Russian women's self-confidence was also enhanced by the new phase of the women's movement from the late 1880s until 1917.[7] Whereas Catriona Kelly has argued that the number of women writers who actively participated in the women's movement was small, and that "the involvement of Russian women in major public political campaigns was of limited significance to the development of women's writing,"[8] I would lay greater emphasis on the fact that some women realist writers did indeed participate directly in the women's movement, which had a considerable impact on their lives and their writing. Adriana Tyrkova (subsequently Tyrkova-Williams), for example, was both a fiction writer and a prominent campaigner for equal rights for women within the liberal Cadet (Constitutional Democratic) Party. Another active feminist was the novelist Ol'ga Shapir, who joined the Russian Women's Mutual Philanthropic Society, a moderate feminist group founded in the early 1890s, and for the rest of her life participated in campaigns for legal and political reform for women.[9]

In the second half of the nineteenth century, women constituted a substantial minority within the nineteenth-century Russian radical intelligentsia,[10] and women prose writers too played an active part in opposing the tsarist government. Liubov' Gurevich, who had a brief career as a fiction writer up to 1904, intensified her feminist and anti-government activities after the 1905 revolution, publishing pamphlets in favor of civil liberties and women's rights.[11] Other writers participated directly in various branches of the revolutionary movement, which in theory espoused women's emancipation (albeit, after the 1870s, as an issue of secondary importance). Valentina Dmitrieva was arrested for a few months in 1880 for her association with the People's Will, the terrorist wing of the populist movement, exiled to Tver and forbidden to practice medicine from 1886 to 1890. Ol'ga Runova was involved in the progressive social movement of the 1870s, and during the unrest of 1905 was exiled for several years to Saratov. Elizaveta Militsyna and her agronomist husband were subjected to police searches because of their work among the peasantry.

Other women with radical sympathies focused primarily on educational and philanthropic work for women. Ekaterina Letkova, who as a young woman had been involved with Nikolai Mikhailovskii, the theorist of the Russian populist movement, became a member of the Committee on Higher Courses for Women; and Mariia Krestovskaia too gave charitable aid to higher education for women. In 1905, Anastasiia Verbitskaia, who had Bolshevik sympathies, became Chair of the Society for the Improvement of the Lot of Women, helping to publicize the plight of poor women students in St. Petersburg. It could also be argued that many other Russian women writers participated in the "women's movement" in a wider sense through their fiction, translation, criticism, and journalism.[12] Some made an important contribution as role models for other women: most notably the great mathematician Sof'ia Kovalevskaia (herself a writer of fiction), who "extended an immeasurable service to the whole women's movement by her work and reputation."[13] Likewise, Liubov' Gurevich played an important role in inspiring Russian women critics and journalists of the younger generation, such as Elena Koltonovskaia.

Arguably an even more important influence on women's writing was the debate about women's sexuality and identity and the "double standard" of morality which took place in Russian society after the publication of Tolstoy's *Kreutzer Sonata* (1889).[14] From the 1890s, many studies of the psychology, anthropology, and physiology of women were published or translated into Russian, including the works of Havelock Ellis, Sigmund Freud, and, particularly, Otto Weininger's *Sex and Character* (1903), translated into Russian in 1909.[15] Some women contributed to this philosophical debate, such as Elena Koltonovskaia, whose book *Zhenskie siluety* (Women's Silhouettes, 1912), albeit excessively influenced by Weininger's essentialism, nevertheless expresses many interesting views on women's role and creativity.

In the late 1880s, under the influence of the feminist, Symbolist, and Decadent movements, women's right to express the passionate, erotic side of their emotions was openly proclaimed in literature by Russian women writers. One of the first was the poet Mirra Lokhvitskaia (1869–1905), who in the second volume of her poetry (1900) was obliged to defend her "passionate . . . feminine verse" against accusations of antisocial, even pornographic tendencies.[16] Once the theme of women's sexual experience had been opened up in literature, it was developed by other women writers, such as Zinaida Gippius in her poetry of the 1890s,[17] and Mariia Krestovskaia, in her novel *Artistka* (The Actress, published three times between 1891 and 1903), which created a scandal because of its advocacy of a woman's right to "free love." By the early twentieth century, a frank treatment of sexual themes had become fashionable and widespread in Russian literature, notably in Mikhail Artsybashev's *Sanin* (1907), a polemic in favor of extreme individualism and male lechery. Women writers such as Anastasiia Verbitskaia and Evdokiia Nagrodskaia, however, chose to treat erotic themes from a feminine point of view which differed considerably from that of Russian men, exploring female sexual emancipation and fluid gender boundaries through the image of the "new woman." By about 1910, the rise of mass publishing in Russia helped to popularize women's "sensational novels" and turn them into bestsellers.[18]

Charlotte Rosenthal has argued that Russia lacked an earlier tradition of women's prose writing,[19] but by the turn of the century, Russian women writers had a number of role models to emulate, both Russian and foreign. Women had written prose in Russia since the late eighteenth century, and the number of female prose writers had increased significantly during the great age of Russian Realism from the 1830s to the 1880s, when prose had been the dominant genre. There is a certain commonality of themes, patterns, problems, and images in Russian women's prose, different from those in masculine literature, which persist from generation to generation.[20] In the late nineteenth century, Russian women writers were well aware of the existence of their predecessors, as well as of their contemporaries. Verbitskaia, for example, refers in her memoirs to the influence of women writers of the previous generation, such as Nadezhda Khvoshchinskaia, Sof'ia Smirnova, Ol'ga Shapir and "Marko Vovchok" (Mariia Markovich). Some women writers obtained the help and support of female mentors from the older generation of writers (Dmitrieva was encouraged by Khvoshchinskaia and Kapitolina Nazar'eva, and Nagrodskaia was the daughter of another well-known writer, Avdot'ia Panaeva); while others had sisters who were also writers (Verbitskaia and Teffi), or formed close friendships with women writers of their own generation (Ol'nem and Elizaveta Vodovozova, Tatiana Shchepkina-Kupernik and Mariia Chekhova, to name but a few). Some earlier Russian women's writing, notably the work of Karolina Pavlova, was rediscovered by the Symbolists at the turn of the century. Moreover, perhaps more than is generally thought, Russian women writers were influenced by European women writers, such as George Sand and Charlotte Brontë, and, later, by European Modernist and Decadent writings about "the new woman," some of which were published by

Verbitskaia.[21] There is not such a clear tradition in Russian women's prose as there is in poetry, partly, perhaps, because poetry is a more intimate, confessional genre particularly well suited to women's talents, partly because women's prose has frequently been denigrated as a genre devoted exclusively to love and trivial themes, but also partly because Russian women were heirs to a problematic prose tradition in which women were expected to conform to images of "terrible perfection."[22] There is, nevertheless, some evidence of both a Russian and a European women's prose tradition, or "subculture."[23]

One significant influence on Russian women writers was the expatriate Russian artist Mariia Bashkirtseva (1860–1884). Perhaps because of her early death at the age of twenty-four,[24] Bashkirtseva was endowed with a mythical aura by many of her readers, who avidly consumed her diaries,[25] which promoted the model of the new woman, liberated, sexually curious, and concerned with developing her individuality. One male critic directly compared Leont'eva, the heroine of Krestovskaia's novel *The Actress*, with Bashkirtseva, in order to emphasize her alleged immorality.[26]

The advent of Modernism in the 1890s, the period of the Silver Age, promoted artistic creativity as a cause worthy of devotion (as opposed to the sociopolitical activity to which women intellectuals had devoted themselves in the 1860s). This attracted many women into literature, despite the obstacles to such a career and the opprobrium that still accompanied women's transgression of traditional roles. The changing political climate also had a significant impact on Russian women. During the reaction of the 1890s, and subsequently, after the failure of the 1905 revolution, art represented an escape from the general disillusionment with political action.

Most women writers at the turn of the century belonged to one of the two major literary movements of the period, Realism or Modernism. This division reflected the two main intellectual interests of the Russian intelligentsia as a whole – political and social action, and the culture of the Silver Age. These concerns, however, were by no means mutually exclusive. On the one hand, the influence of Nietzsche, the championing of individuality, and the "re-evaluation of all values" prevalent in the Silver Age had an influence even on women writers who did not favor Modernist aesthetics. Many realist writers of a feminist persuasion (such as Gurevich and Tatiana Shchepkina-Kupernik) also espoused values typical of the Symbolists, such as the freedom of the individual, the exploration of personal identity, and the creation of beauty. At the same time, such modernists as Zinaida Gippius and Lydiia Zinov'eva-Annibal treated themes which today would be considered "feminist," such as women's individuality and sexuality.

By the turn of the century, there was greater class differentiation amongst women writers. Previously, nearly all Russian women writers had been members of the landed gentry, but by the 1880s the majority were from urban families of professional men, civil servants, and military officers, while some came from humbler backgrounds: Dmitrieva was born into a family of educated serfs, Militsyna's mother was of peasant origin, and Nadezhda Sanzhar was the daughter of a state peasant and a Don Cossack woman. The woman writer's role was changing: the critic K. F. Golovin emphasized that there was not only an increase in the quantity, but also in the quality of women's fiction,[27] while N. Nadezhdin noted that the content of women's writing was expanding, transcending the confines of purely "feminine themes."[28] Despite some critical praise, however, Russian women writers were still frequently berated for alleged personal immorality, excessive emotionality, or narrow choice of themes. Some such complaints had little to do with the intrinsic merits or demerits of women's prose, but sprang largely from male critics' misogyny and distrust of women's autonomy and sexuality.

Women writers' growing self-confidence nevertheless found reflection in the fact that by this time fewer of them used pseudonyms, particularly male pseudonyms. Those who felt comfortable with the label "woman writer" usually used their own name or a feminine pseudonym, whereas those who used masculine or ambiguous pseudonyms were either reluctant to reveal themselves as women because they were modest about their talents, such as Elena Shavrova ("E. Shavrov" and "E. Shastunov") and Mariia Kiseleva (who used her real name for her children's stories, but the pseudonyms "Pince-nez" for her fiction and "Ego" for translations and reviews), or created prose which deviated from that usually expected of "ladies,"[29] such as Tsekhovskaia (Ol'nem), who wrote penetrating social criticism in a detached manner. As the socialist feminist Aleksandra Kollontai pointed out, when Russian women started speaking "in their own language" about their own "women's issues," their literary works acquired "their own special value and significance."[30]

Many women writers, as in earlier periods, tended to avoid the full-length novel, which was associated with the masculine literary tradition in Russia, in order to concentrate on shorter forms such as the novella (*povest'*) and the short story. After 1880 the "thick journals" were particularly influential in publishing women's realist prose of medium length. Women writers' excursions into the longer, novel form were often less successful artistically, as in the case of Shapir's *V burnie gody* (The Stormy Years, 1906). There is, however, some blurring of these genre boundaries, since such works as Krestovskaia's *The Actress* (1891) and Dmitrieva's *Tuchki* (Clouds, 1904) were relatively long novellas which were serialized in "thick journals." Moreover, the growth of the publishing market in the first decade of the twentieth century encouraged such writers as Verbitskaia and Nagrodskaia to recognize that they could earn good money by publishing novels for a mass audience in separate book editions. The commercialization of the publishing market by firms such as M. O. Vol'f, which was catering to an increasingly large literate population, led to a cult of the writer as celebrity, and the blurring of previous distinctions between "popular literature" (the category generally used to define "women's prose" in Russia) and literature for the intelligentsia.[31]

Another popular genre for women was autobiographical writing – diaries, memoirs, and letters. Some critics have questioned whether the popularity of these genres inhibited women's prose writing, but I would argue that they simply added to the diversity of genres available to women. Some women wrote novellas in letter and diary form (Krestovskaia's *Iz zhenskoi zhizni* [A Woman's Life, 1894–1903]), or chose to write memoirs as well as novels; and many women's novels contain autobiographical elements. Sometimes the genres of memoirs and fiction converge, as in Dmitrieva's "Po derevniam: Iz zapisok epidemicheskogo vracha" ("Round the Villages: A Doctor's Memoir of an Epidemic," 1896).

Women frequently chose to write detailed documentary or naturalistic prose, and some of their works were openly didactic, stating an obvious moral about social deprivation or the role of women. This is typical, for example, of Shapir and Dmitrieva, whose earnest authorial interventions often spoil the artistic effect of their prose. However, some texts by Verbitskaia, Shapir, and Smirnova contain more elements of humor or satire than is usually recognized, while Teffi established a new genre of women's comic prose.

Works on sociopolitical themes

In nineteenth-century Russia, writers were expected to treat the "accursed questions" of life and death and, in a society where the free expression of political opinion was censored, to be the "conscience of the nation." By the late nineteenth century, many women realists, like their male contemporaries, had inherited the Russian tradition that writers should be politically committed and treat sociopolitical themes in their fiction. As we have seen, some women writers had sympathized with the populist movement of the 1860s and 1870s, and continued to support revolutionary movements after 1905. Such writers may have been trying consciously to avoid specifically "feminine" themes, espousing the populist view that women's issues should be subsumed into a wider radical agenda; they could to some extent be described as "honorary males."[32]

The most popular subject for committed women realist writers was peasant or working-class life. Although, as Catriona Kelly suggests, some stories may have been as dependent on ethnographic texts as on fieldwork experience,[33] some women writers did obtain a close knowledge of the peasant lives they portray. Dmitrieva, for example, became well acquainted with peasants and workers through her experience as a village teacher, doctor, and revolutionary activist, and was able to depict both male and female characters with understanding and compassion.

Many women writers produced convincing portraits of peasant women, notably Nadezhda Bashkevich's "Mashina dolia" ("Masha's Lot," 1883), Letkova's "Bab'i slezy" ("A Peasant Woman's Tears," 1898), and Iuliia Bezrodnaia's "V izbe" ("In the Hut," 1909). Dmitrieva's "Akhmetkina zhena" ("Akhmetkin's Wife," 1881) depicts a *soldatka,* the wife of a conscript, a spirited woman who has to care for two husbands when the first one, whom she had given up for dead, unexpectedly returns; and Militsyna's "Nian'ka" ("The Nanny," 1910) paints a sympathetic portrait of an elderly woman discarded by the family for whom she has worked devotedly for many years.

Women writers who also wrote children's stories were particularly successful at portraying children in their adult fiction, especially those forced into child labor. In "Bol'nichnyi storozh Khves'ka" ("Khves'ka, the Hospital Watchwoman," 1900), Dmitrieva portrays an intelligent, capable peasant girl of thirteen, the head of her family, who becomes an indispensable aide to the new doctor in her village. Although the general rule in her community is that "Girls don't study," Khves'ka is taught to read, and the implication is that many other peasant girls deserve a better education. The difficulties experienced in acquiring such an education are, however, powerfully highlighted in Shapir's "V slobodke" ("The Settlement," 1892).

Dmitrieva also writes about the fate of peasants who migrate to cities. "Dimka" (1900), the story of a ten-year-old peasant boy sold by his parents into slavery in a glass factory in Moscow, provides a vivid evocation of urban deprivation and a detailed description of back-breaking factory work in terrible conditions.

In "Maina-vira" ("Heave-ho!," 1900), Dmitrieva depicts the peasant Mikola Sitnikov who leaves the poor land in Tambov province to find work to feed his starving family, and ends up doing heavy manual labor in the port of Batum, where he drinks away his meager wages and is ultimately crushed by a bale. These powerful short stories, which eschew didacticism, are among Dmitrieva's best works. Her more tendentious *povest'* "Druz'ia detstva" ("Childhood Friends," 1904) contrasts men of two different classes: the upper-class narrator and his childhood friend, the strong, cheerful docker Vas'ka Dokuchaev, who vividly describes his adventures as a ship's stoker, emphasizing the exploitation of his fellow workers and their solidarity in the fight against injustice.

Another successful story of working-class life is Anastasiia Krandievskaia's "Tol'ko chas" ("Only an Hour," 1902) which gives a natura-listic depiction of miners' lives as a living hell, while also conveying the feelings of a woman journalist excited at the prospect of collecting "material" on her new assignment (although the journalist's agonized feelings are dwelt upon in excessive detail).

Revolutionary activity was another theme treated by a number of women writers. The moral fervor and absolute commitment of women populists and terrorists of the 1870s and 1880s such as Vera Figner and Sof'ia Perovskaia had fired women writers' imaginations, as is demonstrated by such works as Dmitrieva's "T'iurma" ("The Prison," 1887), Shapir's *The Stormy Years* and Letkova's "Lishniaia" ("A Superfluous Woman," 1893), which depicts the tragedy of a woman raised with populist ideals not shared by her children. Some writers, however, presented a perceptive analysis of the failure of the populist movement due to the gulf between the peasants and the intelligentsia (Runova's "Oni" ["They," 1912]). Nevertheless, the continuing sympathy of some women writers for revolutionary idealism is illustrated by Dmitrieva's "Dobrovolets" ("The Volunteer," 1889), Militsyna's "Idealist" ("The Idealist," 1904), and Verbitskaia's *Istoriia odnoi zhizni* (Story of a Life, 1903), in which the heroine Ol'ga Devich ultimately joins the revolutionary movement. Some works presented female terrorism in a positive light: Shchepkina-Kupernik's dramatic story "Pervyi bal" ("First Ball," 1907) parodies the conventions of the nineteenth-century "society tale" with its depiction of a girl preparing carefully for a ball, where she takes a gun out of her cleavage and shoots a reactionary politician.

Some radical women produced politically controversial works which were banned by the tsarist censorship. Shapir's novel *The Stormy Years,* which portrayed populist revolutionaries, was completed in 1889, but could not be published until 1906. Two pamphlets written abroad anonymously by Dmitrieva in 1902, "For the Tsar, Faith and Fatherland" by "Ivan Volnyi," dealing with the position of Russian soldiers, and "Lipochka the Priest's Daughter" by "Father Ioann Novokreshchenskii," which depicts the death of an innocent girl raped by a police interrogator, were smuggled back into Russia, where they circulated among students, workers, and peasants. Militsyna's "Zapiski sestry miloserdiia" ("Notes of a Sister of Mercy," 1916), an anti-war account of her experiences during World War I, was prohibited by the censor and never published, and is unfortunately missing from her archive.

The 1905 revolution and the severe reprisals which ensued, along with the easing of censorship in 1906, spurred some women writers to write even franker "protest fiction." One of Dmitrieva's best known stories, "Pchely zhuzhzhat" ("The Bees are Buzzing," 1906) presents a vivid description of a peasant "rebellion" – which simply means that they cut hay on neglected fields belonging to a neighboring monastery. Dmitrieva depicts the brutal floggings to which the peasants are subjected, causing their leader's death, but looks forward to better times when the peasants will overcome their masters.

After 1905, a particularly topical theme of protest fiction by women, as well as by male authors such as Gorky and Korolenko, was capital punishment, which was used by order of Peter Stolypin, Prime Minister from 1906 to 1911, against thousands of rebels and revolutionaries. One of Militsyna's best stories, "V ozhidanii prigovora" ("Awaiting the Verdict," 1910), depicts peasant revolutionaries who are waiting to be sentenced or executed; its most original feature is that it is presented not through the eyes of the condemned men, but from the point of view of their relatives and friends, especially the leader's mother. The story is full of psychological verisimilitude and disturbing naturalistic detail, and the mother's religious sympathies enable the author to draw a parallel between her son's execution and the death of Christ.

The new generation of women realists treated a wider range of sociopolitical themes and were more technically accomplished than many of their predecessors. Their works are distinguished by lively dialogue and direct narratorial involvement, but few use new stylistic techniques, such as interior monologue. Such writers were of equivalent standing to many of their male peers, and although, not surprisingly, they focused more on women's lives, some also ventured successfully onto "masculine" territory, with stories of revolutionary action and urban and industrial life.

The critical depiction of society

Much realistic prose by women writers is not directly concerned with political issues, although the condition of Russian society forms an essential background to their work. Many women's texts of the 1880s and 1890s evoke an atmosphere of political reaction, while also conveying a sense of social ferment and change, which became more pronounced in works of the early 1900s.

One aspect of women's realistic writing which was frequently underestimated by male critics was its criticism of society in general through a focus on female characters. *Mimochka na vodakh* (Mimi at the Spa, 1891), the second volume of a trilogy by Lydiia Veselitskaia ("Mikulich"), for example, depicts a bored young woman married to an old, bald general; she has an affair with a young man. Mimochka, albeit a superficial character, is not portrayed as a thoroughly bad person – the implication is that society as a whole is to blame for arranging such unsuitable marriages. Similarly, Verbitskaia's *Vavochka* (1898) suggests that Russian society of the 1890s is responsible for creating a generation of scheming women whose only aim is to catch a rich husband.

Varvara Tsekhovskaia, under her pseudonym "Ol'nem," wrote some of the best realist prose by a woman writer in the Silver Age, although her work has been largely neglected or underrated ever since.[34] Her talent for portraiture and dialogue and her elegant style led her to be compared with Chekhov; but her work was undervalued by her contemporaries because it was perceived as "old-fashioned" Turgenevan realism, imbued with the melancholy lyricism of the reactionary 1890s and largely devoid of social commentary, an omission generally regarded as inadmissible after the 1905 revolution.[35] In actual fact, however, she produced interesting novellas on a variety of subjects, which have dated less than some more obviously committed literature, and her portraits of unusual or eccentric characters, especially of strong, complex women, are remarkably modern.

Many of her stories are graphic depictions of the decline of the old gentry class in Russia, featuring "superfluous men" or "superfluous women" (one of her most characteristic stories is entitled "Passivnye" ["The Passive Ones," 1911]. Some contrast a weak-willed man with a lively, more interesting woman. In her first story, "Warum?" ("Why?" 1895), for example, the young engineer Golubin finds lodgings with an ancient aristocratic family now consisting only of an elderly grandmother, her eccentric son Pavel, and her talented granddaughter Liza. Liza's character is poetically evoked: an accomplished artist and pianist dreaming of an artistic vocation, she plays Schumann's "Warum?" "in her own, special way. Her whole playing was nothing but a question, anxiety before an enigma." This unspoken question also permeates the relationship between Liza and Golovin: when he falls in love with her she can respond only with professions of friendship. The question "warum?" haunts the tale of Liza's life as, after the ruin of her family, she is obliged to contract a loveless marriage, her two children die, and she ultimately abandons all artistic ambitions.

A similar pair of characters is featured in one of Ol'nem's best works, the novella "Ivan Fedorovich" (1903), which depicts a large gallery of characters in a Russian provincial town. Ivan Fedorovich, the town judge, possesses considerable intelligence and generous impulses, but also a certain "spiritual flabbiness and weak-willed complaisance." He has an affair with Liza, an uneducated waitress, and when she becomes pregnant, offers to marry her, although his feelings for her are cooling. Liza, on the other hand, is a strong-minded, independent woman who is prepared to bring up her child alone rather than marry a man who does not love her. Ol'nem's portrait of Liza was criticized as too blatant an effort to create a "new woman,"[36] although Liza epitomizes the new type of socially mobile, lower-class woman who was actually emerging in the early twentieth century.

Ol'nem was often regarded solely as a writer of sad stories in a "minor key,"[37] but she was also capable of producing humorous, semi-autobiographical tales about institute girls ("Na poroge zhizni" ["On the Threshold of Life"], "Adres" ["The Appeal"]), lively descriptions of newspaper offices ("Iubilei redaktora" ["The Editor's Anniversary"] and "Muraveinik" ["The Anthill"]),[38] and biting satires of the decadent gentry ("Dinastiia" ["The Dynasty," 1910]). She could also create optimistic stories about successful women: "Pervyi shag" ("The First Step," 1902) portrays a determined young woman, Shura, who seeks her fortune in the city, obtains work as an insurance agent, and manages to persuade the vice-governor to become her first client. This story was attacked by one critic as incredible, "at times sinking into caricature,"[39] whereas in fact it was based on the author's personal experience. Even in Ol'nem's more pessimistic stories, some women characters manage to make the best of their circumstances through honesty and resourcefulness (Inna Plamen' in "Bezzabotnye" ["The Carefree Ones," 1912] and Liza in "Ivan Fedorovich").

Whereas Ol'nem was berated by contemporary critics for allegedly idealizing her female characters,[40] she often portrays negative types, such as the predatory widow in "U teplogo moria" ("By the Warm Sea," 1909) or the dominating old Kokovtseva in "The Passive Ones." A contradictory criticism leveled against Ol'nem was that she treated no "women's themes" in her work.[41] I would, however, contend that her female characters are equally interesting, and that she treats themes which today would be seen as "feminist," such as women longing to escape from stultifying relationships, bringing up children on their own, or succeeding in their careers.

Although Ol'nem frequently depicts neurotic or eccentric characters, her narratorial voice is sane and calm, avoiding explicit moralizing. This led her to be denounced for "rather cold objectivity," which was "perhaps, even excessive"[42] – a telling example of how Russian women writers could sometimes be criticized for being insufficiently "feminine" rather than, as usual, for being too "feminine." Ol'nem's manner is detached, but by no means "cold": she is an acute observer of unconventional human relationships, and is particularly sensitive to the ways in which selfish people entrap one another (as in her stories "Tsepi" ["Chains," 1911] and "Triasina" ["The Quagmire," 1914]). She clearly sympathizes with characters who express genuine feeling or adherence to a higher cause, but her main concern is a subtle exploration of the reality and complexity of human nature, which makes her stories of interest to us today.

Women's issues and feminist writings

As in other countries, the first-wave feminist movement in Russia, and the writings which accompanied it, had been largely forgotten until their recent rediscovery by western feminists and a few Russian literary scholars. During the Silver Age, however, it would have been well-nigh impossible for any educated woman writer who read the "thick journals" to avoid discussion of the "woman question" and the women's movement, even though some prominent writers, notably Gippius, deliberately elected to despise such issues, preferring to write as a "human being" than as a "woman"[43] (an unacknowledged example of her alternative interpretation of women's liberation). There were, moreover, significant links between writers and feminist activists. The socio-political sketches by feminists such as Mariia Pokrovskaia, leader of the Women's Progressive Party and editor of the journal *Women's Herald*, bear a close relation to the almost ethnographic naturalism of such writers as Dmitrieva and Militsyna;[44] while political activists such as Pokrovskaia and Kollontai took a keen interest in literature about the "new woman." It would, however, be unreasonable to expect Russian women writers to engage in much direct involvement in partisan politics, since the women's movement itself did not adopt an explicitly party-political character until 1905. The majority of the female intelligentsia in Russia was not primarily socialist or even interested in male-dominated political parties, but was, rather, public-spirited, concerned with charitable works and social welfare. As in other countries, such as Germany and America, this was one of the principal means by which women were able to participate in the public sphere.[45] Moreover, since the struggle for women's suffrage had little chance of success in Russia, many writers with feminist sympathies chose to devote themselves to other themes which might give them a greater opportunity to exert a beneficial influence, such as women's education, employment, and personal life.

Elaine Showalter has argued that for the new woman of the 1880s and 1890s in Britain, feminine "difference" was the basis of a "developing female aesthetic," and writing fiction was regarded as a "political act of sexual solidarity."[46] The same could be said of feminist writers in Russia, who experienced a sense of solidarity through their writings and fostered similar feelings in their female readers. The question of what exactly women want, what would make them happy, is asked in many texts by women writers. These works contain little outer action, but devote more attention to women's psychology than in the past.

Two authors who are particularly associated with writing about women and women's issues are Ol'ga Shapir and Mariia Krestovskaia. Shapir, who discovered the feminist movement in the 1890s, was one of the first Russian writers to make a deliberate decision to concentrate on women's themes,[47] which improved her writing. At the Women's Congress of 1908, she argued that since unity between women was impossible in a class society, there was a need to concentrate on the inner emancipation of women, the "raising of their consciousness," in order to free them from the shackles of a slave mentality.[48] This subject is treated in many of Shapir's works, such as "Pominki" ("Funeral Feast," 1889) and *Liubov'* (Love), which demonstrate how love can stifle women's individuality and potential. It can be assumed that many other female writers shared similar views. One such was Krestovskaia, whose intense interest in her own psychology enabled her to create convincing women characters through the extensive use of interior monologue. The confessional forms of her works and the sincerity and subtlety of her psychological analysis made critics define her as a "woman writer" par excellence.

The "escape plot" was still an important genre for Russian women realists, who continued to be preoccupied by women's struggle for education and employment. Since by the 1900s women of the gentry class had already attained greater educational opportunities, texts concerned with education tended to focus on lower-class women. Verbitskaia, in such stories as "Oshibka" ("The Mistake," 1900) and "Oni nadeiatsia" ("They Hope," 1901) and her campaigning articles,[49] emphasizes the penury of female students who live in terrible, cramped conditions, with little money for food or heating, but suggests that they prefer such poverty to an arranged marriage and a life of permanent pregnancy in the provinces.

Women writers often provide a more sympathetic portrayal of women's social mobility than male writers.[50] Shapir's "Avdot'iny dochki" ("Avdot'ia's Daughters," 1898), for example, draws an effective portrait of Sasha, the daughter of a cook in the household of a St. Petersburg official, who is attempting to escape from domestic slavery by training to become a midwife. Shapir highlights the energy of the lower classes and the apathy and neurasthenia of the upper classes.

Many authors illustrate the conflict between women's idealistic aspiration to work and what professional life really means. One of Letkova's best stories, "Otdykh" ("The Holiday," 1896), depicts Mariia Nilovna, who, like the disillusioned Irina in Chekhov's *The Three Sisters,* has become a telegraphist, who "lives for work and works to live."[51] On a cruise along the Volga, she has time to contemplate the emptiness of her life, and eventually, unobtrusively, commits suicide. Letkova's story is one example of numerous works of fiction by Russian women writers at this time which do not focus solely on "women's issues," but cast light on a universal human problem (such as unfulfilling work) through the depiction of a female protagonist. This point was not always recognized by male critics of their day.

In her early works Verbitskaia depicts the working conditions for women in a number of different professions: medicine, teaching, midwifery, journalism, writing, translating, and domestic service. In "Pervye lastochki" ("First Signs," 1887), for example, she offers a compelling semi-autobiographical account of a woman's depressing experiences in a succession of editorial offices, as she tries to make enough money to feed her children.[52]

In the first decade of the twentieth century, some writers depicted the "new woman" who, in Kollontai's opinion, really existed, and was different from the typical woman of the 1880s and 1890s. In *Zapiski Anny* (Anna's Notes, 1910), Nadezhda Sanzhar polemicizes with the advocacy of unconstrained male lechery in Artsybashev's novel *Sanin*, portraying a naive, forthright woman intent on finding her own path in life, who regrets that she possesses a woman's body, as she would prefer men to love a more valuable part of her.

Many of Verbitskaia's works illustrate the problems of the "new woman" whose idealistic dreams come into conflict with Russian reality. In *Po-novomu* (In a New Way, 1902), she depicts a teacher, Mar'ia, who has devoted her whole life to her career, shunning marriage and personal happiness. When she falls in love, she tries to establish a new type of marriage: her main requirements are that she and her husband should each have their own room, which the other may not enter without permission. However, when she becomes pregnant she is legally obliged to leave her teaching job, thus forcing the couple into poverty and a more conventional marriage, which culminates in the husband's infidelity and desertion.

The performing arts were one of the few readily accessible and highly visible professions open to Russian women at the turn of the century.[53] Women writers were, therefore, reflecting both the reality of Russian society and the influence of the Modernist movement when they portrayed the woman artist – particularly the actress – as the epitome of the "new," independent, unconventional woman. However, some writers, such as Krestovskaia, who began her career as an actress,[54] paint a more realistic picture of the acting profession, suggesting that a woman's artistic vocation may come into conflict with her personal life. Although some texts depict acting and singing as worthy professions for women (Ol'nem's "Bez illiuzii" ["Without Illusions," 1903], Verbitskaia's *Ch'ia vina?* [Whose Fault Is It?, 1900]), others emphasize the egoism, materialism, and capriciousness typical of many actresses, especially in the provincial theater (Krestovskaia's "Lelia," 1885).

The relationship between mothers and daughters, remarkable for its absence in most masculine fiction, is frequently depicted in women's prose. However, as in masculine literature, there are still many women's texts which depict women growing up without mothers, or with mothers who are hostile to them (Ol'nem's "Dinastiia" [Dynasty, 1910], Gurevich's "Toska i rasseiannost'" ["Anguish and Distraction"], and the memoirs of Verbitskaia and Elizaveta D'iakonova). Such representations confirm the analysis of Barbara Engel, who argues that close mother-daughter relationships often operated conservatively in Russia, as mothers encouraged their daughters to embark on the conventional path of marriage and motherhood. Women of the radical intelligentsia often had to break away from their mothers and the authoritarian family structure for the sake of their own self-development and their devotion to society as a whole.[55] Some women writers suggest that a rejection of family was necessary for women in other professions too. In Ol'nem's "Without Illusions," for example, the heroine has to escape from the baneful influence of her actress mother in order to become a successful actress herself.

The pleasures and problems of an all-female environment are explored more fully than in earlier women's fiction, in stories and memoirs about girls' boarding schools (a generally positive picture is painted by Ol'nem and Verbitskaia, whereas Krestovskaia's "Vne zhizni" ["Outside of Life," 1889] demonstrates the way such schools can deform the personality). A number of works emphasize the great value of female friendship,[56] such as Shchepkina-Kupernik's *Schast'e* (Happiness, 1897), Letkova's *Mukhi* (Flies, 1903), and Dmitrieva's *Clouds*, which depicts the affection and mutual support between a teacher and a doctor's assistant in a remote country area.

A theme treated by some women writers was a frank expression of the sexual discontent, even revulsion, which women could feel in marriage. In Krestovskaia's "Vopl'" ("The Howl," 1900), the protagonist Natasha feels trapped, with no real work, subjected to the will of her husband Sasha whose only interest is money. He refuses to discuss his work with her, and is irritated by women's sufferings: he behaves insensitively when she has a second miscarriage, thinking to comfort her by saying, "it might have been a daughter instead of a son, so it's completely unimportant." Eventually Sasha is unfaithful to her and curtails their time together.

Krestovskaia's story represents a powerful expression of a woman's unhappiness and lack of sexual fulfillment in marriage, which is ahead of its time. It can be considered a "feminist" story, in that its conclusion, depicting the heroine's successful escape from her confining marriage, represents a "call to action" for women readers (although Krestovskaia's hints about the husband's imminent change of heart are less convincing).

Many other works by women writers discuss legal, moral, and emotional problems related to adultery, separation, divorce, and single parenthood, contributing to the contemporary campaign for divorce reform, which can be assumed to reflect widespread dissatisfaction with the institution of matrimony as it was then understood. Sometimes, as in Verbitskaia's *Osvobodilas'!* (She Was Liberated!, 1898), women's writing combines desire for sexual liberation with an aspiration to political liberation. Celibacy' is not now advocated, as it had been in the 1860s; indeed, it no longer seems to be a viable option. Runova's "Nepravda" ("Falsehood," 1912), for example, presents the life of a lonely single woman in a tragic light. There are exceptions to this rule, such as Shchepkina-Kupernik's novel *Happiness*, in which the heroine eventually achieves happiness without a man, through friendship, art, and single motherhood. (Recent archival research, however, suggests that Shchepkina-Kupernik was a lesbian, so her views cannot be regarded as typical.[57]) The majority of texts by Russian women reflect the difficulty for educated or talented women in combining work with a personal life.

Women's quest for dignity and fulfillment was a common theme in female-authored texts, including some condemned by male critics for their alleged concentration on love. This was, for example, the main theme of Krestovskaia's *The Actress*, which portrays a sexually free woman who finally chooses her art instead of her love. On the whole, sheer physicality still tends to be avoided in women's writings, although a few works discuss problems of sexuality and reproduction more frankly than before, such as Verbitskaia's *Story of a Life*, which provides a frank depiction of the physical problems which Ol'ga Devich experiences during pregnancy. Under the influence of Ibsen's *Ghosts* (first performed in 1889), women writers occasionally refer to venereal disease: in Ol'nem's "The Passive Ones," for example, Elena Matal'tseva relates that she bore a deformed child who lived for only two days because she had been infected by her husband.[58]

The problem of illegitimacy was raised by Zinaida Gippius, in her first, realistic story "Zloschastnaia" ("An Unfortunate Woman," 1890), which depicts a poor washerwoman with an illegitimate child as a victim of society's unjust sexual morality.[59] When the subject of prostitution is treated in women's fiction, it is generally presented as a consequence of economic hardship (as in Dmitrieva's "Dimka" and Shapir's "Ne poverili" ["They Did Not Believe Her," 1898]),[60] not romanticized or sensational-ized, as in some masculine fiction.

Abortion and artificial birth control first began to be discussed in the Russian professional press in the 1890s. Although these subjects did not become campaigning issues for the Russian women's movement, in contrast with the feminist movement in the United States which had advocated contraception since the 1870s,[61] they were debated with a remarkable degree of openness in medical and legal circles between 1905 and World War I.[62] At this time there was still no reliable means of con-traception in Russia, and abortion remained illegal, as in other countries, although physicians believed that Russian working-class women were increasingly resorting to illegal and "black market" abortions, especially after 1905. Whereas there is some evidence that women were using abor-tion as a means of birth control, most unskilled working-class women in Russia either could not afford the services, or did not know of them. One popular stereotype propagated by anti-abortion campaigners was the upper-class lady who had an abortion for social reasons.[63] This viewpoint was endorsed by Ol'ga Runova's story "Bez zaveta" ("Nothing Sacred," 1913), which depicts a number of fashionable women in the surgery of an eminent gynecologist who speak frankly about their desire to obtain an abortion in order to retain their jobs and pursue their lives of luxury and sexual gratification. Runova also highlights the problem of male physi-cians' control of female sexuality and reproduction, demonstrating that the gynecologist, who believes that motherhood is women's natural destiny, punishes some of his patients by performing hysterectomies without their consent.

The sensational novel

Whereas sexuality does not figure very prominently in the works of social realists, it constitutes the central focus of the "sensational novel," a new genre which became tremendously popular in Russia after 1910.[64] If this tradition of feminist erotic literature has been discussed at all, it has usually been associated with one writer, Verbitskaia, whose later fiction is generally regarded as synonymous with second-rate "women's prose."[65]

The best known "sensational novels," Verbitskaia's *Kliuchi schast'ia* (The Keys to Happiness, 1909–13) and Evdokiia Nagrodskaia's *Gnev Dionisa* (The Wrath of Dionysus, 1911), both emphasize the value and importance of women's sexual desires, unconstrained by guilt or remorse. Both depict liberated heroines who love two men and have sexual relations with both at the same time. However, as in Britain, the principal feature of these erotic feminist novels is that they are "less concerned with sexuality than with self-assertion."[66] The protagonists – a ballerina and an artist respectively – assert independence from the tedium and injustice of the feminine role in marriage and the family. Another important theme in these novels is the blurring of gender boundaries, and role reversal on the part of both men and women.

Unlike the more positive, professional heroines of some of Verbitskaia's earlier works, Mania in *The Keys to Happiness* is too flawed and ambiguous to be a feminist heroine. On the one hand, she does achieve some artistic success, and is the first Russian heroine to combine sexual liberation with radical ideology. However, on the other hand, she lives through strong men, is doomed to mental illness because of her morbid heredity, and is ultimately self-destructive. By choosing to leave her protector and patron (later, her husband) Baron Steinbach, who supports her professional achievements, and to succumb to her passion for the dominating, anti-Semitic nobleman Nelidov, she fails to live up to the precepts of her mentor Jan, who offered her the "keys to happiness" if she could "accord love a secondary place in life."

In the end, the heroines of Verbitskaia and Nagrodskaia both sink into traditional female roles. However daring these novels may be in the Russian context, ultimately the heroine's rebellion leads either to suicide (as in the case of Verbitskaia's Mania) or to artistic defeat and full-time motherhood (as in the case of Nagrodskaia's Tania). Nagrodskaia's novel is the more optimistic of the two, suggesting that women can have everything – but not at the same time. Although Nagrodskaia and Verbitskaia seem to have been aware of the possible contradictions between sexual liberation and women's liberation, they fail to explore such issues in any depth.

Even in the "sensational novel," women's options are generally limited by a concentration on heterosexuality, although some works of this period did broach lesbian themes, notably Lydiia Zinov'eva-Annibal's *Tridtsat' tri uroda* (Thirty-Three Abominations, 1907)[67] and *Zhenschina na kreste* (Woman on the Cross) by "Anna Mar" (Anna Lenshina), first published in a heavily censored edition in 1916. Mar's work, the most extended treatment of sadomasochism in Russian literature of this period, is an erotic, non-moralistic novel which violates most of our expectations of Russian women's literature, and contains some penetrating, very modern psychological insights.

Silver Age writers after the Revolution

The fate of women prose writers of the Silver Age in their last years and after the 1917 Revolution requires further investigation. It is generally assumed that Mariia Krestovskaia, whose fictional output diminished sharply towards the end of the 1890s, stopped writing due to illness; however, her archive contains a fascinating, detailed journal of her emotional life in the years 1898–1910 which reads like a novel, and raises feminist issues not always treated so explicitly in her fiction, such as the need for equal pay for equal work, and the unfairness of the double standard of morality.[68] This is just one of the many neglected works by prerevolutionary women writers which deserve rediscovery and publication in contemporary Russia.

After 1917, some women writers who had risen to prominence in the prerevolutionary period attempted, with difficulty, to adapt to the new regime: some eventually became respected figures in Soviet literature and publishing, but this was often at the cost of abandoning fiction writing altogether. Letkova, for example, worked as an editor, translator, and reviewer for the World Literature Press, and later for the State Publishing House "Gosizdat"; Militsyna, after the death of her husband and parents in 1919, joined the Communist Party in 1920 and became director of an orphanage for three years before starting to write again, mainly for provincial newspapers; while Gurevich devoted herself to the theater, editing Stanislavsky's memoirs and theoretical writings. Dmitrieva, who almost starved to death in the Civil War, and lost her husband, mother, and three brothers, subsequently became involved in educational and propaganda activities among the peasantry, worked for the government publishing house, and wrote her memoirs (*Tak bylo* [The Way it Was, 1930]).

Some prerevolutionary women writers, such as Dmitrieva and Militsyna, managed to secure the republication of some of their fiction during their lifetime, but this course was only open to those who had written about the repression of the tsarist regime, and could be presented as having some sympathy for the Bolshevik Revolution. Their early stories, largely based on populist, rather than Marxist views, were often critically received: Militsyna, for example, was censured for her misunderstanding of the class nature of the peasantry.

Writers even less congenial to the Soviet regime, such as Verbitskaia, were persecuted in the 1920s,[69] and had to resort to writing children's books, or, like Shchepkina-Kupernik, doing translations. Still others sank into oblivion, sometimes into dire poverty: on June 29, 1921 Ol'nem sent a letter to the Society for Aid to Needy Writers begging for food, since she was receiving no rations, either at her place of work or as a Russian writer.[70] The suppression of women prose writers and their work probably had even more adverse artistic consequences than the persecution of male writers, because women's prose was still a relatively new, fragile development in the Silver Age.

Women realist writers, 1917–29

The Bolshevik Revolution of October 1917 transformed the legal position of Russian women. The Provisional Government of 1917 had already given women the vote, but in 1918 Lenin's new government issued decrees on labor, marriage, and the family which granted women equality in all spheres of public life. This victory for women's liberation, however, meant the end of feminism as a separate movement: feminist organizations, newspapers, and journals were suppressed in 1918. Women's emancipation was initially left to the Women's Section of the Communist Party (*Zhenotdel*), established in 1919. Bolshevik policy, tacitly accepted by most pro-Bolshevik women writers, was that women's emancipation should be subordinated to the greater goal of transforming an entire society.

A number of well-known women prose writers who could not accept the Bolshevik Revolution joined the "first wave" of emigration (Gippius, Teffi, Zinaida Vengerova). Those who chose to take an active part in the cultural activities of the new Soviet state included writers of peasant or proletarian background (Lydiia Seifullina, Anna Karavaeva), idealists of the younger generation (Ol'ga Berggol'ts, Vera Panova, Vera Ketlinskaia), and some prerevolutionary intellectuals who espoused Bolshevism out of personal conviction (Larisa Reisner, Vera Inber, Ol'ga Forsh, and Marietta Shaginian).

Larisa Reisner was one of the few women writers from the prerevolutionary intelligentsia who became actively involved in the Revolution and Bolshevik culture. Along with Mayakovsky, she came to personify the new Soviet writer, who was also expected to be a political activist and to use literature to enlighten the masses. Reisner wrote a series of sketches from the front during the Civil War (*Front*, [The Front, 1924]), and is sometimes credited with establishing the new Soviet genre of the *ocherk* ("sketch," or documentary reportage in quasi-literary form, usually on a topical subject). "Fellow travelers" (intellectuals sympathetic to Bolshevism) such as Shaginian, Forsh, Inber, and Shkapskaia, who had previously dallied with Symbolism, also had recourse to documentary reportage in an effort to achieve the ideological reconstruction the government demanded of them.

The image of the "new Soviet woman," a courageous, energetic heroine totally dedicated to the Bolshevik cause, featured immediately after the Revolution in the "stranichki" (columns) of *Pravda* written by *Zhenotdel* activists, the *Zhenotdel* journal *Kommunistka*, and the short stories, poems, and plays published in the period of War Communism (1917–21).[71] Whereas the first Soviet literature reflected the initial excitement of revolutionary change, writers soon began to demonstrate a greater awareness of the problems involved in implementing the new laws on women's liberation. Millions of Russian women were illiterate, unskilled, and accustomed to being subservient to men. They had to be educated, directed to work outside the home, shown how to change their attitudes and develop a new self-image. The difficulties of achieving these goals were exacerbated by many Russian men who resented the loss of their power over women.

Whereas the image of the "new Soviet woman" was initially drawn from life, she later became more of a propaganda figure based on the Bolshevik ideal of what a woman should be. Some writers of the 1920s, both male and female, joined in the government's consciousness-raising campaign among women by trying to create inspiring role-models – larger-than-life heroines who, with the help of Marxist-Leninist doctrine, would struggle to establish themselves as full and equal citizens of the USSR.[72]

Many women's texts of the 1920s (like feminist writings by Soviet men) emphasized women's liberation by the Soviet regime. Women were presented as men's equal in factory and party: Karavaeva's *Lesozavod* (The Sawmill, 1927), for example, depicts peasant women recruited to work in a sawmill; and in Inber's "Arlen i Ninel'" ("Arlen and Ninel'," 1928) a young girl proclaims: "Nowadays, woman is like a man – she can do anything." Literature of the 1920s generally celebrated working-class women, while denigrating backward peasant women, women of bourgeois origin, and supporters of the New Economic Policy (such as the aristocratic Alina in Shaginian's *Prikliucheniia damy iz obshchestva* [Adventures of a Society Lady, 1923], and the "NEPwoman" Nina in Kollontai's "Vasilisa Malygina," 1923).

Like the female protagonists of nineteenth-century radical fiction, Bolshevik heroines were expected to subordinate "feminine" desires to the cause.

Interestingly, however, women writers sometimes created characters who were more ambiguous than the one-dimensional proletarian heroines depicted in much male-authored fiction.[73] One such is Virineia, the eponymous heroine of Lydiia Seifullina's best-known novella (1924). Seifullina, a member of the Socialist Revolutionary Party from 1917 to 1919, wrote short naturalistic works distinguished by vivid characters and plots, a close knowledge of peasant language and psychology, and a frank representation of the violence and confusion involved in establishing the new order in the countryside. *Virineia* depicts a beautiful orphaned girl who falls victim to the patriarchal sexual customs still prevalent in the Russian village. She is stigmatized for "erotomania" because she has an affair out of wedlock, then abandons her weak, drunken lover who cannot give her a child, and when another admirer is killed by jealous peasants, leaves her village to work on road construction. Although Virineia eventually sinks into drunkenness and promiscuity, Seifullina's aim throughout is to demonstrate that Virineia eventually develops assertiveness and self-respect through her contact with a communist man. However, her novel differs from some male-authored fiction which depicts women as weak before they meet their communist hero (such as Ol'ga in Aleksei Tolstoy's "Gadiuka" ["The Viper," 1924]). Virineia is portrayed as a proud, sensuous woman who is free to select and abandon her male partners, and enjoys the power which her beauty enables her to exercise over men. Some Soviet critics regarded Virineia as too "decadent" to be a typical proletarian heroine, since she is ruled largely by her emotions, struggles against the old order primarily to obtain sexual freedom, and her deepest desire is to be a mother. Even her murder by counter-revolutionary Cossacks is caused because she is a mother – as her enemies anticipate, she is "drawn by her milk to the babe."

Despite its commitment to women's liberation, the Bolshevik revolution was largely a masculine event, accompanied by masculine iconography.[74] Not surprisingly, then, some prominent women writers of the 1920s who enthusiastically embraced Bolshevism harbored an uneasy attitude towards female identity and feminine writing,[75] which made them reluctant to place female characters at the center of their works,[76] or led them to depict women in conventional terms typical of masculine literature.

Aleksandra Kollontai was the woman writer of the 1920s who made the most conscious effort to incorporate women's issues into her fiction, as well as her political policies. She was a tireless campaigner for women's rights who held a number of high government posts after the Revolution, but was demoted due to political disagreements with the Party leaders. It was after her dismissal as head of the *Zhenotdel* (The Women's Section) in 1922 and her banishment to Norway on a minor diplomatic mission that Kollontai turned to fiction as a vehicle for her ideas on women's liberation. Her six stories (all published in 1923) are primarily fictional commentaries on her political writings. Their style is spare and the characters schematic, but the ideas are forcibly expressed. This simple format was deliberately chosen as an appropriate means of appealing to working-class women.

The typical heroine of Kollontai's stories (for example, the eponymous Vasilisa Malygina, and Natasha in "A Great Love") is an intellectual, usually single and childless, not because she is against marriage and motherhood in principle, but because these aspects of a woman's life do not constitute a high priority for her. Her attitude to sex is healthy and principled, not licentious: she will remain faithful to a man as long as she loves him. She is deeply involved with her work, which is usually in politics or social service, sometimes science; she is dynamic, assertive, valued by her colleagues, with a sense of personal dignity. Her one great source of difficulty is in personal relations with men, both because of external pressures and her own "atavistic" emotions inherited from the patriarchal past. Often she has to cope with a lover's possessiveness, insufficient respect for her work, and resentment of her unwillingness to be a housewife. All Kollontai's fictional works deal to some extent with the problem of women's inner struggle to become less vulnerable and more self-sufficient by overcoming excessive emotional dependence on men. Her works are not as simplistic thematically as is sometimes suggested; her own personal experience enabled her to present the conflict between love and work in a compelling manner. Some of the "solutions" she proposes, however, reflect the simplistic utopianism of the 1920s, such as Vasilisa Malygina's decision to bring up her baby within a communist sisterhood.[77]

The best known of Kollontai's stories is "Liubov' trekh pokolenii" ("Love of Three Generations") which explores women's changing attitudes to sexual love from the 1860s to the 1920s. The heroine's mother espoused the populist view of love as a monogamous passion demanding complete emotional commitment and undivided loyalty. The heroine Ol'ga, whose experiences reflect those of the author, regards love as an experience of great, but not paramount, importance; in her generation infidelity to one's chosen partner, though not easily accepted, was tolerated. Ol'ga's daughter Zhenia, an eighteen-year-old Komsomol activist, engages in casual affairs with a number of men, including her mother's lover, claiming that she has no time to fall in love. She resorts to abortion to terminate an unwanted pregnancy, vowing to "use something" next time. Soviet critics often misleadingly quoted Zhenia's views as an alleged expression of Kollontai's own ideas, and ascribed to her the so-called "glass of water" theory – the view that changing sexual partners was a matter of no greater importance than drinking a glass of water when you are thirsty. This crude philosophy has become associated with Kollontai, but in fact her ideal of sexual life was not promiscuous pleasure for its own sake, but a love between two people based on friendship and equality. Her aim was to dissociate sex from the notion of sin, and to combat the hypocrisy of a society which allowed far more sexual freedom to men than to women.[78]

Although before the Revolution Kollontai had been implacably opposed to the Russian feminist movement, the attacks on her conduct and writings in the 1920s demonstrate that her ideas on women's emancipation (which would now be considered "feminist"), were too radical for male critics and Party officials. Evidently, women's liberation in Russia still had to be within male-established bounds. After 1923, Kollontai spent most of her life abroad, which diminished the influence of her writings within the USSR. Her fiction was not republished in the USSR, and her theoretical writings have only recently been rediscovered by feminists, initially in the West, and subsequently in Russia.

Although "women's literature" continued to be denigrated in the 1920s,[79] women's prose of the 1920s was still characterized by some distinctive female voices. Some authors, such as Forsh, Inber, and Shaginian, engaged in stylistic experimentation, even if they primarily chose to adopt a masculine identity (for example, three out of the four voices in Shaginian's KiK [The Witch and the Communist, 1929] are male).[80] By the mid-1930s, however, innovative methods had been largely crushed by the government-sponsored policy of Socialist Realism. In the Stalin period, works of the 1920s which treated women's issues from a feminine point of view, such as Kollontai's stories, Seifullina's Virineia, and Ketlinskaia's "Nat'ka Michurina" (1927), were subject to criticism for their allegedly distorted and superficial approach to sexual and family themes. The abrupt abolition of the *Zhenotdel* in 1930 on the pretext that its work was finished and that the "woman question" was "resolved" spelled the end of independent feminist writing in Russia until the *samizdat* writings of the late Soviet period.[81]

Conclusion

There is a greater diversity of realist and feminist texts by Russian women writers in the period 1881–1929 than has generally been recognized. Individual women writers are also more versatile than is usually imagined. Verbitskaia was not simply a writer of sensational blockbusters, but also wrote many novels on feminist themes. Krestovskaia, usually regarded as a writer concerned solely with women's tempestuous emotional lives, could also write powerfully about male psychology ("Syn" ["The Son," 1893]), and produced two stories about a young couple's happy love ("Deti" ["Children"] and "Pervoe schast'e" ["First Happiness," 1904]). The author of the Silver Age who has been most seriously underrated is Ol'nem, with her restrained portraits of a declining aristocracy, subtle exploration of male and female psychology, and interesting portraits of the "new woman." Writers later known as committed Socialist Realists, such as Seifullina, Forsh, and Shaginian, produced some experimental texts in the prerevolutionary period and the 1920s.

Although many women writers of this period were deeply influenced by the masculine literary tradition, some took issue with the image of women in the works of male writers. Ol'nem's "Ivan Fedorovich," for example, provides a reworking of Karamzin's "Poor Liza" (1792); and heroines of feminist and erotic fiction asserted women's right to sexual freedom and fulfillment, in contrast to the asexuality propagated by Chernyshevsky's *What is to be Done?* and Tolstoy's *Kreutzer Sonata*, and the male lust advocated by Artsybashev.

After the Bolshevik Revolution, the themes of women's prose were not transformed as substantially as might have been expected. The Russian tradition of committed literature persisted, although the cause to which women writers were committed had changed.

Women realist writers of the period 1881–1929 were by no means solely concerned with love, family, and female psychology, but also attempted (with varying degrees of success) to depict the "truth" of Russian society in those years and to illustrate women's continuing struggle to extend their rights and roles. Many of their novels and stories are still interesting and enjoyable today, treating subjects which are relevant to women in the late twentieth and early twenty-first centuries. It is important to reintegrate the lost voices of Russian women into the history of Russian Realism, not to challenge the acknowledged tradition, but to complement it, demonstrating how female authors evoke women's experience more effectively than their male contemporaries.

NOTES

1. V. Chuiko, "Sovremennye zhenshchiny-pisatel'nitsy," *Nabliudatel'* 4 (1889).

2. A. Skabichevskii, "Tekushchaia literatura," *Syn otechestva* 224 (1899), 2.

3. J. Clausen, "Literature and Politics," in E. Hoshino Altbach, J. Clausen, D. Schultz, and N. Stephan (eds.), *German Feminism: Readings in Politics and Literature* (Albany, NY, 1984), 27–38; Helena Forsås-Scott (ed.), *Textual Liberation: European Feminist Writing in the Twentieth Century* (London, 1991), 1–12.

4. Richard Stites, *The Women's Liberation Movement in Russia: Feminism, Nihilism, and Bolshevism, 1860–1930* (Princeton, NJ, 1978), 166–78.

5. See Paula Baker, "The Domestication of Politics: Women and American Political Society, 1780–1920," *American Historical Review* 89 (June 1984), 620–47; Mary Poovey, *Uneven Developments: The Ideological Work of Gender in Mid-Victorian England* (London, 1988); and Nancy R. Reagin, *A German Women's Movement: Class and Gender in Hanover, 1880–1933* (Chapel Hill, NC and London, 1995).

6. Irina Kazakova, "Criticism and Journalism at the Turn of the Century on the Work of Russian Women Writers," in Marsh *Women*. Barbara Engel, *Between the Fields and the City: Women, Work, and Family in Russia, 1861–1914* (Cambridge, 1994), 135, states that according to the census of 1897, the percentage of working women living alone was 86 percent in St. Petersburg, and 93 percent in Moscow.

7. Stites, *Women's Liberation Movement*, 191–231; Linda Edmondson, *Feminism in Russia, 1900–1917* (Stanford, CA, 1984).

8. Kelly *History*, 126.

9. See, for example, Shapir's articles on the rights of women, "Zhenskii s''ezd," *Russkie vedomosti* (1908), 295; "Zhenskoe bespravie," *Birzhevye vedomosti* (June 15, 1916).

10. Barbara Engel, *Mothers and Daughters. Women of the Intelligentsia in Nineteenth-Century Russia* (Cambridge and New York, 1983).

11. See Gurevich's "9-e ianvaria, 1906" (St. Petersburg, 1906; repr. 1926); "Pochemu nuzhno dat' zhenshchinam vse prava i svobody" (St. Petersburg, 1906; repr. 1917).

12. A number of women writers, such as Letkova, Runova, and Verbitskaia, published in the *Sbornik na pomoshch' uchashchimsia zhenshchinam* (Collection in Aid of Women Students, Moscow, 1901).

13. E. A. Koltonovskaia, *Zhenskie siluety* (St. Petersburg, 1912), 7.

14. Peter Ulf Møller, *Postlude to the Kreutzer Sonata: Tolstoy and the Debate on Sexual Morality in Russian Literature in the 1890s*, tr. John Kendal (Amsterdam, 1989); Laura Engelstein, *The Keys to Happiness. Sex and the Search for Modernity in Fin-de-Siècle Russia* (Ithaca, NY and London, 1992).

15. Engelstein, *Keys to Happiness*, 132, n. 10 gives a full list of forensic and sexology texts available in Russian translation before 1900.

16. M. Lokhvitskaia, *Stikhotvoreniia* (St. Petersburg, 1900), cited in Pachmuss *Modernism*, 90.

17. See, for example, Z. Gippius, "Posviashchenie," in *Sobranie stikhov*, vol. I (Moscow, 1904), 3.

18. See Kelly *History*, 149; Jeffrey Brooks, *When Russia Learned to Read* (Princeton, NJ, 1984). Other best-selling writers were Nadezhda Lappo-Danilevskaia, who usually depicted the upper classes and artistic circles, and Lydiia Charskaia, who wrote for children and adolescents.

19. Rosenthal, "Achievement and Obscurity: Women's Prose in the Silver Age," in Clyman and Greene, 164–5.

20. For further discussion of the Russian women's prose tradition, see Rosalind Marsh, "Introduction," in Marsh *Gender*, 10–17.

21. On the influence of Sand and Charlotte Brontë, see Ol'ga Demidova, "Russian Women Writers of the Nineteenth Century," in Marsh *Gender*, 98–9; on Verbitskaia, see Rosalind Marsh, "Anastasiia Verbitskaia Reconsidered," in *ibid.*, 205, n. 67.

22. Heldt.

23. Elaine Showalter, *A Literature of Their Own: from Charlotte Brontë to Doris Lessing* (London, 1982), 11–12.

24. *The Journal of Marie Bashkirtseff*, tr. Mathilde Blind (London, 1985); discussed further in Charlotte Rosenthal, "Achievement and Obscurity," in Clyman and Greene, 151–2; Charlotte Rosenthal, "The Silver Age: Highpoint for Women?" in Linda Edmondson (ed.), *Women and Society in Russia and the Soviet Union* (Cambridge, 1992), 34–6.

25. L. Gurevich, "M. K. Bashkirtseva, Biografiko-psikhologicheskii etiud," *RBog* 2 (1888); "Dnevniki Marii Bashkirtsevoi," tr. L.Gurevich, *SevV* 1–12 (1892). An abbreviated translation, *Iz dnevnika Marii Bashkirtsevoi*, tr. K. Plavinskii (St. Petersburg, 1889) had previously attracted little attention.

26. M. Protopopov, "Iarmarka zhenskogo tshcheslaviia," *RMysl'* 4 (1892), 195.

27. K. F. Golovin, *Russkii roman i russkoe obshchestvo* (St. Petersburg, 1897).

28. N. Nadezhdin, "Zhenshchiny v izobrazhenii sovremennykh russkikh zhenshchin-pisatel'nits," *NM* 92 (1902), 290.

29. Charlotte Rosenthal, "Carving Out a Career: Women Prose Writers, 1885–1917, the Biographical Background," in Marsh *Gender*, 131–2, 137.

30. Aleksandra Kollontai, "Novaia zhenshchina," *Sovremennyi mir* 9 (1913), 151–85 (166).

31. Beth Holmgren, "Why Russian Girls Loved Charskaia," *RR* 54 (January 1995), 94–5.

32. This term was used about George Eliot in Rosalind Miles, *The Female Form: Women Writers and the Conquest of the Novel* (London, 1987), 38, to refer to a woman author who writes "largely assuming the values and processes of the male-created and male-dominated society of her time."

33. Kelly *History*, 141.

34. One exception is Rosenthal, "Achievement and Obscurity," 160–1.

35. Koltonovskaia, *Zhenskie siluety*, 189–90 ; "Viktor Rusakov" (S. F. Librovich), "Ol'nem," *Izvestiia knizhnykh magazinov t-va M. O. Vol'f* 2 (1911), coll. 80–2; "Gudash" (M. V. Morozov), "Sredi zhurnalov," *Vseobshchii ezhemesiachnik* 5 (1910).

36. *Novoe vremia*, no. 9933 (1903).

37. Koltonovskaia, *Zhenskie siluety*, 189.

38. All published in the collection *Ocherki i rasskazy* (St. Petersburg, 1903).

39. "O. N. Ol'nem, *Ocherki i rasskazy*," *RBog* 3 (1904), part 2, 22.

40. "A.", "O. N. Ol'nem, *Ocherki i rasskazy*," *RMysl'* 12 (1903), 414; N. Asheshov, "O. N. Ol'nem. *Ocherki i rasskazy*," *Obrazovanie* 10 (1903), 106.

41. Koltonovskaia, *Zhenskie siluety*, 193.

42. *Ibid.*, 192.

43. Temira Pachmuss, *Zinaida Gippius: An Intellectual Profile* (Carbondale, IL, 1971), 17.

44. Kelly *History*, 142, n. 41; Catriona Kelly, "Life at the Margins: Women, Culture and *Narodnost'* 1890–1920," in *Gender Restructuring*.

45. See Henriette Goldschmidt; see Reagin, *A German Women's Movement*, 1, 26 and Baker, "The Domestication of Politics," 632.

46. Showalter, *Sexual Anarchy. Gender and Culture at the Fin de Siècle* (London, 1995), 64.

47. O. Shapir, "Avtobiografiia," in F. Fidler (ed.), *Pervye literaturnye shagi* (Moscow, 1911), 54.

48. Edmondson, *Feminism*, 100.

49. See, for example, A. Verbitskaia, "Vstrecha," *Severnii kur'er* 54 (December 24, 1899); "Kak zhivet i pitaetsia nasha uchashchaiasia zhenshchina?," no ref. (both in RGALI, fond 1042, opis' 1, delo 37, lists, 2–3, 5–6).

50. See also A. Krandievskaia's "Doch' naroda" (1904).

51. Koltonovskaia, *Zhenskie siluety*, 144.

52. On the plight of women writers, see also A. Verbitskaia, "Nezametnye dramy," in *Prestuplenie Mar'i Ivanovnoi*, 3rd edn. (Moscow, 1908), 97–125; and her article "Neskol'ko slov o nedavnei drame," *Smolenskii vestnik* (November 2, 1891), 3–4, written on the occasion of the suicide of her sister, the writer Aleksandra Sorneva (contained in RGALI, fond 1042, opis' 1, delo 37, list 1).

53. Jeffrey Brooks, *When Russia Learned to Read*, 278; for further discussion, see Catherine Schuler, *Women in Russian Theatre: The Actress in the Silver Age* (London, 1997).

54. Other writers with an acting background included Lydiia Charskaia, Verbitskaia, Nagrodskaia, and Shchepkina-Kupernik.

55. Engel, *Mothers and Daughters*.

56. On women's networks among the radical Russian intelligentsia, see Engel, *Mothers and Daughters*, 115, 201–2.

57. Donald Rayfield, *Anton Chekhov: A Life* (London, 1997), 301–2, 316, 334, 387–8.

58. On tainted heredity, see also Z. Gippius, "Odinokii" (1891).

59. On the problems experienced by working-class women with illegitimate children, see Engel, *Between the Fields and the City*, 146–9.

60. The analysis in Engel, *Between the Fields and the City*, 166–97, suggests that women writers' treatment of this theme reflected the reality of prostitution in Russia.

61. Linda Gordon, *Woman's Body, Woman's Right: A Social History of Birth Control in America* (New York, 1976), 95–115. However, by 1900, the United States was still backward in relation to Holland, where the first birth control clinic had been established in 1882, and France and Germany, where contraception was widely practiced.

62. On abortion and contraception in Russia, see Engel, *Between the Fields and the City*, 111–12, 146–7, 217–18, 241; Laura Engelstein, "Abortion and the Civil Order: the Legal and Medical Debates," in Barbara Evans Clements, Barbara Alpern Engel and Christine D. Worobec (eds.), *Russia's Women: Accommodation, Resistance, Transformation* (Berkeley and Los Angeles, CA, 1991), 185–205.

63. See, for example, G. Ia. Zak, "Umershchvlenie ploda i ugolovnoe pravo," *Pravo* 48 (1910), 2751.

64. For further discussion of these novels, see Kelly *History*, 149–52; Brooks, *When Russia Learned to Read*, 158–60, 278–92 *passim*; Engelstein, *Keys to Happiness*, 359–414.

65. For an attempt to rehabilitate Verbitskaia, see Rosalind Marsh, "Anastasiia Verbitskaia Reconsidered," in Marsh *Gender*, 184–205.

66. Showalter, *A Literature of Their Own*, 161.

67. For a critique of the Decadent treatment of lesbianism in this work, see Diana Lewis Burgin, "Laid Out in Lavender: Perceptions of Lesbian Love in Russian Literature and Criticism of the Silver Age, 1893–1917," in Costlow, Sandler, and Vowles, 182–4.

68. RGALI, fond 2174, opis' 1, edinitsa khraneniia 11–16. In 12, listy 6–7, Krestovskaia requests that her diary should be published, although not in her lifetime.

69. Marsh, "Anastasiia Verbitskaia Reconsidered," 186–7.

70. RGALI, fond 591, opis' 1, edinitsa khraneniia 25.

71. Barbara Evans Clements, "The Birth of the New Soviet Woman," in Abbott Gleason, Peter Kenez and Richard Stites (eds.), *Bolshevik Culture: Experiment and Order in the Russian Revolution* (Bloomington, IN, 1985), 220–37. On literature, see T. Kovnator, "Novaia zhenshchina v revoliutsionnoi literature," *Kommunistka* 5 (1920), 32–5; cf. Xenia Gasiorowska, *Women in Soviet Fiction 1917–1964* (Madison, WI, 1968), 35, who suggests that the very first 'New Woman' in Soviet literature appeared in 1921 in A. Neverov's story "Marya the Bolshevik" (1921).

72. For further discussion, see Gasiorowska, *Women in Soviet Fiction 1917–1964*; Rosalind Marsh, "The Birth, Death and Rebirth of Feminist Writing in Russia," in Forsås-Scott *Textual Liberation*, 142–8.

73. Another interesting, though flawed heroine is the eponymous heroine of Ketlinskaia's "Nat'ka Michurina" (1927), which suggests that the sexual liberation of the 1920s was not always to women's advantage.

74. Elizabeth Waters, "The Female Form in Soviet Political Iconography," in Clements, Engel and Worobec, *Russia's Women*, 225–42; Eric Naiman, "On the Metaphysics of Reproduction in a Utopian Age," in Costlow, Sandler and Vowles, 270–4.

75. Ol'ga Forsh, "Avtobiografiia," in *Sovetskie pisateli: Avtobiografii* (Moscow, 1959), vol. II, 585, 385.

76. Shaginian's only female-centered work is "Prikliucheniia damy iz obshchestva" (1923).

77. A similar view is advocated by a character in Ketlinskaia's "Nat'ka Michurina."

78. Kollontai's views on sex and love are outlined in her article "Dorogu krylatomu Erosu!," *Molodaia gvardiia* 3 (1923), 111–24.

79. See Katharine Hodgson's chapter in this volume.

80. For detailed discussion of *KiK*, see David Shepherd, *Beyond Metafiction: Self-Consciousness in Russian Literature* (Oxford, 1992), 64–89.

81. Tatyana Mamonova (ed.), *Women and Russia: Feminist Writings from the Soviet Union* (Oxford, 1984).

10

Women and gender in post-symbolist poetry and the Stalin era

The idea that women had a significant and specifically feminine contribution to make to Russian poetry was a recurring theme among early twentieth-century literary critics. One of the most striking claims came from Nadezhda L'vova, a poet herself, who predicted that "the twentieth century will probably be known to history as the 'women's century,' the century which saw the awakening of woman's creative self-awareness." Indeed, by about 1910 women poets had begun to win recognition from both readers and reviewers on an unprecedented scale. The early 1920s in particular were a time of considerable achievement and promise. Women who had already established their reputations before the 1917 October Revolution were publishing some of their best work, and had been joined by talented newcomers. Judging by the amount and quality of poetry by women being published towards the end of the 1920s, however, things were starting to look rather different. Some women had stopped writing poetry altogether, and turned to other fields such as journalism or translation. Some had emigrated. Many found that they were no longer able to publish their work, and fell silent, or wrote "for the desk drawer." Almost a quarter of a century later, at the time of Stalin's death in 1953, few of the women who had emerged onto the scene before the late 1920s had managed to publish significant amounts of their work in the Soviet Union. A younger generation who had begun their careers in the late 1920s or early 1930s found themselves hemmed in by censorship and the demands of Socialist Realism. Since 1953, however, and especially since 1988, unpublished poetry written during the Stalin era has gradually come to light, and poets who had fallen into obscurity have been rediscovered. The picture that emerges is one of considerable achievement by women writing poetry in Russia.

This process of rediscovery, which has made it possible to gain a much more complete idea of the range and scope of women's poetry written during this period, allows us to consider the nature of a women's tradition in the first half of the century. I would argue that it is more productive to consider ways in which women pushed back the boundaries of literary convention, extending the possibilities available to the female poetic voice, while still maintaining close contact with a male-dominated literary world, rather than attempting to construct an idea of a separate women's tradition which, in Jan Montefiore's words, risks being imagined as "unrealistically autonomous."[1] Most women considered here chose to adopt a persona that was strongly gender-marked, abandoning the tactic of hiding behind a "neutral" masculine voice and therefore emphasizing the difference between themselves and the male poets whose works made up the canon. Drawing attention to their gender was, in effect, the first step towards negotiating a space within the dominant culture which would allow women to speak as individuals, rather than in accordance with conventional ideas of how women "ought" to speak. In their search for models of the authoritative female voice, some looked back to folklore, where genres such as the lament were traditionally women's exclusive preserve. There is, however, little evidence that they wanted to be part of a separate, female canon. Stylistically and thematically many women poets allied themselves with the dominant cultural heritage, in which women were spoken of, but rarely spoke themselves. Yet while male predecessors and contemporaries were acknowledged as mentors and sources of inspiration, women also began to acknowledge their female contemporaries and to be aware of and respond to one another's work. The tradition of women's poetry that began to emerge is the creation of a loose association of women who were influenced by each other's writing and responded critically to what other women wrote, without feeling the need to separate themselves from the Russian literary tradition as a whole.

Our perception of the breadth and variety of Russian women's poetry has been somewhat obscured by concentration on two contrasting and outstandingly gifted figures, Anna Akhmatova and Marina Tsvetaeva. Presented in isolation from their contemporaries, they risk being viewed as anomalies which are difficult to assimilate into a coherent picture of the development of Russian poetry. As a result, the connections that exist between these two and their contemporaries are lost from sight. It was a combination of talent, self-mythologization, and external circumstances that turned them into the Alpha and Omega by whom subsequent Russian women poets have tended to be judged.[2] When Akhmatova and Tsvetaeva first started their literary careers, however, it was as two young women poets among many, and their voices echoed those of their contemporaries.

As Symbolism, the literary movement which had been dominant at the turn of the century, lost its cohesion around 1910, a number of women poets began publishing work which met with considerable critical interest. This interest was fueled by the Symbolists' view of the feminine as a creative, elemental principle, and an expectation that women might discover their own language to express their own experiences. The work of Mirra Lokhvitskaia (1869–1905) proved to be ground-breaking in its presentation of a poetic persona who was exotic, sensual, self-absorbed, and markedly feminine. Among those who published their debut collections before 1917 were Anna Akhmatova, Adelaida Gertsyk, Elena Guro, Vera Inber, Natal'ia Krandievskaia, Elizaveta Kuz'mina-Karavaeva, Nadezhda L'vova, Sofiia Parnok, Marietta Shaginian and Marina Tsvetaeva. Few were formal members of literary groups, though they were not without male mentors, already established writers, to introduce them to the literary world. The earliest published work of most of these poets concentrates on conveying the emotions and experiences – predominantly unhappy love affairs, with an admixture of religious guilt – of young women from well-off families. In many cases these collections had the appearance of lyric diaries, a form felt to be particularly feminine, giving the impression of unmediated self-expression. This led to readers identifying the persona with the poet, reading the poems as biography rather than art. This kind of reading of the work of Lokhvitskaia and Akhmatova certainly contributed to their popularity. The fact that their poetry was so well received suggests that it met a real need for confessional poetry which recognized specifically female experience. Lokhvitskaia's Decadent female persona and "oriental" voice found echoes in the poetry of, among others, Inber and Shaginian, whose popular 1912 collection *Orientalia*, which drew on exotic eastern and Caucasian motifs, was reprinted six times between 1913 and 1922. The poems in Akhmatova's first two collections focused on conveying her heroine's psychological state, an approach taken up by many of her contemporaries. Akhmatova's early poems are, in the main, short lyrical evocations of moments of emotional tension, in which physical details, for example of the heroine's clothing or surroundings, are used to bring her inner predicament into sharp focus.

Although other women explored different themes, for example Elizaveta Kuz'mina-Karavaeva in her cycle centering on the Old Testament heroine Ruth, or experimented with form, as did Elena Guro, who was close to the Futurists in her playfully inventive use of neologisms, critics soon began to categorize "women's poetry," with some exceptions, as having a very limited range and being of little interest to all except the poet's closest friends. Critics' impatience with the feminine persona felt to be typical of women's poetry reflects their own preconceptions about the restricted range of a clearly marked female voice in poetry, though it was also a reaction to the undoubted shortcomings of work which imitated Akhmatova's use of physical detail, without evoking the psychological depth she revealed in her poems. Moreover, reactions against Symbolism meant that talk of a special "women's language" was replaced by criticism of women poets' technical ineptitude, which emerged forcefully in Valerii Briusov's 1912 collection of reviews of women's poetry. Some of the most severe critical comments, however, came from women themselves.[3] Khodasevich praised those he considered to have succeeded in escaping the narrow confines of "women's poetry": Akhmatova for dealing with the themes of "women's poetry" in the spirit of "not women's, but general human poetics"; and Parnok, who, in her poems, was "not a man, nor a woman, but a human being."[4] Indeed, neither Parnok nor Akhmatova restricted their poetic persona to the one Khodasevich dismissed as a catalog of props – silks, rouge, jewelry, and feathers. If this persona was just a role to be acted out, then other roles could be explored, allowing women to express a diversity of identity beyond the familiar feminine stereotypes.

Against the background of strongly masculine bias that existed in post-Symbolist literary groups, poets set about seeking models for an explicitly gender-marked female voice which could be perceived as having authority. The only Russian woman poet invoked by her early twentieth-century successors seems to have been the nineteenth-century writer Karolina Pavlova, in whom interest was revived by Briusov's 1915 edition of her works. Women were more inclined to look back instead to the oral traditions of folklore, beyond the literary canon and individual authorship. Here was a tradition where women took center stage when speaking of key events such as marriage and death. The ritualized language of laments and enchantments offered women poets a way of transcending everyday reality and speaking with authority as prophets whose words could command both nature and mortals. The intimate and

individual could be subsumed into the universal, archetypal, and impersonal. Adelaida Gertsyk in particular used the language of rural folklore
to convey her persona's magical perception of nature; Gertsyk's work was
to have a deep and lasting effect on Tsvetaeva, whose poetry from 1916
onwards was imbued with the language and themes of Russian folklore.
Here women certainly found a model for the authoritative, powerful
female voice which suited a perception of themselves as literary outsiders,
excluded from "masculine" urban high culture, yet claiming membership of a more ancient "feminine" culture grounded in rural tradition.
Women's adoption of a prophetic voice, drawing on the powerful associations of national tradition – Russia's pre-Christian culture gave the
symbols of Mother Earth and Mother Russia particular weight – can be
seen too as a response to the sense of cultural crisis which a world war,
two revolutions and a civil war made more intense.

The October Revolution of 1917 and the ensuing civil war did not
silence the generation of women who had begun to publish around 1910.
It was only gradually, during the 1920s, that the work of many well-
known women poets began to disappear from public view. Akhmatova's
1922 collection, *Anno Domini MCMXXI*, was the last book she was able to
publish for many years. While her early collections remained enormously
popular, a new note appeared in her work during World War I, casting
the poet as the tragic voice of a suffering nation. A powerful impetus to
Akhmatova's self-mythologization as poet of shared personal and
national tragedy was provided by the execution of her former husband,
the poet Nikolai Gumilev, sentenced in August 1921 for alleged participation in a counter-revolutionary plot. His execution is alluded to both
in the title *Anno Domini MCMXXI* and several of its poems. The note of
national tragedy is also heard strongly in the work of Anna Radlova;
her strongly pacifist poems present an apocalyptic picture of a city and
people devastated by war.

Sofiia Parnok, whose first book was published in 1916, went on to write
some of her finest poetry during the 1920s. Parnok's stylistic innovations
were not as blatantly attention-grabbing as those of male Futurists like
Mayakovsky, but her use of colloquial, prosaic diction, her experiments
with rhyme, and avoidance of metaphor and musicality represent a clear
departure from Russian tradition. Her treatment of gender was also
innovative. Parnok's work came to promote a woman's voice which asserts
its independence from notions opposing masculine and feminine, woman
and humanity. A significant portion of her output is made up of love

poetry addressed to women in which the sixth- to seventh-century BC Greek poet Sappho was an important legitimizing figure. The frequent recourse, in the love poems of her early collections, to figures from classical mythology and references to Sappho, as well as use of the stanzaic form associated with her, suggest that the poet felt a certain amount of anxiety about expressing her lesbianism outside these trappings. Parnok felt herself to be an outsider most of her life because of family circumstances, her Jewish origins, and her sexuality. As the 1920s continued, she found herself increasingly marginalized in the Soviet literary world. The image of the poet-outsider is at the center of two late poems, one of which invokes Karolina Pavlova, little regarded in her own time, but the "glorious great-grandmother" of Russian poetry. The other narrates a dream in which the poet is neither heard nor seen by the people around her. Yet exclusion brought Parnok a greater freedom to express her individuality. Late cycles of poems dedicated to her last love are direct, discarding references to antiquity, and are both wistful and playful in their recognition of both partners' ages. In philosophical poetry, a male-dominated genre, Parnok speaks as a woman, but, by dismissing categories of gender, nationality, and political affiliation, speaks to and on behalf of all humanity.[5]

Marina Tsvetaeva's affair with Parnok between 1914 and 1916 was reflected in both women's work. Parnok's poems to Tsvetaeva observe greater decorum, while in Tsvetaeva's cycle, *Woman Friend* (Podruga, 1976), suppressed during her lifetime, the conventionally feminine persona of her earlier work gives way here to one which expresses the physicality and force of her emotions. Many of her poems express female identity in physical terms; her evocations of the body in love poetry as well as in poems about creativity, are compellingly frank and have no parallel in the work of her contemporaries. Tsvetaeva also questioned received ideas about femininity exemplified in myth and literature, defending Helen of Troy on the charge of having started the Trojan war, and having Ophelia address Hamlet in defense of Gertrude. Conventional ideas about the incompatibility of femininity and creativity, however, inform her epic poem "On a Red Steed" ("Na krasnom kone," 1922). A stern, masculine genius demands sacrifices of the heroine, culminating in the sacrifice of her son. Yet Tsvetaeva's prolific output of the early 1920s shows no lack of artistic confidence. Archaisms, colloquial language, and folkloric formulae abound in cycles of poems dedicated to Blok, Akhmatova, and Moscow, and in verse adaptations of Russian folk tales. Tsvetaeva emigrated to Berlin in 1922 and continued to produce poetry – lyric and narrative – using a variety of styles from neo-classical diction and biblical allusions, to incantations, which was full of verbal creativity and rhythmic innovation. Her work is particularly marked by experiments with unconventional meter, unequaled by any poet writing in Russian. Many of the metrical structures she uses do not feature in the classical repertoire of Russian poetry, but these departures from tradition provide new patterns to which she then rigorously adheres, an unusual approach at a time when others tended to use meter in looser, more flexible ways. Tsvetaeva's style is also characterized by the use of puns and densely textured word play. During the seventeen years she spent as an émigrée in Czechoslovakia and France, she never found acceptance in the Russian émigré community, nor had she concealed her spiritedly anti-Soviet attitude before her emigration, epitomized in her cycle in praise of the White Army, *The Demesne of Swans* (Lebedinyi stan, 1957). In her poetry as well as in her life, Tsvetaeva disrupted convention. Because of this, she has come to be identified by some with dangerously unrestrained femininity, by others as a feminist heroine.

The October Revolution of 1917 brought more than a dash of female emancipation, with laws giving women new political, economic, and social rights. For a brief period feminist issues were allowed to surface, making it easier for women to express their female identity on their own terms. The main literary groupings, both pro-Bolshevik and others, were as before, however, largely masculine concerns. The Serapion Brothers group, for example, set up in the early 1920s to defend the primacy of art over ideology, had just one woman member, the poet Elizaveta Polonskaia. Most of the women included in a major 1925 anthology of poetry were categorized as "not belonging to any particular group."[6] Among the more radical post-1917 newcomers was Anna Barkova, whose first book *Woman* (Zhenshchina), published in 1919, has little in common with the preoccupations of prerevolutionary women's poetry. Barkova's lyric personae range from a cosmic, all-embracing mother to a belligerent Amazon, whose sole weakness is a propensity to fall in love with the enemy, to a rebellious, aggressive, and ultimately self-destructive outsider. Mariia Shkapskaia was less openly "revolutionary" in her choice of subject-matter, but radical in her treatment of what might appear to be a standard woman's theme, motherhood. As the title of her 1921 book *Mater Dolorosa* suggests, Shkapskaia's often guilty and anxious lyric persona has nothing in common with the figure of the strong but sympathetic "heroine-mother" which would become a sentiment-laden mainstay of 1930s Socialist Realism. Her guilt is twofold: as a mother she feels guilt at the death of her stillborn or aborted children, and as a religious believer, guilt at turning Christ away because her children have, for the time being, a greater claim on her attention. Shkapskaia does not shrink from evoking the female body; sex, pregnancy, childbirth, and abortion are described in largely symbolic terms which, nevertheless, seemed excessively physical to some contemporaries. The subjects Shkapskaia addresses are, however, those which most obviously differentiate women from men, and her world is polarized between male – both God and mortal men are remote, cruel, demanding figures – and female – the Mother of God and Eve offer solace and understanding to all women.

The range and variety of work by women poets available to the Soviet reader in the early 1920s reflects the fact that lyric poetry was considered by the authorities to be a part of declining bourgeois culture. By the mid-1920s, however, private publishing houses were beginning to be squeezed out of existence, and literature was subject to increasing censorship and political control. Lyric poetry, centered as it was on individual concerns, was declared to be irrelevant to readers in the "new" society, and women poets, most of whose output was lyric in nature, found their work, which ignored "the collective," was no longer in demand. Marginalized as writers of lyric poetry, they were also marginalized as women, for all that the Soviet state had proclaimed female emancipation. Official attitudes towards women as a backward group, in thrall to the past, religion, and superstition, played a decisive role in the critical response to women's poetry. The more women poets turned towards the language of folklore, the more they were exiled from the increasingly restrictive literary mainstream. Trotsky mocked Akhmatova, Radlova, and Shkapskaia for their bourgeois reliance on the deity to solve their amorous and domestic worries; Briusov attacked Akhmatova's technical incompetence.[7]

As the 1920s progressed, not only Tsvetaeva, but also Kuz'mina-Karavaeva, and a number of young poets, including Irina Odoevtseva and Nina Berberova, emigrated. Some, like Gertsyk, found it impossible to publish and wrote instead "for the drawer," while others stopped writing poetry altogether. Between 1923 and 1940 Akhmatova's work was not published in the USSR, and critics referred to her only as a poet of the past who had lost touch with the present day. Children's poetry provided a relatively safe option, taken up by Polonskaia, among others. Marietta Shaginian became a novelist, while Shkapskaia, realizing that her religious stance was unacceptable to the censors, began a career as a journalist. Radlova, Vera Merkur'eva, who published very few of her own poems in her lifetime, and, eventually, Parnok all turned to literary translation as a way of making a living. Tsvetaeva, too, after her return to the USSR in 1939, tried to make ends meet with translations, while trying, unsuccessfully, to publish a book of her own verse. She took her own life in 1941, as an evacuee far from Moscow.

The formation of the Soviet Writers' Union in 1932 offered women only token positions of influence in the literary establishment. At the Union's first congress in 1934, only 3.7 percent of the delegates were women. The "woman question" (*zhenskii vopros*) had officially been declared solved in 1930; during the decades that followed, officially promoted concepts of gender identity became polarized between the "manly" man and the "womanly" woman. This inevitably had repercussions for women poets. Those who continued to pursue a literary career in the 1930s tended to gravitate towards the margins, as representatives of a Soviet version of women's poetry which supported the image of Soviet women as strong, socially involved but essentially domestic and motherly, and conveyed an acceptably conventional picture of women's interests and identity. Vera Inber, whose early career began with the writing of technically competent "decadent" verse, completed the process of reinventing herself as a Soviet woman poet during the 1930s (see Anna Krylova's chapter). Younger poets, such as Margarita Aliger and Ol'ga Berggol'ts, described the joys (and pitfalls) of combining Komsomol activism with raising a young family. What emerged was a kind of poetic division of labor, with women speaking of private, family matters, without losing sight of the wider social context, while men tended to look across broader horizons.

The position assigned to women poets, based in the domestic sphere, with a responsibility to mediate between private and public life, was in fact an ambiguous one. As Beth Holmgren observes, in Stalinist society the domestic sphere had little status, with the result that while life outside the home was thoroughly orchestrated, inside the home women could take advantage of their low profile to express dissenting views in unofficial works of art.[8] Those writing outside official structures were free to ignore the social and political context and write pure lyric poetry, or to produce poetry of protest and resistance. Mariia Petrovykh, known then only as a translator, composed a number of love poems of high quality, using dense, incantatory language (but avoiding folkloric overtones) to create a harmonious whole. Another translator whose own work was unknown at the time is Vera Merkur'eva; although relatively little of her original poetry is yet published, it reveals a distinctive, "difficult" and intriguing voice and a concern with spirituality which connects her work to that of poets like Gertsyk. Akhmatova continued to write some fine lyric poetry; a cycle of poems on the creative process takes its place alongside evocations of distress and spiritual and physical disorientation, and, increasingly, poems to the dead. For Akhmatova, addressing the dead, as Joseph Brodsky wrote, was "the only way of preventing speech from slipping into a howl."[9] The traditional lament for the dead (*prichi-tanie*) is speech threatened with degenerating into a wordless howl, so Akhmatova's address to the dead might be seen as a way of expressing, on the brink of incoherence, the enormities of the Stalin era. Meanwhile some "official" poets, like Berggol'ts, published poems acceptable to the censors, while writing poems on "forbidden" themes which remained unpublished for many years.

Overlooked as politically insignificant, unless they were Communist Party members, many women escaped the arrests of the late 1930s, and carried on writing in private, their work known only to a few trusted friends. Their marginalized position enabled them to speak authorita-tively on matters mainstream culture preferred not to address. The mass arbitrary arrests which ravaged the cities in the late 1930s confirmed ear-lier fears that the ideals of the Revolution had been comprehensively abandoned. Clearly, Stalin's terror found reflection in the work of many Russian poets, male and female; yet it can be argued that women's poetry derived a special power from women's capacity for identification with the symbolic female representative of the nation, Mother Russia. This figure, her authority derived from tradition, stands as a representative of the Russian people in implicit opposition to the corrupt masculine state. None assumed this role more effectively than Anna Akhmatova in her cycle of poems written between 1935 and 1940 entitled *Rekviem* (Requiem, 1963).[10] Akhmatova's husband Punin and her son from her first marriage with Gumilev were both arrested. *Requiem* vividly evokes her own anguish, but makes it clear she is one of a community of suffering women, wives and mothers of prisoners, on whose behalf she testifies. While the persona Akhmatova adopts alludes to national tradition, in which the suffering nation is often personified in the figure of a suffering woman, it is not easily reduced to Russian nationalistic formulae. The accusatory stance of Akhmatova's persona is a new departure from the conventional figure's almost saintly forbearance. Akhmatova's reshaping of traditional models is particularly evident when she casts herself as Christ's mother at his crucifixion. This mother is silent, still, and terrible; none dare even look at her mutely accusing presence. At the same time, she is the one figure who is able to give voice to what is happening.

Berggol'ts, initially an enthusiastic supporter of communism, found herself excluded from the Party in 1937 and, shortly after her reinstatement in 1938, was arrested and held in prison for several months, where she suffered a miscarriage. In the cycle *Rodine* (To my Motherland, 1965), which contains poems written during and immediately after her imprisonment, Berggol'ts, rather than speaking on the nation's behalf as Akhmatova does, addresses her country first in horrified bewilderment, then anger, demanding a dialogue on equal terms. Among addressees of her prison poem cycle *Ispytanie* (Ordeal, 1961) are her husband and her unborn child; with them she speaks using language and imagery reminiscent of folksong. A tale of near-fatal magical transformation, in which a brother appeals for help to his sister, who is powerless to save him, becomes the basis for a dialogue between the poet and her conscience in "Alenushka" (1965). The mismatch between personal experience and the official version of reality led Berggol'ts to address the real political and social context in a poem of 1940 (published only in 1987) in which she speaks on behalf of her generation, deceived and self-deceiving:

> No, it's not from our miserable books –
> Just like a beggar's bundle,
> That you will find out how difficult,
> How impossible our lives were.
> How we loved bitterly, crudely,
> How, as we loved, we deceived ourselves,
> How, gritting our teeth in interrogations
> We renounced ourselves.
> How, in the stifling air of sleepless cells
> All day and all night through
> Dry-eyed, through cracked lips
> We whispered "Motherland . . . the people . . ."
> And we found justifications
> For our cruel mother,
> Who sent her best sons
> To pointless suffering.
> . . . O days of disgrace and sorrow!
> O, could it be that even we
> Did not plumb the depths of human misery
> In the starless swamps of Kolyma? . . .[11]

This same mixture of confession and self-accusation is found in poems of the time by Petrovykh and Barkova. Petrovykh's husband was arrested, leaving her with a young daughter. Anna Barkova wrote from inside the Gulag, having been arrested in 1934. She spent over twenty years in camps and prisons until her final release in 1965. Even in poems written before her arrest Barkova's tone, epitomized in this poem of 1925 (1989), is aggressive:

> Soaked through with blood and bile
> Are our lives and our actions.
> An insatiable wolf's heart
> Was given us by ominous fate.
> We tear with teeth and claws,
> Kill our mother and father.
> We do not cast a stone at our neighbor –
> We puncture their hearts with a bullet.
> Ah! So there's no need to think about it?
> If there's no need – then would you be so kind:
> Give me universal joy
> On a dish, like bread and salt.[12]

Barkova, Berggol'ts and Petrovykh speak not just as individuals, but on behalf of their generation, both victims and perpetrators, if only through their acquiescence. Even if they would only be heard by a mass audience many years later, women spoke powerfully from the margins of Soviet society during the 1930s, drawing on private experience to challenge public representations of that society.

The relaxation of censorship that accompanied the early years of World War II allowed some women to have their work published. In wartime, at least, public and private sentiment coincided. Akhmatova published a poem in *Pravda*, organ of the Central Committee of the Communist Party, of all places, and Petrovykh was able to see some of her own work in print. The way in which the war was represented, however, sidelined women, despite the fact that they were profoundly involved both as civilians and in the armed forces. As Jean Bethke Elshtain points out, in wartime, traditional ideas about gender reassert themselves, no matter what roles are actually performed by real men and women.[13] The prevailing picture of the war was dominated by the heroic actions of men at the front, while women were portrayed as inspiring figures far away from the battlefield: mothers, wives, Mother Russia. Margarita Aliger's long poem "Zoia" (1942), whose real-life heroine Zoia Kosmodem'ianskaia was

executed by the Nazis for her activities as a partisan, was one of the relatively few works portraying women as soldiers. It does not escape the
general tendency to portray female fighters solely in terms of their moral
and personal qualities, revealing an anxiety about portraying women
who commit violent acts. The poem's imagery suggests that martial
heroism and femininity are fundamentally incompatible.

When women came to write about their own wartime experiences,
however, though they relied partly on conventional images of women as
the antithesis of war and guardians of eternal values, they challenged
Stalinist culture's models of masculine heroism expressed through action
and feminine virtue which, as an essential quality, needed no actions to
illustrate it. It is no coincidence that some of the best poetry written
by women in the war years concerns the siege of Leningrad, in which
soldiers and civilians starved under protracted enemy bombardment, and
where there was little scope for conventional military heroics. The siege
created conditions in which everyday survival tested physical and spiritual resources to the limit. Akhmatova lived through and wrote about the
early stages of the siege before being sent as an evacuee to Tashkent. Vera
Inber produced a long narrative poem, *Pulkovskii meridian* (Pulkovo Meridian, 1942), which assembled finely drawn, almost clinical observations of
life under siege. Most widely known for her poems on the siege is Ol'ga
Berggol'ts; as a regular broadcaster on Leningrad radio she became
familiar to Leningraders, offering encouragement, but unafraid to
acknowledge the harshness of the ordeal she shared with her listeners.
Unknown at the time was Natal'ia Krandievskaia's cycle *V osade* (Under
Siege, 1985); prepared for publication in 1946, orders were given for the
typescript to be destroyed before it could be printed. Krandievskaia, an
accomplished poet, had spent the years 1919–22 in exile with her husband,
the writer Aleksei Tolstoy. Having published three books between 1914
and 1922, she fell silent until her marriage collapsed in 1935. The poet's
persona in *Under Siege* echoes that of Krandievskaia's earlier work,
bemused and, at times, amused by her complete inability to conform to
expected behavior. In a compelling and understated account, elevated
sentiment is set aside in favor of down-to-earth observations and the
skillful introduction of everyday speech overheard on the street, which
works to emphasize the poet's highly individual perceptions of the city
as a scene of unreality, incongruity, and wonder.

It is notable that throughout the war women seem to have more
license to express emotions of fear and weakness than men. This may well

have been an attempt to maintain conventional gender roles of the "manly" man and "womanly" woman which were threatened by the war. Male poets did, in fact, have some latitude in expressing feelings of fear, vulnerability, and grief, but towards the end of the war, there was strong criticism of younger male poets who were clearly felt to have gone too far. At the same time the poetry written by Galina Nikolaeva, a doctor at the front, was praised for its pleasingly feminine qualities. Her confessions of grief for fallen comrades, and war-weariness were evidently acceptable from a woman. A more relaxed attitude towards female expressions of vulnerability may have depended in part on the tradition of strong, naturally virtuous female characters who abound in nineteenth-century novels. Being more resilient than their male counterparts, the "superfluous men," such heroines could express their emotions without succumbing to them. Nikolaeva and Iuliia Drunina, who also served in front-line army medical units, set up a thoroughly conventional opposition of feminine weakness and masculine strength, their heroines either learning to be "like men" or lapsing into moments of "womanly" emotion. Berggol'ts's Leningrad poems, however, play on the paradox of women's apparent physical weakness and spiritual strength, without feeling the need to equate strength and masculinity.[14]

Any remnants of wartime liberalization were dispelled by the Central Committee resolution of August 1946, instigated by the Leningrad Party chief Andrei Zhdanov, attacking Akhmatova and the humorous prose writer Mikhail Zoshchenko. The years from 1945 to 1953 were, to say the least, uncongenial for writers. However, women's foothold outside official culture continued to allow them to write significant poetry. Furthermore, some of the work that women managed to publish carried subtexts which were not in tune with surface conformity. The most favored genres in published poetry were the lengthy epic poem, or cycle of shorter poems celebrating Soviet achievements. Aliger marked the construction of the vast new Moscow University buildings with appropriate ceremoniousness, while Berggol'ts commemorated the completion of a canal linking the Volga and Don rivers. Her Volga-Don cycle, however, is far from unambiguously optimistic in tone and hints at the canal's slave-labor origins, which emerge more clearly in later versions. Berggol'ts's Stalin Prize winning epic poem about an agricultural commune, *Pervorossiisk* (1950), was written concurrently with poems of 1949 voicing fears of renewed arrest. Like the Volga-Don poems, *Pervorossiisk* is deceptive in its conformist appearance; a 1957 revised version reveals more fully the poet's tragic perception of the events she narrates, as well as a preoccupation with understanding her own life in a wider national and historical context.

This last concern, taking in questions of guilt and responsibility, is one which informs two major late works by Akhmatova: the enigmatic *Poema bez geroia* (Poem Without a Hero, 1960) and the cycle of poems entitled *Severnye elegii* (Northern Elegies, 1961). By the end of the 1940s, the fact that Akhmatova had been publicly condemned by the authorities combined with the enormous respect in which she was held privately to reinforce her status of poet-outsider who has the right to speak as the "true" voice of her country. The first draft of *Poem Without a Hero* was completed while Akhmatova was a wartime evacuee in Tashkent, but additions and revisions to this complex work continued throughout her life. It contains many layers of allusion, to the work of other poets as well as to Akhmatova's own, and conjures up the life of bohemian society before World War I, judging it from the perspective of the present. Akhmatova's persona in *Poem Without a Hero* adds new layers to the poet's self-mythologization, and is more complex than the one presented in *Requiem.* In the *Poem* her persona is enigmatic, in turn possessed by her poem, then speaking as her work's knowing, controlling creator, weighed down by a sense of personal guilt, yet able to survey her epoch from a privileged vantage point in time and space and pass judgment on it. The presence of figures from the past whom the speaker recognizes as her own doubles, including a younger self whom she fears to encounter, contributes to the creation of the poet's myth of herself as the sole survivor of a turbulent epoch.

Akhmatova's reference to herself and her earlier work in *Poem Without a Hero* helps to convey the idea that she is the founder of a women's tradition in twentieth-century Russian poetry, that she "taught women how to speak," as she claimed in an epigram of 1958. It was the poet Innokentii Annenskii, rather than any female predecessor, whom she acknowledged as her teacher. For women starting to write poetry in 1953, however, Akhmatova was only one of an array of "foremothers" who showed women not "how to speak," but that they could speak as individuals, and that speaking as women did not mean that their poetic voice must be limited or trivial. Their work, whether published or circulated in manuscript form, gave the impression of a certain continuity and the presence of shared concerns, something to refer back to and use as a point of departure. At the start of the century, women poets in Russia risked being seen as anomalies merely because they were women; for a woman poet to be seen as an anomaly by the middle of the century required a marked originality in the poetry she wrote, rather than simply in who she was. The work of Kseniia Nekrasova has a distinctive and strongly individual character, but remains little known, partly, it must be suspected, because of the difficulty of assimilating her into any group, or of identifying a predecessor for her. Although Nekrasova was educated in the Stalin-era Gorky Literary Institute in Moscow, she did not incorporate the clichés of Socialist Realism into her poetry, nor is it easy to discern other literary influences in her work. Neither is it marked by folkloric diction, although it is often concerned with the poet's sense of closeness to, and delight in the natural world:

> I met a lilac bush in the garden.
> It was growing as it pleased from the earth,
> simple-heartedly spreading out its leaves,
> and, like naked children,
> it lifted up its flowers,
> not ashamed of its nakedness.
> Where, I wondered,
> does the power of these little circles lie,
> looking like children's drawings,
> born of the earth,
> the power of naive inflorescences,
> and funny petals?
>
> Why are wise men, shepherd boys and poets
> so moved
> by these little crosses on sticks?
> Much have people
> come to understand on the earth
> and they know how to do many things.
> But we are powerless
> to convey the face of a flower.
> And we stand in silence
> and look,
> and turn over our thoughts.[15]

A childlike quality of vision allies Nekrasova, perhaps, with Elena Guro, another idiosyncratic poet. The relationship between creative individuality and femininity clearly presented difficulties for critics of women's poetry in the first half of the twentieth century. Poetry which adhered to the expected feminine stereotype was condemned for being derivative, while innovation, particularly in matters of form, was seen as incompetence or lack of control. Nevertheless, preconceptions about how women should write exercised more influence on how women were read than on how they actually wrote. Far from trying to conceal that they were women, they drew attention to it, giving expression to specifically female experience and using language and imagery from traditional culture to endow themselves with the authority to speak for the whole country. At the same time they showed that they could write poetry in which female identity was compatible with individuality and innovation. That women's poetry was a lot harder to categorize in 1953 than it had been in 1913 is a measure of these poets' achievement.

NOTES

1. Jan Montefiore, *Feminism and Poetry: Language, Experience and Identity in Women's Writing*, 2nd edn (London, 1994), 70.

2. See the article by the poet Iunna Morits, "Byt' poetessoi v Rossii trudnee, chem byt' poetom," *Daugava* 7 (1987), 79. See also Sandler in this volume.

3. See Valerii Briusov, "Zhenshchiny-poety," in *SS*, 7 vols. (Moscow, 1974), VI, 318–21; for women's critical response to other women's poetry, see Sofiia Parnok (writing under her pseudonym Andrei Polianin), "Otmechennye imena," in *SevV* 4 (1913), 111–15, and Anna Akhmatova, "N. L'vova: *Starye skazki*," in *RMysl'* 1 (1914), 27–8. A useful discussion of women writers as critics of other women writers can be found in Catriona Kelly, "Missing Links: Russian Women Writers as Critics of Women Writers," in Faith Wigzell (ed.), *Russian Writers on Russian Writers* (Oxford, 1994), 67–9.

4. For his comments on Akhmatova, see Vladislav Khodasevich, "'Zhenskie' stikhi," in *Koleblemyi treugol'nik* (Moscow, 1991), 579; on Parnok, see his review "Sofiia Parnok: *Stikhotvoreniia*," in *SS*, ed. John Malmstad and Robert Hughes (Ann Arbor, MI, 1990), vol. II, 255.

5. "Otryvok," *Sobranie stikhotvorenii* (Ann Arbor, MI, 1979), 195, and "Mne snilos': ia bredu vpot'makh . . .," *ibid.*, 212. For a fine example of her philosophical poetry, see "V fortochku," *ibid.*, 231–2.

6. *Russkaia poeziia XX veka: antologiia russkoi liriki pervoi chetverti XX veka*, ed. I. S. Ezhov, E. I. Shamurin (Moscow, 1925; repr. Moscow, 1991).

7. Leon Trotskii, *Literature and Revolution* (Ann Arbor, MI, 1960), 41; Valerii Briusov, "Vchera, segodnia i zavtra russkoi poezii," *SS*, vol. VI, 508.

8. Beth Holmgren, *Women's Works in Stalin's Time* (Bloomington, IN, 1993), 9–10.

9. Joseph Brodsky, "The Keening Muse," in *Less Than One: Selected Essays* (London, 1987), 49.

10. See Joanna Hubbs, "Variations on the Myth of Mother Russia: Akhmatova's 'Rekviem'," in *Gender Restructuring*, 117–26.

11. *SS*, 3 vols. (Leningrad, 1989–1990), vol. I, 169. Нет, не из книжек наших скудных, / подобья нищенской сумы, / узнаете о том, как трудно, / как невозможно жили мы. // Как мы любили — горько, грубо. / Как обманулись мы, любя, / как на допросах, стиснув зубы, / мы отрекались от себя. / И в духоте бессонных камер, / все дни и ночи напролет, / без слез, разбитыми губами / шептали: «родина . . . народ . . .» / И находили оправданье / жестокой матери своей, / на бесполезное страданье / пославшей лучших сыновей. / . . . О, дни позора и печали! / О, неужели даже мы / тоски людской не исчерпали / в беззвездных топях Колымы?..

12. "Propitany krov'iu i zhelch'iu . . .," *Vozvrashchenie* (Ivanovo, 1990), 97. Пропитаны кровью и желчью / Наша жизнь и наши дела. / Ненасытное сердце волчье / Нам судьба роковая дала. / Разрываем зубами, когтями, / Убиваем мать и отца. / Не швыряем в ближнего камень — / Пробиваем пулей сердца. / А! Об этом думать не надо? / Не надо — ну так изволь: / Подай мне всеобщую радость / На блюде, как хлеб и соль.

13. Jean Bethke Elshtain, *Women and War* (Chicago, IL, 1987), 4.

14. For an account of women's poetry in wartime, see K. Hodgson, *Written with the Bayonet: Soviet Russian Poetry of World War Two* (Liverpool, 1996), 207–56.

15. "Lilac" ("Siren'"), *Ia chast' Rusi: stikhi* (Cheliabinsk, 1986), 40. Встретила я куст сирени в саду. / Как угодно он рос из земли, / простодушно раскинув листы. / И, как голых детей, / поднимал он цветы, / обнажений своих не стыдясь. / В чем же, думала я, / сила этих кружков, / по ребячим рисункам / рожденных землей, / и наивных соцветий, / и смешных лепестков? / Почему мудрецов, / пастушат и поэтов / так волнуют / на палочках крестики эти? / Многое люди постигли на свете / и умеют многое делать они. / Но нет силы у нас / передать лик цветка. / И мы молча стоим и глядим, / и ворочаем думы свои.

11

Writing the female body politic (1945–1985)

She wore a pinafore when she cooked their meals, and to look at her one would think that she had never known any other life but that of a happy housewife bustling about her own home.

Life turned out to be full of happiness and wonders. Love had transformed Lena: she had a different walk and posture, her voice had become deep and cooing, and her eyes, their colour enhanced, seemed to have a secret lurking in their languid depths. She glowed with jubilance, men turned to look at her in the street, and she glowed all the more.[1]

VERA PANOVA, *The Train*

The visual propaganda of Socialist Realism has accustomed us to the spartan female body of Stalinism – the stern face, strong physique, plain dress, and powerful forward motion of Vera Mukhina's famous statue of the collective farm worker.[2] Her pairing with an equally muscle-bound, action-packed male worker accentuated both her likeness and subservience to a stereotypically masculine model. In the Stalinist mindset, it seemed, the good body was the hard body, the most desirable mien that of energetic commitment, and the correct attire strictly functional. Much like Nazi Germany and fascist Italy, an industrializing, militarizing Soviet Union relied on such uniform regimentation to fashion its human material into productive tools and eventual soldiers.[3]

We know now that these visions of the body were not even then monolithic. Feminist scholarship on 1930s Germany and Italy has traced the telltale discrepancies in women's artistic representation, not only the expected differences between propaganda and women's own stories, but also between the various producers of public images (propagandists, marketers).[4] The anti-capitalist Soviet system tolerated much less disjuncture between political and mass cultures; no market contended or collaborated with the state to package alternative notions of "consumable" femininity, especially those of public art. Yet within the wholly planned cultural production of Soviet Socialist Realism, *belles lettres*, even of the official sort, proffered more concretely situated and temporally mutable visions. Which brings me to the proper scope of this essay – the course of Soviet women's writing from 1945 to the glasnost period. In the broad sweep of Soviet cultural and Soviet *women's* history, literature holds a special place as a forum for articulating private life, individual perception, and all manner of difference – both in orthodox publications and manuscripts written "for the drawer."

I have argued elsewhere that the Stalinist period, with its emphasis on physical prowess, technological achievement, and public activity, tacitly cast dissident value into the domestic sphere, the domain left to women's control, and I have illustrated, on various examples, how women were empowered as writers and protagonists through this conflation of dissidence with the domestic.[5] I want to modify and expand that claim here. The postwar era (1945–1985) proved to be a propitious moment for *all* Soviet women writers, not just those valorized by political persecution. This is perhaps the first period in Russian literature when women signify as a major and distinctive group. Three women, Vera Panova (1907–1973), Antonina Koptiaeva (1909–1991), and Galina Nikolaeva (1911–1963), were recipients of the Stalin Prize, Panova in 1947, 1948, and 1950, Koptiaeva in 1949, and Nikolaeva in 1951.[6] A few years later Panova and the poet Ol'ga Berggol'ts (1910–1975) played key roles in precipitating the intermittent thaw in Soviet literature, advocating and demonstrating a greater emphasis on sincerity and emotional expression in their work.[7] Over the next decade women writers crowded the literary scene on either side of the political fence, bearing witness to repression in dissident non-fiction (see such memoirists as Evgeniia Ginzburg, Lydiia Chukovskaia, Lydiia Ginzburg, Nadezhda Mandel'stam) and conveying the largely apolitical experience of daily life and family relations in realist fiction (Panova, I. Grekova, Inna Varlamova, Natal'ia Baranskaia, among many others). Why this boom?

One predictable answer is socio-economic, the fulfillment, in a sense, of the Soviet promise of egalitarianism. Notwithstanding its use of political terror, the Soviet economic and political system was designed, and, in many instances, enforced to facilitate women's liberation. By 1945 an entire generation of Soviet women had benefited from equal-opportunity education and equal-opportunity employment. We should not underestimate the obvious fact of women's professional encouragement and development – that such a major intellectual force as the critic and writer Lydiia Ginzburg (1902–1990) underwent the same institute training and participated on equal terms with her "brother Formalists," or that the prize-winning and also popular Panova slipped into fiction writing by way of a journalistic career.

Soviet reshuffling of the class hierarchy also elicited some women's writerly ambitions, as Anna Krylova cogently argues in the case of Panova and Koptiaeva. Much as working-class women in the West gained public attention and professional power through union activities, so formerly lower-class women in the Soviet Union found cultural legitimacy and upward mobility through Party membership and identification. The new Soviet intelligentsia, already in evidence in the 1930s, was to be distinguished from its privileged, cultured prerevolutionary counterpart by lower-class pedigree and early hardship, although, as historian Sheila Fitzpatrick demonstrates, it basically subscribed to old intelligentsia notions of cultural worth.[8] At the same time, women in the new intelligentsia, much like women revolutionaries in tsarist times, sensed soon enough that Party identity – the hagio-biography Krylova notes in this volume – censored them even as it empowered them, pruning their life stories and life work of any sort of ideological, psychological, or sexual ambiguity.[9]

Nevertheless, sanctioned Stalinist icons of womanhood, inadvertently ennobled and strengthened by crisis, did afford women writers more differentiated speaking roles than those of their nineteenth-century predecessors. Stalin's socially conservative family policies hallowed Soviet wives and mothers, old-fashioned paragons that somehow coexisted with that of the strong, independent-minded woman worker, and together spawned the strangely hybrid heroines of high Stalinist Socialist Realism – those women who wed socialist zeal and industry with "wholesome" femininity, and invariably supported the starring heroes.[10] The purges then contaminated high Stalinist heroics, and compelled women with very different political pedigrees to a distinctly conventional heroinism of preservation and commemoration. I have already remarked how post-purge demographics drove women to act as surviving witnesses, for, in comparison with men, they either escaped or better endured the horrors of imprisonment and the gulag, and felt both obliged and entitled to testify about what they had seen and those they had lost.[11] The war truly generalized this phenomenon, and also muddied the distinction between legitimist and dissident testimonies. As the psychological trauma of the war prompted the rehabilitation of comforting traditions (the church, the motherland), the images of bereft mother, or, more generally, female mourner, at once attracted and popularized women writers – even those blighted by politically suspect biographies. It is no accident that the once Decadent poet Vera Inber, as Krylova describes her, banked so much on keeping faith with the besieged city of Leningrad and won general kudos for her eyewitness *Leningrad Diary*, or that a figure as scrupulously defeminized as Lydiia Ginzburg ventured her most poignant work, *Notes of a Blockade Survivor*, as a fictional account of the Leningrad siege.[12] In much the same way, the poets Anna Akhmatova and Ol'ga Berggol'ts surfaced in wartime as powerful female mourners in print and on radio. World War II allowed a long-suffering populace to mourn publicly, and the Stalinist cultural establishment actively recruited women to direct the lamenting chorus.

Thus, surprising as it may seem, the Stalinist system proved to be an institutional and iconic enabler of women's writing. It not only mandated women's higher education and equalized opportunities for employment, but it also specified valorized, if stereotyped, role models for women. And this trend predictably snowballed after 1945, given the postwar population and its peacetime preoccupations. The postwar Soviet Union may not have been as vehemently domesticated as the postwar United States, but the necessary economic shift from industrial build-up to industrial maintenance and the psychological easement from wartime sacrifice to resettling home and family resonated strongly in Soviet life and literature. In her seminal typology of the Socialist Realist novel, Katerina Clark charts the literary relaxation from a 1930s high Stalinism, with its strapping heroes and dramatic feats, to postwar accommodation of the normal and the private: "in the forties it was possible to depict more everyday, unexceptional moments, more of the quotidian world than it had been in the thirties."[13] Clark also notes a postwar interest in what she terms "culture," a phenomenon that ranged from a predictable engagement with highbrow art to matters of hygiene, etiquette, and material well-being (fashionable clothes, luxury goods, home furnishings).[14] Sheila Fitzpatrick, in turn, distinguishes the latter, more material concerns of "culture" as *kul'turnost'* or "culturedness," and traces its emergence to the 1930s as *arriviste* professionals from lower-class backgrounds strived to acquire at least the tangible emblems of old intelligentsia "culture" (Fitzpatrick, *The Cultural Front*, 8, 13). Whenever its first manifestations, this generally Stalinist tendency registered most clearly and fully in literature after the war, as the asceticism and self-sacrifice of pre-war Socialist Realism gave way to the admission of creature comforts and, not so coincidentally, the venting of emotions and the pursuit of romance.[15]

The spotlight on the home, the concern for material welfare and personal cultivation, the valorization of romantic love – all of these trends vastly enhanced the prospects of women writers, for these, the very topics previously deemed inessential or politically suspect in high Stalinist literature, coincided with women's socially acknowledged areas of expertise and control. Whatever their specific talents, Soviet women writers were ceded the right to speak authoritatively about family, home, and love affairs. Men could and did write about such subjects, but for the first time in Russian literary history women's domain and perspective were privileged and generalized rather than sidelined. I would even venture to claim that, to a certain extent, the postwar decades saw the feminization of Soviet literature, in contrast and reaction to the 1920s' myth of a new, masculinized society.[16] Themes, plots, casts, and even narrative voices inscribed this transformation. The steelbodied male worker and soldier "softened" and aged into the family man, and the do-all wife and mother stepped into a lead role.

The novels of the generally orthodox Stalinist writer, Galina Nikolaeva – most notably *Harvest* (Zhatva, 1950) and *The Running Battle* (Bitva v puti, 1954) – already display some of these adjustments. If we compare the hero and heroine of *Harvest* to their Socialist Realist prototypes in Fedor Gladkov's *Cement*, we find a hotheaded male leader who must "learn how to smile" in order to get the job done and a model wife and worker who first finds happiness at the side of another, gentler man and is truly reconciled with her husband only after his emotional tempering. The writings of Vera Panova, however, best illustrate this evaluational shift. Her wonderfully low-key portraits of children and young people, embedded in her novels and proffered singly in such novellas as *Serezha* (1955), *Valya* (1959), and *Volodya* (1959), underscore the values of good parenting and simple childhood pleasures in lieu of politically correct education. Her thaw-era novel, *Span of the Year* (Vremena goda, 1953), and autobiography, *A Sentimental Novel* (Sentimental'nyi roman), emphasize the characters' emotional experiences and advocate healthy emotional adjustment. Even her earlier works written to strict Socialist Realist order – *Kruzhilikha* and *The Factory* (Rabochii poselok) – make industrial productivity dependent on emotional fulfillment. In the latter work, the factory director's problems are first flagged by his pregnant wife's death (a double damnation) and seemingly on their way to solution through a new love affair at novel's end.

Most remarkable in this regard is Panova's Stalin Prize-winning first novel, *The Train* (Sputniki, 1945). This work evolved from her official assignment as war correspondent, but its focus is distinctly quotidian and empathetic, delving into the psychological ordeals and family histories of the characters she, as journalist, interviewed on a hospital train. (Its blurred line between fiction and non-fiction makes this piece an especially useful illustration.) The hero Danilov's political task may be keeping the train running, but the narrator strongly implies that it is just as important for him to work through an old romantic obsession and be reconciled to his less-than-perfect family. Indeed, in *The Train's* cast, the sweet family man, Dr. Belov, stands in positive contrast to the vain, manipulative, and misnamed Dr. Suprugov, a confirmed bachelor.[17] The novel is also replete with strong, elaborated female characters, most of whom, interestingly enough, long for some experience of a traditionally feminine lifestyle, whether this involves a hasty trip to a beauty parlor, reading the prerevolutionary "love story" *The Keys to Happiness*, or landing a good husband.[18] Their desires and indulgences flesh out, rather than detract from, their worth. The homely, exacting head nurse Iuliia Dmitrievna indulges in her secret crushes, although she remains utterly assured in her superior nursing skills. The luscious nurse Fainna is a seasoned flirt, but is also deemed to have real professional scope. The character of Lena Ogorodnikova, cited in this chapter's epigraph, represents a veritable fusion of Socialist Realist and soap opera heroinisms as she first shucks her abusive petty-bourgeois past (entrepreneur father, alcoholic mother) and becomes a good Soviet citizen through the offices of a Soviet children's home. Love then transforms her into a little *hausfrau*, although her "glow" ultimately turns ashen when she finds out her husband has betrayed her.

Panova's particular rewriting of the war experience entails domesticating space as well as character. The main setting of a hospital train already indicates the move from "masculine" battlefield to a site of human repair and recuperation. The occupants of this gleaming state-of-the-art facility labor to make it a self-sufficient "home," taking on livestock and attaching dust ruffles to the lamps. It is significant that even the stern Danilov approves the latter flourish, volunteering to buy dye for the ruffles. It is equally significant, however, that such necessary homey touches do not amount to a wholesale endorsement of domestic materialism. The same Lena who relishes her new home with her beloved is shown to recoil from the cloyingly overdecorated cottage of her schoolfriend,

Katia – a place where fifteen embroidered pillows and a flowering bird-cherry tree cannot mask an essential poverty of spirit.

In sum, Panova truly launches the process of what I term writing the female body politic, recording the overwhelming presence and influence of women in postwar Soviet society and especially those exemplars who integrated in themselves the good worker, the good citizen (this can include dissidence), *and* the "whole woman" (maternal, loving, hetero-sexual, attentive to home, family, and friends, susceptible to romance, and reasonably concerned about her looks). The term "body politic" conveys a corporate, organized, politically *significant* entity: Although a body of women could never signify formal political power in the Soviet context, these postwar writings assert an important elision between women's phys-ical prominence and pragmatic industry (in population percentages, in the operation of daily Soviet life) and their leading roles as protagonists and exemplars in the implicitly political forum of Soviet literature. This at once documentary and modeling process generated impressive variations, ranging in character type from ordinary working mothers to political mar-tyrs, and in setting from women's labor camps to beauty parlors. Essential ingredients, nonetheless, were (1) conventional notions of what constitutes "masculinity" (rationality, physical strength and productivity, domestic helplessness) and "femininity" (emotionalism, nurturing and reproduc-tivity, domestic capacity); (2) the admission, within socially prescribed limitations, of the body's needs and pleasures; (3) the assertion of the power of emotions, and especially romantic and maternal love; and (4) the belief in women's basic transformative goodness. Women writers seemed to be envisioning a kinder, gentler postwar Soviet Union shaped in their own wishful self-image. Predictably enough, their manner of presentation almost always implied a realist poetics, a conscientious depiction of real-life mothers, daughters, sisters, friends, superiors, and peers.

The female body politic emerged in print as a curiously powerful con-ception that crossed ideological and class lines. As I have already indicated on Nikolaeva's and Panova's examples, the concern for a somewhat cir-cumscribed "whole woman" in women's postwar writing was not only ventured, but encouraged in the Socialist Realism of Nikolaeva, Koptiaeva, and Panova, although such a figure in effect subverted pre-war literary standards. Eventually, focus on the "whole woman" threatened to dis-place the old Socialist Realist hagiography with "normal" biography, and vaunted conventional biology over strict Party ideology as the stronger, surviving life force. Yet, as we might expect, these tactics were plied most boldly by dissident writers. In her prison and camp memoirs, (*Journey into the Whirlwind* and *Within the Whirlwind* [Krutoi marshrut] 1967–1981), Evgeniia Ginzburg (1904–1977) enacts a kind of reversal of the Socialist Realist *Bildungsroman*, charting her passage from committed communist to tolerant "sister." Her account of her own purge in the dread 1930s recalls the sage advice of her nonpolitical mother-in-law to go into hiding with her children; her chronicle of prison and camp ordeals commemorates the maternal solicitude of a wide variety of fellow prisoners and recognizes the importance of maintaining her womanly identity (making pickles, concealing her brassiere from the authorities). Ginzburg's second volume even develops a romantic plotline as she discovers a soul mate and alternative mentor in her second husband, the kindly Catholic doctor Anton Walter. Her self-portrait of an engagingly positive heroine combines the seemingly disparate elements of political protest, devotional literature, adventure story, and romance.

Ginzburg's text is indubitably inspirational, and her invocation of such high culture texts as the poetry of Aleksandr Blok, Boris Pasternak, Osip Mandel'stam, and others would seem to guarantee her own work's highbrow status. But her work's motley structure – what makes it such a compelling *read* – reveals a rather different and important tendency in postwar women's writing, the fact of its collusion with popular social practices and literary formulae. Especially in Russian culture, which privileges the highbrow and the "authentic" folk over any other art forms, such collusion was a double-edged phenomenon, for, on the one hand, it genuinely enhanced a work's accessibility, and, on the other, it could tarnish that work as aesthetically inferior and morally suspect. It inevitably conjured up the specter of *embourgeoisement* that so often has demoted women's writing from art to product, from a politico-philosophical literature to a mere "literature of everyday life" (*literatura byta*).[19] Indeed, the critic Vera Dunham has levelled this charge against postwar Soviet writing in general, alerting us to the return of execrable "petty-bourgeois taste" (*meshchanskii vkus*) in just such details as Panova's dust ruffles and pinafored heroines.[20] For Dunham, postwar sanction of materialism mainly points up Soviet hypocrisy and corruption.

Dunham is by no means alone in her condemnation. Soviet women writers themselves sensed this sabotage, as we saw in the reaction of Panova's Lena Ogorodnikova. Material indulgence and corporeal corruption loomed as the chief threats to an otherwise flourishing female body politic. Ginzburg also skirts these dangers when she draws a sharp dividing line between the intellectual political prisoners and the crass, promiscuous common criminals. Dissident writer Lydiia Chukovskaia (1907–1996) conveys similar judgments in her fiction and memoirs, upholding art-loving, justice-seeking heroines (Nina Sergeevna in her novel *Going Under* [Spusk pod vodu, 1949–52], the real-life Anna Akhmatova in *Notes on Anna Akhmatova* [Zapiski ob Anne Akhmatovoi, 1939–66]), and either pitying or damning those women whose concern for appearance or worldly goods could only derive from some moral deficiency. Such reactions, I contend, merit analysis, but not endorsement. If critics in the West have been just as liable to tar any connection between women's writing and popular culture and to disdain such phenomena as the "women's novel" or the "women's magazine," we need not repeat the same limiting mistake in our present rewriting of Russian literary history. The fact is that postwar women's literature repeatedly exploits and positively battens on popular "female" pastimes and preoccupations; obvious examples include beauty salon visits, the shopping expedition, the support group, the romance, etc. The moral bane of such connections proved to be a boon in terms of reader engagement and appeal.

Moreover, such connections were drawn not only by women. Many writers of both sexes in the postwar period produced an effective blend of the highbrow (strong political/social message, sophisticated writing style, complex characterizations) with what we have come to term, often pejoratively, the middlebrow – a literature that furnishes "a genial middle ground" of empathetic identification and vaguely consumerist values situated between ultra-formulaic commercial fiction and a too rarefied elite art.[21] It is my hypothesis that a highly qualified middlebrow developed in part from the postwar establishment of a *de facto* middle class concerned with career and possessions, and in part because a short-lived Russian Modernism never succeeded in demoting Realism as a poetics. Much as the *de facto* middle class never had to confront public stigmatization as a bourgeoisie, so a *de facto* middlebrow never lost its artistic respectability; its realism was read as a Sovietized (that is, politically dimmed) continuum of the great Russian realist tradition. Whatever the genesis of this middlebrow, women writers gained proportionately more prestige and currency from the mix. The female body politic they wrote, however well-attired and comfortably accommodated, represented a quite inclusive and validating club for writers and readers.

Natal'ia Baranskaia's (b. 1908) small masterpiece and best work, "Nedelia kak nedelia" ("A Week Like Any Other," 1969), serves as an excellent case in point. It is not at all ironic that its first English translation appeared in a perfectly middlebrow forum, the American women's magazine *Redbook*, despite the fact that its initial Soviet publication was in *New World*, the most prestigious and politically independent journal of its day.[22] Baranskaia came to writing quite late in life, after retiring from her career as a museum researcher, and this, one of her first efforts, trains on the experience of a typical professional woman, a young scientist frantically coping with the double burden of job and family and the Soviet exigencies of long commutes, overcrowded facilities, and scarce consumer goods. Written as a first-person, present-tense chronicle of an everywoman's week, the novella has been lauded aesthetically for its laconic style, breakneck pace, and irresolution, and politically for its frank report on Soviet daily life. But it is just as remarkable that the points of psychological relief in this hectic narrative emanate from the popular practices I noted above. At midweek the protagonist inadvertently "stops time" when she gets a haircut on her lunch break, and her physical transformation from a disheveled working mother into her former boyish carefree self elicits renewed energy, general admiration, and spousal ardor as well as a past-tense romantic reverie. For an everywoman programmed to serve everyone practically everywhere, this makeover constitutes a moment of freedom and self-investment – here even an assay at recovering identity. Rather than reduce the woman to a mere body, Baranskaia's narrative equates attention to the body with concern for the soul.[23]

It is striking that romance only enters this plot as distant history, a recollection of the protagonist's courtship in which she figures as an alien "she." That romance, nevertheless, unfolds according to a predictable pattern with magical first meetings, a mysterious but happily resolved separation, and an Edenic honeymoon in the vacationland of the Crimea. Relief comes elsewhere in the form of supportive female friends – the women who are at once her professional colleagues, shopping network, and emotional support. In contrast to the domestic scenes, in which the narrator largely records household tasks and arguments with her husband, work scenes feature more individuated female characters and interactions that frequently comfort and sometimes empower. At one point the protagonist articulates a sense of strength as she and her kindred "mamas" walk three abreast along the street, sharing heavy

shopping bags and sweeping everyone from their path. This literal support group shores up her function and magnifies her identity.

In postwar women's writing variations of the makeover and the
support group recur under what would seem the most unlikely circumstances, but which, in fact, sanction these experiences as vital and mean-
ingful. The sanatorium and the hospital are staple settings in Soviet
women's fiction, and these furnish overburdened female characters with
much-needed sites of reflection and communion.[24] Even Chukovskaia's
anti-materialist Nina Sergeevna finds solace and unsought-for connections during her stay at a writers' sanatorium. In her solitary quest to "go
under" for true memories of the Stalinist past, she stumbles on unlikely
fellow travelers – the well-upholstered sanatorium manager who literally
drags a package to post to her exiled sister, the orthodox writer who has
been crippled by a camp sentence and almost seduces her with his truth.
In *Mnimaia zhizn'* (A Counterfeit Life, 1978) Inna Varlamova (1922–1990)
immediately dispatches her protagonist to a hospital for breast cancer
treatment, a bodily cure, and there, too, the patient discovers a kind of
freedom and candor missing from her life "outside."[25] In this hospital
tale, however, the heroine goes on an involuntary journey of the body as
well as of the mind, as she scrutinizes the forms and deformities of her
female wardmates, confronts the medical savagery of (de)gendering
(mastectomy, hysterectomy, injections of testosterone), and ultimately
falls in love with a male patient who is about to die. In a sense, the surprise
male love interest – a sensitive soul who was once "one" with his mother
and twin brother and who contrasts most sharply with the heroine's
activist husband – completes the affirming circle of the female support
group, for his final act is to return her femininity to her by kissing the
path of her scar.

It is notable that both Chukovskaia and Varlamova link convalescence
with political disclosure. Soul and body and the body politic are thus
joined and, to a certain extent, jointly redeemed. Iuliia Voznesenskaia's
(b. 1940) major work, (*Zhenskii dekameron*) (*The Women's Decameron*, 1985),
comprises a kind of culminating exercise of this type. She recounts the
revealing and connecting stories of ten women quarantined in a maternity ward with topics that deliberately jumble the trivial with the
dangerously political. Representing a spectrum of Soviet female types
from senior official to vagrant, these characters gradually coalesce into a
support group that liberates the herb-brewing earth mother in the
bureaucrat Valentina and makes over the embittered tramp Zina into

a beloved and loving wife. Such unifying and upbeat resolutions, a standard feature of the middlebrow, are the more noteworthy in Voznesenskaia's work because she creates such distinct and sometimes clashing voices and viewpoints for her separate narrators and clearly designs her text to be a playful artistic experiment rather than a "comfort read."

By strangely natural extension, the settings of camp and prison like-wise serve as sanctioning backdrop for "female" pleasure in Soviet women's literature. Physical satisfaction and emotional nurturing are nowhere so essential. A much more puritanical version of the support group obtains in a non-fiction work roughly contemporary with *Decameron* – the camp memoir, *Seryi tsvet nadezhdy* (*Gray Is the Color of Hope*, 1988) by Irina Ratushinskaia (b. 1954). An account of the author's persecution by and sustained protest against the Brezhnev regime, this memoir practically beatifies a group of female political prisoners who, like religious sectarians, domesticate their Small Zone within the labor camp into a model community by cooking, cleaning, sewing, gardening, and reciting poetry. With greater political tendentiousness and less nov-elistic skill Ratushinskaia echoes Evgeniia Ginzburg in commemorating her campmates' domestic ingenuity, loving solicitude, and spiritual strength, and in quarantining their noble behavior from the vulgarity and promiscuity of the common criminals. Ruth Zernova's little master-piece "Elizabeth Arden" (1978), in turn, celebrates the material with a refreshing irony in lieu of self-righteousness. Once a fairly privileged member of the Soviet professional class, Zernova (b. 1919) was arrested in the postwar anti-semitic purges; her camp experience prompted her writing, but did not succeed in binarizing her sense of self and society. Characteristically, the semi-autobiographical heroine of "Elizabeth Arden" makes no bones about enjoying the good life, and dares to repre-sent her visits to Elizabeth Arden, the famous western cosmetics firm that briefly maintained a Moscow shop after the war, as a quirky symbol of good fortune. Her heroine savors the respite and status of her weekly "treatments," an enormous luxury for the times; she wryly accepts the closure of the shop as a sign of general political doom; the figure of the cosmetician even recurs to her in dreams while she serves her camp sen-tence, almost always foretelling good news. Zernova's narrator relishes this commercial pleasure with neither naivete nor rancor, instead recog-nizing it as a complex signifier of her complex and complicit self.[26]

As the surveyed examples indicate, romance takes center stage only intermittently in postwar women's fiction. It may occupy a predictable first place in the sequence of a heroine's more generally elaborated life or erupt as a complicating/affirming affair for the widowed/divorced/long-married heroine. I have noted illustrations of the former in Panova's and Baranskaia's works. The latter resonates more extensively and variously – as a final spiritual reward in Varlamova's *Life* or, in another example, shown up as an enslaving temptation in Baranskaia's story, "The Kiss" ("Potselui"), in which an older woman renounces an incipient romance with a younger man because it will crowd out daily satisfactions and duties. An interesting variation on this model occurs in Zernova's "Nemye zvonki" ("Mute Phone Calls," 1974), in which a protagonist bent on renouncing the emotional ties that wound ultimately returns to nurse her estranged husband after his heart attack.

These romantic plotlines do not at all replicate the formulae of the popular romance, with its focus on a tempestuous courtship and final consummation-marriage.[27] Their difference may speak to Soviet prudery or the lack of a popular romance tradition in Russian literature (a western tradition that eventually spawned Harlequins). I also submit that the postwar authors' tendency to write romance as part rather than whole and as a matter of ironic reflection rather than indulgent obsession has much to do with real-life experience as well as the earnest therapizing function of the middlebrow. The middlebrow cultivates character-reader identification with the intent of helping the reader cope with the passages and vagaries of life. Unlike popular fiction, which delivers escape on a lavish scale, the middlebrow walks the reader through real-life dilemmas, even of the most prosaic sort, to surer catharses and solutions. It prefers exposition of the continuum and maintenance of life to dwelling on a dramatic, all-consuming fantasy. In Soviet women's experience and realist fiction, the makeover and the support group positively contribute to this maintenance, whereas the romance, albeit an important event, must be contained as a phase that then settles into or gives way to a daily, familial routine.

I. Grekova's fiction fine-tunes this identification and approach. Like Baranskaia, Grekova (b. 1907) debuted late as a writer, and her pseudonym (her real name is Elena Venttsel') insists on her primary career as a mathematician. ("Igrek" is the mathematical symbol for y, the unknown.) As in Baranskaia's case, that career-identification seemed to determine Grekova's writerly conception and thematic focus. Grekova is no self-conscious artist who experiments with structure and style; rather, her narrators and characters most often belong to and reflect on her own professional class. The author projects her generic likeness with her creations *and* her readers, and she describes their shared dilemmas and routines with an irony and a precision that likewise engage a generally educated, but not at all avant-garde, audience. Indeed, her preference for successful middle-aged heroines who maintain a career while raising children alone mirrors a readership most in need of empathy and affirmation. In consequence, many of her plotlines feature makeover episodes and support group scenes. Perhaps her most famous story, "Damskii master" ("The Ladies' Hairdresser," 1963), opens with the middle-aged heroine's miraculous transformation and boldly honors her stylist, a philosophical and melancholy young man, as enigmatic subject. In "Letom v gorode" ("Summer in the City," 1968), the flighty Zhanna endures as the true support of the protagonist, Valentina Stepanovna, and flippantly sums up their relationship: " 'I've sat, smoked, had my cry. How good it is that I have somewhere to cry.' "[28] Grekova also marks the contained course of romance for her heroines. If, for example, the romantic Zhanna in "Summer" treats the men in her life as absorbing and ephemeral entertainments, then the honest Valentina enters and exits romance with definitive seriousness. Her story dispenses early with her disappointing husband and focuses instead on the lesson of her near abortion; frightened to undergo this procedure (it was illegal in Stalinist times), she finds real happiness in maternity.

In comparison with Panova and Baranskaia, Grekova is less sentimental in her characterizations and far bolder in playing the traditional intelligentsia role of social observer and critic. It is important to note here that her novella *Na ispytaniiakh* (*On Maneuvers*, 1967) daringly portrayed secret tests conducted by the Red Army in Stalin's time and ultimately cost her her job at the Zhukovskii Military Aviation Academy. Her later novella, *Vdovii parokhod* (*Ship of Widows*, 1981), even seems to challenge those cardinal beliefs of the female body politic in women's goodness and solidarity. Sketching the different female characters on the title "ship," a shabby postwar apartment building, Grekova traces how this involuntary and oftentimes testy female collective manages to misraise its one "son," the alternately indulged and deprived Vadim, whose horrible neglect of his stroke-impaired mother kills her. But the novella's harsh review of the saintly "good" single mother, voiced by her intellectual co-tenant and an authorial judge, ends on a disconcerting note of uplift. After dreaming about his sins against his mother, Vadim washes them away with his tears, and wakes to a new, presumably virtuous life.

I cite *Ship of Widows* as a useful last example, because it almost completes the turn writers of both sexes would make in the glasnost period. Glasnost ushered in a literature of exposé and "blackness" (*chernukha*); it spelled an end not only to the verities of Soviet progress, but also the good/bad opposition of the dissident/official, and the very possibility of some wholesomeness that survived. I have suggested how the female body politic came into print and power through Soviet women's mass education and professionalization, and the change in sociopolitical values after the war. I think that the demise of this kind of writing began with an eclipsing "chernukha" and hastened with post-Soviet Russia's chaotic transition to capitalism. Over the last decade the real-life prototypes for postwar women's heroines have been forced off the stage by the economy. Pensioners face subsistence, not literary fulfillment; successful middle-aged specialists cope with unemployment; young women opt for the new, distinctly non-intellectual role models of business secretary or foreign-currency prostitute. To a sweeping extent, the professional world Baranskaia and Grekova experienced and invoked has disappeared and, with it, a reliable clientele for their highbrow-middlebrow fare.

Perhaps even more significant for a history of Russian women's literature is the present evidence of a kind of generational revolt. As in so many cultures, Russian women writers over the centuries have left peripatetic traces of association with their predecessors. More often than not, they found it in their best artistic and social interests to dissociate themselves from past and contemporary female "scribblers" and "dilettantes." But the writers who debuted and/or flourished in the glasnost era for once could not ignore the prolific and influential generation before it. And much of their work conveys a complex critique of the good postwar woman and her noble survival strategies. Their critique resembles a familial battle, the long-deferred clash in Russian literature of the Daughters with the Mothers in which the camps are drawn by different historico-philosophical world views rather than by strict chronology.[29] True to a glasnost sensibility, the Daughters are more acknowledging of dark or previously taboo topics – female sexuality, for instance, or family dysfunction, institutional abuse, the failure of *mother* love. They either challenge or deny the postwar writers' bedrock of women's goodness and capacity, and expose the horrors of the home and ostensibly "good" mothers who deceive and destroy.

Their rebellion is also aesthetic, rejecting the Mothers' handholding realism for bold stylistic experiments as they either eviscerate or fantastically ornament "daily life," the *byt* that was the staple of postwar prose. Thus such writers as Liudmila Petrushevskaia (b. 1938) keep watch against any whitewashing flow of emotion with twisted plots, claustrophobic situations, and deliberately inchoate narration. Nowhere is the mother more self-indicting than in her novella, *Vremia: noch'* (*Time: Night*, 1992), in which the protagonist self-righteously professes her obtuseness and abusiveness. In an antithetical act of literary rebellion, Tat'iana Tolstaia (b. 1951) skewers and labels the *lumpenromanticism* of the Soviet professional woman through the conjuring, codifying, condescending voice of the collector – fancifully reducing the dreams of one housewife to ashes ("Fire and Dust") or recapitulating, in the language of an ironic fairy tale, a career woman's ruthless hunt for "a wild, true love" ("The Poet and the Muse").[30] In the Daughters' works, the valiant, weary, occasionally pampered female body is no longer depicted as a reliable source of goodness, but as a grotesque mystery, a battlefield, a boobytrap.

In sum, as the fact of a coherent female body politic has passed, so have its verbal reflection and facilitation. But lest we abide by the Daughters' harsh verdict, their rebellion against the Mothers' easy pleasures, ready empathy, and somewhat homogenized images, it behooves us as historians to remark on the latter's popularity and composite artistry. Whether as good communists or dissidents, producers of therapizing fiction or testifying document, these writers effectively articulated, vented, inspired, and comforted postwar Soviet society. To a great extent, they ministered to and immortalized a woman's world.

NOTES

1. Vera Panova, *The Train*, 51.

2. I refer to Mukhina's "The Worker and the Collective Farm Worker" ("Rabochii i kolkhoznitsa"), the enormous Stalin-era public statue that depicts a male factory worker and female collective farm worker with upraised hammer and sickle. This statue encodes a kind of double subservience, since it displays a female artist's conformity to the legislated "masculine" standard.

3. For discussion of this iconography, see Elizabeth Waters "The Female Form in Soviet Political Iconography," in Barbara Evans Clements, Barbara Alpern Engel, and Christine D. Worobec (eds.), *Russia's Women: Accommodation, Resistance, Transformation* (Berkeley, CA, 1991), 225–42; also Victoria E. Bonnell, "The Representation of Women in Early Soviet Political Art," *RR* 50 (1991), 267–88.

4. In *Mothers in the Fatherland: Women, the Family, and Nazi Politics* (New York, 1987), 116, Claudia Koonz elaborates how the Nazis "remained divided on several key issues" of the Woman Question and notes how desirable female images ranged from icons of motherhood to soft pornography. In *How Fascism Ruled Women in Italy (1922–1945)* (Berkeley, CA, 1992), 227, Victoria de Grazia describes the complex tug of war between fascist government, Catholic church, the fashion industry, and influential women over the proper definition of female beauty. She remarks, moreover, that "fascism was of two minds about the cult of domesticity. At one level, it indulged it; at another it despised it."

5. See *Women's Works in Stalin's Time: On Lidiia Chukovskaia and Nadezhda Mandelstam* (Bloomington, IN, 1993); also "For the Good of the Cause: Russian Women's Autobiography in the Twentieth Century," in Clyman and Greene, 127–48.

6. Nikolaeva is a pseudonym for Volianskaia.

7. The term "thaw" refers to a decade (1953–1963) of relative cultural liberalization following Stalin's death and correlated to Nikita Khrushchev's tenure in power. During the thaw, previously proscribed writers were partially reinstated, a group of openly liberal writers and critics emerged to polemicize with dogmatic Stalinists and Socialist Realists, and writers and critics successfully agitated for greater honesty and personal expression in Soviet literature.

8. Sheila Fitzpatrick, *The Cultural Front: Power and Culture in Revolutionary Russia* (Ithaca, NY and London, 1992), 13: "[The new intelligentsia] were practical people from humble backgrounds who knew little of Marxist theory and were politically loyal rather than politicized. They had no specific cultural agendas when they were mobilized for higher education and the professions. Their purpose was to learn; and their teachers, inevitably, were members of the old intelligentsia."

9. For an analysis of that sort of self-censorship among nineteenth-century revolutionaries, see my article, "For the Good of the Cause: Russian Women's Autobiography in the Twentieth Century."

10. See Xenia Gasiorowska's pioneering study, *Women in Soviet Fiction, 1917–1964* (Madison, 1968), for a survey of these hybrid types.

11. See Carl Proffer's *The Widows of Russia and Other Writings* (Ann Arbor, MI, 1987) and my article "Stepping Out/Going Under: Women in Russia's Twentieth-Century Salons," in Goscilo and Holmgren, 225–46.

12. Characteristically, however, Ginzburg's all-experiencing protagonist in that work is male.

13. Katerina Clark, *The Soviet Novel: History as Ritual* (Chicago, 1980), 199.

14. *Ibid.*, 195, 197.

15. For a trenchant discussion of how sexuality was repressed/expressed in the first decades of Soviet literature, see Eric Naiman's *Sex in Public* (Princeton, 1997).

16. See Eliot Borenstein's *Men Without Women: Masculinity and Revolution in Russian Fiction, 1917–1929* (Durham, 2000), in which he lists the following hallmarks of a traditional masculine ethos: production rather than reproduction, participation in the historic process rather than domestic ahistoricity, heavy industry, construction, and, of course, "the struggle."

17. "Supruga" can be translated as "spouse."

18. It is characteristic that Panova portrays the beauty parlor from the viewpoint of an inexperienced young girl, who is both fascinated and terrified by its strange operations (193–4). The goodhearted vamp Fainna lends one wounded soldier *Keys* from her "private stock of love stories" and is pleased when he praises this book "which none of the personnel took seriously" (116).

19. See Andreas Huyssens's *After the Great Divide: Modernism, Mass Culture, Postmodernism* (Bloomington and Indianapolis, 1986), 49, in which he notes a general European pattern of linking women with a "mass culture [of] serialized feuilleton novels, popular and family magazines, the stuff of lending libraries, fictional bestsellers and the like" in tawdry contrast to a genuine folk culture or masterpieces of fine art. In her excellent study, "Paradigm Lost? Contemporary Women's Fiction," in Clyman and Greene, 205–28, Helena Goscilo remarks on this common distinction between male "philosophical" and female "quotidian" writings (208). Fitzpatrick notes a similar attitude among Soviet Party officials in the 1920s: "Zealous young (male) Komsomols tended to suspect that there was something intrinsically bourgeois about the female sex" (237).

20. Vera S. Dunham, *Middleclass Values in Soviet Fiction* (Durham and London, 1990).

21. I am indebted to Joan Shelley Rubin's fascinating study, *The Making of Middlebrow Culture* (Chapel Hill and London, 1992) for these definitions and the history of the middlebrow in the United States. See also Janice Radway's essay on that important middlebrow institution, the Book of the Month Club, in Cathy N. Davidson (ed.), *Reading in America: Literature and Social History* (Baltimore, 1989), and her monograph *A Feeling for Books: The Book-of-the-Month Club, Literary Taste, and Middle-Class Desire* (Chapel Hill, NC, 1997).

22. "The Alarm Clock in the Cupboard," tr. Beatrice Stillman, *Redbook* (March 1971), 179–201; "Nedelia kak nedelia," *NM* 11 (1969), 23–55.

23. For a marvelous analysis of the role of the beauty parlor in Soviet culture, see Nadezhda Azhgikhina and Helena Goscilo's "Getting Under Their Skin: The Beauty Salon in Russian Women's Lives," in Goscilo and Holmgren, 94–121.

24. See Helena Goscilo's pithy treatment, "Women's Wards and Wardens: The Hospital in Contemporary Russian Women's Fiction," *Canadian Woman Studies* 10:4 (Winter 1989), 83–6.

25. Inna Varlamova was the pseudonym for the writer Klavdia Landau.

26. See also Zernova's story "Kuzka's Mother," ("Kuz'kina mat'"), which depicts the camp experience with similar complexity.

27. For discussions of these formulae, see Tania Modleski, *Loving with a Vengeance: Mass-Produced Fantasies for Women* (Hamden, CT, 1982), and Carol Thurston's *The Romance Revolution: Erotic Novels for Women and the Quest for a New Sexual Identity* (Urbana and Chicago, IL, 1987).

28. Taken from Lauren Leighton's translation of Grekova's "One Summer in the City," *RLT* 11 (1975), 161.

29. See Goscilo, "Paradigm Lost?", 207, for her listing of four generations of women writers in the postwar period.

30. I am grateful to Cary Piper, a doctoral candidate in the UNC Slavic Department, for this inventive coinage.

12

In their own words? Soviet women writers and the search for self

The problems, dangers, and even the possibility itself of what Voltaire in *Candide* termed "seeing into the hearts" of historical subjects have become the subject of much historical and literary inquiry in recent years. As scholars engage in dialogue with voices from other eras through the legacy of fiction, memoirs, diaries, and letters, one of the challenges that presents itself is how to decipher the relationship between an author as a free and autonomous producer of a text and his or her "entrapment" within a system where meaning has already been fixed.[1] If literary works are derivative of cultural discourses, they also serve as the venues through which their authors refract and transform the experience of their particular cultural discourse. Thus the historical and cultural "entrapment" of the author within a particular system of signification does not necessarily exclude the possibility of creative self-expression through that same system.

In Soviet Russia during Stalin's time, the possibility of finding room for autonomous expression within an official literary life may seem especially problematic. Indeed, official Soviet literary life held little interest for western critics who preferred to turn their attentions to those writers on the margins of Soviet society who produced narratives of camp resistance, prison survival, and dissident subversion "for the drawer." The decades-long interest in the latter group on the part of critics in the West is paralleled by a nearly complete silence about the former. Thus three "mainstream" Socialist Realist writers: poet and novelist Vera Inber (1890–1972), and novelists Antonina Koptiaeva (1909–1991) and Vera Panova (1905–1973), whose lives and literary work were at the center of Soviet public life and of the Soviet literary profession have been virtually ignored by western critics. Moreover, the established interpretive categories (resistance, survival, marginality) and conceptual oppositions (private/public, personal/official) make the study of so-called "official" writers irrelevant, since their voices, ostensibly trapped within the official discourse, are denied historical validity and discredited by those who relegate the authentic of the Soviet era to the margins of that society.

A different approach to authority is crucial, if we are to avoid reducing the lives of these three immensely popular women writers to already familiar categories and if we are to question the relationship between the official and personal (*lichnyi*) discourses in Soviet women's writing.[2] In this essay I turn to the women's autobiographical, fictional, memoir, and diary narratives as sources of working paradigms. The categories used to structure my terms of analysis are derived from within the women's narratives themselves, and they vary as the analysis moves from one writer to another and from one historical period to another: the 1930s to the 1940s, and then into the 1970s and 1980s.[3] The method of reading I employ is also guided by a particular notion of the author's self-articulation and self-construction in a more general sense. I do not presume that there is a particular text or genre of texts that reveals an identity more truly than do others. The assumption organizing my analysis is that each text, be it a diary or an official autobiography, is the product of an individual writer, and that no text can (or aspires to) articulate a complete portrait. What a text does is reveal a particular dimension of the author's self, a particular mode of communication and interaction with society, be it identification, interrogating, subverting, or misunderstanding. Such, for example, was the case with the reception of official Party discourse in the 1930s and 1940s.

Having lived through the same historical events, the three writers invested them with different meanings, thereby creating a pronounced difference in their self-representations and in the way they borrowed from and understood official discourses. Vera Inber's articulation of herself within the genre of heroic biography is missing in Antonina Koptiaeva's narratives, which are guided by issues of women's self-realization and cultural inferiority within the upwardly mobile classes. Vera Panova's life story presents the most complicated case, as she changes her interpretive categories in the course of her writing, shifting from idealist language in the 1920s to a religious world view after World War II. Due to the paucity of our knowledge about self-perceptions and self-representations of women who actively participated in Soviet society – their conceptions of and relationship to work, family, and Soviet system – one can only speculate as to what the self-articulations of these three writers may suggest about identity formation among Soviet women in general. The focus of this chapter is thus on lives and life-narratives of these particular writers.[4] Their life stories not only reveal the complex and divergent fates of these women but offer new categories of analysis which will open up the seemingly impenetrable boundaries separating the official from the personal. Further, their stories suggest the multiple levels on which self-articulation could take place within official writing during the Soviet period.

The biography of the century

In her 1928 autobiographical novel *Mesto pod solntsem* (A Place in the Sun), Vera Inber points to a significant distinction between the *life* possessed by everyone, and the *biography* possessed by only a few.[5] The awareness of the existence of something more than a simple life, something called a "biography," is one of the most significant characteristics of Soviet political and popular culture of the 1920s and the 1930s. Within the cultural and political discourses of the time, biography was articulated largely through "the heroic," so that "heroic" and "biography" became an associative cluster with tremendous cultural power.[6] It was counterpoised by "ordinary life," and was reproduced by newspapers in numerous articles, and in smiling photos of heroes of underground work, the revolutionary movement, the Civil War, as well as of the shock workers of the Stakhanovite movement and even, spectacularly, sky-divers.[7] The genre of heroic biography became a common journalistic narrative in central newspapers, but it could be found readily beyond their pages as well. It penetrated fiction and drew the attention of literary critics in the 1920s.[8] The biographic narrative was canonized in the 1930s by Nikolai Ostrovskii in *Kak zakalialas' stal'* (How the Steel was Tempered, 1932–4). Maksim Gorky initiated a collection of materials about factories and workers' lives which resulted in numerous heroic narratives with elements of the biographical genre. This initiative was eagerly supported and, in some cases, even anticipated by workers who wrote their autobiographies on their own or under the guidance of writers and journalists.[9]

To appreciate fully the scope and power of the heroic discourse, we first must consider the place of autobiographical writing in Soviet society. Written autobiographies were required for a multitude of ordinary life events: entering school or university; joining a professional organization, the Komsomol, or the Party; as well as applying for a job. During the course of a lifetime, a citizen might write several autobiographical narratives, even if s/he remained within the same organization. Composing autobiographies every five or ten years required citizens to review and represent their own lives from different historical perspectives, and allowed them to reinterpret themselves and their participation in Soviet "historical" events within the context of new realities. At the same time, the regular (re)writing of one's autobiography was a particular type of control mechanism, a constant report on and evaluation of one's participation in the Soviet project writ large. Written narratives coexisted with oral presentations of life narratives, many of which were integrated into Komsomol and Party meetings and attended by the collective. The organization of Soviet public life, in other words, demanded thinking in terms of biography. It not only created situations in which people had to contemplate their lives as narratives, but also composed and supplied categories for such an undertaking. Within the emerging system of signification, a "heroic biography" was presented as admirable, desirable, and enviable, as something to strive for, while the meaning of "ordinary biography" could vary from boring and shameful to socially alien and dangerous.[10]

Despite the centrality of biographical and heroic discourses, the depth of their penetration into people's lives, and their impact on people's self-narratives and self-perceptions varied dramatically depending on the sociocultural position occupied by these biographies in Soviet society. By the late 1920s, Vera Inber could easily articulate what comprised a "real" biography, and obversely, what her "petit bourgeois" life lacked. A real biography boasted "hard childhood, early years in the revolutionary underground, the year 1905, arrest, prison, exile, escape, vegetative life in emigration, wandering around English and French dockyards, and finally the return, not to Russia but to the Union of Socialist Republics."[11] Inber's clear articulation of the era's social imperatives was simultaneously a confession of her lack of a biography, and of the inadequacy of her former life within new post-revolutionary realities. Thus, seeking the heroic self became Inber's life-long agenda.

"I was not lucky with my biography"[12]

Vera Inber's internalization of the categories of the biographical discourse manifested itself differentially over time, acquiring various forms. She revealed them overtly in her notebooks and diary, hid them behind the rhetoric of optimistic triumph in her official autobiography, and negated them publicly in her many speeches. In her public address to the Plenum of the Organizational Committee of the Union of Writers in 1932, Inber criticized one of her readers (a "clever reader with a retentive memory"), who had asked her to narrate a biography she did not possess and who had thus reminded her of her "petit petit bourgeoisness."[13] Inber explained the clever reader's interest in her biographical data as a result of particular political and literary discourses, which had taught the Soviet readership to think in terms of biography, the heroic, and social origins. Inber demanded to be judged for her present worth as a writer, and also suggested that contemporary literary criticism robbed the reader of serious engagement with literature by reducing the available conceptual framework to the paradigm of biography. She, thus, presented herself as offering solid resistance to this confining discourse and as confident to the point of appropriating dominant categories in order to criticize them.

However, in the pages of her contemporaneous (1920s–30s) notebooks, Inber's public self-representation acquires a new dimension and new significance.[14] The self-articulations in her notebooks are organized around the category of otherness – the position of a "stepdaughter" in Soviet literature.[15] If in her public articulations she demonstrated the ability to separate herself from the biographic imperative through criticism and laughter, in her notebooks she revealed how deeply the public discourse about biography had penetrated her imagination, and how successfully it had destroyed her emotional inner balance. Self-confident critique was replaced by fear of exclusion and by helplessness in front of the "othering" eye of the audience. On March 8, 1932, Inber described her state before an evening shared with I. Utkin and M. Svetlov, "two Komsomol poets," as *fearful (Ia boius')* – not because of a lack of confidence as a writer, but because she was painfully aware of the social otherness that would be further underscored by the "proper" biographies of her co-performers.[16]

An analysis of Inber's life-narratives through her 1920s to 1930s autobiographical sketches reveals yet another Vera Inber, one who this time departs from her critical stance towards the biographical imperative and embraces it fully. Inber recalled a schoolmate of hers, the daughter of a rich factory owner, who was ostracized by her family for participating in a revolutionary circle: "the years of her happy youth were over, but her biography began, a biography that would include prison, exile, escape, and emigration. Everything that I needed so badly." The retrieval of this particular scene from the past was Inber's indirect indictment of herself for not having chosen the right path. Her confession that she was not lucky with her biography is both a discursive move to blame objective conditions, and an admission of guilt and acceptance of responsibility for missing an opportunity to initiate a heroic biography. It also illustrates her strong identification with official discourse – the official had become personal. Inber's answer to the "clever reader" inside herself became a life-long search for a proper biography.[17]

Read through the above outlined politico-cultural discourses, Inber's official autobiographies allow us to comprehend the official autobiographical narrative not only as an authoritative genre through which she mechanically narrated her life in politically correct terms but as texts in which the poet dealt with the problems of self-representation. Such a reading suggests many parallels between Inber's official, fictional, and notebook identities. Though Inber's official autobiography of 1932 evidenced neither indignation at exclusion nor self-accusatory attacks, the problem that drives her official life story migrates there from her other writings – the recognition, explanation, and liquidation of her biographical lack. A good Marxist, she blamed her decadent bourgeois environment – with its "socially harmful art," the "root" which nourished her childhood and youth – for her "dwarfish, laughable, childish" poetry.[18] Prerevolutionary society spoke in Inber's autobiography through her husband, who "taught me that life is short but art is eternal, that any ancient crock is more precious than a modern vase" (2). Here she presents herself as a passive, victimized woman. She delegates the responsibility for her non-heroic youth to her husband, with whom she places the agency – he "who taught me" – thus, making use of patriarchal stereotypes to excuse her biographical inadequacy.

The witty and ironic picture of her prerevolutionary life and art was directly condemned as "socially harmful"; her victimization by it is only suggested. As in her novel *Mesto pod solntsem* and her short stories of the 1920s and 1930s, in the first part of her autobiography, Inber used counterpositional techniques that produced a message not through direct articulation but through inference. Thus, she presents her break with her past by means of a little scene that she inserted in her official autobiography. She moves her narrative into the present (1932) and tells a story about her accidental encounter with a sailor who sang a decadent song (written by Inber during her "dwarfish, laughable, childish" life) to "a Soviet girl" – "'Stop it, comrade,' – I said. – 'Why do you want to sing such nonsense (*chepukha*)?'"(2). The past, represented by her prerevolutionary creative undertaking, is symbolically disavowed and erased by equating it with "nonsense." But such a disavowal only exposes Inber's lack of biography, either in the past or in the present. There was nothing biographically heroic in her life of the 1930s that could have filled the erased years. As a consequence, the 1930s in the 1932 autobiography are presented as a time of search and movement. The author could not offer any tangible biographic accomplishments; her literary work had not yet received public recognition, hence she could not yet call herself a proletarian or Soviet writer. What she could claim was intensive inner work on "herself, her feelings . . . and mistakes." What she could offer was nothing more than an optimistic promise "to move in the right direction towards 'the proletariat'" (3). At the same time, the loss of the past in Inber's narrative was counterbalanced by the acquisition of a new agency that was symbolically presented by her break from a patriarchal relationship. In contrast to her prerevolutionary life as years of passive victimization, Inber's period of searching is characterized as "a whole independent life" in which it was *she* who was making mistakes. In the second part of her autobiography, she turns herself into an actor and puts the blame and responsibilities on herself.[19]

A new period of disavowal and searching was marked in the second part of the official autobiography by a new literary intonation. Inber's habit of "speak[ing] in an undertone"[20] – ironically and wittily, with inferences and omissions – was replaced by a pledge, a categorically optimistic, solemnly enthusiastic direct articulation.[21] This new language served two purposes. It was Inber's shield against her biographic emptiness, and it also became her new personal dialect that penetrated conversations with herself on the pages of her diary. Thus, for example, she wondered why "spiritual disorder" and "falling out of rhythm" occurred in her so quickly. She attributed these phenomena to her "petit bourgeois consciousness" and asked herself how to "fight" it.[22] The fact that she saw the solution to her problems in "struggle" (*bor'ba*) is symptomatic of her identification with the official Soviet thinking of the thirties.

Official language turned personal became increasingly prominent in Inber's notebooks and diary over time, particularly through the war and postwar years. But pledging and internalizing official language and the mentality that accompanied it could not replace the non-existent heroic past. A heroic page in Inber's biography had to be lived and suffered through. The deeply felt biographical inadequacy created by sociocultural realities played a crucial and tragic part in Inber's life. During the Great Patriotic War (World War II), she refused many opportunities to leave besieged Leningrad and go to live with her daughter and grandson who had been evacuated from the city. Unlike the Revolution and the Civil War, the siege of Leningrad was the heroic moment that Inber was unable to pass by.[23] By sending her writings from besieged Leningrad to *Pravda* and literary journals, she recruited witnesses – clever readers – to her heroic moment. The image of a small, fragile woman in a small frozen apartment, starving and yet writing and morally defeating the enemy through her poetry was publicly recognized and admired, became part of the popular discourse on war heroism and survived into the postwar years.[24] In her official autobiography of 1949, Inber divided her life into preface and the "writer's true biography" but, like most heroic biographies, hers did not commence without sacrifice. It was during the blockade that her grandson died. The fact that she was unwilling to leave Leningrad to go and join her daughter and grandson and care for them is connected powerfully in Inber's imagination with the grandson's death. She justified remaining in Leningrad but also realized what it had cost her: "I do need this justification. I indeed paid for Leningrad with the life of [her daughter] Zhanna's child. This I know for sure."[25] This admission of guilt must be one of the most terrifying examples of how "time" can take possession of people.[26] Inber's life after the war became her escape from guilt into work.

Problems close to a woman's heart[27]

Antonina Koptiaeva's life-narratives take us in a different direction and open up an under-researched topic – the ways in which the millions of women from "proper" social classes who, having been brought up in poor prerevolutionary households, were pushed upward into new sociocultural milieux by the Revolution, and spent much of their lives searching for new identities and fighting complexes of cultural inferiority. If Inber structured her narratives in relation to and through the dominant biographical and heroic discourses, attempting to renegotiate the terms of her social and biographical exclusion, Antonina Koptiaeva organized her autobiographies, fiction, and memoirs around issues which occupied a significant place in the public debates of the 1920s to 1940s – though they could never compete with the biographical / heroic discourse in terms of sheer volume of media coverage. The issues at the center of Koptiaeva's literary work were how Soviet women negotiated their relationship to education, to the conflicts between work and personal happiness, and to the Soviet family during the period of rapid upward mobility of the 1920s to 1940s. What set Koptiaeva apart from other Soviet writers and attracted to her numerous female readers were less the themes of infidelity, divorce, and female self-realization than her articulation and critique of women's issues from an avowedly female perspective.[28]

Her life-narratives reveal the often ignored complexities, contradictions, pains, and traumas of those who, willingly or unwillingly, intentionally or unintentionally, became part of the enormous social and cultural restructuring of society in the 1930s, and who, over a period of fifteen to twenty years traveled a sociocultural distance that usually requires generations. Koptiaeva's autobiography gives scholars a valuable resource with which to set about exploring the particular experience of peasant, working, and lower middle-class women who "stepped out" of their original social groups, became part of the new Soviet intelligentsia, and in some cases, made striking careers. To document their careers, the bureaucracy had to invent two new entries in its registration forms (*uchetnaia kartochka*): social origin and present social position. In 1946, Koptiaeva indicated her social origin as "a daughter of a gold-digger, from the lower middle class" and her present social position as "writer."[29] The distance between these two bureaucratic classifications embodied Koptiaeva's life and literary work.

Having acquired a semblance of a real biography through birth – a "hard childhood," to use Inber's definition – Koptiaeva did not evidence much anxiety over her non-heroic youth in her 1946 official autobiography. The daughter of a self-employed gold-digger in the Far East who was killed when she was three years old, Koptiaeva lived with her mother, a semi-literate peasant woman from Tomsk, and five siblings.[30] Since her mother was unable to pay for her schooling, Koptiaeva made the extra money she needed in order to be able to attend school by washing the school floors. Life remained hard, however, and one winter she could not go to school because she did not have proper shoes. Koptiaeva created an image of herself as a gifted, energetic, and independent girl who wrote bad poetry, was obsessed with unsystematic reading due to a lack of guidance, and who was responsible for her family as well as her own maintenance. At the age of seventeen, she quit school and walked 750 kilometers to the Aldanskii goldfield to look for a job. Her autobiography partitioned her life into periods of varying lengths all interpreted within the framework of overcoming. Yet, what she means by "overcoming," changes over time in her autobiographical narrative. Through her late-twenties, her self-portrait is adorned with heroic touches: hard work at the age of twelve, walking 750 kilometers across the taiga, the general conquest of objective difficulties. After 1939, when she entered the Literary Institute in Moscow, her life became "awfully interesting." In her 1952 autobiography, she equated her years as a thirty-year-old student with a "second birth," during which a semi-literate woman from the Far East firmly acquired new self-respect and a new identity, and entered the realm of "cultured people." Her later autobiography reinterprets her pre-1939 heroic achievements as a dull, though heroic struggle, relegates her pre-institute life to the margins of Soviet experience, and marks it as a period of exclusion.[31]

The "second birth" at the Literary Institute is presented in official autobiography as an unproblematic, enthusiastic, and joyful triumph. Such an interpretation becomes less central within the corpus of Koptiaeva's extended literary legacy, which goes beyond the official life-narrative, allowing us to interpret the silences in her autobiographical self. Operating also within the paradigm of the "second birth" in her fiction, Koptiaeva invested different meanings in her experiences at the Institute; she never negated her official account but rather enriched and complicated it. The writer attempted in her fiction to master and conceptualize the monumental sociocultural changes of the 1920s to 1940s, which manifested themselves in feelings of inferiority typical of people finding themselves in new political and societal roles without the "proper" education and background to ease the transition into this new reality. A rapidly industrializing Stalinist Russia, which attempted to surpass historical time itself – changing villages into ruralized towns and cities into urbanized villages, building the new through the destruction of the old – replicated its dynamics and disruptions – its second birth – in millions of individual lives. This "catastrophic" period demanded an unprecedented measure of adaptability and was almost inevitably accompanied by anxieties over one's exposed inadequacies and by psychological breakdowns.[32] In 1946, Antonina Koptiaeva could admit and work through her shame about her lack of learning and culture only in fictional form.

The emotional complexity of Koptiaeva's experience of leaving the cultural margins and entering a new sociocultural group makes itself felt most strongly in her 1946 sketch *Kollektiv entuziastov* (The Collective of Enthusiasts), the autobiographical nature of which the writer revealed only in the 1970s.[33] In *Kollektiv entuziastov* Koptiaeva articulated another dimension of her 1940s' personality: the fear, shame, and rudeness of a semi-educated working woman – herself – in unfamiliar cultural surroundings. Koptiaeva represented the moment of cultural crossing through her initial entrance into the Lenin Library, which she figured as her "promised land" – a place where she did not yet belong but which she had come to conquer. The bright electric light exposed "all the darns on her old dress," her feet felt awkward in her worn-out shoes. She fought against the physically-felt otherness in the world of learning with "determination and even anger," with strong belief in herself, and with rudeness towards those who doubted her.[34] Out of this struggle emerged a new person, solid, changed, empowered, and enriched by books. The official self re-emerged at the end of the sketch, as a result of the long and painful process of acculturation which faced those who were upwardly mobile.

Yet for Koptiaeva the interpenetration between the official and fictional went deeper, and the trope of the "second birth" acquired new and more personal significance. Reading her autobiography and fiction of the 1940s against each other, the meaning of the writer's rebirth conforms neither to the painful struggle for the new self nor the triumphant and unproblematic embrace of the future. The rebirth in *Kollektiv entuziastov* was also presented as a desperate escape from the past self towards a complete reconstruction of personality, while the sketch itself became a deconstructive commentary on Koptiaeva's official autobiography.

> Yes, I had children. A husband, also . . . My soul is like this corridor – a lot of empty space. I have to redo myself all over again, I have to create myself anew. Yes, that is right . . . to create![35]

The dialogue above was another comment, in fictional form, on Koptiaeva's 1946 autobiography: "got married, gave birth to and buried my child"; "on the eve of 1938 [first husband] Zeite was arrested and later died in prison"; "buried my second daughter."[36] The dry enumeration of personal calamities in the autobiography is exposed in the fictional narrative as a deep, devastating family trauma in the context of which Koptiaeva's search for knowledge became not only her struggle with an inferiority complex but also an attempt to escape "emptiness," to heal her pain, and to redirect her attention from her family trauma to her self-(re)building. This sketch on cultural inferiority, thus, was a piece of *therapeutic writing* in which Koptiaeva articulated her pain, shared it with readers, and mourned her losses.

But Koptiaeva's relationship to her husband and her attitude to his death were highly ambivalent. In her 1946 official autobiography, she singled out the one period in her life that did not conform to the logic of "overcoming" and described it instead in the following manner: the 1930s begins with her marriage. She describes the subsidiary role she played in her husband's career path, a role that is captured expressively in the text of her autobiography. Her husband studied at the *Promakademiia* (Industrial Academy) in Moscow, while she was "wasting time studying draftsmanship and the English language." In 1932, the family moved to Kolyma, her husband's assigned workplace, where Koptiaeva "worked as a secretary." Through such textual counterpositions, Koptiaeva alludes to the difference between work as derivative of someone else's life, as it was for her during this period, and work as the development and enrichment of one's own self through independent pursuit of individual potential. Her social position as an appendage to her husband's life is a nominal, deceptive inclusion that masks her own feeling of exclusion and her lack of independence. In her official autobiography, Koptiaeva symbolically counterpoised the arrest of her husband with the beginning of a new period in her life: "On the eve of 1938 Zeite was arrested and later died in prison ... while I moved to the city of Miass and started writing a novel." The disappearance of Zeite from her life is thus interpreted by Koptiaeva as the end of her life as a *follower* and the beginning of a life in which she acquires independent agency.

Though only suggested in her official autobiography through textual counterpositions, the problematic of the following female became the central theme in Koptiaeva's mature fiction. In her 1947 Stalin Prize-winning novel *Ivan Ivanovich*, she created a female protagonist whose choices for the future and paths towards self-growth (*rost*) are circumscribed by her husband's career moves.[37] The way out suggested in the novel is to separate from the loving, respectful, but self-focused husband, thereby disrupting the cycle of following. In her later official autobiography of 1952, Koptiaeva expresses admiration for her female protagonist's ability to decipher the deception of her position and for her character's refusal to live as "a wife provided for by a well-positioned husband."

Koptiaeva's self-representations in official, autobiographical, and fictional narratives of different periods reveal a complex relationship between her fictional, official, and autobiographical selves as well as an overlapping of both official and non-official discourse. The re-emergence of the official self in Koptiaeva's fiction of the 1940s, and the emerging significance of the 1946 sketch as a key autobiographical text in her writing in the 1970s suggest a complex, multidimensional identity, in which the official is not necessarily opposed to or in negation of the truly autobiographical, and in which the boundaries between different selves are fluid and interdependent.

The recuperation of self and its rescue from cultural and gendered otherness became Koptiaeva's main theme in her fiction. Her books on "themes close to a woman's heart" brought her in the 1940s and 1950s both great popularity and much criticism. *Literaturnaia gazeta* (Literary Newspaper) accused Koptiaeva of propagating pornography and privileging physical love, and of an inability to see normal family relationships without infidelity and divorces.[38] At the same time, hundreds of female readers wrote to Koptiaeva to thank her for articulating the "emotional experience" of women, and both men and women expressed gratitude for her serious study of the personal realm of Soviet life.[39] It is crucial to point out, however, that despite criticism and disagreement, there was one image uncontested by all participants in these debates – namely the belief that the interaction of the public and the personal in the lives of women was vital to their harmonious development and full self-realization.

Through the lives of her fictional heroines, Koptiaeva insisted on the crucial significance of public life and work as the way for women's personalities to be most completely developed, and as a defense mechanism against calamities in the family – from divorce, infidelity, or death of a family member. Indeed, she followed this prescription herself. Her second husband and the major love of her life, Fedor Panferov, died in 1960. In her memoirs, she recalled how close she was to complete demoralization after his death. As in Inber's case, her literary career became her salvation and life after his death.[40]

"How many kind people I see looking back . . ."[41]

For many women such as Koptiaeva who found themselves in upwardly mobile social groups in the Soviet Union, the lines between different kinds of texts are blurry, their themes and languages intertwine. The solemnly enthusiastic language of the 1940s, usually associated with official impersonal language, is encountered again in Koptiaeva's memoir and autobiographical writing of the 1970s and late 1980s, where it acquires the features of personal narrative.[42] This official-language-turned-personal and its continuous, "dehistoricized" presence throughout

Koptiaeva's long literary career is the most striking difference between her writing and that of Vera Panova. Panova relegated the official Soviet language of enthusiasm and idealism to its proper historical time and place; in other words, she historicized it. Its reality was not negated, but was given the power to express feelings and thoughts proper only to the 1920s and 1930s. For other periods of Soviet history, that language was foreign and false. Panova underlined this foreignness by using her own expressive language and avoiding sovietisms. This historical perspective was a product of much thought and suffering.

Belonging to the upwardly mobile generation whose youth coincided with the 1920s and 1930s, Panova inevitably shared much of its excitement, anxiety, and hope. Like many of her contemporaries who left their traditional sociocultural environments for new ones, she became acutely aware of what she called in her 1970 memoirs a particular "aesthetic and vocabulary circle" that was inherited from her lower middle-class family and that "circumscribed her." In her official autobiographies, fiction, and memoirs, Panova carefully, step by step, outlined her extrication from this circle, her gradual internalization of the new cultural paradigms of correct speech and writing, and proudly figured herself as a self-made person.[43] Her portrayal of the family varied from a categorical denial of its worth to a much more appreciative picture in her later memoirs.[44] However, the theme of the self-made, self-educated, self-mannered, and self-corrected Vera Panova remained central in all of her narratives. Panova's characterization of her education in her registration form for the Union of Soviet Writers as "self-education" is a terse signifier of a fundamental part of her identity and life-long anxiety.

At the age of twelve and after less than two years of education, Panova left the gymnasium (secondary school) in 1917 due to lack of funds, and embarked on reading textbooks and literature for fear of "staying completely uneducated and unpolished."[45] In 1922 she became a journalist at *Trudovoi Don* (Toiling Don) where she prided herself on her rapid learning of the journalistic craft. In her official 1946 autobiography she noted that she had always worked at several newspapers at the same time because she was in high demand, thanks to her well-known and highly praised style. In her memoirs, Panova added to her self-portrait more details that did not contradict her official 1920s self-representation. She portrayed herself as a strong-willed, independent, and opinionated woman who constantly evaluated her accomplishments, enriched herself with what "was not given to her in right time," and constantly pushed herself forward with rebukes and accusations.[46]

Panova's reminiscences offer frequent and direct references to her published fictional work as viable autobiographical material. The novel that she referenced most often is the 1958 *Sentimental'nyi roman* (Sentimental Novel), which she characterized as autobiographical.[47] There is an interesting symbiosis between Panova's memoirs of the 1970s and this novel. Not only did Panova frequently refer to *Sentimental'nyi roman* in her memoirs as an equally reliable autobiographic source, and cited it as such, but the two works are marked by a similar perspective on the Soviet Union of the 1920s and early 1930s. Moreover, in her memoirs she explained and drew connections between her fictional and memoir selves and the fictional and memoir representations of the people she knew in the 1920s. In *Sentimental'nyi roman* she wrote herself into Sevast'ianov, who adores his newspaper and editorial office and is bored outside it; her first husband appeared as Semka, a devoted, selfless fighter against the petit bourgeois. Many of Panova's friends and acquaintances, who dreamt of heroic biographies and came to work "as if the fate of the republic depended" on them, likewise appear and reappear on the pages of her fiction and reminiscences.[48]

The gentle irony with which Panova constructs her characters plays a complicated role in her novel. It both distances her from the events, the people, and her 1930s self–particularly from their/her selfless dedication and naive enthusiasm–and simultaneously suggests her nostalgia for her youth, while also exposing an unbridgeable emotional and conceptual gap between her 1920s self and the one who writes *Sentimental'nyi roman* in the late 1950s. The same ironic, distancing tone is present in her memoirs. As in *Sentimental'nyi roman*, the language of the 1920s and 1930s is used symbolically to represent the break between Panova's pre-war self and that of the 1970s. In contrast to the novel, however, the language of the memoirs is infused with Panova's own new postwar voice that clearly articulates her distance from her youth. She presents the reader with a new language or "vision" and new categories of "kind people" and "fate" with which she evaluates her life in retrospect in the 1970s. Her memoirs are completely devoid of identification with stock solemn Soviet generalizations such as country (*strana*), people (*narod*), revolution, Soviet power, Party – all of which permeate Koptiaeva's memoir writings. She concretizes these official Soviet abstractions and invests value in particular individuals. The Party, for example, appears on the pages of her memoirs as a kind woman, the secretary of the district Party committee who helped Panova during the war. That kindness is not metonymic for the Party as a whole. Kind people acquire a mystical dimension in her memoirs: they are presented as carriers of her fate. It is the sudden appearance of these new people in her life that signifies for Panova the new stages on which she is embarking in her life.

Over the years Panova thus withdrew her life from the official version of Soviet history encased in official language, and offered readers her own history and explanations. The language of her novel and memoirs, ironic, in some places categorical, with religious and mystical undertones, expresses fully the fundamental change that she underwent between the 1930s and the 1950s. This transformation was attributed by Panova to a deep personal trauma, the arrest in 1935 of her second husband, Boris Vakhtin, and his subsequent death in a camp. In her memoirs, her pain and transformation are articulated in an imaginary conversation with Vakhtin. Panova identifies "this eternity of [their] separation" as a time of learning, more often bitter than joyful but, occasionally, happy; as the destruction of her idealistic, bookish knowledge of life; and as the discovery of "what I am and what my calling in the world is."[49] This process of self-discovery, of Panova's formation as a writer, and of mourning over the pain of the loss, which, in her case, was cumulative, resulted in rethinking the idealistic beliefs of her youth. This re-evaluation appears in her memoirs, O moei zhizni, knigakh i chitateliakh (About my Life, Books, and Readers).[50]

The period from the 1920s through the 1950s was thus one of considerable transformation for Panova. From an uncultured meshchanka, (member of the lower middle class) to use her self-definition, she became a well-educated woman and an accomplished writer. She also developed from an idealistic young woman in tune with the spirit of the 1920s into a writer with her own vision, language, and system of values that went their own way from official discourse. The process by which Panova broke with the world view of her youth and acquired a new perceptual framework can hardly be documented in terms of concrete dates. However, the stages of her disillusionment can be traced in her 1952 official autobiography by reading it in light of the problematics of her fiction and memoirs outlined above. Panova's language and the themes on which she focuses change as she describes different periods of her life in her autobiography. Her representation of the 1920s as a time of ideals, enthusiasm, and growth has already been discussed. The part of her narrative that covers the middle and late-1930s – the immediate years after her husband's arrest – can be characterized as a time of hope and belief. She describes her misfortunes and hardships after 1935 – dismissal from the newspaper, concealment of her husband's fate, responsibilities of a mother of three young children – and finally her decision to write to Stalin and ask him for help. In discussing her letter to Stalin, Panova appropriates the official Soviet language for addressing the leader: "I asked Iosif Vissarionovich to give me an opportunity to work, to bring me back into the society out of which I was thrown without a fault on my part." She creates an image of herself as a conscientious, wrongly treated Soviet citizen who reveres Stalin.[51]

In the final section of her official autobiography, Panova turns to detailed descriptions of people she met during her life on the occupied territory during the war. In detailing these characters and the support and help they provided her, she demonstrates her new conceptual framework. Her reverent tone switches from the abstract figure of Stalin to a local inhabitant of the village, introduced in her autobiography by her full name, M. V. Koshevaia, a woman who "gave me a little room." In this last part of her autobiography, Panova's language is strikingly reminiscent of the language of her memoirs and expresses the inner process by which she came to re-evaluate her earlier beliefs and principles.[52] Panova's official autobiography is fascinating because one cannot find a trace of a compromise with the official discourse. She unravels her life story stage by stage carefully designating different periods by the change in her language, and in the categories and themes she employs. Like Koptiaeva's writings, Panova's are characterized by a fluidity of language and theme penetrating her different narratives and migrating between them.

While Koptiaeva and Panova appropriated official discourse in very different ways, we should not overlook significant similarities in their self-representations, in the way they conceptualized the relationship between the public and the private, and in the way they depicted Soviet women. These similarities suggest moments of contiguity between Panova's vision and those of the official and the popular. For Panova, as for Koptiaeva, the fear of wasted personal potential was a consciously articulated anxiety. The symbol of failure in Panova's life was her grandmother, who was "a strikingly gifted person . . . though life let her realize not one of her capabilities."[53] The path towards Panova's ideals – interesting work, steady income, fame – lay in the public realm. Its temporary termination in her life when she was fired from her newspaper after her husband's arrest in 1935 was experienced by her as the half-death of her personality. In her memoirs of the 1970s, she remembers how intense her pain was at being liquidated as a worker. Such an expulsion from public life endangered Panova's most fundamental image of herself as a confident, independent, self-made woman. Thus, after the arrest of her husband, Panova experienced two traumas and two losses, both personal: the loss of the most sustaining love in her life, Vakhtin, and the loss of her familiar working self. Her self-cure was contingent on being allowed "back into society," and thus Panova aggressively sought any type of job. Employment meant not only an income for her family but a reunification with her former persona. She remembers the healing effects that even accidental work had on her: it allowed her to recapture the feeling of being needed somewhere outside of the home.[54]

Panova's autobiography and memoirs reveal to students of Soviet women new dimensions of the complex emotional trauma experienced by those whose husbands were persecuted and who, consequently could not find jobs for many years. As Panova's life story and self-representation demonstrate, their traumas were constituted not only through the destruction of private selves but also of public personae. The expulsion from the public was perceived by many as a deeply felt personal trauma.

Panova's ultimate cure was to pursue seriously a literary career after 1939 when she left her two sons and her mother in the village of Shishaki near Rostov-na-Donu. She started her search for her "literary fate" in Moscow, living with friends and relatives, renting little rooms, and writing on kitchen tables at night. Her travel to her "fate" was a manifestation of her daring will as well as her attempt to refind her former self, which was once in the center of public activity.

Panova's favorite female characters understandably have much in common with their creator.[55] Through them Panova offered to both her male and female readers her ideal of happiness and a fully realized life, which she situated between enriching work, family happiness, and love. This ideal, despite her active literary career, unity with her children, and her third marriage, was never fully realized. She never stopped mourning the separation from and loss of her second husband, "the radiant revelation of my life."[56] In accordance with her will, she was buried in the Christian tradition, hoping to reunite with him in the other world.

Conclusion

The diversity of Inber's, Koptiaeva's, and Panova's self-articulations and relationships both within and with Soviet society extend beyond the resistance / subversion paradigm and demonstrate the range and complexity of their experiences in both the public and private realms. Their interactions with the system varied from wishful identification to unquestioned inclusion to gradual disavowal; from resisting certain (gendered) parts of official discourse without questioning its key political elements – as in Koptiaeva's case – to distancing themselves from the official language while still sharing some aspects of official views, as in Panova's case. Like many women from upwardly mobile social groups, Koptiaeva and Panova neither completely broke from nor identified with the official. The absence of clear lines of demarcation between their self-representations in fiction, memoir, and official discourse suggests a greater degree of fluidity within Soviet discourse than was formerly assumed. It is in Inber's writings particularly that the official / personal and public / private dichotomies are most closely scrutinized. By turning the official and the public into the personal, she exposed both the inapplicability of the model to her life as well as its cultural and historical contingency. Similarly, both Koptiaeva and Panova questioned the very categories of the public and private as they related to how Soviet female identity was formed. Both writers perceived themselves and their fictional characters as constituted by work and family, without demarcating either as exclusively personal or public. Clearly, as we begin to re-evaluate how identity was constructed during the Soviet era, the writings once marginalized by western scholars to make way for those works marginalized by the official literary establishment once again assume center stage. And they do so for good reason. Inber's, Koptiaeva's, and Panova's fictional and autobiographical writings not only allow us to investigate how these women constructed and articulated themselves but also suggest the larger issues that were at stake in Soviet identity formation.

NOTES

1. Judith Walkowitz, *City of Dreadful Delight* (Chicago, 1992), 9.
2. In this essay I will avoid using categories such as "private" and "intimate," given their oversaturation with meaning as well as the problem of translating *lichnoe* as either. I translate *lichnoe* as personal and the dichotomy *obshchestvennoe/lichnoe* as public/personal.

3. For work in cultural history that influenced my approach, see Walkowitz, *City of Dreadful Delight*; Mary Poovey, *Uneven Developments: The Ideological Work of Gender in Mid-Victorian England* (Chicago, 1988).

4. For works considering Soviet women's lives from other perspectives, see Gail Lapidus, *Women in Soviet Society: Equality, Development, and Social Change* (Berkeley, 1978); Wendy Goldman, *Women, the State, and Revolution: Soviet Family and Social Life, 1917–1936* (Cambridge, 1993).

5. Vera Inber, *Mesto pod solntsem* (Moscow, 1934), 65.

6. On the notion of "associative cluster," see Poovey, *Uneven Developments*, 15–21. This constellation is also present in memoir and autobiographical writings of later years, see Vera Ketlinskaia, *Vecher. Okna. Liudi* (Moscow, 1974), 424; Vera Panova, *Sentimental'nyi roman* (1958) in *SS*, 5 vols. (Leningrad, 1970), vol. III 320.

7. See *Pravda*, May–Aug, 1931; Oct–Dec, 1935; *Komsomol'skaia pravda*, Aug–Sept, 1934; see also Jeffrey Brooks, "Revolutionary Lives, Public Identities in *Pravda* in the 1920s," in Stephen White (ed.), *New Directions in Soviet History* (Cambridge, 1991).

8. See B. Tomashevskii, "Literatura i biografiia," in *Kniga i Revoliutsiia: Kritiko-bibliograficheskii zhurnal* 4:28 (1923).

9. See the pathbreaking work by S. V. Zhuravlev, *Fenomen "istorii fabrik i zavodov": Gor'kovskoe nachinanie v kontekste epokhi 1930-kh godov* (Moscow, 1997).

10. See Sheila Fitzpatrick, *Education and Social Mobility in the Soviet Union, 1921–1934* (Cambridge, 1979).

11. Inber, *Mesto pod solntsem*, 65.

12. Vera Inber, "Eti piatnadtsat' let" (1932) in *Za mnogo let* (Moscow, 1964), 15.

13. Vera Inber, "Nashe obshchee delo," the speech at the Plenum of the Organizational Committee of the Union of Writers of the USSR, in Inber, *Za mnogo let*, 20.

14. Inber's diaries and notebooks were first published in 1967; an enlarged version came out in 1977; I use the later one, Vera Inber, *Stranitsy dnei perebiraia. Iz dnevnikov i zapisnykh knizhek* (Moscow, 1977).

15. Inber, *Stranitsy dnei*, April 1933, 22.

16. *Ibid.*, 18.

17. Inber, *Za mnogo let*, 16, 15.

18. RGALI, fond 1072, opis' 2, edinitsa khraneniia 96, list 2; in this section, citations are given in the text.

19. RGALI, fond 1072, *ibid.*, list 2, 3.

20. Inber, *Stranitsy dnei* (September 7, 1934), 34.

21. On the general changes in public speech patterns in the 1920s, especially the movement towards a revolutionary language, see Michael Gorham, "Speaking In Tongues: Language Culture, Literature, and Language of State in Early Soviet Russia, 1921–1934" (Ph.D. dissertation, Stanford University, 1994).

22. Inber, *Stranitsy dnei*, March 13, 1936, 40.

23. During the siege of Leningrad, Inber wrote and published in central newspapers her Stalin Prize-winning *Pulkovskii Meridian*; *Pochti tri goda: Leningradskii dnevnik*, and many articles, poems, and short stories; in 1943 Inber also joined the Communist Party.

24. At the IX Plenum of the Union of Writers, 1944, the writer Boris Gorbatov admitted his "envy" of Inber's heroism; see RTsKhIDNI, fond 17, opis' 125, delo 279, list 148.

25. Inber, *Stranitsy dnei*, 108.

26. Arkhiv tvorcheskikh kadrov Soiuza pisatelei (ATKP), lichnoe delo, list 9.

27. Antonina Koptiaeva, "Avtobiografiia" in *Sovetskie pisateli. Avtobiografii* (Moscow, 1988), vol. v, 299.

28. In 1945, A. A. Fadeev called Koptiaeva's novel *Tovarishch Anna* (1945) "the first book about a Soviet family" from a female perspective; see B. Gorbatov's letter to G. M. Malenkov, RTsKhIDNI, fond 17, opis' 125, delo 461, list 38.

29. ATKP, lichnoe delo.

30. RGALI, fond 2537, opis' 1, edinitsa khraneniia 123, list 7.

31. RGALI, fond 2537, *ibid.*, 7, 8, 11, 39.

32. Moshe Lewin, *The Making of the Soviet System: Essays in the Social History of Interwar Russia* (London, 1985). Sheila Fitzpatrick, *Cultural Revolution*.

33. Antonina Koptiaeva, "O samom dorogom," in Antonina Koptiaeva (ed.), *Fedor Panferov. Vospominaniia druzei* (Moscow, 1977), 148.

34. Antonina Koptiaeva, "Kollektiv entuziastov," *Oktiabr'*, 1–2 (1946), 136.

35. *Ibid.*, 138.

36. RGALI, fond 2537, 9–10.

37. Antonina Koptiaeva, *Ivan Ivanovich* (Moscow, 1950), 57.

38. M. Iunovich, "Nizkoprobnaia literatura", *LitGaz* (September 3, 1946); see also "Lzhivyi roman o sovetskoi sem'e," *Krasnaia zvezda* (August 23, 1946).

39. See letters to Koptiaeva, RGALI, fond 2537, opis' 1, edinitsa khraneniia 295, list 1, 15, 48, 58, 78.

40. Koptiaeva, *O samom dorogom*, 173.

41. Vera Panova, *O moei zhizni, knigakh i chitateliakh* (Leningrad, 1980), 189.

42. See Koptiaeva's 1952 official autobiography and her memoirs *O samom dorogom*, 158–60.

43. Panova, *O moei zhizni*, 37.

44. 1952 official autobiography, *Arkhiv tvorcheskikh kadrov Soiuza pisatelei, lichnoe delo*, 1952 avtobiografiia, 1952 uchetnaia kartochka.

45. Panova, *O moei zhizni*, 49.

46. *Ibid.*, 74, 84.

47. *Ibid.*, 88.

48. Panova, *Sentimental'nyi roman*, 322–31.

49. *O moei zhizni*, 159.

50. Vera Panova, *O moei zhizni, knigakh i chitateliakh* (written 1971–2, first published 1975; 2nd edn, 1980); Panova's secretary in her memoirs attests to the rejection of atheism by Panova at the end of her life and her spiritual transformation: see Serafima Iur'eva, *Vera Panova: Stranitsy zhizni. K biografii pisatel'nitsy* (Tenafly, NJ, 1993), 104–5.

51. ATKP, 1952 avtobiografiia.

52. *Ibid.*

53. *Ibid.*, 138, 52.

54. *O moei zhizni*, 123–4.

55. See the female protagonist in her 1947 novel *Kruzhilikha* to whom Panova "felt a big magnetic force" in Panova, *O moei zhizni*, 228–9; see also Vera Panova, *Sputniki. Kruzhilikha. V kotoryi chas?* (Leningrad, 1985), 344–5, 378.

56. Panova, *O moei zhizni*, 105.

13
_____

Women's poetry since the sixties

During the last four decades of the twentieth century, Russian women poets have drawn creative energy from the changing world around them despite often living and writing at odds with that world. They have endured the thaw, with its temporary recovery from years of war and terror, then stability and stagnation in the 1970s and early 1980s, turbulent reforms in the late 1980s, the Soviet Union's collapse in 1990, and, most recently, the emergence of a new Russian state. The poets in question experienced nearly all these historical stages, although some came to consciousness only after the sixties (Nina Iskrenko, Irina Ratushinskaia, Tat'iana Shcherbina, and Olesia Nikolaeva, born after 1950), and others met untimely deaths (Kari Unksova in 1983, Nina Iskrenko in 1995) or emigrated before the demise of the Soviet Union (Natal'ia Gorbanevskaia, Elizaveta Mnatsakanova, and Marina Temkina). A few are long-lived women who survived World War II and Stalin's Terror (Inna Lisnianskaia and Iunna Morits), whereas others (Mnatsakanova, Iskrenko, Ry Nikonova) are bold experimenters whose work traditional- ists barely regard as poetry.

Despite differences in age, experience, poetic school, and aesthetic taste, these poets share complex views of Russian experience and Russian identity. Either because they witnessed dramatic political change, or because they left Russia, or because they always felt alienated from offi- cial life, they have found the question of Russian identity unresolved and often disturbing. This dilemma of identity is not always grounded in material or historical reality: some of the best recent poetry, including that of Elena Shvarts and Ol'ga Sedakova, sidesteps historical realia to reinvent Russia's poetry of the spirit. History, however, suffuses most self-consciously Russian poems, some of which seem written from the margins, as Bella Akhmadulina, Morits, and Gorbanevskaia did in the 1960s when alternative poetry flourished. Self-styled poets of the underground in the 1970s and early 1980s often have followed their lead.

The era of the late 1980s and 1990s has witnessed alienation from privatization and capitalism (as in Shvarts and Lisnianskaia's songs of a holy fool), but also enthusiasm for novel opportunities and for a chance to jettison entirely the poet's traditional burden of national spokeswoman (Shcherbina). The 1990s have been good years for poets, despite the occasional denigration of poetry in an age of electronic communication and mass media. New routes to publication have opened and some recent poetic experiments are truly inspired. Contact with western feminism, the rediscovery of Russia's heritage of women's activism, and an awareness of Russia's tradition of great women poets have expanded the repertoire of experiences that poets give their feminine personae.

Few would like being grouped as "women poets" (the derogatory sting of the term *poetessa* remains offensive). Akhmadulina shares more with the liberal young poets of the post-Stalin era Evgenii Evtushenko and Andrei Voznesenskii, and Shvarts with Viktor Krivulin, Mikhail Kuzmin, and Nikolai Zabolotskii, than they do with each other. Women poets' primary allegiance is not to other women poets, and none of them makes genuine and complete sense outside the context of their male contemporaries and precursors. But contemporary women poets require separate attention because surveys still do not integrate them into the history of Russian culture. This is a surprising omission given the acknowledgment of women poets' significant, valuable work.[1] Until criticism loses its largely unexamined emphases and preferences, separate accounts of women's contributions to poetry are needed if we are to know their work at all. Separate study also lets one ask what it means that these poets write and are read as women. The answer to that question cannot be unitary, for some poets explore feminine identity with curiosity and passion, while others find the very idea oppressive and uninteresting. But ignoring the question of gender diminishes our appreciation of the achievements of many remarkable poets. This essay treats questions of feminine and national identity by examining the kinds of poems women poets have written since the 1960s. Its ordering is largely thematic, with some poets treated in more than one category.

History, politics, national identity

In a period of turbulent political change, we might expect poets to reflect on public events in their works, yet Russia's notorious habit of politicizing culture has virtually ensured an apolitical stance in many poets. Those poets who best draw historical and political themes into their work do so with self-consciousness and irony, either dramatically retreating into the distant past to write allegories of the present or reporting with unsentimental clarity on their day-to-day lives. Their political positions widely differ. There are activists, like Gorbanevskaia, arrested in the 1960s for demonstrating on Red Square, and Ratushinskaia, imprisoned for anti-Soviet activities in the 1970s. Both wrote detailed and politically effective statements of their beliefs in prose, but their poems reflect the psychic consequences of imprisonment as well as the disillusionment and brutality that pushed them into emigration. Each penned original verses that indict Russia's violent indifference to human life, as in Gorbanevskaia's fine poem "Naznach' mne svidanie" ("Fix a time to meet me"), which transforms a love poem by Mariia Petrovykh into a bitter meditation on the twentieth century's history of terror.

Lisnianskaia underwent a different kind of political initiation after the *Metropol'* affair.[2] Early lyrics convey her inner experiences, but her post-glasnost poetry explores life in a time of chaotic transformation and deep-seated prejudices. Poems speak of earlier massacres in order to lament present-day violence in a waning empire.[3] For Lisnianskaia, Russians live in a time of decline,[4] and, like Akhmatova's writings after 1921, her terse poetry bears the trace of her culture's suffering. She is particularly eloquent in poems to exiled and dead friends, where her grief at their absence also indicts the culture that turned them away.

Morits has long written of suffering; her poems retain undimmed memories of war's destruction, but also curiously distanced ruminations on how poorly poetry marks loss, and how slowly societies learn to be less warlike. Although Morits's earliest poems include personal and moving accounts of the war, her work published after 1990 exudes a more powerful sense of what it has meant for her to live through her country's history.[5] Morits laments her nation's hidden losses as well, famously in her poem on the execution of the Georgian poet Titsian Tabidze ("Na Mtskhetu padaet zvezda" ["A star falls over Mtskheta"]).

Younger poets have written of history in still more disquieting ways. Inna Kabysh expresses ambivalence about national identity in her pungent lyrics – for her the country pushes its citizens to live on its imaginative boundaries and then makes them feel superfluous. Even when set in the past, her poems reflect the disturbances of the present, for example in one poem's dreadful images of womb, fetus, birth, and abortion that retell the murder of the young Tsarevich Dimitry.[6] Elena Ignatova, author of a history of Leningrad, mixes past and present through personal references, as in her poem "Rodstvenniki" ("Relatives"), a family history with an interesting admixture of folklore. Iskrenko addresses directly the social decline of the Brezhnev and Gorbachev years, but she conceives of that devaluation as the deformation of language itself. Her poems sprawl across the page in a loud mix of styles and jargons, languages and symbols, codes and conversations. We can expect such experiments in historical poetry to continue.

The natural world

When poets write nature poems, they also resort to radical experiment to revitalize what seems a traditional theme. Iskrenko uses graphic illustrations in her "Antil'skie ostrova" ("The Antilles Islands"), showing the railroad tracks as ("$-x-x-x-$") and coral reef, lake, and waterfall as tiny inserted drawings; she includes a line of musical notation in "Pesn' zhavoronka" ("Song of the Lark").[7] Such experiments typically come from poets prone to seek the new, as in Mnatsakanova's cycle *Vremena neba* (Times of the Sky), where one poem ends with metrical notation rather than words.

```
    - ´ --
      - ´ ---
    - ´ -
          - ´ ´ -8
```

Formally more traditional poems about the natural world were written by young poets in the 1960s and 1970s as a near initiation rite. Morits, Gorbanevskaia, Lisnianskaia, and others of their generation found the theme safe (from overt ideology) and promising (of a realm in which to explore spiritual values and new poetic lexicons). Especially intriguing is Morits's volume *Mys zhelaniia* (Cape of Desire) about her expedition to the North Pole: her landscape poems have unforgettable huge birds and looming ships.

Landscape poetry may also be a poet's enduring genre. Akhmadulina has stayed with it throughout her career, exploring favorite locales

(Peredelkino, Tarusa, and Georgia) and objects (house, snow, rain, cricket, garden, cherry tree). Although the places are familiar, Akhmadulina writes slightly estranged poems, often choosing to talk about the poem's words – their sound, spelling, and resonance with others' words. She begins "Sad" ("The Garden"), for example, by declaring, "I went out into the garden, but luxuriant overgrowth / lives not there, but in the word *garden*" ("Я вышла в сад, но глушь и роскошь / живут не здесь, а в слове «сад»").[9] Rather than a description, "Sad" offers an aesthetic depiction of a garden. Akhmadulina's natural world brims over with poets – fall is Pushkin's, Tarusa Tsvetaeva's, rain Pasternak's. The familiar theme will not let her go, particularly in poems about the creative process, where Akhmadulina inevitably relies on natural images to evoke inner experiences.[10] Nature is not infinitely solacing, however; doubts about the garden's vivacity in "Sad" yield a meager affirmation – that the poet has written the simple sentence "I went out into the garden."

Gorbanevskaia and Sedakova also wonder whether language can encompass the natural world, but they counter skepticism with a sense of religious faith. There the similarity between them ends, for Sedakova exudes wonder and pleasure in the world around her, while Gorbanevskaia seems easily overcome with grief. She commands anxiety to grow within her, heavy like white clouds, or hears an echo and then wonders why all is exhausted into silence.[11] Sedakova's natural world buzzes with life and movement; its wind, water, sky, air, stone, and mountains greet the poet in generosity; she delights in domestic nuances like cats and needles, scoops and candles that feel archaic but weightless, as if they were poised in the air outside rather than inside a house or a room. She ends her lovely "Kitaiskoe puteshestvie" ("Chinese Journey"), "Let us praise our earth, / let us praise the moon on the water, / and that which is with no one and with all, / that is nowhere and everywhere –."[12] Her praise has religious and philosophical dimensions, but Sedakova's radiant calm emerges as well in the joyful attention she accords all that she contemplates.

Religious visions

Sedakova is the most erudite among a large group of poets who write on religious themes. Some speak boldly of religious experience, spiritual growth, and self-exploration; others prefer allusion to religious motifs in the context of a broader skepticism about God, church, and moral truth.

Catriona Kelly has argued that much of this verse conventionally repeats the "repentant sinner" motif familiar from Silver Age poets, particularly Akhmatova.[13] Kelly's exceptions to the rule include Lisnianskaia, who shows the resentments that religion's requisite self-deprecations elicit, and Shvarts, whose unpredictable rhythms of sin and confession can verge on parody. Less problematic from an Orthodox standpoint is Nikolaeva (often featured in *Novyi mir* and in nationalist publications). In "Na bolote" ("In the Swamp"),[14] Nikolaeva's world mires her in its troubles and pushes toward spiritual journeys of impossible difficulty. Her admiration for saints who withstand what many would deem unendurable suffering lets her affirm human fortitude and express despair when ordinary mortals cannot achieve it.

Nikolaeva's "Zealots and Old Believers" vividly contrast with the saints in Sedakova's poems. "Legenda dvenadtsataia: Sergei Radonezhskii" ("Twelfth Legend: Sergei of Radonezh") has none of Nikolaeva's ecstasy and exhortation, but rather a calm recollection of people and things once able to attest to the life of Sergei.[15] In Sedakova's retelling, events are witnessed by the soul, which circles around what is seen as if in blossom. Her lucid, flourishing images are unlike the darkness of Nikolaeva's poem. Nikolaeva sees her verse and her readers as "twisted through with the serpents of passion," whereas Sedakova quietly personifies the vanished saint in the rainy weather, the pine forest, and the startled air, which visibly bow to her respectful reader.

Possessed by an exuberant faith, Shvarts freely mixes religious traditions. She combines the darkness we noted in Nikolaeva with the light-filled celebration typical of Sedakova. Shvarts's near-novel in verse, *Trudy i dni Lavinii* (Days and Works of Lavinia), describes an errant soul in search of religious faith who stumbles upon experiences of spiritual tribulation and insight. In *Days and Works of Lavinia* and in her shorter lyrics, Shvarts writes lovingly of demons, who inspire poetry as often as they cause evil. Shvarts shows her pagan side in poems about seances and otherworldly experiences; this playfulness concerning demons, ghosts, and spirits challenges the discipline of Orthodoxy,[16] making her poems of faith necessarily ambivalent.

Poetic selves

When Shvarts writes in *Lavinia* of the travails of her novice nun, she does so in the first person, taking on Lavinia's naïvete, passion, curiosity, and wit. Some of her other poems purport to be written by Cynthia, an ancient Roman woman, or Arno Tsart, an Estonian poet; the latter is an invention, and Cynthia, the beloved of Sextus Propertius, left no poems of her own. Shvarts calls these impersonations a form of "masked speech," using a theatrical metaphor to describe herself as watching from the wings.[17] But her poems do not fully conceal their author: she vulnerably exposes the scars not only of abusive relationships and drunken wildness, but also of her historical surroundings. Some poems that successfully combine the individual and social realms are grounded in Russia's history, such as "Detskii sad cherez tridtsat' let" ("Kindergarten After Thirty Years"); others achieve searing results more abstractly, as in "Elegii na storony sveta" ("Elegies on the Four Corners of the World"). The former is particularly striking because Shvarts writes only occasionally of children, or of herself as a child.

Contemporary women poets often recall childhood in their lyric poems, perhaps to counter the culture's dominant image of them as mothers. (Strikingly, many of these poets have no children, an absence movingly recorded in Akhmadulina's "Zavidna mne izvechnaia privychka" ["I find enviable the age-old habit"]; ambivalence about mothering marks Lisnianskaia's work in "Docheri" ["To My Daughter"].) Kabysh's seemingly autobiographical volume *Detskii mir* (A Child's World) fuses free-verse lyrics into an idyll of childhood impressionability and adult clarity. The guitar poet Veronika Dolina, whose songs show her enacting various quintessential women's roles, wished in earlier songs for children from past lovers and friends, but she confronts the reality of children's maturation as well. She maps the fate of mother onto daughter in "Razgovor" ("Conversation"), and in "Dochke" ("To My Little Daughter"), she offers her poems as an inheritance, yet the gesture mixes tenderness with danger because poetry is associated with injury to her child.

Other aspects of women's daily lives let poets create personae familiar to readers who know these experiences all too well. Marina Tsvetaeva's memorable fury at *byt* has not stood in the way of later poets who intertwine details of daily life with more profound meditations, bracingly so in the work of Unksova. She writes with self-irony about a lovely woman who washes dishes rather than standing idle in her loveliness ("Stsenarii" ["Scenario"]), and Akhmadulina's poem about a vending machine, Gorbanevskaia's about a city bus and laundry, and Lisnianskaia's about a vacuum cleaner similarly come to mind.[18] In Kabysh's poem "Galina," a woman laden with grocery bags waits to see the Mona Lisa, sits in a freezing cold lecture hall, and lights a candle in a church. Kabysh tellingly juxtaposes the daily needs of food and warmth with the spiritual experience of hearing a great scholar of religion and culture (Sergei Averintsev) and of mourning a murdered priest (Aleksandr Men') – names which firmly locate the poem in early post-Soviet reality. A similar contrast informs "Argumenty i fakty" ("Arguments and Facts") by Iskrenko. The title names a prominent post-Soviet newspaper, but the poem punctuates its indictments of cynicism and bloodlessness with untimely interjections, creating an internal argument that has more to do with the appropriate subject matter for poetry. The poem verges on a parodic romantic encounter (what it calls "Five Minutes of Love"), but settles into a confession: "My planet – is the door to an open sea / My sculpture – is the air between words / My work – is self-objection / I object".[19] These twists and turns are typical of Iskrenko, as is the agile mix of self-revelation and distancing parody.

Others have juxtaposed the spiritual self with an all too material world, including Ella Krylova in a poem on the "orphaned material world" ("сиротский мир материальный").[20] Elena Kriukova, who often writes on religious themes, also wonderfully embodies this contrast in "Zakupliu v magazinakh nekhitruiu sned'" ("I will buy simple sustenance in stores"):

> I am a page in the book of Being!
> Each line is a celebration. Each line is drudgery.
> But beneath the velvet raincoat is my body.
> Bare,
>   as always.[21]

The poem ends with the tart hope that the speaker will not trip on her high heels. The ending recalls that of Aleksandr Blok's "Unizhenie" ("Humiliation," 1911), but Kriukova gives voice to the silent temptress on whom Blok once cast his gaze. Small wonder that the poet remains poised tensely between body and spirit. Others similarly bring the body into poems about women's purported spiritual identity; Nikolaeva's "Pered zerkalom" ("In Front of the Mirror") comments that women's self-contemplated beauty has been trivialized by poets and philosophers as ephemeral, but she ends in celebration, as the woman poses before eternity itself, which is blind to her beauty.

Philosophical lyrics

The lucid management of argument in Iskrenko and Nikolaeva stands as their contribution to another poetic mode, the philosophical. These contributions are especially noteworthy because women have traditionally been deemed unable to write "high" philosophical poetry. Philosophical dimensions inform the clear-headed reflectiveness of Marina Temkina's poetry, for example, and Sedakova, in a series of long and short poems, poses questions about being, thinking, essence, identity, and meaning. As in the genre of religious poetry, Sedakova's learnedness and sheer inventiveness make her philosophical poems particularly important. Her "Stely i nadpisi" ("Stellae and Inscriptions") interpret nearly effaced markings on stone, speculating on the experiences and emotions of those pictured. These poems treat a traditional epistemological problem – how do we know something to be true – but will not choose between sensory stimulation and imagination as the chief source of knowledge. More ambitious are Sedakova's five great odes named "Stansy" ("Stanzas"); "Piatye stansy" ("Fifth Stanzas") contemplates the Heideggerian question of what is a thing, using imagery that is beautifully tangible.[22]

A similarly meditative temperament inflects much of Unksova's work, often in language more colloquial than Sedakova's. In "Ia pozdno poliubil tebia, Krasota" ("I belatedly came to love you, Beauty"),[23] Unksova irreverently embeds an erotic appeal into her reflections on the philosophical concept of beauty. Taking the existentialists as her point of departure, she criticizes their "mania for self-indictment," yet she pauses over St. Augustine (who also informs Sedakova's "Piatye stansy"), feeling the lure of his confessional mode, only to reject him as well. Unksova transforms Augustine's suspicion of the beautiful into a suspicion of philosophy itself.

Unksova is wonderfully irreverent, but when read side by side with Shcherbina, she seems almost cautious. Shcherbina can write with grotesque mode images, and, like Shvarts and Iskrenko, she often jolts the reader with her juxtapositions of different linguistic registers, indeed, different languages, and disparate forms of experience. The philosophical conclusions implicit in her poetry are postmodern: Shcherbina has noted that the old oppositions that founded the Modernist avant-garde have been rearranged in the contemporary period.[24]

Poems of love and sickness

Contemporary poems about romance and the body also explore post-modern possibilities. After the overshadowing innovations of Tsvetaeva and Akhmatova, poets have been reluctant to merely copy their approaches to the love lyric, and one alternative has been to exceed their boldness. Shcherbina, for example, blithely searches for a metaphor to describe the taste of semen ("Eros Poesis," 1987), but then adds an affectionate address to her poetry, retreating to a safer if also erotic theme (if one wants to express love, poetry is always a worthy object). Consistently and charmingly outrageous is Temkina's "Kategoriia lifchika" ("The Brassiere Category"), which mixes high philosophical language with vulgar Soviet jargon, and dry reportage with hilariously inappropriate comparisons; throughout, she contrasts women's experiences of their bodies with men's perceptions. Temkina subtitles the volume containing this poem "Gendernaia lirika" ("Gendered Lyrics"), and she shows unusual insight into the dynamics of gendered identity throughout her work.

These poems seem all the bolder when compared to more traditional erotic elegies, a genre we find in nearly every poet's oeuvre. Tatiana Bek self-consciously recreates the world of early Akhmatova elegies in "Ne zametil (poskol'ku privyk)" ("You didn't notice [since you're so used to me]") and "Ia znaiu, chto ty izmuchen" ("I know you're tormented"). She fuses the erotic theme with the question of national identity in "Ia liubila tebia namnogo sil'nei, chem nado" ("I loved you much more intensely than was necessary"). With an intonation that recalls Tsvetaeva and Brodsky, Bek bitterly celebrates her freedom to walk in other lands, but metaphors of entrapment suggest ties that can never be severed.

Akhmadulina's poems have long described such psychological constraint. "Oznob" ("Chills") famously portrays the poet beset by chills that vibrate through an apartment house and scare the neighbors. Disease is a common metaphor for love's sickness, but a poem that escapes such clichés (and learns from Pasternak's abstractions of illness) is Sedakova's two-part poem "Bolezn'" ("Illness"), where concrete objects and human beings lack tangible materiality, but pain does not. A headache arises of its own will, casts its glance around, and strides off like a fairy-tale hero. Sedakova responds with confidence in her self-discoveries ("I believe that there, where I am not, / I will meet myself" ["Я верю, что там, где меня уже нет, / я сам себя встречу . . ."]),[25] and with gratitude for all the illness teaches.

Less metaphysical, and more in protest against pain is the work of Lisnianskaia, for whom physical ailment has long been coupled with psychic anguish. Lisnianskaia often gives suffering a moral explanation: as in Akhmatova's early work, her poems link the soul's anguish to its sins. Lisnianskaia's later work more frankly addresses the social sources of suffering, freeing her to treat the body and its woes ironically. In "Oda sosedu po kommunalke" ("Ode to My Neighbor in the Communal Apartment"), she sardonically embraces images of death:

> The head of the morgue
> On his days off
> Ecstatically used to display me
> To his visitors
> Once a month.[26]

Aging is also treated symbolically, as when her muse is said to gray,[27] and Lisnianskaia seems to write knowingly of themes that provoke pathos as well as a smile of satisfaction in her readers.

Poems about poems

Indirectly, many of the poems about poets' bodies, pleasures, and illnesses also refer to the experience of writing poetry. Akhmadulina's "Oznob" tells of inspiration as disease, and Ushakova's "Posle grippa" ("After the Flu") celebrates the return of clear hearing. Ushakova writes extravagantly about poetry, perhaps in self-consciousness at the idiosyncracy of her long lines of pure accentual verse (itself the topic of "K aktsentnoi rechi" ["To Accentual Speech"]). In a poem about intonational patterns, she prosaically describes herself as a detective reading books about linguistics, but her poem ends in wonder at the mysteries of language and the sweetly bitter pleasure of the "melody of unaddressed speech."[28] Despite that last epithet, many of Ushakova's poems are dedicated to Russian intellectuals and friends, and more than any other woman poet in the 1990s she writes directly to and about Joseph Brodsky, probably the most influential Russian poet of the period. Her quotations from Silver Age poets are also unabashed and refreshing—no doubt she is freed from the fear of seeming to repeat their themes because her poems so dramatically reaccentuate familiar lines.

The anxiety of repeating predecessors' work is not unknown to women poets of this period, however; indeed, most have been seen as writing in the shadow of Tsvetaeva or Akhmatova (or both).[29] The poet Tat'iana Bek follows this habit when introducing Kabysh's *Detskii mir*, although Kabysh's poetry points toward quite different models (like Ushakova's, her accentual verse recalls that of Kuzmin). The fusion of Akhmatova and Tsvetaeva, because both were women, reflects nothing so much as the continuing sexism of Russian culture, and canny poets may rightly see them as monstrous alternatives, as in Morits's "Mezhdu Stsilloi i Kharibdoi" ("Between Scylla and Charybdis"), with its brilliant epigraph that ends with the quip: "the unit of female force in Russian poetry is one *akhmatsvet*."[30] Tasks facing scholars of the contemporary period include disentangling the legacies of the two poets (Catherine Ciepiela's essay in this volume argues for the greater impact of Tsvetaeva on émigré poets, for example), studying the use of their poems as sub-texts alongside poetic material by other poets, and understanding the way their poetic careers became seductive models or taboo examples – or both.

While there is no evidence that any significant poet of this period experienced Russian poetry as having a separate tradition of women poets, each of them has at some point been turned into a "poetessa" by a critic or reader. All of the themes and forms associated with women, from love lyric to poems to one's child, from incantation to poems of domestic detail, have now been used with great self-consciousness and irony, and it is to the considerable credit of the poets discussed here, and others too numerous to mention, that such dangerous ground has been traversed intrepidly, and with great style.

NOTES

The author thanks Helena Goscilo for excellent editorial and substantive comments.
1. See, for example, I. Falikov, "Stekliannyi chulan: Zapiski stikhotvortsa," *VopLit* (September-October, 1997), 55–86; esp. 83–6; compare the otherwise excellent survey by Mikhail Aizenberg, "Nekotorye drugie," in Aizenberg, *Vzgliad na svobodnogo khudozhnika* (Moscow, 1997), 38–109, where the only woman to receive even a paragraph of attention is Elena Shvarts (84).
2. In 1979, twenty-three Moscow writers unsuccessfully tried to publish the almanac *Metropol'*. The event resulted in the exile of some participants (e.g., Vasily Aksyonov) and the internal suppression of others. The almanac soon appeared in the West in English and Russian versions.
3. For example, "A kak on byl liubim – " and "Dekabr' devianostogo goda" (Lisnianskaia, *Posle vsego*, 93, 57).
4. See "Prodolzhaetsia vremia raspada" (Lisnianskaia, *Iz pervykh ust*, 330).
5. Examples include "Poeziia zhiva svobodoi i liubov'iu," in *Contemporary Russian Poetry*, 148–9, and "Monolog Vintika," *Oktiabr'* 1 (1989), 130–1.
6. "Kogda k Borisu Godunovu v ocherednoi raz," DN 6 (1997), 75.

7. Iskrenko, *Neskol'ko slov*, 40–1; *Interpretatsiia momenta*, 41.

8. Mnatsakanova, *Shagi i vzdokhi*, 7–32, quotation from "Zimnee utro," 21; but see the entire book for her experiments with visual poetry, often in poems about nature.

9. Akhmadulina, *Taina*, 5.

10. Sonia Ketchian, *The Poetic Craft of Bella Akhmadulina* (University Park. PA, 1993), 25–48.

11. Gorbanevskaia, *Stikhi*, 85; *Chuzhie kamni*, 19.

12. Похвалим нашу землю, / похвалим луну на воде, / то, что ни с кем и со всеми, / что нигде и везде — Sedakova, *Stikhi*, 296.

13. Kelly *History*, 379.

14. Nikolaeva, *Na korable zimy*, 85.

15. Sedakova, *Stikhi*, 89–90. Sergei of Radonezh, a venerated fourteenth-century saint, led the development of Russian monasticism.

16. Shvarts, *Opredelenie v durnuiu pogodu*, 98–113 and the poem "Natal'ia Shishigina" in *Stikhi*, 1990, 31–2.

17. Shvarts, *Mundus imaginalis*, 108–9.

18. Akhmadulina, "Gazirovannaia voda," *Sny iz Gruzii*, 67; Gorbanevskaia, "Oda 83-mu avtobusu," *Chuzhie kamni*, 62 and "Voskresen'e," *Poberezh'e*, 66; Lisnianskaia, *Iz pervykh ust*, 117.

19. Моя планета дверь в открытом море / Моя скульптура воздух между слов / Моя работа само-возражение / Я возражаю. Iskrenko, *Neskol'ko slov*, 75.

20. "Prisutstvie Tvoe poroi," *DN* 9 (1997), 3.

21. Я—страницею в книге твоей, Бытие! / Строчка—праздник. Строчка—страда. / А под бархатом плащика—тело мое. / Обнаженное, / как всегда. *Ogonek* 10 (1990), 16.

22. Kelly *History* 429–32, includes a feminist reading of "Piatye stansy."

23. Unksova, *Izb*, 139–41.

24. *Third Wave*, 14.

25. Sedakova, *Stikhi*, 61.

26. Заведующий моргом / Вне трудового дня / Своим гостям с восторгом / Показывал меня / Раз в месяц. *NM* 2 (1998), 65.

27. Lisnianskaia, "Evterpa," *Posle vsego*, 100.

28. Ushakova, "I kogda chitala o tom, chto terminal'nye tony," *Zvezda* 5 (1997), 41–2. Ushakova has said that "Poetry's destiny is to immortalize the fleeting, momentary, purely locutionary acts of speech, in the first instance its intonation" (Valentina Polukhina, *Brodsky Through the Eyes of His Contemporaries* [New York, 1992], 96).

29. See Carol Ueland's examples in Clyman and Greene, 242–3.

30. *Contemporary Russian Poetry*, 138–43 (English and Russian).

14

The persistence of memory:
women's prose since the sixties

The period in Soviet literary life since Stalin's death in 1953 through glasnost in the mid-1980s has been one of the most volatile in Soviet letters. The thaw (*ottepel'*) that followed on the heels of Stalin's death brought with it under Khrushchev a period of relative relaxation in literary censorship, allowing writers to write about formerly forbidden topics such as the camps, the purges, anti-Semitism, and the response of the leadership to World War II. The liberal reforms were soon followed, however, by a conservative backlash that came increasingly to characterize literary life under Brezhnev. The era was marked by the birth of the dissident movement, *samizdat* (self-publishing), and *tamizdat* (works published abroad), the preferred venues for those who refused to bend to the more conservative literary trends of the day and chose instead to publish outside the official literary establishment. Although the term *zastoi* (stagnation) has since the mid-1980s been used to describe the state of cultural and literary life during the Brezhnev era, it was also true that from time to time important and honest works (those by I. Grekova and Iurii Trifonov, for example) found their way into print through official literary channels in response to increased pressure from the writers themselves for greater latitude in speaking their minds. Similarly, new literary schools such as the village prose writers (*derevenshchiki*) came into being, depicting with nostalgic longing the rural life of Russia that lay outside the domain of official Party-mandated life. Thus, it may be more accurate to term the Brezhnev era part of a long though admittedly uneven continuum wherein Soviet writers were waging the slow and often subtle battle to distance themselves from the ideological rigors imposed upon them ever since the late 1920s. When the policy of glasnost or openness was first publicly enunciated for writers in 1986 under Gorbachev, it was, in effect, not so much a break from the past as the adoption by the Party of a policy of candor towards which Soviet writers both within and outside the official literary establishment had been moving, albeit fitfully, since the death of Stalin.[1]

This chapter explores the ways in which the lives and works of Soviet women prose writers were irrevocably bound to these events. Traditional histories of Soviet literature have tended to view the period since Stalin's death as one in which the official literary venues vied with a non-official sector and with the literature of dissent for control over the moral conscience of Soviet men and women. Moreover, as Anna Krylova states in her chapter, non-official and dissident literature has tended to be valorized in the West at the expense of works written by members of the official literary establishment. I would argue that by looking at this era through the lens of women's literary productions – both fiction and non-fiction – these traditional divisions acquire a different shading, informed by acts of memory, by the reconfiguration of identities, and by the reformation of public and private spaces. In writing both present and past through memoir and fiction, the women writers discussed in this chapter find ways of reclaiming identities and narratives that were unavailable to them in Stalin's Russia.

In one sense, the Soviet period in Russian history was not conducive to the fostering of memory. The early Bolsheviks created a utopian vision of the socialist state, merging the plots of life and politics in a drive towards what came to be known as the radiant future. During the Stalin era certain kinds of memory – of the camps, the purges, certain aspects of the war, in short, those moments from history that strained Party ideology – were deemed off limits by Party ideologues. It was precisely because of these constraints that memory became a kind of moral obligation among many Soviets. Indeed, beginning with the thaw after the death of Stalin, the desire and necessity to write memoirs became paramount in Soviet literature. Many Russian women writers, reflecting perhaps Anna Akhmatova's terror that she would forget the events she had lived through, sat down to record their memoirs. Although women did not produce the volume of prison camp memoirs penned by men,[2] those penned by Evgeniia Ginzburg made an indelible mark on Soviet literature. Her two-volume account of the Soviet camp system (*Krutoi marshrut*, translated into English as *Journey into the Whirlwind* and *Within the Whirlwind*) recorded her experiences in the camps from 1939 to 1947 and from 1949 to 1955, detailing her growing realization of the extent of the terror under Stalin, and showing the strength and resilience of the human spirit under impossibly repressive conditions. Ginzburg began making notes for her memoirs only after returning to the "mainland" from Kolyma in the late 1950s. Prior to that time, many of her recollections were shared orally with her son, the emigré writer Vasily Aksyonov. Her memoirs circulated underground through *samizdat* and were published abroad in 1967. Unfortunately she died before either volume could be published officially in her own country.

Ginzburg's memoirs not only witness and recreate the horror of the camps but are an investigation into the relationship between memory and survival. During her initial imprisonment, she struggled to keep her own memories of her husband and children at bay, fearing what the Soviet poet Vera Inber called the "zone of memory" where "the lightest touch wounds mortally."[3] As the years dragged on, however, the memories she had suppressed came increasingly to be the key to surviving in the camps: "During the long months and years I spent in various prisons, I was able to observe the virtuosity that human memory can develop when it is sharpened by loneliness and complete isolation from outside impressions."[4]

Among the prisoners, great importance was placed on remembering and retracing the course of events that led to their incarceration. The act of memory became a way of creating meaning in a world void of any semblance of rationality. No one was able to understand the rationale behind the arrests, the killings, the terror. Ginzburg at one point says: "What wouldn't I have given in those days to understand the meaning of what was going on?"[5] Deprived of any ability to comprehend the larger picture, Ginzburg focuses on trying to create meaning within her circumscribed environment. She strives, for example, to understand the semiotics of the jail cell, and to understand what it meant, for example, when someone was summoned "without her things," or what the tapping on the neighboring cell wall meant.

Ginzburg also informs a cruel and senseless experience with meaning by seeing herself as part of a literary continuum, as part of the cultural tradition of Russia's past. Often she sees her survival as dependent on her ability to remember and recite out loud the Russian classics. She builds a wall between herself and the madness of the Gulag by reciting the poetry of Blok, Akhmatova, Pasternak, and others. Early in her prison sentence, an entire page from the memoirs of the Russian revolutionary

Vera Figner (1852–1942) suddenly springs to mind, helping Ginzburg decipher the prison alphabet and communicate with her fellow prisoners.

Among the many camp memoirs that were written since the 1960s are Irina Ratushinskaia's memoirs *Gray is the Color of Hope* (Seryi tsvet nadezhdy, 1988) and *In the Beginning* (1991). Ratushinskaia recounts the three years she spent in a labor camp between 1983 and 1986 for preparing and disseminating anti-Soviet materials.[6]

For some, the act of memoir writing arose out of their experiences during the terror in the thirties. One of the most important of the authors who recorded these years was Lydiia Chukovskaia, daughter of the literary critic and children's writer Kornei Chukovskii. Chukovskaia chose to chronicle these years in fictional form through her two novels *Sofia Petrovna* (1939–40) and *Going Under* (Spusk pod vodu, 1949–57). In *Sofia Petrovna* she examines how the terror permeated the lives of average citizens, detailing the process by which these same people slowly came to understand precisely what was going on. Chukovskaia saw her works recounting the years of the terror not so much as literary productions as what she termed "pieces of evidence."[7] Thus, her own function as author combined ethnography, curatorship, and legal work, as she set out to document the times.

Chukovskaia's memoir of her childhood, *Pamiati detstva* (To the Memory of Childhood, 1983), is written in a very different vein. Composed later in her life, the memoir presents an idyllic picture of her childhood in the Finnish village of Kuokkala, where her life was both enriched and complicated by the enormous presence of her father. The figure of Chukovskii is presented at once as the strong patriarchal presence who completely eclipses the figure of Lydiia Chukovskaia's mother and as the literary figure whose own persona instilled in his daughter the tendency to see herself in the role of a literary care-giver rather than a major literary figure in her own right. From her father Chukovskaia came to understand literature as a moral and religious undertaking, a belief that would color her future relationship to literary authorship.[8]

Yet, in chronicling the lives and works of literary figures during her time, Lydiia Chukovskaia became, like her contemporary Nadezhda Mandel'stam, a literary personage in her own right. Particularly telling in this regard is her portrait of Anna Akhmatova, which she compiled between 1938 and 1962. Chukovskaia's father, Kornei Chukovskii, understanding the mythic stature that Akhmatova had already assumed, insisted that his daughter keep a chronicle of Akhmatova's every word. Thus, Chukovskaia's initial relationship to Akhmatova was a combination of scribe and pupil. For many women during this time, whether writers or not, Akhmatova was a moral barometer of sorts. For those who had lived through the purges and lost loved ones, particularly children, Akhmatova's suffering became symbolic of a nation in mourning. Akhmatova served as Chukovskaia's moral guide through the purges and the war. Chukovskaia was struck by how Akhmatova responded to the years of the terror and to the arrest and imprisonment of her own son. She recalls how Akhmatova internalized her grief, preferring to talk about literature rather than the almost unspeakable horrors of the war. If, as Katharine Hodgson notes (211), Akhmatova was engaged in a certain amount of self-mythologizing, Chukovskaia, in contrast, loved what was human about her. At a time when reality seemed slowly and persistently to be dissolving, Akhmatova was for Chukovskaia the only person who remained real for her.[9]

The relationship between the two women, however, was not without its tensions. Between 1941 and 1952, there was a hiatus in their relationship. Even later when they re-established communication, there were things about Akhmatova that bothered Chukovskaia – her almost obsessive need, for example, to suffer more than her contemporaries such as Pasternak, as well as her occasional rudeness. But the moral dilemmas that she sometimes experienced did not deter her from her essential loyalty to Akhmatova. From her, as from her father, Chukovskaia acquired a finely tuned sense of the relationship between art and ethics, and of the almost sacred importance of the written word at a time when language had become cheapened by Party rhetoric.[10]

Alongside Chukovskaia, Nadezhda Mandel'stam, the widow of the poet Osip Mandel'stam, set about recapturing in her two volumes of memoirs, *Hope Against Hope* (Vospominaniia, 1970) and *Hope Abandoned* (Vtoraia kniga, 1972), the lives of the intelligentsia under Stalin, the final years she spent with her husband, and his subsequent arrest and deportation. Assuming the role of preserver of her husband's poetry which, during his arrest and deportation, risked disappearing along with him, she recalls in *Hope Against Hope* sitting in her apartment in Moscow after Mandel'stam's arrest, spending long hours committing his poetry to memory before the next wave of KGB searches.[11] Mandel'stam also became a chronicler and interpreter of daily life under Stalin, earning the same disapprobation of the official Soviet literary establishment which made it impossible for her, as for Chukovskaia, to publish her works within official literary channels. Like Chukovskaia, Mandel'stam also engaged with the figure of Akhmatova in her work, choosing to de-mythologize rather than venerate her.[12] For Mandel'stam, this desire to humanize Akhmatova was part of a more general desire to strip away the mask of lies and falsity that characterized Stalinist and Soviet society both during and after the terror.

Not surprisingly, other women memoirists also turned to the figure of Akhmatova as the moral and literary mainstay in a world gone wild. Returning to the Soviet Union in 1947 from the Harbin emigration, Natal'ia Il'ina, who would subsequently become a well-known satirist and feuilletonist in her homeland, initially fell under the sway of Stalin-ist propaganda because it seemed part of finally living in a place where she had roots. It was almost a decade after her return before Il'ina allowed herself to see Soviet society for what it was. In her memoirs *Dorogi i sud'by* (Roads and Fates, 1985), Il'ina draws a portrait of Akhmatova as surro-gate mother figure who believed that Il'ina was going to have to learn the lessons of Soviet society for herself. During the Pasternak affair in 1958, when Boris Pasternak came under heavy fire for the fact that his novel *Dr. Zhivago* was published abroad (in Italy) before it came out in the USSR, Il'ina sided with those critical of Pasternak. During all of this, Akhmatova listened quietly to Il'ina's vituperations against Pasternak. "Once only," reported Il'ina, "did she utter in a slow voice, dryly and distinctly: 'A POET IS ALWAYS RIGHT.'"[13] The rest Il'ina had to learn for herself. She came to understand that for Akhmatova the lessons of history are essentially non-transferable. Unfortunately, it required much longer for Il'ina to absorb the historical lessons that had caused Akhmatova's grief and loss than to understand and appreciate the poet herself.

Among the women of the intelligentsia who were engaged in memoir writing, one of the most remarkable figures was Lydiia Ginzburg (1902–1990), literary theorist and writer. From the 1920s up through the 1980s, Ginzburg kept a series of journals whose entries (*zapisi*) reflect her belief in "intermediate genres." Unlike many of her contemporaries, whose memoirs were uniquely informed by a desire to rewrite and memorialize the past, Ginzburg was writing a history of the present, extending the form she had found in the writings of the nineteenth-century writer and historian Prince Viazemskii (1792–1878). Like Viazemskii's literary journal, Ginzburg's *zapisi* often begin with a snatch of conversation heard – an old woman debating with herself on how she would prefer to die, a daily schedule posted on the Dom tvorchestva (House of Creativity), a fragment from a story, a quote from one famous writer to another. Using them as stepping stones to discussions ranging from a sociological analysis of Soviet society, to reflections on her own identity within the historical circumstances in which she finds herself, Ginzburg created a genre combining philosophical reflection with a detailed record of daily life in Soviet society.[14]

As can be seen from the above, the tendency among many women writers to view the work of memory as moral imperative extended not only to the act of writing memoir but to the content of what they wrote. Nowhere is the moral obligation to record as clearly seen as in Frida Vigdorova's transcriptions of the trial of the poet Joseph Brodsky in 1964. Trained as a teacher and a journalist, Vigdorova (1915–1965) was, like many of her contemporaries, convinced that her best contribution to the times in which she lived lay in setting the record straight. Like those of Chukovskaia and Mandel'stam, her writings were also informed by deeply ethical questions. Much of her pedagogical essays and journalism dealt with the ethics of exclusion, specifically why some were treated unfairly and victimized by the system while others were not. Under intense scrutiny and fear of reprisals, Vigdorova managed to record the proceedings of the Brodsky trial in 1964, creating the first transcription of a political trial without official sanction.[15]

Since the 1960s women's memoirs have been incorporated increasingly into prose fictions. In particular, the works of I. Grekova (pseudonym of Elena Sergeevna Venttsel), considered by many the grande dame of Soviet women writers, and to a lesser extent those of her contemporary Natal'ia Baranskaia, have engaged with the dynamics and persistence of memory. Grekova is widely known for her stories and novellas dealing with the daily life of women of the intelligentsia bringing up children on their own, balancing home and profession. Baranskaia shares a similar predilection for describing daily Soviet life though her characters represent a broader spectrum of the population than do Grekova's. Surely part of the reason for the retrospective nature of what they write lies in the fact that both women came to writing relatively late in their lives. Grekova began writing only after having established herself in another career, mathematics. She had long been considered one of the pioneers of probability theory in the Soviet Union, and it was only in 1960 when she was fifty-five, that her first story "Za prokhodnoi" ("Beyond the Gates") was published in *Novyi mir*, inaugurating her literary career. Baranskaia had formally "retired" from publishing and museum work and was fifty-eight when she submitted her first stories to *Novyi mir*. Both women had lived through the Revolution, the Civil War, the purges, and World War II, events that had both formed and torn at the fabric of personal and professional identities, gender relations, and the texture of daily life in Soviet history. Thus, it is not surprising that when they began to write, their material was the past and its persistence in the present.

Grekova has always refused to define herself as a writer, seeing herself first and foremost as a scientist. When, after the success of her first published stories, Aleksandr Tvardovsky, the editor of *Novyi mir*, suggested she take up writing full time, the response was tart: "What me, a respectable mother of three? I might as well go out on the streets."[16] Beyond the obvious irony of her remarks, Grekova may well have been elliptically referring to the fate of both female and male writers in the Soviet era who frequently had to prostitute themselves to the Party in order to get published. But other reasons led her to avoid a close identification with the literary sphere. For one thing, she came from a family of scientists and naively believed that it was easier to live in Soviet society as a scientist than as a writer. In her view, the scientific community continued to provide its members with a degree of protection that the field of literature never could. Moreover, as a scientist at a military academy doing sensitive work, she was forbidden to publish anything in the press. If she wished to publish, she was going to have to conceal her own name. Thus, from the time she began writing, she signed herself I. Grekova, a name taken from the Russian form of the mathematical symbol for an unknown quantity, *igrek*.

Some of Grekova's fictions are explicitly retrospective. For example, "Pervyi nalet" ("First Raid," 1960) looks at the fate of a mother and her small children during the war as they nervously prepare to be evacuated to the Urals. One of her most successful recreations of a difficult time in Soviet history is her novella "Na ispytaniiakh" ("On Maneuvers," 1967), which concerns a division of the Red Army conducting secret atomic tests during the last year of Stalin's life (1952). Grekova deliberately avoided using the usual *lakirovka* or "gloss" (a device used by Soviet writers to depict an optimistic and glowing portrait of Soviet life) in her depiction of the Red Army, an organization that was traditionally off limits to any kind of satire or critique. Further, she drew a striking portrait of a Jewish army officer, an intellectual, whose fate hung in the balance as the Soviet Union stood poised on the verge of yet another round of purges.[17]

More frequently, however, Grekova incorporates the past elliptically into her texts, preferring to look at how historical events and the concomitant rupture of family and gender relations have left their mark on her protagonists. In "Malenkii Garusov" ("Little Garusov," 1969), she provides a sustained account of the damaging effects of deprivation and loss during the war years on the developing personality of the child. The story concerns a young boy and his mother who eke out a daily existence in Leningrad during the blockade. The father, a victim of the purges, has disappeared. One day Garusov's mother, like many others at that time, goes out for bread and never returns. Wild with fear and hunger Garusov, age seven, plunges into the streets of Leningrad in a fruitless search for his mother. Grekova narrates the next fifteen years of Garusov's life from his evacuation from Leningrad with the other war orphans to his eventual return to his city, all the while still searching for his mother. On a conscious level he eventually abandons his search, but on an unconscious plane his searching never ends. So obsessed is he with guilt over his mother's disappearance that he is never able to bond with women, never able to function other than as a provider, remaining forever emotionally distant and defended. Similarly, in her novella *Vdovii parokhod* (Ship of Widows, 1981), set in Moscow over a twenty-year period beginning in 1943, Grekova not only revisits the war and postwar years but casts a critical eye on the effects of a collective upbringing on a young boy reared in a communal apartment by five widows. As she charts the development of the young man Vadim, who turns into an angry, petulant egotist, Grekova takes to task the whole socialist myth that life in the collective produces a more socially adjusted, less egocentric personality. She also implicitly undercuts the hallowed tradition of the mother in Russian cultural history by providing a disturbing portrait of the product of the mothers' overindulgence and suffocation.[18]

Grekova's most successful and best known story about the effect of the past on the present is "Damskii master" (Ladies' Hairdresser, 1964). On the surface the narrative traces the developing friendship between Mariia Vladimirovna, a middle-aged director of an institute who is also the single mother of two teenaged boys, and a young hairdresser named Vitalii, whose goals combine Marxist rhetoric with artistic subversion. Grekova interweaves three story lines—Mariia Vladimirovna's life at the institute, her life at home, and her relationship with Vitalii—in a way that brings into focus how the ruptures in Soviet society have affected women of the intelligentsia. Mariia Vladimirovna gravitates between the home from which she is completely alienated and where she no longer fulfills the traditional role of mother, the institute with its daily problems, and somewhat spectacularly, the beauty parlor where she discovers young Vitalii. Ironically, what bonds Mariia Vladimirovna to the budding hairdresser is that despite differences in age, background, and status, both are outsiders to the social relations and structures that had come into being in the Soviet Union. Vitalii is an artist, stuck in a society that does not reward real creativity and ends up capitulating to the system. Mariia Vladimirovna, while part of the system, feels as if she has lost control both over her family life and over her work at the institute. Like many women of her generation, she is caught in the conflicting social, political, and family policies of Soviet history which initially exhorted women to put social and political over personal concerns, to go out into the workplace, and then, in the 1930s and 1940s urged them to return to their roles as wives and mothers. Seeking occasional refuge from this bind in the local beauty parlor, Mariia Vladimirovna nevertheless also finds herself distanced from the women there, who are "all involved in some kind of peculiarly female ritual."[19]

The autobiographical impulse has always been a felt presence in Grekova's writings. Perhaps the most clearly autobiographical of her stories is "Bez ulybok" ("Without Smiles," written in 1970 but not published until 1986), a thinly fictionalized chronicle of the period of prolonged chastisement (*prorabotka*) to which Grekova was subjected at the Military Academy, where she taught, after her story "Na ispytaniiakh" was published in *Novyi mir*. Through its protagonist M.M., Grekova's fictional counterpart, the story recounts a woman's experience of suddenly becoming a non-person among her colleagues and details the resources on which she drew in order to survive that experience. Exploring the politics of naming, Grekova has her protagonist recall that whereas formerly her male cohorts always referred to her as M.M., now they suddenly speak of her only as "she." In what seems to be a conciliatory gesture, another colleague suggests that they go easy on M.M. because she is a woman: "Where is our chivalry, comrades?" M.M.'s response suggests Grekova's own wry contempt for the gender codes that would diminish her: "At this point I purposely blew my nose – very loud, very unfeminine."[20]

The majority of Grekova's prose fictions reflects her own autobiographical impulse. She rarely departs from her own persona. Virtually all her female protagonists are, like Grekova herself, members of the intelligentsia, often the scientific intelligentsia, whose family situations mirror that of the author. Unlike Baranskaia, whose narratives speak in the voices of many women from many different classes and social back-grounds, Grekova prefers to speak with one ever-modulating voice.[21] Significantly, when she does change voices, adopting a male persona as in "On Maneuvers," that voice remains ultimately her own in terms of background and social class.

While Natal'ia Baranskaia is best known in the West for her novella *Nedelia kak nedelia* (A Week Like Any Other, 1969), it is in her novel *Den' pominoveniia* (Day of Remembrance, 1989) that the penchant for memoir slips imperceptibly into memorialization. Because of problems with the censors, the novel was completed several years before it was actually published. What proved difficult about this novel for Party ideologues was the detail Baranskaia provided about the quality of life of the women left at home with children during the war. Her grim account highlights the deprivation, hunger, cold, lack of shelter, and dreadful conditions that these women had to face during the evacuation. The novel begins on May 9, 1979, the thirty-fourth anniversary of the end of World War II. As a train carries a group of women with a throng of other passengers to the memorial site where they will honor the dead, Baranskaia allows each woman to tell her own story. Using a language that reflects the different social and geographical background of each woman, the narrative about the Day of Remembrance of the dead becomes instead a memorial and a tribute to the women themselves, whose hardships had often gone unrecorded in war narratives. Ironically, in the act of traveling to the place where they will memorialize their husbands, Baranskaia's narrators unconsciously become engaged in a kind of self-memorializing through narrating the stories of both self and others. One of the narrators, for example, tells the story of a man she saw at a railway station in the provinces as winter was approaching. The man wore a coat but was walk-ing around barefoot. Selflessly the woman dug into her suitcase and gave him the new boots she had bought for her oldest son. The onlookers were appalled that she could give away an item on which one's survival depended. In such acts, recounts the narrator, resided the miracles which sustained people in impossible times.[22]

As we move from the 1960s to the 1980s, we find that memory engages the younger generation of writers differently than it did Grekova or Baranskaia. Born after the purges and the war, younger writers such as Tat'iana Tolstaia seem to skip several generations, recalling in their prose fictions impossibly otherworldly types whose roots remain deep in the prerevolutionary era. In "Sweet Shura" ("Milaia Shura"), one of her most evocative stories, Tolstaia glances back to another era to tell the story of an old woman who is a throwback to prerevolutionary Russia, a time associated with values which had no place in Soviet life in the 1980s. Shura lives her life for the intimate joys of her personal life and loves. Tolstaia's narrator memorializes Shura through a portrait engraved in affection. Unable to contain herself, the narrator steps into Shura's plot, rewriting the end of one of her romances for her. In Tolstaia's hand, Shura becomes an iconographic portrait of a life vanished, a world whose only permanence lies in the narrator's and in Tolstaia's capacity to imprint upon it the permanency of narrative. As the narrator looks at Shura's possessions, thrown into a garbage heap by her neighbors after her death, she muses:

> What can I do with all this? Turn around and leave. It's hot. The wind chases the dust around. And Alexandra Ernestova, sweet Shura, as real as a mirage, crowned with wooden fruit and cardboard flowers, floats smiling along the vibrating crossing, around the corner, southward to the unimaginably distant shimmering south, to the lost platform, floats, melts, and dissolves in the hot midday sun.[23]

Post-Stalinist women's prose works have largely been characterized by a return to themes such as home, family, romance, and descriptions of daily life shorn of their Stalinist varnishing. Stalinist novels downplayed personal romance, giving way to the greater romance of the state. Thus, it was no surprise that the years immediately following Stalin's death witnessed a surge of what can best be described as romantic potboilers. One of the more salacious of these offerings was Ksenia L'vova's 1955 novel *Elena*, in which the author narrates the near fatal love between a young woman chemist and her colleague, both of whom are married to others. L'vova's novel is a narrative of anti-domestic bliss which explores the doubts and dilemmas of the female protagonist as she slowly realizes that for all his admirable qualities, she simply does not love her husband. While stylistically flawed, the novel cashed in on the new climate of literary freedom, providing readers with a welcome respite from the tractor and harvest novels of the 1930s and the patriotic novels and films dutifully ground out during the war.[24] L'vova reintroduced themes of infidelity, passion, and sexuality in a way that critics saw as depressing reminders of the Sentimentalist fiction produced early in the century by Verbitskaia (see Marsh).[25] Despite critical disapprobation, however, *Elena* enjoyed considerable popularity among a reading public yearning for something steamier than romance with a tractor. But it was also precisely this kind of novel that made many women writers bristle and refuse the label "woman writer". The charges leveled at Akhmatova in the 1940s as "half nun, half harlot" imprinted themselves upon the memories of Soviet women writers, who now took pains to distance themselves from anything that could conceivably be construed as women's writing. Indeed, this is one reason why writers from Grekova to Tolstaia and Petrushevskaia have persistently denied any link between writing and gender in their own literary productions – a denial not unlike that of their nineteenth-century female literary predecessors.

Alongside the tendency to de-Stalinize romance, many post-Stalinist women writers have sought to reclaim and recoup the lost family. Many of their fictions are, in fact, domestic narratives reflecting the shift of ideological winds away from the nationalist myth of the great Stalinist family (with Stalin as *pater familius*) back to the personal nuclear family. This is not to say that there was an absence of domestic novels during the Stalin period; novels aplenty dealt with the family theme. The difference is one of emphasis. Whereas in the Stalinist period the home and domestic life become mirror reflections of the state, in post-Stalinist women's writing the home and family once again occupy center stage, and the focus shifts to give greater credence to female protagonists' inner life and psychological travails. One of the important features of Natal'ia Baranskaia's "A Week Like Any Other" is not only that it presents the infamous double burden (*dvoinaia nosha*) within which Soviet women were trapped but that Baranskaia explores the inner life of her protagonist Ol'ga. Ol'ga is a typical product of the Soviet years, caught between work and the deadening weight of domestic chores on the home front. As one critic has recently noted, Ol'ga also longs nostalgically for a world in which time stands still. Ironically, the world she yearns to return to is a world she has never known, and thus becomes what Thomas Lahusen calls "transcendental":

> I long to walk freely, with no baggage and no aim. Just to walk, to take my time, peacefully, very slowly. To walk along the wintry Moscow boulevards, along the streets, to stop at shop windows, to look at photographs, books, slippers, to read posters without rushing, to think about where I want to go, to lick a choc-ice and somewhere in a square, under a clock, to wait for Dima. All that was such a long time ago, so dreadfully long ago that it feels as if it wasn't me but some other she. . . .[26]

The return to the nuclear family in women's fiction has also brought with it in women's prose fictions a focus on *byt*. A word virtually untranslatable into English, *byt* connotes the everyday, but the everyday with a particularly Soviet twist – the endless lines, the communal apartments, the lack of privacy, products in deficit, the countless hours taken up with shopping – a phenomenon so omnipresent that it virtually defined the context of daily life for most Soviet citizens.

There were several reasons why *byt* became so omnipresent in Soviet literature from the 1960s on. For one thing, with the gradual relaxation in ideological correctness, writers were drawn to describing life as it was rather than life as it was becoming. And the reality of life as it was included lines, birthing houses, hospitals, doctors' offices, crime, food deficits, to name but a few. Further, normal, everyday life in Stalin's time had become, in Sheila Fitzpatrick's words a "luxury."[27] The hardships, the upheavals, the persistent propaganda, made it hard to conduct a normal, daily life. Thus, when the reforms of the Khrushchev era made it possible to return to a semi-normal life, it was the very texture of that life – from the non-politicized random encounters between two people to descriptions of days in which nothing particularly happens – that attracted writers such as Natal'ia Baranskaia, Viktoria Tokareva, and Irina Velembovskaia.

And yet, the focus on *byt* has been no less ideologically laden than the grand Soviet narratives these writers were rejecting. Even a writer such as Lydiia Ginzburg used *byt* as a way of discussing what has happened to social relations in the Soviet era. She takes her reader on a Soviet passenger vessel and shows how the hierarchies of class still predominate, influencing everything from service in the restaurant to one's ability to get a good night's sleep.[28] Even in recent fiction in the 1990s *byt* becomes implicated in larger philosophical concerns. In the novella *Evgesha and Annushka*, written by Marina Palei (1990), Palei presents a sobering portrait of two old women living in a communal apartment in Leningrad.[29] Narrated by their neighbor, the story presents a harrowing portrait of how *byt* has come to define their lives and spiritual makeup:

> I remember once some distant relatives called her [Annushka] around November 7th and how, embarrassed by this telephone toy, she spoke into the receiver: "They gave me a rouble seventy five more on my pension."
>
> After that she just kept asking about the children because she didn't have anything else to communicate.
>
> So that was it: 57 roubles minus the rent, the electric, the gas, the telephone, plus a rouble 75, minus the essentials, and unpredictable expenses ("mustard-plasters, thread, money for the bus, light bulbs, stockings; Lord, you can never keep a supply of all this on hand!")

> But no matter what, Annuskha nevertheless somehow managed to
> put away enough for her funeral, and this accomplishment gave her
> incomparable happiness.[30]

Palei's story suggests what happens when the lives of her characters
become too thoroughly enmeshed in the deadening and slowly dehumanizing effects of the everyday. On the one hand, she sees a general
lowering of the old women's consciousness, crushed by the conditions
within which they have been forced to live, throughout their entire lives,
from dorms to corners to train stations and finally to this communal
apartment of their old age. Oddly, a touchingly misdirected faith sustains
them. Evgesha, who remembers very little now, still recalls the story of
the piece of bread (perhaps some Christmas present) she found under the
pillow of her hospital bed during the blockade of Leningrad in World War
II. Thus, every day, upon returning to her hospital room, she would dive
under her pillow, knowing that one of these days she would eventually
find that heavenly present again. That faith in those crumbs of bread
sustained her then as memory sustains her now.

Written in 1990 during the last year of the Soviet state, Palei's story
interweaves daily life with memory in a way unlike that of her predecessors who lived through these times. Palei memorializes some of the worst
aspects of Soviet reality – the relentless and demeaning pressures of daily
life – by recording the minutest details of the underbelly of Soviet society, digging down into what Irving Howe calls "the ashcan of history" in
order to make permanent not the heroic but its opposite: the grinding
dehumanizing realities that were an intrinsic part of the fabric of Soviet
society, yet frequently written out of it. If Baranskaia's tendency is to
memorialize and thus to heroicize, Palei takes a very different look at
the function of memorialization in Soviet history, finding beneath the
mythic monuments to the past the bleak reality of physical and existential
poverty.

Palei's stories are not defined by the poverty of *byt* alone. In "Cabiria
from the Obvodny Canal" ("Kabiria s Obvodnogo Kanala") and in her
stories about hospitals ("Otdelenie propashchikh" ["The Losers' Division"] and "Den' topolinogo pukha," ["Day of the Poplar Flakes"]),
Palei infuses her narratives with a spirit of transcendence. Alongside the
disquieting reality of the hospital wards and the communal apartments
where her characters often fetch up, is their remarkable ability of transcendence, fantasizing other worlds even as their own lie crumbling
beneath them.

The tendency of Russian women writers to shift their focus internally, concentrating on the nuclear family and on personal relationships, both finds its apogee and takes a peculiar shift in the works of Liudmila Petrushevskaia. In the early 1970s, Petrushevskaia began writing stories frequently narrated by a female speaker who overhears snatches of a conversation, gossip among neighbors, or the tortuous family romances that occur in Petrushevskaia's stories. The characters in these stories are frequently tormented, alienated from their surroundings, and suffer from a pervasive sense of anomie. Shorn of nostalgic longing, her stories reveal the trauma, displacement, and dysfunctionality formerly suppressed in official Soviet literature. Indeed, Petrushevskaia's fictional world is the site of the dysfunctional family romance par excellence. Rape, incest, beatings, botched abortions, alcoholism, suicide: small wonder that *Novyi mir* initially rejected her early stories as "too gloomy."[31]

Because Petrushevskaia so persistently interweaves themes of memory and identity, a brief examination of her work is perhaps a fitting conclusion to this chapter. In one sense, Petrushevskaia's characters have no memory. They are uprooted from family, friends, and any sense of their own belonging. Their worlds are shut tight, despite their desperate attempts to forge relationships or to find someone to listen to their stories. For example, in "Rasskazchitsa" ("The Story Teller") the female protagonist tells preposterous and intimate details of her life to her co-workers because ultimately she has no one else to tell. Another story, "Medea," consists of a series of parallel, non-intersecting monologues between a cabbie and his fare, neither one of whom has the slightest interest in the other's story. Yet, for all the limitations of Petrushevskaia's characters, the stories themselves are sophisticated explorations into what has happened to the female voice during the past forty years of Soviet history.

Petrushevskaia's narrators struggle in vain to get their stories told, most of the time against insurmountable odds. Seldom do the stories reach their intended audience, a fact Petrushevskaia underscores by titling many of her prose works *"monologi"* (monologues). Among Petrushevskaia's narrators, there is the same constant monologue that has been noted in the works of Marina Tsvetaeva: "not the monologue of a heroine, but a monologue as a consequence of having no one to talk to."[32] Other reasons abound for narrative silencing. Often her narrators, though garrulous, do not understand the tale that they are constructing. Indeed, their very loquaciousness may mask their lack of comprehension. In stories such as "The Story of Clarissa" ("Istoriia Klarissy"), or "The Story Teller," the narrators fill their stories with detail, making the reader a complicit listener to their gossip. "The Story of Clarissa," for example, offers an account of an ordinary young woman, her three marriages, her search for the right man and her efforts to bring up her child. The narrator, a schoolmate of Clarissa's, artificially forces a happy ending onto the tale as Clarissa settles down with husband number three, a pilot, to the family life she has always sought. The narrator seems unaware that the contrived conclusion makes mockery of both the sentimental romance and the prescriptive happy endings of Socialist Realism:

> And one could consider that everything stabilized and flowed towards a natural, healthy maturity, towards a series of winters and vacations, purchases and a feeling of the fullness of life, if you didn't take into account the fact that on flight days Clarissa, left alone, was capable of calling the airport for hours on end to procure information about the flight and that Valery Petrovich on returning would have to listen to comments about his wife's phone calls. Only this clouded the bright horizon of Valery Petrovich and Clarissa's life, only this.[33]

Like many of Petrushevskaia's other fictions, "The Story of Clarissa" in fact becomes self-reflexive, a story about the narrator herself who fails to grasp the crux of the tale she is telling.

Why do Petrushevskaia's narrators have such trouble telling their stories? The question has no easy answer. Barbara Heldt in her classic study *Terrible Perfection* makes the point that women were idealized and emulated but never fully described or given their voice in nineteenth-century Russian male-authored fictions. Petrushevskaia may be carrying Heldt's thesis one step further by exploring the effects of literary and social silencing on the female voice precisely at the point when it begins to lay claim to its own story. Interestingly, whatever the disconnectedness we find in Petrushevskaia's narrators, they do, in fact, manage to tell their stories. For many of them, their problems begin because they do not narrate their stories in a way that conforms to accepted narrative conventions. Petrushevskaia may be looking here at the more recent constraints under which all writers of conscience were forced to work in the Soviet Union: the necessity to work with a plot, Socialist Realism, that had already been created for them.

Perhaps more than any other Russian woman writer of recent memory Petrushevskaia has been engaged in trying to find her identity as a
writer vis-à-vis the male literary tradition. Like writers from Grekova to
Tolstaia, she was educated on the classics of Russian literature. Whereas
a writer such as Grekova acknowledges Tolstoy and Dostoevsky as her
"bread" (khleb), Petrushevskaia takes the tradition on, playing with it,
rewriting it, as she simultaneously writes herself into and distances
herself from it. In one of her most successful stories, "Svoi krug" ("Our
Crowd"), a story about a young woman slowly dying, no longer loved by
her husband, an outsider to her own circle, Petrushevskaia chronicles her
protagonist's efforts to tell her story and to see that her son is provided
for after her death. In this story Petrushevskaia engages in dialogue with
Dostoevsky's Underground Man – an alienated superfluous being – by
turning her female narrator and chief protagonist into the Underground
Woman. Like most of Petrushevskaia's narrators, this one has suppressed
her own story. It hovers in the background as she recounts the lives of the
other characters. Slowly the narrator's story takes over this text, becoming its central concern. Departing from Dostoevsky by refusing to
manipulate the readers' sympathies, this young woman recovers her own
text, reclaiming her story for herself and never reaching out in a feeble
gesture of self-pity.

The literary fortunes of Russia's women writers since the late 1950s
have been no less complex than the times in which they have lived. As I
have suggested in this chapter, the tendency among many of them to look
back has reflected their need not only to record the past and place it in
perspective but to understand how that past has shaped their identity
both as women and as writers. Clearly, their sense of themselves as women
writers (pisatel'nitsy) has been enormously complicated by the nineteenth-
century male literary tradition to which these women are indebted. There
has also been the troubling notion for many of these women that to write
like a woman was to be consigned to the world of potboilers and sentimental trivia. Yet, as the figure of Akhmatova reveals, writers play much
more than purely literary roles in each other's lives. For writers such as
Chukovskaia, Mandel'stam, and Il'ina, Akhmatova was more than a mere
literary presence. Whether mythologized or humanized, she sculpted the
response to terror and loss, putting into words what most had no vocabulary for. Increasingly too, Russia's women writers have had to confront
a world without the ideological structures of the past. In returning to
the familiar structures and images from Russia's past – the family, the

mother figure, daily life – they have had to confront a reality completely transformed from the one they imagined. If some have chosen to look back on the war and on the terror, others have focused their sights on an equally problematic present. What to do with both past and with the very recent present – one marked by the passing of an entire era and an entire social and political system – will be one of the many important directions for women's writing in Russia in the post-Soviet era.

NOTES

I would like to thank Susan Aiken, Jehanne Gheith, and Stephanie Sandler for keeping me on track.

1. See Stephen Lovell and Rosalind Marsh's cogent overview of literature after Stalin "Culture and Crisis: The Intelligentsia and Literature after 1953" in Catriona Kelly and David Shepherd (eds.), *Russian Cultural Studies: An Introduction* (Oxford, 1998), 56–87.

2. More recently a collection of memoirs by women who had either been imprisoned, sent to labor camps, or exiled (mostly during the thirties though some later) has appeared entitled *Dodnes' tiagoteet: Zapiski vashei sovremennitsy.* In English it appeared under the title *Until My Tale is Told: Women's Memoirs of the Gulag*, ed. Simeon Vilensky, tr. John Crowfoot *et al.* (Bloomington, IN, 1999). See also the recently published volume by Sheila Fitzpatrick and Yuri Slezkine (eds.), *In the Shadow of Revolution: Life Stories of Russian Women from 1917 to the Second World War* (Princeton, NJ, 2000).

3. Quoted in Eugenia Semenovna Ginzburg, *Journey into the Whirlwind*, tr. Paul Stevenson and Max Hayward (New York, 1967), 117. It is also conceivable that she kept herself from thinking of the family because, as a member of the Communist Party, she was schooled in the ideology of the Great Soviet Family.

4. Ginzburg, *Journey into the Whirlwind*, 71.

5. *Ibid.*, 128.

6. Even after Khrushchev's Secret Speech at the 20th Party Congress in 1956, denouncing Stalin and his crimes, the penal colony system still remained in place in the Soviet Union.

7. See Author's Note in *Sofia Petrovna*, tr. Aline Worth (Evanston, IL, 1988), 1.

8. See Beth Holmgren's excellent analysis of Lydiia Chukovskaia's relationship with her father in Holmgren, *Women's Works in Stalin's Time: On Lidiia Chukovskaia and Nadezhda Mandelstam* (Bloomington, IN, 1993), chapter 2.

9. Lydiia Chukovskaia, *Zapiski ob Anne Akhmatovoi*, 3 vols. (Moscow, 1997).

10. See Stephanie Sandler's essay "Reading Loyalty in Chukovskaia's *Zapiski ob Anne Akhmatovoi*," in Wendy Rosslyn (ed.), *The Speech of Unknown Eyes: Akhmatova's Readers on Her Poetry* (Nottingham, 1990), 267–82.

11. See Nadezhda Mandel'stam, *Hope against Hope: A Memoir*, tr. Max Hayward (New York, 1970), chapters 1–3.

12. Beth Holmgren makes this point in her article on "Nadezhda Iakovlevna Mandel'stam" in Tomei, II, 405.

13. Natal'ia Il'ina "Eshche ob Akhmatovoi," *Ogonek* 38 (1987), 28–30.

14. See Jane Gary Harris's excellent article "The Crafting of Self: Lidiia Ginzburg's Early Journal," in Marsh *Gender*, 263–82.

15. See Teresa Polowy's excellent essay on "Frida Vigdorova" in Tomei, II, 1085–93.

16. Quoted in Cathy Porter's introduction to I. Grekova, *The Ship of Widows* (London, 1985), vi.

17. See Barker, "Irina Grekova's 'Na Ispytaniiakh': The History of One Story," *Slavic Review* 48:3 (1989), 399–412.

18. See Helena Goscilo's article "Mother as Mothra: Totalizing Narrative and Nurture in Petrushevskaia," in Sonya Stephen Hoisington, *A Plot of Her Own: The Female Protagonist in Russian Literature*, (Evanston, IL, 1995), 102–13.

19. "Ladies' Hairdresser," tr. Brian Thomas Oles in *Dialogues*, 47.

20. I. Grekova, "Bez ulybok," *Oktiabr'* 11 (1985), 162–79. It has been translated as "No Smiles," in *The New Soviet Fiction*, comp. Sergei Zalygin (New York, 1989), 79–110.

21. See Catriona Kelly's article "I. Grekova and N. Baranskaya: Soviet Women's Writing and De-Stalinisation," *Rusistika* 5 (1992), 39–43.

22. Natal'ia Baranskaia, *Den' pominoveniia* (Moscow, 1989), 96.

23. Tat'iana Tolstaia, "Sweet Shura," from *On the Golden Porch*, tr. Antonina W. Bouis (New York, 1989), 40.

24. A notable exception to this general rule was the film *The Cranes Are Flying* (Zhuravli letiat) made in 1957. The film deals with World War II and with a couple who become affianced just as the young man is called off to war. In a departure from most cinematic and literary productions made during and immediately after the war featuring faithful women waiting for their loved ones to return from the front, this film explores the fate of the young woman who is unfaithful, who does not wait, but who ultimately finds redemption in the viewers' eyes and in her own eyes by film's end. See Aleksandr Prokhorov's excellent chapter "Soviet Family Melodrama of the 1940s and 1950s: from *Wait for Me* to *Cranes are Flying*," in Louise McReynolds and Joan Neuberger (eds.), *Imitations of Life: Two Centuries of Melodrama in Russia* (Durham, NC, 2002).

25. See Natal'ia Il'ina's scathing parody of *Elena* in "Liubov'i kolby," in *Vnimanie opasnost'!* (Moscow, 1960), 9–13. For an example of how critics responded to *Elena*, see T. Smolianskaia's "Poetizatsiia poshlosti" in *Komsomol'skaia pravda* 85 (April 10, 1955), 8; and V. Pankeev's "Ia umru ot vas: o romane Ksenii L'vovoi *Elena*," in *Zvezda* 8 (1955), 174–8.

26. *A Week Like Any Other*, tr. Pieta Monks (London, 1989), 29–30. Thomas Lahusen argues that Ol'ga's desire for home in "A Week Like Any Other" is, in fact, the desire for a transcendental home, fed by her "impersonal" recollection of a paradise lost. "'Leaving Paradise' and Perestroika" in Helena Goscilo (ed.), *Fruits of Her Plume: Essays on Contemporary Russian Women's Culture* (Armonk, NY, 1993), 213.

27. Sheila Fitzpatrick, *Everyday Stalinism: Ordinary Life in Extraordinary Times: Soviet Russia in the 1930s* (New York, 1999), 1.

28. See Lydiia Iakovlevna Ginzburg, *Zapisnye knizhki: novoe sobranie* (Moscow, 1999), 366–75.

29. The apartment Palei describes in this story is her own.

30. Marina Palei, "Evgesha i Annushka," *Znamia* 7 (1990), 14.

31. From "Liudmila Petrushevskaya," by Alma Law in *Clarissa and Other Stories*, tr. Alma Law (Arlington, VA, 1985).

32. Joseph Brodsky, "A Poet and Prose," in *Less Than One: Selected Essays* (New York, 1986), 192–3.

33. "Istoriia Klarissy," in L. Petrushevskaia, *Po doroge boga Erosa* (Moscow, 1993), 36. "The History of Clarissa" appears in translation in *Clarissa and Other Stories*, tr. Alma Law.

15
_____

Perestroika and post-Soviet prose: from dazzle to dispersal*

"Women writers have a lot to overcome
within themselves and a lot of work to do."
        NATAL'IA IVANOVA (1986)

"The aggression and naturalism saturating
'women's prose' are explained simply and
are rooted in the nature of a woman's soul."
        PAVEL BASINSKII (1991)

"The literary establishment in Soviet Russia
was so clearly a male domain."
        SVETLANA VASILENKO (1997)

"If a feminist is a woman who considers
herself no worse than a man, then I'm
unquestionably a feminist."
        ALEKSANDRA MARININA (1998)

Politics and prose

Russia's official divestment of communism vividly illustrates ideology's capacity to shape history, make mock of geographies, and reverse ostensibly sacrosanct trends and traditions. The turmoil and trauma of the dozen-odd years spanning perestroika and the post-Soviet era have reconfigured the map not only of Russia, but also of recent women's fiction. A reader versed in women's prose of the 1970s and early 1980s now contemplates a radically altered fictional landscape – within a society that currently gives short shrift to Literature and other high culture genres consecrated by the Soviet establishment. With Literature no longer a supreme category of ideological and cultural self-definition, its practitioners have forfeited status and state subsidies. They now compete for a readership with authors of pulp fiction and translations of western bestsellers in a book market driven by customer demand. Not ideological rectitude, but the muse of solvency presides over publishing, film production, recordings, and stage performance. Accordingly, like all forms of Russian culture today, women's texts – as well as their authors' professional standing – reflect the far-reaching consequences of a systemic, and seismic, transformation.

Glasnost marked a veritable boom in women's culture, witnessing the debut of several notable literary talents: Tat'iana Tolstaia, Marina Palei, Valeriia Narbikova, Ekaterina Sadur, and Liudmila Ulitskaia – the last shortlisted twice for the Russian Booker Prize, presented with the prestigious Medici award in France, and quickly translated amidst lavish praise in Germany. While women's clubs and organizations proliferated, conferences and competitions vitalized women's creativity, art exhibits showcased their canvasses, and collaborative anthologies of their writings followed hard and fast: the inanely-titled *Zhenskaia logika* (Female Logic, ed. L.V. Stepanenko, 1989), *Chisten'kaia zhizn'* (A Pure Life, ed. Anatolii Shavkuta, 1990), *Ne pomniashchaia zla* (She Who Bears No Grudge, comp. Larisa Vaneeva, 1990), *Novye Amazonki* (The New Amazons, comp. Svetlana Vasilenko, 1991), and *Abstinentki* (The Abstinents, comp. Olga Sokolova, 1991). Desovietization, however, stemmed this rush and ultimately exerted a centrifugal influence on women's cultural production. Members of "collectives" drifted apart; the escalation in costs of book publishing measurably worsened authors' chances of negotiating contracts; devaluation of the ruble and stratospheric leaps in prices of consumer goods led some women to seek greater financial security in spheres other than literature.

Politics and economics account for unexpected dislocations and relocations, as well as the curtailment of literary careers: Svetlana Vasilenko's current position as head of the Russian Writers' Union,[1] Larisa Vaneeva's temporary withdrawal from literature, followed by her move to Estonia, Dina Rubina's and Elena Makarova's emigration to Israel, and Tat'iana Nabatnikova's lucrative, voluntary demotion from prize-winning author to translator of German materials, then to employee of Limbus Press. Despite the publication in 1997 of I. Grekova's miraculously preserved novel, *Svezho predanie* (The Legend Is Fresh, written in 1962), thirty-five years after its submission to the liberal journal *Novyi mir*, Grekova, along with Natal'ia Baranskaia, Maiia Ganina, and Nadezhda Kozhevnikova, has effectively abandoned literature. In the case of Grekova and

Baranskaia this has largely been due to age and ill health. Tolstaia, who after her 1983 debut on the pages of *Avrora* became the West's perestroika author of choice, ceased writing fiction approximately when the Soviet Union disintegrated – more or less when Nina Katerli opted for social cause over creativity, launching a prolonged battle with anti-semitism in court and in print, instead of penning the acerbic narratives deriding *idées reçues* that had made her reputation. In short, by the mid-1990s, the euphoria of glasnost and its fertile creative chaos had rapidly dissolved into the haze of a remote, semi-forgotten dream. Literary creativity had become a luxury affordable for authors either blessed with other means of material support or willing to eke out a minimal livelihood through paltry payments by undersubscribed thick journals and small runs of book editions.

Glasnost: poetic flight and psychic laceration

During the heady atmosphere of glasnost, the feverish, massive recuperation of formerly proscribed works by writers ranging from Tsvetaeva, through Daniil Kharms, to Vladimir Nabokov overshadowed achievements in contemporary literature.[2] Yet readers and critics keenly registered two exciting novelties in original women's fiction: the emergence of Tolstaia as a prosaist of formidable imaginative power and the long-delayed appearance of Petrushevskaia's sizable drawer-stuffing oeuvre. The multifacetedness and stylistic sophistication of both impressed even those skeptics underwhelmed by the predilection for a quasi-journalistic, anodyne prose that had earned Soviet women's fiction the derogatory label of "trolleybus reading."

Tolstaia's meteoric career coincided with glasnost, the last of her twenty-one stories ("Siuzhet") appearing in *Sintaksis* the year the Soviet Union formally ended. An unrivaled mistress of metaphor, Tolstaia voluptuously showcased the iridescent richness of language in a rhythmic prose that meditates on the soul, art, imagination, memory, and mortality. Simultaneously dense yet digressive, lyrically poetic yet ironic, playful yet plangent, her synesthetic, vividly textured narratives seduce all the senses in a manner redolent of 1920s ornamentalism. Invoking poetry, folklore genres, urban romances, and social clichés, Tolstaia elegised wondrous childhoods (" 'Na zolotom kryl'tse sideli . . .' " ["On the Golden Porch"], "Svidanie s ptitsei" ["Rendezvous with a Bird"]); waxed mordantly sardonic over terminally self-absorbed pragmatists ("Okhota na mamonta" ["Hunting the Wooly Mammoth"], "Poet i muza" ["The Poet and the Muse"], "Krug" ["The Circle"], "Plamen' nebesnyi" ["Heavenly Flame"], "Spi spokoino, synok" ["Sweet Dreams, Son"]); and in alternately tender and satiric registers mocked physically grotesque idealists ("Sonia," "Samaia liubimaia" ["Most Beloved"]), decrepit nostalgic dreamers ("Milaia Shura" ["Sweet Shura"]), and bohemian fantasts ignited by an inner vision ("Ogon' i pyl'" ["Fire and Dust"], "Fakir"). Her lush, magical tales exploded stale preconceptions about female fiction in Russia, a fiction with which Tolstaia categorically disclaimed all ties. Hailed by western admirers as a brilliant woman writer, Tolstaia vehemently repudiated gender's relevance to creativity and denounced feminism as misguided at best, half-witted at worst.

If the extravagant opulence of Tolstaia's style offered readers displaced compensation for her fictional characters' sorrows and disillusionments, Petrushevskaia's gynocentric litanies of unabating despair diffused universal gloom via the calculatedly withholding, cryptic narrative voice that is her instantly recognizable signature. Whereas Tolstaia garnished and decorated, Petrushevskaia camouflaged, at key junctures maintaining an eloquent silence more unsettling than screams.[3] Her stories and plays published during perestroika feature an unmitigatedly bleak vision of the world; the exploration of such traditionally taboo topics as alcoholism ("Strana" ["A Country"]), physical violence ("Girlianda ptichek" ["A Garland of Birds," 1990], "Pesni vostochnykh slavian" ["Songs of the Eastern Slavs," 1990]), murder and suicide ("Medeia" ["Medea," 1989], "Gripp" ["Flu"]), sexuality in all its manifestations, including prostitution ("Doch' Kseni" ["Ksenia's Daughter"]), casual copulation, rape, incest ("Otets i mat'" ["Father and Mother"]), pedophilia, impotence ("Svoi krug" ["Our Crowd"]), and homosexuality; situational leitmotifs and character-types that compactly signal comprehensive psychological and physical desperation – seamy orgies and group scandal scenes reminiscent of Dostoevsky, countless pregnancies, which inevitably end in abortions, the hospitalized, insane or crippled mother, the fist-wielding father, husband or son ("Syraia noga" ["A Raw Leg"]), the abandoned wife, the habitually unfaithful spouse ("Takaia devochka" ["A Girl Like That," 1988]), the destitute alcoholic who pilfers from his or her own family ("Ali Baba" [1988]), and the sick or neglected baby; complex narrative strategies, particularly the *skaz* of her preponderantly female narrators, which derives from Dostoevsky's Underground Man's dialogized monologue with its allusion, irony, self-contradiction, flaunted omissions, defensively misplaced emphases, red herrings, and purple patches. Petrushevskaia's is a highly rhetorical discourse that patches together lexicon and structures from disparate, frequently incompatible walks of life where temporal diffusion operates in tandem with precise, semantically freighted spatial specification.

These quintessentially Petrushevskaian features find exemplary condensation in her superb story "Our Crowd" ("Svoi krug," 1988, written in 1979). A corrosive decrowning, in Petrushevskaia's characteristic tragic vein, of the Soviet technical intelligentsia, "Our Crowd" simultaneously demythologizes romantic love, "family values," intellectual pretensions, medical professionalism, and hallowed cultural institutions.[4] Unlike Tolstaia's, Petrushevakaia's style confirms the irreparability of what she perceives as the inarticulate and inescapable suffering that defines the human condition. Her authorial manner, vision of existential devastation, and unremitting focus on specifically women's lives overlapped with the fiction of a much younger generation of women that came to the fore during perestroika (Vasilenko, Vaneeva, Palei, Narbikova), whose writing earned the ostensibly innocent, but in practice defamatory, sobriquet of New Women's Prose.

Unheavenly bodies: New Women's Prose

New Women's Prose drew fire from the male-dominated critical establishment after three collections produced by women, whose philosophical and stylistic heterogeneity posed no obstacles to bona fide group projects, saw print: *Ne pomniashchaia zla* (She Who Bears No Grudge), *Novye amazonki* (The New Amazons), *Abstinentki* (The Abstinents). Implicitly challenging the conciliatory stance favored by previous generations of women eager for acceptance by the literary male oligarchy (Baranskaia, Grekova, Ganina, Viktoriia Tokareva), they endorsed literature as a gender-inflected entity, featured unsubmissive female protagonists, and highlighted women's concerns; all focused on contemporary life; most relied to varying degrees on modernist techniques. Their chief common denominator, which disturbed critics already uneasy at the prevalence of *chernukha* (see Holmgren, 239) on the page and screen,[5] was an uncensored preoccupation with what Bakhtin characterized as the grotesque body, a disruptive site of apertures and appetites. Their refusal to gloss over physiological realia – disease, aging, abortion, rape, physical violence, substance abuse, compulsive eating – offended the sensibilities of critics and readers habituated to a euphemized denial of such "filthy" phenomena.[6]

Whereas Petrushevskaia marketed herself as a male writer in woman's guise, inasmuch as her unaccommodating "tough" prose (*zhestkaia proza*) abjured the fabled "feminine" ingredients of romance and sentiment, authors of New Women's Prose, and notably Vasilenko, Vaneeva, Narbikova, Palei, Nina Sadur, and Elena Tarasova, embraced their female identity, while the somber, gritty outlook and often repellent physiological particulars inscribed in their texts struck readers as distressingly "unfeminine" – that is, brazenly unsanitized. Elaborating narrative techniques not unlike Petrushevskaia's, but grounded in a vastly different, less Soviet, sense of gender, they debunked cobwebbed gender stereotypes (Palei's "Svidanie" ["Rendezvous"], Sadur's "Chervivyi synok" ["Worm-Eaten Sonny"], Nina Gorlanova's "Novella"), crediting women with will, reasoning powers, and sexual hunger free from emotional attachment (Vasilenko's "Shamara," Vaneeva's "Parad planet" ["Parade of Planets"] and "Venetsianskie zerkala" ["Venetian Mirrors"], Tarasova's "Ne pomniashchaia zla," and Narbikova's *Ravnovesie sveta nochnykh i dnevnykh zvezd* [Day for Night, 1990]).

In addition to travestying images of unassailable virility propagated by mainstream culture, New Women's Prose hypothesized a world driven less by males' self-seeking desires and fantasies than by female subjectivity. The bracing irreverence of New Women's Prose, its complete lack of "ladylike" squeamishness, and its refractory confrontation of life's brutal, seamy side sounded an original and disquieting note that had its counterpart in Kira Muratova's films, notably *Astenicheskii sindrom* (Asthenic Syndrome, 1989). Three narratives from the early 1990s, varying in conception and impact, stand out by virtue of their originality, scope, and profundity: Palei's *Kabiriia s Obvodnogo Kanala* (Cabiria from the Bypass Canal, 1991), Ulitskaia's *Sonechka* (1992) and Petrushevskaia's *Vremia noch'* (The Time: Night, 1992). They share a strongly articulated female subjectivity, amplitude of scale, stylish and thematic complexity, and deftly wrought psychological portraits. While *Vremia noch'* culminates Petrushevskaia's gallery of maternal monsters, the memorable protagonists of Palei's and Ulitskaia's novellas refurbish two polar paradigms of womanhood.

Palei draws on the tradition, underdeveloped in Russia, of robustly, joyously "loose" heroines – epitomized in Defoe's Moll Flanders and Henry Fielding's Molly Seagrim (*Tom Jones*) – for the sexual adventures of her insouciant, irrepressible, and insatiable Mon'ka Rybnaia, the Fellini-inspired Cabiria of the title. With unflagging zest and humor, *Kabiriia* explodes not only the cliché of marriage as a sacred institution, but also the vapid iconography of woman as fragile vessel, irreproachable mother, and stoic martyr of domestic duty. Mon'ka's ebullient sexual energy, like Pipka's in Tolstaia's "Ogon' i pyl'," celebrates female lust as an indomitable life force and on the textual level ensures the work's unflagging narrative momentum.

Whereas in such stories as "Gulia," "Lialin dom" ("Lialia's House"), and "Bron'ka," Ulitskaia likewise gives female sexuality its full due, the eponymous heroine of her *Sonechka*[7] incarnates all the spiritual qualities signaled by her culturally overdetermined name. Amply endowed with the meekness, generosity, and forgiving wisdom distilled through previous literary Sonias into iconic features, Ulitskaia's Sonechka nonetheless emerges as a psychologically credible flesh-and-blood creature. In a manner reminiscent of Tolstaia's Sonia (a being equally and perhaps overstatedly devoid of physical beauty), she quite simply lives the principles that her more intellectual artist-husband attempts to fathom and depict on canvas. If on first glance Ulitskaia seems to subscribe to the traditional gendered dichotomy whereby male identity as culture/concept predicates woman's role as nature/matter, by novella's end Sonechka's inseparability from literary texts affirms her capacity to effortlessly straddle both realms. While exploring the nature of multiple art forms, Ulitskaia through her disarmingly integrated protagonist collapses the hackneyed binarism between nature and culture that for a quarter-century feminist theorists have assailed as misogynistically repressive.

The eminently tolerant, civilized conception of humanity at the heart of Ulitskaia's world view ultimately rests on the conviction that, despite pain, cruelty, and struggle, life teems with incalculable bounties. Nothing could be more alien than that belief to the fictional world of Petrushevskaia's *Vremia noch'*, which conceives of existence as relentless psychic nightmare. A Dostoevsky-indebted tour de force of psychological revelation, this chilling first-person narrative subtly discloses the devouring, vampiric aspects of personality through a brilliant interplay between self-justifying dialogism and the totalitarian impulse that compulsively silences other voices in a blind drive for self-assertion. A finalist for the Russian Booker Prize in 1992, this compendium of Petrushevskaian *topoi* – embattled family members enmeshed through hatred and need, overcrowded apartment as locus of carnivalized scandals, crushing poverty, sexual violation, substance abuse, physical brutality and incontinence, unwanted children, the sick, institutionalized mother – offers a terrifying glimpse into the Self's despotic heart of darkness that above all recalls Dostoevsky's *Besy* (The Possessed/Devils).

Plus ça change . . . : historicizing women and feminizing history

Vremia noch' reflects the multi-generational tendency in women's prose of the 1990s, widely manifested on both the textual and the extra-textual level. The feminization of history, which unfolds as the often harrowing interaction between one or more generations of mothers and daughters, constitutes the conceptual backbone of such works as *Vremia noch'*, Vasilenko's "Khriusha" ("Piggy," 1989), Shcherbakova's "Tri 'liubvi' Mashi Peredreevoi" ("The Three 'Loves' of Masha Peredreeva," 1990), "Materi, dochki, ptitsy, ostrova" ("Mothers, Daughters, Birds, and Islands," 1991), and *Ubikvisty* (The Ubiquists, 1992), Ulitskaia's *Medeia i ee deti* (Medea and Her Children, 1996), and Ekaterina Sadur's "Iz teni v svet pereletaia" ("Flying from Shadow into Light," 1994). As a materialized metonymy/ metaphor for temporality, the family has yielded such mainstream Russian "classics" as S. Aksakov's *Semeinaia khronika* (Family Chronicle, 1856), L. Tolstoy's *Voina i mir* (War and Peace, 1869), and M. Saltykov-Shchedrin's *Gospoda Golovlevy* (The Golovlyovs, 1872–76). Post-Stalinist Russian texts, however, bear the additional, indelible imprint of the dominant Stalinist trope, which figured the entire nation as "one big happy family" of kindred socialist enthusiasts, both superseding and giving meaning to the "small" family united through biology instead of ideology.

Recent women's texts such as those noted above implicitly collapse the national family into the domestic unit, registering the perverse, dismal circumstances of Soviet life (a legacy of deprivation, fear, mistrust), but largely relegating them to the background. Consequently, the cumulative vision of life that gradually emerges varies markedly from work to work, often confounding expectations bred by ghastly events, insoluble problems, and seemingly irreconcilable enmities.

Age, doubtless, plays a role here. At the dark pole of the spectrum, Petrushevskaia (born under Stalinism) conceives of family/history as the cyclical repetition of self-destructive patterns, as entrapment in a purgatory of mutual devastation. Both *Vremia noch'* and the author's recently published *Malen'kaia Groznaia* (Little Grozna, 1998), which via such notorious names as Grozny and Stalinka bares the device of historicizing the family metaphor, imply an iron-clad determinism. Less absolute in her pessimism, Shcherbakova nonetheless also shows mothers and daughters as self-absorbed, eternal competitors ("Materi . . ."), divided either by conflicting goals dependent on the values and criteria of each generation or by a sameness of intolerant temperament (*Ubikvisty*, "Tri 'liubvi' . . ."). Vasilenko and Ulitskaia rely on myth for a modern ritual of bloodletting to appease the gods, the cathartic violence enabling their protagonists to attain reconciliation with irretrievable losses and to salvage trans-generational bonds. And, at the opposite pole of the spectrum from Petrushevskaia, Ekaterina Sadur affirms an irrational faith in an elusive, intermittent happiness accessed through a vital inner realm unmarred by the wretchedness of empirical circumstance. Her representatives of three female generations extract from the "shadow" of drunkenness, abject penury, and the degradation of meaningless physical labor the "light" of poetic creativity and the joys of nuanced perception. An inviolable imagination tempers, though it cannot redress, the imperfections of one's immediate environment. In these fictional recreations of an all-female domestic world, continuity vies with and frequently stifles change, conveying a desolate aura of stasis or regression. With rare exceptions, survival at exorbitant psychological cost replaces more exalted aspirations.

Literary mother/daughter narratives currently have their intriguing analogues off the page too. For instance, the critic Alla Latynina's versatile daughter, Iulia, writes essays as a freelance journalist on cultural and social issues, crisp politico-economic analyses as a staff writer for *Ekspert* (Expert), and, for her own pleasure, fantastic fiction geared to a mass audience. Ekaterina Sadur has followed more closely in her mother's footsteps. Readers familiar with Nina Sadur's biography can easily detect the outlines of her persona in Inessa, the hard-drinking, versifying theater cleaningwoman of "Iz teni . . .," as well as her stylistic influence on her daughter's prose in general – an influence Ekaterina readily acknowledges. The creative umbilical cord, however, pulls tightest in the case of Ekaterina Shcherbakova, who reprised her mother's inaugural, vastly successful publication, *Vam i ne snilos'* (You Never Even Dreamed, 1979), for a skeptical polemic in her revisionist continuation, *Vam i ne snilos' – 15 let spustia* (You Never Even Dreamed – Fifteen Years Later, 1996). True to the post-Soviet spirit of disillusionment with the past and cynicism about the present, the daughter's contemporary perspective emphasizes degeneration: the idealistic principles, integrity, and potential for love earlier embodied in and uniting the youthful couple Iuliia and Roman have hardened into a "middle-aged" selfish pragmatism, which under the pressure of current trials and temptations pushes them apart.

Proponents of essentialism intent on explaining women's attraction to literary continuity and continuation by their "inherent nurturing instincts" may find grist for their mill in the wordy two-volume *P'er i Natasha* (1996). The pseudonym of Vasilii Staroi adopted for this unremarkable, profiteering "continuation" of Tolstoy's *War and Peace* hides the authorship of Larisa Vasil'eva, whose notoriety for the gossipy revelations of *Kremlevskie zheny* (Kremlin Wives, 1992) far surpassed her earlier reputation as a Soviet poet. Vasil'eva realized impressively quickly that in Russia's post-ideological era hitching one's star to famous names, as well as servicing an audience hungry for "fun reading" offered a more lucrative alternative to penning "masterpieces" of artistic elegance or moral purity.

Exchanging one's ticket and the mysteries of life

Under the impact of literature's post-Soviet commercialization, Vasil'eva was not alone in exchanging, if not returning, her ticket as a self-appointed priestess of high culture. During the 1990s, Galina Shcherbakova, who formerly had adjusted her awareness of sex and greed as two of life's prime movers to the dictates of Soviet decorum, gave sexuality and materialism freer rein (for instance, in *Zhenshchiny v igre bez pravil* [Women in a Game without Rules, 1996]), sometimes treading a fine line between pulp and "respectable prose."[8] The breakdown in the cultural infrastructures that had ensured a predictable level of security for literati during the Soviet era prompted a pseudonymous migration to popular genres. Nabatnikova and Irina Polianskaia both began writing romances under the rubric of "women's novels," though Polianskaia, unlike Nabatnikova, not only continues to author serious fiction, but has garnered critical praise for her novel *Prokhozhdenie teni* (A Shade's Passing, 1997).[9] The playwright Mariia Arbatova profitably elaborates her ideas about sex and gender across the genres of drama, journalism, and television appearances, not distinguishing between the conventions of high and popular culture.

But the most revolutionary development in post-Soviet writing from the standpoint of gender is women's phenomenal success in pulp fiction, and specifically *detektivy*.[10] The premier genre in the thriving post-Soviet mass market, the murder mystery/crime novel throughout the Soviet period was an exclusively male province, possibly because the nation's sexism viewed the stock qualifications of the professional investigator (logic, analytical skills, passion for justice or for challenges) as innately masculine and incompatible with the "gentler sex." Agatha Christie enjoyed an enthusiastic following within a circle of intelligentsia aficionados, but authors, protagonists, and readers of domestic crime fiction were overwhelmingly men.

The late 1990s, however, have witnessed the extraordinary rise of Aleksandra Marinina, currently the top-selling author of detective novels. With eighteen titles in print, sales exceeding ten million copies, and several-million-dollar contracts with western publishers,[11] Marinina has granted a record number of interviews, attracted the attention of foreign academics, journalists, and mystery fans, and been featured in *Vanity Fair*.[12] A forty-something law enforcement official who until her resignation in February 1998 held the rank of lieutenant colonel at the Ministry of the Interior, where she headed the Law Institute,[13] Marinina harbors a guilty passion for pulp fiction writers such as Jackie Collins and an inexplicable veneration of Sidney Sheldon – her all-time favorite. Although she has out-stripped her male competitors in a genre that shows little sign of satiating its numerous addicted consumers, her debut in 1995 hardly augured fame and fortune: the publisher who accepted her first submission advised her to adopt a man's pseudonym and to feature a male detective.[14]

Marinina's unprecedented popularity evidences the post-Soviet public's receptivity to not only female authors of mysteries, but also female investigators. Indeed, various interviews and surveys indicate that Marinina's "serial" protagonist, Anastasiia Kamenskaia (Nastia), may be the chief attraction in her mysteries, which focus on the moral and especially psychological aspects of criminality. A heavy smoker and inveterate coffee-junkie with a liking for martinis, Nastia bears no resemblance to Soviet *or* post-Soviet ideals of womanhood. A thin, nondescript blonde in her late thirties, she eschews emotional entanglement, suffers from chronic fatigue, and downplays her potential physical allure by neglecting makeup and sporting sex-neuter jeans, sweater, and sneakers. Solving crime is her overriding passion in life, her chief professional assets being a superb memory and brilliant logical analysis. Nastia's incessant musings on "the nature of things" allow Marinina to regularly incorporate observations that any feminist would endorse:

> Humankind is divided into Men and Women. This banal truth,
> instead of simply attesting to a biological fact, has been gradually
> converted into a rule, a guide for action by which humankind oriented
> itself when it began to construct its rickety social structure . . .

Guided by that basic rule, wise humankind began to dream up various degrees of complexity for the game: separately for men, separately for women, and separately for mixed teams. And humankind was so enthusiastic about the process of socio-sexual segregation that it did not notice how the boundaries, which originally had little basis in reality and were more of a ritual, a part of the game, were suddenly transformed from playful into absolutely real, concrete ones that neither the most progressive minds nor the most advanced weapons were capable of breaking down.

A seamstress must be a woman. The investigator of a crime, a man. That's the way it is, come hell or high water . . . There are perhaps more women detectives than men. But investigating a felony is a male domain – and no dumb broad dares encroach upon it . . . For some reason or other, nobody likes to mention the fact that investigating a crime is brainwork, a quiet, imperceptible task.

. . . A woman never, under any circumstances, can turn out to be more intelligent than a man and therefore she can never carry out the brainy part of detective work better than a guy operative.[15]

This classic interrogation of gender stereotypes informs above all Nastia's relationship with her long-time lover, the mathematician Aleksei Chistiakov, which unmistakably reverses standard gender roles. He shops for food and prepares their meals, yearns for the stability of marriage, subordinates his schedule to hers, and provides the comforting domestic environment for which Russians unvaryingly hold women responsible. Anticipating readers' discomfort with a heroine who in her acute reasoning powers and indifference to time-sanctioned signs of "femininity" violates the norms of Soviet and post-Soviet sexism, Marinina astutely cements into Nastia's basic temperamant a self-consciousness about her own heterodoxy.

Although Marinina deserves credit for breaking the gender barrier in Russian detective fiction, she no longer reigns in isolated splendor. Mysteries featuring female sleuths by both Polina Dashkova and Tatiana Poliakova now regularly make the weekly list of ten top bestsellers. Poliakova affects a breezy, fast-paced narrative that skims where Marinina delves, and Dashkova seems a pale, occasionally murky replica of Marinina, but the derivative cast to their work apparently presents no handicap in the enormous market for pulp authors. In short, whereas the intelligentsia-controlled Booker Prize, mired in ingrained Soviet prejudices, has yet to recognize fully women's talent, profit-driven pulp fiction ultimately lacks an analogous gender bias. Sustaining misogynistic traditions, the blinkered seers of high culture have bypassed Petrushevskaia – a dragon, but a

genius of a dragon – and the consistently excellent Ulitskaia in their sentimental rush to confer the Russian Booker Prize on Bulat Okudzhava (1994),
a "soft and sweet" bard, but a mediocre prosaist, and on the "nostalgia"
winner, Georgii Vladimov (1995), author of *Vernyi Ruslan* (Faithful Ruslan,
1981) and *General i ego armiia* (The General and His Army, 1994). Since mass
literature follows only dollar and ruble signs, its publishers and marketers
have no cultural agenda to implement, allowing reader preference to
determine who qualifies as the "winning" writer in any given week. The
discrepancy between the preponderance of women in the list of best-selling
authors and their virtual absence in the roster of nominees for prestigious
literary prizes could lead one to draw unpleasant, but unsurprising,
conclusions about the intelligentsia's attitudes to gender.

Conclusion, with a utopian fantasy

Any generalization about the last thirteen-odd years in Russian women's
fiction courts simplification and inexcusable omissions, for it cannot
accommodate the diversity of that huge corpus. Perceptible trends, however, include an increased engagement with history, a diminishment of
idealism, the inscription of the female body as both trope and visible site
of traumatic experience, and a penchant for "bad girl" heroines possess-
ing sexual appetite, lust for adventure, and a flexible morality. Death,
sickness, violence, destitution, and incessant domestic and romantic
clashes recur with exhausting frequency in contemporary women's fiction, but such writers as Ulitskaia, Vasilenko, and Ekaterina Sadur posit
inspiration, integrity, and spiritual wealth as indivisible from the realm
they depict.

The current nostalgia fuelling the national vogue for memoirs and
(auto)biographies, instanced by Andrei Voznesensky's, El'dar Riazanov's,
Andrei Bitov's, Anatolii Naiman's and Vitalii Amurskii's recent publications, has also inspired reminiscences by women: Bella Akhmadulina's
Mig bytiia (An Instant of Being, 1997), Larisa Miller's *Bol'shaia Polianka*
(1992), Mariia Arbatova's *Menia zovut zhenshchina* (I'm Called A Woman,
1997), and retrospective narratives by Dina Rubina and Irina Murav'eva
that wistfully strive to capture the vanished, ineffable aura of a specific
region, milieu, or historical moment. Similarly, Ulitskaia, Rubina, and
Elena Makarova regularly explore the formerly anathemized topic of
Jewishness in Soviet society – a concern that periodically surfaces in the
prose of Nina Katerli, Nina Sadur, and Larisa Miller.

A brief overview of women's current fiction, however, cannot do justice to the individual stylistic aspects of numerous significant writers that constitute their unique appeal: Valeriia Narbikova's ironic, deconstructive paronomasia; the lexically splintered yet integrative strategies of Vasilenko; the endlessly refined permutations wrought by Petrushevskaia in her narrators' totalizing voices; Nina Sadur's multiple ways of inscribing the inexorability of irrationalism; Ulitskaia's orchestration of tone and rhythm to achieve discursively the reconciliation she philosophically embraces; Vaneeva's recourse to visual genres (for example, Cubist art) as an eloquent "language" for fragmentation; and Palei's sardonic use of accretion and intertexts to deride self-serving time-sanctioned conventions. A thorough examination of these features lies beyond the purview of this essay, but would substantially enrich our appreciation of the aesthetics of current women's fiction.

Prophets, futurologists, and devotees of sweeping hypotheses doubtless wonder how Russian women's writing will fare in the twenty-first century. As the millennium draws near, elitist culture confronts an uncertain future, while the mood of Russian apocalyptism intensifies. Against this dark backdrop shimmers a truly fantastic utopian vision: stimulated by the pioneering entrepreneurship of Anastasiia Verbitskaia, Russia's first best-selling female author, Marinina pays homage through imitation. Like her energetic predecessor, she invests her royalties in a publishing house founded exclusively for women writers. She commissions translations of Rita Mae Brown, Toni Morrison, Adrienne Rich, Alice Walker, and Monique Wittig, which revolutionize Russians' retrograde suppositions about Womanhood (*zhenskoe nachalo*). Her newly acquired status of ideological pathbreaker empowers Marinina to expunge the phrase "*slabyi pol*" (the weak sex), the toast "*za prekrasnykh dam*" (to beautiful ladies), and the apostrophe "*devushka!*" ([hey,] girl!) forever from the Russian language. Finally realizing the perils of grammatical sexism, Russians unanimously endorse a gender operation performed on their country's name. With *Rossiia* neutered into *Ross'e*, the nasty habit of troping Russia as either a whip-wielding slut or a blighted, desexed, ever-welcoming Mother abruptly ceases, thereby ending the careers of Viktor Erofeev, Aleksandr Solzhenitsyn, countless cartoonists, and all Village Prose writers (*derevenshchiki*) . . .

In light of developments since 1985, such a scenario for Russia's foreseeable future seems only marginally more fanciful than an announcement that the Booker Committee has awarded the Prize for fiction to a woman. The spectacular failure of the commission appointed by the government in 1997 to forge a new "Russian idea" in place of the discredited socialist utopia has left an ideological vacuum. The nation desperately needs an inspirational concept. What better candidate to nominate as an equally unattainable but less commonplace ideal than the wild dream of Herland?

NOTES

* Since this essay was completed in early 1999, it does not take into account subsequent publications of important women's texts or any pertinent scholarship that appeared thereafter.

1. Under different circumstances, Vasilenko's position would warrant rejoicing at the historic event of a woman's appointment to that role – for the first time in the history of the Writers' Union. Unfortunately, the very fact that a woman occupies that post merely confirms the demotion of literature in the cultural hierarchy of post-Soviet Russia.

2. For a condensed survey of the period, see the Introduction to *Glasnost: An Anthology of Literature Under Gorbachev*, ed. Helena Goscilo and Byron Lindsey (Ann Arbor, MI 1990); xv–xlv.

3. For an analysis of Petrushevskaia's techniques, see Helena Goscilo, "Body Talk in Current Fiction: Speaking Parts and (W)holes," *Russian Culture in Transition*. Stanford Slavic Studies, 7 (Stanford, 1993) 145–77 and "Speaking Bodies: Erotic Zones Rhetoricized," in Helena Goscilo (ed.), *Fruits of her Plume: Essays on Contemporary Russian Women's Culture* (Armonk, NY, 1993) 135–64; Natal'ia Ivanova, "Bakhtin's Concept of the Grotesque and the Art of Petrushevskaia and Tolstaia," *ibid.*, 21–32; Josephine Woll, "The Minotaur in the Maze: On Lyudmila Petrushevskaya," *World Literature Today* 67:1 (1993), 125–30.

4. For further commentary on the story, see *Glasnost*.

5. *Chernukha* ("grime and slime") as a concept evolved from the root of "black" ("chernyi"), which, when applied to work, suggests mindless, grinding labor under gruelling conditions ("chernyi vkhod" refers to the servants' entrance). During and after perestroika *chernukha* became a catchword for hard-hitting exposés of cynical corruption, sleaze, sexual depravity, "the lower depths" aspects of life, its underbelly – all conveyed in a quasi-naturalistic vein that had no room for idealism.

6. For a sampling of responses to this aspect of New Women's Prose, and an assessment of them, see Helena Goscilo (ed.), *Skirted Issues; The Discreteness and Indiscretions of Russian Women's Prose* (special issue of Russian Studies in Literature) 28:2 (Spring 1992) and her *Dehexing Sex: Russian Womanhood During and After Glasnost* (Ann Arbor, MI, 1996), 70–80.

7. *Sonechka* made the finalists' list for the Russian Booker Prize in 1992, as did *Medeia i ee deti* for 1997.

8. The borderline status of her texts partly clarifies why in the last few years the Moscow publishing house Bukmen has (re)issued her fiction in print runs of 20,000 copies, twice the size of typical print runs for works of "serious literature."

9. Published in *NM* 1 (1997), 7–71 and 2 (1997), 3–78.

10. On Russian pulp fiction and women's place in it, see Goscilo, "Big-Buck Books: Post-Soviet Pulp fiction," *The Harriman Review* 12, 2/3 (Winter 1999/2000) 6–24.

11. In the United States, with Owl Books (the paperback subsidiary of Henry Holt), and in Germany with Fischer Verlag (paperback), Argon Verlag (hardcover) (my appreciation to Anja Grothe for information about the publishers). Marinina has also signed a contract with the Italian publishing house Piemme for an Italian translation of all eighteen novels over the next four years. See Alessandra Stanley, "In Its Dreams, Russia Solves Its Crime Problems," *New York Times* (March 15, 1998).

12. See the August, 1998 issue of *Vanity Fair*, which quotes Marinina's unexpected claim: "I read through opera librettos. In them seethe genuine human passions. I find many of the ideas for my detective novels in them" (102).

13. Interviews with Marinina and brief articles about her have overrun the press during the last two years. For an analysis of Marinina and a selective bibliography of pertinent items, see Goscilo, "Feminist Pulp Fiction: Detecting Murder and Aleksandra Marinina," *Women East-West* 50 (November 1997), 15–16; Goscilo, "Big-Buck Books:"; Catharine Theimer Nepomnyashchy, "Markets, Mirrors, and Mayhem: Aleksandra Marinina and the Rise of the New Russian Detektiv," in Adele Barker (ed.), *Consuming Russia: Popular Culture, Sex, and Society since Gorbachev* (Durham, 1999), 161–91.

14. Since men reportedly accounted for 70 percent of the genre's readers, the publisher's reasoning seemed impeccable. See Mitchell Landsberg, "Russian Crime Writer Reaps Renown," *Associated Press* (November 9, 1997).

15. Aleksandra Marinina, *Igra na chuzhom pole* (Game on Alien Turf, 1997), 188–93.

Bibliographical guide to writers and their works

This guide reflects those authors who have been discussed at some length in this volume. For information on other women writers not found here, see Tomei, *Russian Women Writers* and Ledkovsky, Rosenthal, and Zirin, *Dictionary of Russian Women Writers*.

Akhmadulina, Bella (Izabella) Akhatovna (b. 1937, Moscow). Poet, prose writer, translator, lives in Moscow.
Writings: Struna. Moscow, 1962; *Oznob.* Frankfurt-am-Main, 1968; *Uroki muzyki.* Moscow, 1969; *Stikhi.* Moscow, 1975; *Svecha.* Moscow, 1977; *Metel'.* Moscow, 1977; *Sny o Gruzii.* Tbilisi, 1977; *Taina.* Moscow, 1983; *Sad.* Moscow, 1987; *Stikhotvoreniia.* Moscow, 1988; *Izb.* Moscow, 1988; *Poberezh'e.* Moscow, 1991; *Larets i kliuch.* St. Petersburg, 1994; *Zvuk ukazuiushchii.* St. Petersburg, 1995; *Griada kamnei.* Moscow, 1991; *Sozertsanie stekliannogo sharika.* St. Petersburg, 1997; *SS,* 3 vols. Moscow, 1997; *Odnazhdy v dekabre.* St. Petersburg, 1996 (prose); *Mig bytiia.* Moscow, 1997 (prose); *Zimnaia zamknutost'.* Moscow, 1999; *Vozle elki.* St. Petersburg, 1999; *Nechaianie: Stikhi, dnevnik 1996–1999.* Moscow, 2000.
Interviews: "'Ia iz liudei, i bol'no mne liudskoe . . .': Shest' fragmentov odnoi besedy," *LitGaz* 10:5284 (March 7, 1990), 13; *Brodsky's Poetics and Aesthetics,* ed. L. Loseff and V. Polukhina. New York, 1990, 194–204.
In translation: Fever and Other New Poems, tr. Geoffrey Dutton and Igor Mezhakoff-Koriakin. New York, 1969; *The Garden,* tr. F. D. Reeve. New York, 1990; poems in *Contemporary Russian Poetry,* 124–37; Todd and Hayward, 873–94; prose in *Metropol'.* New York, 1982; selected poems and "To My Readers," tr. Christine Rydel in Tomei, II.

Akhmatova, Anna Andreevna (b. Gorenko, 1889, Bol'shoi Fontan, nr. Odessa; d. 1966, Moscow). A major poet of the 20th century. Member of the Acmeist school. During the Stalinist terror both her husband and son were arrested. Became spokesperson for her people during the war.
Writings: Vecher. St. Petersburg, 1912; *Chetki.* St. Petersburg, 1913; *Belaia staia.* Petrograd, 1917; *Podorozhnik.* Petrograd, 1921; *Anno Domini, MCMXXI.* Petrograd, 1922; *Iz shesti knig.* Leningrad, 1940; *Izb.* Tashkent, 1943; *Izbrannye stikhi.* Moscow, 1946; *Stikhotvoreniia.* Moscow, 1958; *Requiem.* Munich, 1963; *Beg vremeni.* Moscow and Leningrad, 1965; *Stikhotvoreniia i poemy.* Leningrad, 1976; *Soch.* Moscow, 1988; *Soch.* 2 vols. Moscow, 1990.

In translation: *Poems of Akhmatova*, tr. S. Kunitz and M. Hayward. Boston, 1967; *Tale Without a Hero and Twenty-Two Poems by Anna Akhmatova*, tr. J. van der Eng-Liedmeier and K. Verheul. The Hague, 1973; *Selected Poems*, tr. Richard McKane. Newcastle-upon-Tyne, 1989; *The Complete Poems of Anna Akhmatova*, updated and expanded edn. tr. Judith Hemschemeyer, ed. Roberta Reeder. Edinburgh and Boston, 1992; "The Willow," tr. Alan Myers in Kelly *Utopias*.

Aliger, Margarita Iosifovna (b. 1915, Odessa; d. 1992, Moscow). Poet, essayist, translator. Attended Gorky Literary Institute in Moscow. Prolific and loyal poet of the Stalin era; active in literature of the Thaw.

Writings: *SS*, 3 vols. Moscow, 1984–5; *Vstrechi i razluki*. Moscow, 1989; *Tropinka vo rzhi: o poezii i poetakh*. Moscow, 1980.

In translation: poems in *The Heritage of Russian Verse*, ed. Dmitri Obolensky. Bloomington, 1976; *Three Russian Poets: Margarita Aliger, Yunna Moritz, Bella Akhmadulina*, ed. Ellen Feinstein. Manchester, 1979; *Song of a Nightingale: An Anthology of Modern Soviet Short Stories*. Delhi, 1987; poems, tr. Lisa Taylor in Tomei, II.

Andersen, Larissa Nikolaevna (b. 1914, Khabarovsk), married Chaiz. Poet, ballet dancer. Wrote poetry and danced on the stages of Harbin and Shanghai until the early 1950s when she left China first for Tahiti and then France with her French husband.

Writings: *Po zemnym lugam*. Shanghai, 1940.

Andreeva, Tat'iana or Tamara. Poet.

Anisimova, Domna (pseudonym "Blind Domania," b. 1812, Riazan' province; d. after 1868, Riazan province). Daughter of poor village sexton; blind by 20, she dictated her poetry. Collection published by Russian Academy in 1838 received considerable but short-lived attention.

Writings: *Stikhi bednoi devitsy, slepoi docheri derevenskogo ponomaria*. St. Petersburg, 1838. Poems in *Poety iz naroda*. Moscow, 1901.

Annenkova, Varvara Nikolaevna (b. 1795; d. 1866/1870, Moscow). Born into wealthy aristocratic family, with connections to Decembrists. Friend and relative of Lermontov; moved in Moscow literary circles in the 1830s and 1840s; published poetry, unsigned or with initials, in 1830s; 1844 collection widely reviewed.

Writings: *Dlia izbrannykh*. Moscow, 1844; *Stikhotvoreniia 1854, 1855, 1856*. St. Petersburg, 1856; *Chudo-Iudo. Skazka v stikhakh*. St. Petersburg, 1866; *Sharlotta Korde*. St. Petersburg, 1866.

Arbatova, Mariia (b. Gavrilina, 1957, Murom). Writer of drama and screenplays, Arbatova (whose pseudonym is taken from the Arbat, on which she lived, in Moscow) began her publishing career with poetry. Co-host of television talk show *On My Own*.

Writings: Poems in *Moskva* 6 (1977); *NM* 8 (1979); *Al'manakh poezii* 29 (1981), *NM* 3 (1982); *Sny na beregu Dnepra*. 1985; *Seminar u moria*. 1986; *Uravnenia s dvumia izvestnymi* (film script), directed by Nadezhda Repina. 1988; *Seishen v kommunal'ke*. VAAP, 1990; "Alekseev i teni," *Al'manakh "Teplyi stan'"* 1 (1990); *Natural Foods*. With Peter Dedman. 1990; *P'esy dlia chteniia*. Moscow, 1991. Includes *Uravnenie s dvumia izvestnymi, Viktoria Vasil'eva glazami postoronnykh*, and *Zavistnik; Pozdnii ekipazh*. 1991; "Uroki feminizma" (MS); *Vremia i my*, 1995; "Kapustnik," *Moskovskii komsomolets* (September 22, 1996); "Opyt sotsial'noi skul'ptury," *Zvezda* 2 (1996); *Menia zovut zhenshchina*. Moscow, 1997, 1999; *Mne 40 let: avtobiograficheskii roman*. Moscow, 1999; *Vizit nestaroi damy: vpolne roman*. Moscow, 1999; *Po doroge k sebe*. Moscow, 1999; *Mobil'nye sviazi*, Moscow, 2000. For more publications, see http:/www.arbatova.ru/publ/

In translation: "Equation with Two Knowns," tr. Melissa Smith; "My Teachers," tr. Joanne Turnbull. *Glas* 13 (1996); *On the Road to Ourselves*, in *Russian Mirror: Three Plays by Russian Women*, ed. and tr. Melissa T. Smith. Amsterdam, 1998.

Bakunina, Ekaterina Vasil'evna (b. 1889, Tsarskoe selo; d. 1976, Keighley, Yorkshire; married Novoselov; one son). Raised in St. Petersburg; matriculated at School of Agronomy; left for US, worked as a laborer; later entered law program of the Bestuzhev Women's School; left for Khar'kov, 1918, finished degree, worked as secretary of local newspaper. In Petrograd, 1921; worked as tr. and ed. at Institute of Brain Science. Emigrated c. 1922, living in Paris by 1923. Published verse collection, 1931; from 1932, editorial secretary, literary journal *Chisla*; published two popular erotic novels, 1933, 1935. Moved to England after World War II, wrote verse, published little.

Writings: *Stikhi*. Paris, 1931; *Telo*. Berlin, 1933; "Shtorm," *Chisla* 10 (1934); "Osennie list'ia," *Nov'* 7 (1934); *Liubov' k shesterym*. Paris, 1935.

Recent editions: *Liubov' k shesterym*. Moscow, 1994; the latter and *Telo* included in Anna Mar, *Zhenshchina na kreste*. Moscow, 1994.

Baranskaia, Natal'ia (b. 1908, St. Petersburg). Writer of prose fiction. Daughter of revolutionaries, she grew up in the underground and in exile. Upon return to Russia after the 1917 revolution, she studied at Moscow University and worked at the Pushkin Historical Museum in Moscow. She began writing after retirement at the age of 58.

Writings: "Nedelia kak nedelia," *NM* 11 (1969). Also published in Copenhagen, 1973, Paris, 1976; "Muzhchiny, beregite zhenshchin," *LitGaz* 46 (1971); "Chemu raven iks?" *Iunost'* 5 (1974); *Otritsatel'naia Zhizel'*. Moscow, 1977; *Zhenshchina s zontikom*. Moscow, 1981; *Portret podarennyi drugu*. Leningrad, 1981; *Den' pominoveniia: roman, povest'*. Moscow, 1989; "Avtobiografiia bez umolchanii," *Grani* 156 (1990); Avtobus s chernoi polosoi. "Ptitsa Rasskaz," *Grani* 166 (1992); "Vstrecha." "Lesnaia poliana." "Udivitel'nye shariki." "Portret Zoiki na fone dvora," *Grani* 168 (1993); *Stranstvie bezdomnykh*. Moscow, 1999.

In translation: "The Alarm in the Cupboard" (A Week Like Any Other), tr. Beatrice Stillman, *Redbook*, March, 1971; "The Retirement Party," tr. Anatole Forostenko, *RLT* 9 (1974); *The Barsukov Triangle, the Two-Toned Blonde and Other Stories*, ed. Proffer and Proffer; *A Week Like Any Other: Novellas and Stories*, tr. Pieta Monks. Seattle, WA, 1989; *Just Another Week*, ed. Lora Paperno, Natalie Roklina, and Richard Leed. Columbus, OH, 1989; "The Kiss," tr. Wanda Sorgente in *Balancing Acts*; "Laine's House," tr. Gerald Mikkelson and Margaret Winchell, in *Soviet Women Writing*; excerpt from *Day of Remembrance*, tr. Maureen Riley in Tomei, II, 1284–97.

Barkova, Anna Aleksandrovna (pseudonym Kalika Perekhozhaia; b. 1901, Ivanovo-Voznesensk; d. 1976, Moscow). Poet, dramatist. Came from a working-class background and in 1918 enrolled as a member of the Circle of Genuine Proletarian Poets. Suffered repeated arrests and two long periods of exile both during and after the Stalin years. Allowed to return to Moscow in 1967.

Writings: *Zhenshchina*. Petrograd, 1922; *Nastas'ia-Koster*. Moscow and Petrograd, 1923; poems in *Dodnes' tiagoteet*, ed. S. Vilensky. Moscow, 1989; "Stikhi raznykh let" *Lazur'* 1 (1989); "Rovesnitsa veka," ed. A. L. Ageev and L. N. Taganov, *Volga* 5 (1989); *Vozvrashchenie*. Ivanovo, 1990; "Plamia snegov," *LitOb* 8 (1991); *Geroi nashego vremeni*. Moscow, 1992; *Izb: iz gulagskogo arkhiva*, ed. L. N. Taganov and Z. Ia. Kholodova. Ivanovo, 1992.

In translation: six poems, tr. Catriona Kelly, in *Russian Women's Camp Memoirs*, ed. J. Crowfoot and S. Vilensky. London, 1995; poems, tr. Catriona Kelly in Tomei, II.

Bazhenova, Taisiia Anatol'evna (d. 1978, USA). Poet.

Writings: Pesni sibiriachki. Harbin, 1919.

Bek, Tat'iana Aleksandrovna (b. 1949, Moscow). Poet, critic, lives in Moscow, member of the Writers' Union since 1979. Prolific reviewer, only a few examples included below.

Writings: Skvoreshniki. Moscow, 1974; *Snegir'.* Moscow, 1980; *Zamysel.* Moscow, 1987; *Smeshannyi les.* Moscow, 1993; *Oblaka skvoz' derev'ia.* Moscow, 1997; essays and reviews in *DN* 2 (1994), 196–204; *Znamia* 5 (1996), 221–2; *VopLit* (Sept–Oct, 1996), 253–64; *DN* 2 (1995), 165–78; *NM* 11 (1995), 86–92; *DN* 12 (1991), 245–61; *VopLit* 1 (1992), 324–48; *DN* 8 (1989), 5–62 and 9 (1989), 51–105; *LitOb* 3 (1985), 25–8; *NM* 9 (1997), 235–57; *Antologiia akmeizma: stikhi, manifesty, stat'i, zametki, memuary,* comp. and annotated by T. A. Bek. Moscow, 1997.

Berberova, Nina Nikolaevna (pseudonyms: Ivelich, Gulliver, b. Karaulova, 1901, St. Petersburg; d. 1993, Philadelphia; married: 1) Vladislav Khodasevich, 1922; 2) painter N. V. Makeev, 1936; 3) pianist G. A. Kochevitsky, 1954). Raised in St. Petersburg, bourgeois family; studied philology, Rostov-on-Don, 1919–20. In St. Petersburg, 1921; published 1st poem, 1922; attended Gumilev's poetic studio, meetings of Serapion Brothers; member, Union of Poets. With husband Vladislav Khodasevich emigrated on Soviet passport, 1922, resided with Maksim Gorky in Sorrento. To Paris, 1925; Gippius's circle; co-ed. of "Green Lamp" journal *Novyi dom,* 1926; from 1925, correspondent for *Poslednie novosti.* In same, author of stories of émigré life, "Biiankurskie prazdniki," 1928–40; published translations of Laclos, Dostoevsky, Rolland; during 1930s, also published four novels, biographies of Tchaikovsky and Borodin, series of long stories in *Sovremennye zapiski.* Remained in occupied France; after war, established weekly *Russkaia mysl',* published book on Blok. Emigrated to US, 1950; ed. work at *Mosty;* published scholarly edns. of Khodasevich's work, biography of Budberg, vol. of collected verse, study of Russian Masonry. Taught at several universities, mainly Yale, 1958–62, Princeton, 1963–71. International recognition with autobiography in English, 1969; translations of stories bestsellers in France; visited Russia, 1989.

Writings: Poslednie i pervye. Paris, 1930; *Povelitel'nitsa.* Berlin, 1932; *Chaikovskii: istoriia odinokoi zhizni.* Berlin, 1936; *Bez zakata.* Paris, 1938; *Borodin.* Berlin, 1938; *Alexandre Blok et son temps.* Paris, 1948; *Oblegchenie uchasti.* Paris, 1949; "Mys bur" *NZh,* 24–7 (1950–1); *Vladislav Khodasevich, Sobranie stikhov, 1913–1939.* Munich, 1960; repr. New Haven, 1961; *Kursiv moi.* NZh (1967), and Munich, 1972; 2nd edn, New York, 1983; *Zinaida Gippius, Pis'ma k Berberovoi i Khodasevichu.* Ann Arbor, 1978; *Zheleznaia zhenshchina.* New York, 1981; *Vladislav Khodasevich, Izbrannaia proza.* New York, 1982; *Stikhi, 1921–1983.* New York, 1984; *Liudi i lozhi.* New York, 1986; *Neizvestnaia Berberova: roman, stikhi, stat'i.* St. Petersburg, 1998; *Borodin. Mys bur. Povelitel'nitsa.* Moscow, 1998; *Aleksandr Blok i ego vremeni.* Moscow, 1999.

In translation: The Italics are Mine, tr. P. Radley. New York, 1969; *The Accompanist,* tr. M. Schwartz. London, 1987; *The Revolt,* tr. M. Schwartz. London, 1989; *The Tattered Cloak,* tr. M. Schwartz. London, 1991, and *Three Novels,* 2 vols. London, 1990–1; *Alexander Blok: A Life,* tr. Robyn Marsack. New York, 1996; *The Book of Happiness,* tr. M. Schwartz. New York, 1999. For complete listing, see Tomei, II.

Recent editions: "Malen'kaia devochka: P'esa," *Sovremennaia dramaturgiia* 2 (1991); *Zheleznaia zhenshchina.* Moscow, 1991; *Rasskazy v izgnanii.* Moscow, 1994; *IzbS,* 2 vols.

Moscow, 1997; *Neizvestnaia Berberova. Roman, stikhi, stat'i*. St. Petersburg, 1998. *Bez zakata. Malen'kaia devochka. Rasskazy ne o liubvi. Stikhi*. Moscow, 1999.

Berggol'ts, Ol'ga Fedorovna, (b. 1910, St. Petersburg; d. 1975, Leningrad). Poet, writer, and journalist. A witness to and victim of the major cataclysms of Soviet history, Berggol'ts served the state with her poetry, prose and journalism, yet never regimented her lyrical gift. Graduated from Leningrad State University, 1930, with degree in Philology. Embarked on dual career as journalist and creative writer. In late 1930s, ex-husband, Boris Kornilov, executed. Berggol'ts imprisoned for several months. During World War II articulated the sufferings of fellow Leningraders in the blockade – through radio broadcasts, poetry, and plays. After war her work charted shift in cultural values from Stalinism to the Thaw.

Writings: *Stikhotvoreniia*. Leningrad, 1934; *Leningradskaia tetrad'*. Moscow, 1942; *Leningradskaia poema*. Leningrad, 1942, 1976; "Leningradskaia simfoniia," *Komsomol'skaia Pravda* (August 19, 1942); *Leningrad*. Moscow, 1944; *Oni zhili v Leningrade*. Moscow, 1945; *Tvoi put'*. Leningrad, 1945; *Izb*. Moscow, 1948, 1954; *Pervorossiisk*. Moscow, 1952; *SS*, 2 vols. Moscow, 1958; *Dnevnye zvezdy*. Leningrad, 1959, 1971, 1975, 1978; 1985; *Uzel: Novaia kniga stikhov*. Leningrad, 1965; *Vernost': Stikhi i poemy*. Leningrad, 1970; *IzbPr*. Leningrad, 1983. *SS*, 3 vols. Leningrad, 1988; *Govorit Leningrad; Stat' i*, 1985. *P'esy i stsenarii*. Leningrad, 1988; *Ekho Stikhi*, 1990; *Proshlogo-net!: stikhi, poemy, iz rabochikh tetradei*, comp. M. F. Berggol'ts. Moscow, 1999. For a more complete listing, see Tomei, II.

In translation: "Daytime Stars," *SovLit* 12(1961), 27–90; extract from "Daytime Stars" in Kelly *Utopias*; poems in *Russian Poetry: The Modern Period*, ed. John Glad and Daniel Weissbort. Iowa City, IA, 1978, 183–8; "In Memory of the Defenders," in *Three Centuries of Russian Poetry*, ed. E. N. Bannikov. Moscow, 1980, 723; "February Diary," in *Land of the Soviets in Verse and Prose*, ed. Galina Dzyubenko. Moscow, 1982, 201–3; "Conversation with a Neighbour," *SovLit* 5 (1985); prose and poetry, tr. Trina Mamoon in Tomei, II.

Blokh, Raisa Noevna (pseudonyms: M. Leonidovna, R. Noev; b. 1899, St. Petersburg; d. 1943, German concentration camp; married literary scholar Mikhail Gorlin, 1935; one daughter). Father distinguished Jewish lawyer, brother Jacob Blokh, playwright and publisher. Studied medieval history, St. Petersburg University, 1919–20; participant in Mikhail Lozinsky's translation studio; member St. Petersburg Union of Poets, 1920. Emigrated to Berlin, 1922; degree in medieval history, University of Berlin; researcher at publishing house Monumenta Germaniae Historica with medieval historian Brachmann; member poetic circle "tridtsat'" (sic), led by Gorlin; published translations of Gozzi, Machiavelli, Tauler, Heredia; published first book of poetry, 1928. To Paris with Gorlin, 1933; earned money tutoring, doing scholarly piece-work at the Sorbonne; published several essays, medieval culture and politics. Daughter born, 1936; Gorlin arrested, 1939, detained at Potivier, transported to labor camp, Silesia; daughter died en route to Switzerland; Blokh arrested at Swiss border, sent to death in Nazi camp.

Writings: *Moi gorod*. Berlin, 1928; *Tishina*. Berlin, 1935; with Mirra Borodina, *Zavety*. Brussels, 1939; with Mikhail Gorlin, *Izbrannye stikhotvoreniia*. Paris, 1959; *Études littéraires et historiques par M. Gorlin et R. Blokh-Gorlin*. Paris, 1957.

In translation: poem in Todd and Hayward.

Recent editions: *Zdes' shumiat chuzhie goroda*. Moscow, 1996.

Bulich, Vera Sergeevna (b. 1898, St. Petersburg; d. 1954, Helsinki). Father S. K. Bulich, professor St. Petersburg University and director of Women's College; student, History and Philology Dept., St. Petersburg University, 1917; fled with family to estate, Kuolemajaarvi, Finland, 1918; moved to Helsinki after father's death, 1921. Published poems, stories, reviews, poetic translations, literary criticism in émigré journals; wrote plays, ballet librettos. First books collections of fairy tales in Finnish, 1927, and Russian, 1931; published four books of poetry; also published poetry in Swedish and Finnish. From 1932, worked Slavic Division, University library; member, literary society "Svetlitsa"; head of library, Institute for Soviet Studies, 1947; during 1940s–50s, associate, library of Finland-USSR Friendship, and literary ed. of *Russkii zhurnal*, organ of Russian Cultural-Democratic Union. Died of lung cancer.

Writings: Satu pikkirikkisestra ptinsessasta. Porvoo, 1927; *Skazki.* Belgrade, 1931; "Chetvertoe izmerenie." *Zhurnal sodruzhestva* 4 (1934); *Maiatnik.* Helsingfors, 1934; *Plennyi veter.* Tallin, 1938; "O zarubezhnoi russkoi poezii 1937 g.," *Zhurnal sodruzhestva* 6 (1938); *Burelom.* Helsinki, 1947; *Vetvi.* Paris, 1954.

In translation: "On Emigré Russian Poetry, 1937," in *Russian Literature in the Baltic Between the World Wars*, ed. T. Pachmuss. Columbus, 1987; poetry in Kelly *Anthology*; Pachmuss, *Russian Literature in the Baltics,* 394–422.

Bunina, Anna Petrovna (b. 1774, Riazan' province; d. 1829, Riazan' province). Born into old gentry family; raised with limited education by aunts. Moved to Moscow in 1798 and St. Petersburg in 1802, where she pursued literary interests, living independently and writing essays, poetry, prose, and translations. 1815 traveled to England for her health, returning uncured in 1817; literary activities curtailed by painful cancer.

Writings: Pravila poezii. Sokrashchennyi perevod Abbata Bate s prisovokupleniem Rossiiskago stopolozheniia v pol'zu devits. Moscow, 1808; *Neopytnaia muza,* 2 vols. St. Petersburg, 1809–12; *Padenie Faetona.* St. Petersburg, 1811; *Sel'skie vechera.* St. Petersburg, 1811; *Spasenie Fiv. Geroicheskaia povest'.* St. Petersburg, 1811; *Sobranie stikhotvorenii,* 3 vols. St. Petersburg, 1819–21; *Nravstvennye i filosoficheskie besedy Kh. Blera.* Moscow, 1829;

Recent editions: poems in *Poety 1790–1810-kh godov,* ed. Iu. M. Lotman. Leningrad, 1974; Bannikov; *Tsaritsy muz.*

In translation: poems in *RLT* 9 (1974); *Perkins and Cook;* Kelly *Anthology;* tr. Bonnie Marshall in Tomei, I.

Catherine II ("the Great"), Tsaritsa (b. Sophie Frederike Augusta von Anhalt-Zerbst, 1729; d. 1796). Immensely prolific author of satirical journalism, didactic fiction, comedies, histories, memoirs, law codes, etc. Major works include the periodical *Vsiakaia vsiachina* (1769), numerous satirical and other dramas, the outline for a legal codex *Nakaz* (St. Petersburg, 1768–9), a lengthy memoir intended for her sons (dating from the 1790s), and a number of shorter memoirs.

Writings: Soch, ed. V. F. Solntsev. 3 vols. St. Petersburg, 1893; 2nd edn, St. Petersburg, 1895. For complete listing, see Tomei, I.

In translation: Memoirs of the Empress Catherine II, Written by Herself with a Preface by Aleksandr Herzen. New York and London, 1859; also as *Memoirs of Catherine the Great,* tr. Katharine Anthony. New York, 1927; *Voltaire and Catherine the Great: Selected Correspondence,* tr. A. Lentin. Cambridge, 1974; Selections from *Odds and Ends,* tr. Marcus C. Levitt in Tomei, I. For complete listing, see Tomei, I.

Chebotarevskaia, Anastasiia (b. 1876; d. 1921). Critic, editor, playwright and translator.

Writings: "V sumerkakh," *RBog* 6 (1905); "Tvorimoe tvorchestvo," *ZR* 11–12 (1908); "Kholod-nyi sochel'nik," *Slovo*, 1908; as F. Sologub, "Aisedora Dunkan v prozreniiakh Fredrikha Nitsshe," *ZR* 4 (1909); "Zhenshchina nastoiashchego i budushchego," *Trudy pervogo vserossiiskogo zhenskogo s' 'ezda*. St. Petersburg, 1909; "Staryi dom," *Zem-lia* 3(1909); "Put' v Damask," in *Shipovnik*. 1910; "Liubov' nad bezdnami," in *Al' manakh shipovnik*, 1910, and separately St. Petersburg, 1913; *O Fedore Sologube*. St. Petersburg, 1911; as F. Sologub, *Mechtapobeditel'nitsa*. St. Petersburg, 1912; "Zelenyi bum," in *Nebokory: VIII al' manakh ego-futuristov*. St. Petersburg, 1913; "Po povodu nekotorikh iubileev," in *Ocharovannyi strannik, Al'manakh intuitivnoi kritiki i poezii*. St. Petersburg, 1913; ed., *Liubov'v pis' makh vydaiushchikhsia liudei XVII i XIX veka*. Moscow, 1913; *Kamen' broshennyi v vodu*. St. Petersburg, 1915; *Shchit: Literaturnyi sbornik*. Moscow, 1915; ed., *Rossiia v rodnykh pesniakh*. Petrograd, 1915; ed., *Voina v russkoi poezii*. Petrograd, 1915; *Zhenshchina nakanune Revoliutsii 1789 g*. Petrograd, 1922.

Chegrintseva, Emiliia Kirillovna (b. Tsegoeva, 1904, Ekaterinburg; d. 1989, Nachod, Czechoslovakia; married Sergei Chegrintsev, 1932). Raised in Kishinev; graduate gymnasium of Baroness I. P. Geiging. Emigrated with family to Prague, c. 1921. Enrolled in philosophy at Charles University, 1922; attended seminars on Soviet Russian literature, Free Russian University; from 1928, member Alfred Bem's cir-cle "Skit". Published verse in major émigré periodicals, anthologies; two verse collections, 1936, 1938. Last émigré publication, 1939, but continued to write; several late poems published, *Moskovskii Komsomolets*, 1989.

Writings: *Poseshcheniia: Stikhi 1929–1936*. Prague, 1936; *Strofy*. Warsaw, 1938.

Chervinskaia, Lydiia Davidovna (b. 1907; d. 1988, Paris; married to poet Lazar Kel'berin). Fled with family through Constantinople, c. 1920; in Paris, 1922. Mem-ber, Union of Young Poets and Writers; attended "Green Lamp," later "Krug" (1935–9); during 1930s, published poems, articles, reviews in Parisian journals, two books of poetry. Participated in Resistance. After war, published third book of verse; worked for Radio Liberty in Munich. Died in old-age home in Mont-morency, near Paris.

Writings: "My," *Chisla* 10 (1934); *Priblizheniia*. Paris, 1934; "Skuka," *Krug* 1 (1936); *Rassvety*. Paris, 1937; "Ozhidanie," *Krug* 3 (1938); "V posledniuiu minutu," in *Literaturnyi smotr*. Paris, 1939; *Dvenadtsat' mesiatsev*. Paris, 1956.

In translation: poems in Markov and Sparks; Pachmuss, *A Russian Cultural Revival*.

Chukovskaia, Lydiia Korneevna (b. 1907, St. Petersburg; d. 1996, Moscow. married: 1) Tsezar Volpe; 2) Matvei Bronshtein). Memoirist, novelist. Daughter of literary critic and children's writer Kornei Chukovskii. Chronicled lives and events dur-ing the Stalinist terror. Early works able to be published only in *samizdat*. Under glasnost her works were published for the first time in the Soviet Union. First recipient of Sakharov Prize in 1990.

Writings: *V laboratorii redaktora*. Moscow, 1963; "Byloe i dumy," *Gertsena*. Moscow, 1966; *Otkrytoe slovo*. New York, 1976; *Po etu storonu smerti. Iz dvevnika 1936–1976*. Paris, 1978; *Protsess iskliucheniia. Ocherk literaturnykh nravov*. Paris, 1979; Moscow, 1990; *Zapiski ob Anne Akhmatovoi*, 3 vols. Moscow, 1997; *Pamiati detstva*. New York, 1983; Moscow, 1989; *Sof'ia Petrovna. Spusk pod vodu*. Moscow, 1989; *Izbrannoe*. Moscow, 1997; *SS*, 2 vols. Moscow, 2000.

In translation: *The Deserted House*, tr. Aline Worth. New York, 1967; *Going Under*, tr. Peter Weston. New York, 1972; *Sofia Petrovna*, tr. Aline Worth, revised edn, Eliza Kellogg Klose. Evanston, IL, 1988; *To the Memory of Childhood*, tr. Eliza Kellogg Klose.

Evanston, IL, 1988; *The Akhmatova Journals*, vol. I, 1938–1941, tr. Milena Michalski, Sylva Rubashova, and Peter Norman. New York, 1994; excerpt from "The Process of Expulsion," tr. Christine D. Tomei in Tomei, II, 1133–40.

Damanskaia, Avgusta (Avgustina) Filippovna (pseudonym Arsenii Merich; b. Veisman, 1875/77, Popeliukha, Podol'sk province; d. Cormeilles-en-Parisis, near Paris, 1959). Attended school, Odessa. Married, moved to St. Petersburg, 1892/1901; degree, Higher Courses for Women; studied piano, St. Petersburg Conservatory. Began publishing stories, poetry in prestigious journals as A. Fillipov, 1903. Published numerous translations, incl. first Russian translations of Romaine Rolland, Herbert Wells, Octave Mirbeau. After Revolution, worked at "Vsemirnaia literatura", met Evgenii Zamiatin. Emigrated to Berlin, 1920; published anti-Bolshevik pamphlet, two short novels. From 1923, governing member, Union of Russian Translators, Germany; permanent staff of *Poslednie novosti*. Moved to Paris, 1923; published stories, travel sketches, criticism in major émigré periodicals and as separate volumes; articles for American and French press. Postwar stories concern Resistance. Prolific translator of contemporary French, German, Italian, English, and Polish literature.

Writings: *Rasskazy*. Moscow, 1908; *Gde-to tam*. Petrograd, 1918; *Stekliannaia stena: Rasskazy*. Petrograd, 1918, 2nd edn, Berlin, 1921; "V gorakh," *Spolokhi* 1 (1921); "Prosti-proshchai," in *Zhar-Ptitsa* (1921); *Kartochnye domiki sovetskogo stroitel'stva*. Berlin, 1921; *Voda ne idet: Povest'*. Berlin, 1922; "Ochen' prosto: iz peterburgskikh vpechatlenii," *Volia Rossii* 19 (1922); "Ivan Petrovich," in *Tsveten'*, 1922; *Vikhorevy gnezda*. Berlin, 1923; "Plonkheir," *Perezvony* 4 (1925); "Lenia," *Perezvony* 26 (1926); *Zheny: Rasskazy*. Paris, 1929; *Radost' tikhaia: Putevye zametki*. Paris, 1929; "Tania iz Kaira," *Illiustrirovannaia Rossiia* 274 (1930); "Modeli," *Illiustrirovannaia Rossiia* 282 (1930); "Sud'ia," *Novosel'e* 22–3 (1945); "V Savoie," *Novosel'e* 33–4 (1947); *Miranda*. New York, 1953.

Darem, Elena — Elena Nikitina. Poet.

Writings: *U moria*. Harbin, 1938.

Dashkova, Princess Ekaterina Romanovna (b. Vorontsova, 1743; d. 1810). Dramatist, journalist, memoirist. Appointed Director of the Russian Academy of Sciences, 1783. Ed. of *Sobesednik liubitelei russkogo slova* and *Ezhemesiachnye sochineniia*. Major works include *Mon histoire* (1804–5: first published London, 1840).

Writings: *E. R. Dashkova: Literaturnye sochineniia*, ed. G. N. Moiseeva. Moscow, 1990.

In translation: *The Memoirs of Princess Dashkova*, ed. and tr. Kyril Fitzlyon. London, 1958; repr. Durham, 1995; selected prose and poetry, tr. Alexander Woronzoff-Dashkoff in Tomei, I.

Dashkova, Polina (b. 1960). Enrolled in Literary Institute in 1979. Poetry first published in *Iunost'* and *Sel'skaia molodezh'*. In early 1990s worked as head of the literature section of *Russkii kur'er*. Important figure in Post-Soviet genre of detective novel.

Writings: *Krov' nerozhdennykh*, 1996; *Prodazhnye tvari*, 1996; *Legkie shagi bezumiia*, 1997; *Nikto ne zaplachet*, 1997; *Mesto pod solntsem*, 1997; *Obraz vraga*, 1998; *Zolotoi pesok*, 1998; *Kriminal'nye voiny RUOP*, 1999; *Efirnoe vremia*, 1999. A list of her numerous works may be accessed through http://www.eksmo.ru.

Deisha, Elena Al'bertovna (pseudonym Georgii Peskov; b. Repman, 1885, Moscow; d. 1977, near Paris; married to Adrian Deisha; one son). Father well-known Moscow physician. Began writing stories at early age; graduate, Higher Courses for Women, Moscow. Emigrated with husband and son to France through Baltics, 1924. Published stories in émigré journals and newspapers, 1926–32, published two collections. Also wrote in French. Lived near Paris but apart from literary community.

Writings: "Svidanie," *Zveno* 161 (1926); "Shimpanze," *Zveno* 167, 168 (1926); "Vera, nadezhda, liubov'," *Zveno* 179 (1926); "Kurnosaia," *Zveno* 216 (1926); "Zhitets," *Zveno* 3 (1927); "Kum," *Sovremennye zapiski* 38 (1929); *Pamiati Tvoei: Rasskazy.* Paris, 1930; "Konrad Meistergauzen," *Illiustrirovannaia Rossiia* 310–12 (1931); "Zlaia vechnost'," *Sovremennye zapiski* 48 (1931), 49 (1932); "Meduza," in *Pestrye rasskazy,* ed. V. Aleksandrova. New York, 1953; *V rasseianii sushchie.* Paris, 1959; *Arc-en ciel.* Vaduz, 1968; "Sekret Anny Ivanovnoi," in *Russkaia zhenshchina v emigratsii.* San Francisco, 1970; "My i oni. Otryvok iz knigi *Razgovor s soboi,*" *Ekho* 1 (1978).

In translation: "The Customer" in *Tellers of Tales: One Hundred Short Stories,* ed. W. Somerset Maugham. New York, 1939.

Dmitrieva, Elizaveta (pseudonym Cherubina de Gabriak; b. 1887, d. 1928). Poet, prose writer, dramatist, and translator.

Writings: poems in *Apollon.* 1909–10; as E. Vasilievna with S. Marshak, *Teatr dlia detei. Sbornik p'es.* Krasnodar, 1922; *Novyi Robinzon.* Leningrad, 1924; *Avtobiografiia, Izbrannye stikhotvoreniia.* 1927; repr. Moscow, 1989. *Chelovek s luny.* Moscow and Leningrad, 1929; *Domik pod grushevym derevom, NM* 12 (1988). For more complete listing, see Tomei, I.

In translation: poems, tr. Barry P. Scherr in Tomei, I; "The Red Cloak" (and nine other poems), tr. T. Pachmuss, in Pachmuss *Modernism,* 250–60.

Dmitrieva, Faina Leonidovna (b. 1913, Hengdaohezi Station, Chinese Eastern Railway, China; d. 1990, Sverdlovsk, USSR; married name Kononova). Poet. Published in journals and planned a second book of poetry. In the 1950s went to the USSR.

Writings: *Tsvety v konverte.* Harbin, 1940.

Dmitrieva, Valentina Iovovna (b. 1859, Voronino, Saratov province; d. 1947, Sochi; married to revolutionary, Ershov). From family of educated serfs; taught in village school, but dismissed for populist sympathies. Entered Women's Medical Courses, St. Petersburg; graduated 1886, but exiled for four years, forbidden to practice. Wrote more than 70 realist stories and novels, 1880s to early 1900s, and autobiography of early life, 1930.

Writings: *Derevenskie rasskazy.* Moscow, 1892; "Po derevniam," *VE* 10–11 (1896); *Rasskazy.* St. Petersburg, 1896; *Rasskazy i povesti.* St. Petersburg, 1906; *Povesti i rasskazy.* St. Petersburg, 1909; *Chervonnyi khutor.* St. Petersburg, 1912; Khar'kov, 1925; *Rasskazy.* St. Petersburg, 1913; *Povesti i rasskazy,* 3 vols. Petrograd, 1916; *Tak bylo: Put' moei zhizni*: Moscow and Leningrad, 1930. *Povesti i rasskazy.* Moscow, 1976; *Povesti. Rasskazy.* Voronezh, 1983; "Pchely zhuzhzhat," in *Tol'ko chas,* ed. Uchenova. Moscow, 1988.

In translation: *Love's Anvil: A Romance of Northern Russia,* tr. Douglas Ashby. London, 1921; "After the Great Hunger" (extract from "Round the Villages: A Doctor's Memoir of an Epidemic," 1896), in Kelly *Anthology*; from *Notes of a Rural Doctor,* tr. Mildred Davies in Tomei, II.

Dolgorukaia, Princess Natal'ia Borisovna (b. Sheremet'eva, 1714; d. 1771). Memoirist. From a highly-placed aristocratic family; her exile with her husband, Ivan Dolgorukii, to Siberia, his execution and her subsequent impoverished existence form the substance of her memoirs (*Zapiski,* written in the late 1760s, and published in 1810).

Dolina, Veronika Arkad'evna (b. 1956, Moscow) Poet and singer-songwriter, lives in Moscow.

Writings: *Stikhi*. Paris, 1987; *Moia radost'*. Moscow, 1988; *To li koshka, to li ptitsa* . . . Tallin, 1988; *Vozdukhplavatel'*. Moscow, 1989; *Neletal'noe*. Moscow, 1993; *Viden'e o roze*. St. Petersburg, 1997.

Donbrovskaia, Rozaliia Iogannovna (b.1896, Russia – ?). Novelist.

Writings: *Vchera i segodnia*. Harbin, 1934; *Stepan Chertorogov*. Harbin, 1935; *Kniazhny Zardeevy*. Harbin, 1936, 1937; *Raspiataia Rossiia*. Harbin, 1938.

Drunina, Iuliia Vladimirovna (b. 1924, Moscow; d. 1992, Moscow). Poet and translator. Worked during the war as an officer in a medical battalion. Studied at Gorky Literary Institute in Moscow. Elected deputy of Supreme Soviet in 1989. In despair over personal loneliness and over the fate of her country, she took her own life.

Writings: *Trevoga: izbrannye stikhi 1942–1962*. Moscow, 1963; *Strana Iunost'*. Moscow, 1966; *Izb*, 2 vols. Moscow, 1989; *Polyn': stikhotvoreniia i poemy*. Moscow, 1989.

In translation: poems in *SovLit* 6 (1967), 5 (1985), and in *Land of the Soviets in Verse and Prose*, I, ed. Galina Dzyubenko. Moscow, 1982.

Durova, Nadezhda Andreevna (pseudonyms: A. Aleksandrov, Kavalerist-devitsa; b. 1783, Ukraine; d. 1866, Elabuga; married name Chernova). Soldier (1807) and officer (1808–16) in the Russian light cavalry. Author of prose fiction and autobiography. Best known for her *Notes of a Cavalry Maiden* (1836), an account of her service in the Napoleonic wars, first published 1836 in Pushkin's *Sovremennik* (The Contemporary) with his preface.

Writings: *Kavalerist-devitsa*. 1836; *God zhizni v Peterburge ili Nevygody tret'ego poseshcheniia*. 1838; "Nekotorye cherty iz detskikh let," *Literaturnoe pribavlenie k "Russkomu invalidu,"* 41, 44 (1838); *Zapiski Aleksandrova (Durovoi). Dobavlenie k "Devitse-kavalerist"*. Moscow, 1839; *Gudishki*, 4 vols. St. Petersburg, 1839; *Povesti i rasskazy*, 4 vols. St. Petersburg, 1839; *Igra sud'by, ili protivozakonnaia liubov'*. 1839; *Pavil'on*. 1839; *Iarchuk, sobaka-dukhovidets*. 1840; *Klad*. St. Petersburg, 1840; *Nurmeka*. 1840. *Ugol*. St. Petersburg, 1840. For more bibliographical information, see Mary Zirin's translation of Durova's *The Cavalry Maiden*.

In translation: "The Sulphur Spring," in Andrew; *The Cavalry Maiden: Journals of a Russian Officer in the Napoleonic Wars*, ed., intro., and tr. Mary Fleming Zirin. Bloomington, 1988; "From *Notes of Aleksandrov: Supplement to A Cavalry Maiden*," tr. Christine D. Tomei in Tomei, I.

Engel'gardt, Liudmila Nikolaevna (b. 1911, Smolensk, Russia; d. 1988, Tashkent, USSR, married name Sherever). Poet. Emigrated with widowed mother to Harbin and became a pharmaceutical chemist. In the 1930s moved to Shanghai, married a British subject. During World War II was interned in a Japanese camp for foreign nationals, where she lost a young son. After the war, she and her husband moved to Australia and soon divorced. She and her daughter returned to Shanghai and went to the USSR in 1956.

Writings: *Ostyvshie nochi*. Shanghai, 1941.

Fedorova, Nina (Antonina Fedorovna Podgorinova; b. 1895, Lokhvitsa, Ukraine; d. 1985, Oakland, California). Prose writer. Shortly before the Revolution moved to Harbin where in 1923 married a historian V. Riazanovskii. The family lived in Tianjin, and in 1938 moved to the USA, where in the 1940s she wrote short stories and several novels in English and in Russian, some of which depict Russian émigré life in China.

Writings: *Sem'ia* (Family). Boston, 1940 in English; New York, 1952 in Russian; *Deti* (Children). Boston, 1942 in English; Frankfurt, 1958 in Russian; *Zhizn'* (Life). Washington, 1964–6.

Fuks, Aleksandra Andreevna (b. c. 1805, Apekhtina; d. 1853, Kazan). Born into family with ties to merchantry; raised by aunt; married German-born physician in 1821; of five children, one daughter survived. Made Kazan home a literary center in 1830s and 1840s; in the 1830s traveled to Moscow and introduced to writers, including Pushkin. Published poems in Kazan and St. Petersburg journals. Combined literary interests with ethnography.

Writings: Pis'ma iz Moskvy v Kazan. Kazan, 1833; *Poezdka iz Kazani v Cheboksary.* Kazan, 1834; *Stikhotvoreniia.* Kazan, 1834; *Osnovanie goroda Kazani: Povest' v stikhakh vziataia iz tatarskikh predanii.* Kazan, 1836; *Ona pokhudela.* Kazan, 1837; with P. A. Zhmakin, *Tsarevna Nesmeiana.* Kazan, 1838; "Chernaia koza," *BdCh* 28 (1838); *Zapiski o chuvashakh i cheremisakh Kazanskoi gubernii.* Kazan, 1840; *Kniazhna Khabiba.* Kazan, 1841.

Gan, Elena ("Zeneida R-va"; b. Fadeeva, 1814; d. 1842; married Petr Gan, an artillery captain, 1830). Two daughters, one son; both daughters became writers (Elena Blavatskaia and Vera Zhelikhovskaia). Gan's friendship with Osip Senkovskii, the notorious author and ed. of *BdCh*, led her to publish most of her work in that journal beginning with *Ideal* in 1837. Despite her slim literary output (only 11 tales in all), she was regarded as one of Russia's most famous female authors by Vissarion Belinsky, Ivan Turgenev, and others.

Writings: "Ideal", *BdCh*, 1837; *Vospominaniia Zheleznovodska.* 1837; *Dzhellaledin, BdCh* 1837; *Utballa.* 1838; *Sud sveta, BdCh* 1839; *Teofaniia Abbiadzhio, BdCh* 1841; *Liubin'ka, OZ* 1842; *PSS.* 6 vols. St. Petersburg, 1905; *Ideal,* in *Russkaia romanticheskaia povest',* ed. V. I. Sakharov. Moscow, 1992; *Sud sveta,* in *Dacha; Naprasnyi dar,* in *Serdtsa.*

In translation: The Ideal, Society's Judgement in Andrew; "From *The Reminiscences of Zheleznovodsk*," tr. Veronica Shapovalov in Tomei, I; excerpt from *Sud sveta* in Bisha et al.

Ganina, Maiia Anatol' evna (b. 1927, Moscow). Writer of prose fiction, travelogues, and essays. Received a technical education. She graduated from the Gorky Literary Institute in 1954, the same year she published her first novella. Explores subjects ranging from love relationships to the conflict between personal life and professional career. In addition to her fiction, she has authored a sociological study of women in an industrial town on the Kama River.

Writings: Pervye ispytaniia. Moscow, 1955; first published in NM (1954); *Razgovor o shchast'e: ocherki i rasskazy.* Moscow, 1959; *Matvei i Shurka: rasskazy.* Moscow, 1962; *Ia ishchu tebia, cheloveka: rasskazy i povest'.* Moscow, 1963; *Slovo o zerne gorchichnom.* Moscow, 1965, 1971; *Rasskazy.* Moscow, 1966; *Zachem spilili kashtany?* Moscow, 1967; *Zapiski o pogranichnikakh.* Moscow, 1969; *K sebe vozvrashchaius' izdaleka: ocherki.* Moscow, 1971; "Teatral'naia aktrisa," NM 10 (1971); "Tiapkin i Lesha: povest'," *Znamia* 12 (1971); Moscow, 1977; *Povest' o zhenshchine: povesti, rasskazy, ocherki.* Moscow, 1973; *Dal'naia poezdka: rasskazy.* Moscow, 1975; *Sozvezdie bliznetsov: povesti i rasskazy.* Moscow, 1980, 1984; *Dorogi Rossii: vstrechi na dorogakh Rossii s zhivshimi nedavno i nyne zhivushchimi.* Moscow, 1981; *Izbrannoe: rasskazy i povesti.* Moscow, 1983; "Esli budem zhit'," *Oktiabr'* 6 (1983); *Sto zhiznei moikh: roman, povest'.* Moscow, 1983; "Poka zhivu-nadeius'," *Oktiabr'* 10 (1986) and 11 (1987); *Poka zhivu-nadeius': roman, rasskazy, publitsistika.* Moscow, 1987, 1989; *Kamazonki na rabote i doma (Ocherki o zhenshchinakh Naberezhnykh Chelnov).* Moscow, (n.d.); "Opravdanie zhizni. Sub"ektivnaia epopeia," *Moskva* 10–12 (1995).

In translation: The Road to Nirvana. Moscow, 1971; "Stage Actress," tr. Helena Goscilo in *Balancing Acts.*

Gertsyk, Adelaida (b. 1874, d. 1925). Poet, prose writer, translator.

Writings: "Ideal," *Mir bozhii* 11 (1898); "Religiia krasoty," *RBog* 1 (1899); "Iz mira detskikh igr," *Russkaia shkola* 3 (1906); "Emil Vekharn. Stikhi o sovremennosti v perevode V. Briusova," *Vesy* 8 (1906); "Stikhotvoreniia," *RMysl'* 8 (1909); *Stikhotvoreniia.* Moscow, 1910; "O tom chego ne bylo," *RMysl'* 5 (1911); "Aleksei Remizov. Posolon," *RMysl'* 5 (1911); *Stikhi i proza*, 2 vols. Moscow, 1993.

In translation: from *About That Which Never Was* and poems, tr. Kathleen Dillon in Tomei, I.

Ginzburg, Evgeniia Semenovna (b. 1904, Moscow; d. 1977, Moscow). Memoirist and educator. A political activist and teacher who had rejected her middle-class family background for a life dedicated to the Communist Party, Ginzburg's new world fell apart when she and her first husband, a prominent Party bureaucrat, were arrested in 1937. Her surviving son from this marriage, Vasilii Aksyonov, later became famous as a talented dissident writer. She endured 18 years in jail, camp, and exile, and bore coherent, eloquent witness to her ordeal in the two-volume memoir *Krutoi marshrut* (the first volume is translated as *Journey into the Whirlwind*, the second as *Within the Whirlwind*).

Writings: *Krutoi marshrut: Khronika vremen kul'ta lichnosti*, 2 vols. Milan, 1967, 1979; Frankfurt/Main, 1967; New York, 1985; Riga, 1989; Moscow, 1990.

In translation: *Journey into the Whirlwind*, tr. Max Hayward and Paul Stevenson. New York, 1967, 1989; *Within the Whirlwind*, tr. Ian Boland. New York, 1981, 1988.

Ginzburg, Lydiia Iakovlevna (b. 1902, Odessa, d. 1990). Literary and cultural critic, writer, memoirist. The lone female member among the influential Formalist group, Ginzburg developed into a prominent literary scholar whose innovative critical work focused on the complex interactions between literary creation, life experience, and spiritual values. A keen interpreter of non-fiction, Ginzburg also produced a trenchant journal-memoir of her own experiences and observations on Soviet culture, *Chelovek za pis'mennym stolom* (At One's Desk, 1982), and an extraordinary analysis in fiction of the Leningrad siege, *Zapiski blokadnogo cheloveka* (Notes of a Blockade Survivor, 1984). In the 1980s Ginzburg truly flourished as a public intellectual, at last able to publish her more provocative and personalized writing, and serving as an intellectual conduit between pre- and post-Stalinist generations of the intelligentsia.

Writings: *Tvorcheskii put' Lermontova.* Leningrad, 1940. *"Byloe i dumy Gertsena.* Leningrad, 1957. *O lirike.* Leningrad, 1964; 2nd edn, 1974, 1997; *O psikhologicheskoi proze.* Leningrad, 1971, 2nd edn, 1977, 3rd edn, 1999; *Chelovek za pis'mennym stolom.* Leningrad, 1982, 1989; *O literaturnom geroe.* Leningrad, 1979; *O starom i novom.* Leningrad, 1982; *Literatura v poiskakh real'nosti.* Leningrad, 1987; "Zapiski blokadnogo cheloveka," *Neva* 1 (1984); *Pretvorenie opyta.* Riga, Leningrad, 1991; Moscow, 1995; *Zapisnye knizhki: novoe sobranie.* Moscow, 1999.

In translation: "'The Human Document' and the Formation of Character," in *The Semiotics of Russian Cultural History*, ed. Alexander D. Nakhimovsky and Alice Stone Nakhimovsky. Ithaca, NY, 1985; *On Psychological Prose*, tr. Judson Rosengrant. Princeton, NJ, 1991; *Blockade Diary* tr. Alan Myers. London, 1995; from *The Journals*, tr. Jane Gary Harris in Tomei, II.

Gippius, Zinaida (pseudonyms: Anton Krainii, Tovarishch German, Lev Pushchin, Roman Arenskii, Anton Kirsha; b. 1869, d. 1945). Poet, dramatist, short story writer, novelist, literary critic.

Writings: *Novye liudi: Rasskazy, pervaia kniga.* St. Petersburg, 1896; *Zerkala: Vtoraia kniga rasskazov.* St. Petersburg, 1898; *Pobediteli.* St. Petersburg, 1898; *Sviataia krov'. P'esa.* St. Petersburg, 1901; *Tret'ia kniga rasskazov.* St. Petersburg, 1902; *Sobranie stikhov: 1889–1903.* Moscow, 1904; *Alyi mech: Rasskazy, chetvertaia kniga.* St. Petersburg, 1906; with D. Merezhkovskii and D. Filosofov, *Le Tsar et la Révolution.* Paris, 1907; *Chernoe po belomu: Piataia kniga rasskazov.* St. Petersburg, 1908; as Anton Krainii, *Literaturnyi dnevnik 1899–1907.* St. Petersburg, 1908; *Sobranie stikhov: Kniga vtoraia, 1903–1909.* Moscow, 1910; *Chertova kukla.* Moscow, 1911; *Lunnye murav'i. Shestaia kniga rasskazov.* Moscow, 1912; *Roman-Tsarevich.* Moscow, 1913; *Kak my voinam pisali i chto oni nam otvechali. Kniga podarok.* Moscow, 1915; *Zelenoe kol'tso. P'esa.* Petrograd, 1916; *Poslednie stikhi, 1914–1918.* St. Petersburg, 1918; *Pokhodnye pesni.* Warsaw, 1920; *Nebesnoe slovo. Rasskazy, 1897–1900.* Paris, 1921; *Stikhi: Dnevnik 1911–1921.* Berlin, 1922; *Zhivye litsa.* Prague, 1925; *Sinnaia kniga. Peterburgskii dnevnik, 1914–18.* Belgrade, 1929; *Siianiia.* Paris, 1938; ed. with Dmitrii Merezhkovskii, *Literaturnyi smotr: svobodnyi.* Paris, 1939; *Dmitrii Merezhkovskii.* Paris, 1951.

In translation: "Song" and twenty-one more poems, in Markov and Sparks, 56–89; "Heavenly Words" and twelve stories in *Selected Works of Zinaida Hippius*, ed. and tr. Temira Pachmuss, Urbana, 1972; *Between Paris and St. Petersburg: Selected Diaries of Zinaida Hippius*, tr. Temira Pachmuss. Munich, 1972; "Choosing a Sack," in Kelly *Utopias*; poems, tr. Christine Borowec in Tomei, II. For more complete listing, see Tomei, II and *DRWW*.

Glinka, Avdot'ia Pavlovna (b. Golenishcheva-Kutuzova, 1795, St. Petersburg; d. 1863, Tver'). Born into old gentry family; well-educated; married Fedor Glinka in 1829; lived in Moscow 1835–53, St. Petersburg in late 1850s, and Tver' until her death. Salon hostess, poet and translator of German poetry, assisted husband in literary work. Devout and charitable, wrote on religious subjects. Published poems in conservative literary journals and almanacs. After 1850s turned to prose.

Writings: *Pesni o Kolokole F. Shillera.* Moscow, 1832; *Zhizn' Presviatoi devy Bogoroditsy iz knig Chet'i-Minei.* Moscow, 1840; 16th edn, Moscow, 1915; *Stikhotvoreniia Shillera. Zum Dichters 100 Jahrigem Geburtsfest.* St. Petersburg, 1859.

Golovina, Alla Sergeevna (b. Baroness Steiger, 1909, Nikolaevka, near Kiev; d. 1987, Brussels; married 1) sculptor Alexander Golovin, 1929; 2) Philippe Gilles de Pelichy, 1951; one son). Swiss aristocratic family in Ukraine since 1815, father Duma member, brother poet Anatoly Steiger. Emigrated with family through Constantinople, 1920; in Czechoslovakia, 1921; attended Russian school, Moravská Třebová. Married Golovin, 1929; son writer Sergei Golovin. Degree, Russian history and philology, Charles University, 1931; member, Alfred Bem's "Skit," co-ed. almanac *Skit* 2 (1934); participant Khodasevich's "Perekrestok"; published verse collection, 1935. To Paris, 1935. Frequented literary café "Kupol"; friendship with Tsvetaeva. Joined parents, Switzerland, 1939, for duration of World War II. Married Belgian citizen, 1951; to Belgium, 1955. From 1950s, wrote mainly short stories, published little; most of her books appeared posthumously. Visited USSR, met Nadezhda Mandel'stam, 1967.

Writings: *Lebedinaia karusel': Stikhi 1929–1934.* Berlin, 1935; "Chuzhie deti," *Sovremennye zapiski* 68 (1939); "Letnaia koloniia," *Kovcheg* 2 (1942); "Asia: Glava iz Romana Zagrzhevskii," *Opyty* 1 (1953) "Iz perepiski I. A. i V. N. Buninykh s A. Golovinoi (1942–1953)," in *I. A. Bunin i russkaia literatura XX v.* Moscow, 1995.

Recent editions: *Gorodskoi angel: izbrannye stikhi*. Brussels, 1989; *Nochnye ptitsy*. Brussels, 1990. *Villa "Nadezhda": stikhi, rasskazy*. Moscow, 1992.

Gorbanevskaia, Natal'ia Evgen'eva (b. 1936, Moscow). Poet, journalist, political activist. Emigrated from USSR, 1975; lives in Paris.

Writings: Stikhi. Frankfurt, 1969; *Poberezh'e*. Ann Arbor, MI, 1973; *Tri tetradi stikhotvorenii*. Bremen, 1975; *Pereletaia snezhnuiu granitsu*. Paris, 1979; *Angel dereviannyi*. Ann Arbor, MI, 1982; *Chuzhie kamni*. New York, 1983; *Peremennaia oblachnost'*. Paris, 1985; *Gde i kogda*. Paris, 1985; *Tsvet vereska*. Tenafly, NJ, 1993; *Kto chem poet*. Moscow, 1997; *Polden'*. Frankfurt, 1970 (prose). For complete listing, see Tomei, II.

In translation: Poems, The Trial, Prison, tr. Daniel Weissbort. Oxford, 1972; *Red Square at Noon*, tr. Alexander Lieven. Harmondsworth, 1972; *Contemporary Russian Poetry*, 100–11.

Gorlanova, Nina (b. 1947, near Perm). First published fiction in 1980 after abandoning graduate study in philology. After initial success, her works were denied publication until the late 1980s for ideological reasons. Winner of the Russian Booker Prize for 1996.

Writings: Raduga kazhdyi den': rasskazy. Perm, 1987; "Istoriia ozera Veselogo" and "Stariki," in *Ne pomniashchaia zla*; "Kazachii sud," in *Chisten'kaia zhizn'*. "Novella," in *Eros, syn Afrodity*, comp. S. Markov. Moscow, 1991; "Protokol," "Novyi Podkolesin," "Reshenie Valeriia," "Gamburgskii schet," and "Chto-to khoroshee," in *Abstinentki*. Moscow, 1991; "Pokaiannye dni, ili V ozhidanii kontsa sveta," in *Novye amazonki*; "Liubov' v rezinovykh perchatkakh," in *Chego khochet zhenshchina: sbornik zhenskikh rasskazov*; with Viacheslav Buker, "Uchitel' ivrita," *Zvezda* 5 (1994); with Viacheslav Buker, "Roman Vospitaniia," *NM* 8–9 (1995); "Muzhchiny v moei zhizni," *Ural'skaia nov'* 1–2 (1996); *Rodnye liudi: rasskazy*. Perm, 1996; "Vsem postradavshim ot AO 'MMM'," *Piatii ugol* (Cheliabinsk), (December 25, 1996); *Vsia Perm'*. Perm, 1996; "Chetyre rasskaza," *Den' i noch'* 4 (1997). Includes, "Iarostnye kartezhniki," "Liubov' deputata," "Zolotoi kliuchik," and "Diadia"; "Lav stori," *Zvezda* 11 (1998); *Liubov' v rezinovykh perchatkakh*. St. Petersburg, 1999. *Dom so vsemi neudobstvami: povesti*. Moscow, 2000.

In translation: "Confessional Days: In Anticipation of the End of the World," tr. Masha Gessen in *Half a Revolution: Contemporary Fiction by Russian Women*.

Gornaia, Liubov'. Poet.

Writings: Inei. Harbin, 1921.

Gorodetskaia, Nadezhda Danilovna (b. 1901, Moscow; d. 1985, Witney, England). Father journalist D. M. Gorodetskii. Emigrated through Constantinople to Zagreb, 1919; studied Zagreb University. To Paris, 1924; Studio Franco-Russe; friendly with writers, religious philosophers Kuprin, Mat' Mariia, Berdiaev, Paul Bazin. Published two novels, several stories in Russian and French. To England, studied theology, College of the Ascension, Birmingham, and Oxford, 1934–5; published thesis in English, *The Humiliated Christ*, 1938; Ph.D., Oxford, 1944. Taught Oxford, 1941–56; chair, Russian Dept., University of Liverpool. British citizenship; made several visits to USSR.

Writings: "Samoubiistvo: iz dnevnika bezhenki," *Illiustrirovannaia Rossiia* 84 (1926); "Finiki," *Zveno* 228 (1927); *Neskvoznaia nit'*. Paris, 1929; *Mara*. Paris, 1931; "La vie et l'oeuvre de Péguy," in *Les cahiers de la quinzaine*, 1931; with Jean Maxence, *Charles Peguy. Textes suivie de debats au Studio franco-russe*. Paris, 1931; "Belye kryl'ia," *Volia Rossii* 3 (1929); "L'exil des enfants," in *Les cahiers de la quinzaine*, 1936; *The Humiliated Christ in Modern Russian Thought*. London and New York, 1938; *Saint Tikhon Zadonsky, Inspirer of Dostoevsky*. London, 1951.

In translation: *Les mains vides*, intro. A. Kuprin. Paris, 1931; *Les ailes blanches*, tr. M.E. and W. Vogt. Paris, 1932.

Grekova, I. (pen name for Elena Sergeevna Venttsel; b. Dolgintsova, 1907, Revel', Tallin). Prose writer, mathematician. Married D. A. Venttsel, a ballistics expert, three children. Graduate University of Leningrad. Taught at Zhukovsky Military Aviation Academy in Moscow. One of few women scientists to earn the doktorat. Resigned in 1967 in connection with her novella *Na ispytaniiakh*.

Writings: *Pod fonarem*. Moscow, 1966; *Seryozha u okna*. Moscow, 1976; *An'ia i Man'ia*. Moscow, 1978; *Vdovii parokhod*. Paris, 1983, Moscow, 1998; *Kafedra*. Moscow, 1983; *Na ispytaniiakh*. Moscow, 1990; *Svezho predanie*. Tenafly, NJ, 1995; Moscow, 1998; *Damskii master*. Moscow, 1998.

In translation: "The Ladies' Hairdresser," tr. L. Gregg, *RLT* 5 (1973), 223–65; repr. *Ardis Anthology of Recent Russian Literature*. Ann Arbor, MI, 1975, 223–64; *ibid.*, tr. Brian Thomas Oles in *Dialogues*, 44–87; "One Summer in the City," tr. Lauren Leighton, *RLT* 11 (1975), 146–67; *ibid.*, tr. Sigrid McLaughlin in *The Image of Women in Contemporary Soviet Fiction*, 18–48; "The Faculty," tr. Melinda MacLean, *SovLit* 9 (1979), 3–107; 10 (1979), 16–128; "The Hotel Manager," tr. Michel Petrov, in *Russian Women: Two Stories*. New York, 1983, 65–304; *The Ship of Widows*, tr. and intro. Cathy Porter. London, 1985; "Real Life in Real Terms," *Moscow News* 24 (1987), 11; "Masters of Their Own Lives," tr. Dobrochna Dyrcz-Freeman, in *Soviet Women Writing*, 85–105; "Under the Street Lamp," tr. Dobrochna Dyrcz-Freeman, in *Russia According to Women: Literary Anthology*, comp. and preface Marina Ledkovsky. Tenafly, NJ, 1991 45–66; "Rothschild's Violin", tr. Maureen Riley in Tomei, II, 1338–48.

Guro, Elena Genrikhovna (pseudonym Eleonora von Notenberg; b. 1877, St. Petersburg; d. 1913, Uusikirkko, Finland). Poet, prose writer, dramatist, artist. A painter by training, Guro became the only woman to occupy a prominent place in early Futurist literature.

Writings: *Sharmanka*. St. Petersburg, 1909; *Osennii son*. St. Petersburg, 1912; *Nebesnye verbliuzhata*. St. Petersburg, 1914; *Selected Prose and Poetry*, ed. A. Ljunggren and N. A. Nilssen. Stockholm, 1988; *Selected Writings from the Archives*, ed. A. Ljunggren and N. Gourianova. Stockholm, 1995; *Sochineniia*. Oakland, CA, 1996.

In translation: *Soviet Poets and Poetry*, ed. A. Kaun. Berkeley, 1943; *The Little Camels of the Sky*, tr. K. O'Brien Ann Arbor, MI, 1983; from her diary and from *Hurdy-Gurdy*, tr. Juliette Stapanian-Apkarian in Tomei, I.

Iankovskaia, Viktoriia Iur'evna (b. 1909, Vladivostok; d. 1996, San Francisco). Poet, short story writer.

Writings: *Eto bylo v Koree*, Harbin, 1935; *Po stranam rasseianiia*. New York, 1978.

Ievleva, Varvara Nikolaevna (b. 1900, Russia; d. 1960, USSR). Poet, journalist. Emigrated first to Harbin, then Shanghai. Went to the USSR after World War II.

Ignatova, Elena Alekseevna (b. 1947, Leningrad). Poet, screenwriter; lives in Jerusalem.

Writings: *Stikhi o prichastnosti*. Paris, 1975; *Zdes', gde zhivu*. Leningrad, 1983; *Nebesnoe zarevo*. Jerusalem, 1992; *Zapiski o Peterburge: ocherki istorii goroda*. St. Petersburg, 1997.

In translation: poems in *Lives in Transit*, 299–300.

Il'ina, Natal'ia Iosifovna (b. 1914, St. Petersburg; d. 1994, Moscow). Satirist, journalist, memoirist, novelist, and autobiographer. Married to linguist A. A. Reformatskii. Fled with her family to Harbin after the Revolution. Grew up in Harbin and Shanghai where she became a feuilletonist for émigré press. Later worked for pro-Soviet press. Returned to USSR in 1947. Graduated from Literary Institute in

Moscow. Began writing satire for *Krokodil*. In last decades of her life turned to literary memoirs, writing reminiscences of Akhmatova, Vertinskii, Chukovskii, and her husband Reformatskii.

Writings: *Inymi glazami: Ocherki shangkhaiskoi zhizni*. Shanghai, 1945; *Vozvrashchenie*. Moscow, 1957–66; *Vnimanie opasnost'!* Moscow, 1960; *Ne nado ovatsii!* Moscow, 1964; *Chto-to tut ne kleitsia*. Moscow, 1968; *Tut vse napisano*. Moscow, 1971; *Svetiashchiesia tablo*. Moscow, 1974; *Sud' by*. Moscow, 1980; *Dorogi*. Moscow, 1983; *Dorogi i sud' by*. Moscow, 1985, 1988, 1991; *Belogorskaia krepost'*. Moscow, 1989.

In translation: "Anna Akhmatova in the Last Years of her Life," *Soviet Studies in Literature* (Fall, 1977), 27–76; "Five Feuilletons," tr. N.V. Galichenko and C. Partridge, *RLT* 14 (1976), 193–223; "A Haunting Spectre," in *The Best of Ogonyok*, tr. Cathy Porter. London, 1990, 203–8; "Repairing Our Car," tr. Steven W. Nielsen in *Soviet Women Writing*, 145–52.

Il'nek, Nina. Poet.

Inber, Vera Mikhailovna (b. 1890, Odessa; d. 1972, Moscow; married to I. D. Strashun, MD). From intelligentsia family; studied history and philology at the Odessa Higher Courses for Women, left during 2nd year; first published 1910; poet, writer, journalist; member of Union of Soviet Writers, 1934; member of CPSU, 1944; Stalin Prize for *Pulkovskii meridian, Pochti tri goda*, 1946.

Writings: *Pechal'noe vino*. Paris, 1914; *Gor'kaia uslada*. Moscow, 1917; *Mesto pod solntsem*. Khar'kov, 1928; *Amerika v Parizhe*. Khar'kov, 1928; *Soiuz materei. Komediia*. Moscow, 1938; *Pulkovskii meridian*. Moscow, 1942; *Pochti tri goda. Leningradskii dnevnik*. Moscow, 1944; *Kak ia byla malen'kaia*. Moscow, 1954; *Vdokhnovenie i masterstvo*. Moscow, 1957; *Aprel'. Stikhi o Lenine*. Moscow, 1960; *Stranitsy dnei perebiraia. Iz dnevnikov i zapisnykh knizhek*. Moscow, 1967.

In translation: "Pulkovo Meridian," in *Russian Literature since the Revolution*, ed. Joshua Kunitz. New York, 1948 and in *Land of the Soviets in Verse and Prose*, ed. G. Dzyubenko. Moscow, 1982; "Nor-Bibi's Crime" and "Spring Cleaning," in *Loaf of Sugar and Other Stories*, ed. Yvonne Kapp. London, 1957; *Leningrad Diary*, tr. Serge M. Wolff and Rachael Grieve. New York, 1971; "Garlic in His Suitcase," tr. M. Schwartz, *Literary Review* 34 (Winter 1991), 259–66; from *A Place in the Sun*, tr. Mary Nichols in Tomei, II.

Iskrenko, Nina Iur'evna (b. 1951, Petrovsk; d. 1996, Moscow). Poet. Studied physics at Moscow University, lived in Moscow until her death.

Writings: *Ili: Stikhi i teksty*. Moscow, 1991; *Referendum*. Moscow, 1991; *Neskol'ko slov*. France, 1991; *Pravo na oshibku*. 1995; *Interpretatsiia momenta: stikhi i teksty*. Moscow, 1996; *Neposredstvennaia zhizn'*. Moscow, 1997; *O glavnom*. Moscow, 1998; *Rasskazy o liubvi i smerti: Zhitie Lysogo i Vermisheli* (prose). Moscow, 1999.

In translation: "Special Troikas: A Corps," *Conjunctions* 23 (1994), 145–49; *Women's View, Glas* 3 (1992), 151–61; *Third Wave*, 89–100; *Mapping Codes, Five Fingers Review* 8–9. San Francisco, CA, 1990, 32–6, 174–85; Todd and Hayward, 1019–22.

Iunge, Ekaterina Fedorovna (b. 1843, d. 1913). Artist, half-sister of Kamenskaia, whose memoir, *Vospominaniia (1843–1860 gg.)* came out in 1914, after partial publication in 1905 and 1911.

Izvekova, Mariia Evgrafovna (married name Bedriaga; b. 1789?, d. 1830). Daughter of an army officer; prolific author of novels, poetry, fiction.

Writings: *Emiliia, ili pechal'nye sledstviia bezrassudnoi liubvi*. Moscow, 1806; *Milena, ili redkii primer velikodushiia*. St. Petersburg, 1811; and *Al'fons i Florestina, ili shchastlivyi oborot*. Moscow, 1807.

Kabysh, Inna. (b. Moscow). Poet, teacher of literature.

Writings: *Lichnye trudnosti* (1994); *Detskii mir.* Moscow, 1996; poems in *Ogonek* 10 (1990), 16; *NM* 1 (1996), 41–9; *DN* 6 (1997), 74–7; *DN* 8 (1996), 8–12; *DN* 3 (1994), 72–5.

Kamenskaia, Mariia Fedorovna (b. Tolstaia, 1817, d. 1898). Author of sporadic fiction based on her own life or family tradition ("Piat'desiat let nazad," *Otechestvennye zapiski* 10–12 [1860] and "Znakomye," *Vremia* 10 [1861]). Her memoir, "Vospominaniia," was first published in *Istoricheskii vestnik* 1–10, 12 (1894) and has recently been reissued in Russia (Moscow, 1991).

Katerli, Nina Semenovna (b. 1934, Leningrad). Holds a degree in engineering from a technical institute in her native St. Petersburg (Leningrad). First prose published in 1973. Activist against anti-Semitism.

Writings: *Okno: rasskazy.* Leningrad, 1981; "Treugol'nik Barsukova," *Glagol* 3 (1981); "Polina," *Neva* 1 (1984); *Tsvetnye otkrytki: rasskazy i povesti.* Leningrad, 1986; "Kurzal," *Zvezda* 11 (1986); "Zhara na severe. Povest," *Zvezda* 4 (1988); "Solntse za steklom," *Zvezda* 4 (1989); *Kurzal. Povesti.* Leningrad, 1990; "Sennaia ploshchad'," *Zvezda* 7 (1991), (reissue of "Treugol'nik Barsukova"). Published separately, St. Petersburg, 1992; *Isk.* Samara, 1998; (ms. 1991); "Sindrom 'P.' Povest'," *Zvezda* 11 (1994); "Piramida Tsukermana," *Zvezda* 10 (1995); "V-4-52-21," *Zvezda* 10 (1997); "Vozvrashchenie," *Zvezda* 4 (1998); "Tot svet," *Zvezda* 2, 3 (1999); *Tot svet.* Moscow, 2000.

In translation: "The Profited Land," in Hoisington, *Out Visiting*; "The Barsukov Triangle," tr. David Lapeza in *The Barsukov Triangle, the Two-Toned Blond and Other Stories*; "Between Spring and Summer" and "The Farewell Light," tr. Helena Goscilo and Valeria Sajez in *Balancing Acts*; "The Monster," tr. Bernard Meares in *Soviet Women Writing*; "Victory," in *Soviet Literary Culture in the 1970s*, ed. and tr. Anatoly Vishnevsky and Michael Biggins. Gainesville, FL, 1993; "Slowly the Old Woman . . .," tr. John Beebe in *Lives in Transit*.

Khaindrova, Lydiia Iulianovna (originally in Georgian, Khaindrava; b. 1910, Odessa, Russia; d. 1986, Krasnodar, USSR; married name Serebrova). Poet.

Writings: *Stupeni.* Harbin, 1939; *Kryl'ia.* Harbin, 1941; *Razdum'ia.* Harbin, undated, early 1940s; *Na rasput'e.* Shanghai, 1943; *Serdtse.* Shanghai, 1947; *Daty, daty.* Krasnodar, 1976; *Shchedrost'.* Krasnodar, 1986.

Kheraskova, Elizaveta Vasil'evna (b. Neronova, 1737, d. 1809). Poet. Married neoclassical poet and Freemason Mikhail Kheraskov in 1759. Published a small number of poems in journals such as *Poleznoe uveselenie* and *Aonidy.* Mentor to Anna Labzina (see below).

Khvoshchinskaia, Nadezhda Dmitrievna (pseudonyms: V. Krestovskii-psevdonim, V. Porechnikov, N. Vozdvizhenskii; b. 1820?, Riazan' province; d. 1889, St. Petersburg, married name Zaionchkovskaia [m. 1865]). Poet, prose writer, essayist. Began her literary career publishing poetry in the 1840s. Much of her prose satirizes the provinces (e.g. her 1850s trilogy, *Provintsiia v starye gody*), and many of her works are deeply ironic.

Writings: *SS V. Krestovskogo (Psevdonim)*. 5 vols. St. Petersburg, 1892, and 1912–13; Also published literary criticism under various pseudonyms, including the series "Provintsial'nye pis'ma o nashei literature" ("Provincial Letters about Our Literature" in *Otechestvennye zapiski*, 1861–3).

Recent editions: *Povesti i rasskazy.* 1963, 1984; *Svidanie*, in *Svidanie*; poems in *Poety 1840–1850-kh godov*, ed. B. Ia. Bukhshtab. Leningrad, 1972; Bannikov; *Tsaritsy muz.*

In translation: *On the Way: A Sketch*, in Andrew; *After the Flood*; tr. Karla Thomas Solomon in Tomei, I; *The Boarding-School Girl*, tr. Karen Rosneck. Evanston, IL, 2000.

Khvoshchinskaia, Sof'ia Dmitrievna (pseudonym Iv. Vesen'ev b. 1828?, Riazan province, d. 1865.) Artist, poet, critic, author. A talented painter and author, she is deservedly known for her fine irony and psychological probing.

Writings: *Znakomye liudi*, *OZ* 91 (1856); *Nasledstvo tetushki*, *OZ* 3 (1858); *Mudrennyi chelovek*, *OZ* 6–8 (1861); *Vospominaniia institutskoi zhizni*, *RV* 9–10 (1861); *Gorodskie i derevenskie*, *OZ* 3–4 (1863); also appears in *Svidanie*.

In translation: *Reminiscences of Institute Life*, tr. Valentina Baslyk, in Clyman and Vowles.

Khvostova, Aleksandra Petrovna (b. 1767, d. 1852). Author of prose, prose poems, and translations. Niece of Elizaveta Kheraskova (see above). Hostess of a salon in the 1800s. Major works include the runaway success *Otryvki* (St. Petersburg, 1796).

Klimenko-Ratgauz, Tat'iana (b. Ratgauz, 1909, Berlin; d. 1993, Riga; married: 1) Aseev; 2) actor V. V. Klimenko, 1936). Father poet Daniil M. Ratgauz; raised in Kiev, Moscow; emigrated with father to Berlin, 1921; father published two books of poetry, 1922, 1927. To Prague, 1923; degree, College of English; studied dramatic studio of L. S. Il'iashenko; performed in local productions of Gorky, Meierhold; member, Czech Union of Russian Actors, 1927. Published first poems in *Studencheskie gody*, 1925; from late 1920s, member, Alfred Bem's "Skit poetov," literary circle "Daliborka". Joined Russian Dramatic Theater, Riga, 1935–46; with husband Klimenko applied for Soviet citizenship, refused. Poetry published in Soviet Russia since late 1970s; first vol. of collected verse, 1987, incl. memoir of father.

Recent editions: *Vsia moia zhizn': stikhotvoreniia i vospominaniia ob otse*. Riga, 1987.

Kniazhevich, Lydiia (Lydiia Nikolaevna Ul'shtein; b. 1895, Saratov, Russia; d. 1939, Shanghai). Novelist, playwright, actress.

Writings: *Liubov' po ob'iavleniiu*. Shanghai, 1930s; *Model' No. 115*. Shanghai, 1930s; *Zhenshchina, o kotoroi ne govoriat*. Shanghai, 1930s.

Kniazhnina-Sumarokova, Ekaterina Aleksandrovna (b. 1746, d. 1797). Poet. Daughter of the major neoclassical poet Aleksandr Sumarokov, married to the playwright, poet and translator Iakov Kniazhnin. Hostess of an important salon: undoubtedly the author of works that have not survived.

Knorring, Irina Nikolaevna (b. 1906, Elshanka, Samara province; d. 1943, Paris; married poet Iurii Bek-Sofiev, 1928; one son). Aristocratic family, father historian; raised in Khar'kov; writing poetry at age of eight. Emigrated with family, 1920; lived Tuapse, Simferopol, Sevastopol, Bizerte (Tunisia), completed high school education. To Paris, 1925; studied Franco-Russian Institute; active in Paris literary circles. Diagnosed with diabetes, 1927; married Bek-Sofiev, 1928; son, 1929. Published 1st vol., 1931, 2nd, 1939, despite illness; poems written during German occupation published by father Nikolai N. Knorring, 1949. Bek-Sofiev repatriated after war, father in 1955, to Alma-Ata; organized publication of Knorring's poetry in *Prostor*, 1962, *Den' poezii*, 1965, and as separate vol., *Novye stikhi*, 1967.

Writings: *Stikhi o sebe*. Paris, 1931; *Okna na sever*. Paris, 1939; *Posle vsego*. Paris, 1949; *Novye stikhi*. Alma-Ata, 1967.

Recent editions: *Posle vsego: Stikhi 1920–1942*. Alma-Ata, 1993.

Kollontai, Aleksandra Mikhailovna (b. Domontovich, 1872, St. Petersburg; d. 1952, Moscow; married: 1) cousin V. Kollontai, 1893 [separated 1898, one son]; 2) P. Dybenko, Commissar of Navy, 1918 [separated 1922]). Illegitimate daughter of aristocratic parents; studied economics in Zurich; began writing on women's emancipation, 1905. Joined Mensheviks, 1903; Bolsheviks, 1915; arrested by Provisional Government, 1917. After Revolution, became highest-ranking woman in Lenin's government as Commissar for Social Welfare (1917–18); head of Women's Department of Communist Party (*Zhenotdel*), 1921–2; dismissed 1922 for membership in Workers' Opposition. 1922–30, diplomatic service in Norway and Mexico; 1930–45, Soviet ambassador to Sweden. In 1920s turned to fiction; writings after 1927 less interesting.

Writings: *Sotsial'nye osnovy zhenskogo voprosa*. St. Petersburg, 1909; "Novaia zhenshchina," *Sovremennyi mir* 9 (1913); *Obshchestvo i materinstvo*. Petrograd, 1916; *Novaia moral' i rabochii klass*. Moscow, 1918; "Dorogu krylatomu Erosu!," *MGv* 3 (1923), 111–24; *Liubov' pchel trudovykh*. Petrograd, 1923; as A. Domontovich, *Zhenshchina na perelome*. Moscow, 1923; *Bol'shaia liubov'*. Moscow and Leningrad, 1927; *Izbrannye stat'i i rechi*. Moscow, 1972.

In translation: *Autobiography of a Sexually Emancipated Woman*, tr. S. Attanasio, ed. E. Fetscher, preface by Germaine Greer. New York, 1971; *The Love of Worker Bees*, tr. Cathy Porter. London, 1977; *Selected Writings of Alexandra Kollontai*, ed. and tr. Alix Holt. Bristol and New York, 1977; *A Great Love*, tr. Cathy Porter. London, 1981; *Alexandra Kollontai: Selected Articles and Speeches*, ed. Cynthia Carlile. New York, 1984; "Thirty-Two Pages," tr. Rimma Volynska in Tomei, II.

Kolosova, Marianna (Rimma Ivanovna Vinogradova; b. 1903, Altai, Russia; d. 1964, Santiago, Chile; married name Pokrovskaia. Pseudonyms Marianna Kolosova, Elena Insarova, Dzhungar). Poet. For more bibliographical data, see *DRWW*, 310.

Writings: *Armiia pesen*. Harbin, 1928; *Gospodi, spasi Rossiiu*. Harbin, 1930; *Perezvony*. Harbin, 1930; *Ne pokorius'!* Harbin, 1932; *Na zvon mechei*. Harbin, 1934; *Mednyi gul*. Shanghai, 1937.

Kondratovich, Alla. Poet. Sister of Vera Kondratovich. Went to the USSR in the 1950s.
Kondratovich, Vera (married name Sidorova). Poet. Went to the USSR in the 1950s.
Writings: *Otpechatki mgnovenii*. Novosibirsk, 1990.

Koptiaeva, Antonina Dmitrievna (b. 1909, Iuzhnyi, Far East; d. 1991, Moscow; married: 1) manager K.Ya. Zeite [arrested, 1938, died in prison]; 2) writer F. Panferov). From lower middle class (*meshchane*); Komsomol member, 1926–8; began writing sketches, 1935; member of Union of Soviet Writers, 1944; writer; member of CPSU, 1944; graduated Moscow Literary Institute, 1947; Stalin Prize for *Ivan Ivanovich*, 1949.

Writings: *Kolymskoe zoloto*. Moscow, 1936; *Byli Aldana*. Moscow, 1937; *Tovarishch Anna*. Moscow, 1946; *Ivan Ivanovich*. Moscow, 1950; *Druzhba*. Moscow, 1954; *Derzanie*. Moscow, 1958; *Dar zemli*. Moscow, 1958; *Na Ural-reke*. Moscow, 1971.

In translation: *Ivan Ivanovich*, tr. Margaret Wettlin. Moscow, 1952.

Korostovets, Mariia Pavlovna (b. Popova; d. 1980s). Poet. Daughter of a Russian consul in Mongolia and Sinologist P. Popov, wife of a son of the diplomat I. Ia. Korostovets. Lived in Beijing, in 1943 moved to Shanghai. In the 1950s the family went to Australia.

Kozhevnikova, Nadezhda (b. 1949, Moscow). Moscow native, daughter of Soviet writer Vadim Kozhevnikov, and graduate of Moscow's Gorky Institute of Literature. First published fiction in 1967.

Writings: *Chelovek, reka i most. Povesti i rasskazy*. Moscow, 1976; *Okna na dvor*. Moscow, 1976; *Bremia molodosti (ocherki)*. Moscow, 1978; *Vorota i novyi gorod. Ocherki*. Moscow, 1978;

Doma i liudi. Moscow, 1979; *O liubvi materinskoi, dochernei, vozvyshennoi i zemnoi. Povesti, rasskazy, ocherki.* Moscow, 1979; *Elena Prekrasnaia.* Moscow, 1982; *Postoronnie v dome. Povesti.* Moscow, 1983; *Vnutrennii dvor.* Moscow, 1986; *Posle prazdnika.* Moscow, 1988; *Printsessa.* Moscow, 1999.

In translation: "The Stone Mason," *Soviet Literature* 1 (1981); "Rush Hour," tr. Valentina Jacque, *Soviet Literature* 3 (1984); "Home," tr. Marina Astman in *Balancing Acts*; "Vera Perova," tr. Rebecca Epstein in *Lives in Transit*.

Krandievskaia, Anastasiia Romanovna (b. Tarkhova, 1865; d. Stavropol, 1938; married publisher V. Krandievskii in 1880s; three children). Mother of poet Natal'ia Krandievskaia and great-grandmother of prose writer Tat'iana Tolstaia. Educated at Moscow Higher Courses for Women; worked as journalist, 1880s; first published 1896. Produced several collections of didactic short stories: most famous, "Tol'ko chas," 1902. Later tried short philosophical pieces and a political novel. Stopped publishing after Revolution.

Writings: *To bylo ranneiu vesnoi i drugie rasskazy.* Moscow, 1900; 2nd edn, 1905; "Noch'," in *Sbornik na pomoshch' uchashchimsia zhenshchinam.* Moscow, 1901; "Tol'ko chas," *Mir bozhii* 3 (1902), also in *Tol'ko chas i dr. rasskazy.* Rostov, 1903; other edns: 1905, 1906, 1917, 1918, and Uchenova, *Tol'ko chas.* Moscow, 1988; *Nichtozhnye*, 2 vols. Moscow, 1905; *U svezhei mogily.* St. Petersburg, 1911; "Aforizmy bessonitsy," in *Utrenniki*, 1915; "Taina radosti," *RMysl'* 1–7 (1916); *Okhranitel'.* Moscow, 1917; 2nd edn, 1918.

Krandievskaia, Natal'ia Vasil'evna (b. 1888, Moscow; d. 1963, Leningrad; m. Krandievskaia-Tolstaia). Poet, children's writer and memoirist. An accomplished lyric poet many of whose best verses were produced during the war and the Leningrad blockade.

Writings: *Stikhotvoreniia.* Moscow, 1913; *Stikhotvoreniia* II. Odessa, 1919; *Ot Lukavogo: tret'ia kniga stikhov.* Berlin, 1922; *Vospominaniia.* Leningrad, 1977; *Vechernii svet.* Leningrad, 1972; *Doroga.* Moscow, 1985; *Grozovyi venok.* St. Petersburg, 1992.

Krestovskaia, Mariia Vsevolodovna (b. 1861, St. Petersburg; d. 1910, Marioki, Finland; married E. A. Kartavtsev, 1891). Daughter of writer V. Krestovskii; parents divorced. Became actress at 17; had illegitimate son at 19; first published, 1885. Gave charitable aid to higher education for women; established health center for writers on estate at Marioki. Stopped publishing fiction 1901, but continued writing diary; contracted cancer.

Writings: "M. Kh.," "Ugolok teatral'nogo mira," *RV* 2 (1885); "Lëlia. Rasskaz iz teatral'nogo byta," *RV* 8–9 (1885); "Rannie grozy," *RV* 8, 10–12 (1886); *Rannie grozy.* St. Petersburg, 1889; 2nd edn, 1892; 3rd edn, 1904; "Nemudrenye," *RV* 9 (1889); *Romany i povesti*, 2 vols. St. Petersburg, 1889; 1892; "Artistka," *VE* 4–12 (1891), and St. Petersburg, 1896; 2nd edn., Moscow, 1903; "Syn," *VE* 11–12 (1893); "Zhenskaia zhizn'. Povest' v pis'makh," *SevV* 11–12 (1894), 1 (1895), and *Mir bozhii* 2–4 (1903); *Syn i drugie rasskazy.* Moscow, 1904; *Romany i povesti*, 2 vols. St. Petersburg, 1896; 2nd edn., Moscow, 1904; "Vopl'," *RMysl'* 1–2 (1900), in *Ispoved' Mytishcheva.* Moscow, 1903, and in *Tol'ko chas.*

Krichevskaia, Liubov' Iakovlevna (c. 1800–after 1841). Khar'kov-based author of poetry, fiction, plays. After her father's death in the 1810s, became responsible for the care of her whole family (her career as a writer probably had economic promptings). Never married, owing to the absence of a dowry. Major works include *Moi svobodnye minuty* (Khar'kov, 1817), *Dve povesti: Korinna i Emma* (Moscow, 1827).

Kriukova, Elena, (b. 1956, Gorky). Poet, graduated from Moscow Conservatory as well as Literary Institute; began publishing in 1984.

Writings: Kupol. Gorky, 1990; poems in *Ogonek* 10 (1990), 16; *DN* 3 (1992), 35–8; *DN* 3 (1995) 19–24; *DN* 9 (1996), 3–8; *Iunost'*, *Volga*, *NM*, *Neva*; *Sotvorenie mira.* Nizhnii Novgorod, 1997.

In translation: Todd and Hayward, 1048–9.

Kriukova, Ol'ga Petrovna (b. 1815/17, Simbirsk province; d. 1885, Simbirsk). Of uncertain origin, apparently an orphan raised by a poor woman landowner. Published lyric verse and narrative poems in early 1830s and after 1859 (primarily in *Razvlechenie*).

Writings: Donets. Moscow, 1833; *Starina.* Moscow, 1839; *Danilo Besschastnyi.* St. Petersburg, 1876.

Krüdener, Baroness Juliane-Barbare von (b. von Vietinghoff, 1764, d. 1824). From a Baltic German noble family; married at 14, and toured Europe with her husband, a Russian diplomat. Later became famous as a mystic; for a while, the confidante of Aleksandr I. Major works include *Valérie* (Paris, 1803).

Kruk, Nora (b. 1920, Harbin). Lived in Harbin, Shanghai, and Hong Kong, then settled in Sydney. Writes poetry in Russian and English.

Writings: "Even though . . . Poems." Hong Kong, 1975. "Nam ulybalas' Kvan ln'. Litsa skvoz' vremia," *Rossiiane v Azii* 7 (2000), 151–97. Also memoirs.

Kruzenshtern-Peterets, Iustina Vladimirovna (b. 1903, Russia; d. 1983, San Francisco; married names: Stepanova; Peterets). Journalist, prose writer, poet. Pseudonyms Snorre, Sibilla Ven, T. Stern, Merry Devil, Mary Kruzenshtern. A descendant of the famous explorer I. F. Kruzenshtern, she grew up in Harbin where her father, an officer, served in the Zaamurskii District Border Guard at the Chinese Eastern Railway. In the 1920s, Kruzenshtern became a journalist and writer in Harbin and continued her career in the second half of the 1930s and 1940s in Shanghai. Together with her second husband, Harbin poet Nikolai Peterets, she took an active part in Russian literary life in Shanghai. In the early 1950s, she went first to Brazil and then to the USA where she worked for the "Voice of America" and Russian émigré newspapers.

Writings: Stikhi. Shanghai, 1946; *Antigona.* Shanghai. 1948; *Ulybka Psishi.* Toronto, 1969; "U kazhdogo cheloveka est' svoia rodina. Vospominaniia," *Rossiiane v Azii* 1 (1994), 17–132; "Vospominaniia," *Rossiiane v Azii* 4 (1997), 124–209; 5 (1998), 25–83; 6 (1999), 29–104; and 7 (2000), 91–149.

Krylova, Ella

Writings: Poems in *Znamia* 1 (1997), 80–5; *DN* 9 (1997), 3–6; *DN* 4 (1996), 3–10.

Kul'man, Elisaveta Borisovna (b. 1808, St. Petersburg; d. 1825, St. Petersburg). Daughter of officer of German descent; eighth of nine children; father died soon after her birth; grew up with mother in poverty in St. Petersburg. Prodigious linguistic talents recognized and encouraged by tutor Karl Grossgeinrikh, who found her other teachers; poverty alleviated by small court pension awarded 1821; died at 17 of consumption. Manuscripts edited and published in Russia and abroad by former tutor.

Writings: Piiticheskie opyty Elisavety Kul'man. St. Petersburg, 1833; *Sammtliche Dichtungen*, 4 vols. St. Petersburg, 1835; Leipzig, 1844, 1884; Frankfurt, 1851, 1853, 1857; *Polnoe sobranie russkikh, nemetskikh i italiianskikh stikhotvorenii. Piiticheskie opyty Elisavety Kul'man.* St. Petersburg, 1839; 2nd edn, 1841; *Skazki*, 3 vols. St. Petersburg, 1839; *Dichtungen von Elisabeth Kulman.* Heidelberg, 1875. Poems in *Bannikov*; *Tsaritsy muz.*

In translation: poem in Kelly *Anthology.*

Kuz'mina-Karavaeva (Skobtsova), Elizaveta (b. Pilenko, 1891, Riga; d. 1945, Ravensbruck, Germany; also Mat' Mariia; pseudonym Iurii Danilov; married 1) D. V. Kuz'min-Karavaev, 1910–16; 2) D. E. Skobtsov-Kondrat'ev, 1918–27; two daughters, one son). Raised on family estate, Black Sea; on father's death, family moved to St. Petersburg, 1906; studied philosophy, Bestuzhev School. Married Kuz'min-Karavaev, Duma member, leader Poets' Guild, 1910; Symbolist circles, friendship with Aleksandr Blok; published first book of verse, 1912. Daughter Gaiana, 1913; divorced, 1916. Studied St. Petersburg Theological Academy, as woman, *in absentia*; proclaimed religious vocation in collection *Ruf'*, 1916. Arrested during post-revolutionary period; married Cossack Skobtsov, 1919; emigrated through Constantinople; son Iurii Skobtsov, 1920. To Belgrade; second daughter, Anastasia, 1922. In Paris, 1923; published novel about revolutionary period, articles on politics as Iurii Danilov, 1924–7. Daughter Anastasia died, separation from husband, began active religious vocation, 1926; published under married name saints' lives, books on religious thinkers, numerous articles on theology, ethics; from 1930, traveling representative of RSKhD among émigré communities. Took monastic vows, name Mat' Mariia, 1932; cared for mentally ill, organized women's shelters, sanatorium for tubercular patients; established philanthropical society "Pravoslavnoe delo," members Nikolai Berdiaev, Sergei Bulgakov; participant literary circle "Krug", mid–1930s. Daughter Gaiana returned to Soviet Union, died, 1935. Arrested by Nazis for harboring Jews, 1943; sent to Ravensbruck, died in gas chamber. Vol. of prison documents, writings from 1930s, published posthumously, 1947. Novel based on life by Elena Mikulina, *Mat' Mariia* (Moscow, 1983; 2nd expanded edn 1988).

Writings: Skifskie cherepki. St. Petersburg, 1912; *Ruf'*. Petrograd, 1916; "Ravnina russkaia," *Sovremennye zapiski* 19–20 (1924); "Klim Semenovich Baryn'kin," *Volia Rossii* 7–10 (1925); *Zhatva dukha (Zhitiia Sviatykh)*, 2 vols. Paris, 1927; *A. S. Khomiakov*. Paris, 1929; *Dostoevskii i sovremennost'*. Paris, 1929; *Mirosozertsanie Vladimira Solov'eva*. Paris, 1929; *Stikhi*. Berlin, 1937; *Mariia. Stikhotvoreniia, poemy, misterii, vospominaniia ob areste i lagere v Ravensbriuke*. Paris, 1947; *Stikhi*. Paris, 1949.

In translation: poems in Kelly *Anthology*.

Recent editions: Izb. Moscow, 1991; *Vospominaniia, stat'i, ocherki*, 2 vols. Paris, 1992; *Zhatva dukha*; repr. Tomsk, 1994; *Nashe vremia eshche ne razgadano: Stikhi, vosp., pis'ma*. Tomsk, 1996.

Kuznetsova, Galina Nikolaevna (b. 1900, Kiev; d. 1976, Munich; married White Army officer D. M. Petrov). Raised in Kiev; married after school graduation, 1918. Emigrated with husband through Constantinople, 1920; to Czechoslovakia, 1921. Studied French Institute, Prague; published first poem in Prague journal, 1922. In Paris, 1924; joined household of Ivan and Vera Bunin, 1927, for 15 years, Paris and Grasse; diary of experience later published as *Grasskii dnevnik* (first in *NZh* 74, 1963). First book a collection of stories, second a novel, third a collection of verse, 1930s. To Germany with opera singer Margarita A. Stepun, 1945, then to US, 1949; worked at Russian section of UN, New York, from 1955; American citizenship, 1956. Worked European section of UN, Geneva, 1959–63; retired in Munich.

Writings: "Vostochnyi prints," in *Studencheskie gody*, 1 (1922); "Zygmus'," *Novyi dom*, 3 (1927); "Pervyi liubovnik," *Illiustrirovannaia Rossiia* 283 (1930); *Utro*. Paris, 1930; *Prolog*. Paris, 1933; *Olivkovyi sad: Stikhi 1923–29*. Paris, 1937; "Na vershine kholma," in

Pestrye rasskazy, ed. V. Aleksandrova. New York, 1953; "Potselui svidaniia," *NZh* 36 (1954); *Grasskii dnevnik.* Washington DC, 1967.
In translation: excerpt, *Grasse Diary,* in *The Bitter Air of Exile,* ed. Simon Karlinsky. Berkeley, CA, 1977.
Recent editions: *Grasskii dnevnik. Rasskazy. Olivkovyi sad.* Moscow, 1995.

Labzina, Anna Evdokimovna (b. Iakovleva, 1758; d. 1828). Memoirist. Labzina's autobiography, written in 1810, records her childhood in a minor gentry family in Siberia, her unhappy first marriage to the hypocritical Aleksandr Karamyshev, and contact with the circle of Kheraskova (see above). Her 2nd marriage to the religious philosopher Aleksandr Labzin took her into the heart of Russian Masonic circles, where her work was acknowledged by the gift of a pair of white gloves, symbolic attribute of a virtuous wife.

Lanskaia-Villamova, Elizaveta Ivanovna (b. Villamova, 1764; d. 1847). Poet. Wife of Privy Councillor and Senator S. S. Lanskoi; daughter of a German poet and inspector of Petropavlovsk School; sister of the State Secretary Grigorii Ivanovich Villamov (1773–1842), tutor of Grand Duchess Aleksandra, daughter of Paul I. Her "Poslanie Derzhavinu" appears in vol. III of his *Soch,* ed. Grot, 516–17. A volume in French, *Mélanges littéraires, dediés à l'indulgence, par m-me de Lanskoy-Willamow,* appeared in St. Petersburg in 1830.

Latynina, Alla. Literary critic; graduated from Dept. of Philology, Moscow University. Received postgraduate degree from Faculty of Philosophy also at MGU. Writes about contemporary literary developments; chaired the first Russian Booker Prize jury in 1992.
Writings: *Vsevolod Garshin: tvorchestvo i sud'ba.* Moscow, 1986; *Znaki vremeni: zametki o literaturnom protsesse, 1970–80-e gody.* Moscow, 1987; *Za otkrytym shlagbaumom: literaturnaia situatsiia kontsa 80-kh.* Moscow, 1991; "Tvorets i kommentator. Roman R. Ivanychuka 'Orda'," *LitOb* 5–6 (1994); "Patent na blagorodstvo: vydast li ego literatura kapitalu?" *NM* 11 (1993); "Posle srazheniia s dubom," *LitGaz* 36 (September 9, 1998).

Latynina, Iuliia (b. 1966). Writer of prose fiction and essays. Journalist. Daughter of Alla Latynina.
Writings: "V ozhidanii Zolotogo Veka." *Oktiabr',* 6 (1989); *Irov den'.* Moscow, 1992; "Dedal i Gerkules, ili neskol'ko rassuzhdenii o pol'ze i bespoleznosti," *NM* 5 (1993); "Demokratiia i svoboda," *NM* 6 (1994); "Iskusstvo striazhaniia," *Znanie-sila* 1 (1995); *Kolduny i imperiia.* Saratov, 1996; "Povest' o blagonravnom miatezhnike," *Zvezda* 3 (1996); *Sto polei.* St. Petersburg, 1996; *Kolduny i ministry.* St. Petersburg, 1997; "Kak general Dzhekson s amerikanskim Tsentrobankom voeval," *Zvezda* 2 (1998); *Okhota na iziubria.* Moscow, 1999; *Insaider.* Moscow, 1999; *Delo o propavshem boge.* Moscow, 1999; *Razbor poletov.* Moscow, 2000; *Stal'noi korol'.* Moscow, 2000; *Sarancha.* Moscow, 2000; *Zdravstvuite, ia vasha "Krysha."* Moscow, 2000.
In translation: "Waiting for the Golden Age," tr. Bob Greenall, *Women's View, Glas* 3 (1992).

Lesnaia, Irina (Irina Igorevna Lesevitskaia; b. 1913, Khailar, China; d. 1999, Paraguay). Poet.

Letkova, Ekaterina Pavlovna (b. 1856, St. Petersburg; d. 1937, Leningrad; married architect N. V. Sultanov, 1884; one son). Daughter of military man and female landowner. Studied at Moscow Pedagogical Courses and Higher Courses for Women. First contributed to journals as a student. 1870s: associated with populists; involved with Nikolai Mikhailovskii, theorist of Russian populist movement. 1889–1918: member of Committee for Higher Courses for Women and representative of courses' library committee. After Revolution, worked for World Literature Press and State Publishing House; from 1921, member of Literary Fund Committee; on board of directors of House of Writers. Wrote more than 60 works of fiction and memoir of feminist Anna Filosofova; after Revolution, published memoirs of writers she had known.

Writings: *Povesti i rasskazy*, 2 vols. St. Petersburg, 1899; *Povesti i rasskazy*, 3 vols. St. Petersburg, 1900–03; *Rasskazy*. St. Petersburg, 1913; "Iz pisem N. K. Mikhailovskogo. Komentarii E. L.," *RBog* 1 (1914), 370–98; *Ocherki i rasskazy*. Petrograd, 1915; "Krasivaia zhizn' (Iz vospominanii ob A. P. Filosofovoi)," in *Sbornik pamiati Anny Pavlovny Filosofovoi*, vol. II. Petrograd, 1915, 26–34; *I. S. Turgenev: Obshchedostupnaia biografiia i kharakteristika k 100-letniiu so dnia rozhdeniia*. Petrograd, 1918; "Slepye i glukhie. Vospominaniia o V. Korolenko," in *V. G. Korolenko. Zhizn' i tvorchestvo. Sbornik statei*. Petrograd, 1922; "O F. M. Dostoevskom: Iz vospominanii," *Zven'ia* 1, Moscow and Leningrad, 1932, 459–77; "Pro Gleba Ivanovicha," *Zven'ia* 1, Moscow and Leningrad, 1935, 682–731.

Lisitsyna, Mariia Alekseevna (b. 1810?, d. 1842?). Poet, novelist. Probably the daughter of the well-known Moscow actor Aleksei Lisitsyn. Friend of the Teplova sisters (see below). Major works include *Emilii Likhtenberg* (Moscow, 1826) and *Stikhi i proza Marii Lisitsynoi* (Moscow, 1829).

Lisnianskaia, Inna L'vovna (b. Baku, 1928). Poet, critic, lives in Moscow. Participant in Metropol affair.

Writings: *Eto bylo so mnoi*. Baku, 1957; *Vernost'*. Moscow, 1958; *Ne prosto – liubov'*. Moscow, 1963; *Iz pervykh ust*. Moscow, 1966; *Vinogradnyi svet*. Moscow, 1978; *Dozhdi i zerkala*. Paris, 1983; *Stikhotvoreniia: Na opushke sna*. Ann Arbor, MI, 1984; *Vozdushnyi plast*. Moscow, 1990; *Stikhotvoreniia*. Moscow, 1991; *Posle vsego*. St. Petersburg, 1994; *Odinokii dar*. Moscow, Paris and New York, 1995; *Iz pervykh ust*. Moscow, 1996; *Veter pokoia*. St. Petersburg, 1998; *Muzyka "Poemy bez geroia" Anny Akhmatovoi*. Moscow, 1991, revised as *Shkatulka s troinym dnom*. Kaliningrad, 1995 (literary criticism); *Izbrannoe*. Rostov-na-Donu, 1999; *Muzyka i bereg*. St. Petersburg, 2000.

In translation: poems, tr. H. William Tjalsma in *Metropol'. Literary Almanac*. New York, 1982; poems, tr. Walter Arndt in *Lives in Transit*, 309–12; Todd and Hayward, 897–8; poems, tr. Ronald Meyer in Tomei, II.

Lokhvitskaia, Mirra (Mariia) (b. 1869/70, d. 1905). Poet and dramatist.

Writings: *Stikhotvoreniia*. Moscow, 1896; *Stikhotvoreniia* I–II. Moscow, 1900; *Stikhotvoreniia* III. St. Petersburg, 1900; *Stikhotvoreniia* IV. St. Petersburg, 1903; *Stikhotvoreniia* V. St. Petersburg, 1904; *Pered zakatom*. St. Petersburg, 1908.

In translation: poems, tr. Christine D. Tomei in Tomei, I.

L'vova, Kseniia

Writings: *Rasskazy*. Moscow, 1939; *Na lesnoi polose*. Moscow, 1950, 1951; *Elena*. Moscow, 1961; 1963; *Vysokii veter*. Moscow. 1968.

L'vova, Nadezhda Grigor'evna (b. Poltoratskaia, 1891, Podol'sk; d. 1913, Moscow). Poet, translator, critic. Influenced by both Symbolists and Futurists.

Writings: *Staraia skazka*. Moscow, 1913; 2nd expanded edn, 1914; "Kholod utra: neskol'ko slov o zhenskom tvorchestve," *Zhatva* 5 (1914), 249–56; poems in *Tsaritsy muz*.

Magnitskaia, Aleksandra Leont'evna? (b. 1784, d. 1846), poet and translator, and **Magnitskaia, Natal'ia Leont'evna?**, poet and translator: active 1790s. The sisters of the brilliant Moscow intellectual and poet Mikhail Leont'evich Magnitskii, who also published in *PPPV* and *Aonidy*.

Makarova, Elena (b. 1951, Baku). Author of prose fiction and essays. Daughter of poet Inna Lisnianskaia. Studied at Surikov Institute of Art and the Gorky Institute of World Literature in Moscow. Art therapist and teacher of art to handicapped children. Emigrated with her family to Israel in 1990.

Writings: Katushka: povesti. Moscow, 1978; *Perepolnennye dni: rasskazy i povesti*. Moscow, 1982; *Osvobodite slona*. Moscow, 1985; *Leto na kryshe*. Moscow, 1987; *Otkrytyi final*. Moscow, 1989; "Poslezavtra v San-Frantsisko," *Daugava* 9 (1989); *V nachale bylo detstvo*. Moscow. 1990; *From Bauhaus to Terezin: Friedl Dicker-Brandeis and Her Pupils*. Jerusalem, 1990; *Gde sidit fazan; Stuchit-gremit; Obsession; Nachat' s avtoportreta*. Jerusalem, 1993; *Smekh na ruinakh. Roman, Znamia* 3–4 (1995); *Friedl Dicker-Brandeis; ein Leben für Kunst und Lehre: Wien, Weimar, Prag, Hronov, Theresienstadt, Auschwitz*. Vienna, 2000.

In translation: "Herbs from Odessa," tr. Helena Goscilo in *Balancing Acts*; "Uncle Pasha," tr. Lise Brody in "*From the Soviets*," Special issue of *Nimrod* 33: 2 (Spring/Summer 1990); "Rush Job," tr. Lise Brody in *Lives in Transit*; "Needlefish," tr. Lise Brody in *Dialogues*.

Mandel'stam, Nadezhda Iakovlevna (b. 1899, Saratov; d. 1980, Moscow). Artist, memoirist, cultural critic. Trained as an artist. Met the poet Osip Mandel'stam in 1919. Preserved works and memory of Mandel'stam after he perished in 1938 in a labor camp. After death of her husband completed a doctorate in linguistics. Began writing memoirs of the Stalin years. In her writings of major literary figures became one in her own right.

Writings: Vospominaniia. New York, 1979, Paris, 1982; Moscow, 1999; *Vtoraia kniga*. Paris, 1987; Moscow, 1990, 1999; *Moe zaveshchanie i drugie esse*. New York, 1982; *Kniga tret'ia*. Paris, 1987; "Ob Akhmatovoi," *Literaturnaia ucheba* 3 (1989), 134–51; *Vospominaniia, proizvedeniia, perepiska*. St. Petersburg, 1999.

In translation: Hope against Hope, tr. Max Hayward. New York, 1970; *Mozart and Salieri*, tr. Robert A. McLean. Ann Arbor, MI, 1973; *Hope Abandoned*, tr. Max Hayward. New York, 1974.

Mar, Anna (b. Anna Iakovlevna Brovar, 1887, St. Petersburg; d. 1917, Moscow; married Lenshin, 1903, but marriage quickly broke up). Daughter of artist Ia. Brovar; left home for Khar'kov, aged 15, attracted to Catholicism. Helped to publish by V. Briusov. Participated in women's movement; answered readers' letters to *Journal for Women* under pseudonym "Princess Daydream." Poisoned self because of unhappy love affair, reputedly with the writer Vlasii Doroshevich.

Writings: Miniatury. Khar'kov, 1906; *Nevozmozhnoe*. Moscow, 1912; *Idushchie mimo*. Moscow, 1914; 2nd edn., Moscow, 1917; *Lampady nezazhennye*. Petrograd and Moscow, 1915; "Tebe edinomu sogreshila," in *My pomnim Pol'shu*. Petrograd, 1915; *Zhenshchina na kreste*. Moscow, 1916; 2nd edn, Moscow, 1916; 3rd edn, Moscow, 1918.

Recent editions: Zhenshchina na kreste. Moscow, 1994.

Marinina, Aleksandra (pseudonym of Marina Anatol'evna Alekseeva, b. 1957, Leningrad). One of most popular writers of detective fiction in post-Soviet Russia. Moved to Moscow in 1971 where she studied jurisprudence at Moscow State University. The author of more than 30 scholarly publications, she worked for the Ministry of Internal Affairs until retiring in 1998. Selected the "Writer of the Year" at the 1998 Moscow International Book Fair. Marinina's website <http://www.marinina.ru> lists numerous articles about her that have appeared in the Russian press as well as biographical and publication information.

Writings: with Aleksandr Gorkin, *Shestikrylyi serafim*. Moscow, 1992; *Stechenie ob-stoiatel'stva*. Moscow, 1993; *Igra na chuzhom pole*. 1994; *Ukradennyi son*. Various edns, Moscow, 1995–8; *Ubiitsa po nevole*. Various edns, Moscow, 1995–8; *Smert' radi smerti*. Various edns, Moscow, 1995–7; *Shesterki umiraiut pervymi*. Various edns, Moscow, 1995–7; *Smert' i nemogo liubvi*. Various edns, Moscow, 1995–8; *Chernyi spisok*. Various edns, Moscow, 1996–8; *Posmertnyi obraz*. Various edns, Moscow, 1996–8; *Za vse nado platit'*. Various edns, Moscow, 1996–8; *Chuzhaia maska*. Various edns, Moscow, 1996–8; *Ne meshaite palachu*. Various edns, Moscow, 1996–7; *Stilist*. Various edns, Moscow, 1996–7; *Illiuziia grekha*. Various edns, Moscow, 1996–7; *Svetlyi lik smerti*. Various edns, Moscow, 1997–8; *Imia poterpevshego – Nikto*. Various edns, Moscow, 1997–8; *Muzhskie igry*. Various edns, Moscow, 1997; *Ia umer vchera*. Various edns, Moscow, 1997–8; *Rekviem*. 2 edns, Moscow, 1998; *Prizrak muzyki*. Moscow, 1998; *Kogda bogi smeiatsia*. Moscow, 2000. *Tot, kto znaet*, 2 vols. Moscow, 2001. For more information, see http://www.eksmo.ru or http://www.rsl.ru.

Mat' Mariia, see Kuzmina-Karavaeva.

Mendeleeva-Blok, Liubov' (b. 1881, d. 1939). Stage actress, memoirist, and author of articles on the ballet.

Writings: *I byl i nebylitsy o Bloke i o sebe*. Bremen, 1979.

Merkur'eva, Vera Aleksandrovna (b. 1876, Vladikavkaz; d. 1943, Tashkent). Poet, translator. Published only 15 poems during her lifetime. Made her living exclusively from translation. "Discovered" only in the 1980s.

Writings: Poems in *Oktiabr'* 5 (1989); translations of Percy Bysshe Shelley in *Izbrannye stikhotvoreniia* (1937); "Vera Merkur'eva (1876–1943): stikhi i zhizn'," in *Litsa* 1 (St. Petersburg, 1995).

In translation: "The Grandmother of Russian Poetry: A Self Portrait," in Kelly *Anthology*; poems in Tomei, II.

Militsyna, Elizaveta Mitrofanovna (b. 1869, Ostrogozhsk, Voronezh province; d. 1930, Voronezh; married: 1) steward Kargin, 1889; 2) supportive agronomist N. A. Militsyn). Helped to publish 1896 by Korolenko and Gorky. Persecuted by police; third vol. of collected works censored, 1913. Worked as nurse in World War I; joined Russian Communist Party, 1920; published little fiction after Revolution.

Writings: *Rasskazy*. Moscow, 1905; *Rasskazy*, vols I–III. St. Petersburg and Moscow, 1910–13; *V ozhidanii prigovora*. Moscow, 1924, and in *Tol'ko chas; Izbrannye rasskazy*. Voronezh, 1949.

In translation: *The Village Priest and Other Stories from the Russian of Militsyna and Saltykov*, tr. Beatrix L. Tollemache. London, 1918.

Miller, Larisa (b. 1940, Moscow). Writer of poetry and prose. Graduate of the Foreign Language Institute.

Writings: *Bezymiannyi den': stikhi*. Moscow, 1977; *Zemlia i dom*. Moscow, 1986; *Bol'shaia Polianka*. Moscow, 1991; *Pogovorim o strannostiakh liubvi*. Vilnius, 1991; *Stikhi i proza*. Moscow, 1992; *V ozhidanii Edipa: Stikhi i proza*. Moscow, 1993; "I drugoe, drugoe, drugoe . . . —" *VopLit* 6 (1995); *Stikhi o stikhakh*. Moscow, 1996; *Zametki, zapisi, shtrikhi*. Moscow, 1997; "Uiutnyi dom s vidom na bezdnu," *NM* 6 (1997); *Splosh-nye prazdniki*. Moscow, 1998; *Mezhdu oblakom i iamoi*. Moscow, 1999.

In translation: "Bolshaya Polyanka: A Childhood in Post-War Moscow," tr. Ivan Chulaky, *Women's View, Glas* 3 (1992); "Home Address" (excerpt), tr. Raisa Bobrova, *Glas* 6 (1993); "Springtime in Broad Daylight," tr. Jose Alaniz, *Glas* 13 (1996); *Dim and Distant Days*, tr. Kathleen Cook and Natalie Roy, *Glas: New Russian Writing*, 2000.

Mnatsakanova (occasional pen name Netzkowa) Elizaveta Arkad'evna (b. 1922, Baku). Poet, graphic artist, essayist, and musicologist. Lives in Vienna.

Writings: *Shagi i vzdokhi: Chetyre knigi stikhov*. Vienna, 1982; *U smerti v gostiakh*. Vienna, 1982; *Metamorphosen*. Vienna, 1988; *Das Buch Sabeth*. Vienna, 1988; Literary essays: "O roli detskogo vospominaniia v psikhologii khudozhestvennogo tvorchestva: Na primere prozy Mariny Tsvetaevoi i dvukh otryvok iz romana F. M. Dostoevskogo *Brat'ia Karamazovy*," *Wiener Slawistischer Almanach* 10 (1982), 325–49; "Khlebnikov: Predel i bespredel'naia muzyka slova," *Sintaksis* 11 (1983), 101–56; "Znachenie i rol' vospominaniia v khudozhestvennoi praktike. Freid—Dostoevskii—Geine," *Wiener Slawistischer Almanach* 16 (1985), 37–80.

In translation: poems, tr. Gerald Janacek in Tomei, II.

Morits, Iunna Petrovna (b. 1937, Kiev). Studied at Gorky Literary Institute and in Riga. Poet, essayist, translator, children's writer. Lives in Moscow.

Writings: *Razgovor o schast'e*. Moscow, 1957; *Mys zhelaniia*. Moscow, 1961; *Schastlivyi zhuk*. Moscow, 1969; *Loza*. Moscow, 1970; *Surovoi nit'iu*. Moscow, 1974; *Malinovaia koshka*. Moscow, 1976; *Pri svete zhizni*. Moscow, 1977; *Poprygat'-poigrat'*. Moscow, 1978; *Tretii glaz*. Moscow, 1980; *Izb*. Moscow, 1982; *Sinii ogon'*. Moscow, 1985; *Domik s truboi*. Moscow, 1986; *Na etom berege vysokom*. Moscow, 1987; *V logove golosa*. Moscow, 1990; *Muskul vody*. Moscow, 1990; *Sobaka byvaet kusachei*. Moscow, 1998; *Litso: stikhotvoreniia*. Moscow, 2000; *Takim obrazom: Stikhotvoreniia*. St. Petersburg, 2000.

In translation: *Three Russian Poets*, tr. Elaine Feinstein. Manchester, 1979; *Contemporary Russian Poetry*, 138–55; Todd and Hayward, 932–9; poems, tr. Jonathan Chaves in Tomei, II.

Morozova, Galina Vsevolodovna (b. 1915, Omsk, married name, Loginova). Novelist.

Writings: *Lana*. Harbin, 1939.

Morozova, Ol'ga Aleksandrovna (b. Kolesova, 1877, Khar'kov, Ukraine; d. 1968, San Francisco). Novelist. Pseudonym M. Aleksandrov. Graduate of Khar'kov Institute, she established schools for peasant children in Russia; during World War I was in charge of the office responsible for procuring meat from Asia for the Russian army, and during the Civil War organized a hospital. She emigrated to western China, then moved to Tianjin and later Shanghai. In 1951 she and her daughter came to the USA via a refugee camp on Tubabao, Philippines. For more bibliographical data see M. Ledkovsky *et al.* (eds), *DRWW*, 443–4.

Writings: *Nevozvratnoe*. Harbin, 1932; *Nora*. China, date not known; *Mechty i zhizn'*. China, date not known; *Sud'ba*. Harbin, 1934; repr. San Francisco, 1984.

Moskvina, Elisaveta Osipovna (married name Mukhina) and **Mariia Osipovna** (active 1800s): poets, authors of *Aoniia* (Moscow, 1802).

Murzina, Aleksandra (active 1790s): poet, author of *Raspuskaiushchaiasia roza* (Moscow, 1798).

Nabatnikova, Tat'iana (b. 1948, Altai region). Writer of prose fiction. Grew up in the country, graduated from the Novosibirsk Electrochemical Institute in 1971, attended the Gorky Institute of Literature, 1975–81. Began publishing fiction (several prize-winning collections) while living in Cheliabinsk.

Writings: *Rasskazy*. Novosibirsk, 1982; *Domashnee vospitanie. Rasskazy, povest'*. Moscow, 1984; *Kazhdyi okhotnik. Roman, Sibirskie ogni* 1–3 (1987); Moscow, 1989; "Nezametnaia rabota," *Novoe russkoe slovo* 6 (1987); "Zadumyvaias' nad proshlym," *Literaturnaia Rossiia* 27 (July 8, 1987); "Gde sidit fazan?" *LitGaz* (November 25, 1987); "Krug zabluzhdenii," *Literaturnaia Rossiia* 11 (March 13, 1988); *Zagadai zhelanie*. Moscow,

1990; "Govori, Mariia!" and "Domokhoziaika," in *Chisten'kaia zhizn'*, "Govori, Mariia!" also appears in *Novye amazonki*; *Dar Izory*. Moscow, 1991 and *Voin Rossii* 3 (1998); *Gorod v kotorom —: roman, povest', rasskazy*. Cheliabinsk, 1991; *Ne rodis', krasivoi*. Rostov-on-Don, 1995; "Proisshestvie," *Realist. Literaturnyi al'manakh* 1 (1995); *Prokhozhdenie teni*. Moscow, 1997.

In translation: "Alina's Seagull," tr. Vladimir Korotky. *SovLit* 9 (1989); "In Memoriam," tr. Catharine Nepomnyashchy, in *Soviet Women Writing*; "A Bus Driver Named Astap," and "The Phone Call," tr. Helen Burlingame, in *Lives in Transit*; "Speak, Maria!" tr. Masha Gessen in *Half a Revolution*.

Nagrodskaia, Evdokiia Apollonovna (b. 1866, St. Petersburg; d. 1930, Paris; married high official V. Nagrodskii). Maternal grandparents were actors at Aleksandrinskii Theater; daughter of writer Avdot'ia Panaeva and journalist Apollon Golovachev. Possibly worked in theater, 1880s. Her first novel *The Wrath of Dionysus* (1910), went through 10 editions by 1916. After Revolution, emigrated to Paris; published historical novels influenced by her work in Masonic movement.

Writings: *Gnev Dionisa*. St. Petersburg, 1910; 10th edn, 1916; Riga, 1930; *Bronzovaia dver'*. St. Petersburg, 1911; *Bor'ba mikrobov*. St. Petersburg, 1913; *Belaia kolonnada*. St. Petersburg, 1914; 4th edn, Riga, 1931; *Reka vremen*. Berlin, 1924–6; poems in *Tsaritsy muz*; *Gnev Dionisa*, repr. St. Petersburg, 1994.

In translation: *The Wrath of Dionysus: A Novel by Evdokia Nagrodskaia*, tr. and ed. Louise McReynolds. Bloomington, IN, 1997.

Narbikova, Valeriia (b. 1958, Moscow). Writer of prose fiction and artist. First published fiction in 1989, winning the prize for best publication of the year in the journal *Iunost'*.

Writings: "Plan pervogo litsa: I vtorogo," in *Vstrechnyi khod: Sbornik*. Moscow, 1989; "Vidimost' nas," *Strelets* 3 (1989), and in *Litsei na Chistykh Prudakh. Moskovskii krug. Sbornik*. Moscow, 1991; *Ravnovesie sveta dnevnykh i nochnykh zvezd*. Moscow, 1990, excerpted in *Iunost'* 8 (1988); "Ad kak Da/aD kak dA," in *Ne pomniashchaia zla*; comp. L. Vaneeva; "Okolo ekolo . . .," *Iunost'* 3 (1990); "Probeg—pro beg," *Znamia* 5 (1990); "Velikoe knia," *Iunost'* 12 (1991); "Skvoz'" (MS); *Okolo ekolo—: povesti*. Moscow, 1992. Title story also appears in *Novye amazonki*; ". . . i puteshestvie," *Znamia* 6 (1996); "Devochka pokazyvaet," *Znamia* 3 (1998); *Vremia v puti*. Moscow, 1997.

In translation: "In the Here and There," tr. Masha Gessen, in *Half a Revolution; In the Here and There*, tr. Masha Gessen. Ann Arbor, MI 1997; *Day Equals Night*, tr. Seth Graham. Ann Arbor, MI, 1998.

Nedel'skaia, Elena Nikolaevna (b. 1912, Iaroslavl'; d. 1980, Sydney). Poet. Left Harbin in the 1950s and lived in Australia.

Writings: *U poroga*. Harbin, 1940; *Belaia roshcha*. Harbin, 1943; *Nash dom*. Sydney, 1978.

Neelova, Natal'ia Alekseevna (married name Makarova). Pioneer prose writer. Probably the sister of the minor writer Pavel Neelov. Author of *Leinard i Termiliia, ili zloschastnaia sud'ba dvukh liubovnikov*. St. Petersburg, 1784.

Nekrasova, Kseniia Aleksandrovna (b. 1912, Urals; d. 1956, Moscow). Poet. Little known in her early years. Lacked a conventional education. Lived during the war years in Tashkent where she was discovered by Akhmatova. Published only one work during her lifetime.

Writings: *A zemlia nasha prekrasna*. Moscow, 1956; 2nd edn, 1960; *Stikhi*. Moscow, 1971; *Sud'ba*. Moscow, 1981; *Ia chast' Rusi*. Cheliabinsk, 1986.

In translation: poems, tr. Diana Burgin, intro. S. Poliakova, *Boulevard* 4:3 and 5:1 (1990).

Nikolaeva, Galina Evgen'evna, (b. 1911, v. Usmanka, West-Siberian rgn; d. 1963, Moscow; married M. Sagalovich, 1930). From rural intelligentsia; graduated from Gorky Medical Institute, 1935; doctor, worked in hospital during war; transported wounded from Stalingrad; began writing poetry, 1944; first published, 1945; poet, writer; member Union of Soviet Writers; Stalin Prize for *Zhatva*, 1951.
Writings: *Skvoz' ogon'. Stikhi*. Moscow, 1946; *Kolkhoz "Traktor"*. Gorky, 1948; *Zhatva*. Moscow, 1951; *Povest' o direktore MTS i glavnom agronome*. Moscow, 1954; *Bitva v puti*. Moscow, 1958; *Rasskazy babki Vasilisy pro chudesa*. Moscow, 1962; *Nash sad. Korotkie povesti i rasskazy*. Moscow, 1966; *SS*, 3 vols. Moscow, 1972–3.
In translation: *The Traktor-Kolkhoz*, Moscow, 1950; *Harvest*. Moscow, 1952; New York, 1953; *The New Comer. The Manager of an MTS and the Chief Agronomist*, tr. David Skvirsky. Moscow, 1955.

Nikolaeva, Olesia (Ol'ga) Aleksandrovna (b. 1955, Moscow). Poet, lives in Moscow.
Writings: *Sad chudes*. Moscow, 1980; *Na korable zimy*. Moscow, 1986; *Smokovnitsa*. Tbilisi, 1990; *Zdes'*. Moscow, 1990; *Kliuchi ot mira*. Moscow, 1990; *Nichego, krome zhizni*. Moscow, 1990; *Amor fati*. St. Petersburg, 1997; "Invalid detstva: povest'," *Iunost'* 2 (1990), 34–61; "Progulki s Siniavskim," *LitGaz* 41 (October 9, 1996), 5; *Sovremennaia kul'tura i Pravoslavie*. Moscow, 1999.
In translation: poems in *SovLit* 3 (1989), 134; *Lives in Transit*, 306–8.

Nikonova, Ry (Reia; Anna Aleksandrovna Tarshis; b. 1942, Eisk). Poet, artist, theorist.
Writings: *PANV und andere Zeichenchimare*. W. Berlin, 1988; *Transfurism*. Leipzig, 1989; *Protsess nad shotlandstem traktion*. Trento, 1989; with Sergei Sigei, *Transponance Transfurismus, oder kaaba der abstraktion*. Seigen, 1989; with Sergei Sigei, *Zaum*. Vienna, 1990.

Odoevtseva, Irina Vladimirovna (pseudonym Zinaida Shekarazina; b. Iraida Gustavovna Geinike, 1901, Riga; d. 1990, Leningrad; married: 1) lawyer Popov-Odoevtsev; 2) poet Georgii Ivanov, 1921; 3) novelist Iakov Gorbov, 1978). Father St. Petersburg lawyer. Protégée Nikolai Gumilev, member "Poets' Guild"; noted for ballads; first book vol. of poetry, 1922. Emigrated with Ivanov to Berlin, 1923, then Paris; wrote popular short fiction, several novels; Biarritz during German occupation, returned to Paris; wrote three plays in French and new poetry, early 1950s. After Ivanov's death, 1958, correspondent *RMysl'*, two vols. of memoirs about prerevolutionary St. Petersburg (1919–22) and émigré Paris (1920s–70s). Moved to Leningrad, 1987.
Writings: *Dvor chudes: stikhi, 1920–21*. Petrograd, 1922; "Serdtse Marii," *Zveno* 157 (1926); "Epilog," *Zveno* 163 (1926); "Dom na peske," *Zveno* 173–4 (1926); "Zhasminovyi ostrov," *Zveno* 193 (1926); "Rumynka," *Zveno* 200 (1926); "Putanitsa," *Zveno* 206 (1927); "Sukhaia soloma," *Novyi dom* 3 (1927); "Eliseiskie polia," *Zveno* 212–13 (1927); "Zhizn' madam Diuklo," *Zveno* 6 (1927); *Angel smerti*. Paris, 1927, 1938; "Prazdnik," *Illiustrirovannia Rossiia*. 209 (1929); "Valentin," *Illiustrirovannia Rossiia* 219 (1929); "Roza na snegu," *Illiustrirovannia Rossiia* 250 (1930); *Izol' da*. Paris, 1929; Berlin, 1931; *Zerkalo*. Brussels, 1939; *Kontrapunkt: stikhi*. Paris, 1951; *Stikhi, napisannye vo vremia bolezni*. Paris, 1952; *Ostav' nadezhdu navsegda* (novel). New York, 1954; "God zhizni," *Vozrozhdenie* 63–8 (1957); *Desiat' let*. Paris, 1961; *Odinochestvo*. Washington DC, 1965; "Na beregakh Nevy," *NZh* (1962–4) and Washington DC, 1967; *Zlataia tsep': stikhi*. Paris, 1975; *Portret v rifmovannoi rame: stikhi*. Paris, 1976; "Na beregakh Seny," *RMysl'* (1978–81) and Paris, 1983.
In translation: *Out of Childhood*, tr. D. Nachshen. New York, 1930; *All Hope Abandon*, tr. F. Reed. New York, 1949; poetry in "Days With Bunin," tr. K. Gavrilovich, *RR*

(1971); Markov and Sparks; Pachmuss, *A Russian Cultural Revival*; and Todd and Hayward.

Recent editions: *Na beregakh Nevy*. Moscow, 1988; *Na beregakh Seny*. Moscow, 1989; *Izbr.* Moscow, 1998.

"Ol'nem, O. N." (Tsekhovskaia, Varvara Nikolaevna; b. Men'shikova, 1872, Bobrov, Voronezh province; d. 1941). Daughter of officer from gentry; mother, daughter of priest, died 1886, while she was still studying at Kremenchug Women's Gymnasium. Became journalist in Kiev, 1889. Published first story, 1899; published regularly for only 15 years. Ed. journal *Russkoe bogatstvo* (later renamed *Russkie zapiski*), 1914–16. Last publication: 1923 biography of writer Elizaveta Vodovozova.

Writings: "Warum?" *RBog* 2 (1899); "Na poroge zhizni. Stranichka iz biografii dvukh sovremennits," *RBog* 4 (1900); "Iubilei redaktora," *RBog* 5 (1900); "Pervyi shag," *Obrazovanie* (1902); "Ivan Fedorovich," *RBog* 1 (1903); "Bez illiuzii," *RBog* 11–12 (1903); *Ocherki i rasskazy*. St. Petersburg, 1903; 2nd edn, 1912; "U teplogo moria," *RBog* 7–8 (1909); "Dinastiia," *RBog* 4–6 (1910), repr. *Bez illiuzii* (1911), and in Uchenova, *Tol'ko chas*. Moscow, 1988; *Bez illiuzii. Rasskazy*. St. Petersburg, 1911; *Tsepi–pered rassvetom*. St. Petersburg, 1911; "Bezzabotnye," *RBog* 5–7 (1912); "Iz reporterskikh vospominanii," *Golos minuvshego* 7–8 (1913); "Triasina," 8–9 (1914); *Rasskazy*. Moscow, 1919; "Elizaveta Nikolaevna Vodovozova-Semevskaia," *Golos minuvshego* 3 (1923).

Palei, Marina (b. Spivak, 1955, Leningrad). Writer of prose fiction. Professional training in medicine. Abandoned medicine. Graduated with honors from Gorky Literary Institute, 1991. One of the most talented new writers, Palei's works evoke both nostalgia and the absurd in her renderings of the Soviet everyday.

Writings: "Tvoia nemyslimaia chistota," *LitOb* 6 (1987); "Figurka na ogolennom pole," *NM* 11 (1988); "Pust' budet dver' otkryta," *LitOb* 2 (1988); "Otpechatok ognia," *LitOb* 12 (1989); "Kompozitsiia na krasnom i sinem," *Sobesednik* 12 (1989); "Evgesha i Annushka," *Znamia* 7 (1990); "Den' topolinogo pukha," in *Novye amazonki* and *NZh* 180 (1991); "Kabiria s Obvodnogo Kanala," *NM* 3 (1991); *Otdelenie propashchikh*. Moscow. 1991; "Skazki Andersena," in *Moskovskii krug*. Moscow, 1991. "Den' imperii," *Zvezda* 7 (1993); "Pritvorotnoe zel'e," *Volga* 12 (1993); "Reis," *NM* 3 (1993); "Mestorozhdenie vetra," *NM* 12 (1994); *Mestorozhdenie vetra*. St. Petersburg, 1998; *Long Distance, ili Slavianskii aktsent*. Moscow, 2000.

In translation: "The Bloody Women's Ward," tr. Arch Tait, *Women's View, Glas* 3 (1992); "The Losers' Division," tr. Jehanne Gheith in *Lives in Transit*; "The Day of the Poplar Flakes," tr. Masha Gessen in *Half a Revolution*; "Rendezvous," tr. Helena Goscilo in *Lives in Transit*. "Cabiria of the Obvodny Canal," tr. Brian Thomas Oles (ms).

Panaeva, Avdot'ia Iakovlevna (pseudonym N. Stanitskii; b. Brianskaia; 1819/20, d. 1893. name [2nd marriage] Golovacheva). Writer, memoirist, and central figure in the circle around the journal *The Contemporary* which her husband Ivan Panaev co-edited with the poet and prose writer Nikolai Nekrasov. Daughter (2nd marriage) became an author (Evdokiia Nagrodskaia). Although she is today mainly known for her memoirs, Panaeva was also an accomplished author of fiction.

Writings: "Bezobraznyi muzh," *Sovremennik* 8 (1848); "Zhena chasovogo mastera," *Sovremennik* 13 (1849); "Zhenskaia dolia," *Sovremennik* 92–93 (1862); *Roman v Peterburgskom polusvete*, 1869; and two novels co-written with Nikolai Nekrasov, *Tri strany sveta*, 1849, and *Mertvoe ozero*, 1851.

In translation: *The Young Lady of the Steppes*, in Andrew; from *Memoirs*, tr. Ruth Sobel in Tomei, I.

Recent editions: *Semeistvo Tal'nikovykh*. Leningrad, 1992; *Russkie povesti XIX veka: 40–50 godov*, 2 (1952); *Tri strany sveta, Mertvoe ozero*, in N. A. Nekrasov, *PSS*, vols. IX, X. Leningrad, 1984–5; *Vospominaniia* (1889, 1890; various edns from 1927–1972); *Stepnaia baryshnia*, in *Dacha*; *Rasskaz v pis'makh*, in *Serdtsa*.

Panova, Vera Fedorovna (b. 1905, Rostov-on-Don; d. 1973, St. Petersburg; married: 1) journalist A. V. Starosel'skii; 2) journalist B. Vakhtin (arrested, 1936, died in camp); 3) writer D. Ya. Dar). From lower middle class (*meshchane*); left gymnasium during 2nd year, self-educated; journalist, 1920s–30s; started writing late 1930s; member of Union of Soviet Writers, 1946; writer, playwright, screenwriter; Stalin Prizes for *Sputniki*, 1947; *Kruzhilikha*, 1948; *Iasnyi bereg*, 1950.

Writings: *Sputniki*. Moscow and Leningrad, 1946; *Kruzhilikha*. Molotov, 1947; *Iasnyi bereg*. Leningrad, 1949; *Vremena goda*. Moscow, 1954; *Sentimental'nyi roman*. Leningrad, 1958; *Valya Volodia. Rasskazy*. Moscow, 1960; *Liki na zare. Istoricheskaia povest'*. Leningrad, 1965; *Pogovorim o strannostiakh liubvi. P'esy*. Leningrad, 1968; *Zametki literatora*. Leningrad, 1972; *O moei zhizni, knigakh i chitateliakh*. Leningrad, 1975. For complete listing, see Tomei, II.

In translation: *The Train*, tr. E. Manning and M. Budberg. London, 1948; *The Factory*, tr. Moura Budberg. London, 1949; *Bright Shore*, tr. B. Isaacs, *SovLit* 3 (1959), 3–142; *Looking Ahead* (Kruzhilikha), tr. David Skvirsky. Moscow, 1955; *Span of the Year*, tr. Vera Traill. London, 1957; *Serezha and Valya*. New York, 1964; *Selected Works*, tr. Olga Shartse and Eve Manning. Moscow, 1976; from *Bright Shore*, tr. Ruth Kreuzer in Tomei, II. For complete listing see Tomei, II.

Parkau Aleksandra Petrovna (b. 1889, Novocherkassk; d. 1954, USSR; married Nilus). Poet, satirist. The earliest woman poet in Harbin, she settled there during World War I with her husband, Colonel E. Kh. Nilus, a military lawyer and historian. In the 1920s, Parkau's poetry often appeared in Harbin periodicals, and she held a literary salon. In 1933 in Shanghai she continued to write poetry and participate in literary circles; in the late 1940s, she followed her son and his family to the USSR.

Writings: *Ogon' neugasimyi*. Shanghai, 1937; *Rodnoi strane*. Shanghai, 1942.

Parnok, Sofiia Iakovlevna (pseudonym Andrei Polianin; b. Parnokh, 1885, Taganrog; d. 1933, Karinskoe). Poet, critic, opera librettist, translator.

Writings: *Stikhotvoreniia*. Petrograd, 1916; *Rozy Pierii*. Moscow and Petrograd, 1922; *Loza*. Moscow, 1923; *Muzyka*. Moscow, 1926; *Vpolgolosa*. Moscow, 1928; *Sobranie stikhotvorenii*. Ann Arbor, 1979; poems in M. L. Gasparov, *Russkii stikh*. Daugavpils, 1989; and *Tsaritsy muz*.

In translation: Poems in Markov and Sparks; *Conditions*, 6 (1980); Perkins and Cook; Kelly *Anthology* and Tomei, I. From 'Noted names' in Kelly *Utopias*.

Pavlova, Karolina Karlovna (b. Jaenisch/Ianish, 1807, Moscow; d. 1893, Dresden). Of German, French, English and Russian extraction. Daughter of physics professor; well-educated at home; moved in Moscow literary circles in 1820s; failed romance with Adam Mickiewicz in late 1820s profoundly influenced life and later poetry; married writer Nikolai Pavlov in 1837, by whom she had one son; active as translator in 1820s and 1830s; wrote original Russian poetry from late 1830s until mid-1860s; salon hostess c. 1839–52; endured political and marital troubles from late 1840s onward; separated from husband, went to Dorpat in 1853, and settled in

Dresden 1858. Little is known of her life, but from this point on apparently wrote little Russian poetry, although continued literary activities until death.

Writings: Das Nordlicht. Dresden, 1833; *Les préludes.* Paris, 1839; *Stikhotvoreniia.* Moscow, 1863; *SS.* 2 vols., ed. Valerii Briusov. Moscow, 1915; *Polnoe sobranie stikhotvorenii.* Moscow and Leningrad, 1964; *Stikhotvoreniia.* Moscow, 1985. Poems in *Bannikov; Tsaritsy muz; Moskovskaia muza 1799–1997,* ed. G. D. Klimova. Moscow, 1998.

In translation: A Double Life, tr. Barbara Heldt Monter. Ann Arbor, MI, 1978; 3rd, revised edn, Oakland, CA, 1996; poems in *The Penguin Book of Russian Verse,* ed. Dimitri Obolensky, 1962; repr. London, 1969; Perkins and Cook; *The Portable Nineteenth-Century Russian Reader,* ed. George Gibian. New York, 1993; Kelly *Anthology;* Tomei, I.

Petrovskaia, Nina (b. 1884, d. 1928). Writer of short stories, feuilletons, and reviews.

Writings: "Lozh'," in *Korabli.* Moscow, 1907; "Iz tsikla "Pesni liubvi," in *Almanakh Kristall.* Khar'kov, 1908; *Sanctus Amor.* St. Petersburg, 1908; *Nakanune.* Unpublished, 1922–4.

Petrovskaia, Ol'ga. Poet.

Writings: Kryl'ia vzmakhnuvshie. Harbin, 1920.

Petrovykh, Mariia Sergeevna (married name Golovacheva; b. 1913, Norskii posad; d. 1979, Moscow). Poet, translator of Armenian poetry. Instrumental in helping poets such as Akhmatova get published but published little herself during her lifetime. Her poetry was collected for publication only in 1968.

Writings: Dal'nee derevo. Erevan, 1968; *Prednaznachenie.* Moscow, 1983; *Cherta gorizonta.* Erevan, 1986; *Izb.* Moscow, 1991; *Koster v nochi.* Iaroslavl', 1991.

In translation: poems in *RLT* 5 (1972); poems in Tomei, II.

Petrushevskaia, Liudmila Stefanovna (b. 1938, Moscow). Playwright, journalist, and prose writer. Left Moscow with family during repression. Spent part of childhood in orphanages. Returned 1956. Graduated Moscow State University where she studied journalism. Worked for Moscow Radio and Moscow Television. Began writing in 1960s. Prior to perestroika ran into trouble with the censorship apparatus for the gloomy nature of her writing. One of most important voices to emerge in late Soviet and post-Soviet period. Currently resides in Moscow.

Writings: Skazki bez podskazki. Moscow, 1981; *Bessmertnaia liubov'.* Moscow, 1988; *Pesni dvadtsatogo veka.* Moscow, 1988; *Tri devushki v golubom.* Moscow, 1989; *Svoi krug.* Moscow, 1990; *Lechenie Vasiliia i drugie skazki.* Moscow, 1991; *Vremia: noch',* NM 2 (1992); *Po doroge Boga Erosa.* Moscow, 1993; *Taina doma: povesti i rasskazy.* Moscow, 1995; *Bal poslednego cheloveka.* Moscow, 1996; *SS,* 5 vols. Khar'kov, 1996; *Nastoiashchie skazki.* Moscow, 1997, 1999; *Dom devushek: rasskazy i povesti.* Moscow, 1998, 1999; *Malen'kaia Groznaia,* Moscow, 1998; *Naidi menia, son.* Moscow, 2000; *Karamzin derevenskii dnevnik.* St. Petersburg, 2000.

In translation: Four by Petrushevskaya, tr. Alma Law. Scarsdale, NY, 1984; *Clarissa and Other Stories,* tr. Alma Law. Scarsdale, NY, 1985; "Our Crowd," tr. Helena Goscilo, *Michigan Quarterly Review* (Fall, 1998); "Nets and Traps," tr. Sigrid McLaughlin, in *The Image of Women in Contemporary Soviet Fiction,* ed. McLaughlin. New York, 1989; *Three Girls in Blue* in *Stars in the Morning Sky: Five Plays from the Soviet Union,* tr. Michael Glenny. London, 1989; "Mania," tr. Helena Goscilo in *Balancing Acts;* "The Violin," tr. Marina Ledkovsky in *Balancing Acts;* "Our Crowd," in *Glasnost: An Anthology of Literature under Gorbachev.* Ann Arbor, MI, 1990; "The Overlook," tr. Dobrochna Dyrcz-Freeman in *Soviet Women Writing;* "The New Family Robinson," tr. G. Bird in *Dissonant Voices: The New Russian Fiction*, ed. Oleg Chukhontsev. London, 1991; *Cinzano: Eleven Plays*, tr. Stephen Mulrine. London, 1991. *The Time: Night*, tr. Sally Laird. London, 1994; *Immortal Love*, tr. Sally Laird. London; "That Kind of Girl," tr. Lise Brody in *Dialogues*, 1995. "Fairy Tales for Grownup Children," tr. Jane Taubman in *Glas* 13 (1996). For more complete listing, see Tomei, II and *DRWW*.

Poliakova, Tat'iana. Graduate of Ivanovo State University with a degree in language and literature. Writer of ironic detective fiction.

Writings: Den'gi dlia killera. Moscow, 1997, 1998; *Tonkaia shtuchka*. Moscow, 1997; *Ia-vashi nepriiatnosti*. Moscow, 1997; *Stroptivaia mishen'*. Moscow, 1998; *Ee malen'kaia taina*. Moscow, 1998, 1999; *Zhestokii mir muzhchin*. Moscow, 1998; *Kak by ne tak*. Moscow, 1998, 1999; *Moi liubimyi killer*. Moscow, 1999; *Nevinnye damskie shalosti*. Moscow, 1998; *Sestrichki ne promakh*. Moscow, 1998; *Chego khochet zhenshchina*. Moscow, 1999; *Kapkan na sponsora*. Moscow, 1999; *Chumovaia damochka*. Moscow, 1999; *Otpetye plutovki*. Moscow, 1999; *Cherta s dva*. Moscow, 1999; *Ovechka v volch'ei shkure*. Moscow, 2000; *Ia-vashi nepriiatnosti*. Moscow, 2000; *Baryshnia i khuligan*. Moscow, 2000. For more references, see http://www.eksmo.ru.

Polianskaia, Irina (married name Kravchenko; b. 1952, Kasli, the Urals). Writer of prose fiction. The daughter of a survivor of a German prison camp, of Kolyma, and exposure to radiation. Studied music and then theater before entering the Gorky Institute of World Literature from which she graduated in 1980. First published fiction in 1983.

Writings: Predlagaemye obstoiatel'stva. Moscow, 1988. Title story also included in *Chisten'kaia zhizn'*, comp. A. Shavkuta; *Poslannik*. Moscow, 1990; "Ploshchad'," "Sel'va," and "Zhizn' dereva," in *Ne pomniashchaia zla*, comp. L. Vaneeva; "Chistaia zona," *Znamia* 1 (1990) also in *Novye amazonki*; "Bednoe serdtse Mani," *LitGaz* (September 5, 1990); "Mama," *LitOb* 11 (1990); *Chistaia zona*. Moscow, 1991; "Rasskazy," *Znamia* 5 (1993) (cycle of stories including "Penal," "Son," and "Zhizel'"); "Sneg idet tikho-tikho." "Perekhod." Rasskazy, *Znamia*, 12 (1994); "Tikhaia komnata. Rasskaz," *NM* 3 (1995); "Prokhozhdenie teni," *NM* 1–2 (1997).

In translation: "Mitigating Circumstances," tr. Michele Berdy in *Soviet Women Writing*; "The Pure Zone," tr. Rachel Osorio and Joanne Turnbull, *Glas* 13 (1996); "The Clean Zone," tr. Masha Gessen in *Half a Revolution*; "Where Did the Streetcar Go," tr. Julie Barnes in *Lives in Transit*; "The Game," tr. Ayesha Kagal and Natasha Perova in *Present Imperfect*.

Polonskaia, Elizaveta Grigor'evna (b. Movshenzon, 1890, Warsaw; d. 1969, Leningrad). Poet, translator, journalist, children's writer, and memoirist. Member of the Serapion Brothers group, trained as a doctor in Paris, returned to Russia in 1915. Served as a doctor during World War II while continuing to write.

Writings: Znameniia. St. Petersburg, 1921; *Pod kamennym dozhdem*. St. Petersburg, 1923; *Goda: izbrannye stikhi*. Leningrad, 1935; *Novye stikhi*. Leningrad, 1937; *Izb*. Moscow and Leningrad, 1966. For more complete listings, see Tomei, II.

In translation: poems in Tomei, II.

Pospelova, Mar'ia Alekseevna (b. 1780, d. 1805). Author of poetry and prose. From an impoverished gentry family in Vladimir; died young from consumption. Major works include *Luchshie chasy zhizni moei* (Moscow, 1798), for which she was rewarded with a diamond ring from Paul I; and *Nekotorye cherty prirody i istinny* (Moscow, 1801).

Pregel, Sofia (b. 1894/7, Odessa; d. 1972, Paris). Jewish descent, daughter of wealthy industrialist; mother Rosa Glazer pianist, singer. Attended progressive Chudnovskii Gymnasium; began writing poetry as schoolgirl. Mikhailovsky theater studio; performed for two seasons, Odessa; studied voice, Petrograd Conservatory. Emigrated with family to Berlin, 1922; participant in literary circle "Kruzhok poetov"; published verse in major émigré periodicals. To Paris, 1932; contributor to *Sovremennye zapiski, Chisla*; published three verse collections, 1935–8. At start of World War II, left for US, New York; American citizenship; established literary journal *Novosel'e*; published several short stories. To Paris, 1948; helped establish publishing house "Rifma", main venue for émigré poetry; published three more verse collections before death by cancer; a fourth appeared posthumously, also 3-vol. memoir of prerevolutionary life.

Writings: *Razgovor s pamiat'iu*. Paris, 1935; *Solnechnyi proizvol*. Paris, 1937; *Polden'*. Paris, 1939; "Krymskaia mozaika," *Novosel'e* 1 (1942); "Potonuvshee zakholust'e," *Novosel'e* 2 (1942); "Gnom," *Novosel'e* 3 (1942); "Zapisnaia knizhka," *Novosel'e* 6 (1942); *Berega*. Paris, 1953; *Vstrecha*. Paris, 1958; *Vesna v Parizhe*. Paris, 1966; *Poslednie stikhi*. Paris, 1973; *Moe detstvo*, vols I–II. Paris, 1973; vol. III, 1974.

In translation: poem in Todd and Hayward.

Prismanova, Anna Semenova (b. Prisman, 1892, Libau, Latvia; d. 1960, Paris; m. poet Aleksandr Ginger; two sons). Jewish Russian family, mother died young, raised by stepmother, Libau. To Moscow c. 1918, joined group "Literaturnyi osobniak"; to St. Petersburg c. 1920; by 1921 member of Union of Poets. Emigrated to Berlin, 1922, joined group "Chetyre plius odin," published in Bely's *Epopeia*. To Paris, 1924; married Ginger, 1926, two sons. Active in émigré literary organizations; helped found Union of Young Poets and Writers (1925), involved in "Kochev'e" (early 1930s), "Krug" (1935–9). First verse collection, 1937, with poems from 1924–36. In Paris through Occupation; Soviet citizenship in 1946, did not return. Headed postwar "formist" group; published three more vols. of poetry, several stories in French and Russian. Died of heart disease.

Writings: *Ten' i telo*. Paris, 1937; "Les coqs," *Cahiers du Sud* 331 (1942); *Bliznetsy*. Paris, 1946; "Les fleur et couronnes," *Cahiers du Sud* 353 (1946); *Sol'*. Paris, 1949; *Vera: liricheskaia povest'*. Paris, 1960; "O gorode i ogorode," *Mosty* 12 (1966).

In translation: poems in Markov and Sparks; Pachmuss *A Russian Cultural Revival*; Todd and Hayward; poetry and story in Kelly *Anthology*; poem tr. C. Kelly, *New Poetry Quarterly* 2 (1995).

Recent editions: *SS*. The Hague, 1990.

Puchkova, Ekaterina Naumovna (b. 1792, d. 1867). Poet, essayist. Friend of Anna Bunina, to whom she addressed a valedictory poem on the latter's departure to England. Major works include *Pervye opyty v proze* (St. Petersburg, 1812). Work reprinted with laudatory comments in *Damskii zhurnal* during the 1820s.

Rachinskaia, Elizaveta Nikolaevna (b. 1904, Helsingfors; d. 1993, London; married name Gusel'nikova). Poet, short story writer, journalist. Emigrated to Harbin in 1918. Left China for Australia and Great Britain.

Writings: *Kliuchi*. Harbin, 1926; *Dzhebel'-Kebir*. Harbin, 1937; *Komu v Kharbine zhit' khorosho*. Harbin, 1940; *Pereletnye ptitsy*. San Francisco, 1982; *Kaleidoskop zhizni*. Paris, 1990.

Radlova, Anna Dmitrievna (b. Darmolatova, 1891, St. Petersburg; d. 1949, Shcherbakov). Poet, critic, and accomplished translator of the classics from

English and French. Little of her works survived as a result of her persecution under Stalin. Died in a labor camp.

Writings: *Soty*. Petrograd, 1918; *Korabli*. Petrograd, 1920; *Krylatyi gost'*. Petrograd, 1922; *Bogoroditsyn korabl'*. Berlin, 1923.

In translation: poems in Tomei, II.

Ratushinskaia, Irina Borisovna (b. 1954, Odessa). Poet, memoirist, political activist. Lives in England.

Writings: *Stikhi. Poems, Poèmes*. Ann Arbor, 1984; *Ia dozhivu*. New York, 1986; *Vne limita. Izb.* Frankfurt, 1986; Prose: *Skazka o trekh golovakh*. Tenafly, NJ, 1986; *Stikhi*. Chicago, 1988; *Seryi tsvet nadezhdy*. London, 1989; *Odessity*. Moscow, 1996; *Ten' portreta*. Moscow, 2000.

In translation: *No, I'm Not Afraid*. Newcastle upon Tyne, 1986; *A Tale of Three Heads*, tr. Diane Nemec Ignashev. Tenafly, NJ, 1986; *Beyond the Limit*, tr. Frances Padorr Brent and Carol J. Avins. Evanston, 1987; *Pencil Letter*. Newcastle upon Tyne, 1988; *Gray is the Color of Hope*, tr. Alyona Kojevnikov. New York, 1988; *In the Beginning*, tr. Alyona Kojevnikov. New York, 1991; *Dance with a Shadow*, tr. David McDuff. Newcastle upon Tyne, 1992; *Wind of the Journey: Poems*. Chicago, 2000.

Reznikova, Nataliia Semenovna (b. 1908, Irkutsk, Russia; d. 2000, New York, married names: Tarby; Deriuzhinskaia). Novelist, poet, journalist. See *DRWW*, 536–7.

Writings: *Izmena*. Harbin, 1935; *Pushkin i Soban'skaia*. Harbin, 1936; *Raba Afrodity*. Harbin, 1936; *Pobezhdennaia*. Harbin, 1937; *Pesni zemli*. Harbin, 1938; *Ty*. Harbin, 1942.

Rostopchina, Evdokiia Petrovna (pseudonym Iasnovidiashchaia; b. Sushkova, 1811; d. 1858, Moscow; married Count Andrei Fedorovich Rostopchin 1833.) Poet, prose writer, salon hostess. Two daughters and one son; daughter Lydiia later wrote and publ. poetry. Born and raised in Moscow; 1836 moved to St. Petersburg. Her Saturday salon included Pushkin, Zhukovsky, Petr Pletnev. R. was virtually exiled to Moscow for her ballad "Nasil'nyi brak" ("The Forced Marriage," 1846) an allegory of Russian-Polish relations. In the last ten years of her life, R. wrote mainly novels and plays incl. *Vozvrat Chatskogo v Moskvu* (1856) and the novel in verse *Dnevnik devushki* (1840s and 1850s).

Writings: *Ocherki bol' shogo sveta*. St. Petersburg, 1839; *Stikhotvoreniia*. St. Petersburg, 1841; *Stikhotvoreniia*, 2 vols. St. Petersburg, 1856–8; *U pristani. Roman v pis' makh*, 4 vols. St. Petersburg, 1857; *Dnevnik devushki*. St. Petersburg, 1866; *Soch*, 2 vols. St. Petersburg, 1890; *SS*. St. Petersburg, 1910. Poems, in *Poety 1840–1850-kh godov*; Bannikov; *Tsaritsy muz; Moskovskaia muza*, ed. G. D. Klimova.

In translation: "Rank and Money," tr. Helena Goscilo in *Russian and Polish Women's Fiction*, ed. Helena Goscilo. Knoxville, TN, 1985; *SEEJ* 30:2 (1986); Perkins and Cook; Kelly *Anthology*; poems and the play *Chatsky's Return to Moscow* excerpted in Tomei I.

Recent editions: "Dom sumasshedshikh v Moskve v 1858g," in *Epigramma i satira: iz istorii literaturnoi bor' by XIX veka*. Moscow and Leningrad, 1931–21; repr. Oxford, 1975; *Stikhotvoreniia. Proza. Pis' ma*, ed. Boris Romanov. Moscow, 1986; *Talisman: izbrannye liriki*. Moscow, 1987. *Schastlivaia zhenshchina: Literaturnye sochineniia* (1991); "Poedinok," in *Russkaia romanticheskaia povest'*. Moscow, 1992; *Palazzo Forli* (1993).

Rubina, Dina (b. 1953, Tashkent). Studied music at the Tashkent Conservatory. Began publishing prose fiction in her teens. Moved to Moscow in 1984; emigrated to Israel in 1988. In 1991 awarded the Arie Dulchik Prize for Literature.

Writings: *Kogda zhe poidet sneg?…* Tashkent, 1980; *Zavtra, kak obychno*. Plovdiv, 1985; *Otvorite okno*. Tashkent, 1987; *Dvoinaia familiia*. Moscow, 1990; "Doch' Bukhary," *NM* 1

(1993); "Vo vratakh Tvoikh," *NM* 5 (1993); *Odin intelligent uselsia na doroge.* Jerusalem, 1994; "Itak, prodolzhaem!.. Monolog naturshchitsy," *Dialog* 1 (Moscow, 1996); *Kamera naezzhaet.* Moscow, 1996; "'Vot idet Messiia!..'" *DN* 9–10 (1996); *Angel konvoinyi.* Moscow, 1997; *Uroki muzyki.* Moscow, 1998.

In translation: "Recapitulation," tr. Alex Miller, *SovLit* 6 (1987); "That Strange Man Altukhov," tr. June Goss and Elena Goreva, *SovLit* 3 (1989); "The Double-Barreled Name," tr. Marian Schwartz, *From the Soviets*, Special issue of *Nimrod* 33: 2 (Spring/Summer 1990); "The Blackthorn," tr. Nicholas Short, *SovLit*, 1988; "The Blackthorn," tr. Brittain Smith in *Lives in Transit*; "On Upper Maslovka," tr. Marian Schwartz, *Glas* 13 (1996).

Runova, Ol'ga Pavlovna (b. Meshcherskaia, 1864, Smolensk province; d. 1952; married: 1) Runov, 1882; 2) Bogdanov, 1889). Precocious daughter of provincial gentry. 1879, attended teachers' college for women, St. Petersburg; sympathy for radical movement. First published 1887; and in 1890, by Tolstoy's publishing house "Posrednik" ("Intermediary"); stories on peasantry demonstrate influence of Tolstoyanism. 1905, exiled to Saratov for several years for revolutionary activity. After Revolution, wrote pamphlets on revolutionary women; last collection of stories published 1927.

Writings: "V noch' pered Rozhdestvom," suppl. to *Nedelia* 1 (1887); *Likhie podarki.* 1890; 8th edn., 1912; "Pastoral," in *Sbornik na pomoshch' uchashchimsia zhenshchinam.* Moscow, 1901; *Pavliuk.* Saratov, 1904; 3rd edn, Moscow, 1912; "*Utrennichki" i drugie rasskazy.* Moscow, 1905; *Letiashchie teni. Rasskazy.* St. Petersburg, 1912; "Bez zaveta," *Sovremennyi mir* 10 (1913); "Lunnyi svet," *RMysl'* 4–5 (1914); *SS*, vol. I *Lunnyi svet*; vol. II *Mudrost' zhizni.* Petrograd, 1916; *Babushka kommunizma Klara Tsetlin.* Moscow, 1924; *Bol'shaia dusha (N. K. Krupskaia).* Moscow and Leningrad, 1924; *U kornia. 1904–1906.* Moscow and Leningrad, 1926; 2nd edn, Moscow, 1927; *Polden'. Rasskazy.* Moscow and Leningrad, 1927.

In translation: Russian Boy. Fragment of an Autobiography from 1916–1924. London, 1942; "The Thief," in *Soviet Stories of the Last Decade*, tr. Elizaveta Fen. London, 1945.

Saburova, Irina Evgen'evna (b. 1907, Riga; d. 1979, Munich; married: 1) poet, journalist A. M. Perfil'ev; 2) Baron von Rosenberg). Raised in Riga. Began writing early, published first story at 16. Contributed to Riga journals, mostly fairy tale-novellas. Emigrated after Soviet occupation of Baltic, 1940; lived nomadic life; camp for displaced persons near Munich, 1946; produced own books on linotype machine, incl. account of camp life, *Dipilogicheskaia azbuka*, later incorporated into *O nas.* Published several more collections of fairy tales, single vol. of verse, anti-utopian tale *Posle...*, illustrated monograph on poet Anna Pavlova, historical novel about Russian life in Baltics. In Munich until death.

Writings: "Chezare," *Zhurnal sodruzhestva* 9 (1935); "Proshchenoe voskresen'e," *Zhurnal sodruzhestva* 2 (1936); "Izumrudnyi persten'," *Zhurnal sodruzhestva* 6 (1936); "Plant goroda Sankt-Peterburga," *Zhurnal sodruzhestva* 7 (1936); "Zheleznye tiul'pany," *Zhurnal sodruzhestva* 8–9 (1936); "Praktiki radi," *Zhurnal sodruzhestva* 5 (1937); "Oleni," *Zhurnal sodruzhestva* 7 (1937); "Alesha," 8–9 (1937); "Vstrecha," *Zhurnal sodruzhestva* 11 (1937); "Na elke u printsa," *Zhurnal sodruzhestva* 12 (1937); "Pis'mo poeta," *Zhurnal sodruzhestva* 38 (1938); *Ten' sinego marta.* Riga, 1938; *Dama tref. Sbornik rasskazov.* Munich, 1946; *Dipilogicheskaia azbuka.* Munich, 1946; *Korolevstvo Alykh Bashen'. Rozhdestvenskie rasskazy.* Munich, 1947; "Professor istorii," *Literaturnyi sovremennik* 3 (1952); "Vara," *Grani* 19 (1953); *Bessmertnyi lebed' (Anna Pavlova).* New

York, 1956; *Razgovor molcha. Sbornik stikhov.* Munich, 1956; *Kopilka vremeni. Rasskazy.* Munich, 1957; *Posle...* Munich, 1961; *Korabli starogo goroda. Istoricheskii roman iz zhizni russkoi Baltiki 1924–1944.* Munich, 1963; *Gorshochek nezhnosti,* 1965; *Schastlivoe zerkalo. Rasskazy.* Munich, 1966; *O nas. Roman.* Munich, 1972; *Korolevstvo.* Munich, 1976.

In translation: stories in Pachmuss, *A Russian Cultural Revival* and *Russian Literature in the Baltic Between the World Wars.*

Recent editions: Alykh Bashen' korolevstvo. Moscow, 2000.

Sadur, Ekaterina (b. 1973, Novosibirsk). Writer of prose fiction. Moved to Moscow in 1985 with her mother Nina Sadur.

Writings: "Chuzhoi dnevnik," *Novaia iunost'* 5–6 (1994); "Iz teni v svet pereletaia," *Znamia* 8 (1994); *Prazdnik starukh na more.* Vologda, 1998.

In translation: "Kozlov's Nights," tr. Rachel Osorio in *Present Imperfect.*

Sadur, Nina (b. Kolesnikova, 1950, Novosibirsk). Writer of prose fiction and plays. Moved to Moscow in 1978 where she completed a program of study at the Institute of Literature in 1983. Entered the Soviet Union of Writers in 1989 as a playwright. Experienced difficulties publishing before the 1990s. Nominated for the Russian Booker Prize in 1993. Won the "Znamia" Prize in 1997 for her story "Nemets."

Writings: "Eto moe okno," *Sibirskie ogni* 7 (1977); "Novoe znakomstvo," *Teatr* 4 (1986); *Poka zhivye.* VAAP, 1987; *Chudnaia baba.* Moscow, 1989, staged in US as "Wonderbroad"; "Devochka noch'iu," in *Vstrechnyi khod.* Moscow, 1989. Issued separately, Moscow, 1992; "Ekhai," *Teatr* 6 (1989); *Ved'miny slezki: kniga prozy.* Novosibirsk, 1990; Moscow, 1994; "Pronikshie," in *Ne pomniashchaia zla* (a suite of stories including "Blesnulo," "Milen'kii, ryzhen'kii," "Kol'tsa," "Dve nevesty," "Shelkovistye volosy," "Chervivyi synok," "Zlye devushki," "Siniaia ruka," "Zamerzli," and "Ved'miny slezki"); "Krasnyi paradiz" and "Morokob," *Siuzhety* 1 (1990); "Chto-to otkroetsia," in *Vidimost' nas.* Moscow, 1991; "Krasnyi paradiz (P'esa v I akte)," in *Novye amazonki;* "Cherti, suki, komunnal'nye kozly . . .," *Teatr* 6 (1992); "Iug," *Znamia* 10 (1992); "Milen'kii, ryzhen'kii," *Teatr* 8 (1992); Stories in *Soglasie,* 1992 and *Ural,* 1993; *Devochka noch'iu.* Moscow, 1993; "Slepye pesni," *Znamia* 10 (1995) (the third part of her novel *Sad*); "Zaikusha. Povest'," *Strelets* 2 (1995); *Nemets. Roman, Znamia* 6 (1997); "O realizme prizrachnogo," *Zolotoi vek* 10 (1997); *Sad.* Vologda, 1997; "Som-s-usom," *Zolotoi vek* 10 (1997); *Obmorok: kniga p'es.* Vologda, 1999; "Zapreshcheno," *Znamia* 2 (1999); *Chudesnye znaki.* Moscow, 2000.

In translation: "Touched: Little Stories," tr. Masha Gessen in *Half a Revolution;* "Wicked Girls," tr. Wendy Fornoff in *Lives in Transit;* "Worm-eaten Sonny," tr. Wendy Fornoff in *Lives in Transit;* "Witch's Tears," tr. Alexander Maidan in *Present Imperfect;* excerpts from "Witch's Tears," tr. Alexander Maidan, *Women's View, Glas* 3 (1992); "Irons and Diamonds," tr. Andrew Bromfield, *Glas* 6 (1993); *Frozen* (one-act play) in Kelly *Anthology; Witch's Tears and Other Stories,* tr. Cathy Porter. London, 1997.

Sedakova, Ol'ga Aleksandrovna (b. 1949, Moscow). Poet, educated at Moscow State University and the Institute of Slavic and Balkan Studies, with a candidate's dissertation on Slavic mythology (1982). Teaches on Philosophy Faculty, Moscow State University, lives in Moscow. Prolific scholar and translator, selected examples given below.

Writings: "Shkatulka s zerkalom. Ob odnom glubinnom motive A. A. Akhmatovoi," *Uchenye zapiski Tartusskogo gosudarstvennogo universiteta* 641 (Trudy po znakovym sistemam), 17 (1984), 93–108; *Vrata, okna, arki: izbrannye stikhotvoreniia.* Paris, 1986; *Kitaiskoe puteshestvie, stely i nadpisi, starye pesni.* Moscow, 1990; "O granitsakh poezii. Velimir Khlebnikov v noveishikh zarubezhnykh issledovaniiakh," in *Russkaia literatura v zarubezhnykh issledovaniiakh 1980-kh godov.* Moscow, 1990, 46–75; "O pogibshem literaturnom pokolenii: pamiati Leni Gubanova," *Volga* 6 (1990), 135–46; "Mednyi vsadnik: kompositsiia konflikta," *Rossiia-Russia* 7 (Marsilio Editori, 1991), 39–55; "Vospominaniia o Venedikte Erofeeve," *Teatr* 9 (1991), 98–103; "Zametki i vospominaniia o raznykh stikhotvoreniiakh, a takzhe POKHVALA POEZII," *Volga* 6 (1991), 135–64; with M. Gasparov, "Dialogi o Bakhtine," *Novyi krug* 1 (Kiev, 1991), 113–17; "Znak, smysl, vest'," in *Nezamechennaia zemlia.* Moscow and St. Petersburg, 1992, 249–52; "Puteshestvie v Briansk," *Volga* 5–6 (1992), 138–57; "Muzhestvo i posle nego: zametki perevodchika *Muzhestva byt'* P. Tillikha," *Strana i mir* 3: 69 (May–June, 1992), 159–70; *Stikhi.* Moscow, 1994; "Frantsisk, chelovek tainstvennyi," *LitOb* 3–4 (1994), 69–76; "Rassuzhdenie o metode," *NLitOb* 27 (1997), 177–90; "V Geraklitovu reku vtoroi raz ne voidesh'," *Znamia* 6 (1998), 190–5; with V. Bibikhin, *et al., Nashe polozhenie: obraz nastoiashchego.* Moscow, 2000.

Translations: Paul Claudel, *Izbrannye stikhi.* Moscow, 1992; "Rainer Maria Rilke," *Rodnik* 8 (1988), 13–18; Ezra Pound, *Izbrannye stikhotvoreniia.* Moscow, 1992; "Ezra Paund: 1885–1972–1995," *LitOb* 6 (1995), 52–5.

In translation: Poems in *Third Wave*, 129–36; "A Rare Independence," *Brodsky Through the Eyes of His Contemporaries*, ed. V Polukhina. Basingstoke, 1992, 237–59; *Contemporary Russian Poetry*, 268–79; *Glas* 4 (1993), 221–7; "Fifth Stanzas," in Kelly *Anthology*; *The Silk of Time*, ed. Valentina Polukhina. Keele, 1994; *The Wild Rose*, tr. Richard McKane. London, 1996; poems, tr. Catriona Kelly in Tomei, II; essay: "The Vacancy for a Poet," in *Rereading Russian Poetry*, ed. Stephanie Sandler, New Haven, CT, 1999, 71–7.

Seifullina, Lydiia Nikolaevna (b. 1889, nr. Magnitogorsk; d. 1954, Moscow; married to critic and journalist V. Pravdukhin). Daughter of peasant woman and Tatar father, village priest. Started working at 17; first published 1917. Member of Socialist Revolutionary Party (1917–19); 1920 graduated from Moscow Higher Pedagogical Courses. Husband executed, 1939; Seifullina also possibly arrested. Published best experimental prose in 1920s; subsequently more active as dramatist, journalist and educator, later fiction displays constraints of Socialist Realism.

Writings: *SS*, 3 vols. Moscow, 1925; *SS*, 6 vols. Moscow and Leningrad, 1929–31; *SS*, 4 vols. Moscow, 1968–9; *Soch*, 2 vols. Moscow, 1980.

In translation: "The Old Woman," in *Azure Cities. Stories of New Russia*, ed. Joshua Kunitz. New York, 1929; "The Lawbreakers," in *Soviet Literature*, ed. George Reavey and Marc L. Slonim. New York, 1934; excerpt from *The Lawbreakers*, tr. Lisa Taylor in Tomei, II.

Serebrennikova, Aleksandra Nikolaevna (b. Petrova, 1883, Macha, Lenskie Goldfields; d. 1975, San Francisco). Poet, journalist.

Writings: *Tsvety kitaiskoi poezii* (translations of Chinese poetry from English translations, with her husband I. I. Serebrennikov). Tianjin, 1938; *Velikaia legenda*. San Francisco, 1967.

Shaginian, Marietta Sergeevna (b. 1888, Moscow; d. 1982, Moscow). Poet, prose writer, journalist, dramatist. Born into a family of Armenian intelligentsia, Shaginian wrote prolifically. Embraced the Bolshevik Revolution and became associated with the official Soviet literary establishment.

Writings: *Pervye vstrechi*. Moscow, 1909; *Orientalia*. Moscow, 1913; *Mess-mend, ili Ianki v Petrograde*. Leningrad, 1927; *Kik*. Leningrad, 1929; *Gidro-tsentral'*. Leningrad, 1931; *SS*, 5 vols. Moscow, 1971–5; *Chelovek i vremia*. Moscow, 1980. For more complete listing, see Tomei, II.

In translation: "Three Looms," in *Azure Cities*, ed. J. Kunitz. New York, 1929; *Creative Freedom and the Soviet Artist*. London, 1953; *Journey through Soviet Armenia*. Moscow, 1954; *Retracing Lenin's Steps*. Moscow, 1974; "Seeing in the Twentieth Century," in *Always a Woman*. Moscow, 1987; "Man and Time," *SovLit* 9 (1989); *Mass Mend: Yankees in Petrograd*. Ann Arbor, 1991; "The Corinthian Canal," in Tomei, II.

Shakhova, Elizaveta Nikitichna (b. 1822, St. Petersburg; d. Staraia Ladoga, 1899). Daughter of naval officer who encouraged literary interests; father d. 1834; compared to Kul'man when published first book at 15. Visited Glinkas' and Maikova's homes; friends included Turgenev and Benediktov; published in journals late 1830s–50s. 1845 entered Spaso-Borodinskii Monastery in Moscow; 1863 took the veil, and adopted name Mother Mariia. Continued writing mainly on religious subjects until her death.

Writings: *Opyty v stikhakh piatnadtsatiletnei devitsy Elisavety Shakhovoi*. St. Petersburg, 1837; *Stikhotvoreniia*. St. Petersburg, 1839; *Stikhotvoreniia*. St. Petersburg, 1840; *Povesti v stikhakh*. St. Petersburg, 1842; *Mirianka i otshel'nitsa*. St. Petersburg, 1849; "Pamiatnye zapiski o zhizni igumenii Marii, osnovatel'nitsy Spaso-borodinskogo obshchezhitel'nogo monastyria," *Strannik* 5–6 (1865); *Iudif*. Moscow, 1877; *Sochineniia v stikhakh*, 3 vols., ed. N. N. Shakhov. St. Petersburg, 1911. Poems in Bannikov; *Tsaritsy muz*.

In translation: Kelly *Anthology*.

Shakhovskaia, Zinaida Alekseevna, Princess (pseudonyms: "Jacques Croisé", Z. Sarana; b. 1906, Moscow; married S. S. Malevskii-Malevich, 1926). Brother Dmitrii Shakhovskoi, later Bishop of Russian Orthodox Church in San Francisco. Raised in Moscow and estate Matovo, Tula province; fled Russia with family from Novorossiisk to Constantinople, 1920; American College in Turkey, 1921–3; to Brussels with brother Dmitrii, 1923; began writing poetry, participated in literary group "Edinorog"; finished studies, Paris, 1925–6. In Belgian Congo, 1926–8, settled in Belgium, 1928; participated in Paris literary life of 1930s, close to "Paris Note" writers; reporter for Belgian newspaper; ed. Belgian literary journal. During war, French Army Red Cross; participated in Resistance; to London, 1942, ed. French Information Agency; news correspondent in Europe, 1945–8, at Nuremburg trials; decorated by Belgium and France. To Paris, 1949; won Prix de Paris for novel *Europe et Valérius*, 1949. Visited Russia on diplomatic passport, 1956–7, inspiration for 4-vol. memoir in French. Head of French and Russian broadcasting, French Radio Television, 1961–8; twice won Prix Therouanne de l'Academie Française for historical works, 1964, 1968. Chief ed. *RMysl'*, 1968–78; co-ed. *Russkii al'manakh*. Member Société des Gens de Lettres de France, French Pen Club; since 1986, Commandeur dans l'Ordre des Arts et des Lettres for literary activities. Most notable for prose works in French, though returned to writing poetry, memoirs, criticism in Russian, 1970s.

Writings: *Dvadtsat' odno*. Brussels, 1928; *Ukhod*. Brussels, 1934; *Doroga*. Tallin, 1935; *Vie d'Alexandre Pouchkine*. Brussels, 1937; *Insomnies. Poèmes*. Brussels, 1939; *Europe et Valérius*. Paris, 1949; *Sortie de secours*. Paris, 1952; *Le dialogue des aveugles*. Paris, 1955; *La parole devient sang*. Paris, 1955; *Jeu des massacres*. Paris, 1956; *Ma Russie habillée en*

U.R.S.S. Paris, 1958; *La vie quotidienne à Moscou au XVIIe siecle.* Paris, 1963; *La vie quotidienne à St. Petersbourg a l'époque romantique.* Paris, 1967; *Tel est mon siècle: I. Lumières et ombres.* Paris, 1964; II. *Une manière de vivre.* Paris, 1965; III. *La folle Clio.* Paris, 1966; IV. *La drôle de paix.* Paris, 1967; *Pered snom.* Paris, 1970; *Otrazheniia.* Paris, 1975; *Rasskazy, stat'i, stikhi.* Paris, 1978; *V poiskakh Nabokova.* Paris, 1979.

In translation: The Privilege Was Mine. London, 1958; New York, 1959; London, New York, 1964; *The Fall of Eagles: Precursors of Peter the Great.* New York, 1964.

Recent editions: V poiskakh Nabokova. Otrazheniia. Moscow, 1991.

Shapir, Ol'ga Andreevna (b. Kisliakova, 1850, Oranienbaum; d. 1916, Petersburg; m. doctor and revolutionary L. Shapir, 1872). Daughter of former serf, estate manager who worked for Decembrist Pestel'; mother of aristocratic Swedish descent. Educated at Aleksandr Gymnasium, St. Petersburg, 1863, and public Vladimir courses. In 1870s, closely associated with liberal and radical circles in St. Petersburg. First published 1879; well-known writer for next 35 years. In 1890s joined Russian Women's Mutual Philanthropic Society, moderate feminist group. Member of commission in first Duma to draw up petition for women's rights; helped to organize First All-Russian Congress of Women, 1908.

Writings: Povesti i rasskazy. St. Petersburg, 1889; *Ee siiatel'stvo.* St. Petersburg, 1890; 3rd edn, 1905; *Avdot'iny dochki.* St. Petersburg, 1901, and in Uchenova, *Tol'ko chas.* Moscow, 1988. *Invalidy i novobrantsy.* St. Petersburg, 1901; *Drug detstva.* St. Petersburg, 1903; "V burnie gody," *RMysl'* 1–8 (1906) and St. Petersburg, 1907; 2nd edn, 1910; "Zhenskii s"ezd," *Russkie vedomosti* 295 (1908); *SS*, 10 vols. St. Petersburg, 1910–11; "Avtobiografiia" in F. Fidler, *Pervye literaturnye shagi.* Moscow, 1911; "Zhenskoe bespravie," *Birzhevye vedomosti,* June 15, 1916.

In translation: "The Settlement," in Kelly *Anthology.*

Shchepkina-Kupernik, Tat'iana L'vovna (b. 1874, d. 1952; m. name Polynova). Prose writer, playwright, translator, memorist, poet, journalist, actress. Important in Russian theater world before Revolution; author of prize-winning plays. First collection of poetry *Iz zhenskikh pisem* (From Women's Letters, 1898). Wrote many journalistic articles and reviews; also short stories and numerous memoirs. Received Order of the Red Banner of Labor (1944). Translations include plays by Hugo, Molière, Lope de Vega, Shakespeare.

Writings: "Letnaia kartinka," *Artist* 23 (1892); *Schast'e.* St. Petersburg, 1898; *Stranichki zhizni.* St. Petersburg, 1898; *Iz zhenskikh pisem. Stikhotvoreniia.* Moscow, 1898; *Nezametnye liudi.* Moscow, 1900; *Na solntse i v teni.* Moscow, 1904; *Neotpravlennye pis'ma i drugie rasskazy.* Moscow, 1906; *Schastlivaia zhenshchina.* Moscow, 1911; *Oblaka.* Moscow, 1912; *Dramaticheskie perevody* 2–3. Moscow, 1911–1914); *Otzvuki voiny.* Moscow, 1915; *Dni moei zhizni.* Moscow, 1928; *Ermolova.* Moscow, 1972; "Pervyi bal," in *Tol'ko chas.*

In translation: "A Vision of the War," and "Deborah," tr. J.D. Duff in *The Soul of Russia,* ed. Winifred Stephens Whale. London, 1916; "First Ball," tr. Melissa Merrill, in Bisha *et al.*

Shcherbakova, Ekaterina (Klim-Shcherbakova). Daughter of Galina Shcherbakova. *Writings: Vam i ne snilos'* . . . *Piatnadtsat' let spustia* in *Vam i ne snilos'.* Moscow, 1996.

Shcherbakova, Galina (b. Rezhabek, 1932, Dzerzhinsk). Writer of prose fiction. Trained as a journalist in Rostov University. Lives in Moscow. Laureate of the "Novyi Mir" Prize for 1995. Nominated by editorial board of *Novyi Mir* for the State Prize of the Russian Federation in literature and art for 1998.

Writings: Sprava ostavalsia gorodok. Moscow, 1979; *Roman i Iul'ka: P'esa-razmyshleniia.* Moscow, 1982; *Vam i ne snilos'.* Moscow, 1983; *Dver' v chuzhuiu zhizn'.* Moscow, 1985. Reissued in 1997 by "AST" Press; *Otchaiannaia osen': Povesti.* Moscow, 1985; "Krushenie," *Zhurnalist* 1, 2 (1987); *Sneg k dobru.* Moscow, 1988; "Ei vo vred zhivushchaia," in *Chistye prudy.* Moscow, 1989; *Krushenie.* Moscow, 1990; *Anatomiia razvoda.* Moscow, 1990; "Tri 'liubvi' Mashi Peredreevoi," in *Chistye prudy.* Moscow, 1990; "Emigratsiia po-russku [sic] . . .," *Ogonek*, 9 (1991); "Dochki, materi, ptitsy i ostrova," *Soglasie* 6 (1991); "Puteshestviia," *Ogonek* 20–21 (1992); "Ubikvisty," *Soglasie* 2 (1992); "Radosti zhizni," *NM* 3 (1995); "Kostochka avokado," *NM* 9 (1995); "Love-storiia," *NM* 11 (1995); *God Aleny: romany.* Moscow, 1996; *Vam i ne snilos'.* Moscow, 1996; *Zhenshchiny v igre bez pravil.* Moscow, 1996; *Mandarinovyi god: povesti i rasskazy.* Moscow, 1997; "Mitina liubov'," *NM* 3 (1997); *Prichudy liubvi.* Moscow, 1997; *Provintsialy v Moskve: romany.* Moscow, 1997; *Armiia liubovnikov, NM* 2, 3 (1998); *Otchaiannaia osen'.* Moscow, 1998; "Aktrisa i militsioner," *NM* 3 (1999); "Liudi stol'ko ne zhivut, skol'ko ia khochu rasskazat'," *NM* 1 (1999).

Screenplays: "Fe Li Ni": Fedoseeva Lidiia Nikolaevna. Moscow, 1989.

In translation: "The Wall," tr. Helena Goscilo, in *Balancing Acts;* "Uncle Khlor and Koriakin," tr. Mary Zirin, in *Lives in Transit;* "The Three 'Loves' of Masha Peredreeva," tr. Rachel Osorio, *Women's View, Glas* 3 (1992) and in *Present Imperfect.*

Shcherbina, Tat'iana Georgievna (b. 1954/6 Moscow). Poet, essayist. Studied at Moscow University in the French department, with some graduate work in theater studies; has worked for Radio Liberty in Moscow and Munich.

Writings: Lebedinaia pesnia. Moscow, 1981; *Tsvetnye reshetki.* Moscow, 1982; *Novyi Panteon.* Moscow, 1983; *Natiurmort s prevrashcheniiami.* Moscow, 1985; *Nol' nol'.* Moscow, 1987, includes selections from first four books; *Ispoved' shpiona.* Moscow, 1988; *Prostranstvo.* Moscow, 1989; *Shcherbina.* Moscow, 1991; *Zhizn' bez: Stikhi.* Moscow, 1997.

In translation: poems in *Lives in Transit,* 294–8; *Glas* 1 (1991), 237–46; *Third Wave,* 13–22.

Shchirovskaia, Elena Nikolaevna (d. Paris 1937). Novelist.

Writings: Sbornik rasskazov, miniatiur i pr. Harbin, 1912; *Po puti zhizni.* Harbin, before 1921; *Pered voinoi.* Harbin, 1921.

Shendrikova, Klavdiia Vasil'evna (b. 1882, Viatka, Russia; d. 1955, San Francisco). Prose writer, playwright.

Writings: Iz-za vlasti. Shanghai, 1932; *Kreshchenskii vecherok.* Shanghai, 1932; *Sem'ia Kuznetsovykh.* Shanghai, 1936; *Zhenshchina iz bara.* Shanghai, undated, 1930s; *V pautine Shanghaia.* Shanghai, 1937.

Shkapskaia, Mariia Mikhailovna (b. Andreevskaia, 1891, St. Petersburg; d. 1952, Moscow). Poet, journalist. Mother had been born a serf. Looked after herself from age 11. Arrested and exiled for socialist activity in 1913. Returned to Russia in 1916. Chiefly known for her journalistic prose and her poems de-mythologizing and reconceptualizing motherhood.

Writings: Mater dolorosa. Petrograd, 1921, 2nd edn, Berlin-Riga, 1922; *Baraban strogogo gospodina.* Berlin, 1922; *Chas vechernii.* Petrograd, 1922; *Iav'.* Moscow, 1923; *Krov'-ruda.* Petrograd and Berlin, 1922, 2nd edn, Moscow, 1925; *Zemnye remesla.* Moscow, 1925; *Sama po sebe.* Leningrad, 1930; *Piatnadtsat' i odin.* Moscow, 1931; *Stikhi.* London, 1979.

In translation: It Actually Happened. A Book of Facts. Moscow, 1942; *The Mother and the Stern Master: Selected Poems.* Nottingham, 1998; "No Dream," in Kelly *Anthology;* poems in Tomei, II.

Shvarts, Elena Andreevna (b. 1948, Leningrad). Poet, lives in St. Petersburg.
Writings: Tantsuiushchii David. New York, 1985; *Stikhi.* Leningrad, 1987; *Trudy i dni Lavinii, Monakhini iz Ordena Obrezaniia Serdtsa.* Ann Arbor, 1987; *Storony sveta. Stikhi.* Leningrad, 1989; *Stikhi.* Leningrad, 1990; *Lotsiia nochi.* St. Petersburg, 1993; *Pesnia ptitsy na dne morskom.* St. Petersburg, 1995; *Mundus Imaginalis.* St. Petersburg, 1996; *Zapadno-vostochnyi veter.* St. Petersburg, 1997; *Opredelenie v durnuiu pogodu.* St. Petersburg, 1997; *Solo na raskalennoi trube.* St. Petersburg, 1998; *Stikhotvoreniia i poemy.* St. Petersburg, 1999; *Dikopis' poslednego vremeni.* St. Petersburg, 2001.
In translation: "Coldness and Rationality," *Brodsky Through the Eyes of His Contemporaries,* ed. Valentina Polukhina. London, 1992, 215–36; *Paradise: Selected Poems,* tr. Michael Molnar. Newcastle upon Tyne, 1993; poems in *Lives in Transit,* 289–93; *Contemporary Russian Poetry,* 246–57; *Women's View; Glas* 3 (1992), 163–74; *Third Wave,* 211–22; *Mapping Codes,* 56–57; "Sale of a Historian's Library," in Kelly *Anthology;* poems, tr. Sibelan Forrester in Tomei, II.

Skopichenko, Ol'ga Alekseevna (b. 1908, Syzran'; d. 1997, San Francisco), married name Konovalova. Poet, short story writer. Emigrated to Harbin, then moved to Shanghai.
Writings: Rodnye poryvy. Harbin, 1926; *Budushchemu vozhdiu.* Tianjin, 1928; *Put' izgnannika.* Shanghai, 1932; *Pro zaitsa, lisu i ezha.* Shanghai, 1930s; *U samogo sinego moria.* Tubabao, 1949; *Nasha zhizn'.* Tubabao, 1950; *Neugasimoe.* USA, 1954; *Pamiatka.* San Francisco, 1960s; *Rasskazy i stikhi.* San Francisco, 1994.

Sofonova, Ol'ga Vasil'evna (b. 1907, St. Petersburg; d. 1992, Sydney). Poet, prose writer. Emigrated to Harbin, then moved to Shanghai; in both cities worked as a journalist and translator. Went to Australia in 1949, continued to publish poetry and articles in émigré journals.
Writings: Tainyi kliuch stikhov. Sydney, 1966; *Puti nevedomye.* Munich, 1980.

Sokhanskaia, Nadezhda (Pseudonym "Kokhanovskaia," b. 1823, d. 1884). Author of prose fiction and autobiography, journalist, ethnographer. Graduated with honors from a boarding school in Khar'kov. On the advice of Petr Pletnev, then ed. of *The Contemporary,* she wrote an autobiography in a series of letters to him (1847–8, first published 1896). Sokhanskaia was most prolific in the late 1850s and early 1860s. She had ties to the Slavophiles and published many of her works in Ivan Aksakov's *Den'* (Day) and *Rus'.*
Writings: Grafinia D**** (1848); *Posle obeda v gostiakh, RV* 8:2 (1858); *Iz provintsial'noi gallerei portretov, RV* 5 (1859) and in *Dacha;* "Stepnoi tsvetok na mogilu Pushkina: Kriticheskii etiud," 1859; "Gaika," *Russkoe slovo* 4 (1860); *Starina: Semeinaia pamiat',* 1861; *Kholera: Kamennye baby,* 1861; "S khutora. Pis'mo o sviatykh gorakh," 1864; *Sumerechnye rasskazy. Staroe vospominanie tetushki,* 1885.
In translation: A *Conversation after Dinner,* in Andrew; *An After-Dinner Visit,* tr. Andrea Lanoux in Tomei, I

Solov'eva, Poliksena (pseudonym Allegro; b. 1867, d. 1924). Poet, prose writer, author of children's stories, editor and publisher of children's magazine.
Writings: Stikhotvoreniia. St. Petersburg, 1899; *Inei.* St. Petersburg, 1905; ed. *Tropinka.* 1906–12; *Plakun-trava.* St. Petersburg, 1909; tr. Lewis Caroll, *Prikliucheniia Alisy v strane chudes.* St. Petersburg, 1909. *"Tainaia pravda" i drugie rasskazy.* Moscow, 1910; *Perekrestok. Povest' v stikhakh.* St. Petersburg, 1913; *Prikliucheniia Kroli. Stikhi.* St. Petersburg, 1914; *Krupenchika.* St. Petersburg, 1915; *Chudesnoe kol'tso. Narodnye skazki.* Moscow, 1915; *Kuklin dom. Rasskaz v stikhakh.* St. Petersburg, 1916; *Poslednie stikhi.* Moscow and St. Petersburg, 1923.

In translation: poems, tr. Nancy Lynn Cooper in Tomei, I.

Stolitsa, Liubov' (b. 1884, d. 1934). Poet and dramatist.

Writings: *Rainia*. Moscow, 1908; *Lada*. Moscow, 1912; *Rus': Tret'ia kniga stikhov*. Moscow, 1915; *Elena Deeva*. Moscow, 1916; *Golovoi kover*. Unpublished, 1916; *Sviataia blud-nitsa*. Unpublished, c. 1917; *Dva Ali*. Unpublished, 1926; *Rogozhskaia Charovnitsa*. Unpublished, 1928; *Golos nezrimogo*. Sofia, Bulgaria, 1934.

Sumarokova, Natal'ia Platonovna (b. 1765, d. 1814). Poet, sister of the Tobol'sk writer and journalist Pankratii Platonovich Sumarokov, in whose journal *Irtysh'* she published her epigrams and lyric poems.

Sundueva, Ekaterina. Poet.

Writings: *Pushinki*. Harbin, 1927.

Sushkova, Mar'ia Vasil'evna (b. Khrapovitskaia, 1752; d. 1803). Poet, prose writer, translator. From a distinguished gentry family (her brother Aleksandr, also a poet, was a highly-placed official at the court of Catherine II). Contributed many poems and translations to periodicals, beginning in 1769.

Svin'ina, Anastas'ia Petrovna. Poet; **Svin'ina, Ekaterina Petrovna** (married name Bakhmeteva, b. 1778 or 1779, d. 1841). Poet, translator. From the family of a highly-placed state official, apparently residing in Pereslavl'-Zalesskii. Published quite widely in late eighteenth-century periodicals, especially *PPPV*.

Tarasova, Elena (b. 1959, Rostov-on-Don). Writer of prose fiction. Grew up in Makhahk-ala on the Caspian Sea.

Writings: "Ne pomniashchaia zla," in *Ne pomniashchaia zla*, comp. L. Vaneeva. Moscow, 1990; "Ty khorosho nauchilsia est', Adam," in *Novye amazonki*.

In translation: "She Who Bears No Ill," tr. Masha Gessen in *Half a Revolution*.

Tauber, Ekaterina (b. 1903, Khar'kov; d. 1987, Mougin; married Konstantin Starov, 1936). Father lawyer, professor at Khar'kov Business School. Emigrated with parents to Belgrade, 1920; graduate girls' school, Khar'kov Institute, 1922. From mid-1920s participant in Lermontov Literary Circle, and Russian-Serbian group "Stupen'"; published first verse, 1927; from 1928, member Belgrade filial of Khodasevich's "Perekrestok". French Department, Belgrade University, 1924–8; taught French and German in Serbian school. Member, Belgrade Union of Russian Writers and Journalists; from 1934, participant in circle "Literaturnaia sreda"; tr., co-ed. anthology of Yugoslavian verse. First book of poetry, 1935. To Mougin, near Cannes, 1936; French citizenship, 1949; taught Russian Carnot Lycée, Cannes, 1955–71. Continued publishing verse collections, stories, reviews of émigré and Soviet writers throughout lengthy career.

Writings: ed., *Antologiia novoi iugoslavskoi liriki*. Belgrade, 1933; *Odinochestvo*. Berlin, 1935; *Pod sen'iu olivy*. Paris, 1948; *Plecho s plechom*. Paris, 1955; "Vozvrashchenie," *NZh* 42 (1955); "U poroga," *NZh* 53 (1958); "Sosny molodosti," *NZh* 59 (1960); "Chuzhie," *NZh* 70 (1962); "Annushka," *NZh* 89 (1969); "Posledniaia loshad' Arzhevilia," *Mosty* 13–14 (1968); *Nezdeshnii dom*. Munich, 1973; *Vernost'*. Paris, 1984.

Teffi (b. Nadezhda Aleksandrovna Lokhvitskaia, 1872, Volyn' province; d. 1952, Paris; married Buchinskii, 1890; three children). Gentry family of distinguished writers; father a famous wit; sister poet Mirra Lokhvitskaia. Secondary school, St. Petersburg; married Polish aristocrat, 1890; left husband for literary career in St. Petersburg, 1900. Published comic poems, stories from 1901; during 1910s, eight vols. prose and poetry. Participant in Symbolist literary circles; short plays staged in St. Petersburg theaters, widespread popularity. To Kiev after

Revolution, emigrated through Constantinople, 1919, in Paris, 1920. Organized first émigré literary salon; participant in Gippius's "Zelenaia lampa." Published stories, feuilletons weekly, esp. in *Poslednie novosti*. 1920s, published two vols. of poetry, three vols. of stories about émigré life. 1930s, several vols. of mystical/ psychological stories, a novel, memoir of flight from Russia, portraits of contemporaries. War years in Biarritz.

Writings: Sem' ognei. St. Petersburg, 1910; *Sol' zemli* (1910); *Iumoristicheskie rasskazy*, 2 vols. St. Petersburg, 1910–11; *I stalo tak.* St. Petersburg, 1912; *Vosem' miniatiur.* St. Petersburg, 1913; *Dym bez ognia.* St. Petersburg, 1914; *Karusel'.* St. Petersburg, 1914; *Miniatiury i monologi*, 1915; *Nichego podobnogo*, 1915; *Zhit'e-byt'e*, 1916; *Nezhivoi zver'.* Petersburg, 1916; repr. as *Tikhaia zavod'.* Paris, 1921; *Vchera*, 1918; *Vostok i drugie rasskazy.* Shanghai, 1920; *Rasskazy*, 2 vols. Kharbin, c. 1921; *Tak zhili.* Stockholm, 1921; *Chernyi iris.* Stockholm, 1921; *Sbornik izbrannykh rasskazov.* Paris, 1921; *Sokrovishche zemli.* Berlin, 1921; *Stambul i solntse.* Berlin, 1921; *Rys'.* Berlin, 1923; *Shamram.* Berlin, 1923; *Passiflora.* Berlin, 1923; *Vechernii den'.* Prague, 1924; *Provorstvo ruk.* Moscow and Leningrad, 1926; *Gorodok.* Paris, 1927; *Tango smerti.* Moscow and Leningrad, 1927; *Parizhskie rasskazy.* Moscow, 1927; *Kniga iiun'.* Belgrade, 1931; *Vospominaniia.* Paris, 1931; *Baba-iaga.* Paris, 1932; *Avantiurnyi roman.* Paris, 1932; *P'esy.* Paris, 1934; *Ved'ma.* Berlin, 1936; *O nezhnosti.* Paris, 1938; *Zigzag.* Paris, 1939; *Vse o liubvi.* Paris, 1946; *Zemnaia raduga.* New York, 1952; *Rasskazy.* Moscow, 1971.

In translation: "The Dog", tr. E. Haber, *RLT* 9 (1974); "Time," tr. E. Haber, in *The Bitter Air of Exile.* Berkeley, 1977; stories in Pachmuss *Modernism* and *A Russian Cultural Revival; All About Love*, tr. D. Goldstein. Ann Arbor, 1985; one-act play, story in Kelly *Anthology*; "A Small Town on the Seine," "Huron" in Kelly *Utopias*; "The Pipe," in Tomei, II; poem in Todd and Hayward.

Recent editions: Nostal'giia: rasskazy, vospominaniia. Leningrad, 1989; *Iumoristicheskie rasskazy.* Moscow, 1990; *Vybor kresta.* Moscow, 1991; *Zhit'e-byt'e: Rasskazy, vospominaniia.* Moscow, 1991; *Smeshnoe v pechal' nom.* Moscow, 1992; *Demonicheskaia zhenshchina.* Moscow, 1995; *SS*, 5 vols. Moscow, 1998.

Tel'toft, Ol'ga Iaroslavovna (b. 1915, Russia; d. 1945, Harbin; married name Slobodchikova). Poet.

Writings: Brennye pesni. Harbin, 1943.

Temkina, Marina (b. 1948, Leningrad). Poet and artist, emigrated in 1978, lives in New York.

Writings: Chasti chast'. Paris, 1985; *V obratnom napravlenii.* Paris, 1989; *Kalancha: Gendernaia lirika.* New York, 1995; with Alfred Corn and Michel Gérard, *Geomnesic Observatory.* Metz, 1990.

Teplova, Nadezhda Sergeevna (b. 1814, Moscow; d. 1848, Zvenigorod). Born into merchant family; she and sister Serafima (married name Pel'skaia) received good education; published in journals and almanacs from late 1820s until death; literary mentor Mikhail Maksimovich assisted in getting all her collections published. Married Teriukhin in 1837; widowed in 1845; two of her three children d. 1846. Became increasingly devout before her own death.

Writings: Stikhotvoreniia. Moscow, 1833; revised edn, 1838; revised and enlarged, 1860. Poems in *Poety 1820–1830-kh godov*, ed. L. Ia. Ginzburg and V. E. Vatsuro. 2 vols., Leningrad, 1972, vol. I; Bannikov; *Tsaritsy muz*; V. E. Vatsuro, "Zhizn' i poeziia Nadezhdy Teplovoi," in *Pamiatniki kul'tury. Novye otkrytiia. Ezhegodnik 1989.* Moscow, 1990, 16–43; poems in *Moskovskaia muza*, ed. G. D. Klimova.

In translation: RLT 9 (1974); Perkins and Cook; poems in Tomei, I.

Titova, Elizaveta Ivanovna (b. 1780–?). Playwright. Married into the prominent Titov musical and military family. Major works include *Gustav Vaza* (St. Petersburg, 1809) and *Adelaida i Vol'mar* (St. Petersburg, 1811).

Tokareva, Viktoriia (b. 1937, Leningrad). Writer of prose fiction and film and television scripts. Holds a degree in scriptwriting from the Moscow State Institute of Cinematography (1967). Began publishing stories while a student at the institute. Has received awards for her film writing.

Writings: *O tom, chego ne bylo*. Moscow, 1969. Reissued Moscow, 1996; *Kogda stalo nemnozhko teplee*. Moscow, 1972; *Zanuda*. Tallin, 1977; *Letaiushchie kacheli*. Moscow, 1978. Reissued Tallin, 1982 and Moscow, 1996; *Nichego osobennogo*. Moscow, 1983. Reissued Moscow, 1997; "Mezhdu nebom i zemlei," 1985; "Dlinnyi den'," *NM* 2 (1986); *Letaiushchie kacheli*. *Nichego osobennogo*. Moscow, 1987; "Dva Rasskaza ('Piat' figur na postamente' and 'Pasha i Pavlusha')," *Oktiabr'* 9 (1987); "Pervaia popytka," *NM* 1 (1987); "Kirka i ofitser," *Ogonek* 10 (March 1991); "Kak ia ob"iavil voinu iaponii," *Krokodil* 12 (April 1991); *Skazat'–ne skazat'*. Moscow, 1991; *Staraia sobaka*. Moscow, 1991; "Ia est'. Ty est'. On est'. Rasskaz," *NM* 9 (1991); *Dzhentl'meny udachi*. Moscow, 1993; *Korrida*. Moscow, 1993. Reissued Moscow, 1995; *Den' bez vran'ia*. Moscow, 1994; *Kheppi end*. Moscow, 1995; "Lavina. Povest'," *NM* 10 (1995); *Lavina*. Moscow, 1996; *Na cherta nam chuzhie: povesti i rasskazy*. Moscow, 1995; *Shla sobaka po roialiu*, 2 vols. Moscow, 1995; *Vmesto menia*. Moscow, 1995; 1996; *Loshadi s kryl'iami*. Moscow, 1996; *Ne sotvori*. Moscow, 1996; *Rimskie kanikuly*. Moscow, 1996; "Sistema sobak," *Oktiabr'* 3 (1996); *Koshka na doroge*. Moscow, 1997; *Mezhdu nebom i zemlei*. Moscow, 1997; *Mozhno i nel'zia*. Moscow, 1997; *Nakhal*. Moscow, 1997; *Odin kubik nadezhdy: povesti, rasskazy*. Moscow, 1997; *Sentimental'noe puteshestvie*. Moscow, 1997; *Skazhi mne chto-nibud' –: povesti i rasskazy*. Moscow, 1997; *Telokhranitel': (rasskazy)*. Moscow, 1997; *Kino i vokrug*. Moscow, 1998; *Odin iz nas*. Moscow, 1998; *Samyi schastlivyi den'*. Moscow, 1998; *Nu i pust'*. Moscow, 1998; *Etot luchshii iz mirov*. Moscow, 1999; *Gladkoe lichiko*. Moscow, 1999; *Lilovyi kostium*. Moscow, 1999; *Perelom*. Moscow, 1999; *Rozovye rozy*. Moscow, 1999; *Banketnyi zal*. Moscow, 1999; *Zvezda v tumane*. Moscow, 1999; *Malo li chto byvaet*. Moscow, 1999; *Vse normal'no, vse khorosho*. Moscow, 2000.

Screenplays and scripts: with Georgii Daneliia, *Dzhentl'meny udachi: neliricheskaia komediia*. Moscow, 1971; with Georgii Daneliia, *Sovsem propashchii*; with Revaza Gabriadze and Georgii Daneliia, *Mimino*. Moscow, 1978; *Eksprompt-fantaziia*. Moscow, 1982.

In translation: "Oh, How the Mist Came Stealing," *SovLit* 6 (1970); "On the Set," *SovLit* 3 (1975), 66–73; "That's How It Was," *SovLit* 3 (1978), 91–102; "Sidesteps," *SovLit* 6 (1986), 184–8; "Thou Shalt Not Create ..." *SovLit* 3 (1989), 48–65; "Between Heaven and Earth" and "The Happiest Day of My life (The Story of a Precocious Girl)," in *The Image of Women in Contemporary Soviet Fiction*, ed. Sigrid McLaughlin; "Between Heaven and Earth" and "Nothing Special," tr. Helena Goscilo in *Balancing Acts*; "Dry Run," tr. Michael Glenny. *Granta* 33 (1990); "The Happiest Day," tr. Carol Lynn Ecale. *Massachusetts Review* 31 (Autumn 1990); "Hello," *SovLit* 8 (1990); "Centre of Gravity," tr. Michael Glenny. *Granta* 30 (1990); "Five Figures on a Pedestal," tr. Debra Irving in *Soviet Women Writing*; *The Talisman and Other Stories*. London, 1993; "First Try," in *Lives in Transit*; "One, Two, Three . . ." and "A Ruble Sixty Isn't Much," in *Soviet Literary Culture in the 1970s: The Politics of Irony*, ed. A. Vishnevsky and M. Biggins. Gainesville, FL, 1993.

Tol'staia, Tat'iana Nikitichna (b. 1951, Leningrad). Novelist, short story writer and critic. Granddaughter of Aleksei Tolstoy, Tolstaia grew up in a family of Leningrad intelligentsia. Graduated in 1974 from Dept. of Languages and Literatures at Leningrad State University. Best known for her highly figurative use of language and for her depictions of characters – dreamers, misfits, the elderly – who exist on the fringes of society, Tolstaia has emerged as one of the most talented in the new generation of writers since the mid-1980s. Married with two sons, she divides her time between Russia and the United States.

Writings: Na zolotom kryl'tse sideli. Moscow, 1987; *Liubish' ne liubish'.* Moscow, 1997; *Sestry* (with Natal'ia Tolstaia). Moscow, 1998; *Reka Okkervil: rasskazy.* Moscow, 1999; *Kys': roman.* Moscow, 2000.

In translation: "Peters," tr. Mary Zirin in *Balancing Acts*; "Night," tr. Mary Zirin in *Glasnost: An Anthology of Literature under Gorbachev.* Ann Arbor, MI, 1990; *On the Golden Porch,* tr. Antonia Bouis. New York, 1989; "Sleepwalker in a Fog," tr. Jamey Gambrell in *Soviet Women Writing; Sleepwalker in a Fog,* tr. Jamey Gambrell. New York, 1990; for full cites see *DRWW* and Tomei, II.

Triolet, Elsa (b. Ella Iurevna Kagan, 1896, Moscow; d. 1970, St. Arnoult-en-Yvelines, France; married: 1) André Triolet, 1918; 2) Louis Aragon, 1939). Raised in Moscow; with sister Lily Brik, friend of Vladimir Mayakovsky. Left Moscow to marry French citizen, 1918; trip to Tahiti, 1919, letters to Shklovsky published in his *Zoo.* Separated from husband, resident in Paris hotel from c. 1919 until meeting Aragon, c. 1924. Published three novels in Russian in Soviet Russia during 1920s. Fourth book, fact-novel about French fashion industry, censored by Soviets, despite Triolet's membership in French Communist Party. Began writing novels in French, published 17; won Prix Goncourt, 1945, for *Le premier accroc côute deux cents francs,* set in France during the German occupation. Also published several books on Mayakovsky, self-portrait as a writer *La mise en mots* (1969), translations of Celine, and of Russian Modernist poets.

Writings: Na Taiti. Leningrad, 1925; *Zemlianichka.* Moscow, 1926; *Zashchitnyi tsvet.* Moscow, 1928; *Six entre autres: nouvelles.* Lausanne, 1945; *Maiakovski, poete russe.* Paris, 1945; *L'écrivain et le livre.* Paris, 1948; *Oeuvre romanesques croisées.* Paris, 1964.

In translation: The White Charger, tr. Gerrie Thielens. New York, 1946; *A Fine of 200 Francs.* New York, 1947, 1986; *The Inspector of Ruins,* tr. Norman Cameron. London, 1952; New York, 1953.

Tsvetaeva, Anastasiia Ivanovna (b. 1894; d. 1993). Sister of the poet Marina Tsvetaeva and author of a corpus of chiefly autobiographical works, many of which have been published or reissued in recent years.

Writings: Vospominaniia. Moscow, 1971; 3rd expanded edn, 1983, 1995; *Amor. Roman i povest' Moia Sibir'.* Moscow, 1991; *O chudesnom.* Moscow, 1991; *Neischerpaemoe.* Moscow, 1992; and a collection of poetry *Moi edinstvennyi sbornik.* Moscow, 1995.

Tsvetaeva, Marina Ivanovna (b. 1892, Moscow; died 1941, Elabuga; married White Army officer Sergei Efron; two daughters, one son). Raised in Moscow; father Ivan Tsvetaev, founder Pushkin Museum; pianist mother died young. Published first vol. of poetry at age eighteen; joined circle of Maximilian Voloshin, visited Koktebel'. Married Efron, daughter Ariadna, 1912. Intro. to St. Petersburg literary world, affairs with poets Sophia Parnok, Osip Mandel'stam, 1916. During civil war years, involved in Vakhtangov studio, wrote verse dramas. Second daughter Irina died of starvation, 1919. Emigrated to Berlin, joined Efron, 1922; beginning of correspondence with Pasternak; published eight vols. of poetry written during teens, early twenties. In Prague 1923–5; new lyrics, long poems, verse tragedies; affair with Rodzevich; son Georgii (Mur), 1925. To Paris, late 1925. Correspondence with Rilke, critical scandals, 1926; late 1920s/early 1930s, turned to autobiographical, critical essays. Daughter Ariadna returned to Soviet Russia; Efron returned 1937, after involvement in NKVD plot. Followed with son Mur, 1939; family arrested; homeless existence in Moscow until German invasion; evacuated, suicide in Elabuga.

Writings: *Vechernii al'bom.* Moscow, 1910; *Volshebnyi fonar'.* Moscow, 1912; *Iz dvukh knig.* Moscow, 1913; *Versty* I. Moscow, 1922; *Versty* II. Moscow, 1921, 1922; *Konets Kazanovy.* Moscow, 1922; *Razluka.* Moscow and Berlin, 1922; *Stikhi k Bloku.* Berlin, 1922; *Tsardevitsa.* Moscow, 1922; *Psikheia.* Berlin, 1922; *Remeslo.* Moscow and Berlin, 1923; *Molodets.* Prague, 1924; *Posle Rossii.* Paris, 1928; *Lebedinyi stan.* Munich, 1957; *Lettre à l'Amazon.* Paris, 1979; *IzbPr.* Moscow, 1965; *Izbr. proza,* 2 vols. New York, 1979; *Stikhotvoreniia i poemy,* 4 vols. New York, 1980–3.

In translation: *Selected Poems,* tr. E. Feinstein. Oxford, 1971, 1986 and New York, 1987, 1994; *A Captive Spirit* (essays), tr. J. M. King. Preface by Susan Sontag, London, 1983 and Ann Arbor, 1980, 1994; *The Demesne of Swans,* tr. R. Kemball. Ann Arbor, 1980; *Letters, Summer 1926,* tr. M. Wettlin and W. Arndt. San Diego, 1985; *Selected Poems,* tr. D. McDuff. Newcastle, 1987, 1991; *Art in the Light of Conscience* (essays), tr. A. Livingstone. Cambridge, MA, 1992; *After Russia,* tr. M. Naydan and S. Yastremski, ed. M. Naydan. Ann Arbor, 1992; "Staircase," in Kelly *Anthology;* "Letter to the Amazon," in *Artes* 3 (1996); poems and letters, tr. Jane Taubman and Sibelan Forrester in Tomei, II. *Poem of the End. Selected Narrative and Lyrical Poetry,* tr. Nina Kossman, Dana Point, CA. 1998; *The Ratcatcher,* tr. Angela Livingstone. London, 1999; "In Praise of the Rich," tr. Mimi Khalvati in Kelly *Utopias; The Letters of Marina Tsvetaeva* (forthcoming); For complete listing, see Tomei, II.

Recent editions: *Pis'ma 1926 goda.* Moscow, 1990; *Stikhotvoreniia i poemy.* Moscow, 1990; *SS,* 7 vols. Moscow, 1994–5. *Neizdannoe. Svodnye Tetradi.* Moscow, 1997.

Tur, Evgeniia (Countess Elizaveta Vasil'evna Sailhas de Tournemire, b. Sukhovo-Kobylina, 1815; d. 1892, m. 1837.) Three children, two daughters, one son, Evg. Sal'ias, who became an author of historical prose. From the late 1850s, published critical essays incl. articles on Charlotte Brontë, Victor Hugo, and George Sand as well as Dostoevsky, Tolstoy, and Turgenev. Founded and edited a periodical, *Russkaia rech'* (Russian Speech), in 1861. From the mid-1860s, she wrote children's literature.

Writings: "Antonina," *Kometa* (1851); *Plemiannitsa,* 1851; *Dolg, Sovremennik* 11 (1851); *Dve sestry, OZ* (1851); *Tri pory zhizni,* 1854; "Krymskie pis'ma," *SPVed,* (1853–1854); *Zakoldovannyi krug, OZ* 1–2 (1854); *Starushka, RV* 1 (1856); Writings for children include: *Semeistvo Shalonskikh,* 1880; *Kniazhna Dubrovina,* 1886; *Sergei Bor-Ramenskii,* 1888; *Zhizn' Sviatogo Makariia Egipetskogo,* 1885, and a reworking of Bulwer-Lytton's *The Last Days of Pompeii* (Poslednie dni Pompei, 1883, 1991).

Recent editions: *Dolg,* in *Serdtsa.*

In translation: *Antonina,* tr. Michael Katz. Evanston, 1996; excerpts from *Crimean Letters,* tr. Jehanne Gheith in Tomei, I; "Reminiscences and Ruminations," tr. Sibelan Forrester, http://ash.swarthmore.edu/Slavic/turr&r.html.

Ulitskaia, Liudmila (b. 1943, Davlekanovo in Bashkiria). Writer of prose fiction and film scripts. Holds a degree in biology from Moscow State University. First publication was an academic work in the field of genetics. In the 1980s published her first works of prose fiction, first in the West and then in Russia. Laureate of the Russian Booker Prize in 1993 and 1997 and the "Prix Medicis étranger" (France, 1996).

Writings: "Bron'ka," *Ogonek* 52 (1989); "Za kapustoi," *Krest'ianka* 2 (1989); "Bumazhnaia pobeda" and "Schastlivyi sluchai," *Krest'ianka* 3 (1990); "Doch' Bukhary," *RMysl'* (1990) also in *Ogonek* 2 (1991); "Genele-Sumochnitsa," *Novoe russkoe slovo* (April 20, 1990); "Narod izbrannyi," *Kontinent* 65 (1990) also in *Piatyi ugol*, ed. Sergei Kaledin. Moscow, 1991; "Vtorogo marta togo goda," *RMysl'* (July 26 and August 9, 1991); "Sonechka," *NM* 7 (1992); "Devochki," *NM* 2 (1994); "Gulia," *Oktiabr'* 2 (1994); *Bednye rodstvenniki* (sbornik). Moscow, 1994; 1995; "Medeia i ee deti," *NM* 3–4 (1996); *Medeia i ee deti: Povesti*. Moscow, 1996, 1997; *Lialin dom: Povesti i rasskazy*. Moscow, 1999; *Veselye pokhorony: Povest' i rasskazy*. Moscow, 1998, 1999 and *NM* 7 (1998); *Medeia i ee deti; Sonechka*. Moscow, 1999; with G. Shcherbakova and others, "Vyrazhaetsia sil'no rossiiskii narod!" *NM* 2 (1999); *Kazus kukotskogo*. Moscow, 2000.

In translation: "March Second of That Year," in Hoisington, *Out Visiting*; "Lucky," tr. Helena Goscilo, *From the Soviets*, *Nimrod* 33: 2 (special issue of spring/summer 1990) and *Wild Beach*; "The Chosen People," tr. Isabel Heaman, and "Gulia," tr. Helena Goscilo in *Lives in Transit*; "March, 1953," tr. Arch Tait in *Present Imperfect* and *Glas* 6 (1993); "Barley Soup," tr. Andrew Bromfield. *Glas* 6 (1993); Excerpt from "Sonechka," tr. Cathy Porter. *Glas* 7 (1994); "Sonechka and Other Stories," tr. Arch Tait in *Glas* 17 (1998); *The Funeral Party*, tr. Cathy Porter. New York, 2001.

Ulybysheva, Elizaveta Dmitrievna (18??–18??). Poet and prose writer in French and Russian.

Writings: *Etincelles et cendres*. Moscow, 1842; *Pensées et soucis, suivies de La Sylphide-pöete*. Moscow, 1843; *Epines et lauriers, suivis du "Juif errant," de "La nonne sanglante" et de quelques essais de vers russes*. Moscow, 1845; *Journal d'une solitaire*. Moscow, 1853; *Posledniaia pesn' lebedia. Russkie i frantsuzskiia stikhotvoreniia*. St. Petersburg, 1864.

Unksova, Kari (b. Alma Ata, 1941; d. Leningrad, 1983). Poet, graduate of Geography Faculty at Leningrad University, feminist activist, killed by a car just before she was to emigrate to Israel.

Writings: *Izb*. Tel-Aviv, 1985.

In translation: "An Uphill Battle," in *Women and Russia*, ed. Tatyana Mamonova. Boston, 1984: 93–106.

Urusova, Princess Ekaterina Sergeevna (b. 1747, d. after 1817). Poet. From an aristocratic Russian family, cousin of Mikhail Kheraskov (see under Kheraskova above). Major works include *Polion* (St. Petersburg, 1774), *Iroidy, muzam posviashchennye* (St. Petersburg, 1777), *Stikhi* (St. Petersburg, 1817). In 1811, became honorary member of Shishkov's Society of Lovers of the Russian Word (Beseda liubitelei russkogo slova).

Ushakova, Elena. Poet, lives in St. Petersburg.

Writings: *Nochnoe solntse*. St. Petersburg, 1991; poems in *NM* 10 (1995), 91–3; *NM* 4 (1997), 64–7; *Zvezda* 5 (1997), 40–2.

Interviews: V. Polukhina (ed.), *Brodsky Through the Eyes of His Contemporaries*. New York, 1992, 94–9.

Vaneeva, Larisa (b. 1953, Novosibirsk). Writer of prose fiction. Graduate of the Literary Institute in Moscow. Was not able to publish until the changes of the 1990s.

Writings: "Priznak odnogo tallintsa, ili Gebel' Odessy" and "Razvenenie rybok," *Zhenskaia logika*, ed. L.V. Stepanenko and A.V. Fomenko. Moscow, 1989; *Iz kuba: Rasskazy, povest'*. Moscow, 1990; *Ne pomniashchaia zla*, comp. L. Vaneeva. Moscow, 1990. Includes the compiler's story, "Mezhdu Saturnom i Uranom (*Teni*)"; *Skorb' po ploti. Kubicheskii traktat i rasskazy*. Moscow, 1990; "Venetsianskie zerkala," *Chisten'kaia zhizn'; Igra tuchi s dozhdem*. Moscow, 1991; "Antigrekh," in *Novye amazonki;* "Snovidets (. . . snov)," in *Eros, syn Afrodity*, comp. S. Markov. Moscow, 1991; *Igra tuchi s dozhdem*. Moscow, 1991; "Proshchenoe voskresen'e," *Novaia Evropa* 7 (1995); "Novye rasskazy," *Den' i noch'* 3 (1996), includes "Sestra-bludnitsa," "Dom na bolote," and "Ulovka kontseptsii"; "Dva rasskaza," *Oktiabr'* 1 (1998); "Takuiu ne znaiu; Zdes' i seichas proizkhodit takoe," *Literaturnaia ucheba* 2 (1998); "Dom na bolote," *Zolotoi vek* 13 (1999).

In translation: "Parade of the Planets;" tr. Diane Nemec Ignashev in *Soviet Women Writing*; "Lame Pigeons," tr. Rosamund Bartlett in *Dissonant Voices: The New Russian Fiction* ed. Oleg Chukhontsev and Nina Sadur. New York, 1991; "Venetian Mirrors," tr. Valentina Baslyk in *Lives in Transit*.

Vangai, Galina. Poet.

Vasilenko, Svetlana (b. 1956, Kapustin Iar). Writer of prose fiction and film scripts. Grew up in the security zone around a rocket launch site. 1983 graduate of the Gorky Institute of World Literature in Moscow. Worked as a fruit hauler and post-woman to support herself. Continued her education at the institute in film directing. First published story in 1982. Winner of a *Novyi Mir* prize for 1998. President of Russian Writers' Union.

Writings: "Den' smerti," in *Vstrechnyi khod.* Moscow, 1989; "Suslik," "Za saigakami," "Zvonkoe imia," "Schast'e," "Kto ikh poliubit?" "Tsaritsa Tamara," in *Zhenskaia logika*, comp. Stepanenko and Fomenko. Moscow, 1989; "Zvonkoe imia," in *Chisten'kaia zhizn'*, comp. A. Shavkuta. Moscow, 1990; *Novye amazonki*. (includes the compiler's story "Duratskie rasskazy"); *Shamara*. Moscow, 1991; *Zvonkoe imia.* Moscow, 1991; "Dva rasskaza," *NM* 9 (1997); "Durochka," *NM* 11 (1998); *Durochka*. Moscow, 2000.

In translation: "Going After Goat-Antelopes," tr. Elisabeth Jezierski in *Lives in Transit*; "Piggy," tr. Andrew Bromfield in *Present Imperfect*; "Shamara," tr. Andrew Bromfield, *Women's View, Glas* 3 (1992). *Shamara and Other Stories*, ed. and intro. Helena Goscilo. Evanston, IL, 2000.

Vasil'eva, Larisa (b. Kucherenko, 1935, Khar'kov). Poet, essayist, novelist. Also writes under the pseudonym Vasilii Staroi.

Writings: *Ognevitsa: stikhotvoreniia i poemy*. Moscow, 1969; *Lebeda*, 1970; *Den' poezii Rossii*, comp. with M. P. Shevchenko. Moscow, 1972; *Al'bion i taina vremeni: rasskazy*. Moscow, 1978; 2nd edn, Moscow, 1983; *Listva: kniga stikhov*. Moscow, 1980; *Izbrannoe: stikhotvoreniia i poemy*. Moscow, 1981; *Derzost': sbornik stikhov*. Moscow, 1984; *Kniga ob ottse: roman-vospominanie*. Moscow, 1984; *Moskvorech'e: stikhotvroreniia i poemy*. Moscow, 1985; *O sokrovennom: razgovor s chitatelem.* Moscow, 1987; *Oblako ognia*. Moscow, 1988; *Izbrannye proizvedeniia v dvukh tomakh.* Moscow, 1989; "Zhenshchina. Zhizn'. Literatura," *LitGaz* (December 20, 1989); *Kremlevskie zheny: fakty, vospominaniia, dokumenty, slukhi, legendy i vzgliad avtora*. Moscow, 1992; 2nd edn, 1998; *Deti Kremlia*. Moscow, 1996; as Vasilii Staroi. *P'er i Natasha: prodolzhenie romana L. N. Tolstogo "Voina i mir."* Moscow, 1996; "Moe kredo – ne feminizm a garmoniia mezhdu muzhchinoi i zhenshchinoi" (interview), *Voin Rossii* 3 (1999); *Zhena i Muza: taina Aleksandra Pushkina: fakty, daty, dokumenty, vospominaniia, pis'ma, slukhi, legendy, stikhi i vzgliad avtora*. Moscow, 1999.

In translation: "A Glimpse of Diplomacy from the Sideline," *International Affairs* (Moscow); "I Stand as Witness," *Soviet Life* 7 (1989); "So Shall My Life Proceed," *SovLit* 3 (1981); *Kremlin Wives*, tr. Cathy Porter. London, 1994.

Velembovskaia, Irina (b. Shugalter, 1922, Moscow; d. 1990, Moscow). Prose writer. Spent most of her life in Moscow with exception of war years. Graduated Gorky Institute of World Literature in 1959. Wrote prose fictions about average Soviet women attempting to deal with work and family.

Writings: *Lesnaia istoriia*. Moscow, 1965; *Zhenshchiny*. Moscow. 1967; *Tretii semestr*. Moscow, 1973; *Vid s balkona*. Moscow, 1981; *Vse prokhodit*. Moscow, 1990; *Sladkaia zhenshchina*. Moscow, 1994.

In translation: "Through Hard Times," tr. Joseph Kiegel in *Balancing Acts*.

Verbitskaia, Anastasiia Alekseevna (b. Ziablova, 1861, St. Petersburg; d. 1928, Moscow; m. surveyor A.V. Verbitskii, 1882, three sons). Daughter of colonel, hereditary nobleman and mother from acting family; sister of writer A. Sorneva, who committed suicide, 1891. Educated at private women's institute and studied singing at Moscow Conservatoire. Worked as teacher; began journalistic career, 1893. First published fiction, 1887; full-time writer from 1894; own publishing house from 1899. 1905, Chair of Society for Improvement of Lot of Women; lent house to Bolsheviks during Moscow uprising. 1909–13: achieved unprecedented popularity for best-selling novels. After Revolution, novels banned; attempt of prominent Bolsheviks to help her failed.

Writings: *Osvobodilas'!* Moscow, 1898; *Vavochka*. Moscow, 1898; *Sny zhizni*. Moscow, 1899; *Pervye lastochki*. Moscow, 1900; *Ch'ia vina*. Moscow, 1900; "Avtobiografiia," in *Sbornik na pomoshch' uchashchimsia zhenshchinam*. Moscow, 1901, 84–91; *Po-novomu: roman uchitel'nitsy*. Moscow, 1902; *Istoriia odnoi zhizni*. Moscow, 1903; *Zlaia rosa*. Moscow, 1904; *Schast'e: novye rasskazy*. Moscow, 1905; *Dukh vremeni*. Moscow, 1907; *Prestuplenie Marii Ivanovnoi, i drugie rasskazy i ocherki iz zhizni odinokikh*, 3rd edn, Moscow, 1908; *Moemu chitateliu*, I: *Detstvo. Gody ucheniia*. Moscow, 1908; II: *Iunost', Grezy*. Moscow, 1911; *Kliuchi schast'ia*, 6 vols. Moscow, 1909–13; *Igo liubvi*, Parts 1 and 2. Moscow, 1914–16; Moscow, 1992, 1993; Part 3, 1920, unpublished, in Russian archives, RGALI, fond 1042, for a new, abridged edn, see *Kliuchi schast'ia*. Kiev, 1995; for recent fuller edns, see *Kliuchi schast'ia*. Kiev, 1995; *Igo liubvi*. Kiev, 1995.

In translation: "Mirage," in Pachmuss, 120–74; *The Keys to Happiness*, tr. Beth Holmgren and Helena Goscilo. Bloomington, 1999; from *My Reminiscences: Youth. Dreams*, tr. Natasha Kolchevska in Tomei, I.

Vigdorova, Frida Abramovna (b. 1915, Orsha; d. 1965, Moscow; married names: Kulakovskaia, Raskina). Pedagogue, journalist, and novelist. Began work as journalist in 1938. Traveled throughout Russia, keeping copious notes and travel diaries. Defender of those victimized by the system. Transcribed Brodsky Trial in 1964.

Writings: *Moi klass*. Moscow, 1949; *Doroga v zhizn'*. Moscow, 1954; *Chernigovka*. Moscow, 1959; "Glaza pustye i volshebnye," *Tarusskie stranitsy*. Kaluga, 1961; *Semeinoe schast'e*. Moscow, 1962; *Dorogaia redaktsiia. Ocherki*. Moscow, 1963; *Liubimaia ulitsa*. Moscow, 1964; "Zasedanie suda nad Iosifom Brodskim. Dokumental'naia zapis' " in *Vozdushnye puti* 4 (1965) and in E. Etkind, *Zapiski nezagovorshchika*. London, 1977, 437–67; *Doroga v zhizn'. Eto moi dom. Chernigovka*. Moscow, 1966; *Minuty tishiny*. Moscow, 1967; *Doroga v zhizn'. Povesti*. Moscow, 1969; *Kem vy emu prikhodites'?* Moscow, 1969; "Sudilishche," *Ogonek* 49 (1988), 26–31.

In translation: *Diary of a Schoolteacher*, tr. Rose Prokofieva. Moscow, 1954; "Empty Eyes and Magic Eyes," in *Pages from Tarusa*. Boston, 1964, 301–9; "The Trial of Iosif Brodsky," *New Leader* (August 31, 1964), 6–17, and *Encounter* (September, 1964), 84–91; "A Question of Ethics," tr. F.F. Snyder, *RLT* 5 (1973), 406–13; "Five Lives and the Committee," tr. Teresy Polowy in Tomei, II, 1093–1101.

Vil'kina, Liudmila (b. 1873, d. 1920). Poet, prose writer, and translator.

Writings: *Moi sad*. Moscow, 1906; "Odno i to zhe," *Severnye tsvety na 1902*. Moscow, 1902; - "Osvobozhdenie (iz zhenskikh sonetov)," *Severnye tsvety* 3 (1903); as Nikita Bobrinskii, "Pafos zhizni," *Novyi put'*, 3 (1904); poems in *Almanakh Grif*. Moscow, 1914; *P'esy*. Moscow, 1958.

Vizi, Mariia Genrikhovna (Vezey, Mary Custis; b. 1904, New York; d. 1994, San Francisco; m. Tourkoff). Poet.

Writings: *Stikhotvoreniia I*. Harbin, 1929; *Stikhotvoreniia II*. Shanghai, 1936; *Golubaia trava*. San Francisco, 1973.

Vladi, Elena – Elena Vladimirovna Nikobadze (b. 1927, Harbin; d. 1990, Tashkent, USSR; m. Kim). Poet. In 1956 went to the USSR.

Writings: *Ia khochu krasotu podarit'*. Moscow, 1992 (posthumously).

Volkonskaia, Princess Zinaida Aleksandrovna (b. Belosel'skaia-Belozerskaia, 1789; d. 1862, Rome): Poet, fiction writer in French and Russian. Wealthy socialite, organizer of a famous salon in 1820s Moscow; continued to be a center of Russian literary life after her emigration to Rome in 1829.

Writings: poems in Bannikov; *Tsaritsy muz*; poems in *Moskovskaia muza*, ed. G.D. Kumova.

Volkova, Anna Alekseevna (b. 1771, d. 1834). Poet. Daughter of State Councillor; from 1817 an honorary member of Shishkov's Society of Lovers of the Russian Word. Published a large number of poems in periodicals.

Voloshina, Margarita (b. Sabashnikova, 1882; d. 1973). Poet, artist, and anthroposophist.

Writings: *Lesnaia svirel'*. 1907.

Vovchok, Marko (Mar'ia Aleksandrovna Markovich, b. Vilinskaia, 1833; d. 1907; 2nd marriage Lobach-Zhuchenko). Prose writer and translator. Educated at home and in a Khar'kov boarding school. Known for her tales of peasants and, later, satires of provincial life; in both, female characters often play a central role. Her first folk tales, published in 1857, were written in Ukrainian and based on her ethnographic work with her first husband. In 1859, moved to Petersburg and published 2-vol. *Ukrainian Folk Tales* (Ukrainskie narodnye rasskazy); these were translated into Russian by Ivan Turgenev.

Writings: *Sochineniia Marka Vovchka v dvukh tomakh*. St. Petersburg, 1867; *Sochineniia Marka Vovchka v chetyrekh tomakh*. St. Petersburg, 1870; *PSS Marka Vovchka v semi tomakh*. Saratov, 1896–1899; translations of Jules Verne, Charles Darwin, and others.

In translation: *Sasha*, tr. Pamela Chester in Bisha et al. *The Plaything*, tr. Jane Costlow (unpubd.); *Karmelyuk*, tr. Oles Kovalenko (orig., 1863, tr. Dnipro, 1981); *Ukrainian Folk Stories*, tr. N. Pepan-Popil. Saskatoon, Saskatchewan, 1983; *Katerina*, tr. Lisa Taylor in Tomei, I.

Recent editions: Marko Vovchok. *Tvory v semy tomakh*. Kiev, 1964–66; *Lyst y do Marka Vovchka v dvokh tomakh*. Kiev. 1979, 1984; *Tri doli* in *Svidanie*. *Institutka*, in *Serdtsa*.

Zaitseva, Sofia Artem'evna (b. Avanova, 1899, St. Petersburg; d. 1945, Beijing). Novelist. Emigrated to Prague, then Paris. Married Professor K. I. Zaitsev and in 1935 went with him to Harbin where he taught in the Law Faculty. After her death from tuberculosis, her husband published the last two parts of her trilogy.

Writings: Detskimi glazami na mir. Harbin, 1937; Shanghai, 1947; *U poroga v mir.* Harbin, 1942; Shanghai, 1947; *Put' cherez mir.* Shanghai, 1946.

Zavadskaia, Nina (b. 1928, Harbin; d. 1943, Harbin). Poet.

Writings: Svetloe kol'tso, Harbin, 1944 (posthumously).

Zhadovskaia, Iuliia Valerianovna (b. 1824, Iaroslavl' province; d. 1883, Kostroma province; m. Seven). Poet, prose writer, translator. Precursor to Symbolists and Acmeists. Overcame serious physical disabilities (she had no left arm and only three fingers on her right arm) in order to write. Like Rostopchina, her poems constitute a kind of lyric diary. Her autobiographical novel *V storone ot bol' shogo sveta* (Apart from the Great World, 1857) was widely read. Her prose was reviewed by other women in the nineteenth century. "Ni t'ma, ni svet" ("Neither Dark, Nor Light," 1848) is one of her stronger stories. Nature and thwarted love (repeating her own drama with her tutor) are two common themes in her work.

Writings: Stikhotvoreniia. Moscow, 1846; *Stikhotvoreniia.* St. Petersburg, 1858; *PSS,* 4 vols. St. Petersburg, 1885–6; 2nd revised edn, 1894; *Izbrannye stikhi.* Iaroslavl', 1958. *Zhenskaia istoriia* and *Otstalaia,* in *Vremia,* 1861; poems in *Poety 1840–1850 kh godov;* Bannikov; *Tsaritsy muz.*

Recent editions: "Perepiska" in *Dacha.*

Zhemchuzhnaia, Zinaida Nikolaevna (b. Volkova, 1887, Alapaevka, Russia; d. 1961, Wollongong, Australia). Prose writer.

Writings: My i nashi deti. Harbin, 1934; *Ot vosemnadtsati do soroka.* Tianjin, 1939; *Povest' ob odnoi materi.* Tianjin, 1939; *Puti izgnaniia* (memoirs). Tenafly, NJ, 1987 (posthumously).

Zhukova, Mar'ia Semenovna (b. Zevakina, 1804; d. 1855). Prose writer, travel sketches. Raised mainly in Tambov province, befriended by the Korsakov family who were instrumental in her education. Husband died in 1830, leaving her with many debts. Her literary career spanned 20 years.

Writings: Vechera na Karpovke, 1837–8; *Moi kurskie znakomtsy,* 1838; *Samopozhertvovanie,* 1839; *Oshibka,* 1841; *Ocherki iuzhnoi Frantsii i Nitstsy. Iz dorozhnykh zapisok 1840–1842 godov,* 2 vols., 1844; *Dacha na Petergofskoi doroge,* 1845–1850s; *Naden'ka,* 1853. *Baron Reikhman* (from *Vechera na Karpovke*), in *Russkaia romanticheskaia povest'; Dacha na Petergofskoi doroge,* in *Dacha; Vechera na Karpovke.* Moscow, 1986; *Naden'ka,* in *Serdtsa.*

In translation: Self-Sacrifice; from *Evenings by the Karpovka: Baron Reichman, The Locket,* in Andrew; from *My Acquaintances from Kursk,* tr. Rebecca Bowman, in Tomei, I.

Zinov'eva-Annibal, Lydiia (b. 1866, d. 1907). Writer of plays, short stories, novels, fictionalized memoirs, prose poems, and literary criticism. Second husband was poet-philosopher Viacheslav Ivanov. With husband hosted the St. Petersburg "Tower" Salon in early 1900s.

Writings: Kol'tsa. Moscow, 1904; "Net! Liricheskie tseny," *Fakely* 1 (1906); "Pevuchii osel'." *Tsvetnik Or.* St. Petersburg, 1907; *Tridtsat'-tri uroda.* St. Petersburg, 1907; *Tragicheskii zverinets.* St. Petersburg, 1907; *Plamenniki.* Incomplete and unpublished; *Velikii kolokol.* Incomplete and unpublished.

In translation: The Head of the Medusa, tr. Carol Ueland in Tomei, I; *The Tragic Menagerie,* tr. Jane Costlow. Evanston, IL, 1999; "The Whip," in Kelly *Utopias.*

Zoroastra, Kzhishanna (Izidora [or Izida] Tomashevna Orlova). Poet.

Writings: Chernye immorteli. Harbin, 1929; *Misticheskie rozy.* Shanghai, 1946.

Guide to further reading

In assembling this guide we have tried to provide the reader with representative books and articles primarily in English and Russian which deal with general topics as well as with specific writers. For a more complete guide, we urge the reader to consult the excellent lists of secondary works which appear in Tomei and DRWW.

Anthologies in Russian

Bannikov, N.V. (ed.), *Russkie poetessy XIX veka*. Moscow, 1979.

Dzhangirov, Karen (ed.), *Antologiia russkogo verlibra*. Moscow, 1991.

Ezhov, I. S., and E. I. Shamurin (eds.) *Russkaia poeziia XX veka: antologiia russkoi lirike pervoi chetverti XX veka*. Moscow, 1991.

Gasparov, M. L., *et al.* (eds.), *Sto odna poetessa serebriannogo veka: antologiia*. St. Petersburg, 2000.

Gorlanova, Nina, *et al.* (eds.), *Chego khochet zhenshchina: sbornik zhenskikh rasskazov*. Moscow, 1993.

Gumilevskii sbornik. Harbin, 1937.

Iakushin, N. I. (ed.), *"Serdtsa chutkogo prozren'em". . . Povesti i rasskazy russkikh pisatel'nits XIX v*. Moscow, 1991.

Literaturnyi kruzhok "Akhme" (ed.), *Lestnitsa v oblaka*. Harbin, 1929.

Mitropol' skii, A. I. (ed.), *Lira*. Harbin, 1945.

Ostrov. Shanghai, 1946.

Pereleshin, V. (ed.), *Izluchiny*. Harbin, 1935.

Semero. Harbin, 1930.

Shavkuta, Anatolii (comp.), *Chisten'kaia zhizn'*. Moscow, 1990.

Sokolova, Ol'ga (comp.), *Abstinentki*. Moscow, 1991.

Stepanenko, L.V. and A.V. Fomenko (comps.), *Zhenskaia logika*. Moscow, 1989.

Uchenova, V. (ed.), *Dacha na Petergofskoi doroge*. Moscow, 1986.

 Svidanie. Moscow, 1987.

 Tol'ko chas. Moscow, 1988.

 Tsaritsy muz: russkie poetessy XIX – nachala XXvv. Moscow, 1989.

Vaneeva, Larisa (comp.), *Ne pomniashchaia zla*. Moscow, 1990.

Vasilenko, Svetlana (comp.), *Novye amazonki*. Moscow, 1991.

Anthologies of translations

Andrew, Joe (ed. and tr.), *Russian Women's Shorter Fiction: An Anthology, 1835–60*. Oxford, 1996.

Bisha, Robin, Jehanne Gheith, Christine Holden, William Wagner (eds.), *Russian Women, 1698–1917: Experience and Expression. An Anthology of Sources*. Bloomington, IN, 2002.

Clyman, Toby W. and Judith Vowles (eds.), *Russia Through Women's Eyes: Autobiographies from Tsarist Russia*. New Haven, CT and London, 1996.

Cook, Albert and Pamela Perkins (eds.), *The Burden of Sufferance: Women Poets of Russia*. New York, 1993.

Decter, Jacqueline (ed.), *Soviet Women Writing*. New York, 1990.

Foster, Edward and Vadim Mesyats (eds.), *The New Freedoms: Contemporary Russian and American Poetry*. Hoboken, 1994.

Gessen, Masha (ed.), *Half A Revolution*. Pittsburgh and San Francisco, 1995.

Goscilo, Helena (ed.), *Balancing Acts*. Bloomington, IN, 1989.

(ed.), *Lives in Transit*. Ann Arbor, MI, 1995.

(ed. and tr.), *Russian and Polish Women's Fiction*. Knoxville, TN, 1985.

Goscilo, Helena and Byron Lindsey (eds.), *Glasnost: An Anthology of Literature under Gorbachev*. Ann Arbor, MI, 1990.

Wild Beach and Other Stories. Ann Arbor, MI, 1992.

Hoisington, Thomas H. (ed. and tr.), *Out Visiting and Back Home*. Evanston, IL, 1998.

Johnson, Kent and Stephen M. Ashby (eds.), *Third Wave: The New Russian Poetry*. Ann Arbor, MI, 1992.

Kagal, Ayesha and Natasha Perova (eds.), *Present Imperfect*. Boulder, CO, 1996.

Karlinsky, Simon (ed.), *The Bitter Air of Exile: Russian Writers in the West 1922–1972*. Berkeley, CA, 1977.

Kelly, Catriona (ed.), *An Anthology of Russian Women's Writing*. Oxford, 1994.

Kelly, Catriona (ed. and tr.), *Utopias: Russian Modernist Texts, 1905–1940*. London, 1999.

Kuprianova, Nina (comp.), *Always a Woman: Stories by Soviet Women Writers*. Moscow, 1987.

Mapping Codes / Five Fingers Review 8–9. San Francisco, CA, 1990.

Markov, Vladimir and Merrill Sparks (eds.), *Modern Russian Poetry: An Anthology with Verse Translations*. Indianapolis, IN, 1967.

McLaughlin, Sigrid (ed. and tr.), *The Image of Women in Contemporary Soviet Fiction: Selected Short Stories from the USSR*. New York, 1989.

Mortimer, Peter and S. J. Litherland (eds.), *The Poetry of Perestroika*. Newcastle upon Tyne, 1991.

Pachmuss, Temira, (ed.) *A Russian Cultural Revival: A Critical Anthology of Emigré Literature Before 1939*. Knoxville, TN, 1981.

Women Writers in Russian Modernism: An Anthology. Urbana, IL, 1978.

Perova, Natasha (ed.), *Women's View, Glas* 3 (1992).

A Will and a Way, Glas 13 (1996).

Smith, Gerald S. (ed.), *Contemporary Russian Poetry*. Bloomington, IN, 1993.

Solo 13 (1994). Special Women's Issue.

Todd, Albert C. and Max Hayward (eds.), *An Anthology of Twentieth Century Russian Poetry*, selected by Evgenii Evtushenko. New York, 1993.

Vilensky, Simeon (ed.), *Till My Tale Is Told: Women's Memoirs of the Gulag*. Bloomington, IN, 1999.

General studies and reference works

Aiken, Susan, Adele Barker, Maya Koreneva, and Ekaterina Stetsenko (eds.), *Dialogues/ Dialogi: Literary and Cultural Exchanges between (ex-) Soviet and American Women*. Durham, NC, 1994.

Barta, Peter, *Gender and Sexuality in Russian Civilisation*. Newark, NJ, 2001.

Buck, Claire (ed.), *Bloomsbury Guide to Women's Writing*. London, 1992.

Chester, Pamela and Sibelan Forrester (eds.), *Engendering Slavic Literatures*. Bloomington, IN, 1996.

Clyman, Toby W. and Diana Greene (eds.), *Women Writers in Russian Literature*. Westport, CT, 1994.

Cornwell, Neil (ed.), *Reference Guide to Russian Literature*. London and Chicago, 1998.

Costlow, Jane T., Stephanie Sandler, and Judith Vowles (eds.), *Sexuality and the Body in Russian Culture*. Stanford, 1993.

Efimov, Nina, Christine D. Tomei, and Richard Chapple (eds.), *Critical Essays on the Prose and Poetry of Modern Slavic Women*. Lewiston, NY, 1998.

Fitzpatrick, Sheila and Yuri Slezkine (eds.), *In the Shadow of Revolution: Life Stories of Russian Women from 1917 to the Second World War*. Princeton, NJ, 1999.

Göpfert, Frank, *Russland aus der Feder seiner Frauen zum femininen Diskurs in der Russischen Literatur*. Munich, 1992.

Goscilo, Helena and Beth Holmgren (eds.), *Russia. Women. Culture*. Bloomington, IN, 1996.

Heldt, Barbara, *Terrible Perfection*. Bloomington, IN, 1987.

Hoisington, Sonya Stephan, (ed.), *A Plot of Her Own: The Female Protagonist in Russian Literature*. Evanston, IL, 1995.

Hubbs, Joanna, *Mother Russia: The Feminine Myth in Russian Culture*. Bloomington, IN, 1988.

Jones, Malcolm V. and Robin Feuer Miller (eds.), *Cambridge Companion to the Classic Russian Novel*. Cambridge, 1998.

Kasack, Wolfgang, ed. *Dictionary of Russian Literature since 1917*, tr. Maria Carlson and Jane T. Hodges. New York, 1988.

Kelly, Catriona, *A History of Russian Women's Writing 1820–1992*. Oxford, 1994.

"Women's Writing in Russia," in Cornwell, *Reference Guide*.

Ledkovsky, Marina, Charlotte Rosenthal, and Mary Zirin (eds.), *Dictionary of Russian Women Writers*. Westport, CT, 1994.

Liljeström, Marianne, Eila Mäntysaari, and Arja Rosenholm (eds.), *Gender Restructuring in Russian Studies*. Slavic Tamperensia 2 (Tampere, 1993).

Marsh, Rosalind (ed.), *Gender and Russian Literature. New Perspectives*. Cambridge, 1996.

(ed.), *Women and Russian Culture: Projections and Self-Perceptions*. New York, 1998. (Studies in Slavic Literature, Culture, and Society, 2).

Nikolaev, P. A. (ed.), *Biograficheskii slovar'*. 4 vols. Moscow, 1989–99.

Sandler, Stephanie (ed.), *Rereading Russian Poetry*. New Haven, CT, 1999.

Tomei, Christine D. (ed.), *Russian Women Writers*, 2 vols. New York and London, 1999.

Studies of women in old Russian literature and culture

Atkinson, Dorothy, *et al.* (eds.), *Women in Russia*. Stanford, 1977.

Balzer, Marjorie Mandelstam (ed.), *Russian Traditional Culture: Religion, Gender, and Customary Law*. Armonk, NY, 1992.

Barker, Adele Marie, *The Mother Syndrome in the Russian Folk Imagination*. Columbus, OH, 1986.

Bernshtam T. A., "Russian Folk Culture and Folk Religion," in Balzer (ed.), *Russian Traditional Culture*, 34–47.

Clement, Barbara Evans, Barbara Alpern Engel, and Christine Worobec (eds.), *Russia's Women: Accommodation, Resistance, Transformation*. Berkeley, CA, 1991.

Conte, Francis, "Paganism and Christianity in Russia: 'Double' or 'Triple' Faith?" in *The Christianization of Ancient Russia. A Millennium: 988–1988*. Paris, 1992, 207–15.

Dewey, H. W. and A. M. Kleimola, "Muted Eulogy: Women Who Inspired Men in Medieval Rus'," *Russian History* 10:2 (1983), 188–200.

Eremin, I. P., *Literatura drevnei Rusi*. Moscow, 1966.

Fedotov, G. P., *The Russian Religious Mind. Vol. I. Kievan Christianity: The Tenth to the Thirteenth Centuries*. Cambridge, MA, 1966.

Franklin, Simon and Jonathan Shepherd, *The Emergence of Rus 750–1200*. London, 1996.

Glasse, Antonia, "The Formidable Woman: Portrait and Original," *RLT* 10 (1974), 433–53.

Grossman, Joan Delaney, "Feminine Images in Old Russian Literature and Art," *California Slavic Studies* 11 (1980), 33–70.

Ivanits, Linda J., *Russian Folk Belief*. Armonk, NY, 1989.

Kollman, Nancy Shields, "The Seclusion of Elite Muscovite Women," *Russian History* 10:2 (1983), 170–87.

 Kinship and Politics: the Making of the Muscovite Political System 1345–1547. Stanford, 1987.

 Major Problems in Early Modern Russian History. New York, 1992.

Levin, Eve, "Women and Property in Medieval Novgorod," *Russian History* 10:2 (1983), 154–69.

 Sex and Society in the World of the Orthodox Slavs, 900–1700. Ithaca, NY, 1989.

Levy, Sandra, "Women and the Control of Property in Sixteenth-Century Muscovy," *Russian History* 10:2 (1983), 201–12.

Likhachev, D. S., *Chelovek v literature Drevnei Rusi*. Moscow, 1958.

 "The Type and Character of the Byzantine Influence on Old Russian Literature," *Oxford Slavonic Papers* 12–13, (1965–67), 14–32.

 Poetika drevnerusskoi literatury. Leningrad, 1971.

 Velikii put': stanovlenie russkoi literatury XI–XVII vekov. Moscow, 1987.

Pushkareva, N. L., *Zhenshchiny Drevnei Rusi*. Moscow, 1989.

 Zhenshchiny Rossii i Evropy na poroge novogo vremeni. Moscow, 1996.

Pushkareva, N. L. and Eve Levin, *Women in Russian History from the Tenth to the Twentieth Century*. Armonk, NY, 1997.

Zenkovsky, Serge A. (ed. and tr.), *Medieval Russia's Epics, Chronicles, and Tales*. New York, 1974.

Ziolkowski, Margaret, "Women in Old Russian Literature," in Clyman and Greene, 1–15.

Studies on women writing in imperial Russia

Andrew, Joe, *Women in Russian Literature: 1780–1863*. Basingstoke, 1988.

 Narrative and Desire in Russian Literature, 1822–49: The Feminine and the Masculine. New York, 1993.

Aplin, H. A., "M. S. Zhukova and E. A. Gan. Women Writers and Female Protagonists. 1837–1843," Ph.D. diss., University of East Anglia, 1988.

Astman, Marina (Ledkovsky), "Avdotya Panaeva: Her Salon and Her Life," *RLT* 9 (1974), 423–32.

Bennett, Sandra Shaw, "'Parnassian Sisters' of Derzhavin's Acquaintance: Some Observations on Women's Writing in Eighteenth-Century Russia," in L. Hughes and M. di Salvo (eds.), *A Window on Russia: Papers from the V International Conference of the Study Group on Eighteenth-Century Russia*. Turin, 1996, 249–56.

Bernstein, Lina, "Women on the Verge of a New Language: Russian Salon Hostesses in the First Half of the Nineteenth Century," in Goscilo and Holmgren, 209–24.

Brown, William E., *History of Russian Literature of the Romantic Period*. Ann Arbor, MI, 1986.

Bukhshtab, B. Ia., "Russkaia poeziia 1840–1850-kh godov," in B. Ia. Bukhshtab (ed.), *Poety 1840–1850-kh godov*. Leningrad, 1972.

Engel, Barbara Alpern, *Mothers & Daughters. Women of the Intelligentsia in Nineteenth-Century Russia*. Cambridge and New York, 1983.

Engelstein, Laura and Stephanie Sandler (eds), *Self and Story in Russian History*, Ithaca, NY, 2000.

Fainshtein, M. Sh., *Pisatel'nitsy pushkinskoi pory: Istoriko-literaturnye ocherki*. Leningrad, 1989.

Fusso, Susanne and Alexander Lehrman (eds.), *Essays on Karolina Pavlova*. Evanston, IL, 2001.

Gheith, Jehanne, "The Superfluous Man and the Necessary Woman: A 'Re-vision'," *RR* (April 1996), 226–44.

    Finding the Middle Ground: Krestovskii, Tur, and the Power of Ambivalence in Nineteenth-Century Russian Women's Prose (forthcoming).

Göpfert, Frank, *Dichterinnen und Schriftstellerinnen in Russland von der Mitte des 18. bis zum Beginn des 20. Jahrhunderts: eine Problemskizze*. Munich, 1992.

Greene, Diana, "Gender and Genre in Pavlova's *A Double Life*," *SR* (Fall 1995), 563–77.

Greenleaf, Monika, and Stephen Moeller-Sally (eds.), *Russian Subjects: Empire, Nation and the Culture of the Golden Age*. Evanston, IL, 1998.

Gregg, Richard, "A Brackish Hippocrene: Nekrasov, Panaeva, and the 'Prose of Love'," *SR* 34: 4 (December 1975), 731–51.

Grenier, Svetlana, "'Everyone Knew Her, No One Noticed Her': The Fate of the Vospitatel'nitsa (Female Ward) in Nineteenth-Century Russian Literature," Ph.D. diss., Columbia, 1991.

Harussi, Yael, "Women's Social Roles as Depicted by Women Writers in Early Nineteenth-Century Russian Fiction," in J. Douglas Clayton (ed.), *Issues in Russian Literature before 1917: Selected Papers of the Third World Congress for Soviet and East European Studies*. Columbus, OH, 1989, 35–48.

Hoogenboom, Hilde Maria, "A Two-Part Invention: The Russian Woman Writer and Her Heroines from 1860–1917," Ph.D. diss., Columbia 1996.

Karlinsky, Simon, *Russian Drama from its Beginnings to the Age of Pushkin*. Berkeley, CA, 1985, 83–92 (on Catherine II); 192–3 (on Titova).

Khvoshchinskaya, Nadezhda, *The Boarding-School Girl*, tr. Karen Rosneck. Evanston, IL, 2000.

Meehan-Water, Brenda, "The Authority of Holiness: Women Ascetics and Spiritual Elders in Nineteenth-Century Russia," in Geoffrey Hosking (ed.), *Church, Nation and State*. London, 1991, 38–51.

    Holy Women of Russia: The Lives of Five Orthodox Women Offer Spiritual Guidance for Today. San Francisco, 1993.

Nikolaev, P.A. (ed.), *Russkie pisateli 1800–1917. Biograficheskii slovar'* vols. I–IV (of a projected five). Moscow, 1989–99.

Platt, Kevin M. F., *History in a Grotesque Key: Russian Literature and the Idea of Revolution*. Stanford, 1997 (ch. 2 on Khvoshchinskaia).

Rosenholm, Arja, "Auf den Spuren des Vergessens: Zur Rezeptionsgeschichte der russischen Schriftstellerin N. D. Chvoscinskaja," *Studia Slavica Finlandensis* 4 (1989), 63–91.

    Gender Awakening: Femininity and the Russian Woman Question of the 1860s. Helsinki, 1999.

Rosslyn, Wendy, "Anna Bunina's 'Unchaste Relationship with the Muses': Patronage, the Market and the Woman Writer in Early Nineteenth-century Russia," *SEER* 74:2 (1996), 223–42.

Anna Bunina (1774–1829) and the Origins of Women's Poetry in Russia. Lewiston, Queenstone, Lampeter, 1997.

Facts of Agreeable Usefulness: Translations by Russian Women 1763–1825. Fichtenwald, 2000.

Saks, A., *Kavalerist-devitsa. Shtabs-rotmistr A. A. Aleksandrov (Nadezhda Andreevna Durova)*. St. Petersburg, 1912.

Savkina, Irina, *Provintsialki russkoi literatury: (zhenskaia proza 30–40-kh godov XIX veka)* (FrauenLiteraturGeschichte, 8). Wilhelmshorst, 1998.

"Pishu sebia: Avtodokumental'nye zhenskie teksty v russkoi literature pervoi polovinoi XIX veka," Ph. D. diss., University of Tampere, 2001.

Semenko, I. M., *Poety pushkinskoi pory*. Moscow, 1970.

Todd III, William Mills, *Fiction and Society in the Age of Pushkin. Ideology, Institutions and Narrative*. Cambridge, MA, 1986.

Wachtel, Andrew, *The Battle for Childhood: Creation of a Russian Myth*. Stanford, 1990.

An Obsession with History: Russian Writers Confront the Past. Stanford, CA 1994, chapter 1 (on Catherine II's historical writing).

Zirin, Mary Fleming, "A Woman in the 'Man's World': The Journals of Nadezhda Durova," in Marilyn Yalom and Susan Groag Bell (eds.), *Revealing Lives: Gender in Autobiography and Biography*. Albany, NY, 1990, 43–51.

Studies of women's writing in the late imperial period

Aikhenval'd, Iu., "E. Militsyna. Rasskazy, v. 3," *Rech'* 324 (1912).

Amfiteatrov, A., "Literaturnye vpechatleniia. (E. Militsyna, *Rasskazy*, vv. 1–2)," *Sovremennik* 2 (1922).

Antalovsky, Tatjana, *Der russische Frauenroman: exemplarische Untersuchungen*. Munich, 1987.

Balin, Carole B., *To Reveal Our Hearts: Jewish Women Writers in Tsarist Russia*. Detroit, 2000.

Briusov, V., "Adelaida Gertsyk, 'Stikhotvoreniia,'" *RMysl'* 8 (1910), 247–8.

"Zhenshchiny-poety," *Dalekie i blizkie*. Moscow, 1912.

Brooks, Jeffrey, *When Russia Learned to Read*. Princeton, NJ, 1984.

Burgin, Diana, "Laid Out in Lavender: Perceptions of Lesbian Love in Russian Literature and Criticism of the Silver Age, 1893–1917," in Costlow, Sandler, and Vowles, 177–203.

Chebsheva-Dmitrieva, E., "Ol'ga Andreevna Shapir. Ee zhizn' i deiatel'nost'," *VE* 9 (1916), part 2.

Chester, Pamela, "Male and Female Sense of Self in the 'Childhoods' of L. N. Tolstoi and A. I. Tsvetaeva," *Tolstoy Studies Journal* 2 (1989), 53–9.

Cioran, Sam, "The Russian Sappho: Mirra Lokhvitskaia," *RLT* 9 (1974), 317–35.

Clowes, Edith W., *The Revolution of Moral Consciousness: Nietzsche in Russian Literature, 1890–1914*. DeKalb, IL, 1988.

Costlow, Jane, "The Gallop, the Wolf, the Caress: Eros and Nature in *The Tragic Menagerie*," *RR* 56:2 (April 1997), 192–208.

Dalton, Margaret, "A Russian Best-Seller of the Early Twentieth Century: Evdokiya Apollonovna Nagrodskaya's *The Wrath of Dionysus*," in Julian W. Connolly and Sonia J. Ketchian (eds.), *Studies in Russian Literature in Honor of Vsevolod Setchkarev*. Columbus, OH, 1986, 102–12.

Demidova, Ol'ga, "Memuary pisatel'nits russkoi emigratsii (po materialam Bakhme-tevskogo arkhiva," in *Ei ne dano prokladyvat' novye puti . . . ? Iz istorii zhenskogo dvizheniia v Rossii, vypusk 2. Sbornik nauchnykh trudov*. St. Petersburg, 1998.

Dorotin, S., "Gospozha Nagrodskaia i eia roman," *Izvestiia knizhnykh magazinov T-va M. O. Vol'f* 11 (1911).

Edmondson, Linda, *Feminism in Russia, 1900–1917*. Stanford, 1984.

Engelstein, Laura, *The Keys to Happiness. Sex and the Search for Modernity in Fin-de-Siècle Russia*. Ithaca, NY and London, 1992.

Fainshtein, M. Sh. (ed.), *Russkie pisatel'nitsy i literaturnyi protsess v kontse XVIII–pervoi treti XXvv. Sbornik nauchnykh statei*. Wilhelmshorst, 1995.

Forrester, Sibelan, "Reading for a Self: Self-Definition and Female Anxiety in Three Women Poets," *RR* 1 (1996), 21–36.

"Wooing the Other Woman: Gender in Women's Love Poetry in the Silver Age," in Chester and Forrester, 107–34.

Gornfel'd, A. G., "E. Letkova, *Rasskazy*," *RBog* 8 (1913).

Gove, Antonina Filonov, "Gender as a Poetic Feature in the Poetry of Zinaida Gippius," *American Contributions to the VIIIth International Congress of Slavists, vol. I: Linguistics*. Columbus, OH, 1978, 377–407.

Gracheva, A. M., "Estetika russkogo moderna i zhenskaia proza nachala XX veka (A.A. Verbitskaia)," in Frank Göpfert (ed.), *Dichterinnen und Schriftstellerinnen in Russland von der Mitte des 18. Jahrhunderts bis zum Beginn des 20 Jahrhunderts: eine Problemskizze*. Munich, 1992.

"'Zhiznetvorchestvo' Anny Mar," in *Litsa. Biograficheskii al'manakh, 7*. Moscow/ St. Petersburg, 1996.

Grossman, Joan Delaney, "Valery Briusov and Nina Petrovskaia: Clashing Models of Life in Art," in Irina Paperno and J. D. Grossman (eds.), *Creating Life: The Aesthetic Utopia of Russian Modernism*. Stanford, CA, 1994, 122–50.

Hoogenboom, Hilde, "Mat' Gogolia i otets Aksakovykh: Kak Nadezhda Sokhanskaia nashla rodnoi iazyk," in Nataliia Kamenetskaia (ed.), *Fenomen pola v kul'ture*. Moscow, 1998, 149–59.

Ianovskii, N., *Lidiia Seifullina: Kritiko-biograficheskii ocherk*. Moscow, 1959; 2nd edn, 1972.

Johanson, Christine, *Women's Struggle for Higher Education in Russia, 1855–1900*. Kingston, Ontario, 1987.

Kardin, V., *Dve sud'by: Lidiia Seifullina i ee povest' 'Virineia'*. Moscow, 1975.

Karlinsky, Simon. "Introduction: Who was Zinaida Gippius?" in Vladimir Zlobin (ed.), *A Difficult Soul: Zinaida Gippius*, tr. and intro., Simon Karlinsky. Berkeley, CA, 1980, 1–21.

Kelly, Catriona, "Reluctant Sibyls: Gender and Intertextuality in the Work of Adelaida Gertsyk and Vera Merkur'eva," in Sandler (ed.), *Rereading Russian Poetry*. New Haven, CT, 1999, 129–45.

Khodasevich, Vladislav, "Konets Renaty," in *Nekropol'*. Paris, 1976 (essay dated 1928).

Kogan, P. S., "Iz zhizni i literatury: Intelligentnaia zhenshchina v rasskazakh g-zhi Krandievskoi," *Obrazovanie* 2 (1902), 31–8.

Koltonovskaia, E. A., "Iz zhizni i literatury," *Obrazovanie* 9 (1907), 74–88.

"Tvorchestvo, utverzhdaiushchee zhizn'," *Novaia zhizn'*, St. Petersburg, 1910.

Kriticheskie etiudy. St. Petersburg, 1912.

Zhenskie siluety. St. Petersburg, 1912.

Kondakov, N., "Rasskazy E. M. Militsynoi," *Sbornik otdeleniia russkogo iazyka i slovesnosti*, 84 (1908), part 2, 103–8.

Kozlova, L. N., *Starost' – molodosti: Anastasiia Ivanovna Tsvetaeva v zhizni.* Moscow, 1992.

Larsen, Susan, "Girl Talk: Lydia Charskaia and Her Readers," in Laura Engelstein and Stephanie Sandler (eds.), *Self and Story in Russian History.* Ithaca, NY, 2000, 141–167.

Lunacharskii, A., "Zhurnal zametki," *Obrazovanie* 3 (1905).

Makovskii, Sergei, "Cherubina de Gabriak," in *Portrety sovremennikov.* New York, 1955.

Maksimov, D., "Liubov' Dmitrievna," ed. K. M. Azadovskii and A.V. Lavrov. *NlitOb* 35 (1999), 257–80.

Marsh, R. J., "The Birth, Death and Rebirth of Feminist Writing in Russia," in Helena Forsås-Scott (ed.), *Textual Liberation: European Feminist Writing in the Twentieth Century.* London, 1991, 130–63.

"Anastasiia Verbitskaia Reconsidered," in Marsh *Gender,* 184–205.

"Sex, Religion and Censorship in Anna Mar's *Zhenshchina na kreste,*" in Peter Barta (ed.), *Gender and Sexuality in Russian Civilisation.* Newark, NJ, 2001.

Matich, Olga, *Paradox in the Religious Poetry of Zinaida Gippius.* Munich, 1972.

"Dialectics of Cultural Return: Zinaida Gippius' Personal Myth," in Boris Gasparov, Robert P. Hughes, and Irina Paperno (eds.), *Cultural Mythologies of Russian Modernism: From the Golden Age to the Silver Age.* Berkeley, CA, 1992, 52–72.

"Gender Trouble in the Amazonian Kingdom: Turn-of-the-Century Representations of Women in Russia," in John E. Bowlt and Matthew Drutt (eds.), *Amazons of the Avante-Garde.* New York, 2000, 75–93.

McReynolds, Louise, "Female Journalists in Prerevolutionary Russia," *Journalism History* 4 (1987), 104–10.

"Reading the Russian Romance: What Did the *Keys to Happiness* Unlock?" *Journal of Popular Culture* 31:4 (1998), 95–108.

Mikhailovskii, N. M., "Literatura i zhizn'," *RBog* 8 (1899), 161–82.

Mirtov, O., "E. Militsyna. Rasskazy," *Obrazovanie* 3 (1905).

"A. Krandievskaia. *Rasskazy,*" *Obrazovanie* 7 (1905).

Møller, Peter Ulf, *Postlude to 'The Kreutzer Sonata': Tolstoj and the Debate on Sexual Morality in Russian Literature in the 1890s.* Leiden/New York, 1988.

Nagrodskaya, E., *The Wrath of Dionysus,* tr. Louise McReynolds. Bloomington, IN, 1997.

Nikolaeva, M. N., "Prevysprennye geroini," *RBog* 12 (1891).

Nikolskaia, T., "The Contemporary Woman in Early Twentieth-Century Russian Literature," *Irish Slavonic Studies* 8 (1987), 107–13.

Norton, Barbara T. and Jehanne Gheith, (eds), *An Improper Profession: Women, Gender, and Journalism in Late Imperial Russia.* Durham, NC, 2001.

Ovsianiko-Kulikovskii, D. N., "Predislovie," in Olga Shapir, *SS,* vol. I. St. Petersburg, 1910.

Pachmuss, Temira, *Zinaida Hippius: An Intellectual Profile.* Carbondale, IL, 1971.

(ed. and tr.), *Women Writers in Russian Modernism.* Urbana, IL, 1978.

Pil'skii, P., "A. N. Sologub-Chebotarevskaia," *Segodnia* (1921), 231.

"K tragicheskoi smerti A. N. Chebotarevskoi-Sologub," *Russkii kur'er* (Latvia, 1922), 295.

Presto, Jenifer, "The Androgynous Gaze of Zinaida Gippius," *RL* 48: 1 (July 2000), 87–115.

"Reading Zinaida Gippius: Over Her Dead Body," *SEEJ,* vol. 43, no. 4 (1999), 621–35.

Primakov, A.V., "Valentina Iovovna Dmitrieva i ee knigi," in V. I. Dmitrieva, *Povesti i rasskazy.* Moscow, 1976.

Ramdas, Mallika U., "Through Other "I"s: Self and Other in Russian Women's Autobiographical Texts," Ph.D. diss. Columbia University, 1996.

Rosenthal, Charlotte, "The Silver Age: High Point for Women?" in Linda Edmondson (ed.), *Women and Society in Russia.* Cambridge, 1992, 32–47.

Savel'ev, S. N., *Zhanna d'Ark russkoi religioznoi mysli: intellektual'nyi profil'*, Z. Gippius. Moscow, 1992.

Savkina, Irina, "Zhenstvennoe i muzhestvennoe v proze Nadezhdy Durovoi," *Studia Slavica Finlandensia* 12 (1995), 126–40.

Schuler, Catherine, "Zinaida Gippius: An Unwitting and Unwilling Feminist." In *Theatre and Feminist Aesthetics,* ed. Karen Laughlin and Catherine Schuler. Madison, NJ, 1995, 131–47.

Shaginian, Marietta, *O blazhenstve imushchego: poeziia Z.N. Gippius.* Moscow, 1912.

Skabichevskii, A. M., *Sochineniia.* St. Petersburg, 1903.

Smirnova, L., *Literaturnoe nasledie Lidii Seifullinoi.* Moscow, 1967.

Sologub, F., "A. N. Sologub-Chebotarevskaia," *LitZ* 1 (1922), 12–14.

"Staryi i novyi zavet zhenshchiny. ('Bez zaveta O. Runovoi)," *Biulleteni literatury i zhizni* 7 (1913).

Stites, Richard, *The Women's Liberation Movement in Russia: Feminism, Nihilism, and Bolshevism, 1860–1930.* Princeton, 1978.

Zhukovskaia, T. N., and E. A. Kallo (comps.), *Adelaida i Evgeniia Gertsyk i ikh okruzhenie: Materialy nauchno-prakticheskoi konferentsii v g. Sudake, 18–20 sentiabria 1996 goda.* Moscow and Sudak, 1997.

Zinovieva-Annibal, Lydia, *The Tragic Menagerie,* tr. Jane Costlow. Evanston, IL, 1999.

Studies of writing in exile

Agenesov, V., and K. Tolkachev (eds.), *Poetessy russkogo zarubezhiia. Sbornik stikhotvorenii Lidii Alekseevoi (1909–1989), Ol' gi Anstei (1912–1985), Valentiny Sinkevich (rod. 1926g.).* Moscow, 1998.

Bakich Olga, "Charbin: 'Russland jenseits der Grenzen' in Fernost," in Karl Schlögel (ed.), *Der grosse Exodus. Die russische Emigration und ihre Zentren 1917 bis 1941.* Munich, 1994.

Beaujour, Elizabeth Klosty, *Alien Tongues: Bilingual Russian Writers of the "First" Emigration.* Ithaca, NY, 1989.

Broe, Mary Lynn and Angela Ingram (eds.), *Women's Writing in Exile.* Chapel Hill, 1989.

Clements, Barbara Evans, *Bolshevik Feminist: The Life of Aleksandra Kollontai.* Bloomington, IN, 1979.

Diao Shao-hua, "Khudozhestvennaia literatura russkogo zarubezh'ia v g. Kharbine za pervye 20 let (1905–1925)," *Rossiiane v Azii* 3 (Fall 1996), 57–109.

Farnsworth, Beatrice Brodsky, *Aleksandra Kollontai: Socialism, Feminism and the Bolshevik Revolution.* Stanford, 1980.

Harbin and Manchuria: Place, Space, and Identity. Special issue of *South Atlantic Quarterly,* ed. Thomas Lahusen, 99:2 (2000).

Ingemanson, Birgitta, "The Political Function of Domestic Objects in the Fiction of Alexandra Kollontai," *SR* 48 (1989), 71–82.

Karlinsky, Simon (ed.), *The Bitter Air of Exile.* Berkeley, CA, 1977.

Kelly, Catriona, "Writing an Orthodox Text: Religious Poetry by Russian Women, 1917–1940," *Poetics of the Text,* Studies in Slavic Literature and Poetics, vol. 17. (1992), 153–70.

Kruzenshtern-Peterets, Iu., "Churaevskii pitomnik (O dal'nevostochnykh poetakh)," *Vozrozhdenie* 204 (1968), 45–70.

Mokrinskaia, Nina, *Moia zhizn' (detstvo v Sibiri, iunost' v Kharbine – 1914–1932 gody)*. New York, 1991.

Moia zhizn'. Vospominaniia. Kniga vtoraia. New York, 1995.

Murav'ev V., "Zhenskaia dusha v poezii. Muzy kharbinskogo Parnassa," *Rubezh* 40:297 (1933), 16–17.

Pachmuss, Temira, "Five Women Poets in Early Russian Emigre Literature," in *Zapiski russkoi akademicheskoi gruppy v S.Sh.A.* New York, 1967, 187–200.

Russian Literature in the Baltic between the World Wars. Columbus, OH, 1988.

Pereleshin Valerii, "Dva polustanka. Vospominaniia svidetelia i uchastnika literaturnoi zhizni Kharbina i Shangkhia," published under the title *Russian Poetry and Literary Life in Harbin and Shanghai 1930–1950. The Memoirs of Valerij Perelesin.* Amsterdam, 1987.

Porter, Cathy, *Alexandra Kollontai: A Biography.* London, 1980.

Raeff, Marc, *Russia Abroad: A Cultural History of the Russian Emigration.* New York, 1990.

Sel'kina, D.G. and E.P. Taskina (comps.), *Kharbin. Vetka russkogo dereva.* Novosibirsk, 1991.

Sentianina, E., "Kharbinskie pisateli i poety," *Rubezh* 24:645 (June 8, 1940), 5–8.

Smith, G. S., "The Versification of Russian Emigré Poetry, 1920–1940," *SEER* 1 (1978), 32–46.

Sofonova O., *Puti nevedomye. Rossiia (Sibir', Zabaikal'e), Kitai, Filippiny.* Munich, 1980.

Stephan, John, *The Russian Fascists. Tragedy and Farce in Exile, 1925–1945.* New York, 1978.

Struve, Gleb, *Russkaia literatura v izgnanii.* 3rd expanded edn, Paris and Moscow, 1996.

Suleiman, S.R. (ed.), *Exile and Creativity: Signposts, Travelers, Outsiders, Backward Glances.* Durham and London, 1998.

Taskina, E. P., "Poety russkogo Kharbina," *Problemy Dal'nego Vostoka* 3 (1989), 120–30, and 4 (1989), 118–26.

Neizvestnyi Kharbin. Moscow, 1994.

(ed.), *Russkii Kharbin.* Moscow, 1998.

Yakobson, Helen, *Crossing Borders. From Revolutionary Russia to China to America.* New York, 1994.

Studies of women's writing in the Soviet and post-Soviet periods

Ageev, A. L., and L. N. Taganov, "Rovesnitsa veka," *Volga* 5 (1989), 165–8.

Akhmatova, A., "O stikhakh N. L'vovoi," *RMysl'* 1 (1914), 27–8.

Aleksandrova, A., "Na iskhode real'nosti," *Grani* 168 (1993), 302–17.

Aliger, M., "Chto takoe podvig?" in *Tropinka vo rzhi.* Moscow, 1980, 119–23.

Amert, Susan, *In a Shattered Mirror: The Later Poetry of Anna Akhmatova.* Stanford, CA, 1992.

Annenskii, I., "O sovremennom lirizme," *Apollon* 3 (1919).

Babenysheva, S., "Dokument epokhi: o dnevnikakh Ol'gi Berggol'ts," *Vremia i my* 57 (1980), 272–5.

Banjanin, M., "The Prose and Poetry of Elena Guro," *RLT* 9 (1974), 303–16.

"Of Harlequins, Dreamers and Poets: A Study of an Image in the Works of Elena Guro," *RLJ* (1982), 123–4.

"Nature and the City in the Works of Elena Guro," *SEEJ* 30 (1986).

Bank, Natal'ia, *Ol'ga Berggol'ts: kritiko-biograficheskii ocherk.* Moscow and Leningrad, 1962.

Barker, Adele, "Irina Grekova's 'Na ispytaniiakh': The History of One Story," *SR* 48 (1989), 399–412.

"Women Without Men in the Writings of Contemporary Soviet Women Writers," in Daniel Rancour-Laferriere (ed.), *Russian Literature and Psychoanalysis*. Amsterdam and Philadelphia, 1989, 431–49.

Bethea, David, "What Does a Six-Winged Seraphim Taste Like?" *Parnassus* 14:2 (1988), 310–23. (on Ratushinskaia).

Bobel, Avgusta, "Zachatnyi chas Marii Shkapskoi," in Göpfert (ed.), *Russland aus der Feder seiner Frauen*. Munich, 1992, 9–20.

Boym, Svetlana, *Death in Quotation Marks: Cultural Myths of the Modern Poet*. Cambridge, MA, 1991, 192–240.

Briusov, V., "Sredi stikhov," *Pechat' i revoliutsiia* 2 (1922), 143–9.

"Vchera, segodnia i zavtra russkoi poezii," *Pechat'i revoliutsiia* 7 (1922), 65.

Brooks, Jeffrey, "Revolutionary Lives, Public Identities in *Pravda* in the 1920s," in Stephen White (ed.), *New Directions in Soviet History*. Cambridge, 1991, 27–40.

Brown, Deming, *The Last Years of Soviet Russian Literature: Prose Fiction, 1975–1991*. Cambridge and New York, 1993.

Brown, Edward J., *Russian Literature Since the Revolution*. Cambridge, 1982.

(ed.), *Canadian-American Slavic Studies* 28: 2–3 (1994). Special issue on Lydiia Ginzburg.

Bulatov, D. (ed.), *Eksperimental'naia poeziia: Izbrannye stat'i*. Königsberg, 1996.

Buldeev, A., "N. L'vova. Staraia skazka," *Zhatva* 5 (1914).

Bulin, E., "Otkroite knigu molodykh," *Molodaia gvardiia* 3 (1989), 237–48.

Burgin, Diana Lewis, "After the Ball is Over: Sophia Parnok's Creative Relationship with Marina Tsvetaeva," *RR* 47 (1988), 425–44.

"Sophia Parnok and the Writing of a Lesbian Poet's Life," *SR* 51:2 (1992), 214–31.

Sof'ia Parnok: the Life and Works of Russia's Sappho. New York, 1993.

Chashchina, Liudmila. "Put' vozvrata: k 80-letiu so dnia rozhdeniia Ol'gi Berggol'ts," *Iskusstvo Leningrada* 5 (1990), 21–8.

Chernetsky, Vitaly, "Epigonoi, or Transformations of Writing in the Texts of Valeriia Narbikova and Nina Iskrenko," *SEEJ* 38:4 (Winter 1994), 655–76.

"Nina Iskrenko: The Postmodern Poet and Her Few Words," in Stephanie Sandler (ed.), *Rereading Russian Poetry*. New Haven, CT, 1999, 104–25.

Chukovskaia, Lidiia, *Zapiski ob Anne Akhmatovoi*, vols. I–II. Paris, 1976–80.

The Akhmatova Journals, vol I, tr. Milena Michalski, Sylva Rubashova, Peter Norman. New York and London, 1994.

Clark, Katerina, *The Soviet Novel: History as Ritual*. Chicago, 1981.

Cook, R., "The Poetry of Irina Ratushinskaya," *Journal of Russian Studies* 53 (1987), 8–15.

Cooper, Nancy L., "Secret Truths and Unheard-of Women: Poliksena Solov'eva's Fiction as Commentary on Vladimir Solov'ev's Theory of Love," *RR* 56: 2 (April 1997), 178–91.

Dalton-Brown, Sally, "A Map of the Human Heart: Tatyana Tolstaya's Topographies," *Essays in Poetics* 21 (1996), 1–18.

Epshtein, Mikhail, "Metamorfoza (o novykh techeniiakh v poezii 80-kh godov)" in Epshtein, *Paradoksy novizny*. Moscow, 1988, 139–76.

Ermolin, Evgenii, "Zhit' i umeret' v Permi," *NM* 12 (1997). Review of Nina Gorlanova's *Vsia Perm'*.

Feiler, Lily, *Marina Tsvetaeva: The Double Beat of Heaven and Hell*. Durham, NC and London, 1994.

Feinstein, Elaine, *A Captive Lion: The Life of Marina Tsvetaeva*. London, 1987.

Forrester, S., "Bells and Cupolas: The Formative Role of the Female Body in the Poetry of Marina Tsvetaeva," *SR* 51: 2 (1992), 232–46.

Garros, Veronique, Natalia Korenevskaya, and Thomas Lahusen, *Intimacy and Terror: Soviet Diaries of the 1930s*. New York, 1995.

Gasiorowska, Xenia, *Women in Soviet Fiction, 1917–1964*. Madison, WI, 1968.

Gasparov, M. L., "Iz literaturnogo naslediia: Kassandra," *Oktiabr'* 5 (1989), 149–59. Introduction to publication of poems in *Litsa* 1. St. Petersburg, 1995.

Gertsyk, Evgeniia, *Vospominaniia*. Paris, 1973.

Goscilo, Helena, "Women's Wards and Wardens: The Hospital in Contemporary Russian Women's Fiction," *Canadian Woman Studies* 10 (Winter 1989).

"Coming a Long Way, Baby: A Quarter-Century of Russian Women's Fiction," *The Harriman Institute Forum* 6:1 (September 1992).

"Perspective in Tatyana Tolstaya's Wonderland of Art," *World Literature Today* 67:1 (Winter 1993), 80–90. This issue also contains an interview with the author.

"Mother as Mothra: Totalizing Narrative and Nurture in Petrushevskaia," in Sonya Stephan Hoisington (ed.), *A Plot of Her Own: The Female Protagonist in Russian Literature*. Evanston, IL, 1995, 102–13.

Dehexing Sex: Russian Womanhood During and After Glasnost. Ann Arbor, MI, 1996.

The Explosive World of Tatyana N. Tolstaya's Fiction. Armonk, NY, 1996.

(ed.), *Skirted Issues: The Discreteness and Indiscretions of Russian Women's Prose*. Special issue of *Russian Studies in Literature* 28:2 (Spring 1992).

(ed.), *Fruits of Her Plume: Essays on Contemporary Russian Women's Culture*. Armonk, NY, 1993.

"Big-Buck Books: Pulp Fiction in Postsoviet Russia," in *Russian Culture of the 1990s*, ed. Helena Goscilo, 23:1 (Winter 2000). Special issue of *Studies in 20th Century Literature*.

Gove, A. F., "Stereotype and Beyond: Role Conflict and Resolution in the Poetics of Marina Tsvetaeva," *SR* 2 (1977) 231–56.

Greber, Erika, "Carnivalization of the Short Story: Tatyana Tolstaya's *The Poet and the Muse*," *Essays in Poetics* 21 (1996), 50–78.

Grinberg, I., *Vera Inber: kritiko-biograficheskii ocherk*. Leningrad, 1961.

Gumilev, N., *Pis'ma o russkoi poezii*. Petrograd, 1923, 144–6.

Hackel, S., *Pearl of Great Price: The Life of Mother Maria Skobtsova 1891–1945*. London, 1982.

Haight, Amanda, *Anna Akhmatova: A Poetic Pilgrimage*. Oxford, 1990.

Halfin, Igal, "From Darkness to Light: Student Communist Autobiography During NEP," *Jahrbücher für Geschichte Osteuropas* 45 (1997), 210–36.

Harris, Jane Gary (ed.), *Autobiographical Statements in Twentieth Century Russian Literature*. Princeton, NJ, 1990.

Heaton, Julia, "Russian Women's Writing – Problems of a Feminist Approach, with Particular Reference to the Writing of Marina Palei," *SEER* 75:1 (January 1997), 63–85.

Heldt, Barbara, "The Burden of Caring," *The Nation* 244 (June 13, 1987), 820.

"Motherhood in a Cold Climate," *RR* 3 (1992), expanded version in Costlow, Sandler, and Vowles.

"Gynoglasnost: Writing the Feminine," in Mary Buckley (ed.), *Perestroika and Soviet Women*. New York, 1992.

Hodgson, Katharine, "Kitezh and the Commune: Recurrent Themes in the Work of Ol'ga Berggol'ts," *SEER* 74:1 (1996), 1–18.

Written with the Bayonet: Soviet Russian Poetry of World War II. Liverpool, 1996.

Holmgren, Beth, *Women's Works in Stalin's Time: On Lidiia Chukovskaia and Nadezhda Mandelstam*. Bloomington, IN, 1993.

"Why Russian Girls Loved Charskaia," *RR* 54 (1995), 91–106.

"Stepping Out/Going Under: Women in Russia's Twentieth-Century Salons," in Goscilo and Holmgren, 225–46.

Isenberg, Charles, "The Rhetoric of *Hope Against Hope*," in Jane Gary Harris (ed.), *Autobiographical Statements in Twentieth-Century Russian Literature*. Princeton, NJ, 1990.

Jensen, K. B., *Russian Futurism, Urbanism and Elena Guro*. Aarhus, 1977.

Kalina-Levine, V., "Through the Eyes of the Child: the Artistic Vision of Elena Guro," *SEEJ* 25:2 (1981), 30–43.

Karlinsky, Simon, *Marina Tsvetaeva: The Woman, Her World and Her Poetry*. Cambridge, 1985.

Kataev, V., "Vechernii svet", *Znamia* 6 (1972), and preface in Krandievskaia, *Doroga*. Moscow, 1985.

Kelly, Catriona, "I. Grekova and N. Baranskaia: Soviet Women's Writing and De-Stalinisation," *Russistika* 5 (June 1992), 39–43; 6 (1992), 14–18.

Ketchian, Sonia, *The Poetry of Anna Akhmatova: A Conquest of Time and Space*. Munich, 1990.

Khrenkov, D., *Ot serdtsa k serdtsu: o zhizni i tvorchestve Ol'gi Berggol'ts*, 2nd edn, Leningrad, 1982.

Kolesnikoff, Nina, "The Generic Structure of Ljudmila Petruševskaja's 'Pesni vostochnykh slavian,'" *SEEJ* 37:2 (1993), 220–30.

Kovalev, V. A. (ed.), *Tvorchestvo Marietty Shaginian*. Leningrad, 1980.

Lahusen, Thomas, "Leaving Paradise and Perestroika: 'A Week Like Any Other and *Memorial Day* by Natal'ia Baranskaya; in Goscilo (ed.), *Fruits of Her Plume*, 205–24.

Lakshin, V., "Ol'ga Berggol'ts," in *Otkrytaia dver'*. Moscow, 1989, 332–61.

Makarov, A., "Vera Inber," in Inber, *SS*, vol. I. Moscow, 1965, 5–42.

Makin, Michael, *Marina Tsvetaeva: Poetics of Appropriation*. Oxford, 1993.

Manuilov, V., preface in Krandievskaia, *Vechernii svet*. Leningrad, 1972.

Markov, V., *Russian Futurism: A History*. Berkeley, 1968.

McLaughlin, Sigrid, "Contemporary Soviet Women Writers," *Canadian Woman Studies* 10: 4 (Winter 1989), 77–80.

"An Interview with Viktoria Tokareva," *Canadian Woman Studies* 10:4 (Winter 1989), 76.

Mirsky, D. S., "O sovremennom sostoianii russkoi literatury," *NZh* 131 (1978); repr. D. S. Mirsky, *Uncollected Writings on Russian Literature*, ed. G. S. Smith. Berkeley, CA, 1989.

Naiman, A., *Rasskazy ob Anne Akhmatovoi*. Moscow, 1989; in English as *Remembering Anna Akhmatova*. London, 1991.

Nepomnyashchy, Catharine Theimer, "Markets, Mirrors, and Mayhem: Aleksandra Marinina and the Rise of the New Russian Detektiv," in Adele Barker (ed.), *Consuming Russia: Popular Culture, Sex, and Society since Gorbachev*, Durham, NC, 1999, 161–91.

"The Seduction of the Story: Flight and 'Fall' in Tolstaya's Heavenly Flame," in Karen L. Ryan and Barry P. Scherr (eds.), *Twentieth-Century Russian Literature: Selected Papers from the Fifth World Congress of Central and East European Studies, Warsaw, 1995*. New York, 2000, 193–205.

Nikol'skaia, T. L., "Tema misticheskogo sektanstva v russkoi poezii 20-kh godov XX veka," *Trudy po russkoi i slavianskoi filologii Tartuskogo universiteta. Literaturovedenie* 883 (1990).

"Novaia Eva," *Iskusstvo Leningrada* 8 (1991).

Ninov, A., "Real'nost' geroia," *Zvezda* 7 (1967), 192–202.

Oskotskii, V., "Kak khoroshi, kak svezhi byli rozy...," *DN* 4 (1977), 272–5.

Ovanesian, E., "Tvortsy raspada," *MGv* (April 3, 1992), 249–62

Palei, M., "Tvoia nemyslimaia chistota," *LitOb* 6 (1987), 1–64.

Peterson, Nadya L., *Subversive Imaginations: Fantastic Prose and the End of Soviet Literature, 1970–1990s.* Boulder, CO, 1997 (ch. 10 on Petrushevskaia, Sadur, Tolstaia, Narbikova).

"Games Women Play," in Goscilo (ed.), *Fruits of Her Plume*, 165–83.

Pittman, Riitta H., "Valeriya Narbikova's Iconoclastic Prose," *Forum for Modern Language Studies* 28 (1992), 376–86.

Poliakova, S., "Vstupitel'naia stat'ia," in Parnok, *Sobranie stikhotvorenii.* Ann Arbor, MI, 1979, 7–106.

Nezakatnye oni dni: Tsvetaeva i Parnok. Ann Arbor, 1983.

Porter, Robert, *Russia's Alternative Prose.* Oxford, 1994.

Pratt, Sarah. "Lydia Ginzburg and the Fluidity of Genre," in Jane Gary Harris (ed.), *Autobiographical Statements in Twentieth-Century Russian Literature.* Princeton, NJ, 1990, 207–16.

Rancour-Laferrière, Daniel, Vera Loseva and Aleksej Lunkov, "Violence in the Garden: A Work by Tolstaja in Kleinian Perspective," *SEEJ* 39 (1995), 524–34.

Reeder, Roberta, *Anna Akhmatova: Poet and Prophet.* London, 1995.

Roll, Serafima (ed. and tr.), "A Contemporary Textual Psychology (Interview with Valeriia Narbikova)," in *Contextualizing Transition: Interviews with Contemporary Russian Writers and Critics.* New York, 1998, 85–93.

Rosslyn, Wendy, *The Prince, the Fool and the Nunnery: the Religious Theme in the Early Poetry of Anna Akhmatova.* Nottingham, 1984.

Rozhdestvenskii, Vs. Preface in Krandievskaia, *Vospominaniia.* Leningrad, 1977.

Sandler, Stephanie, "The Canon and the Backward Glance," in Goscilo (ed.), *Fruits of Her Plume*, 113–33.

"Cultural Memory and Self-Expression in a Poem by Elena Shvarts," in Sandler (ed.), *Rereading Russian Poetry*, 256–69.

"Thinking Self in the Poetry of Olga Sedakova," in Marsh *Gender*, 302–25.

Schaffner-Baumgartner, Sabine, *Die Autobiographie einer sowjetischen Dichterin: Mythisierungen in Ol'ga Berggol'c Dnevnye zvezdy.* Bern, 1993.

Schweitzer, Viktoria, *Tsvetaeva.* London, 1992.

Shcherbina, Tat'iana, "Medeia ne ubivala svoikh detei," *Kommersant-daily* 197 (November 15, 1997). (On Ulitskaia.)

Shepherd, David, "Facts versus Figures: Marietta Shaginian," in Shepherd, *Beyond Metafiction: Self-consciousness in Soviet Literature.* Oxford, 1992, 64–89.

"Canon Fodder: Problems in the Reading of a Soviet Production Novel," in C. Kelly, M. Makin, and D. Shepherd, *Discontinuous Discourses in Modern Russian Literature.* Basingstoke, 1989, 39–59.

Shneidman, N. N., *Russian Literature 1988–1994: The End of an Era.* Toronto, 1995.

Shteinman, Z., "Svetlaia zhizn'," *Literaturnaia zhizn'* (June 24, 1960).

Shustov, A., "Zhizn' i tvorchestvo E. Iu. Kuz'minoi-Karavaevoi," *RLit* 4 (1981).

"Doch' Rossii," in Liliia Dobrinskaia (comp.), *Belye nochi.* Leningrad 1985, 198–227.

Simmons, K. A., "Zhenskaia Proza and the New Generation of Women Writers," *Slovo* 3:1 (May 1990), 66–78.

Siniavskii, Andrei, "The Poetry and Prose of Olga Berggolts," in Abram Terts, *For Freedom of Imagination*, tr. Laszlo Tikos and Murray Peppard. New York, 1971.

Skorino, L., *Marietta Shaginian – khudozhnik*. Moscow, 1981.

Skvortsov, L. I., "V zhanre damskoi povesti (o iazyke i stile povesti I. Grekovoi *Na ispytaniiakh*," *RRech'* 1 (1968), 26–35.

Smith, Melissa T., "Profiles: A New 'Voice of Authority': Nina Sadur," *Theater Three* 10–11 1992.

Startseva, N., "Sto let zhenskogo odinochestva," *Don* 3 (1989), 58–65.

Stolitsa, Liubov', "Poetessa-veshchun'ia," *Vozrozhdenie* (September 1, 1925).

Taganov, L., "'Zhenshchina' Anny Barkovoi," *Na poeticheskikh meridianakh*. Iaroslavl, 1975, 37–47.

"Anna Barkova: sud'ba i stikhi," in Barkova, *Vozvrashchenie*. Ivanovo, 1990.

"*Prosti moiu nochnuiu dushu...*": *Kniga ob Anne Barkovoi*. Ivanovo, 1993.

Taubman, Jane. *A Life through Poetry: Marina Tsvetaeva's Lyric Diary*. Columbus, OH, 1989.

Trofimova, Elena, "Sovetskaia zhenshchina 80-kh godov: Avtoportret v poezii," *VopLit* 2 (1994), 30–44.

Tschöpl, Carin, *Die Sowjetische Lyrik-Diskussion: Ol'ga Berggol'c Blockadedichtung als Paradigma*. Munich, 1988.

Vasil'evskii, Andrei, Review of *Stikhi o stikhakh* [Larisa Miller], *NM* 5 (1997).

Velichkovskaia, T., "O poezii Materi Marii," *Vozrozhdenie* (1969), 205.

Verblovskaia, I., "Poet tragicheskoi sud'by," *Neva* 4 (1989), 206–7 (on Barkova).

Vilenkin, V., *V sto pervom zerkale*. Moscow, 1987.

Vishnevsky, Anatoly and Michael Biggins (eds.), *Soviet Literary Culture in the 1970s: The Politics of Irony*. Gainesville, FL, 1993.

Voronskii, A., "Pesnia severnogo rabochego kraia," *Krasnaia nov'* 2 (1922), 216, 221 (on Barkova).

Vygodskii, D., "O sbornike Goda," *Zvezda* 2 (1936), 169–70.

"O sbornike *Pod kamennym dozhdem*," *Kniga i revoliutsiia* 3 (1923).

Woll, Josephine, "The Minotaur in the Maze: Remarks on Lyudmila Petrushevskaya," *World Literature Today* 67:1 (1993), 125–30.

Zekulin, Nicholas, "Changing Perspectives: The Prose of Natal'ia Baranskaia," *Canadian Slavonic Papers* 35 (Fall 1993).

Zhirmunskii, V., *Tvorchestvo Anny Akhmatovoi*. Leningrad, 1973.

Zholkovsky, Alexander, "Anna Akhmatova: Scripts not Scriptures," *SEEJ* 40:1 (1996), 135–41.

"The Obverse of Stalinism: Akhmatova's Self-Serving Charisma of Selflessness," in Engelstein and Sandler (eds.), *Self and Story in Russian History*. Ithaca, NY, 2000, 46–68.

Zolotusskii, I., "Faust i fiziki," *VopLit* 11 (1965), 50–68.

Index

The name and subject index covers the periodicals section of the list of abbreviations, the introduction, chapters 1–15, authors in the Bibliographical Guide to writers and their works and the Guide to further reading. Page references in **bold** type refer to the biobibliographies. All names of works mentioned in chapters 1–15 are included under the relevant author. Titles of works and first lines are entered in italics or within quotation marks (" ") as in the text. Endnotes are referred to by n and note number e.g. 23n8. Please see also note on transliteration, p. xiv.